FOURTH EDITION

Greenhouse Operation and Management

Paul V. Nelson

Department of Horticultural Science
North Carolina State University

PRENTICE HALL
Englewood Cliffs, New Jersey 07632

Library of Congress Cataloging-in-Publication Data

Nelson, Paul V.
Greenhouse operation and management / Paul V. Nelson.—4th ed.
p. cm.
Includes bibliographical references and index.
ISBN 0-13-365198-3
1. Greenhouse management. 2. Floriculture. I. Title.
II. Title: Greenhouse operation and management.
SB415.N44 1991
635.9'823—dc20 91-133
CIP

Cover: A premiere crop of poinsettias at Van Wingerden International, Inc., in Fletcher, NC 28732.

Acquisitions Editor: Robin Baliszewski
Editorial/production supervision and interior design: Laura Cleveland
Buyers: Mary McCartney/Ed O'Dougherty

A Simon & Schuster Company
Englewood Cliffs, New Jersey 07632

Printed in the United States of America
10 9 8 7 6 5 4 3 2

ISBN 0-13-365198-3

Prentice-Hall International (UK) Limited, *London*
Prentice-Hall of Australia Pty. Limited, *Sydney*
Prentice-Hall Canada Inc., *Toronto*
Prentice-Hall Hispanoamericana, S.A., *Mexico*
Prentice-Hall of India Private Limited, *New Delhi*
Prentice-Hall of Japan, Inc., *Tokyo*
Simon & Schuster Asia Pte. Ltd., *Singapore*
Editora Prentice-Hall do Brasil, Ltda., *Rio de Janeiro*

Contents

CHAPTER 6
Root-Media Pasteurization 209

CHAPTER 7
Watering 231

CHAPTER 8
Fertilization 257

CHAPTER 9
Alternative Cropping Systems 317

Preface

The greenhouse production industry was easier to characterize before World War II than it has been since. That was the era prior to plastic or panel greenhouses, localized heating systems, soil-less root media, root-media pasteurization, automatic watering and fertilization, wide-scale automation, and, in America, the mass market. Much of the drive for these innovations occurred after World War II, when the vast military technology was redirected toward peacetime applications. During the thirty years subsequent to World War II, technological improvements were impressive and steady. When the first edition of this book was published in 1978, a second revolution in production and marketing technology was in its early stages. It gained momentum during the 1980s. The current pace of change is unequaled in any prior era of the greenhouse industry.

A number of factors came together to force this latest revolution. The oil embargo during the early 1970s stimulated worldwide research into energy conservation. These studies began to come to fruition in the late 1970s in the forms of new energy-efficient greenhouse coverings, high-efficiency boilers and heaters, new concepts in floor heating systems, and even in greenhouse designs.

Development of extensive floral production in Africa and eastern Europe put pressure on the western European markets. The untapped potential of the American floral market provided hope for European and Israeli producers faced with their saturated markets and for Latin American nations that lack a large domestic market. New colors and forms of old crops along with new crops, introduced largely through imports but quickly assimilated by domestic producers, have stimulated consumer purchasing. The mass market has come into its own during the past fifteen years to help absorb the increase.

To offset the relatively lower prices brought on by international competition, producers have been forced to seek greater production efficiency. Computers now present in many greenhouses are used to monitor and control the environment. The result is less labor expended, energy savings through more precise control, and the capability to engage in even higher levels of technological development not possible with manual controls. The past ten years have seen the deployment of robotics in greenhouse production. Bench modules of plants move automatically to outside growing areas during the day and back inside at night to a two-tiered arrangement for greater utilization of expensive greenhouse facilities. Bench modules also move automatically along rails from production to packing areas where species and cultivar mixes are mechanically assembled. Machines have recently appeared on the market for transplanting seedlings. Other machines place potted plants at their proper spacing on benches after planting. Later these machines lift and re-space plants as they grow. This is only the beginning of a trend that may ultimately see the exclusion of all human activity from the plant-growing area. Labor stations would be restricted to the service building.

While this change is exciting, it also carries a warning. Change can be beneficial or harmful. The person who can recognize change and prepare for it is invariably the one who benefits because he or she directs change. Many steadfast flower growers will perish in this period of escalating floricultural change, only to be replaced by others with a vision to the future who will find the next years very profitable.

It would be a fallacy to prepare for a career in horticultural production by merely learning how to grow crops. Whether you own your own business or work for someone else, your well-being will depend upon your ability to manage materials, money, and time—both your own and those of others. Without this ability, the application of your technical knowledge of growing crops ultimately will not be profitable and rewarding. You must become knowledgeable in cost accounting, business management, and marketing. Because an appreciation of these areas is not common in the young student entering the floriculture field, this book is written in such a way that these principles are developed and presented in context with cultural instructions.

The outline for this book anticipates the decisions in the order in which they occur for a person entering the floricultural production business. Initially, the decision to enter the field is dealt with in a chapter on the worldwide perspective of floriculture. Decisions involving the physical arrangement of a greenhouse business are taken up in successive chapters considering site selection, greenhouse types, and heating and cooling systems. Considerations then turn toward the type of root media in which the crops are to be grown; pasteurization of the root media; maintenance of disease-free conditions in the greenhouse; watering principles and automated systems; fertilizer formulations and methods of application; alternative systems of production such as NFT, rock wool, and ebb and flow; injection of carbon dioxide gas into the greenhouse atmosphere; light; temperature; chemical growth regulation; pest control; postproduction handling of crops; and cost accounting. These are the main categories of decisions with which you will be faced as you design, build, and operate a greenhouse business.

CHAPTER 1

Floriculture—A Dynamic Industry

Flowers are grown wherever humans have established themselves. In tropical climates, they are grown outdoors, and limited quantities grown by amateurs and businesses alike enter the local sales channels there. The compulsion to purchase floral products is greater in temperate and frigid climates, where natural floral plants are not as abundant and where there is a need to establish ties with nature during the dormant winter season. A few tropical regions have recognized this need and have developed impressive export businesses. In nontropical areas, vast quantities of floral products are produced under protected environments.

The leading centers of production are in the northern countries of Western Europe, Japan, and America (*America* refers to Canada and the United States collectively in this book). Moderate quantities of floral products are produced in the Soviet Union, the Eastern European countries, Australia, and New Zealand. Recently, tropical countries in Central America, as well as the countries of Colombia, Israel, Kenya, and South Africa, have become important production areas, sending most of their products to the markets of Western Europe and America.

ORIGIN OF THE GREENHOUSE INDUSTRY

The greenhouse industry as we know it today probably originated under circumstances similar to those that existed in Holland during its Golden Age, the 1600s.

Figure 1–1

Lilacs were one of the first floral crops grown in The Netherlands, and they are still grown today. (a) Dormant bushes are dug in the late fall and stored. (b) Periodically during the winter, bushes are brought into the greenhouse for forcing.

During the first half of the seventeenth century, The Netherlands became the world's foremost sea power. Its merchant fleet tripled to the point where The Netherlands provided half the world's shipping, and Amsterdam became the world's leading commercial city. The Dutch standard of living was the highest in the world. In 1602, the Dutch East India Company was founded, and in 1621, the Dutch West India Company; both expanded trade throughout a vast colonial empire. Conflict existed also during this period, beginning in 1581 with a declaration of independence from Spain and continuing through the Thirty Years' War (1618–1648), which involved most of Europe. At the culmination of the Thirty Years' War, The Netherlands won its cause and became an independent nation.

The royal courts of Europe at this time had a taste for elegance and the means to afford it. Spring flowers in the winter and fruit out of season were very enticing. The productive capacity of the large middle class and the trade channels of the merchant segment soon gave birth in The Netherlands to what is today the largest greenhouse industry in the world. Grapes were grown along rock walls in western Holland under glass enclosures constructed in a lean-to fashion. These greenhouses conserved the energy of the sun during the winter and permitted early crops of grapes. Today, a vast greenhouse vegetable and cut flower industry exists, with its center in the Westland area, as a direct descendant of this initial business.

In the region near Amsterdam, field-grown lilac bushes were dug in late fall prior to freezing of the ground and were stored outside. Periodically during the winter, bushes were moved into greenhouses where they broke dormancy and flowered (Figure 1–1). The cut blooms graced the palaces of seventeenth-century royalty in Great Britain, France, Germany, and other countries. Even today this industry persists, although much of this region, centered around Aalsmeer, is involved in pot plant culture in general.

AMERICAN DEVELOPMENT

Development of the greenhouse industry in America followed much later because of its dependence on the economic growth of this new land. Greenhouse technology brought in by emigrants from Europe was used to establish an industry that began to flourish during the nineteenth century. Actually, the first reported greenhouse in the United States was that of James Beckman in 1764 located in New York City (Kaplan 1976). Floriculture first started around the population centers of Boston, New York, Philadelphia, and, later, Chicago. In those days, prevailing modes of transportation necessitated production in close proximity to the markets.

As trucks became commonplace in the early part of the twentieth century, transportation posed less of a problem. The populated areas of eastern Massachusetts, Connecticut, and the New York City region, particularly Long Island, became major centers for carnation production. Rose production became especially important in the northeastern urban areas as well as in Chicago. Pot plant production continued to spread across America following population centers.

These trends were shaken during the 1950s. Air transportation had developed to the extent that shipping cut flowers to any point in America was possible. The growing of cut flowers (hereafter referred to as *fresh flowers*) outdoors in warm climates, for shipment to distant markets, became a possibility. Production of cut chrysanthemums expanded at a startling rate in Florida, southern California, and, to a lesser extent, Texas. Crops were (and are still) grown year round under shade fabric supported on inexpensive frames (Figure 1–2). No heating or cooling was required. The increased cost of transportation was more than offset by lower production costs—cheaper growing facilities, no heating expense, and less expensive labor.

The production of *stock* (a cut flower crop of secondary importance) essentially came to a halt in northern greenhouses since nearly all the demand was met by southern California growers (Figure 1–3). Northern chrysanthemum growers feared that they too would soon become a relic of the past. Interestingly, chrysanthemum production in the field reached a plateau during the 1960s and came into balance with the rest of America. The attainment of this position caused many greenhouse growers to turn away from the production of this crop.

Those northern growers who foresaw the trends improved the quality of their product to give themselves a competitive edge over poorer-quality flowers grown during periods of harsh weather conditions in the fields. Particularly in the northern areas, near the ends of the distribution lines from the southern fields, chrysanthemum growers established year-round production schedules to guaran-

Figure 1–2

Large areas of crops, particularly fresh flowers such as this chrysanthemum crop in Florida, are grown outdoors under shade fabric in Florida and California.

tee a steady 52-week supply of flowers. Where it was not possible to meet the competition of southern spray-type chrysanthemums during the winter months, astute growers switched to standard greenhouse-grown chrysanthemums, which at that time did not grow well in the fields.

The equilibrium between field- and greenhouse-grown chrysanthemums was further supported by the lack of control over natural factors in the weather-dependent field environment. Frosts, tropical storms, winds, periods of excessive moisture, and sudden infestations of insects were (and are) all very difficult and sometimes impossible to control in the field. When these forces came into play, the market demands for quantity and quality were not met, and the door was opened for controlled-environment (greenhouse) crops. Roses are a good example of this point. They are particularly prone to powdery mildew disease and spider mites as well as to any adversity in handling. Because of the quality factor, field production of roses as a fresh flower has not developed.

Based on the value of a controlled environment coupled with the need to minimize production costs, a mammoth fresh flower greenhouse industry has developed in California over the past 30 years (Figure 1–4). According to the National Agricultural Statistics Service of the U.S. Department of Agriculture, in 1976 and in 1989, California produced the following percentages of the total number of fresh flowers sold out of 28 leading states in the United States: 52 and

Figure 1–3

Relatively inexpensive field culture, such as this crop of field-grown stock in California, replaced greenhouse crops in the northern states. (*Photo courtesy of* R. A. *Larson, Department of Horticultural Science, North Carolina State University, Raleigh,* NC 27695–7609)

82 percent pompon chrysanthemum, 71 and 82 percent standard chrysanthemum, 69 and 82 percent standard carnation, 46 and 67 percent tea rose, and 30 and 53 percent sweetheart rose. Of the total fresh flowers in the United States, 57 percent was produced in California. These statistics clearly show that the proportion of fresh flowers produced in California has increased steadily to the present. Of all the remaining floral products produced in the United States, 19 percent was produced in California in 1989. This is close to the 23 percent proportion that existed 10 years earlier in 1979. The 28 states from which these statistics were derived accounted for more than 90 percent of the U.S. production.

The predominance of California is due to several factors: Heating costs are low in its mild climate, a large market in the Southwest and the Northwest is available to California, and cultural conditions are favorable. Also of great importance at the time the movement got under way were the favorable airfreight rates to the East. The predominant movement of air cargo in 1950 was westward, resulting in partially empty planes returning eastward. To fill these planes, lower rates were offered for eastward transport. This effectively opened the eastern markets to western growers and at the same time protected the western markets against competition from eastern growers.

It is interesting to compare airfreight rates from San Francisco to Chicago between 1950 and 1990 (see Table 1–1). The influence of these rates on horticultural development in the Southwest is immediately evident. A reduction from \$21.47 per 1,000 cut carnation flowers in 1950 to \$12.65 in 1965 constituted a

Figure 1–4

The past three decades have seen a dynamic expansion in greenhouse-grown fresh flowers in California. (*Photo courtesy of* Hall-Manatee Greenhouses, Encinitas, CA)

strong motivation. Nothing is static in our existence, however, and by 1972 the rate had risen to $15.15. Although not as high as the 1950 rate, this rate was critical because it occurred at a time when imported carnations from Latin America began to constitute serious competition for the San Francisco and Denver production areas. The airfreight rate continued to rise to $20.75 in 1980. This tipped the scale in favor of truck shipment.

Developments in precooling and packaging technology offered a partial solution to the airfare problem by increasing the feasibility of truck shipment. Whereas in 1975 more than 90 percent of fresh flowers was shipped via air from California, in 1980 about 70–80 percent was shipped by truck. During the 1980s, truck rates rose faster than air rates so that today air rates are only modestly higher. Due to the faster shipping time and the impact it can have on flower quality, air shipment once again predominates. In 1990, about 60 percent of fresh flowers were shipped from California to the East via air.

The rapid rise in the fresh flower industry has ended in California. Floral production in total in California is now advancing with the rest of the country. Rising transportation costs and the steady growth in imports of fresh flowers present a formidable challenge to a floral production region that relies so heavily on fresh flower production. Individual firms, as well as the California industry as a

Table 1–1

Airfreight Rates from San Francisco to Chicago*

Year	*Rate*
1950	$21.47
1957	13.03
1965	12.65
1969	13.40
1972	15.15
1980	20.75
1990	25.00

*Per 1,000 cut carnation flowers.

whole, will continue to hold their position as long as (1) quality flowers are produced; (2) the midwestern and eastern markets are properly serviced; and (3) higher levels of production and marketing efficiency are achieved as new technology becomes available. Market servicing includes the guarantee of ample flowers 52 weeks per year and a reasonable spectrum of cultivars, as well as innovations in new species, cultivars, shipping methods, packaging, and so on. It is not likely that fresh flower production will change back from a centralized to a localized status. The main question is, Where will the geographical centers of flower production be in the future?

A very interesting chapter of American floriculture is seen in the carnation industry. Production centers prior to 1950 were located in New England and New York. Through the efforts of forward-thinking individuals like Professor W. D. Holley of Colorado State University, more satisfactory environments were identified that came closer to fitting the requirements of this crop, which calls for 52°F (11°C) night and 75°F (23°C) day temperatures, high light intensity, and a 12-hour daylength. The Denver, Colorado, region offered more temperate summer temperatures and a high light intensity because of its high elevation. From an essentially nonexistent floral industry in 1950, an impressive carnation industry grew, which accounted in 1964 for 23 percent and in 1976 for 26 percent of the number of blooms sold in the leading 27 states.

Carnation production followed quickly in the San Francisco Bay Area. The poorer light intensity of this area was offset by more temperate winter and summer temperatures and a greater availability of labor. Of the total U.S. carnation plants, 44 percent was grown in California in 1964, 69 percent in 1976, and 83 percent in 1981. Development of the California industry had its repercussions in that carnation production in Colorado dropped back to 15 percent of U.S. production by 1981. The phenomenal expansion in Colorado and later in California had a devastating effect upon the eastern production areas.

IMPORTED FLOWERS

The carnation story goes one step further. Two carnation ranges begun in 1966 in Bogotá, Columbia, in South America, produced quality carnations at an incredibly low price. They were joined in 1969 by an American firm, and others followed. Today, there are over 300 firms in the Bogotá area. While about 80 percent of the floral production of the country is around Bogotá, the total area of floral production in the country is 6,700 acres. Greenhouses are primarily covered with polyethylene. Bogotá enjoys a daylength close to 12 hours year round because of its location near the equator. Evening temperatures are in the 40–50°F (4–16°C) range, and day temperatures are in the 60–70°F (16–29°C) range in all seasons. The area offers high light intensity because of its high altitude. All these factors contribute to high-quality flowers. Additionally, the cost of labor is low, and there is no expense for heating because flowers are produced in unheated plastic houses in Colombia (Figure 1–5).

Colombian carnations constituted a modest 0.5 percent of all carnations sold in the U.S. market in 1970, but by the end of 1974 the figure was a stunning 25 percent. While the level waned a bit in 1975 because of a politically motivated shift of emphasis to the European market, it regained its strength in 1976, making up about 29 percent and in 1978, 1979, 1981, and 1988 about 40, 46, 60, and 76 percent, respectively, of total sales. This new competitor has necessitated an increase in efficiency in California and Colorado and, together with these states, has all but annihilated the carnation-growing industry in the rest of the United States. The values of floral exports from Colombia to various countries are presented in Table 1–2. The major market, the United States, received 81.5 percent of Colombia's floral exports in 1987. The amounts of each fresh flower crop exported from Colombia in 1988, expressed as a percentage of the combined value of all flowers exported, are presented in Table 1–3. Carnations are the leading export crop, followed by roses and then by chrysanthemums.

U.S. floral imports are primarily in the fresh flower category. Besides carnations, 71 percent of the pompon chrysanthemums, 38 percent of the standard chrysanthemums, and 34 percent of the roses sold in the United States in 1988 were imported. Countries from which U.S. flower imports originated in 1988 are shown in Table 1–4. The leading source was Colombia, which supplied 61.9 percent of total imports, followed by The Netherlands with 22.4 percent.

The once vast field-production areas of fresh flowers in Florida have nearly disappeared during the past 10 years because of import pressures. Much of the former domestic orchid production has given way to imports from around the world. Several other crops now imported include alstroemeria, freesia, cut lilies, and cut spring-flowering bulb crops from Holland; statice, gypsophila, and daisies from Colombia; protea from tropical regions; and cut palms for floral arrangements from Mexico and Guatemala. All of these crops were produced in sizable quantities in the United States in prior times.

Figure 1–5

Carnation production in the Bogotá area of Colombia, South America.

Table 1–2

Global Distribution of Fresh Flowers Exported from Colombia in 1987 in Terms of U.S. Dollars*

Country	*Value ($ mil)*	*Percent of Total*
United States	141.77	81.5
United Kingdom	8.98	5.2
West Germany	6.17	3.6
Canada	4.05	2.3
Sweden	2.78	1.6
The Netherlands	1.57	0.9
Switzerland	1.43	0.8
Other	7.13	4.1
Total	173.88	100.0

*From *Grower Talks* (1989).

It is worth considering the rose import situation since it has developed more recently. Rose imports for 1975, 1978, 1981, 1984, and 1988 were 1.0, 7.8, 15, 25, and 34 percent, respectively, of domestic U.S. sales in terms of number of blooms. Rose imports lagged behind carnation and chrysanthemum imports because their production requires more sophisticated greenhouse structures, production handling, and marketing. The Latin American industry, in the early stage of development, found it difficult to address these needs. This, however, was a temporary obstacle. The growing conditions in countries such as Colombia are conducive to quality production. Mexico has been the most recent country of sizable potential

Table 1–3

Crop Breakdown of Fresh Flowers Exported from Colombia in 1988 Expressed as a Percentage of Total Fresh Flowers Exported*

Crop	*Percent*
Carnation (standard)	40.1
Rose	20.9
Chrysanthemum (pompon)	18.5
Carnation (miniature)	6.1
Alstroemeria	4.3
Chrysanthemum (standard)	3.0
Gypsophila	2.7
Statice	0.8
Other	3.6

*From *Grower Talks* (1989).

Table 1–4

Sources of Fresh Flowers Imported into the United States in 1988 and Their Quantity in Terms of U.S. Dollars and as a Percentage of Total Imports*

Country	*$ million*	*Percent of Total Imports*
Colombia	175.571	61.9
The Netherlands	63.571	22.4
Mexico	7.275	2.6
Canada	6.110	2.2
Costa Rica	5.936	2.1
Israel	3.907	1.4
Ecuador	3.885	1.4
Thailand	2.798	1.0
Peru	2.762	1.0
France	2.295	0.8
Guatemala	2.111	0.7
Italy	1.268	0.4
Other	6.016	2.1
Total	277.489	100.0

*From Johnson (1990).

to enter the American market. Exports of roses and other fresh flowers are growing rapidly from there.

Flower imports originate primarily from parts of the world along established trade routes. Israel and Africa are the likely origins of floral imports into Western Europe because of the established trade between these two parts of the world. Similarly, North America and South America are logical trade partners. Well-established means of transportation exist along each of these routes. The cost of shipping in these channels is inexpensive relative to shipping between parts of the world in different channels. While there are well-established trade channels between Japan and the United States, as well as Europe and the United States, the United States is not the recipient of significant quantities of floral imports from Japan. The reason is that production and marketing costs do not vary enough between these areas to generate a sufficiently high profit incentive. Labor is expensive in both areas, energy inputs are high, and shipping costs are significant.

The situation is different between America and The Netherlands. What was a moderate flow of floral imports into the United States 10 years ago developed into the second major source of fresh flower imports (Table 1–4). This situation was able to occur in spite of high wages and energy inputs in The Netherlands for several reasons. The auction market system in The Netherlands allows growers to specialize in single or related crops requiring similar facilities, equipment, and temperatures. The numerous types of fresh flowers and potted plants are combined at the auction to offer to the wholesaler the required mix; thus, the grower is left free to focus mainly on production. In America, marketing is an important part of each firm's responsibility; thus, management is more diverse. In America, individual growers commonly grow a wide range of crops to satisfy the wholesalers and retailers they directly service. This further increases the complexity of management and leads to lower production efficiency. Even if an American firm is large by Dutch standards, it may still be unable to automate as extensively as its Dutch counterpart because it is divided into small areas for each crop. Each area requires its own unique form of automation. One exceptional area in America is in the Vancouver region of Canada where the establishment of a very successful flower auction is permitting the same type of crop specialization that is seen in The Netherlands.

The saturated market in Europe has imposed a level of competitiveness that, in turn, has led to a higher level of production automation. The great potential for expanding markets in America will continue to attract floral imports. Those segments of the floral production industry that achieve high production and marketing efficiency and that avail themselves of innovative marketing systems will share in the prosperity—be they American or otherwise.

Fresh flower imports can be combated through pricing. Profit is the difference between production–marketing costs and sales revenue. Increasing profits by raising prices works only in the short run. This attracts foreign imports because it more fully covers their transportation costs. Profits can likewise be increased by reducing production–marketing costs. This is the safest course to be followed by the domestic industry. Price stabilization works a hardship on the foreign producer. Cost reduction is achieved through more efficient management of personnel and the business as a whole, energy conservation, and substitution of capital for labor (automation). (These subjects will be discussed later in this book.)

Cost reduction is not the only way of combating imports. Market servicing is equally important. Maintenance of profits in the marketplace depends on a steady supply of flowers, high-quality flowers, a proper selection of flowers, and new marketing innovations. This last point applies to the rose situation, where there is a need for longer-lasting cultivars. For the mass-marketing channels, smaller flowers are desirable, which opens the door to breeding for higher productivity and new colors and forms.

The demand for fresh flowers continues to increase in the industrialized world. The question remains, Will the demand be met by domestic or foreign producers? The answer lies in the ability to adopt new management, production, and, in particular, marketing technology.

PRODUCTION-AREA DETERMINANTS

From the preceding discussion, it should be obvious that the floral production industry is far from static. Three forces govern its location: (1) cost of produc-

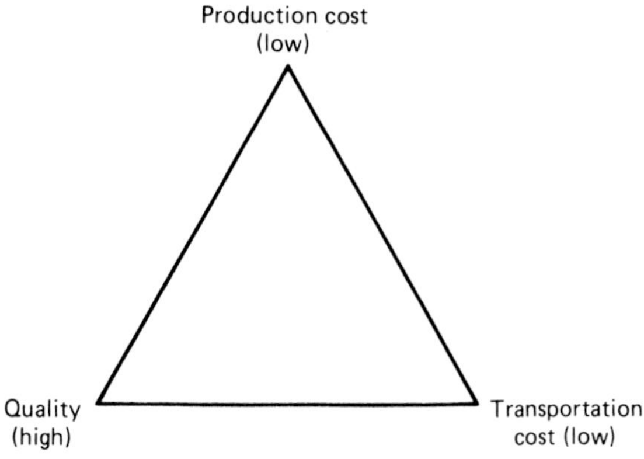

Figure 1–6

Crop-production areas often can be explained on the basis of three factors: production cost, quality, and transportation cost. If all three factors are ideal, then the area is safe from competition. If conditions are less than ideal, as is usually the case, the weakness of any one factor must be offset by the strengthening of one or both of the others in order for the production area to meet outside competition.

tion, (2) quality, and (3) cost of transportation (Figure 1–6). For example, prior to 1950, carnations were grown primarily in the northern states in spite of poor quality achieved during the dark winter months. When long distance transportation became reasonable, carnation production shifted to Colorado, where high quality could be achieved. The shift in chrysanthemum production to the fields of Florida and California was in response to lower costs of production in those areas. The savings in production costs were greater than the added transportation costs; thus, the shift occurred. Field-grown flowers did not completely replace greenhouse-grown flowers because field quality was not consistently high. Colombian production has become a stable situation because production costs are lower than those in Colorado, quality is reasonably high, and transportation costs are modest. Under present technology, it would be very difficult to cause a further shift in carnation production.

Roses continue to be produced in greenhouses because of the quality factor. Any attempts thus far to reduce production costs by abandoning the controlled greenhouse environment have resulted in an unacceptable reduction in quality. Flowering pot plants are produced near their markets because of quality and cost considerations in shipping.

The triangle in Figure 1–6 should be fixed in your mind as you read the rest of this book. It will have a great bearing on the location and greenhouse types you select for your business from Chapter 2 and on the degree of automation and type of production systems you decide upon from the remaining chapters. Keep in mind that a "love of flowers" alone does not justify your business involvement; you must realize a profit as well.

AMERICAN PRODUCTION

An effort is under way to categorize greenhouse crops under the following headings:

1. *Fresh flowers*—flowers that are cut from the plant prior to sale.
2. *Flowering plants*—plants bearing flowers that are sold in a pot.
3. *Green plants*—plants sold in a pot and valued more for their foliage than for their flowers.
4. *Bedding plants*—young plants sold for planting around the home (including vegetable seedlings).
5. *Vegetables*—produce grown to maturity.

Fresh Flowers

Consumer demand for fresh flowers has risen over the past two decades. However, American production has been in decline. The expansion in retail sales has been primarily met by imported flowers. Note in Figure 1–7 that U.S. production of standard carnations dropped for a decade and then held at that low level. Standard and pompon chrysanthemum production remained level for a period after the advent of imports but then for more than a decade fell. Hybrid tea rose production declined through the 1970s but in the 1980s increased.

The pressure of imported chrysanthemums and carnations has reduced the profitability of producing these crops for many growers in America. Consequently, they have switched to the production of potted and bedding plants, where competition is generally localized. Notice in Table 1–5 the significant drop in numbers of growers producing various floral crops in the United States. The increase in domestic rose production has been the result of increased efficiency of production through automation, a switch to a heavier proportion of colors in addition to red, and the adoption of novelty cultivars.

The outlook for fresh flowers in the 1990s is positive. Dutch imports have been comprised primarily of crops either not grown at all or not grown extensively in America. Such crops include alstroemeria, freesia, cut hybrid lilies, ranunculus, gerbera, and liatris. Introduction of these crops to the consuming public has met with success and has cultivated a demand for more of the same and for new flowers. Today, there is a developing market for cut annuals and perennials. Fresh flowers now being grown commercially include the following: *Achillea*, ageratum, aster, alstroemeria, *Aquilegia*, calendula, celosia, carnations from the garden cultivars, *Carthamus*, cosmos, *Craspedia*, delphinium, *Echinacea*, *Eryngium*, *Godetia*, *Gomphrena*, *Kalanchoe*, *Lisianthus*, *Lupinus*, rudbeckia, sedum, *Verbena*, and *Veronica*. The list is not nearly complete. The optimism in such a list lies in the wide range of climatic conditions required for growth. Growers in all regions should be able to find crops in the future well adapted to their conditions.

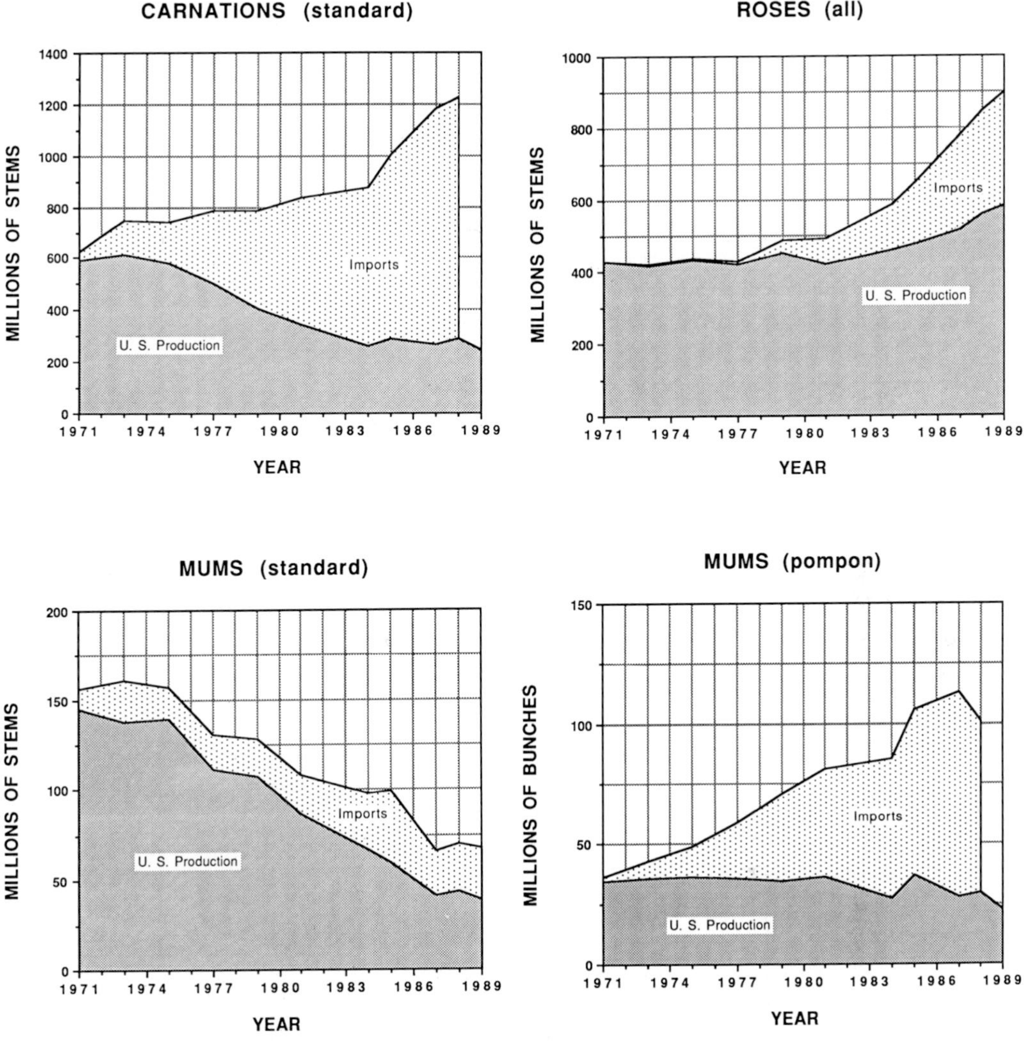

Figure 1–7

Number of blooms, or bunches in the case of pompons, of various fresh flowers produced in and imported into the United States per year from 1971 through 1989. (U.S. *production data are from* Agricultural Statistics Board, USDA, 1972 through 1990. *Import data are from* Johnson 1990.)

Flowering Pot Plants

Notable among the flowering pot plants are pot mums (chrysanthemum, including indoor and garden types), poinsettia, geranium, and lilies (including Easter and hybrid types). The production value of these crops has increased steadily in the United States (Figure 1–8). The market, in recent times, has seen the resur-

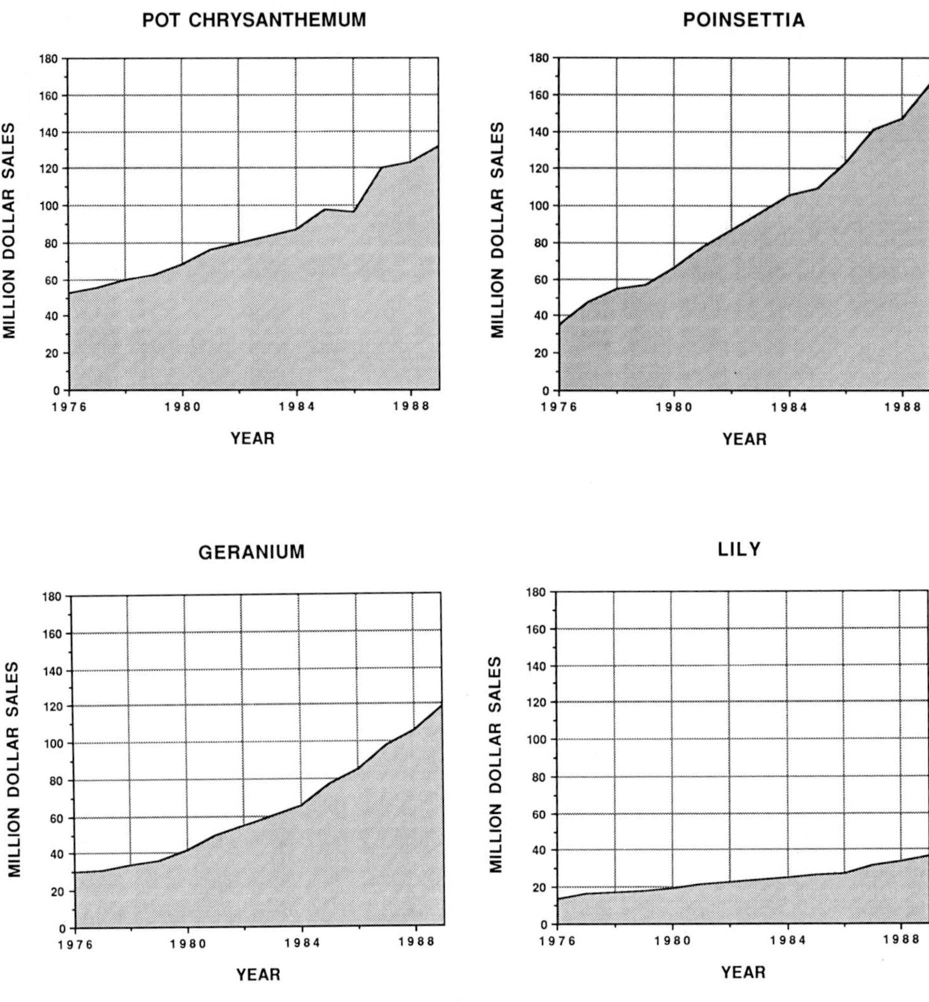

Figure 1–8

Wholesale value of major flowering pot plant crops produced in the United States from 1976 through 1989. (From *Agricultural Statistics Board*, USDA, 1977 *through* 1990)

gence of several flowering plants that lost popularity during the first half of this century. *Kalanchoe, Calceolaria,* cineraria, and *Cyclamen* are some examples. Some new crops have also been introduced, including Rieger begonia, clerodendron, *Exacum,* and *Gerbera*. These crops are not new, however, to Europe, where a much wider variety of plants is grown commercially.

Although the present looks promising for flowering pot plants, there is concern for the future. Quarantines aimed at preventing the influx of disease and insect problems have served to keep the import of pot plants to a minimum. Exemptions from such regulations are being sought by European and Latin American producers. Partly because of the relatively inert, soil-less root media used today, such exemptions will undoubtedly increase. It was possible for fresh flower growers to shift to the vast area of pot plants when import competition occurred. Such fertile fields do not exist for pot plant producers. It is becoming ever more important for American growers to increase their production and marketing efficiency. In short, we are moving steadily toward a single international floriculture industry in which production of each commodity category will go to that group of growers who can best manage costs.

Bedding Plants

Bedding plants are a unique group of plants. Fifty or more plant species are grown, ranging from vegetables such as tomato, eggplant, and cabbage to flowers such as petunia, marigold, and impatiens. These plants are established in small containers, flats, or small pots and are sold for use in home gardens, window boxes, or displays. Sales have increased by over 15 percent per annum since the mid-1970s. The wholesale value of this crop in the United States in 1989 was $867 million, or 36 percent of total floral sales.

The future looks excellent for bedding plants. A significant change in greenhouse technology in this past decade was the production of seedlings in "plugs." In this system, seeds are mechanically sown in flats containing from 268 to more than 600 small cells. One plant is produced in each cell, as opposed to broadcasting seed in an open flat and later digging the seedlings out for transplanting. Customarily, plug seedlings are germinated in ideally controlled growth rooms. From there, the plug flats are moved to the greenhouse, where they remain at a high density for several more weeks depending upon the plant species. Automatic spray booms deliver water and fertilizer, and again conditions are idealized for this second stage of growth. Such plug seedlings may be used by their propagator or sold to smaller firms that cannot afford the equipment and facilities for producing plugs. The highest labor input into bedding plant production is the transplanting of seedlings. Plug seedlings lend themselves to a high level of automation of this step. Flats into which the plug seedlings are to be transplanted can be automatically filled with a root medium and a hole made in each cell to receive a plug. Plug flats move along a conveyor belt to a point where plugs are mechanically removed. At this point, workers transfer the plugs to the depressions in the finishing flats.

Plug technology is revolutionizing the bedding plant industry and greatly aiding those flowering and green pot crops that are propagated from seed. The advantages include lower overhead costs (because the seedlings can be held at high densities for a considerable time), a better chance to establish ideal cultural conditions during the early stages of growth for the purpose of reducing crop time, less transplanting shock, and reduction in sowing and transplanting labor.

As with most technological advancement, the firms that first adopt it are able to translate the advantage into large profits. As the technology is more widely adopted, the savings are passed on to the consumer in terms of lower prices. This stems from those producers who are trying to gain a greater local market share by lowering their prices below their competitors'. After this point is reached, the remaining producers must adopt the technology simply in order to maintain their current profitability. Individuals entering the bedding plant field should study the currently changing plug technology in order to assimilate it into their business.

Green Plants

Green plants, also commonly referred to as *foliage plants,* made up about 20 percent of the U.S. floral production in 1989. They include philodendrons, dracena, ficus, croton, a wide range of hanging basket plants, and many others. The size of this crop was very stable through 1970 with a wholesale value of about $25 million. After that, it exploded to a value of $282 million in 1978 (Figure 1–9). The area in production expanded 308 percent from 1968 through 1978, while the wholesale value increased 968 percent! In 1978, the market began to saturate, prices leveled off, and many marginally efficient producers perished. This stress fostered change through the surviving innovative growers. Attention to quality, acclimatization of plants to better guarantee their survival in the consumer envi-

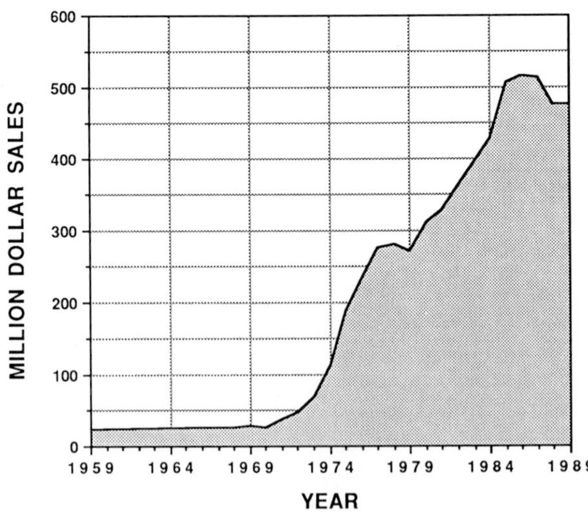

Figure 1–9

Wholesale value of green (foliage) plants produced in the United States from 1959 through 1989. (*From Agricultural Statistics Board,* USDA, 1960 *through* 1990)

Table 1–5

Total Number of Growers Producing Various Floral Crops in the Leading States Accounting for Perhaps 90 Percent or More of the U.S. Production*

	Number of Growers			*Percentage*
Crop	*1971*	*1979*	*1989*	*of Change*
Chrysanthemum, pompon	2,168	999	477	−78
Chrysanthemum, standard	2,134	829	397	−82
Carnation, standard	1,525	418	254	−83
Rose, hybrid tea	323	238	285	−12
Pot chrysanthemum	1,394	1,424	1,090	−22
Green plants	835	1,687	2,094	+151
Bedding plants	—	2,819	4,458	—
Poinsettia	—	1,977	3,069	—

*From Agricultural Statistics Board, USDA (1972, 1980, 1990).

ronment, and sensitivity to the changing desires of the consuming public all led to new increases in demand for the years 1980 through 1985. The wholesale value climbed to $508 million in 1985. In 1986, the green plant industry entered another period of adjustment and has had essentially zero growth since. One contributing factor was the large number of growers who were attracted to this commodity by the former boom period (Table 1–5).

Of the U.S. production of green plants, 58 percent was grown in Florida, 19 percent in California, and 5 percent in Texas in 1989. These are the three leading states in production. Except for hanging basket plants, only a modest number of green plants are grown in other states. Many of these plants are of tropical origin and can be produced more economically in subtropical areas.

Northern areas, where heated greenhouses are required, have found a future in green plants, although it is more modest than that of the subtropical regions. Premium hanging basket plants, being large in volume and cumbersome to handle, are expensive to ship. They are best grown close to their terminal markets. The cost of production of hanging basket plants is low since many of the fixed costs such as greenhouse depreciation and heat are shared with another crop on the benches or ground below. Hanging baskets offer a means for utilizing nearly 100 percent of the equivalent floor space of a greenhouse (Figure 1–10).

Many greenhouse enterprises in temperate regions purchase green plants in the final stage of development from the tropical regions and grow them to larger sizes in their greenhouses until they can sell them to the network of retail outlets they service. Other green plant crops are purchased in various intermediate stages of development and are grown to the finished market stage in the temperate-region greenhouses.

Figure 1–10

The expense involved in producing hanging basket plants is shared with other crops since the baskets occupy space over the walks not formerly used. It is possible to achieve 100 percent utilization of the equivalent floor area of a greenhouse with such a production program.

THE GROWING DEMAND FOR FLORAL PRODUCTS

Anyone who has traveled in Europe is awestruck by the extensive use of flowers. In several European countries, where apartment dwellings abound, the occupants have literally taken to indoor gardening. The apartments are constructed with plants in mind, making use of large windows and deep sills on the sides where light intensity is high. A veritable plant paradise exists within most dwellings. Numerous customs enhance the use of flowers. For example, since it is generally an offense to arrive at the home of a host without a gift, most often a plant or flowers are brought along by guests. Floral products are exchanged regularly between loved ones—in Holland, quite often on a weekly basis. Flowers are a part of daily life—from decoration in a street intersection, a vacant lot, or on a light pole to vases in a wedding coach or on the dashboard of an automobile.

Some would say that Americans do not have the same inclinations for flowers as Europeans do; however, recent years have proven this idea wrong. Dormitories on American campuses abound with plants regardless of whether the occupants are male or female. Flowers and plant sales have made their appearance in drug, food chain, and discount stores from coast to coast. People never before reached have become repeat customers. In short, Americans, given the proper exposure, can be as ardent about floral products as Europeans.

According to the National Agricultural Statistics Service of the U.S. Department of Agriculture, which surveys the industry annually, the wholesale value of floral production in the United States in 1969, 1979, and 1989 was $228, $838, and $2,430 million, respectively. A separate set of figures collected every 10 years by the U.S. Census of Horticultural Specialties traditionally runs about 50 percent higher. This latter census includes all growers in all states. The former organization surveys growers over a specified size and in only 28 states. Increasing the 1989 USDA figure by 50 percent brings the wholesale value of floral production to $3.645 billion. Assuming an average mark-on of 200 percent, the retail value was about $10.9 billion in 1989.

Social changes of many extremes have all been kind to the floral industry. The environmental movement nurtured an awareness of nature and a desire to bring plants into personal lives. The recession of the early half of the 1970s would certainly have been thought to be injurious to the floral industry, as it was to so many others. Instead, diverted from their former expensive pastimes, many people took to gardening, both indoor and outdoor. The oil embargo, while reducing the number of people driving along pleasure routes, swelled the ranks of plant hobbyists. Now, the continued urbanization of America threatens our biological roots and causes people to hold tenaciously to them. These forces have effected the escalation of horticulture courses taught in high schools and in adult education programs.

CHANGING MARKET CHANNELS

The Conventional Florist

Traditionally, Americans have purchased their floral products at full-service retail flower shops. These shops were characterized in the past by nonspontaneous purchases. Eighty-five percent of fresh flower sales went into funeral and wedding orders in the early 1950s. Traditional holiday sales accounted for another heavy proportion of fresh flower and pot plant sales, including such demands as Easter lilies at Easter, poinsettias at Christmas, and roses at Valentine's Day. Apart from the strongly motivated wedding, funeral, and floral holiday customers, routine customers represented only a small percentage of the American public—about 25 percent.

Full-service retail flower shops generally purchase fresh flowers from wholesalers who, in turn, purchase them from the growers. The wholesaler retains an average 25 percent of the wholesale price charged to the retail florist and returns 75 percent to the grower. Flowering pot plants are customarily delivered directly to the retail florist by the grower. The grower does not pay a sales commission, but he or she must meet the expenses of transportation and sales.

The full-service retail florist, in addition to selling floral products, sells service. Fresh flowers are professionally arranged beyond the competence of the average consumer. Pot plants are wrapped in foil and tied with a bow. These products carry the prestige of the flower shop's name. The convenience of home delivery is an important part of the service. Through the services of organizations referred to as *wire houses*, such as *American Floral Services, Florifax, Florists Clearing Network, Florists' Transworld Delivery, Gold Medal Florists, Sears Flowers by Wire*, and *Teleflorist*, a customer is able to telephone a local florist and place an order for flowers or plants that will be arranged and delivered nearly anywhere in the world by a florist in that locality.

Services cost the retail florist dearly in trained personnel and in physical overhead such as buildings and trucks. These costs must be passed on to the consumer. It is not uncommon for floral products to be marked up to a retail price 3 or 4 times the wholesale price paid for them. While this markup may seem exorbitant, it is not. It is fair in light of the overhead expenses of the flower shops and is acceptable to the customers who frequent these outlets. The emotional effect of a gift of flowers sent by a son to his mother some 3,000 miles away on her birthday is very significant. The impact of a florist's van pulling up to the home of a hostess to deliver flowers for an elegant evening gathering is as great as that of the flowers alone.

The Mass Market

Not everyone places emphasis on prestige and service, nor can everyone afford the prices that a full-service florist must charge. As is the case with so many other commodities in American society, methods have been found to increase the availability and decrease the retail price of floral products, making repeat purchases possible for a larger proportion of the American public—the 75 percent of the population who were not reached in the past.

Mass marketing is the sale of floral products in high-traffic locations such as supermarkets, large discount stores, shopping malls, busy street corners, airport terminals, and so on (Figure 1–11). The objective is a high-volume business. Since purchases are usually spontaneous, prices must be sufficiently low to attract a customer's discretionary dollars (money remaining after the necessities of life are purchased). Thus, costly services such as floral arranging and delivery are avoided. Such business is generally cash-and-carry.

Floral mass marketing was developed long ago in Europe, where it is now highly perfected. It has only begun to develop in the past 25 years in the United States. The potential of mass marketing, however, was recognized well before that time. The results of the Northeast Regional Marketing Project NEM–8 conducted in the 1950s (Zawadzki et al. 1960) indicated optimistic prospects for mass marketing of fresh flowers through nonfloral outlets regularly patronized by consumers. Initial development was slow, partly because of the initiative and re-

Figure 1–11

This street-side outlet for fresh flowers in San Francisco is one of the forms mass marketing has taken in recent years. Others include no-service cash-and-carry shops in supermarkets, airports, and shopping malls. (*Photo courtesy of* J. C. *Raulston, Department of Horticultural Science, North Carolina State University, Raleigh,* NC 27695–7609)

sources needed to bring about such a change in production and marketing and partly because of resistance within the industry. Many conventional florists in the 1950s and 1960s boycotted growers who sold in the mass-marketing channels. Taken at face value, mass marketing appeared as a great threat to the continued existence of the conventional florist market system. Lower prices and high volume struck a chord of fear in spite of optimistic predictions coming out of market studies. Such studies indicated that flowers purchased from mass-marketing outlets would be for a different purpose than those purchased through the already established florists' outlets. These studies further indicated that mass-marketing sales would help to create a greater appreciation and desire for flowers in America and thereby enhance sales in the conventional florists' channel.

About half of the current 30,400 supermarkets in the United States have a floral department. The value of retail sales in 1989 was $1.6 billion. This is about 16 percent of the total retail floral sales in the United States and an increase from the 14 percent held in 1986. The outlook is very optimistic for the expansion of mass marketing in the future. A current trend within supermarkets is to offer more services. Thirty-one percent of supermarket chains offer custom arrangements. Twenty-five percent of floral departments now have a full-time designer. Retail prices are typically 1.5–2 times the wholesale price. This is a highly profitable margin for these stores. The sales breakdown includes 30 percent fresh flowers, up from 20 percent in 1982; 53 percent flowering plus green plants; and 17 percent made up by bedding plants, dried flowers, silk flowers, and supplies.

In addition to supermarkets, there are many other categories of mass-marketing outlets including discount stores, department stores, and plant boutique shops located in the middle of shopping malls, in airport lobbies, and on carts along the side of city streets. Some estimate that about 60 percent of the number of units of green plants, flowering pot plants, and bedding plants move through the mass market, while perhaps 30 percent of fresh flowers are sold through this channel. The proportion of the value of these products moving through the mass market is much smaller than the proportion of units since unit prices are lower in the mass market than in the specialized retail market channel.

The interesting point is that the industry is not bound by traditionalism. New customers are purchasing new crops, are accepting new colors, forms, and sizes, and are eager to do so through new outlets. As a grower or a marketer, you are free to set your imagination to work, and your chances of success are great. Your objective might be to produce shorter-stem flowers in less time at a lower cost. Or, you might choose to produce the many species of plants, including garden flowers and wild flowers, as mentioned earlier, that could be grown outside and in greenhouses. The field is wide open for the breeding of new cultivars. Rather than growing large premium flowers, your goal could be producing numerous smaller flowers per plant in shorter time. In the mass market, consumers are not tradition bound; thus, a wide range of plant species, colors, and forms could be appropriate for this market. Popular music, clothing styles, and entertainment are constantly changing to maintain sales. Why not flowers? Flowers can be geared to meet the needs of holidays, personal events, social and political occurrences, and any other mood of the times.

The overall expansion of floral sales has been educational to the public, showing them ways to enhance their personal lives. It has generated yet other uses for floral products and will continue to do so. For example, an interesting business in recent times is that of interior plantscaping, an enterprise involved partly in growing and partly in merchandising. Such firms decorate commercial buildings, malls, and so on, providing plants on a contract basis. As these plants are returned to greenhouses for rejuvenation, new plants take their place.

FUTURE DIRECTION OF PRODUCTION

Increased Production and a Lower Sales Price at a Reasonable Profit

The future holds much optimism for American production. The market will continue to expand rapidly, bringing an even greater demand for floral production. Systems are currently available that will lend efficiency to production and postproduction handling to ensure America's place in production and at the same time guarantee a respectable profit. Three factors attest to this potential.

1. *Advertising can be more fully exploited.* The Society of American Florists (SAF), serving as a parent organization to all segments of the industry, including growing, transportation, wholesaling, and retailing, has made great efforts through the American Florists' Marketing Council (AFMC) to collect voluntary contributions from all segments for the purpose of promoting floral products nationally. The wire services and full-service florists have allocated funds for promotion. But, when one takes into consideration the whole floral industry in America, probably less than 1 percent of the retail value is spent on promotion. No other viable industry would attempt to promote itself on such a weak basis. More must be done nationally. Fortunately, this need is recognized and is being pursued. Undoubtedly, the market of floral products will expand even more rapidly and bring with it a tremendous opportunity for growers.

2. *Production efficiency can be improved.* Current production is profitable but is still not highly efficient. Systems exist for further increasing efficiency and profit. Inefficient greenhouse ranges composed of several freestanding small greenhouses that cannot be properly automated or managed are giving way to newer, reasonably priced ridge-and-furrow designs. The new designs take advantage of the many systems of automation discussed in this book. Systems for growing pot plants on movable benches, which serve also as the internal transport system in the greenhouse, permit more efficient handling of plants and a growing area of 95 percent or more rather than the traditional 67 percent of the heated greenhouse area. Thermal blankets and high-efficiency heaters can reduce energy costs. Computerized environmental control can further reduce energy costs and improve yield. Finally and perhaps most importantly, the motivating mentality, a love for plants, which has accounted for many floral growers, is now expanding to include the satisfaction of sound business management.

3. *Postproduction handling of floral crops has considerable room for improvement.* A study sponsored by Ohio State University (Staby et al. 1976) examined handling of fresh flowers, particularly after harvest. The findings were that 5 percent of fresh flower crops were not harvested and that 20 percent of those flowers that were harvested ended up unsuitable for final sale. Technology exists to reduce this level significantly.

Great horizons exist for the prepackaging of floral products, which would improve sales and increase shelf life. Pot plants in transparent packages can continue to receive light while remaining in a moist atmosphere where they are not injured by drying and do not require watering during the normal period of sales. The package itself can carry information for the consumer, including instructions for the care of the plant, along with further enticement to purchase the product.

Fresh flowers sell much better in the mass-marketing outlets when a picture of flowers is offered and a stem of greenery is included. When the package is opened, one has an instant bouquet. Packaging of such combinations permits handling by the customer in self-service outlets and affords a place to present a brand name, information, and price. A stated price and accessibility to the customer are important sales incentives.

Competition from other parts of the world will continue to grow as political and geographical boundaries continue to dissolve. More and more, the world moves toward the model situation described by the Dutch Nobel Prize winner Jan Tinbergen in 1969, which calls for production of each product in the location and by the society in which it can be produced the most efficiently at the required quality level. This competition will be the driving force to bring about efficiency in production and marketing in America. Many growers who are unable to accept change will perish while the others will prosper. Numerous large nonhorticultural firms can be expected to enter the industry, bringing with them sound principles of management and marketing in order to develop and enjoy the great profit potential that exists.

Profile of Future Growers

What form will production take from here on? This question is perhaps easiest to answer by discussing (1) production for full-service florists' shops, (2) production for the mass market, and (3) new production businesses.

Production for full-service florists' shops will continue in its current trends. Fresh flowers will be produced for the most part in specific areas where satisfactory quality can be achieved at a low production cost. American production will continue to have competition and will depend upon increased efficiency of production and postproduction handling as well as new crops.

Flowering pot plant production for full-service retail florists' shops will remain for a while near the markets throughout America. The high costs of transportation for heavy pot plants and the need for a controlled environment to produce the quality level required for these outlets necessitate proximity to market channels.

Green plants of tropical origin are all adapted to our subtropical field conditions and can be produced cheaply and at high quality in these regions. Increased competition will come from other subtropical and tropical countries. The key to success here will lie in freedom from diseases and insects, a high level of quality, and plants that have gone through a special period of acclimatization to the low-light, slow-growth conditions they will face in the consumer environment. Such plants will offer a greater assurance of success to the consumer, thus encouraging success in the marketplace. New types of plants and sizes will be needed to meet the desires of the various groups of consumers.

The second category of production, production for the mass market, comprises better than half of our floral output now. Eventually, it will probably encompass 80 percent of total production. This increase will not be achieved at the expense of retail florists' outlets since their sales will continue to rise as the population expands and the economy improves. The increase in production for the mass market will be supported by the large segments of our public who have not before been steady floral customers.

Fresh flower production for the mass market will change toward shorter stems and a wider variety of species as already listed. The most important aspects of this production will be (1) a steady year-round supply of fresh flowers of high keeping quality, (2) the capability to expand production for periods of peak demand, (3) modest prices, and (4) special prepackaging to extend shelf life.

Potted plant production for the mass market also will deviate from that for retail florists' shops. A much wider range of crops will be grown. Many crops important in Europe will be developed in America. The mass-marketing chains will encourage the growth of large greenhouse production ranges that can fill the contract for a large number of outlets. The large ranges, in turn, will be able to produce efficiently and sell at a low price. This evolution will make it difficult for small growers to produce the major pot plant crops unless they are producing exceptional quality and an unusual size of the product or can provide delivery to rather remote outlets.

The third category of production involves the new production businesses. Today, the greatest opportunity to enter floral production lies in pot plant crops. The return per square foot is generally too low for fresh flowers to justify a small range. Bedding plants afford a particularly good avenue for entry. This crop is labor intensive, but the labor can be provided by the person starting the business while it is still small. Two crops or more can be turned over within the season of January through May in some parts of the country to bring in income before the season ends. At the same time, the initial cash outlay is not great. Cold frames can be used later in the season to supplement the greenhouse and bring the overhead costs down, but they require more labor and are seldom used in northern areas.

When pot plant production becomes more efficient in the future, it may become difficult to enter the business by growing any of the major crops. The margin of profit will be too low for a small range to compete when it is unable to hold the cost of production down through automation. Such a producer will find opportunity in the low-demand specialty crops. Since the production of these crops will not have been worked out on a production-line basis, the margin of profit will be respectable for smaller, less automated growers. New crop introductions and plants with regional appeal will fit this category. Labor-intensive crops will be a good possibility as well. Such crops are difficult to mass-produce. Terrarium plants, for instance, involve numerous types of plants, each with a different cultural program. The volume of any one is not great.

Becoming a combination grower–retailer will provide a beginner with an avenue of entry into the floral production business. This is actually two separate businesses, and eventually, as they grow, they should be treated as such to determine where the profits lie. At the beginning, however, this combination can provide the profits necessary to keep going. Most people have a natural inclination to browse about in greenhouses and pick their own plants. Even in a small town, there are sufficient customers to support such a business. After a period of time, the volume of sales could become large enough to profitably enter the wholesale market channel.

YOUR PROSPECTS IN FLORAL PRODUCTION

The situation today and prospects for tomorrow indicate that now is a good time to be in the floral business. The continual growth of traditional markets and the potential of the still unrealized mass market present an enticing profit picture for the future.

It cannot be emphasized too strongly that a technical knowledge in floriculture is only half of what it takes to succeed in the floral production business. You must become equally well versed in principles of business management and marketing. While the foundation for this education lies in formal courses, ideally it will be built upon by an educational process that you will maintain throughout your career. You can do this by reading books on the subject, by subscribing to business periodicals, and most importantly, by establishing communications with people in other phases of the floral industry. Knowledge of the responsibilities of these people is your responsibility, even though you are not directly involved in their work. In addition to attending your local flower growers' association's meetings and short courses, you should become accustomed to participating in conferences held by floral associations representing other areas such as transportation, wholesaling, and retailing. The Society of American Florists is such an organization.

No knowledge is of value unless there is a human mind to assemble it into a plan and a spirit to activate it. If you feel a glow when you handle a plant, or a thrill when you walk into a greenhouse, then you are in the right field of endeavor. Make up your mind now that this is your field and that you will succeed. Do not waste further energy doubting yourself. Invest your efforts in learning how to succeed and in formulating a plan. Sit down now and write on paper what it is you want to achieve in life. This book will take you through many of the decisions you face ahead. As you study the facts, reflect on how they can fit into your plan. Seek further knowledge to fill in your plan by perusing the references listed at the end of each chapter, by attending local growers' short courses, by establishing a relationship with commercial people, and, best of all, by taking a job in the area of your choice—perhaps part time during your school year or during the summer. Sooner or later, you must gain practical experience to supplement your book learning if you are going to be able to apply it. It is not your background or your current aptitude that will bring you success but rather your knowledge of what you want out of life, your belief in yourself, and the persistent effort you are willing to put forth to achieve your goal.

REFERENCES

1. Agricultural Statistics Board. 1990. Floriculture crops, 1989 summary. Natl. Agr. Statistics Ser. Sp. Cir. 6–1 (90). USDA, Washington, D.C. (Available annually except in 1983 and 1984.)
2. Ball, V. 1976. Early American horticulture. *Grower Talks* 40 (3):1–56.
3. ______. 1980. Trends. *Grower Talks* 44 (5):1–19.
4. ______. 1985. *The Ball Red Book,* 14th ed. Reston, VA: Reston Publishing.
5. Johnson, D. C. 1990. Floricultural and environmental horticulture products: A production and marketing statistical review: 1960–88, Commodity Economics Div., Economic Res. Ser., USDA, Statistical Bul. No. 817.
6. Kaplan, P. 1976. Origins of commercial floriculture in U.S. found to predate Declaration of Independence. *Florist* 10 (2):39–46.
7. Kiplinger, D. C., and R. W. Sherman. 1962. Florist crops for mass market outlets. Ohio Agr. Exp. Sta. Res. Bul. 928.
8. Miller, R. 1989. From Bogota to Miami, Colombian cut flowers continue to rise. *Grower Talks* 53 (6):32, 34, 36–38.
9. Robertson, J., B. Behe, S. Born, P. Holness, T. Prince, and B. Raudsep. 1984. 1984 foliage market survey. *Florists' Review* 174 (4512):38, 41–44, 46.
10. Staby, G. L., J. L. Robertson, D. C. Kiplinger, and C. A. Connover. 1976. *Proc. National Floricultural Conference on Commodity Handling.* Ohio Florists' Assoc., 2001 Fyffe Ct., Columbus, OH 43210.
11. Voigt, A. O. 1984. The shop, the nation, and the consumer. *Florists' Review* 174 (4502):30–32.
12. Zawadzki, M. I., W. E. Larmie, and A. L. Owens. 1960. Selling flowers in supermarkets. Univ. of Rhode Island Agr. Exp. Sta. Bul. 355.

CHAPTER 2

Greenhouse Construction

The term *greenhouse* refers in the United States to a structure covered with a transparent material for the purpose of admitting natural light for plant growth. The structure is usually heated artificially and differs from other growing structures, such as cold frames and hotbeds, in that it is sufficiently high to permit a person to work from within. The European definition of a greenhouse differs in that it refers to a structure that receives little or no artificial heat. The term *glasshouse* is used in Europe to refer to an artificially heated structure. Quite frequently, two or more greenhouses in one location are referred to as a *greenhouse range*. A building associated with the greenhouses that is used for storage or for operations in support of growing of plants but that is not itself used for growing plants is referred to as a *headhouse* or *service building*. Greenhouses are to be found in many designs including the conventional A-shaped, Quonset, and gutter-connected types. The transparent coverings are as varied as the designs. Originally, glass was used, but now film plastics, fiberglass-reinforced plastic (FRP), acrylic panels, and polycarbonate panels are used as well. The future holds promise of new covering materials that will reduce the burden of heating and cooling and also of new frame designs that will be more economical.

LOCATION

The first consideration in establishing a greenhouse range is that of location. Several factors to be considered follow.

Room for Expansion

A parcel of land larger than the immediate needs should be acquired. The ultimate size of the range should be predicted. Area should then be added to this predicted figure to accommodate service buildings, storage, and access drives. (Doubling the area covered by greenhouses would constitute a bare minimum.) Finally, extra space should be allotted to cover unforeseen needs. For instance, it may become necessary to engage in stockpiling of supplies as fostered by shortages of materials, or the future may call for holding ponds for water effluent from the range in order to reduce the nutrient content before releasing it into streams or the groundwater table.

The floor area of service buildings required for small firms is equal to about 13 percent of the greenhouse floor area. This requirement diminishes with increasing firm size to an area equal to 7.5 percent of the growing area for large firms with 400,000 square feet (ft^2) (37,000 m^2) of area. On the average, service buildings are equal to 10 percent of the growing area (Brumfield et al. 1981).

Topography

The building site should be as level as possible to reduce the cost of grading. A level site permits the construction of large greenhouse blocks that can be easily automated. The site should be well drained. Because of the extensive use of water in greenhouse operations, providing a drainage system is always advisable. Where drainage is a problem, it is wise to install tiles below the surface prior to constructing the greenhouses. It is also advisable to select a site with a natural windbreak, such as a tree line or hill, on the north and northwest sides. In regions where snow is expected, trees should be 100 feet (30 m) away in order to keep drifts back from the greenhouses. To prevent shadows on the crop, trees located on the east, south, or west sides should be set back a distance of 2.5 times their height.

Land-Use Prediction

Local zoning and tax laws are subject to changes brought on by development pressures. Such changes have brought about the termination of many greenhouse businesses, as witnessed by the extensive disbandment of the once vast greenhouse industry immediately east of New York City. The past development of the location in question should be carefully studied in order to assess its future direction. Some local governments classify greenhouses as agricultural businesses to protect them from prohibitive property taxation due to zoning shifts. Others, in order to change the occupants within a zone, have denied expansion permits to floral production businesses.

Climate

As indicated earlier, climatic conditions have dictated worldwide geographical shifts in horticulture. Such forces are also at work within local regions. Areas where there is frequent fog or inclement weather or shadows from the north slope of tall mountains are poor for crops in general. The better light intensity of higher altitudes is particularly advantageous for carnation and rose crops but has little benefit for crops with a requirement for low light intensity such as African violet, begonia, gloxinia, and most green plants. The greenhouse site should be selected with specific crops in mind. The greenhouses of one carnation range that was forced to terminate operations on Long Island, New York, were disassembled and trucked to carefully selected high elevation sites in the Appalachian Mountains in the southeastern United States and then reconstructed. These sites were located well above the customary morning fog layer of this region and enjoyed high light intensity and cool summer temperatures—conditions ideal for carnation growth. Subsequent production records testified to the successful selection of these sites.

Labor Supply

Present and future labor needs should be assessed and should be in accord with the labor supply of the area. Procurement of a labor supply has been a perennial problem in the horticulture industry. While the solution has appeared to rest in locating close to an urban area, this does bring on a problem of wage level. Traditionally, greenhouse wages have been low, which has given the labor recruitment advantage to the more technologically advanced industries. The solution appears to lie in meeting the competition directly through higher wages. Higher wages can be compensated through automation, which reduces the number of employees but increases the productivity of each.

Accessibility

A site should be selected where shipping routes are easily accessible. Marketing of floral crops costs approximately one-quarter of the gross wholesale return. Minimization of shipping costs by close proximity to markets for the earlier stages of business development as well as to long-distance shipping routes such as bus, truck, or air terminals for the later and more successful stages of development will go a long way toward alleviating this burden. At the same time, local carrier costs for goods received will be reduced.

Site location is often the deciding factor in the type of fuel used. In some regions, natural gas is a cheaper source of energy than other fuels. Some greenhouse ranges are able to take advantage of this factor because their location is at a prohibitive distance from the gas line, while the competition located near the line can enjoy this advantage. In one situation where a greenhouse range was built at a high altitude to take advantage of light conditions, the remoteness of the location necessitated the transfer of oil from large tank trucks to smaller trucks during delivery, thus raising the cost of the oil.

Water

Water is one of the most frequently overlooked commodities in the establishment of a greenhouse business. Before a site is purchased, the available water source should be tested for quality (see Chapter 7) and quantity. There are several cases where businesses located in coastal and riverbed regions have been compelled to move to new locations to obtain water of suitable quality. The cost of removing ions such as sodium, chloride, and bicarbonate can be prohibitive, but failure to do so results in plant injury. Water quantity is equally important since as much as 2 quarts of water can be applied to 1 ft^2 (20 l/m^2) of growing area in a single application. Well water is the desired source since municipal water is often too costly and may contain harmful fluoride (as discussed in the "Water Quality" section of Chapter 7). Pond or river water is subject to disease organisms and may require expensive chlorination.

Orientation

Shadows are cast by the greenhouse frame. The magnitude of the shadows depends upon the angle of the sun and thus upon the season of the year. The effect can be most detrimental to growth in the winter when light is often limited.

Single greenhouses located above 40°N latitude in the Northern Hemisphere should be built with the ridge running east to west so that low-angle light of the winter sun can enter along a side rather than from an end where it would be blocked by the frame trusses. Below 40°N latitude, the ridge of single greenhouses should be oriented from north to south since the angle of the sun is much higher. Ridge-and-furrow greenhouses (greenhouses connected to one another along their length) at all latitudes should be oriented north to south in order to compensate for a shadow that occurs from the north roof and gutter of each adjacent greenhouse. The north–south orientation permits this shadow to move across the floor during the day, whereas the east-west orientation does not.

L. G. Morris made the calculations presented in Table 2–1 in England at a latitude of about 50°N. They leave little doubt that the ridge of a single greenhouse should run from east to west. The difference in light intensity due to orientation is not great during the summer, when the angle of the sun is large. A difference shows up in the winter, when light is an important issue.

Table 2–1

Effect of Greenhouse Orientation on Light Transmission in the Midsummer and Midwinter at a Latitude of Approximately 50°N

	Percent Transmission	
Orientation	*Midsummer*	*Midwinter*
N–S	64	48
E–W	66	71

FLOOR PLAN

It is important to develop a greenhouse floor plan that allows for more future expansion than will likely occur. This consideration best ensures that an efficient operation will always be possible. If there is a slope to the land, construction should begin at the midpoint (average elevation). In this way, the soil excavated will provide the fill needed during each expansion. In the end, there will be one final elevation for the entire greenhouse range. A plan, as pictured in Figure 2–1,

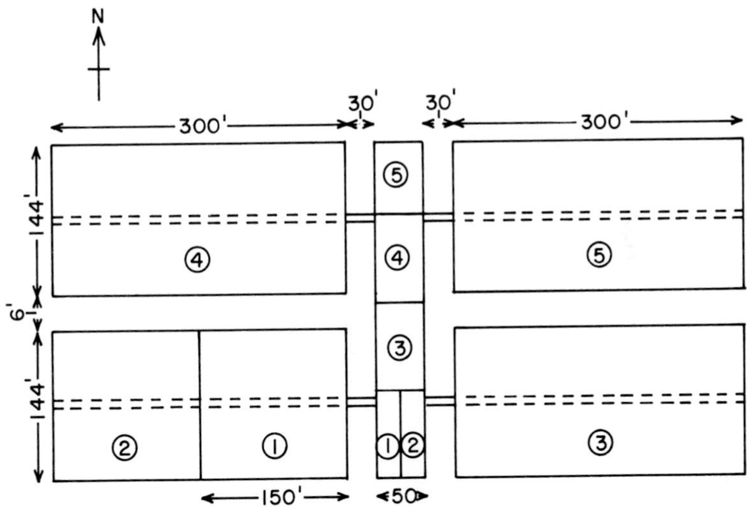

Figure 2–1

This floor plan for a greenhouse firm allows for construction in five phases. The design employs a single, central service building. Building phases are numbered consecutively. The adjacent greenhouse or service building walls between each building phase are removed. Greenhouses are separated from the service building by transparent corridors 30 feet (9 m) long to prevent shadows in the growing area.

allows for the addition of service buildings and greenhouses without removal of previous buildings or the accumulation of multiple service buildings. The service building is centrally located in a nearly square design, which minimizes distances that plants and materials need to be moved. The whole firm is on one elevation and is internally connected so that an internal transport system can be used.

Doors between the service building and the greenhouse should be 10 feet (3 m) wide by 9 feet (2.7 m) high. The drive through the corridor and greenhouse should be 8 feet (2.4 m) wide to accommodate internal transport systems such as tractors. It would be well to have the greenhouse gutters 10 feet (3 m) or higher above the floor to accommodate automation and thermal blankets and still leave room for vehicles. The greenhouse gutters need to be oriented north to south. A greenhouse block length (gutter length) of 144 feet (44 m) coincides well with the most common standard gutter unit length of 12 feet (3.7 m) and the maximum effective summer cooling distance of approximately 150 feet (46 m). The service building should have 16 foot (4.9 m) eaves to allow for doors 12 feet (3.7 m) wide by 14 feet (4.2 m) high needed to accommodate trailer trucks for both receipt of goods and shipping of plants. All plant loading should be carried out from a central point inside the service building.

GLASS GREENHOUSES

Only glass greenhouses existed prior to 1950. They are one of the more expensive types today. Although such structures have been known to last 100 years and longer with proper maintenance, their average cost per year is still more than that of film plastic greenhouses because of fuel costs.

Several styles of glass greenhouses are designed to meet specific needs. A *lean-to* design is used when a greenhouse is placed against the side of an existing building (Figure 2–2a). This design makes best use of sunlight and minimizes the requirements for roof supports. An *even-span* greenhouse is one in which the two roof slopes are of equal pitch and width (Figure 2–2b). By comparison, an *uneven-span* greenhouse has roofs of unequal width, which make the structure adaptable to the side of a hill (Figure 2–2c). This style is seldom used today because such greenhouses are not adaptable to automation. Individual greenhouses standing free of one another are well adapted to cold climates since snow easily slides from their roofs.

A *ridge-and-furrow* design refers to two or more A-frame greenhouses connected to one another along the length of the eave (Figure 2–2d). The eave serves as a furrow or gutter to carry rain and melted snow away. The side wall is eliminated between greenhouses, which results in a structure with a single large interior. Consolidation of interior space reduces labor, lowers the cost of automation, improves personnel management, and reduces fuel consumption because there is less exposed wall area through which heat can escape. The snow load must be

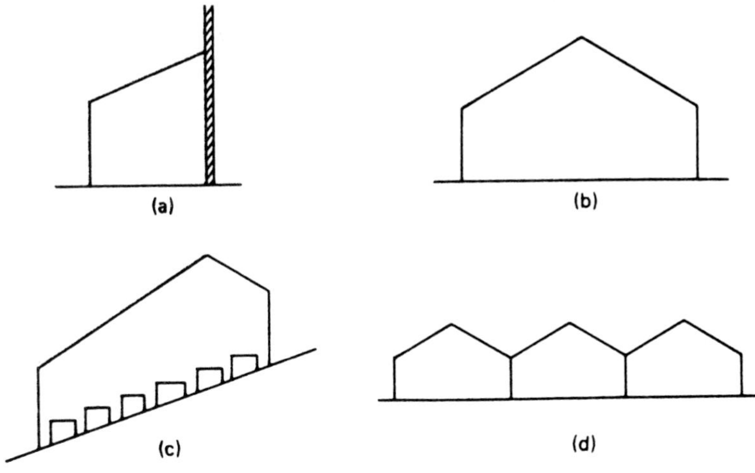

Figure 2–2

Four basic greenhouse styles: (a) lean-to, (b) even-span, (c) uneven-span, and (d) ridge-and-furrow.

taken into account in the frame specifications of these greenhouses. Snow cannot slide off the roofs, as in the case of individual freestanding greenhouses, but must melt away. Heating pipes are generally located beneath the gutters for this purpose. In spite of snow loads, ridge-and-furrow greenhouses are effectively used in the northern countries of Europe and in Canada.

Basically, three frame types have been used with various combinations of these greenhouses. *Wood frames* were used for greenhouses under 20 feet (6 m) in width. Side posts and columns were constructed of wood without the use of a truss. Wider houses required sturdier frames. *Pipe frames* served well for greenhouses up to a width of about 40 feet (12 m) (Figure 2–3a). The side posts, columns, cross ties, and purlins were constructed from pipe. Again, a truss was not used. The pipe components did not all interconnect but depended on attachment to the sash bars for support. Some greenhouses under 50 feet (15 m) in width and most over this width were and are built on *truss frames* (Figures 2–3b, 2–4). Flat steel, tubular steel, or angle iron are welded together to form a truss encompassing the rafters, chords, and struts. Struts are support members under compression, while chords are support members under tension. Angle-iron purlins running the length of the greenhouse are bolted to each truss. The frame thus constructed can stand without support of sash bars. Columns are used only in very wide truss-frame houses of about 70 feet (21 m) and wider.

Today, glass greenhouses are primarily of the truss-frame type. Truss-frame greenhouses are best suited to prefabrication, which has made the construction of greenhouses more economical over the years. Automation has also fostered wider houses, which require the strength of truss frames.

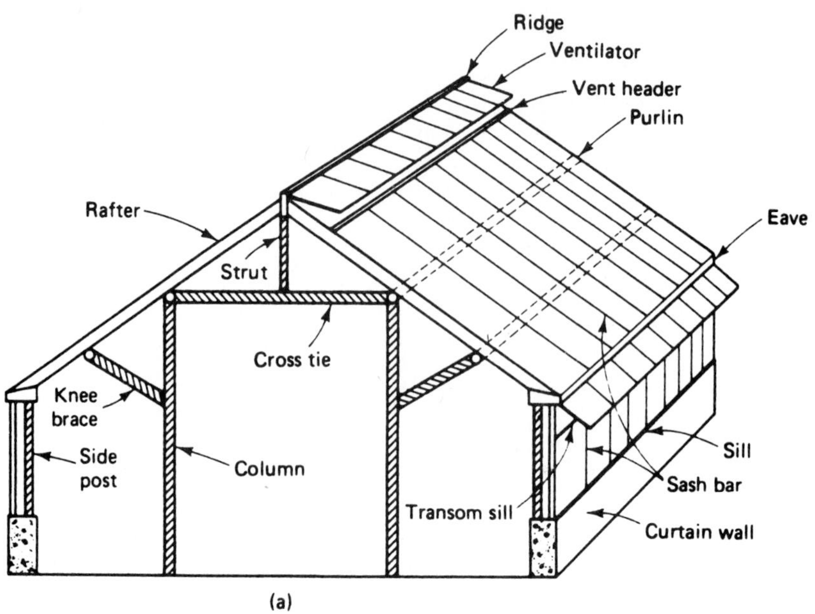

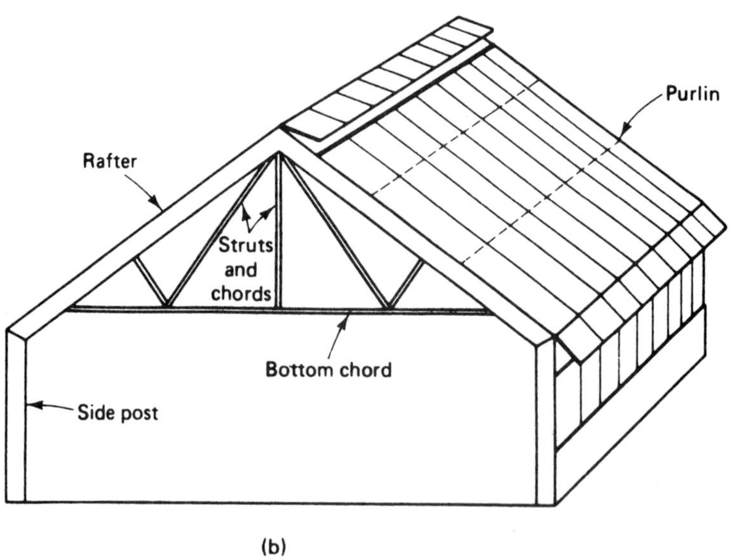

Figure 2–3

Structural components of (a) a pipe-frame greenhouse and (b) a truss-frame greenhouse. In the house in part (b), the side posts, rafter, chords, and struts are one unit known as a *truss*.

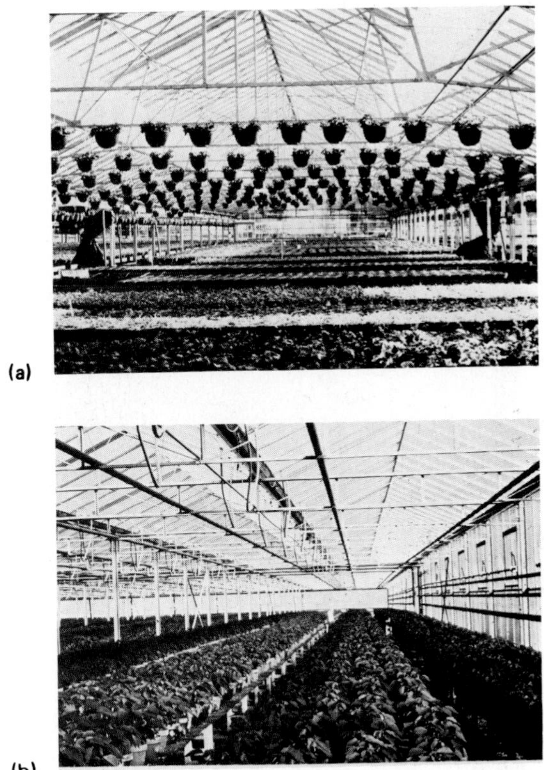

Figure 2–4

(a) A high-profile, ridge-and-furrow, truss-frame greenhouse. (b) A low-profile, truss-frame greenhouse.

The glass on the greenhouse is attached to sash bars. In earlier days, sash bars were made exclusively of wood, primarily cypress and redwood. Wood required periodic painting to protect it against rot. Ideally, exteriors were painted every two years and interiors every five to seven years. This practice was costly. Aluminum sash bars and ventilators were introduced in the early 1950s. The resultant all-metal greenhouses were very expensive at the outset but quickly became competitive with houses having wooden sash bars. All-metal greenhouses proved cheaper to maintain since they required no painting. Virtually all glass greenhouse construction is of the metal type today.

Application was also found for aluminum on greenhouses with wooden sash bars. Aluminum barcaps were developed that covered the portion of the sash bar exterior to the glass, thus eliminating most of the exterior painting needs (Figure 2–5). A considerable effort was required to cover a greenhouse with barcaps, but the advantages made it well worthwhile. Prior to the use of barcaps, panes of glass

Figure 2–5

Aluminum barcaps are installed on wooden sash bars to protect them from the elements and eliminate the need for painting. Shading compound on the glass reduces the interior light intensity during the summer.

were usually installed in a staggered rather than in a parallel fashion to increase greenhouse strength. Since the lower end of each barcap is crimped downward to hold the lower edge of the glass panes on either side of the sash bar from sliding, the glass must now be in parallel rows and only full panes can be used. It has been necessary to reglaze many greenhouses prior to installing barcaps.

The structural members of the greenhouse cast shadows that reduce plant growth during the dark months of the year. Aluminum sash bars can be made stronger than wooden ones, and thus wider panes of glass can be used with the aluminum bars.

The original 16 inch (41 cm) width of glass has evolved over the years to widths of 20 inches (51 cm), 24 inches (61 cm), 29 inches (73 cm), 36 inches (91 cm), and 39 inches (1 m), a width that is now available in Europe. The original length of 18 inches (46 cm) is now commonly 30 or 36 inches (76 or 91 cm) but can range up to 57 inches (1.45 m) in America and 65 inches (1.65 m) in Dutch greenhouses. Mostly double-strength float glass of ⅛ inch (3.175 mm) thickness is used in American greenhouse designs. It currently sells for about $0.85/ft^2$. The larger panes of Dutch greenhouses are triple-strength glass of 0.157 inch (4 mm) thickness. The reduction in structural material plus the reflectance of aluminum have given these metal greenhouses a great advantage over wooden greenhouses in terms of interior light intensity. Hammered glass (glass with a rough, uneven surface) has been used to a moderate degree in Dutch-design greenhouses. This glass scatters the light so that intensity is more uniform across the inside of the greenhouse, which leads to more uniform crop growth. Little hammered glass is used today because of its high rate of breakage during shipping and handling. Low-iron-content glass is often used in rose greenhouses because of its higher light transmission, which is 90–92 percent versus 88 percent for float glass. Low-iron glass costs about $1.00/ft^2.

Today's glass greenhouse construction can be categorized as *high profile* (Figure 2–4a) or *low profile* (Figure 2–4b). The low-profile greenhouse is most popular in The Netherlands. Eaves are approximately 10.5 feet (3.2 m) apart, and single panes of glass extend from eave to ridge. The lower profile slightly reduces exposed surface area, thereby reducing the heating cost. It is suggested, however, that these greenhouses are more expensive to cool in warm climates where fans are required. Ventilator cooling during intermediate seasons is not as effective due to the lower height from ground to ventilator; thus, fan cooling may be used more extensively. In North America, both low- and high-profile greenhouses are currently popular. Price appears to be a dominant factor in the relative popularity of these greenhouse types. The price advantage has shifted back and forth in America.

High-profile greenhouses are available with special sash bars that hold two or even three layers of glass. This layering produces one or two dead-air spaces to cut heat loss (see Table 3–1 for heat loss specifications).

FILM PLASTIC GREENHOUSES

Role

Flexible films of plastic including polyethylene, polyester, polyvinyl chloride, and polyvinyl fluoride have been used for greenhouse coverings. Polyethylene is principally used today for two reasons. First, film plastic can be used on permanent greenhouse frames at a considerable savings in the cost over a glass greenhouse. Even greater savings can be realized when film plastic is applied to less permanent frames such as in Quonset greenhouses. Second, film plastic greenhouses are popular because the cost of heating them is approximately 40 percent lower compared to single-layer glass or FRP greenhouses.

Polyethylene film was developed in the late 1930s in England, and its use as a greenhouse covering was pioneered about the middle of this century. The expanded use of polyethylene for greenhouses has been very rapid and continues to be so. In the United States alone, about 40 acres (16 ha) of plastic greenhouses were in use in the mid-1950s, about 2,300 acres (920 ha) by the mid-1960s, and 4,800 acres (1,920 ha) in 1977. Polyethylene film greenhouses constitute the largest portion of new greenhouse construction in the United States today. Their popularity, however, is not very great in northern Europe.

Some disadvantages occur along with the advantages of film plastic. These covering materials are short-lived compared to glass and FRP. The highest-quality, ultraviolet (UV) light-resistant, 6 mil thick (6 one-thousandths of an inch, 0.15 mm) polyethylene films last four years. UV light from the sun causes the plastic to become brittle and dark in color. Ultimately, it breaks. While the time required to cover a 30 foot by 100 foot (9.1 m by 30 m) Quonset-design house is minimal (about eight labor hours), the task is never ending and carries implicit costs of management and the use of equipment. However, under proper management, the savings in fuel as well as the lower initial purchase price give the film plastic greenhouse a lower overhead than that of a glass greenhouse.

Types of Film Plastic

Polyethylene Polyethylene has always been and still is the principal choice of film plastic for greenhouses. Nearly all current greenhouses have two layers. The outer layer is customarily 6 mil thick, while the inner layer may be 4 or 6 mils thick (0.1 or 0.15 mm). All polyethylene used for covering year-round production greenhouses has a UV inhibitor in it; otherwise, it would last for only one heating season. The common life expectancy is three years, although a four-year product has recently become available. UV-grade polyethylene is available in widths up to 50 feet (15.2 m) in flat sheets and up to 25 feet (7.6 m) in tubes. Several standard lengths include those of 100, 110, 150, and 220 feet (30.5, 33.5, 45.7, and 67.0 m). Some companies provide custom lengths as well.

A polyethylene covering is colder in the winter than the air inside the greenhouse. When warm, moist greenhouse air contacts the cold polyethylene, it cools. As a result, water vapor condenses on the polyethylene surface. The surface is repellent to water; thus, the water forms into beads. With time, the water beads slide downward into one another and form larger beads that drop off to the plants below. The wet foliage fosters disease development, while the constantly wetted soil becomes water-logged and oxygen deficient. If the plastic surface were not as repellent to water, the condensing water would form smaller droplets that would quickly flow over the surface to the ground. Spraying with a surfactant (detergent) will give this beneficial effect, but the surfactant washes off quickly. A liquid (Sun Clear®) is available that, when diluted with water and sprayed on the inner surface of film plastic and rigid-panel greenhouses, will persist. This material costs \$0.007/ft^2 (\$0.075 m^2) of surface treated. Another benefit derived from this treatment is that of reducing the barrier to light transmission that is caused by the layer of condensation on the plastic surface. Today, polyethylene as well as rigid FRP, acrylic, and polycarbonate panels are available with an antifog surfactant built into the surface of the film or panel.

Warm objects, such as plants, radiate infrared (radiant) energy to colder bodies, such as the sky at night. This condition creates a large source of heat loss in greenhouses. Polyethylene is a poor barrier to radiant heat. Polyethylene with infrared- (IR-) blocking chemicals formulated into it during manufacture will stop about half of the radiant heat loss. On cold clear nights, as much as 25 percent of the total heat loss of a greenhouse can be prevented in this way. On cloudy nights, only about 15 percent is saved.

Light that is utilized in photosynthesis is termed *photosynthetically active radiation* (PAR) and comprises the wavelengths from 400 nm to 700 nm. Transmission of PAR through polyethylene can vary with the brand of and the chemical additives in polyethylene (Table 2–2). UV-stablilized polyethylene, on average, transmits about 87 percent of PAR. IR-absorbing polyethylene, which reduces radiant heat loss, transmits about 82 percent of PAR. The amount of light passing through two layers of a greenhouse covering is approximately the square of the decimal fraction of the amount passing through one layer. Where 87 percent (0.87) passes through one layer of UV-inhibited polyethylene, only 76 percent

Table 2–2

Light Transmission Values for Various Greenhouse Coverings

Covering	*Number of Layers*	*Percent Transmission*[1]
Glass (double-strength float, 3.2 mm)	1	88
	2	77
Glass (low-iron, 3.2 mm)	1	90–92
	2	81–85
FRP (clear, 0.640 mm)	1	88
	2	77
Polyethylene	1	87
(4 or 6 mil, 0.10 or 0.15 mm, UV-stabilized)	2	76
Polyethylene	1	82
(4 or 6 mil, 0.10 or 0.15 mm, IR-absorbing)	2	67
Vinyl, clear[2]	1	91
Vinyl, hazy[2]	1	89
Polyvinyl fluoride film (4 mil, 0.10 mm)	1	92
	2	85
Acrylic panels (8 or 16 mm)	2	83
Polycarbonate panels (6 or 8 mm)	2	79

[1]Light transmission values for photosynthetically active radiation (PAR, 400–700 nm) and for single sheets are from Amer. Soc. Agr. Engineers (1990), unless otherwise indicated. Transmission for two layers was computed by squaring the single-layer values.

[2]Manufacturers' specifications.

(0.87 × 0.87) passes through two layers. PAR transmission through two layers of IR-absorbing polyethylene is 67 percent.

While two layers of polyethylene transmit less light than one layer of glass, it is questionable whether there is less light in a polyethylene greenhouse. Kozai et al. (1978) developed a simulation model for a glass-covered greenhouse located at 30°41′N latitude. Although they indicated a light transmissivity of 86 percent at a zero angle of incidence for the glass itself, the light transmissivity for the entire greenhouse varied from 50 percent to 60 percent, depending on season and orientation of the greenhouse. The difference between 60 percent and 86 percent was due to the angle of incidence of light, sash bars, and structural members. Polyethylene greenhouses have less structural material and no sash bars. This could compensate in great part for the lower light transmissivity through a double layer of polyethylene compared to a single layer of glass.

The latest technology in polyethylene production makes use of the coextrusion process. Three liquid resins are extruded simultaneously such that a single layer of film can have three different chemistries across it. In the present tri-extruded films, the inner core contains the antifog surfactant. This chemical is not entirely compatible with polyethylene. The repelling forces cause it to slowly bleed out of the core through the overlying zones of polyethylene that do not contain it. In this way, it can last a few years.

The IR-blocking chemical is also placed in the core. Typically, this chemical weakens polyethylene. If polyethylene containing it is stretched, it can turn cloudy. By confining the IR block to the core, a zone of unusually strong and clear polyethylene can be developed over each side of the core, which alleviates much of the clouding problem. It also gives the film an overall strength greater than that of standard three-year film of the same thickness. Some tri-extruded film is warranted for four years when it is 6 mils thick (0.15 mm) and is on either the outer or the inner covering of the greenhouse. Four mil (10 mm) can also be warranted for four years if it is used under a 6 mil, UV-inhibited film. The 4 mil tri-extruded film is sufficiently strong to equal the life of the current 6 mil, three-year film.

Average prices per square foot for 6 mil, three-year polyethylene film are 7.0¢ for UV-inhibited, 8.0¢ for UV-inhibited plus antifog, and 9.5¢ for UV plus IR block ($.075, $0.86, and $1.02/m^2). For tri-extruded, 6 mil, four-year film, the equivalent prices are 7.3¢, 8.3¢, and 10.1¢ ($0.79, $0.89, and $1.09/m^2). Several greenhouse construction companies can be hired to re-cover polyethylene greenhouses. Prices vary from 10¢ to 20¢ per square foot of ground covered. The lower price applies to greenhouses covered with a tube of plastic since in one step both layers of plastic can be applied. Gutter-connected greenhouse designs also frequently contribute to the lower price because less surface area per unit of ground area is exposed as compared to Quonset greenhouses. The use of channel locks for attaching the plastic as opposed to staples and batten strips can further reduce the price.

Vinyl Ultraviolet light-resistant vinyl (polyvinyl chloride) films of 8 and 12 mil (0.20 and 0.30 mm) thicknesses are guaranteed for four and five years, respectively. This guarantee was a decided advantage years ago when polyethylene lasted for only one or two years. With the recent advent of four-year polyethylene, the advantage is nearly gone. The cost of 12 mil vinyl is 21.5¢/ft^2, which is 3 times that of 6 mil (0.15 mm) polyethylene. Although vinyl film is produced in rolls up to 50 inches (1.27 m) wide, any width can be purchased since the supplier can seal strips of vinyl together. The vinyl films tend to hold a static electrical charge, which attracts and holds dust. This, in turn, reduces light transmittance until the dust is washed off. Vinyl films are not used to a large extent in America.

Polyester Mylar®-brand polyester film for a time offered the strong advantage of durability. Films of 5 mil (0.13 mm) thickness were used for roofs and lasted four years, while 3 mil (0.08 mm) films were used on vertical walls and had a life expectancy of seven years. Although the cost of Mylar® was higher than that of polyethylene, it was offset by the extra life expectancy. Other advantages included a level of light transmittance equal to that of glass and freedom from static electrical charge, which collects dust. Other industrial uses were found for Mylar® in the mid-1960s, and soon its price increased out of the practical realm for floriculture. Polyester is still used frequently, however, in heat retention curtains because of its high capacity to block radiant energy.

Polyvinyl Fluoride (PVF) The most recent category of greenhouse film plastic covering to appear is polyvinyl fluoride (PVF), available as Tedlar® (Figure 2–6). Actually, this film has had an application as the protective covering on FRP panels for many years. The anticipated life expectancy is 10 years or longer. The light transmission of 4 mil (0.10 mm) PVF is 92 percent and is greater than that of float glass customarily used on greenhouses. PVF is available in tubes comprised of a 4 mil plus a 2 mil (0.10 mm + 0.05 mm) layer or a 3 mil plus a 2 mil (0.08 mm + 0.05 mm) layer. The 3 + 2 mil combination is used in general situations, while the 4 + 2 mil combination is used under conditions of high light intensity or wind. Four mil PVF has 4 times the tensile strength of 6 mil (0.15 mm) polyethylene. Tubes of PVF are available in widths of 8.5, 10, and 10.5 feet (2.6, 3.0, and 3.2 m) and in lengths up to 220 feet (67 m).

The current price for the 3 + 2 mil combination film is \$0.73/ft^2 (7.86/m^2). A double, 6 mil (0.15 mm), antifog, three-year life expectancy tube of polyethylene costs about \$0.16/ft^2 (2 square feet of film) (\$1.72/m^2). A modest savings could be realized with PVF because of elimination of the need to re-cover 2.33 times over the 10 years and because of greater growth under higher light conditions. On the basis of a square foot of greenhouse surface area (not floor area), re-covering a double-layer polyethylene greenhouse carries an average cost of about \$0.10 for labor plus \$0.16 for plastic (\$1.08 + \$1.72/m^2). Thus, the total cost of polyethylene for the 10 years would be the initial purchase of material plus 2.33 re-coverings for a total cost of $0.77/ft². A major drawback to PVF use is its narrow widths and the need to use attachment rails to splice pieces together on the greenhouse.

PVF film can be preshrunk onto frames to form panels ideal for reglazing glass or FRP greenhouses (Figure 2–6). The PVF film is wrapped over the frame to form two layers and is attached with tape. Exposure to a temperature of 250–275°F (121–135°C) will cause shrinkage and pull the surface taut in 5–10 minutes.

Film Plastic Greenhouse Designs

When polyethylene first entered the horticultural scene, it was relegated to temporary functions. Accordingly, inexpensive frames were sought. Pine wood was commonly used. Various frames were designed through the 1950s and 1960s. The A-frame (Figure 2–7) was one of the more popular. The scissors-truss frame (Fig-

(a)

Figure 2–6

(a,b) A greenhouse at Elliott and Williams Roses in Dover, NH, covered with a double layer of Tedlar® film plastic. Note the double clamping rails running the length of the greenhouse to which the 10 foot (3 m) wide sheets are attached. The lowermost sheet of film plastic on either side is polyethylene. (c) A wooden greenhouse formerly covered with FRP in the process of being reglazed with panels of double-layer Tedlar® on galvanized metal frames at Tagawa Greenhouse in Brighton, CO. (*Photos courtesy of Du Pont Co., Wilmington,* DE 19898)

(b)

(c)

ure 2–8) was particularly strong. These and other designs, including the exterior gusset, were used for greenhouses ranging from 20 feet to 30 feet (6.1 m to 9.1 m) wide.

A single layer of film plastic was generally used until the early 1960s. Then, fuel costs entered into the picture. Double coverings of film plastic were desired to

Figure 2–7

An inexpensive but temporary A-frame film plastic greenhouse very popular in the early days of film plastic greenhouses.

Figure 2–8

A scissors-truss film plastic greenhouse designed at Virginia Polytechnic Institute. This is a particularly strong design.

bring about a savings of about one-third of the fuel cost. At first, the second layer was applied from the inside of the greenhouse. This task was difficult in greenhouses with columns. Stronger truss designs were sought to eliminate columns.

Next, the width of the dead-air space became a consideration. Ideally, the dead-air space should be 0.5–4 inches (1.25–10 cm) thick (U.S. Housing and Home Finance Agency 1954). When it exceeds 4 inches (10 cm), air currents can become established inside and reduce the insulating property of this space. Warm air immediately above the inner covering rises up into contact with the outer covering, and here it gives up heat. As it cools, the air becomes heavy and drops back to the inner covering to pick up more heat. This loss does not become very significant until a space of 18 inches (46 cm) is reached. Below 0.5 inch (1.25 cm), the insulating property again diminishes, and when the two layers touch, the insulation value is totally lost. In houses that had support columns, holes were cut in the inner layer of plastic to maneuver it around the columns. The holes were generally not sealed and thus left avenues of entry for warm air into the dead-air space, which further reduced the insulating property. A-frame and scissors-truss designs necessitated dead-air spaces several feet thick. To avoid this problem, the Gothic-arch greenhouse was developed at Virginia Polytechnic Institute (Figure 2–9). Greenhouses up to 30 feet (9.1 m) wide with a frame thickness of 4.5 inches (11 cm) could then be constructed without columns.

Figure 2–9

A Gothic-arch greenhouse of the type designed at Virginia Polytechnic Institute. The trusses used are fabricated during the construction of the greenhouse. This greenhouse offers a pleasing appearance and is devoid of internal columns.

The greenhouses thus far discussed were constructed of short-life wood, which required frequent painting to prevent rotting. White paint was usually used to increase interior light intensity. Today, as in the past, when paint is applied in or on a greenhouse, a mercury-base paint should be avoided. Mercury will volatilize from the paint for a considerable length of time and thus cause damage to the crop. Paints sold specifically as greenhouse paints are safe; however, other paints may be used as long as those with a mercury base are avoided. If mercury-base paint is used by mistake, injury can be avoided by painting over it with a weight mixture of 5 parts lime–sulfur fungicide and 10 parts wheat flour in 100 parts water.

Posts and other wood in contact with the ground should be treated with a wood preservative. Treated wood may be purchased for this purpose, or the wood may be treated at the time of use. Several treatments are available, but not all are safe. Pentachlorophenol and creosote should not be used. Creosote in contact with roots and foliage can burn them. Pentachlorophenol produces fumes that can last for more than a year and that are toxic to plants. Entire crops can be killed by moving them into a new house with treated posts. A single treated board can cause abnormal growth throughout the house. A very suitable wood preservative is copper naphthenate, which is sold under several trade names. Generally used as a 2 percent solution of copper naphthenate, it can be sprayed, dipped, or applied with a brush. It is an excellent preservative for frame members as well as for wooden benches and flats. Lumber pressure-treated with Wolman Salts is safe for greenhouse use (Beese 1978).

With time, the price of wood became objectionably high relative to metal. The cost of continual painting was an added burden. By 1970, film plastic greenhouse designs were mainly of two styles. The first, and least expensive, which persists to this day, is the Quonset-style greenhouse (Figure 2–10). Quonset houses can be purchased prefabricated or can be fabricated on the site. Often, the trusses are constructed from water pipe that is bent to fit a 180° arc modified for somewhat more vertical sides. In greenhouses 20 feet (6.1 m) wide, 0.75 inch pipe is used; 1 inch pipe is used for a 30 foot (9.1 m) greenhouse width. An aluminum electrical conduit should not be used since it does not have sufficient strength to support a snow load. Slightly larger pipe is driven into the ground into which the pipe arches are inserted for support. A 2 inch by 8 inch (5 cm by 20 cm) wooden plank is attached to the base of the pipe arches such that it runs along the ground partially buried. This provides a basal point of attachment for the film plastic. The pipe arches, or trusses, are supported by pipe purlins running the length of the house. Trusses are spaced 30–36 inches (75–90 cm) apart. The width of film plastic required to cover a Quonset greenhouse of given width can vary according to the height and shape of the trusses. A 20 foot (6.1 m) wide greenhouse generally requires a 32 foot (9.8 m) wide sheet of plastic. The covering width for a 30 foot (9.1 m) wide Quonset greenhouse varies greatly; the more common widths are 40 feet and 42 feet (12.2 m and 12.8 m).

Figure 2–10

A metal-frame, Quonset-style greenhouse very popular today with users of film plastic. This greenhouse is very inexpensive, does not require painting, and is well suited to a double covering of film plastic.

Quonset houses are either constructed in a freestanding style or may be arranged in an interlocking ridge-and-furrow manner as depicted in Figure 2–11. In this latter case, the trusses overlap sufficiently to place a bed of plants between the overlapping portions of adjacent houses. A single large interior thus exists for a set of houses, an arrangement that is better adapted to the movement of labor and to automation.

The gutter-connected house is the second currently popular film plastic greenhouse design (Figure 2–12). The gutters can be placed at greater heights than is possible in ridge-and-furrow Quonset ranges. This permits a roadway in either direction within the greenhouse to accommodate tractors as well as trucks. Gutters, depending upon the manufacturer, can occur at 12–40 foot (3.65–12.2 m) intervals. Columns can be placed in greenhouses with gutters spaced 12 feet (3.65 m) apart and the columns placed under each, every other, or every third gutter. A 36 foot (11 m) spacing between rows of columns, while more expensive, greatly enhances the ease with which the shading of plants with black cloth can be accomplished.

Gutter-connected greenhouses greatly minimize the exposed surface area and, consequently, the heating cost. Only 20 feet (6.1 m) of film plastic is required to span a 17 foot (5.2 m) bay. Gutter-connected bays of 12, 17, 21, 22, and 30 foot (3.7, 5.2, 6.4, 6.7, and 9 m) widths can be covered by film plastic sheets

Figure 2–11

An interconnecting arrangement of Quonset greenhouses offering a single large interior for several greenhouses. This greenhouse arrangement is in harmony with the current needs for automation and efficiency of movement.

14, 20, 24, 35, and 36 feet (4.3, 6.1, 7.3, 10.7, and 11.0 m) wide. When additions are made, the film plastic can be removed from an existing side wall and the new houses connected at that point without any resulting discontinuity. In this way, a modest initial investment, unadaptable for automation, can be developed through expansions into a structure well suited to automation.

The gutter-connected greenhouse brings us full circle to the category of permanent metal-frame greenhouses of which the glass greenhouse is a member. The major portion of new construction in America today, whether for temporary or permanent use, is film plastic.

Double-Layer Covering

Today, virtually all film plastic greenhouses make use of the air-inflated system. Two layers of film plastic, one applied directly on top of the other from the outside, are held apart by a cushion of air maintained at low positive pressure. Single sheets of plastic, wide enough to span the entire truss from ground to ground, are rolled out the length of the greenhouse and are attached to the greenhouse along its length at the ground level on both sides of Quonset greenhouses and in the gutters of gutter-connected greenhouses. The ends of the sheet overlap the green-

Figure 2–12

Exterior and interior view of the gutter-connected polyethylene greenhouse range of Mr. Aart van Wingerden in Horse Shoe, North Carolina.

house ends by a few inches and are attached at that point. No attachment is made to the trusses. Two sheets of plastic are attached to each end of the greenhouse as well. Sometimes, plastic is attached to Quonset greenhouses by placing a batten strip over it and nailing or stapling through it. Some growers use thick plastic strips about 1 inch (2.5 cm) wide obtained from greenhouse supply companies; others use strips of wood. Most greenhouses are equipped with metal or plastic channel locks. The layers of film plastic are laid over the channel, and then a metal rod or plastic bead is placed over the film plastic and pushed into the channel, locking the plastic in place. The outer layer of plastic should be 6 mils (0.152 mm) thick, while the inner needs to be only 4 mils (0.102 mm) thick because of the lower UV light level. A polyethylene tube, available in widths up to 25 feet (7.6 m), is often used to cover narrower greenhouses. In this way, both layers are applied in one step, thus significantly reducing the labor cost.

The tension under which the plastic is installed is important since film plastics contract and expand to a considerable degree with temperature shifts. When it is applied on a cold day, the film should be pulled taut. On a warm day, with temperatures near 80°F (27°C), about 2–3 inches (5–8 cm), of slack should be

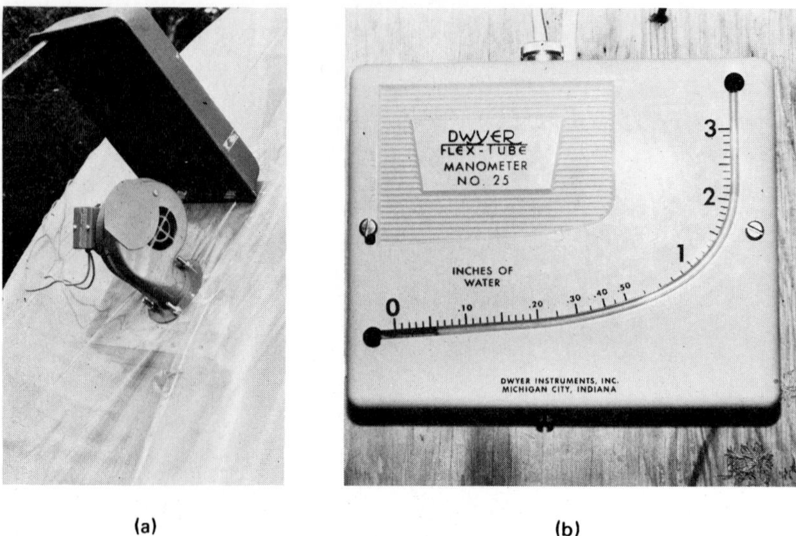

(a) (b)

Figure 2–13

(a) A squirrel-cage fan used to inflate the space between two layers of plastic. The plate on the side can be moved to adjust the air supply to the fan and, consequently, the pressure between the two coverings on the greenhouse. (b) A manometer used to measure the air pressure between the two plastic covers.

left in the covering all the way along one side of a Quonset greenhouse 20 feet (6.1 m) wide to permit contraction over the truss when cold weather comes. If this slack is not allowed, the film will tear loose from the points of attachment when it contracts during cold weather. Conversely, if it is not pulled taut when it is applied on a cold day, excess slack will occur during warm weather, resulting in an excessive air space between the two layers.

A small squirrel-cage fan is installed inside the greenhouse to inflate the space between the two film plastic layers (Figure 2–13). Air is maintained between 0.2 inch and 0.3 inch (5.1 mm and 7.6 mm) of water-column pressure. Even higher pressures have been used—up to 0.5 inch (13 mm)—under conditions of heavy wind. The high pressure should not be maintained because the plastic will stretch. The fan should have an adjustable door on the air inlet for adjusting the pressure between the two films. For a greenhouse measuring 26 feet by 96 feet (8 m by 29 m), a fan delivering air at 200–400 cfm (5.7–11.3 cmm) at a static water pressure of 0.5 inch (13 mm) (about 1 ampere, 115 watts) is sufficient. During a snowstorm when snow sticks to the roof, it may be necessary to turn off the fan. This will allow the two polyethylene layers to come together, thus eliminating the insulating effect of the dead-air space. More heat will escape through the covering to melt snow and clear it from the roof.

The fan is generally mounted on the end wall of the greenhouse. A hole is cut in the end wall adjacent to the fan so that air feeding the fan is drawn in from outside. Outside air is colder than the air between the plastic layers. As the cold air warms in the roof cavity, it dries. This helps to control condensation between the layers of plastic. Such condensation leads to light reduction as well as corrosion problems. If warm moist air from inside the greenhouse were used, it would cool and water would condense in the roof cavity.

A flexible tube, such as that used for a clothes dryer, is installed between the fan and the inner layer of plastic to be inflated. A +-shaped cut is made in the inner layer of plastic, and the tube is inserted through it. The four points of plastic resulting from the cut are pulled out over the tube and taped to it to make an airtight seal. Air is conducted from the fan to the inner space through this tube. This system is sufficient to inflate the entire roof of a Quonset-style greenhouse. Generally, the two layers of plastic pull tight at the ridge of an A-frame greenhouse, thus separating the roof into two inflatable portions. In this case, air from the fan can be divided in a 4 inch (10 cm) stovepipe tee and introduced to each side of the roof through flexible tubing immediately below the ridge. Side or end walls can be inflated as well without adding additional fans. Pieces of garden hose can be inserted between the layers of plastic to connect the roof cavity to the end or side wall cavities, or flexible connectors sold for this purpose can be used.

The pressure between the layers of plastic should be sufficient to hold the layers apart under conditions of wind and yet low enough to avoid tearing the sheets. A manometer can be purchased from greenhouse supply companies for measuring this pressure. The manometer is a simple device and can be easily fabricated by the grower as follows:

1. Bend a 2 foot (61 cm) long piece of clear plastic tube into the shape of a U and attach it to a board.
2. Make a +-shaped cut in the inner layer of plastic and insert one end of the plastic tube.
3. Seal the film plastic to the tube with plastic tape.
4. Put about 8 inches (20 cm) of water in the tube such that it settles at the bottom of the U. Leave both ends of the tube open.
5. Attach a ruler to the board behind or alongside the plastic tube.

Pressure between the layers of plastic will push the water down on the film plastic side of the U and up on the opposite side of the U. A rise in water level of 0.2–0.3 inch (5.1–7.6 mm) indicates the desired pressure. Coloring the water will help make it more visible.

The air-inflated system offers the easiest method for covering a greenhouse with two layers of film plastic. It has another very decided advantage of long life expectancy because the outer layer of plastic rests on a cushion of air. Plastic applied by techniques other than the air-inflated system is constantly chafed against the trusses by the lifting and dropping action of the wind. This reduces its life expectancy in many cases to one heating season. Polyethylene in the air-inflated double-layer system lasts three years and often four heating seasons.

RIGID-PANEL GREENHOUSES

Polyvinyl Chloride

Polyvinyl chloride (PVC) rigid panels have, for the most part, been dropped from use. Initially, they showed promise as an inexpensive covering (about 40 percent of the cost of long-lasting FRP). They had a life expectancy of five years or better at a time when polyethylene lasted one year. Commercial use of these panels soon indicated that this life expectancy was much shorter, sometimes as little as two years. This was unacceptable because the cost of PVC panels was 4–5 times that of polyethylene film and because they required much more time to install. Rigid PVC, like its film plastic counterparts, was subject to the deteriorating effect of UV light, which caused it to turn dark and become brittle. At first, light transmission was reduced; later, the panels would break apart. Rigid PVC was purchased in corrugated panels 26 or 28 inches (66–71 cm) wide and 8, 10, or 12 feet (2.4–3.7 m) long. The panels were available in various colors; however, clear panels were used for general greenhouse culture.

Fiberglass-Reinforced Plastic

Role Fiberglass-reinforced plastic (FRP) was more popular as a greenhouse covering in the recent past than it is today. Like PVC, corrugated panels were used because of their greater strength. Flat panels are occasionally used on the end and side walls where the load is not as great. Panels are available in 51 ½ inch (1.3 m) widths, lengths up to 24 feet (7.3 m), and a variety of colors. The panels are flexible enough to conform to the shape of Quonset greenhouses, which makes FRP a very versatile covering material.

FRP can be applied to the inexpensive frames of film plastic greenhouses (Figure 2–14) or to the more elaborate frames of glass-type greenhouses (Figure 2–15). In the former case, the price of the FRP greenhouse lies between that of a film plastic greenhouse and that of a glass greenhouse, but the cost is offset by elimination of the need for replacement of film plastic. In the latter case, the FRP greenhouse costs about the same as the glass greenhouse.

FRP and glass greenhouses each have advantages and disadvantages, and growers are divided as to their preference. FRP is more resistant to breakage by factors such as hail or vandals. Sunlight passing through FRP is scattered by the fibers in the panels, with the result that light intensity is rather uniform through-

Figure 2–14

A Quonset greenhouse being covered with sheets of corrugated FRP.

Figure 2–15

A permanent iron-frame greenhouse with FRP covering.

out the greenhouse by comparison with a glass covering. Plants on the north sides of beds, and particularly in the north beds, as a whole, grow much better. Hammered glass, however, offers a similar light-scattering benefit.

There are disadvantages as well. The acrylic surface of FRP panels is subject to etching and pitting by dust abrasion and chemical pollution. Thus, glass fibers become exposed and subject to fraying, and they begin to collect dust as well as harbor algae. The resultant effect is a darkening of the panels and a subsequent reduction in light transmission. The situation can be corrected by scrubbing the FRP surface clean with a stiff brush or steel wool and then painting on a new surface of acrylic resin. The material is inexpensive, but the labor is extensive. The need for refinishing varies with the grade of FRP purchased. Some grades do not carry a guarantee and may last only five years or so. Other grades carry guarantees of various lengths of time up to 20 years. Those with a UV light-resistant protectant hold the longest life expectancy. The guarantee generally protects the level of light transmission and compensates for the unused portion of the term of the guarantee. By contrast, glass can last as long as a grower's life or longer, while FRP is guaranteed to cover about half that time. The decision between glass and FRP is not clear-cut. Some northern growers have been known to cover only the north slope of a glass greenhouse with FRP to increase the light intensity within. A portion of the sun's rays impinging upon the north roof are then transmitted inward rather than being deflected off.

Light Transmission The total quantity of light transmitted through clear FRP is roughly equivalent to that transmitted through glass (Table 2–2) but diminishes in relation to its color. For greenhouse crops in general, only the clear FRP permits a satisfactory level of light transmission (88–90 percent). Colored FRP has found a limited use in greenhouses used for growing some house plants that require low light intensity and in display greenhouses used for holding plants during the sales period.

Heat Transmission FRP has the distinct advantage over glass of being easier to cool. In an experiment conducted at Colorado State University with two greenhouses of identical size and style, one was covered with clear FRP and the other with glass. The length of time that the cooling fans operated in each greenhouse was recorded for the period June 4, 1961, through June 14, 1962. Fewer hours of cooling were required in the FRP greenhouse month by month. At the end of the 13 months, a total of 2,066 hours of cooling had been required in the glass greenhouse versus only 1,668 hours in the FRP greenhouse. This represented a reduction of 19 percent. The winter heat requirement of corrugated FRP greenhouses is about equivalent to that of structurally tight glass greenhouses.

Construction FRP greenhouses require fewer structural members than glass greenhouses since sash bars are not needed. The construction labor input is accordingly lower for an FRP greenhouse. Both high-quality, 5 ounce FRP and double-strength glass cost about \$0.85/ft². FRP panels are 50.5–52.6 inches (1.28–1.34 m) wide but, with overlap, have an effective covering width of only 48 inches (1.22 m). The thickness of FRP is measured in terms of weight per square foot. Where a snow load is expected, 5 ounce weights (37 mils, 0.94 mm thick) are used on peak roofs. The 4 ounce weight (30 mils, 0.76 mm thick) is common on arch roofs and vertical walls. Trusses are spaced 8–10 feet (2.4–3.0 m) apart and purlins 4 feet (1.2 m) apart.

The greenhouse must be constructed as airtight as possible. Corrugated plastic closures (Figure 2–16) are available for insertion between the FRP panel

Figure 2–16

A corrugated plastic closure strip in place, sealing off the outer air at the point of attachment of a corrugated FRP panel to the frame member.

and frame components such as the eave and the sill to seal off outer air. Flashing is used at the ridge to cover the exposed ends of the FRP panels for the purpose of preventing water entry. The flashing can be constructed from aluminum or corrugated FRP. The FRP panels are attached to the purlins by aluminum screw nails or by aluminum wood screws. These nails and screws have a rubber washer immediately beneath the head to seal the hole made by the shaft.

When condensation flows along the inner surface of FRP, it does so along the corrugation valleys. If the FRP panels are attached directly to the purlins, the corrugation valleys are in contact with the purlins. Condensation, upon reaching this point, flows onto the purlin and drips from its lower edge, thus causing harm to plants beneath. The FRP panel must be elevated away from the purlin. Metal U-shaped supports are placed between the purlin and the corrugation ridges of the FRP panel. The nail or screw attaching the panel to the purlin passes through the support (Figure 2–17).

Fire Hazard Many greenhouse structures are insured. One cause of destruction is fire, which is not a significant danger in glass greenhouses but is a very definite concern in FRP greenhouses. The glass fibers themselves do not burn, but the polyester and acrylic resins binding them together do. A few years ago, a fire be-

Figure 2–17

U-shaped metal supports are placed between the purlin and FRP panel to provide a space so that condensation water can flow along the inner surface of the panel to the ground or to a gutter. The pot label was inserted to demonstrate this space.

lieved to have originated from a faulty electrical wire beneath a sheet of black shade cloth spread to the FRP covering of a ridge-and-furrow range on a windy night. More than an acre of greenhouses was consumed within 20 minutes. Insurance rates are assessed according to the risk involved, which is greater for FRP greenhouses. Fire-retardant FRP panels are available and carry the best rating for building materials (Class I). These panels offer no support for sustainment to flame even when they are directly attacked. Benefits associated with standard greenhouse FRP are not associated with fire-retardant FRP by manufacturers; thus, these panels are not commonly used for greenhouses.

Acrylic and Polycarbonate

Acrylic and polycarbonate, double-layer, rigid panels have been available for about 10 years for greenhouse use. A number of research institutions have installed these panels. There has been gradual acceptance in the commercial industry. The heaviest commercial use thus far has been for glazing side and end walls on film plastic greenhouses and for retro-fitting old glass and FRP greenhouses. A modest number of new buildings have been completely glazed with these panels. While the acrylic panels are highly flammable, the polycarbonate ones are not flammable.

Acrylic panels are available in thicknesses of 16 mm (0.63 in.) and 8 mm (0.3 in.). The thicker panels cannot be bent, but the thinner panels can be bent to fit curved-roof greenhouses. Panels are available with a coating to prevent condensation drip. The two acrylic layers of these panels are held apart by ribs spaced approximately 0.6–0.9 inch (16–24 mm) apart. The panels have a width of 47.25 inches (120 cm) and come in lengths up to 39 feet (11.9 m). The effective covering width of the panel is 48 inches (122 cm) since the metal support member takes up space between panels. Heat loss (U) values for 8 mm and 16 mm panels are 0.65 and 0.58 Btu per hour per square foot per degree Fahrenheit (Btu/hr/ft^2/°F) temperature differential from inside to outside the greenhouse, respectively (3.68 and 3.29 W/m^2 • K). The heat loss value for glass is 1.13 Btu (6.40 W), which is nearly double this. PAR light transmission is 83 percent. The thinner panels carry a limited warranty against loss of more than 3 percent light transmission in 10 years. The 8 mm panels sell for \$1.60/ft^2 (\$17.22/m^2), while the 16 mm panels sell for approximately \$2.00/ft^2 (\$21.53/m^2).

Polycarbonate panels come in thicknesses of 4, 6, 8, 10, and 16 mm (0.16, 0.24, 0.31, 0.39, and 0.63 inch). The thinner panels can be bent to fit curved-roof greenhouses, while the thicker ones cannot. Their skin thicknesses and rib dimensions are similar to those of acrylic panels. Depending on the manufacturer, panels are available with a coating to prevent condensation drip and also with an acrylic coating for extra protection from UV light. Panels are available in widths from 4 feet to 8 feet (122 cm to 244 cm). Lengths are available up to 32 feet (9.75 m). Heat loss values are 0.65 and 0.58 Btu/hr/ft^2/°F (3.69 and 3.29 W/m^2 • K) for the thin and thick panels, respectively. PAR transmission is 79 percent. The loss in light transmission is anticipated at 1 percent per year in the thin panels. The 6 mm and 8 mm panels sell for \$1.35/ft^2 and \$1.60/ft^2 (\$14.53/m^2 and \$17.22/m^2), respectively.

BENCHES AND BEDS

Fresh Flowers

The first choice in growing fresh flowers is whether to grow them in raised benches or in ground beds. If the crop is of moderate height, such as chrysanthemum and snapdragon, raised benches can be used; however, these benches should be located close to the ground to keep the plants at a practical level for disbudding, spraying, and harvesting. Rose plants are grown for about five years and become exceedingly tall during this time. Most are grown in ground beds to minimize height. Carnations are grown from one to two years and also become very tall. Years ago, they were commonly grown in ground beds without bottoms, but the occurrence of a bacterial wilt disease nearly destroyed this business in the northeastern United States, and since then they have been grown in raised benches. (It was not possible to pasteurize the root medium deep enough in the bottomless ground beds, and the disease continually recurred.)

If ground beds are selected, they should be constructed in a manner that isolates the root medium contained within from external soil. In this way, the root medium can be thoroughly pasteurized on a routine schedule, thus reducing the possibility of disease. Concrete is very suitable for ground beds (Figure 2–18). The bottom should be V-shaped with the longitudinal center at least 1.5 inches (4 cm) lower than the sides. A half tile should be placed in the center over the V, and the bed sloped 1 inch per 100 feet (1 cm per 1,200 cm) to ensure drainage of water. The bottom of the bed should be filled level with gravel to ensure lateral movement of water into the tile. At the point where the tile contacts the lower end of the bed, a hole should be located to permit drainage of water. The drainage tile serves another valuable purpose since steam introduced through the tile will percolate up through the root medium and pasteurize it.

Other less expensive ground beds can be constructed as well (Figure 2–19). Side walls can consist of treated wood or cement blocks. The wall should be at least 8 inches (20 cm) deep and extend down to a well-drained foundation substance, such as a sandy subsoil. If the base substance is not well drained, drainage tile should be installed in this substance below each bed. Walks should be filled with gravel; paved walks should be sloped for drainage. It is important that walks be separated from beds to ensure (1) that soil in them, easily contaminated by soil carried in on shoe bottoms, does not spread into the beds and (2) that water remains where it is applied rather than running off into the walks.

Figure 2–18

A concrete ground bed used for cut flower production. The bed is sloped and has a V-shaped bottom. A half tile runs the length of the bed at the lowest point to conduct water to a drain hole at the end of the bed. A concrete trough running across the greenhouse collects water from all beds and carries it out of the greenhouse. Steam can be injected into the drain hole for pasteurization of the bed between crops.

Ground beds are well suited for tall crops, such as roses and carnations. If raised beds are preferred for cut flowers, they should be situated close to the ground. An 8 inch (20 cm) concrete block serves as a good post to separate the bench from the ground. The bottom should have abundant drainage holes along its length. Raised bottoms should be as level as possible to prevent wet and dry areas. Benches are most commonly constructed from concrete or treated wood. Concrete benches can be poured in place or assembled from precast concrete boards. One board is used for each side; several boards, running lengthwise, are used for the bottom. The bottom boards have a ½ inch (1.3 cm) space between them for drainage. Galvanized iron brackets are used to bolt the sides to a pipe frame or concrete cross support beneath the bench floor.

The preferred woods for bench construction are cypress, redwood, locust, and cedar because of their resistance to decay. Wooden benches should be

Figure 2–19

(a) Drainage tiles imbedded in gravel beneath a ground bed. (b) Ground beds with treated wood sides. The root medium is placed on the gravel base containing the drainage tile.

painted with a copper naphthenate preservative. The natural preservative in redwood is corrosive to iron and steel; therefore, nails, screws, or bolts should be made of other types of metals such as aluminum, brass, or zinc.

The preferred widths of cut flower benches and beds are 3.5 feet and 4.0 feet (1.1–1.2 m). Roses are conveniently grown in 4 foot (1.2 m) wide beds because bushes are planted 1 foot (30 cm) apart in each direction. This permits four plants across the bed. The other cut flower crops may be found in either width of bed. Except in very wide greenhouses, benches run the length of the greenhouse. The beds and benches should be 8 inches (20 cm) deep to accommodate 7 inches (18 cm) of root media. Rose beds, which should be 1 foot (30 cm) deep, are an exception. Eighteen inch (46 cm) walks should be used between all benches except in the center of the greenhouse, where a 2 foot (61 cm) walk should be established. This *longitudinal* arrangement of benches allows for the use of about 67 percent of the floor area for growing.

Pot Crops

Raised benches are generally used for pot plant crops. They should be 32–36 inches (81–91 cm) high for convenience of working. Benches should not exceed a 3 foot (91 cm) width if they are against a wall or a 6 foot (1.83 m) width if they are accessible from both sides. It is difficult to handle plants in the center of wider benches, and labor becomes inefficient. It is important to have air circulation around each plant to reduce the incidence of condensation on foliage and thus the possibility of disease. Pot plant benches should not have sides. The floor of the bench should be as open as possible. Redwood lath in woven wire similar to snow fencing but manufactured more precisely for benches makes excellent bench floors and is sold for this purpose. The redwood lath can be supported with a 2 inch by 4 inch (5 cm by 10 cm) wooden frame (Figure 2–20) or by a pipe frame. The frame itself is often supported by concrete blocks. One inch (2.5 cm) square, 14-gauge welded-wire fabric and expanded metal also make excellent bench floors. These benches permit proper circulation of air.

A special category of pot plant benches is used for ebb-and-flow culture. These benches are watertight to accommodate periodic flooding with fertilizer solution and are plumbed to a tank below them for holding the solution when it is not in use. (See Chapter 9 for details.)

Cut flower benches generally run lengthwise in a greenhouse to minimize the number of end posts needed for supporting plants and the time necessary to attach and tighten support wires. Since support is not a consideration in pot plant benches, these benches usually run across the greenhouse to minimize handling of heavy pots. A 3–4 foot (0.9–1.2 m) wide center aisle is provided along the length of smaller greenhouses to permit motorized carts to be used for transporting plants and materials. In larger greenhouse ranges, an 8 foot (2.4 m) center drive should be provided for larger internal transport

Figure 2–20

A raised pot plant bench using redwood lath for the floor and 2 inch by 4 inch (5 cm by 10 cm) lumber frame. Cement blocks are used for legs.

equipment. Side walks should be 18 inches (46 cm) wide at most and should end 3 feet (91 cm) in from the side walls. Benches are located at the ends of the walks. Benches in this arrangement are known as *peninsular* benches and can result in as much as 80 percent growing area as opposed to 67 percent in the longitudinal arrangement.

A more recent concept in space efficiency for greenhouses equipped with pot plant benches is seen in the various *movable-bench* systems. Such a system can increase production space up to about 90 percent of the floor space. By turning a crank at the end of the bench or by simply pushing the bench, the bench platform can be moved to either side. As a bench is moved from right to left, an aisle on the left side closes and a new aisle opens up on the right side (Figure 2–21). When several movable benches are used, only one aisle is needed, which can be shifted to any position.

The number of benches permitted per aisle is a difficult question. In a stationary-bench arrangement, a production operation could be carried out in each aisle simultaneously. This would be a benefit for crops requiring constant attention, such as frequent respacing, disbudding, pinching, or selection of plants for market. A crop such as Easter lily or poinsettia, which does not require as

(a) (b)

Figure 2–21

An aisle-eliminator bench system: (a) The bench on the right is in its extreme right position; (b) the bench on the right has been moved to its left position, thus shifting the aisle to the right of this bench. (*Photos courtesy of Simtrac, Inc., Skokie,* IL 60076)

many production operations and is marketed over a short period, is well adapted to movable benches. As many as five benches may be used per 2 foot (61 cm) aisle for such a crop.

Benches are an expense that is often forgotten in the pricing of a greenhouse firm. Prefabricated benches are available in many designs and cost \$1.80–\$3.50/ft^2 (\$19.38–\$37.67/m^2) of bench. An additional cost of \$0.50–\$1.00/ft^2 (\$5.38–\$10.76/m^2) is required to have them installed.

A recent concept for ridge-and-furrow ranges with a large single interior calls for paving the floor with porous asphalt or concrete and growing pot plants directly on the floor (Figure 2–22). Water percolates through the pavement to a gravel bed beneath, while weeds are unable to grow through this layer. Standard asphalt paving with a reduced quantity of binder can be used, or porous concrete made from a mixture of 2,800 pounds (1 cu yd, 0.76 m/^{3}) of ⅜ inch (10 m) dust-free gravel, 5.5 bags (94 lb, 43 kg, each) of cement, and 23.4 gallons (88 l) of water can be used (Aldrich and Krall 1978; Aldrich and Bartok 1989). Porous concrete is generally poured in a layer 4 inches (10 cm) thick. It will withstand a working compressive strength test of 600 pounds per square inch (psi) (4,137 kPa). Light vehicles may be driven over the floor for setting up and removing crops. This system makes it possible to use 90 percent of the floor area for growing. A disadvantage is found with crops requiring relatively extensive hand labor operations because working at ground level is fatiguing and takes its toll on labor efficiency. Bedding plants, azalea liners, some green plants, and possibly poinsettias are well suited to this system.

Figure 2–22

A ridge-and-furrow range in which pot plants are grown on a pavement of water-porous asphalt. Growing space is maximized in this greenhouse, and tractors or trucks can be used for moving plants and materials.

COST OF GREENHOUSE CONSTRUCTION

Table 2–3 presents the range of commercial 1990 construction prices for 20,000 ft^2 (1,858 m^2) of various types of greenhouses. Included in the basic structure category are the total frame, vent coverings for the cooling pads, greenhouse ends, doors, and erection labor including placement of the heating and cooling systems. The heating systems are of the forced-air unit heater type. Central hot water and steam systems can cost \$1.50–\$3.00/ft^2 (\$16–\$32/m^2) of greenhouse. The cooling systems include a pressurized convection tube for winter cooling and a cross-fluted cellulose pad-and-fan system for summer. Thermal screens, also known as heat curtains, and thermal blankets vary widely in price according to the number of zones in a given area.

The basic price of a polyethylene greenhouse can be as reasonable as \$1.50/ft^2. This figure, however, does not include the covering, end walls, erection labor, heating, cooling, wiring, and plumbing. When these items are added, the polyethylene greenhouse can cost \$5.40–\$7.86 ft^2 (\$58–\$84/m^2). If benches and thermal screens are desired, the price goes up to \$8.20–\$14.35/ft^2 (\$88–\$154/m^2). Missing yet are the prices of land, grading, service buildings, access drives, and parking areas, which could easily add another \$2.50/ft^2 of greenhouse for a total

Table 2–3

Range of Prices ($/ft² of floor area) for 20,000 ft² (1,858 m²) of High-Profile Glass; Low-Profile Glass; and Gutter-Connected, Double-Layer Polyethylene Greenhouses[1]

Item	*Glass, HP*	*Glass, LP*	*Polyethylene*
Basic structure (including labor)	$ 8.50–11.00	$ 5.00–5.75	$2.75–4.00
Heating system[2]	0.50–1.00	0.50–1.00	0.50–1.00
Cooling systems[2]	1.15–0.75	1.15–0.75	1.15–0.75
Plumbing	0.50–1.00	0.50–1.00	0.50–1.00
Wiring	0.50–1.10	0.50–1.10	0.50–1.10
Subtotal	11.15–14.85	7.65–9.60	5.40–7.85
Benches	1.80–3.50	1.80–3.50	1.80–3.50
Thermal screen	1.00–3.00	1.00–3.00	1.00–3.00
Total	13.95–21.35	10.45–16.10	8.20–14.35

[1]Prices derived from a broad range of greenhouse suppliers in America in 1990. $1.00/ft² = $10.76/m².

[2]The lowest heating and highest cooling prices are associated to represent firms in warm regions while the opposite combination represents cold regions. Heating systems are of the forced-air unit heater type. Cooling systems include the summer fan-and-pad system plus the winter fan–tube system.

of $10.70–$16.55 ft² ($115–$178/m²). Glass greenhouses increase the price further. Other greenhouse coverings are not included in the table. Acrylic and polycarbonate panels on permanent frames could cost more than glass greenhouses. FRP on permanent frames would be priced similarly to glass greenhouses. Quonset polyethylene greenhouses might be as low as half the basic price of a gutter-connected polyethylene greenhouse.

Selection of a greenhouse should not be based solely on the total purchase price. Maintenance, such as re-covering polyethylene every 3 years, PVF every 10 years, or FRP every 20 years, must be assigned a cost. The 40 percent fuel savings in a double-layer film plastic greenhouse, or the nearly 50 percent fuel savings of acrylic and polycarbonate panels compared to single-layer glass, must enter into the decision. The predominant choice of the industry today is film plastic. There are, however, regions of the world where glass still predominates for reasons including tradition, belief that light intensity is higher inside, and strength to hold up against snow and wind loads. PVF film may change these decisions based on light intensity. With the numerous options available and the differences in prices for greenhouse frames, coverings, heat conservation systems, and heating systems, it is extremely important that a greenhouse operator study the available information and perform the appropriate cost analysis. This is an easy time to go bankrupt from the purchase of too much cost-saving technology.

NEW GREENHOUSE DESIGNS

There is considerable room for improvement in greenhouse design when one considers the poor thermal insulation in current designs relative to other buildings such as homes. Consider a home wall consisting of siding, 0.5 inch plywood, 3.5 inch fiberglass insulation, and 0.5 inch gypsum board. The *R* value for heat transfer through this wall is about 14.5. By comparison, the *R* values for greenhouses covered with either glass or double-layer polyethylene are only 0.93 and 1.43, respectively. The higher the *R* value, the more resistant the wall is to heat movement outward in the winter and inward in the summer. The polyethylene greenhouse transmits heat at 10 times the rate of the home wall described.

The possibility of improvements in greenhouse energy efficiency is strengthened by the fact that while all of the available sunlight is required for some crops in the winter, half or less is used in the summer. One company, Optimum Greenhouses, Inc., has designed a "greenhouse" with walls and much of the roof constructed from steel and heavy insulation with an overall insulating *R* factor of over 30. Only 20 percent (southern California at Gubler Orchids) (Figure 2–23) to

(a)

Figure 2–23

(a) The exterior elevation of the Optimum Greenhouse at Gubler Orchids in Landers, CA. Since light enters only through the roof, any exterior style may be used to blend into the commercial surroundings. (b) The roof of an Optimum Greenhouse. The smaller light emitting vaults in the foreground provide an interior intensity of 1,500 fc (16 klux) while the larger vaults provide 3,000 fc (32 klux). Other light levels are feasible. (c) A commercial crop of orchids inside the Optimum Greenhouse at Gubler Orchids. (*Photos courtesy of Optimum Greenhouses, Inc., 2823 N. Locust Ave., Rialto, CA 92376*)

(b)

(c)

50 percent (Canada) of the roof needs to be open to sunlight. The open portions of the roof are covered with transparent vaults running from east to west and measuring from 18 inches to 36 inches wide across their bases. The *R* factor for the vaults is about 2.25, which is much better than that for double-glazed greenhouses.

Vaults are constructed with an outer layer of fiberglass-reinforced plastic. A reflector is attached to the inside north wall of this layer to catch and reflect sunlight into the greenhouse. A double floor is designed into the vault. The upper floor consists of a double-layer polycarbonate panel. Then there is an air space, and below that an acrylic sheet. The acrylic sheet is a light diffuser, which serves to scatter the light so that the shadowing effect of the opaque portion of the roof is essentially nullified inside the greenhouse. Vault dimensions are dictated by the latitude at which the greenhouse is located as well as by the desired inside light intensity. The vertical height of the vault allows for interception of all of the light that would be received by the entire roof of a conventional greenhouse. However, in this vault-design greenhouse, only 20–50 percent of the roof needs to be open, the rest lending itself to a high level of insulation. Vaults are spaced sufficiently far apart to prevent shadowing from one another on the shortest day of the year.

Light intensity is far more constant throughout the day inside a vault-design greenhouse. In the morning and late afternoon, the angle of sunlight is best oriented with the vault reflector for maximum transmission into the greenhouse. Thus, far more light is received than in a conventional greenhouse. As the angle of incidence of sunlight rises through the day, less is intercepted by the reflector and some begins to strike the opaque portion of the roof. Light intensity is likewise equalized to a greater degree throughout the year. In December in the Northern Hemisphere, sunlight is at a low angle; thus, nearly all light reaching the roof is captured by the vault collectors. In June when the sun is nearly perpendicular to the earth's surface, much of the excess light is blocked by the opaque portions of the roof. Also a portion of the sunlight that reaches the collector is intercepted because the curved top of the reflectors blocks part of the vault openings.

Heat loss during the heating season and heat gain during the cooling season can be from one-sixth to one-tenth that of a conventional greenhouse, which cuts the cost of energy by this amount. The first part of the climate control system continuously circulates the moist greenhouse air through heat exchangers in the soil beneath the greenhouse floor. During times of cooling, moisture in the warm greenhouse air condenses, further aiding the soil's cooling of this air. When the cooled air returns to the greenhouse and warms, it is drier. The drier air, in turn, enhances the evaporative cooling from plant foliage. During cool periods, the greenhouse air is warmed by the soil, which also dries it for better disease control. The floor in this optimum greenhouse is metal, but concrete may also be used. It is important that the floor is covered by a moisture barrier to prevent unwanted evaporative cooling.

The second part of the climate control system constantly exchanges inside air with outside air at the very low rate necessary to maintain a near-ambient carbon dioxide level. Further cooling is accomplished through two thermostatically controlled systems when the soil heat exchanger fails to handle the load. The first system cools through dehumidification. Air is not exchanged with the outside. The second system exhausts air to the outside. When heat requirements are not met by solar radiation and the soil exchanger, a backup heating system is used. It is possible to install a solar collector in the south wall for this purpose since that wall is not used for light entry.

SUMMARY

1. Greenhouse location is as important as the greenhouse design itself. Factors to be sought in a location are as follows:
   a. Room for expansion.
   b. A level, well-drained site.
   c. Reasonable tax structure at present and in the future.
   d. A climate favorable for the crop intended.
   e. Available labor.
   f. Reasonable proximity to utilities and shipping routes.
   g. A plentiful supply of good-quality water.
2. Glass greenhouses are permanent and can last as long as the owner's life or longer. The material expense and labor of periodically replacing the covering is eliminated with glass, but the overall cost of a glass structure is higher. There are two general styles: the high-profile American greenhouses, which can be freestanding or connected in a ridge-and-furrow fashion, and the low-profile Dutch-type greenhouses, which are constructed in a ridge-and-furrow style only because of their narrow bay width of 10.5 feet (3.2 m).
3. Film plastic greenhouses are the least expensive to build. They lend themselves well to temporary business ventures, businesses operated for only one season of each year, and locations where there is a tax advantage for non-permanent structures. Film plastic greenhouses offer an inexpensive means of entering the flower-growing business. However, film plastic ranges can be built on permanent, metal, ridge-and-furrow frames, permitting the full degree of automation and efficiency of any glass or FRP range. Polyethylene is the most common film plastic in use and is usually applied as an air-inflated double layer. The insulating property of the double layer reduces fuel consumption by about 40 percent over a greenhouse with a single covering of polyethylene, glass, or FRP, which makes the double-layer polyethylene greenhouse less expensive to purchase and operate in spite of the periodic labor and the cost of replacing the plastic. Film plastic greenhouses constitute the greater portion of new construction.
4. A third type of greenhouse is the FRP (fiberglass-reinforced plastic) panel greenhouse. FRP panels can be bent to fit most film plastic greenhouse frames. This reduces the labor of replacing film plastic since FRP, depending

on grade, will last 5–20 years. FRP is also used on permanent metal-frame greenhouses. In this latter case, the overall structure generally costs about the same as a glass greenhouse. The FRP covering does not last as long as glass, but it is more resistant to breakage, is cheaper to cool in the summer, and has a more uniform light intensity throughout the greenhouse. FRP greenhouses lost popularity in the late 1970s and early 1980s but are holding their market share at present. The highest concentration of use is in California.

5. Acrylic and polycarbonate double-layer panels are gaining popularity. Thick, 16 mm (0.63 in.) panels can reduce heat loss by 50 percent compared to single-layer glass. Heat savings are moderately less with thinner panels. High cost, uncertainty about life expectancy, and, in the case of acrylic, its flammability are tempering their acceptance. The thinner panels of 6 and 8 mm (0.24 and 0.31 inch) can be bent to fit Quonset designs. A large proportion of these panels are being used for side and end walls on glass and film plastic greenhouses and for retro-fitting old glass and FRP greenhouses.
6. Fresh flower crops are grown in either ground beds or raised benches. Such beds are either 3.5 feet or 4 feet (1.1–1.2 m) wide and are generally 8 inches (20 cm) deep, but 1 foot (30 cm) is best for rose beds. Fresh flower beds are oriented along the length of the greenhouse with 18 inch (46 cm) aisles between them. This arrangement of beds allows for 67 percent utilization of floor space for growing.
7. Pot plants can be grown on raised benches or directly on the floor. Raised benches have open bottoms constructed from wire hardware cloth, expanded metal, redwood lath, or treated boards with at least a 1/2 inch (1.3 cm) space between them. Sides are either not used or are low. Benches are usually 5–6 feet (1.5–1.8 m) wide and are arranged in a peninsular style. A central aisle, 3 feet (91 cm) wide or wider, runs the length of the greenhouse. Benches and smaller aisles radiate out from the central aisle to either side. Such an arrangement makes more efficient use of floor space—up to 80 percent growing area—and minimizes the hand-carrying of plants. Some pot crops are grown directly on floors paved with porous asphalt or concrete. Water penetrates the floor, while weed growth is inhibited. This system permits use of up to 90 percent of the floor space.

REFERENCES

Various greenhouse manufacturers offer literature concerning products and technical information.

1. Aldrich, R. A., W. A. Bailey, J. W. Bartok, Jr., W. J. Roberts, and D. S. Ross. 1976. *Hobby Greenhouses and Other Gardening Structures*. Pub. NRAES–2. Northeast Reg. Agri. Eng. Ser., Cornell Univ., 152 Riley-Robb Hall, Ithaca, NY 14853.

2. Aldrich, R. A., and J. W. Bartok, Jr. 1989. *Greenhouse Engineering.* Pub. NRAES–33. Northeast Reg. Agr. Eng. Ser., Cornell Univ., 152 Riley-Robb Hall, Ithaca, NY 14853.
3. Aldrich, R. A., and T. J. Krall. 1978. Compression strength of porous concrete. *Pennsylvania Flower Growers' Bul.* 307:1–6.
4. American Society of Agricultural Engineers. 1991. Engineering practices—Commercial greenhouse design and layout. In *Engineering Standards.* Amer. Soc. Agr. Engineers, St. Joseph, MI 49085-9659.
5. Bartok, J. W., Jr. 1984. Greenhouse startup and expansion. *Greenhouse Manager* 3 (1):57–78.
6. Beese, E. J. 1978. Wood preservatives and treated lumber for use in landscape construction. *Illinois State Florists' Assoc. Bul.* 377 (May–June):20–21.
7. Brumfield, R. G., P. V. Nelson, A. J. Coutu, D. H. Willits, and R. S. Sowell. 1981. Overhead costs of greenhouse firms differentiated by size of firm and market channel. North Carolina Agr. Res. Ser. Tech. Bul. 269.
8. Courter, J. W. 1965. Plastic greenhouses. Univ. of Illinois Coop. Ext. Ser. Cir. 905.
9. Duncan, G. A., and J. N. Walker. 1973. Preservative treatment of greenhouse wood. AEN–6. Univ. of Kentucky, Dept. of Agr. Eng., Lexington, KY.
10. ______. 1973. Greenhouse coverings. AEN–10. Univ. of Kentucky, Dept. of Agr. Eng., Lexington, KY.
11. Godbey, L. C., T. E. Bond, and H. F. Zornig. 1979. Transmission of solar and long-wavelength energy by materials used as covers for solar collectors and greenhouses. *Trans. Amer. Soc. Agr. Engineers* 22 (5):1137–1144.
12. Gray, H. E. 1956. *Greenhouse Heating and Construction.* Florists' Publishing Co., 343 S. Dearborn St., Chicago, IL.
13. Kozai, T., J. Gourdriaan, and M. Kimura. 1978. *Light Transmission and Photosynthesis in Greenhouses.* Center for Agricultural Publishing and Documentation, Wageningen, The Netherlands.
14. Laurie, A., D. C. Kiplinger, and K. S. Nelson. 1979. *Commercial Flower-Forcing,* 8th ed. New York: McGraw-Hill.
15. Robbins, F. V., and C. K. Spillman. 1980. Solar energy transmission through two transparent covers. *Trans. Amer. Soc. Agr. Engineers* 23 (5):1224–1231.
16. Sheldrake, R., Jr., and R. M. Sayles. 1974. *Plastic Greenhouse Manual: Planning, Construction and Operation.* Dept. of Vegetable Crops, New York State College of Agr. and Life Sci., Cornell Univ., Ithaca, NY 14650.
17. U.S. Housing and Home Finance Agency. 1954. The thermal insulating value of air spaces. Res. Paper 32. Office of Administration, Div. of Housing Res., Washington, D.C.
18. Walker, J. N., and G. A. Duncan. 1973. Greenhouse structures, AEN–12. Univ. of Kentucky, Dept. of Agr. Eng., Lexington, KY.
19. ______. 1973. Greenhouse benches. AEN–13. Univ. of Kentucky, Dept. of Agr. Eng., Lexington, KY.
20. ______. 1973. Rigid-frame greenhouse construction. AEN–15. Univ. of Kentucky, Dept. of Agr. Eng., Lexington, KY.

21. ______. 1974. Painting greenhouses and equipment. AEN–14. Univ. of Kentucky, Dept. of Agr. Eng., Lexington, KY.

22. ______. 1974. Greenhouse location and orientation. AEN–32. Univ. of Kentucky, Dept. of Agr. Eng., Lexington, KY.

23. Wiebe, Jr., and R. E. Barrett. 1970. Plastic greenhouses. Ontario Dept. of Agr. and Food. Pub. 40.

CHAPTER 3

Greenhouse Heating

Heat is measured by the *British thermal unit* (Btu), defined as the amount of heat required to raise 1 pound of water 1°F. When the number of Btu's becomes large, as in heating greenhouses, it is more convenient to use the larger unit, *horsepower* (hp). One boiler horsepower is equivalent to 33,475 Btu. To convert from Btu to boiler horsepower, one divides Btu's by 33,475. In the metric system, a *calorie* (cal) is defined as the amount of heat required to raise 1 gram (g) of water 1°C. One *kcal* equals 1,000 cal or 3.968 Btu. In international units, the *joule* (J) is used, which is equivalent to 0.239 cal or 0.00095 Btu. Reciprocally, 1 Btu equals 252 cal or 1,055 J. One *watt* (W) is equal to 1 J per second.

The requirements for heating a greenhouse reside in the task of adding heat at the rate at which it is lost. Most heat is lost by *conduction* through the covering materials of the greenhouse. Different materials, such as aluminum sash bars, glass, polyethylene, and asbestos-cement curtain walls, vary in conduction according to the rate at which each conducts heat from the warm interior to the colder exterior. For instance, aluminum sash bars conduct heat faster than wood, which results in more rapid loss of heat. (Since the upkeep of wood, however, is much greater, its use is not justified.) Glass conducts heat a little faster than flat fiberglass-reinforced plastic (FRP); thus, an FRP greenhouse constructed out of flat sheets is cheaper to heat. When corrugated sheets of FRP are used, there is more than 1 square foot (about 1.09 ft^2) of exposed FRP per square foot of greenhouse covering. This increases the heat loss since conduction loss is related to exposed surface area. Conduction heat loss is slightly higher in corrugated FRP

Table 3–1

Heat Loss through Various Greenhouse Coverings

Covering Material	*Heat Loss (U)*[1] *Btu*	*Heat Loss (U)*[1] *W*	*Radiation Loss*[2] *(% of total)*
Glass (double-strength float or low-iron)	1.13	6.40	4.4
Glass (two layers)	0.70	3.97	
Single film over glass	0.85	4.82	—
Double film over glass	0.68	3.86	—
PVC (rigid)	0.92[3]	5.21	—
FRP (corrugated)	1.20	6.80	1.0
Acrylic or polycarbonate (16 mm panels)	0.58	3.29	—
Acrylic or polycarbonate (8 mm panels)	0.65	3.69	—
Polycarbonate (6 mm panels)	0.72	4.08	—
Polyethylene (single, 6 mil, UV-inhibited)	1.20	6.80	70.8
Polyethylene (double, 6 mil, UV-inhibited)	0.70	3.97	—
Polyester film (Mylar®, single film)	1.05[3]	5.95	16.2
PVF (Tedlar®, single film)	—	—	30.0[4]
PVF (Tedlar®, double film)	0.76[5]	4.31	—

[1]Btu/hr/ft^2/°F, W/m^2·K; *U* is the combined loss of heat due to conduction and radiation. Unless otherwise indicated, from National Greenhouse Manufacturers' Assoc. (1989) as determined by the ASTM C–236 procedure.

[2]Radiation loss is the amount of radiant heat passing through the covering expressed as a percentage of the total radiant heat beaming upon it. From Duncan and Walker (1973).

[3]Manufacturers' specifications.

[4]From Wheeler (1963).

[5]From Sherry (1983).

than it is in glass greenhouses. Table 3–1 lists heat loss (*U*) values for several greenhouse coverings. A greenhouse covered with one layer of polyethylene, for example, loses 1.20 Btu of heat through each square foot of covering every hour when the outside temperature is 1°F lower than the inside. When a second layer of polyethylene is added, only 0.7 Btu is lost. This is a reduction of almost 40 percent of the heat loss.

There are limited ways of insulating the covering material without blocking light transmission. As previously mentioned, a dead-air space between two coverings appears to be the best system. Forty percent of the heat requirement can be saved when a second covering is applied. The savings diminish when the air space between the two coverings increases to the point where air currents can be established in the space—generally when 18 inches (46 cm) or greater is reached—and the insulation value is completely lost when the two layers touch each other.

Although thermopane glass panels (two layers of glass factory-sealed with a dead-air space) significantly reduce heat loss, they have been too expensive to justify. Sash bars are available from some manufacturers that hold two and even three layers of glass. This establishes one or two dead-air spaces between the layers of glass and yields overall U values of 0.70 and 0.47 Btu (3.97 and 2.66 W), respectively. Double-layer, rigid panels of either acrylic or polycarbonate plastic also utilize the concept of dead-air space for heat conservation. Although more expensive than conventional coverings, these materials in 16 mm thick panels have a lower heat loss (U) value of 0.58 Btu (3.29 W).

A second mode of heat loss is that of air *infiltration*. Cracks between panes of glass or FRP and around ventilators and doors permit the passage of warm air outward and cold air inward. A general assumption holds that the volume of air held in a greenhouse can be lost as often as once every 60 minutes in a double-layer polyethylene greenhouse; every 40 minutes in an FRP or a new glass greenhouse; every 30 minutes in an old, well-maintained glass greenhouse; and every 15 minutes in an old, poorly maintained glass greenhouse (see Table 3–2) (American Society of Agricultural Engineers 1990). About 10 percent of the total heat loss from a structurally tight glass greenhouse occurs through infiltration loss.

A third mode of heat loss from a greenhouse is that of *radiation*. Warm objects emit radiant energy, which passes through air to colder objects without warming the air significantly. The colder objects become warmer. Glass, vinyl plastic, FRP, and water are relatively opaque to radiant energy (do not readily permit the passage of radiant heat), whereas polyethylene is not (Table 3–1). Polyethylene greenhouses can lose considerable heat through radiation to colder objects outside unless a film of moisture forms on the polyethylene to provide a barrier.

Table 3–2

Air Infiltration in Greenhouses*

Greenhouse Type	*Air Exchanges per Hour*
Polyethylene, double-layer	0.5–1.0
Glass, new construction or FRP	0.75–1.5
Glass, old construction, good condition	1–2
Glass, old construction, poor condition	2–4

*From Ross et al. (1978).

HEAT SOURCE

A boiler or heater must be provided to supply heat to the greenhouse at the same rate at which it is lost by conduction, infiltration, and radiation. A *central* or a *localized* heat source may be utilized. In the central system, one or more boilers are located in a single position, and the steam or hot water generated is piped to the various greenhouse locations. The localized system makes use of several heaters, usually forced hot air, each located in the area it heats. The typical cost of a central boiler-pipe-coil system, including installation labor, is \$1.50–\$3.00/ft^2 (\$16.15–\$32.29/m^2) of greenhouse. The cost of a localized unit heater system, including installation labor, is usually \$0.50–\$1.00/ft^2 (\$5.40–\$10.76/m^2).

Central Heating System

The localized system has a low initial investment, which suits it to the greenhouse firm that starts small and expands steadily, purchasing heaters as needed. Much of the high initial cost of a large central boiler is not justified until future expansions demand the full capacity of a boiler. A central boiler system is justified for the greenhouse range that starts out large (1 acre or more, 0.4 ha) and makes its expansions in large increments. A boiler can be very inefficient when it is operated at partial capacity. Much heat is required to warm the boiler and its associated plumbing before net heat is received for the greenhouse. As the net heat required increases, the proportion of lost heat diminishes; hence, boiler efficiency goes up. It is important, therefore, to match the boiler to the greenhouse area. Since there is an economy in purchasing large boilers, large greenhouse expansions are suggested.

The extra \$1.00–\$2.00/ft^2 spent on a central heating system compared to a localized system must be made up somewhere. This is easy to do when wood is burned since it costs only 20–25 percent as much as oil. To a lesser degree, some of the extra price can be made up by burning coal or heavy grades of oil. These fuels cannot be burned in automated localized heaters. A large firm can realize some more of the differential in the cheaper maintenance of one or a few large boilers compared to large numbers of localized heaters. Finally, the grower who has crops that would benefit from warmer soil temperatures must have a boiler to generate the hot water that is circulated through the floor or bench. Conclusive economic data to justify one heat source over the other are missing at this point in time.

Years ago, the central system was usually located in a boiler room separate from the greenhouse. Today, boilers may be found in the service building or in the greenhouse. When the boiler is separate from the greenhouse, considerable heat is lost from the boiler jacket, the pipes carrying steam or hot water to the greenhouses, and the return lines carrying condensate or cool water back to the boiler—in spite of proper insulation. When the boiler is in the greenhouse, the escaping heat contributes toward the heat requirement of the crop. There is a disadvantage to locating the boiler in the greenhouse. The high humidity results in corrosion and premature breakdown of switches, pumps, and motors. It is more desirable to locate the boiler in the service building since heat is needed there and the atmosphere is drier than in the greenhouse.

American greenhouse ranges have been heated by steam as well as hot water. In small ranges with less than 20,000 ft^2 (1,850 m^2) of floor area, hot water systems have been used with typical water temperatures of 180°F. Large volumes of water have to be used in these systems because only 1 Btu of heat energy can be obtained from each pound of water as it drops 1°F (1 cal/g water/°C). Circulating pumps are required to move the water through the system.

Larger ranges traditionally have used steam systems since the volume of water needed is much smaller. One pound of water releases 970 Btu of heat energy when it changes from steam at 212°F to water at 212°F and then an additional Btu for each degree it drops below that point. The advantages of a steam system are a smaller boiler, no circulating pumps, and less plumbing.

In the past, small ranges were not as well automated or supervised during the night as larger ranges were; thus, they were more prone to crop loss by freezing. The large volume of water in the hot water system provided a reservoir of slowly available heat that could protect the greenhouse against frost for several hours after boiler failure. The heat of steam, however, is quickly dissipated, placing greater dependency on continual operation of the boiler. Air temperatures in a hot-water-heated greenhouse remain more constant. However, should the air temperature inadvertently drop, a faster corrective response can be obtained from a steam boiler system. Clearly, hot water and steam systems both have advantages.

European systems make far greater use of hot water, even in larger ranges. These are pressurized systems (14.7 psi, 1 atmosphere), which permit a higher water temperature—203°F (95°C) at the point of greenhouse entry—and thus a greater heat capacity than that of low-pressure systems. This factor reduces the required pipe and boiler sizes of the earlier low-temperature American systems. Such high-pressure hot water systems are often used in larger American greenhouse ranges today.

Attention should be paid to the placement and height of the smoke stack in a central system. The stack should be sufficiently tall so that shifting winds cannot sweep emitted gases into the greenhouses, where they can cause plant injury. It is best to place the stack in a position such that the prevailing winds carry the smoke away from the range and also such that the stack does not cast a shadow on the crop. The north side and the northeast corner, for instance, would be good locations for the boiler and stack under conditions of prevailing winds from the west.

Localized Heating System

Numerous heater designs are used in the localized heating system of greenhouses. These heaters fit into three basic categories: (1)*unit* or forced-air, (2)*convection*, and (3)*low-energy radiant* heaters.

Unit Heaters Unit heaters are often referred to as *forced-air* heaters. The price of a unit heater system varies with the climate in which it is located. The typical cost including installation labor is \$0.50–\$1.00/ft^2 (\$5.40–\$10.76/m^2) of greenhouse floor.

These heaters consist of three functional parts as illustrated in Figure 3–1. Fuel is combusted in a firebox to provide heat. The heat is initially contained in the exhaust, which rises through the inside of a set of thin-walled metal tubes on its way to the exhaust stack. The warm exhaust transfers heat to the cooler metal walls of the tubes. Much of the heat is removed from the exhaust by the time it reaches the stack through which it leaves the greenhouse. A fan in the back of the unit heater draws in greenhouse air, passing it over the exterior side of the tubes and then out the front of the heater to the greenhouse environment again. The cool air passing over hot metal tubes is warmed. In short, the metal tubes serve as heat exchangers, absorbing heat from the hot exhaust passing through the inside of them and transferring it to the cool greenhouse air passing over the outside of them.

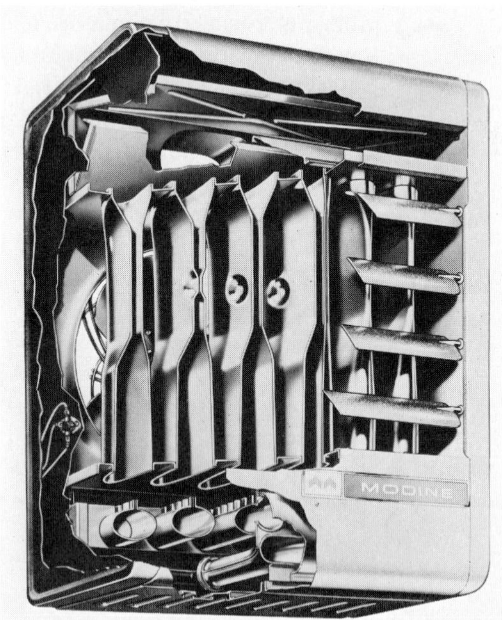

Figure 3–1

Interior view of a horizontal unit (forced-air) heater. Fuel is combusted in the chamber at the bottom. Hot fumes rise inside the heat-exchanger tubes, giving up heat to the walls of the tubes. Smoke exits at the top rear into a stack. A fan behind the unit forces cool greenhouse air over the outside of the tubes, where it picks up heat. (*Photo courtesy of Modine Manufacturing Company, Racine,* WI 53401)

Generally, the fuel supply and fan are connected to a thermostat located in an appropriate area of the greenhouse. Heat is supplied only as needed. Automation is a distinct advantage of unit heaters. Unit heaters burn a variety of fuels, including No. 2 oil, kerosene, LP gas, and natural gas. Fuel types, however, cannot be changed without alteration to the unit heater.

Unit heaters come in vertical as well as horizontal designs (see Figure 3–2) based upon the direction in which the heated air is exhausted from the heater. Vertical heaters take air in from the ridge area of the greenhouse and expel it downward toward the floor. These heaters are purchased in a size capable of heating a square area equal to the width of the greenhouse. They are suspended from the ridge of the greenhouse, well above head height, and are spaced along the length of the greenhouse at intervals equal to its width. When unit heaters first became popular in the 1940s, the vertical type was believed best for greenhouse application. Uneven temperatures and drying of the soil sometimes occurred, which resulted in non-uniform growth. Horizontal units are more widely accepted today. The uneven temperature and drying problems are reduced with horizontal air distribution. It is possible to use fewer but larger heaters, thus reducing the initial cost of the heaters as well as the labor of installation. Horizontal heaters are also adaptable to the newer integrated systems of heating, cooling, and horizontal airflow.

(a) (b)

Figure 3–2

(a) A vertical unit heater typical of the early types used for greenhouse heating. (b) A horizontal unit heater commonly used today.

Whenever fuel is combusted, oxygen is consumed. Old glass greenhouses may or may not have sufficient air leaks to provide the needs of the firebox. Plastic greenhouses are tighter, and there have been many cases where burners have gone out during the night after consuming the available oxygen and causing the crop to freeze. A shortage of oxygen often leads to formation of odorless carbon monoxide gas before the flame goes out. *An employee entering such a greenhouse could lose his or her life.* As a general rule, 1 square inch of opening from the outside should be provided near the heater for every 2,500 Btu capacity of the heater (1 cm^2/114 W). A stovepipe, tile, or flexible clothes dryer tube may be placed near the burner intake, extending outside. It is frequently buried for convenience. An 8 inch diameter pipe would provide the 50 square inches required for a 125,000 Btu heater. The end of the tube should be covered with a screen to prevent the entry of animals.

Unit heaters have an exhaust stack, which generally runs directly through the roof above the heater. The stack must extend above the greenhouse roof sufficiently high to permit dissipation of the smoke without reentry into the greenhouse. The stack should extend 8–12 feet (2.4–3.7 m) above the firebox to ensure a proper air draft.

Convection Heaters Due to their low purchase price, convection heaters are seen in hobby and small commercial greenhouses. They are not satisfactorily automated. These heaters differ from unit heaters in that they do not have a built-in heat exchanger. Fuel of most any type, including wood, coal, oil, or gas, is combusted in a firebox. The resulting hot fumes pass out through an exhaust pipe that is situated along the ground either between ground beds or beneath benches (Figure 3–3).

The exhaust pipe is sufficiently long to permit cooling of the exhaust before it leaves the end of the pipe. The heater is located at one end of the greenhouse, and the exhaust usually exits at the opposite end. The exhaust pipe serves as a heat exchanger, transferring heat from exhaust in the pipe to greenhouse air outside the pipe. The exhaust often is introduced directly into a manifold of large-diameter stovepipe from which several smaller stovepipes feed out. Although stovepipe is frequently used, black polyethylene tubing can be used as well. All joints in the pipe system should be sealed with fire-resistant tape to help prevent leakage of fumes into the greenhouse. To further guarantee against leakage, a low-capacity fan similar to the type used in an oil-fired residential burner should be installed in the outlet of the exhaust system. The fan draws out the exhaust and thus maintains a suction or negative pressure within the system. If leaks exist, air from the greenhouse will enter at these points rather than exhaust escaping. Polyethylene tubing does not work in this system because it collapses under negative pressure.

It is important in all greenhouse heating systems that the exhaust does not contact the crop. When the fuel source is of high purity and is thoroughly combusted, only carbon dioxide and water vapor are produced—but it is rare that

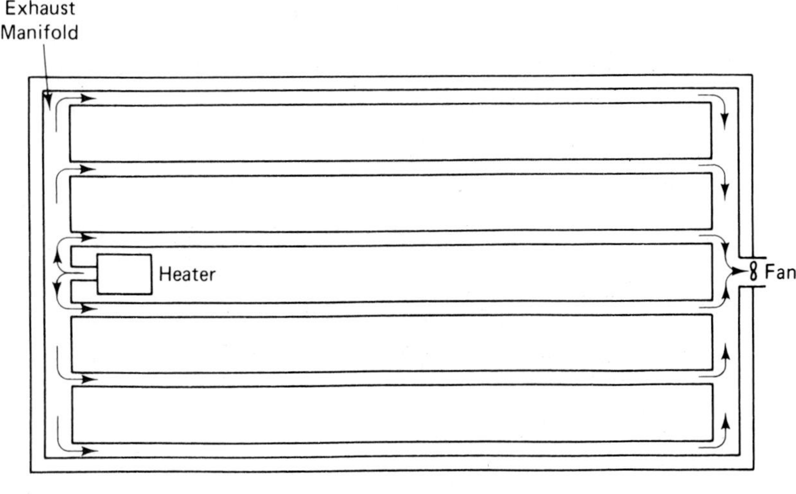

(a)

(b)

Figure 3–3

(a) The physical setup of a convection heating system in a greenhouse. Exhaust from the convection heater enters a large-diameter stovepipe manifold in which it is distributed to several smaller-diameter stovepipes running along the ground between beds or under benches to the opposite end of the greenhouse. There, the exhaust is collected in a manifold and expelled to the outside. A fan located in the outlet draws out the exhaust and maintains a negative pressure in the exhaust-pipe system to prevent fumes from escaping through cracks into the greenhouse. (b) A fan at the end of a stovepipe.

Figure 3–4

Ethylene gas injury to chrysanthemums caused by fumes escaping from an improperly vented unit heater inside the greenhouse. Leaves are distorted and abnormally narrow, and the terminal bud has aborted. (*From* J. W. *Love, Department of Horticultural Science, North Carolina State University, Raleigh,* NC 27695–7609)

fuels are completely combusted. Products of incomplete combustion, including ethylene gas, are injurious to plants (Figure 3–4). Ethylene gas can cause a distorted, corkscrew type of stem growth; curling of leaves; narrow leaves; and abortion of buds. There are also impurities contained in fuels. Sulfur is commonly found in coal, oils, and gases. Upon combustion, it is released as sulfur dioxide gas (SO_2). Sulfur dioxide gas dissolves into moisture films on the plant surfaces and is converted to sulfurous acid and, after oxidation, sulfuric acid, which burns the cells it contacts (Figure 3–5). Small tan spots appear, or in severe cases, the entire leaf may die.

Radiant Heaters Low-energy, infrared radiant heaters have become popular in the past 12 years. Grower reports on fuel savings suggest a 30–50 percent fuel-bill reduction. Infrared radiant heaters are placed overhead in the greenhouse (Figure 3–6). They emit infrared radiation, which travels in a straight path at the speed of light. Objects in the path absorb this electromagnetic energy, which is immediately converted to heat. The air through which the infrared radiation travels is not heated. After objects such as plants, walks, and benches have been heated, they then will warm the air surrounding them. It is the soil and plant temperatures that are important to growth. Air temperatures in infrared radiant-heated greenhouses

Figure 3–5

Sulfur dioxide injury on Rieger begonia foliage. Improperly vented heaters can emit the gas. Carbon dioxide generators burning fuel with an undesirably high sulfur content also produce toxic levels of this gas inside the greenhouse.

can be as much as 7°F (4°C) cooler than in conventionally heated greenhouses with equivalent plant growth. In the conventional system, the air is heated first; the air then heats the plants. Thus, air temperatures tend to be higher than plant temperatures at night. This encourages condensation on plant surfaces. Disease is discouraged by the lesser amount of condensation in infrared radiant-heated greenhouses.

Infrared radiant heaters used in greenhouses are available in sizes from 20,000 to 120,000 Btu/hr (5,860 to 35,160 W) in 20,000 Btu/hr increments. The distance between heaters can be 30–40 feet (9.1–12.2 m). They are placed in tandem overhead along the length of the greenhouse. Above the line of heaters, running the length of the greenhouse, is a deep-dish metal reflector to direct all rays down toward the plants and to give the proper uniformity of heat across the production area. The composition of this reflector is important to ensure that maximum reflectivity is achieved. A high-quality metal for this use is aluminum. Each heater mixes air from the greenhouse with fuel and injects it into a 4 inch (10 cm) pipe. Newer systems ignite the fuel by direct fire ignition rather than by using a pilot light or a spark plug. The pipe heats to a temperature around 900°F (480°C). This is not sufficiently hot to cause the pipe to emit visible red light, which would interfere with the photoperiodic timing of some crops (see Chapter 11). Actually, the temperature can be varied by the manufacturer to suit specific

(a)

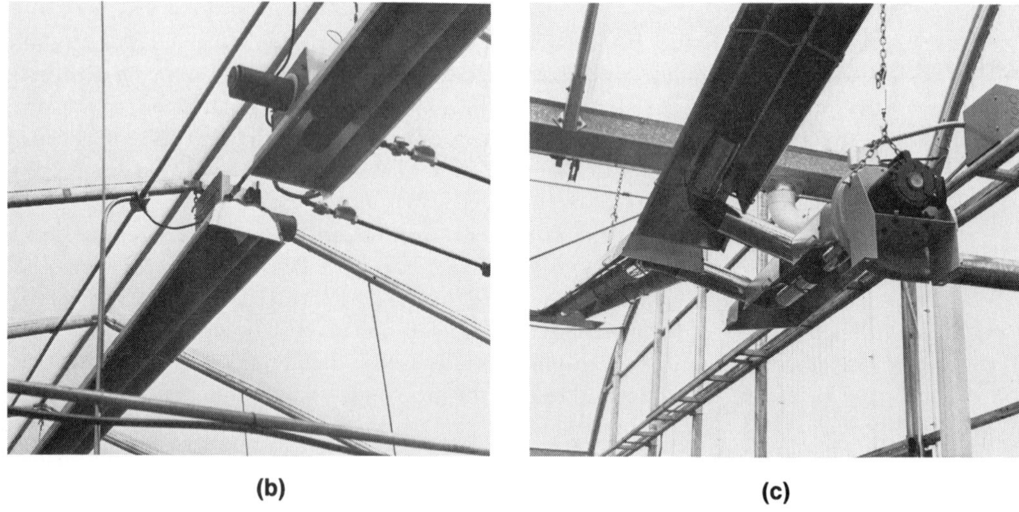

(b) (c)

Figure 3–6

(a) A greenhouse installation of an infrared radiant heating system. (b) Burners installed in two adjacent infrared radiant heating lines. (c) The exhaust fan and outlet port serving two infrared radiant heating lines. (*Photos courtesy of* Infrared Systems, 1719 Old Highway 99 S, Mt. Vernon, WA 98273)

greenhouse spatial needs. The pipe extends the length of the greenhouse, where it exits to the outside. Fumes are drawn along the length of the pipe through a vacuum developed by a pump in the end of the pipe. A vacuum of 2 inches (5 cm) of water column is developed in the pipe. A 0.5 hp (370 W) pump can handle up to 16 smaller heaters. Since the pipe in the vicinity of each heater can be 900°F (480°C), it is important that plants not be placed within 5 feet (1.5 m) of the pipe. Radiant heaters today can heat a width of plant surface up to 3 times the height of the heaters above the plant surface.

Reasons for fuel savings fall into two categories. First, fuel gases in this system exit at less than 150°F (65°C) as opposed to 400–600°F (204–315°C) in conventional greenhouse heaters. Thus, more heat is derived from the combusted fuel. The efficiency of combustion is claimed to be about 90 percent. Second, cooler air temperatures in the greenhouse ensure a smaller temperature differential from outside to inside. Therefore, less heat is lost from the greenhouse. It is important that high-velocity air circulation as generated by convection tubes not be used in infrared radiant-heated greenhouses. Air currents set up by such fans would cool the plants and carry the air warmed by the plants and floor to the cold greenhouse covering. The horizontal airflow (HAF) system (discussed later in this chapter), having a gentler airflow, is apparently acceptable. Another advantage of this heating system is the reduction of about 75 percent in electrical consumption over a conventional unit heater system. The only motor required in the infrared radiant heating system is in the exhaust fan.

Installation and materials for an infrared radiant heating system can range from slightly less than $1.00 in warm southern states to about $2.00/ft^2 of greenhouse floor area in northern states and provinces ($10.76–$21.53/m^2). Although capital costs of this system are higher than those of conventional forced-air unit heaters, the fuel savings could pay for the additional cost over a few years. However, one should be aware that in recent years unit heaters and boilers have become available with low stack temperatures (300°F, 150°C), which allows them to share in part of the benefit that formerly belonged exclusively to radiant heaters. Second, the advantage of the lower inside-to-outside temperature differential across the greenhouse covering offered by radiant heating systems can be achieved in floor heating systems (discussed later). Finally, radiant heaters burn either natural gas or manufactured gas. While natural gas continues to offer a cost advantage over other fuels, manufactured gases have become expensive relative to other fuels in recent years. The grower who must use manufactured gases could be at a disadvantage.

A choice of radiant heating products exists. Factors to consider in selecting one include thermal efficiency, emissivity, reflectivity, fixture efficiency, and pattern efficiency. *Thermal efficiency* is the ratio of heat potential in the fuel consumed to the energy released in the heater. *Emissivity* is a measure of the capacity of the heater tubes to release infrared energy. *Reflectivity* is a measure of the ability of the reflector to redirect energy. *Fixture efficiency* refers to the amount of infrared energy that is absorbed by the heating fixture and is converted to heat ultimately to be convected away. This amount should be as low as possible. *Pattern efficiency* is a measure of the ability of the heater to distribute radiant energy to the space in a manner consistent with the needs of the space. The overall efficiency of the system is a combination of all of these factors.

Solar Heating

Solar heating has recently been the topic of considerable attention as a partial or total alternative to fossil-fuel heating systems. Few solar heating systems exist in greenhouses today. As will be seen, the economics of such a system bear scrutiny. In this section, the fundamental principles and components of solar heating will be considered. The components (Figure 3–7) consist of (1) a collector, (2) a heat storage facility, (3) an exchanger to transfer the solar-derived heat to the greenhouse air, (4) a backup heater to take over when solar heating does not suffice, and (5) a set of controls.

Collector Various solar heat collectors are possible, but the type that has received greatest attention is the flat-plate collector. This consists of a flat black plate (rigid plastic, film plastic, or board) for absorbing solar energy. The plate is covered on the sun side by two or more transparent glass or plastic layers and on the back side by insulation. The enclosing layers serve to hold the collected heat within the collector. Water or air is passed through or over the black plate to remove the entrapped heat and carry it to the storage facility.

A greenhouse itself is a solar collector. Some of its collected heat is stored in the soil, plants, greenhouse frame, walks, and so on. The remaining heat can be excessive for plant growth and is therefore vented to the outside. The excess vented heat could just as well be directed to a rock bed for storage and subsequent

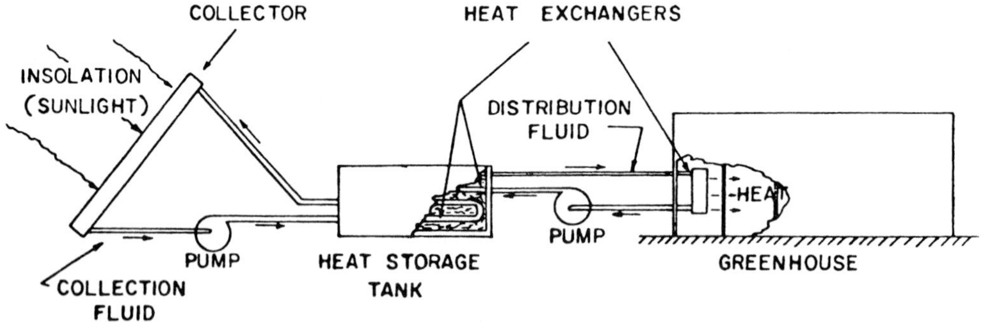

Figure 3–7

A typical solar heating system for greenhouses. (*From* D. H. *Willits, Department of* Biological *and* Agricultural Engi*neering,* North *Carolina State University, Raleigh,* NC 27695–7625)

use during a period of heating. Heat derived in this manner could provide up to half of the total heat requirement for greenhouses in the southern United States and perhaps 10–20 percent of the total requirement in northern states.

Collection of heat by flat-plate collectors is most efficient when the collector is positioned perpendicular to the sun at solar noon. The required angle of tilt with respect to the ground is equal to the latitude on March 21 and September 21 (the spring equinox and fall equinox). The angle should be gradually increased to a maximum of the latitude plus 23° on December 21 (the winter solstice) and then decreased thereafter. Since movable collectors add considerable expense, a stationary compromise angle of the latitude plus 15° is often used (Figure 3–8).

The amount of solar radiation reaching the earth's surface varies with such factors as weather conditions and elevation. Average daily quantities of solar radiation striking a square foot of horizontal surface during July and January are presented in Figure 3–9. While an average solar input of 600 Btu/ft^2 (1,625 kcal/m^2, 6,800 kJ/m^2) of surface per day is expected in the Washington, D.C., area (38°N latitude), not all can be trapped by a solar collector. At solar noon, a flat-plate collector using water can have an efficiency of 65 percent, but the efficiency diminishes at either side of that point to zero percent in the early morning and late afternoon. Considering an overall efficiency of 40 percent, 240 of the 600 Btu impinging on a square foot of collector in a day can be trapped for heating a greenhouse. Based on a heat output of about 100,000 Btu per gallon of oil, 417 square feet of collector would be required to equal the heating capacity of 1 gallon of oil (10.25 m^2 of collector/l oil). At least ½ square foot of collector surface is required per square foot of greenhouse floor area, and in northern areas 1 square foot may be needed.

Heat absorbed by the black plate inside the collector is often removed by water or air. The black plate may be a sheet of black plastic tubes fused together. In this case, water can be passed through the interior of these tubes. If it is a solid

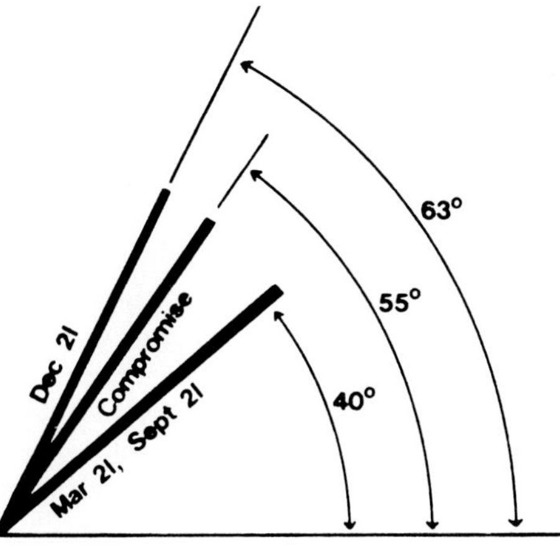

Figure 3–8

The best angle of tilt with respect to the ground for a solar collector at 40°N latitude (Philadelphia, Denver) is 40° on Mar. 21 and Sept. 21. During the 91 days from Sept. 21 to Dec. 21, it increases by 23° to 63°. After Dec. 21, it decreases continually to a value of 40° by Mar. 21. A stationary collector is generally oriented at a compromise angle equal to the latitude plus 15° or 55° in this example.

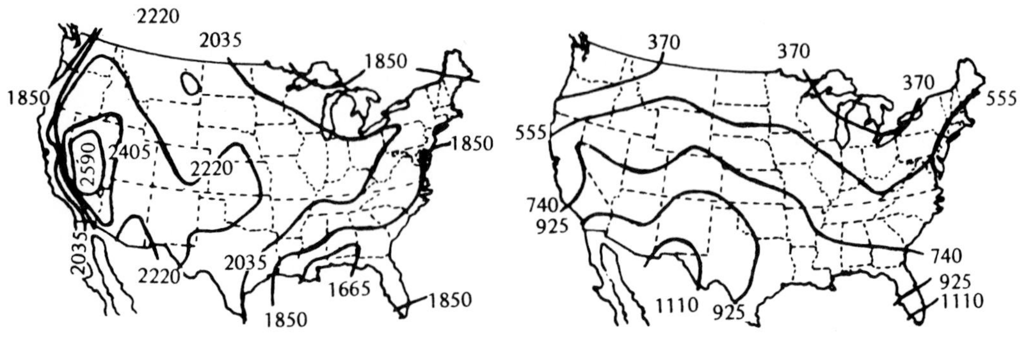

Figure 3–9

Average daily solar radiation received on a square foot of horizontal surface throughout the United States in July and in January. One Btu/ft^2 is equivalent to 2.7 kcal/m^2 or 11.4 kJ/m^2. (*From* Ross *et al.*, 1978)

black sheet, such as polyethylene, water may be passed over its surface. Water picks up the heat and is then transferred to a storage tank. Air may likewise be passed through or over the black plate to remove heat from it. Water collectors require a flow rate of 1–3 gallons per minute (gpm) per 100 square feet (0.4–1.2 l/min/m^2) of collector surface. Correspondingly, air-heating collectors require a flow rate of 5–15 cubic feet per minute (cfm) per square foot (1.5–4.6 cmm/m^2) of collector.

Storage and Heat Exchanger Water and rocks are the two most common storage materials for heat in the greenhouse at the present. One pound of water can hold 1 Btu of heat for each °F temperature rise (4.23 J/g water/°C). Thus, its specific heat is 1. Rocks can store about 0.2 Btu per pound for each °F temperature rise (0.83 J/g rock/°C). The specific heat in this case is 0.2. To store equivalent amounts of heat, a rock bed would have to be 3 times as large as a water tank. A rock storage bed lends itself well to an air-collector and forced-air heating system. In this case, heated air from the collector, along with air excessively heated inside the greenhouse during the day, is forced through a bed of rocks. The rocks absorb much of the heat. The rock bed may be located beneath the floor of the greenhouse or outside the greenhouse, assuming that it is well insulated against heat loss. During the night, when heat is required in the greenhouse, cool air from inside the greenhouse is forced through the rocks, where it is warmed and then passed back into the greenhouse. A clear polyethylene tube with holes along either side serves well to distribute the warm air uniformly along the length of the greenhouse. Conventional convection tubes (such as will be discussed later in this chapter for both heating and cooling greenhouses) can be used for distributing solar-heated air.

A water storage system is well adapted to a water collector and a greenhouse heating system making use of a pipe coil or a unit heater with water coil contained within. Heated water from the collector is pumped to the storage tank during the day. As heat is required, warm water is pumped from the storage tank to a hot water or steam boiler or into the hot water coil within a unit heater. Although the solar-heated water will be cooler than the thermostat setting on the boiler, heat will be saved since the temperature of this water will not have to be raised as high to reach the output temperature of water or steam from the boiler.

Low-temperature solar systems have been the most popular for greenhouses thus far because of their lower price. Solar input during the daytime can cause a storage unit temperature rise in these systems of up to 30°F (17°C) above the evening baseline temperature. Each pound of water can thus supply 30 Btu of heat, and each pound of rock 6 Btu as it cools to 30°F. A 20 foot by 100 foot (6.1 m by 30.5 m) double-layer polyethylene greenhouse has been reported to lose about 3,500 Btu/hr/°F (1,848 W/K) of temperature differential between inside and outside. If an inside temperature of 60°F (16°C) and an average outside night temperature of 35°F (2°C) are experienced and the heating period is considered to be 13 hours long, about 1.1 million Btu (1.17 million kJ) of heat will be required. This would require a 4,400 gallon (16,600 l) water storage tank. (Note that 1,100,000 Btu heat requirement divided by [(Btu/lb × °F) × 30°F × (8.3 lb/gal water)] equals 4,400 gal.) To store the same quantity of heat, about 2,000 cubic feet (ft^3) (57 m^3) of rock would be required.

The water or rock storage unit occupies a large amount of space and a considerable amount of insulation if the unit is placed outdoors. Placing it inside the greenhouse offers an advantage in that escaping heat is beneficial during heating periods. It is detrimental when heating is not required. Rock beds can pose a problem in that they must remain relatively dry. Water evaporating from these beds would remove considerable heat.

Backup Heater Today, a solar heating system is considerably more expensive than a conventional system. Current strategy calls for sizing a solar system to meet the average winter needs. A conventional fossil-fuel backup system is installed to meet the additional heating needs of the coldest nights. This compromise increases the chances of justifying the cost of a solar heating system.

Controls To illustrate typical controls in a solar-heated greenhouse, a water system is considered. The first control activates when water in the collector becomes 10°F (6°C) higher than in the storage tank and cuts off when the differential is 5°F (3°C). Water is pumped from the collector to the top of the storage tank. Cooler water at the bottom of the storage tank returns to the collector. A second control activates the storage tank to the greenhouse heat-exchanger pump when the greenhouse air temperature drops to 63°F (17°C) and turns it off when 65°F (18°C) is achieved. A third control turns on the backup heater at an air temperature of 60°F (16°C) in the event that the solar system fails to hold the desired temperature. A fourth control empties water from the collector into an underground tank when the collector temperature approaches freezing and refills it when the collector temperature rises.

Economics High-capacity collectors capable of raising the storage unit temperature more than 30°F (17°C) have the advantage of requiring less collector area and storage capacity. High-capacity systems are very expensive; thus, low-capacity collectors are more typically used in greenhouses. Costs five years ago for a low-capacity system were about \$4–\$5/ft² (\$43–\$54/m²) for the collector and \$8–\$10/ft² (\$86–\$108/m²) for the total system.

Even at \$8/ft² (\$108/m²) of collector for the total system, the price per acre for a solar heating system is \$348,500 (\$871,000/ha). This is assuming a ratio of 1 square foot of collector per square foot of greenhouse floor area. Such a system might meet total heat requirements in southern regions where 1 gallon of oil is consumed per square foot of floor area per year (41 l/m²/yr) for single-glazed greenhouses. The annual savings in fuel based on \$0.70 per gallon for oil (\$0.19/l) would be \$30.500 per acre (\$75,000/ha). Taking into account interest on invested capital, repairs, electrical consumption, and implicit costs, the payoff period for this system would be well beyond 20 years and highly questionable.

Solar heating systems do, however, exist in commercial greenhouse firms. Generally, these firms are small, and the owner may have been satisfied to overlook portions of the true cost of the system. The owner may have constructed the system personally without placing a value on his or her labor. The firm may have financed the system out of prior profits and failed to calculate an interest cost for the money. The profits could otherwise have been invested and yielded interest. The lost interest is a real *opportunity cost,* which should be added into the total cost of the solar system.

The advent of solar heating does not appear to be on the horizon at this time. Factors that could set the stage would include a return to proportionately high fuel prices, more efficient collectors, and/or an inexpensive, high-capacity heat storage medium.

HEAT DISTRIBUTION

Upon combustion of fuel in the firebox of the heater or boiler, the heat must be transferred to the greenhouse. It is important that only a minimum amount is lost during the transfer and that once inside the greenhouse the heat is evenly distributed across the growing area. Warm air rises to the peak of the greenhouse, where it is of little value, and the cooler air forming at the glass surface drops to the lower area where the plants are growing. This situation raises the price of heating, but fortunately it can be controlled. We have already seen how heat is distributed from radiant heaters and convection heaters and how heat from solar systems is integrated into the heat distribution mechanisms of almost any type of conventional backup heating system. Now, we will focus on heat distribution from (1) steam and hot water and (2) warm air sources.

Steam and Hot Water

Hot water has been customarily supplied at a temperature of 180°F (82°C) in 2 inch (51 mm) pipe in American greenhouses and at a temperature of 203°F (95°C) in 2 inch (51 mm) pipe in Dutch greenhouses. Steam systems, on the other hand, supply steam usually at a temperature of 215°F (102°C), which is 3° above the temperature at which water turns to steam and is possible because the system is under a low pressure of 5 pounds or so. Since there is less resistance to the flow of steam, smaller pipes of 1½ or 1¼ inch (32–38 mm) diameter are used in the greenhouse coil. The amount of pipe needed in a greenhouse coil can be determined by referring to the heat supply values listed in Table 3–3 for various types of pipe. A greenhouse requiring 160,000 Btu of heat per hour would need 1,000 linear feet of 2 inch hot water pipe to provide this heat. This was determined by dividing the total heat requirement for the greenhouse by the amount of heat that 1 linear foot of pipe can provide. In this case, 160,000 Btu/hr is divided by 160 Btu per linear foot of 2 inch hot water pipe, which yields an answer of 1,000 feet of pipe. If a 1½ inch system of steam pipes were used instead, the need would be 160,000 Btu/hr divided by 210 Btu/hr, or 762 feet of pipe.

Placement of heating pipes is very important. If all the pipe is stacked on the side walls and end walls, undesirable patterns of airflow will occur. The cross-sectional view of the greenhouse shown in Figure 3–10a shows that the heat from the side coils of pipe rises along the side wall and part of the roof until it meets a

Table 3–3

Heat Available from Various-Diameter Pipes Heated by Hot Water or Steam*

Heat Source	*Pipe Diameter*	*Heat Supplied*	
		Btu/hr/ft	*W/m*
Steam, 215°F (102°C)	1½ in. (38 mm)	210	202
Steam, 215°F (102°C)	1¼ in. (32 mm)	180	173
Hot water, 180°F (82°C)	2 in. (51 mm)	160	154
Hot water, 203°F (95°C)	2 in. (51 mm)	200	192

*The inside air temperature of the greenhouse is 60°F (16°C).

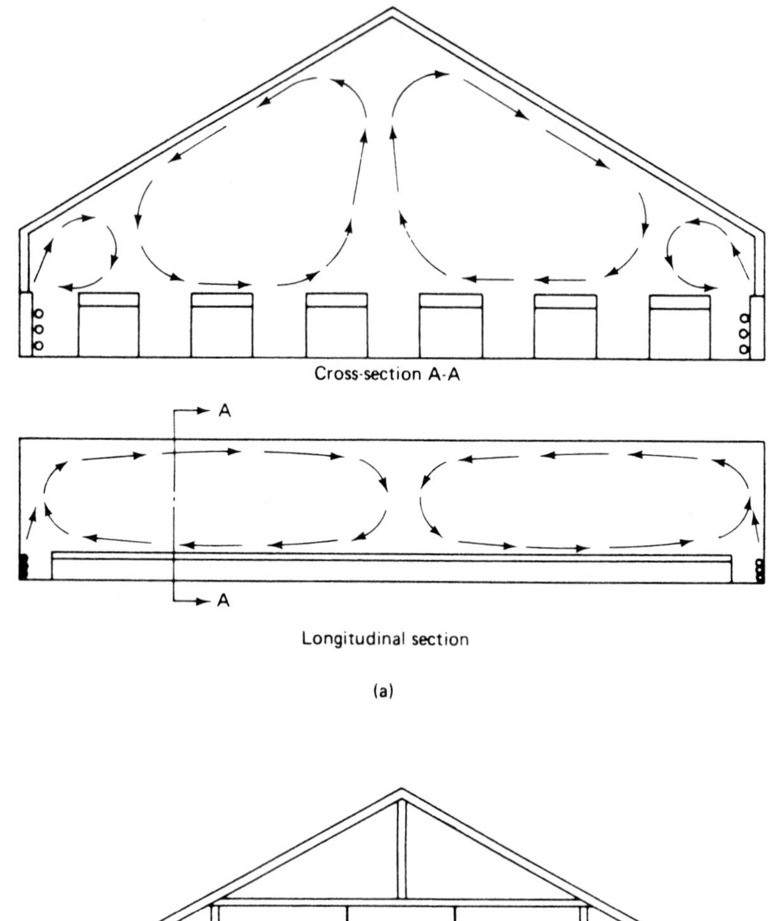

Figure 3–10

(a) Air circulation pattern in a greenhouse using only side coils during the winter. (b) A desirable combination arrangement of overhead pipe and side coils for controlling downdrafts and cold spots in the greenhouse. (*From Gray*, 1956)

stream of air that is being cooled by the glass and is flowing downward under the roof. The two currents mix and drop at this point. Part returns to the pipe coil and part moves toward the center of the greenhouse at plant level, creating a cold spot in the center. In the center of the greenhouse, currents meet from both sides and rise. The longitudinal section shows that heat rises from the end wall coils to the peak, where it travels toward the center of the house and cools as it moves. In the center, the two cool air masses meet and drop to the ground. The growth of plants is delayed where these cold spots occur. Cold spots can be counteracted by the placement of pipe in the regions of the downdrafts. For this reason, about one-third of the pipe is placed across the greenhouse running from end to end as illustrated in Figure 3–10b. The remaining two-thirds of the pipe is placed in stacks along the outer walls. Side pipes should have a few inches of clearance on all sides to permit the establishment of air currents and should be located low enough to prevent blockage of light entering through the side walls. They are generally attached to the curtain wall.

When several pipes are stacked above one another, their effectiveness is reduced. Additional pipes must be added to compensate. Table 3–4 shows the effect. For two pipes, the effect is insignificant. Five pipes in a stack, however, are only as effective as four pipes placed apart from one another. In a heating design where the heat of four pipes is needed in the side coil, five pipes would have to be installed. Overhead pipes are spaced sufficiently far apart to avert the problem.

The expense of pipes and installation became a concern during the 1950s, and alternative materials and designs were sought. Fin pipe became popular as a partial substitute for conventional pipe. Fin pipe is a conventional pipe with numerous thin metal plates radiating outward from it to increase the surface area of the pipe and thus the rate at which it transfers heat from the hot water or steam contained inside to the surrounding air.

Table 3–4

Heat Supply Relationship of Pipes in a Vertical Stack Compared to Pipes Located Separately from One Another*

Number of Pipes in Vertical Stack	*Equivalent Number of Individuals Pipes Giving Same Amount of Heat*
1	1
2	2
3	2⅔
4	3⅓
5	4
6	4⅓
8	5

*From Gray (1956).

Depending on the design, 1 linear foot of fin pipe can be equivalent to 4 or more linear feet of conventional pipe. It should be remembered that heat released from fin pipe is much more intense than heat from conventional pipe. It is therefore important to distribute fin pipes evenly throughout a greenhouse. If a single continuous coil of fin pipe is not needed around the entire greenhouse, then the fin pipe should be alternated with conventional pipe at equidistant intervals.

Pipe coils can be arranged in two styles, either box or trombone (Figure 3–11). Box coils are used in hot water systems. Hot water entering the greenhouse through the pipe main is distributed in a header, or branch tee, to several smaller pipes through which it passes simultaneously to the opposite end of the greenhouse. There, it combines and returns to the boiler to be reheated. There is a resistance to the flow of water in the pipe. The box coil minimizes this resistance by reducing the length of pipe through which any given portion of the water must flow and by increasing the cross-sectional area of the combined pipe through which the water passes.

Trombone coils are used for steam systems. Resistance to flow is not a problem for steam, but the rapid drop in pressure and temperature along the pipe is. If a box coil were used for steam conduction, the entry end would be hot and the exit end much cooler, resulting in an intolerable temperature gradient in the greenhouse. A continuous pipe is used in a trombone coil. Steam enters at the top of the coil and passes to the distant end of the greenhouse. It returns to the entry end in the second pipe down and then back to the distant end in the third pipe down. This arrangement continues until, at the end of the coil, water condensate and steam enter a trap that permits the return of water, but not steam, to the boiler. No temperature gradient exists along the length of the coil. The gradient exists from top to bottom of the coil and is of no consequence. The overhead pipe coil is usually a trombone coil whether hot water or steam is used. In the case of a hot water system, two overhead trombone coils are used to reduce resistance.

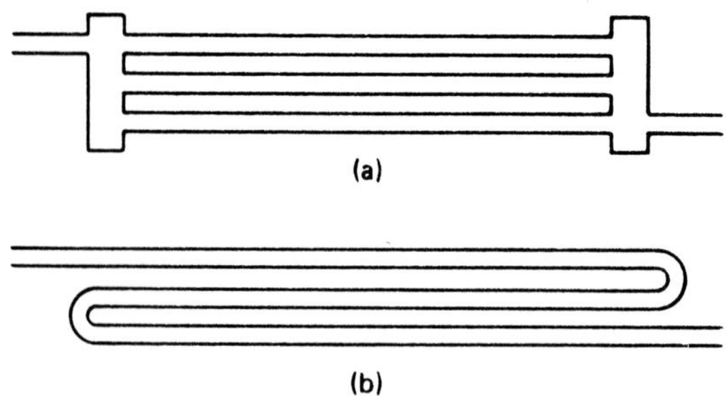

Figure 3–11

(a) Box coil used to distribute hot water through a greenhouse. (b) Trombone coil used in a steam system of heating.

Prior to the middle of this century, heating pipe across the greenhouse was located near the ground either beside ground beds or under benches. The purpose was to heat the soil and plants and minimize the heat loss into the gables. Primarily because of the need for clear space to facilitate automation equipment, after World War II the heating pipes were moved from the floor to the zone above the plants.

Shortly after the shift in heating-pipe location, vertical air-lift fans were introduced to reduce the vertical temperature gradient that occurs in greenhouses heated by pipe coils (Figure 3–12). Since warm air rises, the temperature in the peak can be as much as 1°F warmer for each foot (1.8°C/m) in elevation above ground level. It is only the heat at plant level that counts. Vertical air-lift fans were installed in a row beneath the ridge in greenhouses heated by pipe coils. Warm air from the peak enters the fan from the top and is distributed outward at a gentle downward angle. These fans greatly reduce the vertical temperature gradient, making better use of heat and reducing fuel costs. However, these fans result in very uneven temperatures at plant height. Vertical air-lift fans have not been used with forced-air heating systems.

The next step in the evolution of heat distribution systems stemmed from the high cost of heating pipes. Unit heaters supplied with steam or hot water from

Figure 3–12

Vertical air-lift fan installed in the peak of the greenhouse to transfer warm air down to the plant level.

a central boiler became popular around 1960 as a substitution for the pipe coils. They resulted in considerable cost savings in materials and labor of installation. Because the unit heater contains a fan for heat distribution, vertical air-lift fans are not used with this system. Unit heaters became very popular in America, while pipe coils remained popular in Holland.

Considerable effort has been made in the past decade to bring the heat distribution system back down to the soil level without losing the advantage of clear space. In these situations, pipe coils rather than unit heaters are being used. Pipes are being installed in the framework of benches beneath the table top (Figure 3–13). This arrangement is also possible for movable benches because the frame remains fixed in place. Fresh flower and vegetable beds in Holland are likewise heated with hot water pipes, which are suspended by flexible rubber hoses from overhead mains (Figure 3–14). The heat pipe is confined to the bed and does not cross aisles. For crops such as roses, the pipe may be located in the bed of plants, while for others it is located on either side of each bed. Hot water is used in these systems because temperatures lower than that of steam are required to avoid burning of plants. Hot water also ensures a uniform temperature throughout the greenhouse. To facilitate removal of plants, root-media pasteurization, and replanting, the heating pipes can be lifted and tied overhead without disconnecting them.

Figure 3–13

A 2 inch (51 mm) hot water heat pipe supported by the lower frame of a movable pot plant bench.

Figure 3–14

The hot water pipes heating this tomato crop growing in rock wool are located between the plant rows and just above the floor for maximum efficiency of heat distribution. The hot water pipes are suspended from overhead mains by flexible rubber hoses. This permits the pipes to be raised overhead when the crop is finished for cleaning-up purposes.

Hot water heating pipes are also being installed under slabs of rock wool in this new cultural system to heat the root substrate. The nutrient solution in some nutrient film technique (NFT) hydroponic systems is being heated to deliver heat directly to the roots rather than only to the air above the plants. (Rock wool and other closely related cultural systems are described in Chapter 9.)

The latest approach to heating the root zone takes on two forms. In the first, 0.75 inch (19 mm) diameter pipes are buried in the floor 8–12 inches (20–30 cm) apart depending upon the heat requirement, water temperature, and depth of pipes. The floor may consist of gravel or porous concrete. Polyethylene pipe has commonly been used but has been known to break. PVC pipe can be used but is not popular because of its inflexibility and cost. Polybutylene pipe is now recommended for its flexibility, strength, and high temperature tolerance. Hot water, generally at a temperature of 100°F (38°C), is circulated through the pipe to maintain the desired temperature in the plant canopy. Hot water is pumped the length of the floor and then back to the inlet end to provide a bidirectional flow for the purpose of uniform heat distribution along the length of the greenhouse. In general, heat is applied at the rate of 20 Btu/hr to each square foot (63 W/m^2) of floor. Since the root zone and plant area are heated first, the air temperature above the plants is commonly 5–10°F (3–6°C) lower than in conventionally heated greenhouses with no loss in plant growth. As in the case of radiant heating, this lowers the temperature differential across the greenhouse covering and thereby cuts fuel costs. Floor heating provides one more means of justifying the high cost of central heating systems.

A floor heating system can provide all of the required heat during the fall and spring. On cold winter days, supplemental heating, such as an above-ground pipe coil or unit heaters, will be required. Over the whole year, floor heating may provide from 20–50 percent of the total need and perhaps average out to 25 percent. If the floor is covered with a crop of potted plants or bedding plant flats, a high percentage of the total heat need will be met because the plants are near the heat source and tend to hold the heat down. When plants are grown on benches, the efficiency of this system is reduced. Higher air temperatures are required at the elevation of the plants. Also, heat is able to escape more freely from the uncovered floor to the greenhouse gable, where it is not desired. Hanging baskets reduce the efficiency even more. The total heat requirement cannot be supplied through the floor in cold climates because excessive temperatures could occur in plants on or near the floor. Heat is first supplied via the floor in floor heating systems, and only when this is insufficient are supplemental heaters used. The total system including a porous concrete floor with heating pipes, a hot water heater, controls, and installation labor costs about \$2.00/ft^2 (\$21.50/m^2) of greenhouse floor. This does not include a supplemental heater for the rest of the heat requirement.

Another recent method for heating the root zone is available in various commercial packages (Figure 3–15). Flexible EPDM tubing can be either buried in the floor, placed on the floor, or placed on or beneath the bench surface. It is recommended, however, that it be placed on the floor rather than in it for better heat transfer. Tubes are usually spaced about 2 inches (5 cm) apart along the length of the floor or bench but may be spaced closer or farther apart to meet local heat needs. The inlet and outlet mains for the tubing are located on the same end of the floor or bench to provide bidirectional flow. Tubing is $^5/_{16}$ inch (8 mm) in outside diameter. The tubing is sufficiently strong to withstand burying in concrete or gravel or having pots placed directly on it. Water is circulated through the tubes at temperatures up to 140°F (60°C). The total heat requirement can be met with this system even with a 100°F (56°C) temperature differential from outside to inside.

Figure 3–15

EPDM hot water heat tubing used on the surface of a greenhouse bench for heating a crop of bedding plants. Note that the flats (or pots) are placed directly on the heating tubes. (*Photo courtesy of* Biotherm Co., 421 Second St., Petaluma, CA 94952)

A moderate number of large installations of EPDM tube heating have been made both on the floor and in the bench. Such installations require a large hot water source. Many firms without central hot water boilers have installed EPDM tube heating systems mainly for specialized purposes such as plant propagation. Smaller hot water heaters independent of the primary heat source of the firm are used in these cases for the tube heating system. A tube heating system including heat source, manifolds, tubing, controls, and installation labor costs about \$1.25–\$2.25/ft^2 (\$13.46–\$24.22/m^2) of greenhouse floor.

Warm Air Sources

Unit Heaters Many modern American greenhouses are heated with unit heaters rather than with pipe coils alone. Unit heaters may have a self-contained firebox, or they may derive heat from steam or hot water that is generated in a central boiler and then piped to the heat-exchanging coil within the unit heater. Horizontal unit heaters are used.

Warm air is emitted directly into the greenhouse environment in many small greenhouses. In larger greenhouses, where circulation is a problem, a polyethylene tube is connected to the air outlet (Figure 3–16). The polyethylene tube is installed along the length of the greenhouse above plant height and is sealed at the distant end. Round holes 2–3 inches (5–8 cm) in diameter are located in pairs at opposite sides of the tube every few feet (0.5–1.0 m) along the tube length. Warm air from the heater moves through the tube and out the side holes. The warm air comes out at a high velocity in a jet stream and quickly mixes with the

Figure 3–16

A horizontal unit heater connected to a transparent polyethylene tube with holes along either side for uniform distribution of heat.

surrounding air. This system ensures that heat is distributed from one end of the greenhouse to the other. When neither heating nor cooling is required, many growers keep the fan in the unit heater running without heat so that air from the greenhouse is continually circulated through the tube. Air circulation gives more uniformity of temperature in the greenhouse, conserves heat, and reduces the occurrence of disease by reducing condensation on plant foliage. The polyethylene tube is also used to bring cold air in when cooling is needed during the winter.

Considerable heat is lost through the side walls of the greenhouse. In addition, warm plants radiate heat energy to colder objects outside the greenhouse. The result is a disproportionately high cooling effect in the outer beds of plants. In colder climates, many overhead unit heater systems are supplemented with one or two rows of pipe around the perimeter of the greenhouse. The side coil should have a heat-supplying capacity equal to the heat loss through the walls of the greenhouse. This will generally be one-third or slightly more of the total heat requirement. If more than one row of pipe is required, fin pipe can be used to keep the size of the installation to a minimum. The perimeter pipe coil is generally turned on first and the overhead heaters later when more capacity is required.

Care must be taken to locate unit heaters and air distribution tubes below any thermal screens and photoperiodic shade blankets that may be used in the greenhouse. Some firms have installed the air distribution tubes beneath benches. This is only feasible where long benches are situated in such a manner that tubes do not need to cross aisles.

Horizontal Airflow System A more recent system for establishing uniform temperature in pipe-heated greenhouses is the horizontal airflow (HAF) system developed at the University of Connecticut. This system uses small horizontal fans and moves the air mass with less than half the electricity required by vertical air-lift fans.

The greenhouse may be visualized as a large box containing air. It is difficult to start the air moving, but once it is moving in a circular pattern, like water in a bathtub, it is easy to keep it moving. The horizonal airflow pattern of the HAF system also results in the movement of warmer air from the gable to the plant height and reduces heating costs. Temperatures at plant height are much more uniform with the HAF system than they are in the heat distribution patterns from vertical air-lift fans, which this system replaces.

Minimum and maximum airflow velocities for this system are 40 and 200 feet per minute (fpm) (0.2 and 1.0 m/sec). Below this level, airflow is erratic, and uniform mixing of air cannot be assured. A velocity of 40 fpm (0.2 m/sec) causes slight leaf movement on plants with long leaves, such as tomato. This system should move air at 2–3 cfm/ft^2 of floor (0.6–0.9 cmm/m^2 of floor). Fans of $^1/_{15}$–$^1/_{10}$ hp (62–75 W) and a blade diameter of 16–20 inches (40–50 cm) are sufficient. Commercial, continuous-duty motors should be used. With approximately one fan per 50 feet (15 m) of greenhouse length, fans should be aimed directly down the length of the greenhouse and parallel to the ground. The first fan should be installed 15–20 feet (4.6–6.1 m) from the end of the house; the last one, 40–50 feet (12.2–15.2 m) from the end toward which it is blowing.

Specifications for the HAF system are shown in Figure 3–17 and are described as follows.

1. For individual houses, install two rows of fans along the length of the greenhouse, each row one-quarter of the width of the greenhouse in from the side wall. The row of fans on one side of the greenhouse should blow air opposite to the direction of the row of fans on the other side of the greenhouse to form a circulating pattern. Fans should be 2–3 feet (0.5–1.0 m) above the plants.

2. For ridge-and-furrow houses, install a row of fans down the center of each greenhouse. If the block contains an even number of greenhouses, move air down one house and back in the adjacent greenhouse. In this way, each pair of greenhouses has a circulating air pattern. Connecting gutters must be sufficiently high to permit air movement beneath them. If the block contains an odd number of greenhouses, move air in the same direction in the first and third houses and back the opposite way in the second house.

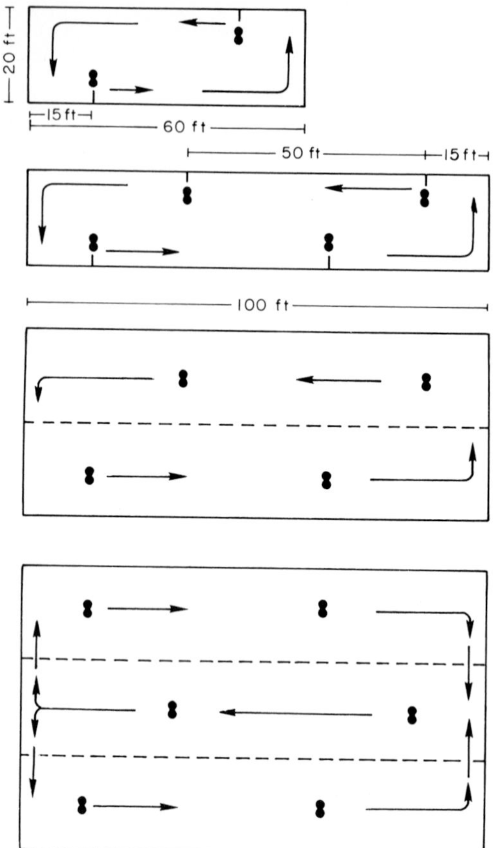

Figure 3–17

Fan arrangements for a horizontal airflow (HAF) system in various greenhouse sizes. Fans are located one-quarter of the width of the greenhouse in from the side walls in the first two single greenhouses illustrated. They are located under the ridge in the ridge-and-furrow greenhouse diagrams. (*Adapted from* Aldrich *and* Bartok, 1989)

The HAF system can also be used where unit heaters are used rather than a pipe coil. A unit heater is substituted for the fan at one or both ends of each greenhouse, depending on the heat requirement of the greenhouse. This places the heat source in the path of the airflow. The fan in the unit heater serves to circulate the air.

GREENHOUSE CLIMATE SENSING AND CONTROL

Cooling and heating systems are controlled by temperature sensors such as thermostats and thermistors. Since temperature gradients exist in greenhouses with even the best of heating systems, placement of the sensor is very important. Its location should reflect the average temperature in the greenhouse. If it were placed in a location near the heater or in a direct flow of warm air, the heater would turn on and off according to conditions in that warm spot and the remainder of the greenhouse would run colder than desired. Consequently, the majority of the crop might be delayed. Sensors are quite often placed near the center of the greenhouse. The height of the sensor placement is also very important with respect to the vertical temperature gradient. The sensor should be located at the height of the growing points of the plants. For pot plant crops, this height is usually 6–12 inches (15–30 cm) above the pot rim. For cut flowers, the height varies, and the sensor should be attached to a post on which it can be raised or lowered.

Direct or indirect rays of sunlight will raise the sensor temperature well above the air temperature. This will prevent the operation of the heater on cold but bright winter days when heat is needed. The sensor should therefore be shielded from the sun's rays. A very desirable system calls for placement of the sensor in a box (Figure 3–18). The outer surface of the box is painted in a reflective color such as white or aluminum to reduce heat buildup. The ends of the box have louvers to permit air passage but prevent entry of the sun's rays. A fan is installed to provide a minimum airflow through the box of 600 fpm (3 m/sec). This

Figure 3–18

An aspirated box that houses the heater thermostat, a low-temperature alarm thermostat, and a thermometer. The box has a reflective outer surface, louvered ends, and a fan to provide a minimum airflow of 600 feet per minute. It is located at the height of the growing points of the plants.

ensures that a large mass of air is continually monitored by the sensor. A housing for climate control sensors is commercially available that can be easily raised and lowered on its suspending chain.

Other instruments should be located in the sensor station. A second sensor set at a low temperature such as 50°F (10°C) should be connected to an alarm in the manager's or owner's home. This will alert someone in the case of heat failure while there is still time to make corrections. The alarm system should be powered by a battery or a standby generator to ensure that it operates during an electrical power failure. When the alarm is to be located a long distance from the greenhouse, it is possible, working through the local telephone company, to use their existing lines.

Thermostats have historically been used for temperature sensing and control in the greenhouse. Most often thermostats have been of the *bimetallic-strip* type. The strip curves to conform to the air temperature because the two metals fused together in the strip have different thermal expansion coefficients. Such a thermostat generally has a switch built into it. It might be a mechanical switch activated by contact with the end of the bimetallic strip, or it could be a mercury switch attached to the end of a bimetallic coil. Depending on the number of settings, such thermostats can cost $200 and up. These thermostats are not highly accurate, nor are they reproducible over time. They need to be routinely calibrated. One problem has been the variation from one thermostat to another within a brand. Even an individual thermostat may slip upward out of calibration one time and downward the next time.

More accurate and reproducible temperature sensing is obtained by those growers who use *thermistors.* The thermistor is a solid-state temperature sensor that changes its voltage output according to the temperature. This sensor requires a circuit to carry the signal to a switch. The switch may be a conventional one for smaller equipment or a relay switch for larger equipment. The circuit can be adjusted to activate switches at specific voltage (temperature) settings. The response is exclusive to temperature, and no other factors are integrated.

The third level of temperature-control equipment also typically includes a thermistor-type sensor. The circuitry, however, contains a microprocessor or even a computer and is termed "intelligent" since decisions can be made within it based on combinations of data received. Such controllers can begin at a cost of $10,000. Their ultimate value lies in the ability to sense several environmental factors, to decide upon the best combination of these factors for optimizing crop growth, and then to send the signals to activate various equipment that will establish this environment. Such controllers should more accurately be called *environmental controllers.*

Factors presently of concern are light intensity, inside temperature, relative humidity, and carbon dioxide (CO_2) concentration in the greenhouse atmosphere. When supplemental lighting is not used, the light level provided by nature is accepted without alteration. The CO_2 level and temperature that will ensure maximum possible growth for the existing light intensity are determined in the computer. The CO_2 generator and the heating or cooling systems are then activated by signals from the computer to establish this optimum balance of growth factors. Such measurements and adjustments are made to maintain growth at its fullest potential without any unnecessary expenditure of energy.

Many environmental computer control systems are preprogrammed. The purchaser is unable to get into the program to alter the environmental factor settings to suit his or her judgment, perhaps to accommodate a new crop not planned in the original program, or even to incorporate new information as it is released from research institutes. Perhaps in time increased sales volume will foster the development of software (programs) that can be custom set for individual growers and that can be altered by the grower.

A major drawback to the development of intelligent environmental controllers is the shortage of integral growth-factor research data. The computer age has caught us with good data for individually setting day or night temperatures, CO_2 level, or light intensity but with little of the necessary knowledge of the almost infinite number of optimum combinations of all of these. We think in terms of day temperatures as 10–15°F (6–8°C) higher than night temperatures. This is probably true on the average but not for each individual day or perhaps for each stage of growth. At what rate and over how many days should night temperatures be lowered to tone a chrysanthemum crop in the reproductive stage? Would it be beneficial to drop from the day to the night temperature gradually over several hours rather than all at once as is currently done? Should the nighttime low temperature differ according to the growing conditions of the previous day? These and many more decisions will one day enter into the computerized decision-making process for greenhouses. The benefits will be seen in improved yield, quality, and energy consumption. Today, we have few answers. One should look carefully at the source of information used to develop the software offered in preprogrammed environmental controllers before investing. A final point worthy of mention is that an intelligent microprocessor type of temperature controller that is not programmed to sense data other than temperature and that cannot be programmed by the grower offers no improvement in control over a non-intelligent thermistor controller but costs much more.

In addition to the services described, environmental controllers, utilizing information from light sensors, are used to draw sunscreens over crops on excessively bright days. Because of the frequent sensing of light conditions, this system may retract and re-cover the crop as often as necessary on partly cloudy days. Information from humidity sensors is used, particularly on winter nights, to activate exhaust systems that briefly expel saturated air and bring in drier air. This averts condensation on foliage, which could lead to disease development. Environmental controllers are used to decide when to apply water and/or nutrient solution to crops. When a predetermined quantity of solar energy is sensed, solenoid valves or pumps are activated. Solar radiation is well correlated to root-media drying.

Many more uses for computers will be found in the near future in the greenhouse industry. They are already assuming an irreplaceable role in keeping firms economically viable. Research direction has shifted and will continue to shift in accordance with the need for computer technology.

EMERGENCY HEATERS AND GENERATORS

The risk of electrical power failure is always present. If a power failure should occur during a cold period, such as a heavy snow or ice storm, crop loss due to freezing is likely. Heaters and boilers depend upon electricity. Solenoid valves controlling fuel entry, safety control switches, thermostats, and fans providing air to the firebox all depend upon electrical energy.

Power failure can be damaging during the summer as well. Temperature control in greenhouses lacking ventilators is dependent upon electrical exhaust fans. It is likely that the temperature will rise to 120°F (49°C) in a closed greenhouse on a clear summer day if a ventilator system is not in effect. High temperatures cause delay in flowering of many crops and, if prolonged for several days, can cause flower bud abortion. Many other types of equipment used in growing crops depend upon electrical power. For these reasons, it is important that a standby electrical generator be installed (Figure 3–19).

The generator can be wired into the greenhouse circuit in such a way that it automatically turns on in the event of a power failure. Some thought should be given to the types of equipment that will be run in this situation. It is rare that the cost can be justified for a generator to handle all power needs. Lights used during the night for control of crop flowering draw considerable power and often cannot be handled by available generators. As will be discussed in Chapter 11, it is possible to use cyclic (flash) lighting in which the crop is divided into three to five zones. Only one zone is lighted at a time, thus reducing the load demand. During the summer, if the entire cooling system cannot be handled, a proportion of the fans should be maintained to ensure against excessive temperatures.

A standby electrical generator is essential to any greenhouse operation. It may never be used, but if required for even one critically cold night, it becomes a highly profitable investment. Generators are available from a number of used-equipment sources, such as government surplus. A minimum of 1 kilowatt (kW) of generator capacity is required per 2,000 ft^2 (184 m^2) of greenhouse floor area.

It is equally likely that the heating system will fail. Temperatures can drop rapidly in a greenhouse if the insulating properties of the coverings are poor. The rate of temperature decline is increased by lower outside temperatures and by increases in wind velocity. Frequently, time is insufficient to seek assistance or repair the heater before the inside temperature reaches the freezing point. In northern latitudes, this period can be as short as three or four hours. Greenhouse owners

Figure 3–19

A standby electric generator (*left*) used in the event of power failure to maintain operation of the boiler (*right*), cooling system, and possibly a portion of the lights used for photoperiodic timing of the crop. (*From* J. W. *Love, Department of Horticultural Science, North Carolina State University, Raleigh*, NC 27695–7609)

using a central boiler system sometimes purchase two boilers to do the job of one. In the event of failure of one, the other can still maintain temperatures above freezing. In greenhouses heated by unit heaters with self-contained fireboxes and by infrared radiant heaters, there is little to fear since there are many heaters. It is unlikely that more than one or two could fail at any one time. Situations where there is only one heater in a given greenhouse or only one central boiler require that a backup heating system be available.

Some growers have installed natural gas or LP gas burners on flexible fuel lines in the greenhouse. When needed, these burners can be moved out into aisles from their storage places under benches or along walls. Because they are already connected to a fuel source and are ready to light manually, no electricity is required.

The Salamander radiant heater, seen in Figure 3–20, is a popular and inexpensive backup. A kerosene supply is maintained in the pot at the bottom. It is combusted within the bottom part of the vertical stovepipe. The fumes rise up the pipe and out the top into the greenhouse. For this reason, a ventilator should be opened about ½ inch (1.3 cm) to prevent concentration of the fumes. The stove-

Figure 3–20

A Salamander heater typical of the type of device that should be held in reserve in the event of heat failure. Kerosene contained in the lower pot burns inside the exhaust stack. Since fumes come out the top, ventilators must be opened a crack when these heaters are used.

pipe turns red and radiates considerable quantities of heat. One heater can raise the temperature of 12,000 ft^3 (340 m^3) of air 25–30°F (14–17°C) and is considered adequate emergency heat for up to 1,500 ft^2 (140 m^2) of greenhouse floor area. The heater burns between ½ gallon and 1 gallon of kerosene per hour. One-gallon cans (3.8 l) have been used as well for emergency heat. The top is removed, and two 1 inch (2.5 cm) holes are cut in opposite sides 2–3 inches (5–8 cm) down from the top to provide air circulation. The can is half filled with alcohol and ignited. Many other systems are feasible. It is important that one be available.

FUEL

Solid, liquid, and gaseous fuels represented by wood, coal, oil, and gas are used for greenhouse heating. Each has advantages and disadvantages. The choice is influenced by antipollution regulations. The use of coal and high-sulfur-content oils has been disallowed in some areas.

Natural gas is the most desirable fuel because the initial installation of a natural gas system is cheaper; storage tanks are not required; and the gas burns clean, which reduces the labor of adjusting and cleaning the boiler. Propane and butane gases have many of the advantages of natural gas but are more expensive.

Oil is generally the next choice. An oil-fueled system is easily automated, but storage tanks are necessary and considerably more ash and soot result. The boiler exhaust passages, or tubes, must be cleaned often, and adjustments are needed at least annually in the firebox. Fuel oils are available in five grades, designated No. 1, 2, 4, 5, and 6. No. 1 is slightly heavier than kerosene and is generally used to heat private homes. The oil becomes heavier (more viscous) as the number increases. No. 6 oil must be preheated before ignition, or it will not flow through the nozzle in the burner. No. 2 oil is used in small greenhouse heaters, and the heavier grades are used in large boilers. The heavier oils cost slightly less and have a higher heat content. Large central boilers, which can burn heavier grades, offer a cost advantage.

Coal is available in many grades. The terms *anthracite* and *bituminous* refer to hard and soft coals, respectively. Many intermediate kinds exist with no distinct lines of demarcation. Materials softer than bituminous also exist, ranging all the way to peat. All are the compacted remains of plant material. Coal requires considerable above-ground storage space, more labor of handling than oil, and yields large volumes of ash, which must be removed and disposed of.

Boilers are commercially available for burning wood. These systems can be completely automated. Owners of moderate-size greenhouses requiring a boiler of 100 hp (980 kW) output and larger could consider this option. A few have done so and are realizing a considerable savings in their heating costs. Fuel can consist of green chips made from entire trees, green chips intended for paper pulp, or sawdust. Green chips have a heat content of about 4,500 Btu per pound (10.5 kJ/g) and a moisture content of about 40–50 percent depending on tree species. Dried wood has a heat content of about 8,500 Btu per pound (19.8 kJ/g) and a moisture content of 18 percent. Taking into account a burning efficiency of 60 percent for wood and 70 percent for oil, a price of $1 per ton for green wood chips is equivalent to 1.8¢ per gallon for oil ($1/metric ton of wood = 0.43¢/l of oil). The current price of $18 per ton for green whole-tree chips is equivalent to an oil price of 33¢ per gallon (9¢/l). This is a little less than half of the current $0.70 per gallon price of oil.

Not all of the fuel-price differential is profit since a more complex fuel-handling system is required for wood. A storage shed is needed to keep rain off the wood. Remember, 1 ton of wood is required for every 56 gallons of oil normally consumed (1 metric ton of wood/233 l of oil). A silo is required to continuously supply wood to an auger, which feeds it into the boiler. An existing coal boiler can often be converted to burn wood. A tractor is needed for moving wood around in the storage shed and into the silo. Finally, a large bin is needed to collect ash from the boiler. Although the system can be automated, additional labor is required to remove ash from the boiler and dispose of it. In spite of these costs and others,

Table 3–5

Typical Heat Contents for Various Types of Fuel Used for Greenhouse Heating[1]

Fuel	*Heat Value*		*Boiler Efficiency (%)*	*Heat Output*	
Moist Coal–Mine Run	*Btu per lb*	*kJ per g*		*Btu per lb*	*kJ per g*
Anthracite (hard)	12,910	30.0	65	8,392	19.5
Semi-anthracite	13,770	32.0	60	8.262	19.2
Low-volatile bituminous	14,340	33.3	65	9,321	21.7
Medium-volatile bituminous	13,840	32.2	60	8,304	19.3
High-volatile bituminous	10,750–13,090	25.0–30.4	55	5,913–7,200	13.7–16.7
Sub-bituminous	8,940–9,150	20.8–21.3	55	4,917–5,033	11.4–11.7
Fuel Oils	*Btu per gal*	*kJ per ml*		*Btu per gal*	*kJ per ml*
No. 1	132,900–137,000	37.1–38.2	70	93,030–95,900	26.0–26.8
No. 2	135,800–141,800	37.9–39.6	70	95,060–99,260	26.5–27.7
No. 4	140,600–153,300	39.2–42.8	68	95,608–104,244	26.7–29.1
No. 5	148,100–155,900	41.3–43.5	67	99,227–104,453	27.7–29.2
No. 6	149,400–157,300	41.7–43.9	65	97,110–102,245	27.1–28.5
Gases	*Btu per cu ft*	*kJ per dm^3*		*Btu per cu ft*	*kJ per dm^3*
Natural	1,000	37.3	75	750	27.9
Manufactured	550	20.5	70	385	14.3
Propane[2]	2,570	95.7	75	1,928	71.8
Butane	3,225	120.1	75	2,419	90.1
Wood	*Btu per lb*	*kJ per g*		*Btu per lb*	*kJ per g*
Green chips	4,500	10.5	60	2,700	6.3
Dried pellets	8,500	19.8	60	5,100	11.9

[1]The heat value is the amount of heat contained in the fuel. The boiler efficiency and heat output are the percentage of the heat value and the actual amount of heat that is obtained from the fuel when combusted in a burner. Efficiency will vary from one boiler design to another; however, these figures give a good relative comparison of energy contents of different fuels.

[2]One gallon of propane has a heat value of 91,690 Btu (25.6 kJ/ml), while one gallon of butane has a heat value of 102,000 Btu (28.5 kJ/ml).

one large greenhouse firm was able to pay back the additional capital cost over an oil system in less than two years and has since realized a considerable savings in heating costs. Modern systems burn wood clean enough to meet federal air pollution standards.

More recently, log-burning boilers have made their way into the greenhouse industry. They can be purchased for heating requirements as small as 200,000 Btu/hr (56,600 W). The firebox can accommodate 6 foot logs, which are loaded by tractor. These open-system hot water boilers generate no pressure. As such, they are free of state inspection requirements for pressurized boilers. The burning efficiency is about 65 percent. The cracked logs, undesirable sizes, and species normally left behind after harvesting the forest can be used for fuel in these boilers. Taking into account the burning efficiencies, 1 cord of wood provides the heat output of 147 gallons of oil (1 m^3 of wood = 148 l of oil). At the current price of $40 per cord, this would be equivalent to buying oil at 26.7¢ per gallon (7¢/l), which is cheaper than the cost of wood chips. For other conversion purposes, it is handy to know that 1 cord of green wood weighs slightly less than 3 tons. Log-burning boilers cost much less than boilers used for burning oil or gas. Logs can be left out in the rain prior to burning, and storage sheds are therefore

Table 3–6

Comparative Costs of Electricity, Oil, and Gas[1]

An Electric Rate of:	Is the Same As If You Heated with			
	Fuel Oil at:		*Gas at:*	
¢/kWh	*¢/gal*[2]	*¢/l*[2]	*¢/therm*	*¢/m³ (natural gas)*[2]
2.0	57.0	15.1	43.8	4.7
2.2	62.7	16.6	48.2	5.2
2.4	68.4	18.1	52.6	5.7
2.6	74.1	19.6	56.9	6.1
2.8	79.8	21.1	61.3	6.6
3.0	85.5	22.6	65.7	7.1
3.2	91.2	24.1	70.1	7.5
3.4	96.9	25.6	74.5	8.0
3.6	102.6	27.1	78.8	8.5
3.8	108.3	28.7	83.2	9.0
4.0	114.0	30.2	87.6	9.4
4.4	125.4	33.2	96.4	10.4
4.8	136.8	36.2	105.1	11.3
5.2	148.2	39.2	113.9	12.3
6.0	171.0	45.2	131.4	14.1
6.8	193.8	51.3	148.9	16.0

[1]Adapted from a table by Clifford M. Tuck and Associates, Athens, GA 30604.
[2]Heat values: kWh = 3,416 Btu; gal = 139,000 Btu; therm = 100,000 Btu.
Boiler efficiency = No. 2 fuel oil at 70%; gas at 75%.

not required. Labor is required to cut the logs and to load them 2–3 times daily into the firebox.

The quantity of fuel required for one night, or for any given period of time, can be predicted by knowing the heat value of the fuel to be used and the heat required in the greenhouse. The heat requirement can be easily calculated (as will be seen later in this chapter). The heat values of the common greenhouse fuels are listed in Table 3–5.

Table 3–5 shows that the heater in a greenhouse requiring 100,000 Btu of heat per hour would burn 11.9 pounds of anthracite coal, or 1 gallon of No. 4 oil, or 133 ft^3 of natural gas. All are equivalent in heat value. Each is determined by dividing the output heat value of the selected fuel into the Btu's of heat required in the greenhouse. In the case of anthracite coal, the 100,000 Btu required in the greenhouse was divided by 8,392 Btu, which is the heat output of 1 pound of coal, resulting in a need for 11.9 pounds of coal.

The cost of fuel is a strong factor in its selection. Equivalent costs of three types of fuel are listed in Table 3–6. The three figures on any line in the table are equivalent. That is, a Btu or a joule of heat would cost the same for each of the three fuels. Taking the eighth line, for example, 3.4¢ per kilowatt hour (kWh) is equivalent to paying 96.9¢ per gallon of No. 2 oil or 74.5¢ per therm of gas. One should check local prices for fuel. If oil is available for 96.9¢ per gallon and electricity for 4¢ per KWh, it is much cheaper to heat with oil. On the other hand, if gas costs 65¢ per therm, each Btu of heat costs less from gas than oil.

CALCULATION OF HEAT REQUIREMENTS

A-Frame Greenhouse

In order to determine the heat requirement, the surface of an A-frame greenhouse must be divided into four components, as illustrated in Figure 3–21. They are the roof, gable, wall, and curtain wall. Heat lost under standard conditions through each of these areas can be found in Tables 3–7 and 3–8. All values in the tables are listed as MBtu, which means thousands of Btu. A figure of 5 in the table, for example, means 5,000 Btu. One MBtu is equivalent to 293 W or 252 kcal/hr. The gable and roof losses can be found in Table 3–7. There are two wall components: (1) the wall covered with a transparent covering and (2) the curtain wall below it, which has a nontransparent covering such as asbestos-cement or concrete block. The heat loss from each is determined separately in Table 3–8. The wall length in each case refers to the total perimeter of the greenhouse since the wall extends around four sides of the greenhouse.

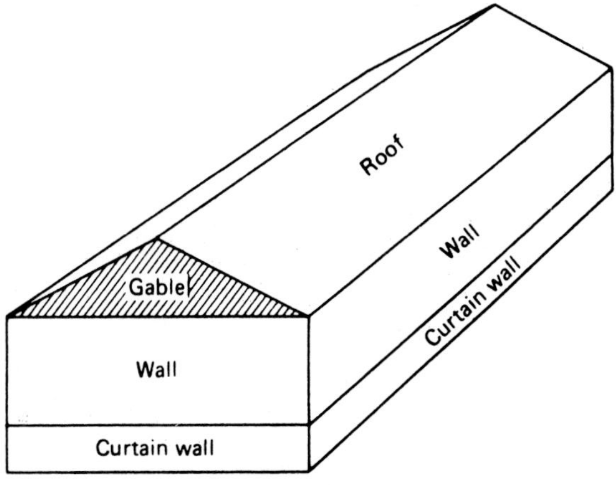

Figure 3–21

Diagram of an A-frame greenhouse showing component areas needed in the determination of the heat requirement of this greenhouse.

All heat losses thus far determined are for standard conditions, which include a 70°F (21°C) temperature difference from the outside to the inside and an average wind velocity of 15 miles per hour (mph) (6.7 m/sec). It is likely that you will have different temperature and wind conditions for a different type of greenhouse construction. You can change the heat loss values in Tables 3–7 and 3–8 by multiplying them by two correction factors. First, determine the difference in temperature between your desired inside night temperature and the coldest outside temperature you expect to encounter during the winter. (Local temperature probabilities can be obtained from the nearest U.S. Weather Bureau Office or by purchasing the most recent Weather Bureau Climatological Data pamphlet from the Superintendent of Documents, Government Printing Office, Washington, D.C. 20042.) Next, determine the average wind velocity for your area. For most areas, 15 mph (6.7 m/sec) will suffice. (However, this too can be checked out with the nearest U.S. Weather Bureau Office.) Select a climate factor, *K*, from Table 3–9 for your particular temperature difference and wind velocity and multiply each heat loss value from Tables 3–7 and 3–8 by the factor. Select a construction factor, *C* from Table 3–10 for the type of greenhouse you have and multiply this by the heat loss values for the gable, roof, and wall (transparent covering only). Determine a curtain-wall construction factor, *CW*, from Table 3–11 and multiply the curtain-wall heat loss value by this factor. All greenhouse component heat losses have now been corrected. The four corrected values should be added together to determine the total heat input required to heat the greenhouse for 1 hour.

Table 3–7

Standard Heat Loss Values for Gables and Roofs of A-Frame Greenhouses[1]

	Greenhouse Width in Feet (m)														
	16 (4.9)	18 (5.5)	20 (6.1)	22 (6.7)	24 (7.3)	26 (7.9)	28 (8.5)	30 (9.1)	32 (9.8)	34 (10.4)	36 (11.0)	38 (11.6)	40 (12.2)	50 (15.2)	60 (18.3)
	Gable Loss (both) in MBtu/hr[2]														
	5	6	8	10	11	13	15	18	20	23	26	29	32	50	72
Greenhouse Length in Feet (m)	Roof Loss (both) in MBtu/hr														
5(1.5)	7	8	9	10	11	12	12	13	14	15	16	17	18	22	26
10(3.0)	14	16	18	19	21	23	25	27	28	30	32	34	35	45	54
20(6.1)	28	32	35	39	42	46	50	53	57	60	64	67	71	88	106
30(9.1)	42	48	53	58	64	69	74	80	85	90	96	101	106	133	160
40(12.2)	57	64	71	78	85	92	99	106	113	120	127	135	142	177	212
50(15.2)	71	80	89	97	106	115	124	133	142	151	159	168	177	222	266
60(18.3)	85	96	106	117	127	138	149	159	170	181	191	202	212	265	318
70(21.3)	99	112	124	136	149	161	173	186	198	211	223	235	248	310	372
80(24.4)	113	127	142	156	170	184	198	212	227	241	255	269	283	354	424
90(27.4)	127	143	159	175	191	207	223	239	255	271	287	303	319	398	478
100(30.5)	142	159	177	195	212	230	248	266	283	301	319	336	354	443	532
200(61.0)	283	319	354	390	425	460	496	531	567	602	637	673	708	885	1,062
300(91.4)	425	478	531	584	637	690	743	797	850	903	956	1,009	1,062	1,328	1,594
400(121.9)	566	637	708	779	850	920	991	1,062	1,133	1,204	1,274	1,345	1,416	1,770	2,124
500(152.4)	708	797	885	974	1,062	1,150	1,239	1,328	1,417	1,505	1,593	1,682	1,770	2,213	2,666

[1]Tables 3–7 through 3–12 adapted from National Greenhouse Manufacturers' Assoc. (1979) and from Bohanon et al. (1989).
[2]One MBtu/hr = 239 W or 252 kcal/hr.

Table 3–8

Standard Heat Loss Values for Greenhouse Walls[1]

Wall Length in Feet (m)	Wall Height in Feet (m)				
	2 (0.61)	4 (1.22)	6 (1.83)	8 (2.44)	10 (3.05)
	Wall Loss in MBtu/hr[2]				
5(1.5)	1	2	2	3	4
10(3.0)	2	3	5	6	8
20(6.1)	3	6	9	13	16
30(9.1)	5	9	14	19	24
40(12.2)	6	13	19	26	32
50(15.2)	8	16	24	32	40
60(18.3)	9	19	28	38	47
70(21.3)	11	22	33	44	55
80(24.4)	13	25	38	51	63
90(27.4)	14	28	43	58	71
100(30.5)	16	32	47	64	79
200(61.0)	32	63	95	128	158
300(91.4)	47	95	142	192	237
400(121.9)	63	127	190	256	316
500(152.4)	79	158	237	320	395

[1]From Bohanon et al. (1989).
[2]One MBtu/hr = 293 W or 252 kcal/hr.

If the heating system is located inside the greenhouse, your calculation is finished. Purchase a boiler with a net rating equal to the heat requirement calculated. If a central heating system is located in a separate building, an additional quantity of heat will be necessary to compensate for heat losses from the delivery and return lines to and from the greenhouse. An engineer should be consulted to determine what this loss is, and it should be added to the heat requirement calculated for the greenhouse.

Example Problem

The following steps are taken to determine the heat requirement for an all-metal, glass-covered greenhouse measuring 30 feet wide by 100 feet long. The curtain wall is 2 feet high and is constructed of 4 inch concrete block. The glass wall above the curtain wall is 6 feet high. An average wind velocity of 15 mph is expected. A 60°F temperature difference is expected between the outside low temperature of 0°F and the inside temperature of 60°F.

1. Set up a chart as illustrated here:

Greenhouse Component	*Standard Heat Loss (MBtu/hr) (from Table 3–7 or 3–8)*	*K (from Table 3–9)*	*C or CW (from Table 3–10 or 3–11)*	*Corrected Heat Loss (MBtu/hr)*
Gable			(C)	
Roof			(C)	
Wall (transparent)			(C)	
Curtain wall			(CW)	
			Total heat requirement	———

Table 3–9

Climate Factors, *K*, for Various Average Wind Velocity and Temperature Conditions*

Inside to Outside Temp. Difference in °F (°C)	**Wind Velocity in mph (m/sec)** 15 (6.7)	20 (8.9)	25 (11.2)	30 (13.4)	35 (15.6)
30(16.7)	.41	.43	.46	.48	.50
35(19.4)	.48	.50	.53	.55	.57
40(22.2)	.55	.57	.60	.62	.64
45(25.0)	.62	.65	.67	.70	.72
50(27.8)	.69	.72	.74	.77	.80
55(30.6)	.77	.80	.83	.86	.89
60(33.3)	.84	.88	.91	.94	.98
65(36.1)	.92	.96	.99	1.03	1.07
70(38.9)	1.00	1.04	1.08	1.12	1.16
75(41.7)	1.08	1.12	1.17	1.21	1.25
80(44.4)	1.16	1.21	1.26	1.30	1.35
85(47.2)	1.25	1.30	1.35	1.40	1.45
90(50.0)	1.33	1.38	1.44	1.49	1.54

*Standard heat loss values from Tables 3–7, 3–8, and 3–12 are multiplied by a factor (*K*) to correct them for local wind and temperature conditions.

From Bohanon et al. (1989).

2. Find the appropriate heat loss value for both gables combined in Table 3–7 immediately below the figure for the greenhouse width. For a 30 foot width, it is 18 MBtu (18,000 Btu) per hour.

3. Find the heat loss value for the combined roofs in Table 3–7 at the point where the 30 foot greenhouse width column and the 100 foot greenhouse length row intersect. It is 266 MBtu in this case.

4. Figure the length of the side wall. It is equal to the perimeter of the greenhouse, which equals 100 + 30 + 100 + 30 feet, or 260 feet. Find the heat loss figure for the transparent wall measuring 6 feet high and 260 feet long and for the curtain wall measuring 2 feet high and 260 feet long in Table 3–8. Since there are no figures in the table for a wall length of 260 feet, look up values for 200 feet and for 60 feet and add them together to arrive at the answer. For the transparent wall, 95 MBtu are lost through a 200 foot wall and 28 MBtu more through an additional 60 feet of the wall. The total loss is equal to 95 + 28, or 123 MBtu/hr. The curtain-wall heat loss is equal to 32 + 9, or 41 MBtu/hr.

Table 3–10

Greenhouse Construction Factors, *C*, for the Common Types of Greenhouses in Use Today*

Type of Greenhouse	C
All metal [tight glass house—20 or 24 in. (51–61 cm) glass width]	1.08
Wood and steel [tight glass house—16 or 20 in. (41–51 cm) glass width—metal gutters, vents, headers, etc.]	1.05
Wood houses [glass with wood bars, gutters, vents, etc.—up to and including 20 in. (51 cm) glass spacing]	
Good tight houses	1.00
Fairly tight houses	1.13
Loose houses	1.25
FRP-covered wood houses	.95
FRP-covered metal houses	1.00
Double glass with 1 in. (2.5 cm) air space	.70
Plastic-covered metal houses (single thickness)	1.00
Plastic-covered metal houses (double thickness)	.70

*Standard heat loss values for transparent components of greenhouses such as gables and roofs in Table 3–7, transparent side walls in Table 3–9, and ends as well as covering in Table 3–12 are multiplied by a factor (C) to correct them for the type of construction.

From Bohanon et al. (1989).

5. Determine a *K* factor from Table 3–9 for a wind velocity of 15 mph and a temperature difference of 60°F. The *K* value is 0.84, which lies at the intersection of the wind velocity column and the temperature difference row. Enter this value in the chart in the appropriate spaces after each of the four greenhouse components.

6. Determine a C factor from Table 3–10 for the type of greenhouse construction. The example greenhouse is constructed with a metal frame and a glass covering and has a C factor of 1.08. Enter this value in the appropriate spaces after the gable, roof, and transparent-wall components. These are the three components constructed with the above materials.

7. Find the C*W* factor for the curtain wall in Table 3–11 and enter it in the chart in the appropriate space in the curtain-wall row. For a 4 inch concrete-block wall, it is 0.58.

8. Correct each of the standard heat loss values in the chart by multiplying each by the *K* factor and then, in turn, by multiplying each answer by the C or C*W* factor in the same row. Enter these four values in the chart.

9. Add the four corrected heat loss values together to arrive at the total heat loss. This value is the amount of heat that must be applied to the greenhouse each hour to maintain the desired temperature if the heater is located in the greenhouse. For the example greenhouse, a heater or boiler with a net rating of 389,128 Btu/hr is needed.

Greenhouse Component	*Standard Heat Loss (MBtu/hr)*		K		C *or* CW		*Corrected Heat Loss (MBtu/hr)*
Gable	18	×	0.84	×	1.08	=	16.330
Roof	266	×	0.84	×	1.08	=	241.262
Wall (transparent)	123	×	0.84	×	1.08	=	111.561
Curtain wall	41	×	0.84	×	0.58	=	19.975
					Total heat requirement		389.128

10. If the heater is located in a building apart from the greenhouse, the loss from the boiler, the steam or hot water mains, and the return lines must be determined and added to the preceding figure.

11. In a mild climate, all heat could be provided by an overhead unit heater system. In a cold climate, a wall coil of pipes should provide an amount of heat equal to the loss through the transparent wall plus the curtain wall. In this

Table 3–11

Curtain-Wall Construction Factor, CW, for Various Types of Coverings Used in the Nontransparent Curtain Wall*

Type of Covering	CW
Glass	1.00
Asbestos-cement	1.00
Concrete, 4 in. (10 cm)	.76
Concrete, 8 in. (20 cm)	.60
Concrete block, 4 in. (10 cm)	.58
Concrete block, 8 in. (20 cm)	.46

*The standard heat loss value for the curtain wall from Table 3–8 is multiplied by this factor to correct it for the type of covering.

example, the requirement would be 111.561 + 19.975, or 131.536 MBtu/hr. The remaining heat, gable plus roof (257.592 MBtu/hr), is provided by the overhead system.

12. If desired, the fuel consumption could be calculated for an hour during the night described. Divide the total heat requirement by the heat output of the fuel used:

Anthracite coal: $\frac{389{,}128 \text{ Btu/hr}}{8{,}392 \text{ Btu/lb coal}} = 46.4 \text{ lb/hr}$

No. 2 oil: $\frac{389{,}128 \text{ Btu/hr}}{97{,}000 \text{ Btu/gal oil}} = 4.0 \text{ gal/hr}$

Quonset Greenhouse

Determination of the heat requirement for a Quonset greenhouse requires a few modifications because of the difference in shape, as diagrammed in Figure 3–22. Quonset greenhouses are covered with film plastic, FRP, or polycarbonate, and a curtain wall is rarely used. The transparent covering usually extends to the ground. Two surface areas are considered in the heat calculation: (1) the two ends collectively and (2) the covering that extends for the length of the greenhouse, which covers the roof and walls but not the ends. Heat loss values under standard conditions through these two components are found in Table 3–12. The values must be corrected for your own conditions in the same way that the heat values for an A-frame greenhouse were corrected. The same K and C factors are located in Tables 3–9 and 3–10, respectively. The end and covering heat loss values are mul-

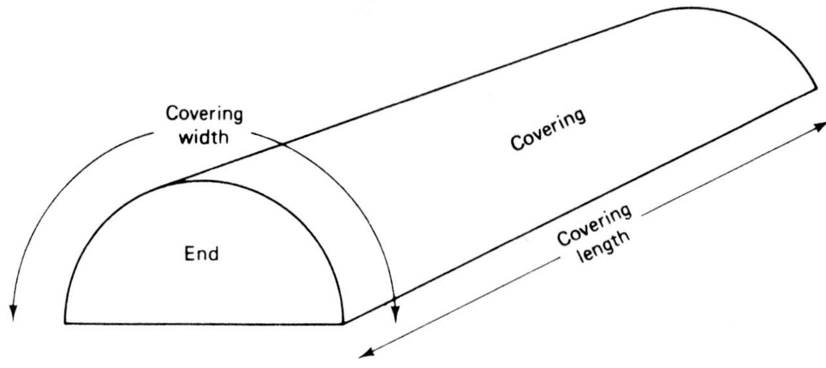

Figure 3–22

Diagram of a Quonset greenhouse showing component areas needed in the determination of the heat requirement of this greenhouse.

tiplied by each of these factors to determine the corrected heat loss values. The two corrected heat loss values are added together to arrive at the heat requirement for the greenhouse.

Example Problem

Listed next are steps to follow in calculating the heat requirement of a metal-frame Quonset greenhouse measuring 30 feet wide by 100 feet long (9.1 m by 30.5 m) and covered with two layers of polyethylene each measuring 40 feet (12.2 m) wide. A temperature difference of 60°F (33°C) and an average wind velocity of 15 mph (6.7 m/sec) are expected.

1. Locate the heat loss value for the two ends combined in Table 3–12. It is the value immediately below the covering width of 40 feet (12.2 m), or 40 MBtu (40,000 Btu) per hour.

2. Locate the heat loss value for the covering in Table 3–12. It is the value located at the intersection of the column below the covering width of 40 feet (12.2 m) and the row for a house length of 100 feet (30.5 m). In this example, the covering heat loss is equal to 316 MBtu/hr.

3. Determine a *K* factor from Table 3–9 for a wind velocity of 15 mph (6.7 m/sec) and a temperature difference of 60°F (33°C). It is equal to 0.84.

Table 3–12

Standard Heat Loss Values from Quonset-Type Greenhouses for the Combined Ends and for the Entire Covering along the Length of the Greenhouse[1,2]

	Covering Width in Feet (m)											
	18 (5.5)	20 (6.1)	22 (6.7)	24 (7.3)	26 (7.9)	28 (8.5)	30 (9.1)	32 (9.8)	34 (10.4)	36 (11.0)	38 (11.6)	40 (12.2)
House Length in Feet (m)	**End Loss in MBtu/hr[3]**											
	8	10	12	15	17	20	23	26	29	33	36	40
	Covering Loss in MBtu/hr[3]											
5(1.5)	7	8	9	9	10	11	12	13	13	14	15	16
10(3.0)	14	16	17	19	21	22	24	25	27	28	30	32
20(6.1)	28	32	35	38	41	44	47	51	54	57	60	63
30(9.1)	43	47	52	57	62	66	71	76	81	85	90	95
40(12.2)	57	63	70	76	82	89	95	101	103	114	120	127
50(15.2)	71	79	87	95	103	111	119	127	134	142	150	158
60(18.3)	85	95	104	114	123	133	142	152	161	171	180	190
70(21.3)	100	111	122	133	144	155	166	177	188	199	211	222
80(24.4)	114	127	139	152	164	177	190	202	215	228	240	253
90(27.4)	128	142	157	171	185	199	214	228	242	256	271	285
100(30.5)	142	158	174	190	206	221	237	253	269	285	301	316
200(61.0)	285	316	348	380	411	443	475	506	538	570	601	633
300(91.4)	427	475	522	569	617	664	712	759	807	854	902	949
400(121.9)	570	633	696	759	822	886	949	1,012	1,075	1,139	1,202	1,265
500(152.4)	712	791	870	949	1,028	1,107	1,187	1,265	1,345	1,424	1,503	1,582

*These values are for standard conditions including a 70°F (39°C) difference from outside to inside temperature and an average wind velocity of 15 mph (6.7 m/sec.).

One MBtu/hr = 293 W or 252 kcal/hr.

From Bohanon et al. (1989).

4. Find a C factor from Table 3–10 for this metal-frame greenhouse covered with a double layer of polyethylene. It is 0.70.

5. Multiply each of the standard heat loss values by the *K* factor and then by the C factor to determine the corrected heat loss values:

$$40 \times 0.84 \times 0.70 = 23.520 \text{ MBtu/hr}$$
$$316 \times 0.84 \times 0.70 = 185.808 \text{ MBtu/hr}$$

6. Add the two corrected heat loss values together to determine the heat requirement of the greenhouse. This is the net load of the heater when it is located within the greenhouse.

Greenhouse Component	*Standard Heat Loss (MBtu/hr) (from Table 3–12)*	K *(from Table 3–9)*	C *(from Table 3–10)*	*Corrected Heat Loss (MBtu/hr)*
Combined ends	40	0.84	0.70	23.520
Covering	316	0.84	0.70	185.808
			Total heat requirement	209.328

Total required kcal/hr = 209.328 MBtu/hr × 252 = 52,750 kcal/hr
Total required W = 209.328 MBtu/hr × 293 = 61,333 W

Gutter-Connected Greenhouse

A gutter-connected greenhouse generally has three components in terms of heat requirement computation. They are the roof, gables, and walls (Figure 3–23). Standard heat loss from the walls is determined from Table 3–8. The wall height is the distance from ground to gutter, while the wall length is the perimeter of the greenhouse. The heat loss from each roof is determined from Table 3–12. The heat loss calculated for one roof is multiplied by the number of roofs in the greenhouse. The heat loss values for ends listed in Table 3–12 yield values too large for the loss from gables. The end of a Quonset greenhouse equates to the gable plus part of the side wall of a gutter-connected greenhouse. Gable heat loss is best determined by calculating the surface area of a gable and then figuring 8 MBtu/hr standard heat loss for every 100 ft^2 (252 W/m^2, 217 $kcal/hr \cdot m^2$). The gable area can be satisfactorily estimated by multiplying the gable height by the gable width and finally by 0.55:

$$\text{height} \times \text{width} \times 0.55 = \text{area of one gable}$$

Actually, a different equation is needed for each manufacturer's design, but this equation will come close enough for all. Be sure to multiply the area of one gable by the number of gables. There are two gables per roof. When the standard heat losses have been determined for the roofs, wall, and gables, each must be multiplied by the appropriate *K* value from Table 3–9 and C value from Table 3–10. The sum of the three corrected heat loss values is the total heat loss for the greenhouse.

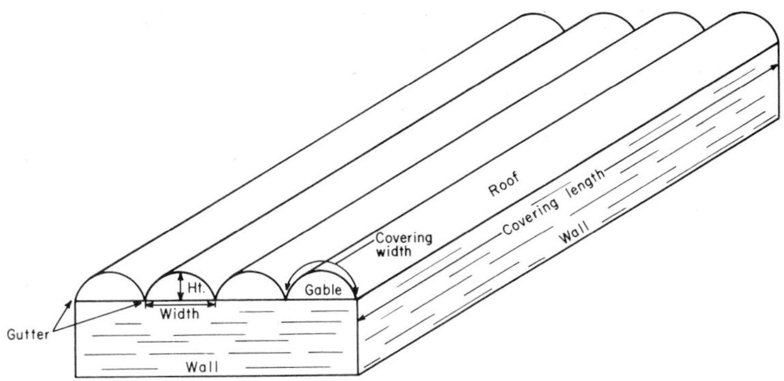

Figure 3–23

Diagram of a gutter-connected greenhouse showing component areas needed in the determination of the heat requirement of this greenhouse.

Significance of K, C, and CW Factors

Standard heat loss factors are multiplied by *K*, *C*, and *CW* factors to correct them for local conditions. When local conditions are the same as the standard conditions under which the heat loss values of Tables 3–7, 3–8, and 3–12 were determined, these factors are equal to 1. Obviously, multiplication by 1 does not change the heat loss values. Note in Table 3–9 that the *K* factor has a value of 1 for an average wind velocity of 15 mph (6.7 m/sec) and a temperature difference of 70°F (39°C).

If the wind velocity remained at 15 mph (6.7 m/sec) and the inside temperature were reduced by 10°F (6°C) so that the temperature difference was now 60°F (33°C) rather than 70°F (39°C), less heat would be required in the greenhouse. This can be seen in the *K* factor, which would become 0.84. When a factor less than 1, such as this factor of 0.84, is multiplied by the standard heat loss value, the heat loss, or in other words the heat requirement, diminishes. The most highly resistant coverings to heat transmission, those that retain heat best in the greenhouse, have the lowest *C* factors in Table 3–10. The same is true for the curtain-wall covering materials in Table 3–11.

HEAT CONSERVATION

Greenhouse Design

Fuel economy can be designed into a greenhouse film. Heat loss is a function of the amount of exposed greenhouse surface area. Quonset greenhouses can have close to 2 square feet of exposed surface per square foot of floor area, while large blocks of gutter-connected greenhouses can approach a ratio of 1.2 square feet of exposed area per square foot of floor area. A sizable decrease in heat loss can be realized through greenhouse design.

Double Covering

A double-layer polyethylene greenhouse will consume about 40 percent less fuel than an equivalent single-layer glass, FRP, or polyethylene-covered greenhouse.

Thermal Screens

Greenhouses with a maximum distance between supporting post rows lend themselves more economically to the installation of thermal screens. A thermal screen is a curtain of material such as polyethylene, polyester film, aluminized polyester film strips, or polyester cloth that is drawn from eave to eave or gutter to gutter as well as around the inner perimeter of the greenhouse each night to box in the crop. It is drawn off in the morning by a motorized mechanism. Polyester is superior to polyethylene because it blocks radiant heat better (Table 3–1). Often, the curtain has an aluminized surface on one side to further reflect radiant heat back to the soil and plants at night so that it cannot leave the greenhouse. Thermal screens serve also to block convection of heat, keeping it around the plants and away from the greenhouse covering. Less heat is lost because the temperature differential across the greenhouse covering is lower. Heat curtains can reduce fuel consumption by 20–60 percent, with 40 percent being a realistic mean value.

Thermal screen systems including installation are available at a cost of $1–$3/ft^2 of floor area covered. The price differential relates to the brand, the number of obstacles within the greenhouse such as supporting post rows, the number of zones to be independently covered, whether the greenhouse was designed to accommodate a screen, whether the screen is drawn from truss to truss or eave to eave (the latter being cheaper), and the type of screen material. This system is not nearly as practical for Quonset greenhouses because the higher price would apply due to the small installation needed for each greenhouse. The composition of screen materials varies depending on the roles the screen is intended to play. There are three roles: (1) heat retention on winter nights, (2) partial sunscreening on bright summer days, and (3) total exclusion of light for lengthening the night in summer for photoperiodic crops (see Chapter 11 for the latter two roles). Screens are available to perform any one of these functions singly. Screens are also available for the combination of heat retention plus sunscreening or for the combination of heat retention plus photoperiodic control. If all three functions were required in a greenhouse, two automatic screen-pulling systems would have to be installed, which is entirely possible.

Firms that grow photoperiodically timed crops (Chapter 11), which require covering with shade cloth to lengthen the night, might be more inclined to install a thermal screen. The mechanism that automatically pulls the thermal screen during the winter is also used to pull the shade cloth from spring to fall. One curtain material can be used for both functions. Thus, a single investment can be recouped in two ways. (Such a system can be seen in Figure 11–12.)

Thermal screens result in a lower greenhouse covering temperature, which reduces the tendency to melt snow. There is a greater risk of collapse from snow load, which can be remedied by leaving the screen open during a snow storm. A snow-sensing device should be installed on the roof for this purpose. Insurance rates may be higher for greenhouses equipped with thermal screens. Some growers have a problem with condensate collecting on the thermal screen, but porous screens are available to solve this problem. Finally, the rush of cold air on the plants when the screen is drawn open in the morning troubles some growers. To get around this problem, many screens have recently been installed immediately below the roof covering material in a way that it is drawn from truss to truss. There is less of a shading problem with this arrangement.

Radiant Heat

Low-energy radiant heaters can also be designed into the heating system for a fuel savings of 30 percent or more where natural gas is available. In high-ridge greenhouses, it is possible to lower the radiant heating system and to install a thermal screen above the radiant heaters.

Wall Insulation

Little benefit is derived from scattered light entering through the north wall of a greenhouse. A 5–10 percent savings in fuel can be realized by constructing a solid, insulated north wall with a reflectorized inner surface. Another 3–6 percent savings can be gained by insulating the foundation (curtain) walls of the greenhouse.

Sealing Air Leaks

A number of techniques for sealing air leaks can be applied to energy-inefficient, existing greenhouses. Several commercial glass greenhouses have been covered with two layers of air-inflated polyethylene for a fuel savings of 40–60 percent. One problem that goes along with this system is the reduction in light transmission. In an Ohio State University study, a solar radiation reduction of 35 percent was measured within a conventional glass greenhouse as a result of glass, sash bars, and frame. An additional 18 percent reduction occurred from a double layer of polyethylene over the glass. For high-light-requiring crops, this situation may be intolerable, but for many others it appears to be acceptable. Considerable heat can be lost through cracks between overlapping panes of glass or sheets of FRP. Aging causes these cracks to open up and may also cause the glazing compound to become brittle and fall away from the area between the glass and the sash bar. Cracks may occur in the glass, with corners falling out, or some panes of glass may slide, opening up holes. Eventually, reglazing of a glass greenhouse becomes necessary. Reglazing should be done as soon as the need becomes evident to prevent heating costs from rising. Under the present fuel situation, it could be false economy to put off a reglazing job. A clear silicon-base sealant can be purchased in tubes and injected into the lap between panes of glass to seal the lap. The cost of labor and material is about 40¢/ft^2 of floor area. The heat savings, ranging from 5 to 40 percent, depend upon the looseness of glass or degree of infiltration loss that exists. This energy-saving option would be exercised in lieu of covering the glass greenhouse with polyethylene film.

Windbreaks

The climate factors in Table 3–9 give a good indication of the effect of wind on the heat requirement. For every 5 mph (2.2 m/sec) rise in average wind velocity above 15 mph (6.7 m/sec), there is a 4 percent increase in heat loss from the greenhouse. The velocity of wind striking a greenhouse can be reduced by providing windbreaks of trees. Fast-growing evergreen trees, such as hemlock, serve well. In some cases, trees are already growing prior to construction of the greenhouse range. Care should be taken to leave these where they can perform a strategic role. While windbreaks are important, they must never cast a shadow over the growing area. This would result in loss of productivity, which would be more costly than the fuel saved by the windbreak. Windbreaks on the east, west, or south side should be located away from the greenhouse a distance equal to 2.5 times the height of the windbreak to prevent winter shadows from interfering with crop growth. In general, a 5–10 percent fuel savings can result from windbreaks.

High-Efficiency Heaters

High-efficiency heaters are available today that have more extensive heat exchangers than previous models. As a consequence, more heat is removed from the exhaust gases. Exhaust temperatures of 600°F (315°C) and higher can now be reduced to about 300°F (150°C). Where one is operating an inefficient boiler, the efficiency can be increased by installing a chimney heat reclaimer in the furnace flue pipe. This consists of a heat exchanger through which air in some models and water in other models is passed. The warmed air may be used to heat the service building or part of the greenhouse, while the warm water may be used for irrigation. Care should be taken not to lower the stack temperature below the manufacturer's recommendation. At low temperatures, water, acids, and other corrosive compounds can condense and cause deterioration of the chimney.

Heater Maintenance

Heaters will consume fuel at varying efficiencies depending upon adjustment of the fuel-to-air ratio. For this reason, heaters should be maintained in good condition. Omission of a periodic service call can cost far more in increased fuel consumption. Soot may build up in the flue passageways of boilers, providing insulation on those iron surfaces that are in actuality the heat exchanger of the boiler. Less heat is transferred to water and more goes up the smoke stack, thus increasing fuel consumption. A soot layer ⅛ inch (3 mm) deep can cause a heat loss of up to 15 percent, and a $^{3}/_{16}$ inch (5 mm) layer can cause a 21 percent loss in heat captured by the boiler. Boilers should be cleaned on a regular basis. Special materials for coating flue tubes can reduce the tendency for soot to adhere to the surface, allowing more to pass out in the smoke effluent. On the average, these tubes are more efficient heat exchangers, assuming a cleaning schedule is still maintained.

Thermostat Maintenance

Many other maintenance possibilities exist for reducing heat loss. Thermostats should be accurately calibrated so that higher-than-desired temperatures are not maintained. This maintenance needs to be done periodically (about every six months) against a calibrated thermometer. Highly precise thermostats should be used. Bimetallic-strip and mercury-bulb thermostats generally activate a heater at the desired temperature setting and turn it off when a higher temperature is reached. The interval between is known as the "dead-load." A dead-load of 2°F (1°C) is quite acceptable for these thermostat types. The dead-load can be 6°F (3°C) or more in a malfunctioning thermostat. Considerable heat is wasted each time the thermostat activates. Such a thermostat should be replaced.

Cool-Temperature Crops

Within some crops are cultivars that can be satisfactorily produced at lower temperatures than others. This is particularly true for poinsettias and chrysanthemums. Greenhouse crops as a whole can be produced at lower temperatures than are generally recommended, but the cropping time is increased. Arguments have been set forth for and against this procedure in reference to fuel conservation. In some cases, the fuel savings are lost in forms such as overhead costs and fuel consumption during the period of extended growth. Before adopting this form of heat conservation, one should test it out and keep accurate records.

Combined Economics

It should be obvious that if several heat-saving options are adopted, the total heat savings will not be equal to the sum of the savings of each option. If a second layer of polyethylene is applied to a plastic greenhouse, a savings of 40 percent might be realized on the original heat bill. The fuel consumption now equals 60 percent of the original. Further installment of a thermal screen, predicted to save 40 percent of the fuel consumption, would not lower the fuel consumption to 20 percent of the original value. It would reduce the fuel consumption after installing the second layer of polyethylene by 40 percent. This would be a 24 percent fuel reduction ($0.40 \times 0.60 = 0.24$).

SUMMARY

1. Heat must be supplied to a greenhouse at the same rate with which it is lost in order to maintain a desired temperature. Heat can be lost in three ways—by conduction, by infiltration, and by radiation. Heat is conducted directly through the covering material in conduction loss. In infiltration loss, heat is lost as warm air escapes through cracks in the covering. In radiation loss, heat is radiated from warm objects inside the greenhouse through the covering to colder objects outside.
2. A central heating system can be more efficient than localized unit heaters in large greenhouse ranges. In this system, two or more large boilers are in a single location. Heat is transported in the form of hot water or steam through pipe mains to the growing area. Central heating systems are most popular in European greenhouses.
3. The localized heating system is the most popular because of its low initial purchase price. In this system, small heaters with self-contained fireboxes are installed in each greenhouse unit as the range is expanded. Ultimately, this system entails a higher cost of maintenance than a central system does.
4. Low-intensity infrared radiant heaters can save 30 percent or more in fuel over more conventional heaters. Several of these heaters are installed in tandem in the greenhouse. Lower air temperatures are possible since the plants and root media are heated directly.
5. Solar heating systems are found in hobby greenhouses and small commercial firms. Both water and rock storage systems are used. The high cost of solar

systems has discouraged any significant acceptance by the horticulture industry to date.

6. Emergency equipment is a necessity and should include a heat source as well as an electrical generator. The generator can be installed to start automatically upon power failure. The need for heat should be signaled by a thermostat-activated alarm system in the manager's or owner's home.

7. Heat can be distributed from central heating systems in hot water or steam carried through coils of pipe. Two-thirds of the pipe is located on the side and end walls and one-third across the greenhouse running from end to end. Pipe across the greenhouse counteracts downdrafts and cold spots. The tendency today is to locate the pipes across the greenhouse at a low level beneath benches, alongside ground beds, or in the floor to ensure warm root-media temperatures. While vertical air-lift fans were used earlier, today the horizontal airflow (HAF) system is often used with pipe coils to reduce the vertical temperature gradient.

   Heat from localized, forced-air systems is distributed either by the HAF system or through convection tubes. Warm air from unit heaters, either with self-contained fireboxes or supplied with heat from a central boiler, is distributed through a transparent polyethylene tube running the length of the greenhouse. Heat escapes from the tube through holes on either side of the tube in small jet streams, which rapidly mix with the surrounding air and set up a circulation pattern to minimize temperature gradients.

8. Temperature sensor placement is very crucial. The sensor should be at the height of the growing point of the plants and in a location typical of the average temperature of the greenhouse. It should be in a light-reflecting box that is aspirated at a minimum airflow rate of 600 fpm (3 m/sec). Also in the aspirated box should be other temperature-sensing controls and a thermometer for testing and correcting the sensors.

9. Relatively easy procedures have been outlined for calculating the heat requirement of greenhouses. Information necessary for determining the heat requirement for an A-frame greenhouse is contained in Tables 3–7 through 3–11 and for Quonset greenhouses in Tables 3–9 through 3–12. Calculations for gutter-connected greenhouses make use of a combination of all tables.

10. The heat requirement of greenhouses can be reduced by installing double greenhouse coverings; by using a greenhouse design with minimal exposed surface area; by using thermal screens; by repairing broken glass, tightening existing glass, or sealing the glass laps; by using a windbreak of trees to reduce wind velocity; by using high-efficiency (low-stack-temperature) heaters and boilers; by periodically adjusting and cleaning heaters, boilers, and thermostats; and possibly by using cool-temperature-tolerant varieties of plants.

REFERENCES

Various manufacturers of heating equipment offer literature concerning products and technical information.

1. Agricultural Development and Advisory Service. 1976. Greenhouse heating systems. Ministry of Agriculture, Fisheries and Food. Mechanization Leaflet 27. Her Majesty's Stationery Office, London.
2. Aldrich, R. A., W. A. Bailey, J. W. Bartok, Jr., W. J. Roberts, and D. S. Ross. 1976. *Hobby Greenhouses and Other Gardening Structures*. Pub. NRAES–2. Northeast Reg. Agr. Eng. Ser., Cornell Univ., 152 Riley-Robb Hall, Ithaca, NY 14853.
3. Aldrich, R. A., and J. W. Bartok, Jr. 1989. *Greenhouse Engineering*. Pub. NRAES–33. Northeast Reg. Agr. Eng. Ser., Cornell Univ., 152 Riley-Robb Hall, Ithaca, NY 14853.
4. American Society of Agricultural Engineers. 1990. Heating, ventilating, and cooling greenhouses. In *Agricultural Engineers Yearbook of Standards*. Amer. Soc. Agr. Engineers, St. Joseph, MI 49085.
5. Badger, P. C., and H. A. Poole. 1979. Conserving energy in Ohio greenhouses. Ohio Coop. Ext. Ser. Bul. 651. The Ohio State Univ., Columbus, OH 43210.
6. Blom, T., F. Ingratta, and J. Hughes. 1982. Energy conservation in Ontario greenhouses. Ontario Ministry of Agr. and Food. Pub. 65.
7. Bohanon, H. R., C. E. Rahilly, J. Stout, and P. E. Bush. 1989. The greenhouse climate control handbook. Form C7S. Acme Engineering and Manufacturing Corp., Muskogee, OK 74402.
8. Boyette, M. D., and R. W. Watkins. 1988. Getting into hot water. North Carolina Agr. Ext. Ser. Bul. AG–398. North Carolina State Univ., Raleigh, NC 27695.
9. Duncan, G. A., and J. N. Walker. 1973. Poly-tube heating-ventilation systems and equipment. AEN–9. Univ. of Kentucky, Dept. of Agr. Eng., Lexington, KY.
10. Gray, H. E. 1956. *Greenhouse Heating and Construction*. Florists' Publishing Co., 343 S. Dearborn St., Chicago, IL.
11. Jacobson, J. S., and A. C. Hill, eds. 1970. *Recognition of Air Pollution Injury to Vegetation: A Pictorial Atlas*. Informative Report No. 1. Air Pollution Control Assoc., Pittsburgh, PA.
12. Jahn, L. G. 1985. Wood energy guide for agricultural and small commercial applications. North Carolina Agr. Ext. Ser. Bul. AG–363. North Carolina State Univ., Raleigh, NC 27695.
13. Laurie, A., D. C. Kiplinger, and K. S. Nelson. 1968. *Commercial Flower-Forcing*, New York: McGraw-Hill.
14. National Greenhouse Manufacturers' Association. 1979. National Greenhouse Manufacturers' greenhouse heat loss standards. *Florists' Review* 164 (4249):132–133.
15. Poole, H. A., and P. C. Badger. 1980. Management practices to conserve energy in Ohio greenhouses. Ohio Coop. Ext. Ser. Bul. 668. The Ohio State Univ., Columbus, OH 43210.

16. Roberts, W. J., J. W. Bartok, Jr., E. E. Fabian, and J. Simpkins. 1989. *Energy Conservation for Commercial Greenhouses*. Pub. NRAES–3. Northeast Reg. Agr. Eng. Ser., Cornell Univ., 152 Riley-Robb Hall, Ithaca, NY 14853.

17. Ross, D. S., W. J. Roberts, R. A. Parsons, J. W. Bartok, Jr., and R. A. Aldrich. 1978. *Energy Conservation and Solar Heating for Greenhouses*. Northeast Regional Agricultural Engineering Services, NRAES–3, 144 Riley-Robb Hall, Cornell Univ., Ithaca, NY 14853.

18. Sherry, W. J. 1983. Which greenhouse cover is for you? *Greenhouse Manager* 2 (2):126–132.

19. U.S. Housing and Home Finance Agency. 1954. Thermal insulation value of air space. Housing Res. Paper No. 32. Housing and Home Financing Agency, Div. of Housing Research, Washington, D.C.

20. Walker, J. N., and G. A. Duncan. 1975. Estimating greenhouse heating requirements and fuel costs. AEN–8. Univ. of Kentucky, Dept. of Agr. Eng., Lexington, KY.

21. ______. 1974. Greenhouse heating systems. AEN–31. Univ. of Kentucky, Dept. of Agr. Eng., Lexington, KY.

22. Whillier, A. 1963. Plastic covers for solar collectors. *Solar Energy* 7 (3):148–151.

Chapter 4

Greenhouse Cooling

Greenhouses require two distinctly different forms of cooling, one for summer and the other for winter. Most localities, with the general exception of those in higher elevations, experience periods of summer heat that are adverse to greenhouse crops. Temperatures inside the greenhouse are frequently 20°F (11°C) higher than those outside in spite of open ventilators. Detrimental effects of high temperatures are typified by loss of stem strength, reduction of flower size, delay of flowering, and even bud abortion. Evaporative cooling systems work well for summer cooling. The evaporative cooling systems are based on the process of heat absorption during the evaporation of water. Excess heat can likewise be a problem during the winter. Even when the outside temperature is below the desired inside temperature, the entrapment of solar heat can raise the inside temperature to an injurious level.

The *fan-and-pad evaporative cooling system* has been available since 1954 and is still the most common summer system in greenhouses (Figure 4–1). Along one wall of the greenhouse, water is passed through a pad that is usually placed vertically in the wall. Traditionally, the pad was composed of excelsior (wood shreds), but today it is commonly made of a cross-fluted cellulose material somewhat similar in appearance to corrugated cardboard. Exhaust fans are placed on the opposite wall. Warm outside air is drawn in through the pad. Water in the pad, through the process of evaporation, absorbs heat from the surrounding pad and frame as well as from the air passing through the pad.

The *fog evaporative cooling system,* introduced in greenhouses in 1980, operates on the same cooling principle as the fan-and-pad system but uses quite a different arrangement. A high-pressure pumping apparatus generates fog containing

(a)

(b)

Figure 4–1

An installation of (a) an evaporative pad and (b) exhaust fans used for evaporative cooling of a greenhouse during the summer.

water droplets with a mean size of less than 10 microns (one-tenth the thickness of a human hair). These droplets are sufficiently small to stay suspended in air while they are evaporating. Fog is dispersed throughout the greenhouse, cooling the air everywhere. People and plants stay dry throughout the process. This system is equally useful for seed germination and cutting propagation since it eliminates the need for a mist system.

Both summer evaporative cooling systems can reduce the temperature of air well below the outside temperature by 25°F (14°C) or more. The fan-and-pad system can achieve temperatures within 3–4°F (1.7°C) of the wet bulb temperature, while the fog system can essentially achieve the wet bulb temperature. Thus, the drier the air, the greater the cooling that is possible (see Figure 4–2). Consider

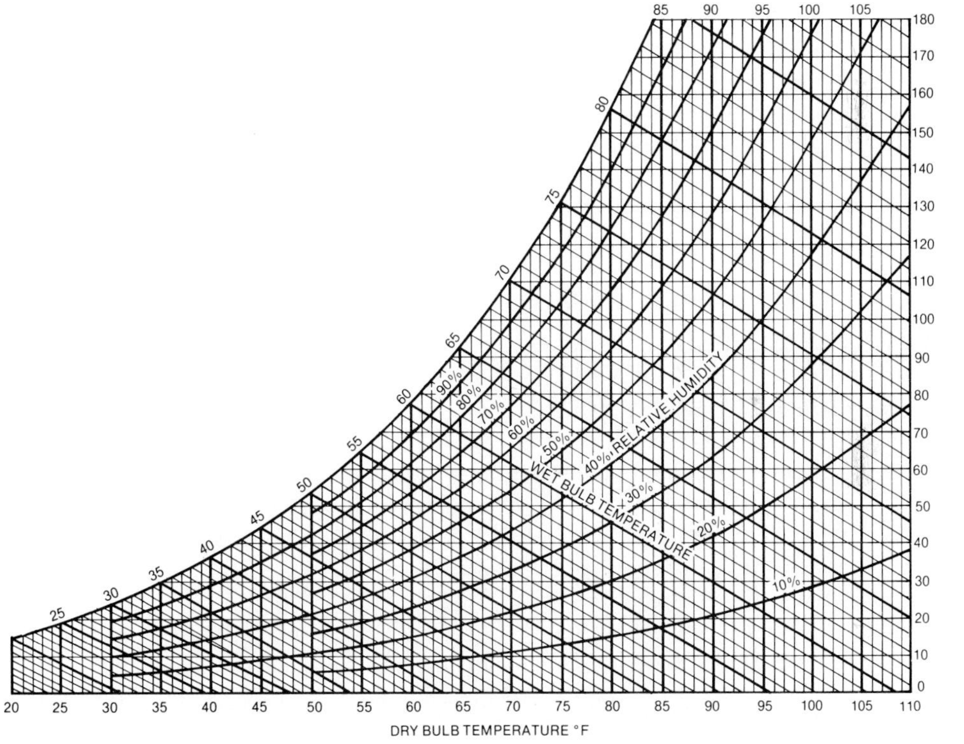

Figure 4–2

The relationship of dry bulb temperature, wet bulb temperature, and relative humidity. To determine the wet bulb temperature (the lowest cooling temperature possible), start with the dry bulb temperature (read on a standard thermometer) along the lower horizontal axis, follow the vertical line above that temperature up to its intersection with the curve for the relative humidity level in the outside air, move from this intersection along the diagonal line toward the upper left corner of the chart until the leftmost curve is reached, and read the wet bulb temperature from this leftmost curve. (*Graph courtesy of* Acme *Engineering & Manufacturing* Corp., P.O. Box 978, *Muskogee*, OK 74402)

air at a dry bulb temperature of 90°F (32°C) but at relative humidities of 20 percent in Arizona and 60 percent in Florida. The wet bulb temperatures (lowest cooling points) would be 63°F and 78°F (17°C and 26°C), respectively.

The fundamental difference between summer and winter cooling systems lies in the temperature of the air that is external to the greenhouse. It is desirable to cool the air during the summer before passing it over the plants. Large volumes of cooled air are introduced directly and uniformly over all plants. During the winter, cold external air must be introduced indirectly and mixed with the undesirable warm air within the greenhouse prior to making contact with the plants in order to prevent cold spots at the plant level. For best results, the flow of incoming air must be smooth in the summer, but in the winter it must be turbulent so as to bring about rapid mixing.

Originally, greenhouses were constructed with ventilators adjacent to the ridge. When cooling was required on winter days, they were opened. Cold air, being more dense than the warm air inside, would drop to the floor beneath the ventilators where it would spread laterally and increase in temperature as it mixed with the warm air. The result was a temperature gradient across the house at plant height. This led to uneven growth rates and subsequently to variation in maturation dates. The *fan–tube ventilation system* used for winter cooling corrects the horizontal temperature gradient problem. It circulates the air in the greenhouse.

GREENHOUSE SUMMER COOLING SYSTEMS

Fan-and-Pad System

The main considerations of the fan-and-pad system, in the order in which they will be discussed, include (1) the rate at which warm air must be removed from the greenhouse to allow cool air to be drawn in, (2) the types of pads used for evaporating water and their specifications, (3) the placement of fans, and (4) the path of the air stream.

Rate of Air Exchange The rate of air exchange is measured in cubic feet of air per minute (cfm) or cubic meters per minute (cmm). Normally, the rate of removal of 8 cfm/ft^2 (2.5 cmm/m^2) of greenhouse floor is sufficient. This applies to a greenhouse under 1,000 feet (300 m) in elevation, with an interior light intensity not in excess of 5,000 foot-candles (fc) (53.8 klux) and a temperature rise of 7°F (4°C) from the pad to the fans.

The rate of air removal from the greenhouse must increase as the elevation of the greenhouse site increases. Air decreases in density and becomes lighter with increasing elevation. The ability of air to remove solar heat from the greenhouse depends upon its weight and not its volume. Thus, a larger volume of air

Table 4–1

Factors Used To Correct the Rate of Air Removal for Elevation Above Sea Level*

	Under								
Feet	1,000	1,000	2,000	3,000	4,000	5,000	6,000	7,000	8,000
Meters	300	300	600	900	1,200	1,500	1,800	2,100	2,400
F_{elev}	1.00	1.04	1.08	1.12	1.16	1.20	1.25	1.30	1.36

*From National Greenhouse Manufacturers' Assoc. (1971).

must be drawn through the greenhouse at high elevations than is drawn through at low elevations in order to have an equivalent cooling effect. Table 4–1 lists factors (F_{elev}) used to correct the rate of air removal for elevation.

The rate of air removal is also dependent upon the light intensity in the greenhouse. As light intensity increases, the heat input from the sun increases, requiring a greater rate of air removal from the greenhouse. Factors (F_{light}) used to adjust the rate of air removal are listed in Table 4–2. An intensity of 5,000 fc (53.8 klux) is accepted as a desirable level for crops in general and is achieved with a coat of shading compound on the greenhouse covering or with a screen material drawn from eave to eave inside.

Solar energy warms the air as it passes from the pad to the exhaust fans. Usually, a 7°F (4°C) rise in temperature is tolerated across the greenhouse. If it becomes important to hold a more constant temperature across the greenhouse, that is, to reduce the rise in temperature, it will be necessary to raise the velocity of air movement through the greenhouse. Factors (F_{temp}) used for this adjustment are given in Table 4–3 for various permissible temperature rises.

The pad and fans should be placed on opposite walls. These walls may be the ends or the sides of the greenhouse. The distance between pad and fans is an important consideration in determining which walls to use. A distance of 100–200 feet (30–60 m) is best. Distances greater than 200 feet (60 m) can result in higher temperature rises across the greenhouse than desired. When the distance

Table 4–2

Factors Used To Correct the Rate of Air Removal for the Maximum Light Intensity in the Greenhouse*

fc	4,000	4,500	5,000	5,500	6,000	6,500	7,000	7,500	8,000
klux	43.1	48.4	53.8	59.2	64.6	70.0	75.3	80.1	86.1
F_{light}	0.80	0.90	1.00	1.10	1.20	1.30	1.40	1.50	1.60

*From National Greenhouse Manufacturers' Assoc. (1971).

Table 4–3

Factors Used to Correct the Rate of Air Removal for Given Pad-to-Fan Temperature Rises*

°F °C	10 5.6	9 5.0	8 4.4	7 3.9	6 3.3	5 2.8	4 2.2
F_{temp}	0.70	0.78	0.88	1.00	1.17	1.40	1.75

*From National Greenhouse Manufacturers' Assoc. (1971).

is reduced below 100 feet (30 m), the cross-sectional velocity of air movement becomes lower and the air often develops a clammy feeling. This situation must be compensated by increasing the size of the exhaust fans or, in other words, the velocity of air movement. This increases the cost of the system. Factors (F_{vel}) used to compensate for this point are listed in Table 4–4.

It is now possible to calculate the rate of air removal required for a specific greenhouse by using the factors given in Tables 4–1 through 4–4. First, determine the rate of air removal required for a greenhouse under standard conditions by the following equation, where L and W represent the greenhouse length and width, respectively. This equation calls for the removal of 8 cfm/ft^2 (2.5 cmm/m^2) of floor area:

$$\text{standard cfm} = L \times W \times 8$$

or

$$\text{standard cmm} = L \times W \times 2.5$$

Now, correct the standard rate of air removal by multiplying it by the larger of the following two factors, F_{house} or F_{vel}. F_{vel} is read directly from Table 4–4. F_{house} is calculated as follows:

$$F_{house} = F_{elev} \times F_{light} \times F_{temp}$$

Thus, the final capacity of the exhaust fans must be

$$\text{total cfm} = \text{standard cfm} \times (F_{house} \text{ or } F_{temp})$$

or

$$\text{total cmm} = \text{standard cmm} \times (F_{house} \text{ or } F_{temp})$$

Table 4–4

Factors Used to Correct the Rate of Air Removal for Various Pad-to-Fan Distances*

Feet	20	25	30	35	40	45	50	55
Meters	6.1	7.6	9.1	10.7	12.2	13.7	15.2	16.8
F_{vel}	2.24	2.00	1.83	1.69	1.58	1.48	1.41	1.35

Feet	60	65	70	75	80	85	90	95	100 and over
Meters	18.3	19.8	21.3	22.9	24.4	25.9	27.4	29.0	30.5
F_{vel}	1.29	1.24	1.20	1.16	1.12	1.08	1.05	1.02	1.00

*From National Greenhouse Manufacturers' Assoc. (1971).

Next, the size and number of exhaust fans must be selected. The fans collectively should be at least equal to the rate of air removal required and should be rated to do so at a static water pressure of 0.1 inch (30 Pa). If slant-wall-housing fans (with the fan outside the louvers) are used, the fans should be rated at a static water pressure of 0.05 inch (15 Pa). The static pressure figure takes into account the resistance the fans meet in drawing air through the pad. Air delivery ratings for various sizes of fans are listed in Table 4–5. Fans should not be spaced more than 25 feet (7.6 m) apart. If the end of the greenhouse is 60 feet (18 m) wide, a minimum of three fans will be necessary. The required capacity of each fan can be determined by dividing 3 into the total cfm (or cmm) of air removal required. It is then a matter of finding fans in the table that are rated for this performance level. These fans should be evenly spaced along the end of the greenhouse, at plant height if possible, to guarantee a uniform flow of air through the plants.

Cross-fluted Cellulose Pad Specifications Originally, excelsior (wood fiber) pads were used that were 1–1.5 inches (2.5–4 cm) thick. They had to be replaced annually. Most cooling pads installed today are constructed of cross-fluted cellulose material (Figure 4–3a). These pads have the appearance of corrugated cardboard. They can last 10 years if properly handled. They should be protected from beating rain and heavy water streams and should be moved only if dry. The cellulose is impregnated within soluble antirot salts, rigidifying saturants, and wetting agents to give it lasting quality, strength, and wettability. Although cellulose pads are more expensive initially, they are cheaper over their 10-year useful life expectancy than are their predecessor, the excelsior pads.

Table 4–5

Air Delivery Ratings and Required Pad Areas for Various Sizes of Steel Fans*

			Pad Area per Fan (ft^2)		
Fan Size (in.)	*Horsepower (hp)*	*cfm at 0.1 Inch Static Pressure*	*Excelsior*	*Cellulose, 4 in.*	*Cellulose, 6 in.*
24	¼	4,500	30	18	13
24	⅓	5,700	38	23	16
24	½	6,500	43	26	19
24	¾	7,600	51	30	22
30	⅓	7,400	49	30	21
30	½	8,800	59	35	25
30	¾	10,200	68	41	29
36	⅓	8,800	59	35	25
36	½	10,600	71	43	31
36	¾	12,700	85	51	37
36	1	14,200	95	57	41
42	½	12,500	84	50	36
42	¾	15,000	100	60	43
42	1	16,800	112	68	48
48	½	14,700	98	59	42
48	¾	17,800	119	72	51
48	1	19,600	131	78	56
54	1	22,900	153	92	66
54	1½	25,800	172	104	74

*Data in first three columns from Acme Engineering and Manufacturing Corp., Muskogee, OK.

Cross-fluted cellulose pads come in units of 1 foot (30 cm) wide and 2, 4, 6, or 12 inches (5, 10, 15, or 30 cm) thick. Heights are available in 1 foot (30 cm) increments of 2–5 feet (0.6–1.5 cm) for the 2 inch (5 cm) thick pad, of 2–6 feet (0.6–1.8 m) for the 4 and 6 inch (10 and 15 cm) thick pads, and of 2–4 feet (0.6–1.2 m) for the 12 inch (30 cm) thick pad. Units are oriented vertically so that each adds 1 foot (30 cm) to the length of the overall greenhouse pad. Four inches is the most common thickness used today. Pads 6 inches thick are useful in walls that are too small to accommodate the greater pad area required for a 4 inch thick pad. One square foot of 4 inch thick pad will accommodate an air intake of 250 cfm (75 cmm/m^2) of pad, while a 6 inch thick pad will accommodate 350 cfm (105 cmm/m^2) of pad. Pads 12 inches thick would be used in excessively hot and humid locations. The required area of 4 and 6 inch thick cellulose pads is only 60 and 43 percent of the area required for excelsior pads, respectively.

The required pad area may be calculated by using the figures in the preceding paragraph or may be read directly from Table 4–5. The cooling pad should extend the entire length of the wall of the greenhouse in which it is installed to

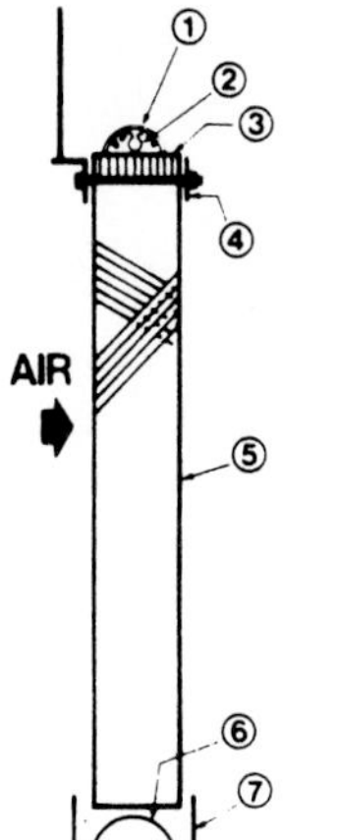

1. Impingement cover
2. Water distribution pipe
3. Water distribution pad
4. Support flashing and bolt
5. Cross-fluted cellulose pad
6. Spacer
7. Gutter

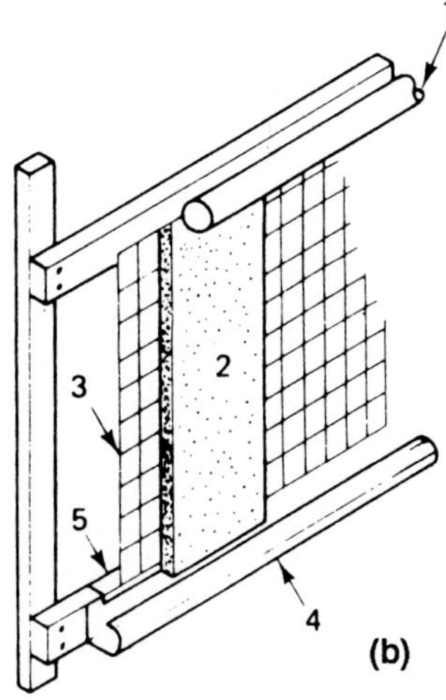

1. Water distribution pipe
2. Excelsior pad
3. Welded wire frame
4. Water return gutter
5. Galvanized flashing

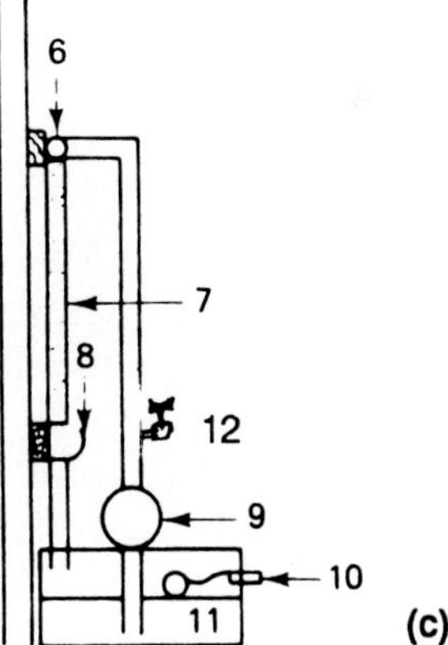

6. Water distribution pipe
7. Excelsior pad
8. Water return gutter
9. Pump
10. Water inlet with float valve
11. Sump
12. Bleed-off valve

Figure 4–3

Diagram of (a) the components of a cross-fluted cellulose pad system for evaporative cooling, (b) the components of an alternative excelsior pad system, and (c) the water distribution system for either cooling pad system including sump, float valve, and pump.

ensure that all plants receive cooled air. The height of the pad is determined by dividing the total area of the pad by the length of the pad. Pads should be placed immediately inside the side or end wall. The pad wall should be equipped with ventilators exterior to the pad to permit air entry during hot weather and for sealing off the outside air during cooler spring and fall nights. In this case, the ventilator arms and gears are located exterior to the greenhouse (Figure 4–4). Exhaust fans must be located in the wall opposite the pad to ensure that an even blanket of cool air passes through all parts of the greenhouse. Pads and fans should be at plant height to keep the cooling air in the plants.

Water must be delivered to the top of a 4 inch (10 cm) thick pad at the rate of 0.5 gpm per linear foot of pad (6.2 l/min/m of pad). For pad lengths of 30–50 feet (9.1–15.2 m), a 1¼ inch (32 mm) water distribution pipe is required, while for lengths of 50–60 feet (15.2–18.3 m), a 1½ inch (38 mm) pipe is needed. Sixty feet (18.3 m) is the longest recommended pipe length. A 120 foot (37 m) pad length could be serviced from a water supply at the midpoint supplying two 60 foot (18.3 m) distribution pipes. At every 3 inches (7.6 cm), ⅛ inch (3 mm) holes should be made in the pipe.

Figure 4–4

An evaporative cooling system arrangement with the pad located inside the greenhouse and the ventilator mechanism exterior to the greenhouse. This system permits cooling on warm autumn days when the evenings are too cold for the side wall to be left open. (*Photo courtesy of* J. W. *Love, Department of* Horticultural *Science, North Carolina State University, Raleigh,* NC 27695–7609)

The flow rate for a 6 inch (15 cm) pad is 0.75 gpm per linear foot of pad (9.3 l/min/m of pad). A 1¼ inch (32 mm) distribution pipe is used for pads 30 feet (9.1 m) and shorter, while a 1½ inch (38 mm) pipe is used for 30–50 foot (9.1–15.2 m) pad lengths. The longest pipe length recommended is 50 feet (15.2 m). Again, ⅛ inch (3 mm) holes are spaced 3 inches (7.6 cm) apart in these distribution pipes.

Holes in the distribution pipes for cross-fluted cellulose pads are oriented upward. An impingement cover is placed over the distribution pipe. Water squirting upward from holes in the distribution pipe strikes the inner side of the impingement cover and is dispersed. Half of a 4 inch (10 cm) plastic pipe provides a good impingement cover. Deflected water drips onto a distribution pad that is 2 inches (5 cm) high and the thickness of the cellulose pad below it. This pad further disperses the water to more thoroughly wet the top of the cellulose pad. It is important that all of the pad be wet. There is less resistance to the flow of air through dry pad; thus, air will channel through dry areas and reduce the overall effectiveness of the pad. A gutter at the base of the pad collects water and permits it to flow to a sump, where it is pumped back to the top of the pad. Between the gutter and the base of the pad is a spacer. Half of a 4 inch (10 cm) plastic pipe provides a good spacer. The sump volume should be 0.75 gallon per square foot (30.5 l/m^2) of 4 inch thick pad and 1 gallon per square foot (40.7 l/m^2) of 6 inch thick pad. These sump volumes are designed for an operating water level at half the depth of the tank and will provide room to accommodate water returning from the pad when the system is turned off.

As much as 1 gallon of water per minute can evaporate from 100 ft^2 of pad (0.4 l/min from l m^2 of pad) on a hot, dry day. Therefore, a water line with a float valve should be plumbed into the sump tank to automatically maintain the water level. As water evaporates from the pad surface, salts in the water are left behind. If this occurs for long, a white salt deposit will solidify on the pad whenever the system is turned off. Depending upon the salt content of the water used, it may be necessary to bleed off 1–2 percent of the recirculating water to avoid a salt buildup. A ⅜ inch (9.5 mm) bleed-off valve can be located on the pump discharge pipe. It should be adjusted to a flow rate that just eliminates signs of scale on the pad. Scale buildup in an excelsior pad is not as noticeable since this pad is used for only one season and water is spilled from the pad as it passes downward.

Algae may build up in cross-fluted cellulose pads after two or three years. Algae buildup does not destroy the cellulose, but it can plug passages in the pad. A 1 percent solution of sodium hypochlorite (bleach) can be injected into the water supply line to the pad. This will provide the required 3–5 parts per million (ppm) free chlorine in the pad. As little as 30 gallons (114 l) of solution per month can keep 100 linear feet (30 m) of 6 inch (15 cm) thick pad free of algae. A problem with bleach is the rise in pH that it causes. The pH level should not go above 9.0 because it will soften the pad, nor should it drop below 6.0. Some growers inject hydrogen peroxide into the water supply line. It does not raise the pH level. Chlorine and hydrogen peroxide break down rapidly and must periodically be applied. Small firms that cannot justify the injection equipment may spray the pads periodically with a chlorine solution. Biocides are also available for cleaning cooling water in various industrial applications that can be added to the sump. Oakite Biocide 20® (Oakite Products, Inc., 50 Valley Rd., Berkeley Heights, NJ 07922), when added once or twice per week to the sump, will control algae, bacteria, and fungi in greenhouse pads. It is used at an initial rate of 2.4–6.0 fluid ounces per 1,000 gallons (20–47 ml/1,000 l) and at a subsequent rate of 0.6–6.0 fluid ounces per 1,000 gallons (4–47 ml/1,000 l).

More recently, Agribrom® tablets (Great Lakes Chemical Corp., P.O. Box 2200, West Lafayette, IN 47906) containing bromine and a lesser amount of chlorine have been used. One injection system makes use of a homemade applicator constructed from 6 inch (15 cm) clear PVC pipe (Figure 4–5). A supply of tablets is maintained in the applicator. For removal of a heavy buildup of algae, a concentration of bromine at the top of the pad of 1–3 ppm should be used. Following cleanup, a maintenance concentration of 0.1–1 ppm bromine is held. A bromine tester is available from Great Lakes Chemical Corporation for about $35. Concentrations can be controlled by adjusting the water inlet valve below the applicator.

The fan-and-pad system can be automated or operated manually. When cooling is demanded in the automated system, the exhaust fans should turn on and the ventilators over the pads should open first. If this does not satisfy the cooling requirement and the temperature continues to increase, the pump providing water to the pads should then be activated. When the cooling requirement is satisfied, the system turns off step by step in the reverse order.

Excelsior Pad Specifications The excelsior pad is about 1 inch thick and is composed of wood fibers (Figure 4–3b). Its life expectancy is generally one year. The pad is contained in a 1 inch by 2 inch (2.5 cm by 5 cm) mesh wire frame for support. Less evaporative surface area is contained within a square foot of excelsior pad than is in an equivalent area of the thicker cross-fluted cellulose pad. Consequently, an excelsior pad area must be greater than that of a cross-fluted cellulose pad to accomplish the same job. The airflow rate through 1 square foot of excelsior pad is 150 cfm (45 cmm/m^2 of pad). This is only 60 percent of the flow rate possible in a 4 inch thick cross-fluted cellulose pad.

Because of the larger required area of excelsior pads, they occasionally do not fit into the wall, particularly the end wall, of a greenhouse. If the required pad area should exceed the area of the greenhouse wall, it is necessary to place it exterior to the greenhouse wall (Figure 4–6). The opening in the greenhouse should be at least half the area of the pad. The pad should be set back from the opening a distance of half the height by which the pad exceeds that of the opening. Ideally, the extra height of the pad should be equally divided above and below the opening. It is important that the pad be connected to the greenhouse on the top and

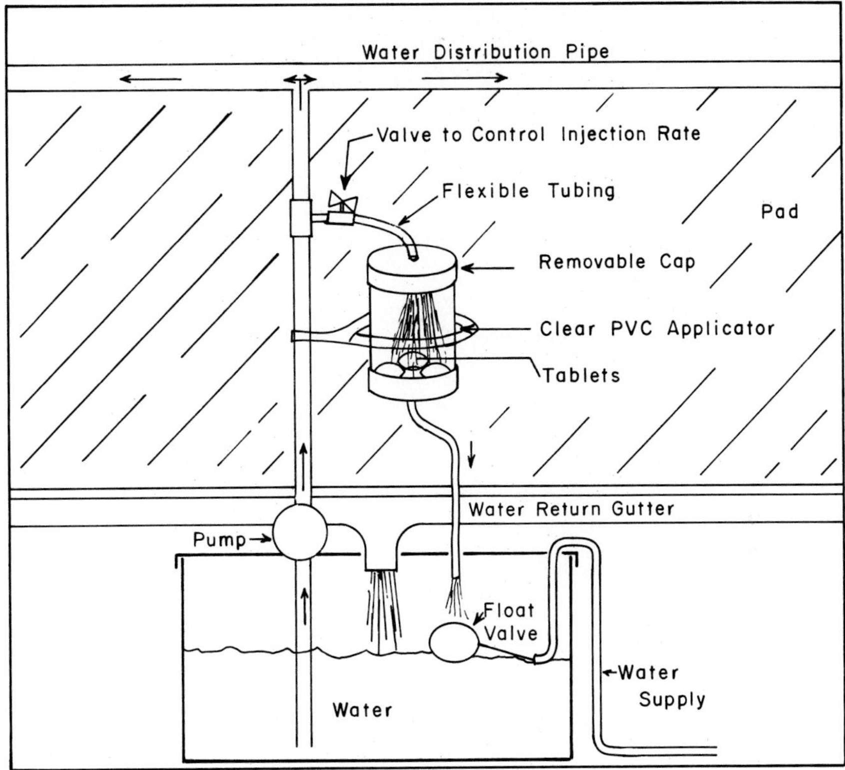

Figure 4–5

Design and installation of a bromine plus chlorine applicator for control of algae in cooling pads. The main body of the applicator consists of a 1 foot long (30 cm) piece of clear PVC pipe to which one cap is cemented at the bottom and a second cap is pressed onto the top. Agribrom® tablets containing bromine plus chlorine can be added to the applicator as previously applied tablets dissolve by removing the top cap. The tablets rest on a wire screen. Each cap is drilled and fitted with a flexible tube. The upper tube is supplied with water from the main leading from the pump to the top of the pad and has a valve on it to control the flow rate. The lower tube permits water that has passed through the applicator and picked up bromine and chlorine to return to the sump tank or to the return gutter.

ends by a transparent covering material to ensure that any air drawn through the pad enters the greenhouse.

Water should be delivered to the top of an excelsior pad at the rate of ⅓ gpm per linear foot of pad (4.1 l/min for each meter of pad) regardless of the height of the pad. Since all water will return to the sump tank when the system is turned off, a sump capacity of 1.5 gallons per linear foot of pad (19 l/m of pad) is required.

Figure 4–6

A cooling pad exterior to the greenhouse. This arrangement can accommodate a pad larger than the wall of the greenhouse. The pad is set back from the wall a distance at least half the excess height of the pad over the wall and is connected to the greenhouse by a transparent covering to ensure that air entering the greenhouse comes through the pad.

Other Pad Materials Cross-fluted cellulose and excelsior are not the only materials from which cooling pads are constructed. Aluminum fiber pads are sold for greenhouse application and can be found in a modest number of firms. Glass fiber pads, commonly used in industrial applications, might also be tried in greenhouses.

Horizontal Pads Horizontal pads are also being tried by growers. A horizontal screen is constructed outward from the greenhouse. One of a variety of materials, including gravel, vermiculite, or excelsior, is placed on the screen to serve as an evaporative surface and yet permit air percolation. Mist nozzles keep the pad wet, and air is drawn from outside through the pad into the greenhouse. Several pads may be installed in a stack along one greenhouse wall, offering an economy of space. Another advantage is the long life expectancy of the pads since more permanent types of materials can be used.

Fan Placement Whenever possible, it is best to place the fans on the leeward side of the greenhouse and the pads on the side toward the prevailing winds so that the winds will assist rather than counteract the cooling system. If fans exhaust into the windward side, their capacity should be increased 10 percent or more. When two or more houses are located adjacent to one another, factors more important than wind direction dictate the placement. Fans from one greenhouse should not exhaust warm moist air toward the pads of an adjacent greenhouse unless it is located at least 50 feet (15.2 m) away.

When fans are located in adjacent walls of greenhouses located within 15 feet (4.6 m) of each other, they should be alternated so that they do not blow directly against each other. Adjacent service buildings can also present a problem. There must be a clearance of one and one-half diameters of the fan between the fan and adjacent obstacles. If this is not possible, special roof-mounted fans should be installed.

A waterproof housing should enclose the fan to protect it from the elements. Air-activated louvers give protection on one side. It is imperative that a screen or welded-wire guard be placed on the other side of the fan to protect workers and visitors from serious injury.

The Air Stream The pads should be located at and slightly above the plant height in order to bring the cool air in on the plants. Because of resistance of the foliage and plant supports, as well as the rising temperature, the air stream will rise at an angle of 7° (1 foot in every 8) and will soon pass over the plants, leaving a pocket of hot air below at the plant height. If air is drawn across ridge-and-furrow or gutter-connected greenhouses, the gutters will keep the flow of air down on the plants. If air is drawn longitudinally the length of the greenhouse, it will rise. In this case, transparent (polyethylene) vertical baffles should be installed in the gable of the greenhouse perpendicular to the air stream to direct the flow of air down to the plants. Baffles should be installed every 30 feet. The bottom of the baffle should be well above the plant height to permit passage of air.

If pads are located near the floor and the benches are tall, considerable air may pass beneath the benches, where little benefit occurs. In this case, baffles should be placed beneath the benches near the pads.

The situation encountered in a greenhouse more than 200 feet (61 m) long and less than 100 feet (30 m) wide can be remedied by placing pads at each end of the greenhouse and exhaust fans in the roof halfway between the ends. In this situation, the greenhouse is cooled by the equivalent of two systems, each half the length of the greenhouse. When roof fans are used, a polyethylene baffle should be installed about 5 feet (1.5 m) before the fan and just above plant height to force the cooling air down into the plants.

Example Problem

The following example illustrates the calculations involved in designing an evaporative cooling system. Consider a single greenhouse 50 feet (15 m) wide and

100 feet (30 m) long located at 3,000 feet (915 m) elevation. The greenhouse has a moderate coat of shading compound on it; thus, the maximum light intensity inside is 5,000 fc (53.8 klux). A 7°F (4°C) rise in temperature can be tolerated from pad to fans. Step-by-step calculations for developing a 4 inch (10 cm) thick cross-fluted cellulose cooling system for this greenhouse follow.

1. Multiply the greenhouse floor width by the length and by 8 to determine the quantity of air to remove per minute under standard conditions:

$$\begin{aligned} \text{cfm}_{\text{standard}} &= L \times W \times 8 \\ &= 50 \times 100 \times 8 = 40{,}000 \text{ cfm} \end{aligned}$$

   or

$$\begin{aligned} \text{cmm}_{\text{standard}} &= L \times W \times 2.5 \\ &= 15 \times 30 \times 2.5 = 1{,}125 \text{ cmm} \end{aligned}$$

2. Determine a factor for the house (F_{house}) by multiplying the three factors together: elevation, light intensity inside the greenhouse, and temperature rise from pad to fans. These factors are found in Tables 4–1 through 4–3, respectively:

$$\begin{aligned} F_{\text{house}} &= F_{\text{elev}} \times F_{\text{light}} \times F_{\text{temp}} \\ &= 1.12 \times 1.0 \times 1.0 = 1.12 \end{aligned}$$

3. Look up the factor for velocity (F_{vel}) in Table 4–4. Select two opposite walls for installation of the pad and fans, which are 100–200 feet (30–61 m) apart or as close to 100 feet (30 m) as possible. The end walls, which are 100 feet (30 m) apart, should be used in this example:

$$F_{\text{vel}} = 1.00$$

4. Multiply the standard cfm value from step 1 by either F_{house} or F_{vel}, using whichever factor is larger—F_{house} in this case. This is the volume of air to be expelled from the greenhouse each minute:

$$\begin{aligned} \text{cfm}_{\text{adjusted}} &= \text{std cfm} \times F_{\text{house}} \\ &= 40{,}000 \text{ cfm} \times 1.12 = 44{,}800 \text{ cfm} \end{aligned}$$

   or

$$\text{cmm}_{\text{adjusted}} = 1{,}125 \text{ cmm} \times 1.12 = 1{,}260 \text{ cmm}$$

5. Determine the number of fans needed. Since they should not be over 25 feet (7.6 m) apart, divide the length of the wall housing the fans by 25 (7.6):

$$\frac{50 \text{ ft}}{25 \text{ ft}} = 2 \text{ fans}$$

or

$$\frac{15 \text{ m}}{7.6 \text{ m}} = 2 \text{ fans}$$

6. Determine the size of the fans needed by dividing the adjusted cfm of air to be removed (from step 4) by the number of fans needed:

$$\frac{\text{cfm}_{\text{adjusted}}}{\text{no. of fans}} = \text{size of fan}$$

$$\frac{44{,}800 \text{ cfm}}{2} = 22{,}400 \text{ cfm per fan}$$

or

$$\frac{1{,}260 \text{ cmm}}{2} = 630 \text{ cmm per fan}$$

7. Purchase two fans of the size determined in step 6 and space them equidistant on one end of the greenhouse. If the fans were to be purchased from the manufacturer of equipment listed in Table 4–5, two 54 inch fans with 1 hp motors would be selected.

8. The pad area is determined next. One square foot of pad is required for each 250 cfm (1 m^2 per 75 cmm) of fan capacity. Divide the capacity of the required fan (22,400 cfm) by 250 cfm to arrive at a required pad area of 90 ft^2 per fan (630 cmm divided by 75 cmm = 8.4 m^2 of required pad per fan). Since there are two fans, a total of 180 ft^2 (16.8 m^2) of pad is required. Approximately the same value could be read directly from Table 4–5.

9. The pad must cover the width of the wall in which it is to be installed—50 feet (15 m) in this example. The height of the pad is determined by dividing the total pad area by its width. A 4 foot (1.1 m) tall pad should be purchased:

$$\text{pad height} = \frac{\text{pad area}}{\text{pad width}}$$

$$= \frac{180 \text{ ft}^2}{50 \text{ ft}} = 3.6 \text{ ft}$$

or

$$\text{pad height} = \frac{16.8 \text{ m}^2}{15 \text{ m}} = 1.1 \text{ m}$$

10. The pump capacity is equal to 0.5 gpm multiplied by the length of the pad in feet (6.2 l/m of pad) and must be selected to have this flow rate for the given head under which it must operate. The head is the distance from the water surface in the sump to the top of the pads:

$$\text{pump capacity} = 0.5 \text{ gpm} \times 50 \text{ ft} = 25 \text{ gpm}$$

or

$$\text{pump capacity} = 6.2 \text{ l/min} \times 15 \text{ m} = 93 \text{ l/min}$$

11. The sump size is equal to 0.75 gallon per square foot of pad (30.5 l/m^2 of pad):

$$\text{sump volume} = 0.75 \text{ gal} \times 200 \text{ ft}^2 = 150 \text{ gal}$$

or

$$\text{sump volume} = 30.5 \text{ l} \times 18.6 \text{ m}^2 = 567 \text{ l}$$

Fog Cooling

The speed of evaporation of water and, consequently, the rate of cooling of air increase proportionately as water droplet size decreases. Mist droplets are in the range of 1,000 microns (0.040 in.) in diameter. If a cup of water was converted to mist, it would have 400 times as much surface area and would evaporate 400 times faster than the same water left in the cup. Mist droplets are large and will settle out of air to wet surfaces of plants, soil, and people. Droplets in a fog are 40 microns or smaller (0.0016 in.). Their surface area and rate of evaporation is 10,000 times greater than the same volume of water in a cup. These droplets stay suspended in air while they evaporate to cool the air. This occurs without water condensing out on surfaces.

Greenhouse fog cooling systems are available that can convert 99.5 percent of water to 40 microns or smaller with an average droplet size less than 10 microns (0.0004 in.) (Figure 4–7). These droplets evaporate at 40,000 times the speed with which water evaporates from a cup. With such a rapid evaporative response, air can be cooled at nearly 100 percent efficiency. The result is that wet bulb temperatures can essentially be obtained. One system that can attain this droplet size is the Mee fog cooling system (Mee Industries, Inc., 4443 N. Rowland Ave., El Monte, CA 91731). It provides a pumping system that is typically operated at 1,000 psi (6.9 MPa) but that can operate at pressures up to 1,500 psi (10.3 MPa).

The fog cooling system can be used in greenhouses built to be cooled by ventilators alone. Fog nozzles are spaced above plants throughout the greenhouse. Fog comes on intermittently to cool air that has entered the greenhouse through ventilators. As the humid cooled air begins to warm and leave the greenhouse through ventilators, more outside air is drawn in and is, in turn, cooled by subsequent fog.

Greenhouses equipped with exhaust fan cooling lend themselves well to fog cooling. Lines of fog nozzles are installed just inside the inlet ventilators. Exhaust fans on the opposite wall draw outside air in through the open ventilators and then through the fog where it is cooled. Only about half the exhaust fan capacity, 4–5 cfm/ft^2 (1.2–1.5 cmm/m^2) of floor, of fan-and-pad systems is used. If there were no more to the system, air would rise in temperature as it crossed the greenhouse, as happens in a fan-and-pad system. To prevent this, a second set of fog nozzles is installed overhead throughout the greenhouse.

Water quality is extremely important. Particles of sand or clay can clog the fog nozzles. Multiple filters capable of screening down to 5 micron particles are used. To prevent scale formation, carbonates and bicarbonates are removed. Sulfur and iron can support growth of slime organisms, which also plug nozzles. All of these factors are assessed, and appropriate filters and chemical treatment are provided by firms supplying fog cooling systems.

Various control systems are used for fog cooling. Timers provide the simplest form of control. A 24-hour timer is used to select the time of day cooling is needed, which is usually the daylight hours. The circuit continues through a recycle timer that is typically set to apply fog from 30 seconds to 4 minutes out of each cycle of 1 to 20 minutes. More consistent control is achieved through the use of a humidistat. When temperature goes up in the greenhouse, humidity goes down. By holding a constant relative humidity, maximum cooling is achieved. The response time of the cooling system is much faster when a humidistat rather than a thermostat is used since air can be cooled 20°F (11°C) or more in 30 seconds.

When fog cooling is used for growing crops to market stage, a relative humidity level is set on the humidistat. This level is often in the range of 80–90 percent. However, growers fine tune this setting by relating relative humidity levels to responses of their crops over time. In this application, visible fog originating from the nozzles generally disappears for a few minutes before coming on again.

(a)

(b)

(c)

Figure 4–7

(a) A nozzle emitting 10 micron fog droplets in an evaporative greenhouse cooling system. (b) A fog system being used in a propagation greenhouse for cooling and for maintaining moisture in cuttings. (c) Water treatment and pumping apparatus for a fog cooling system. (*Photos courtesy of Mee Industries, Inc.*, 4443 N. *Rowland Ave.*, El *Monte*, CA 91731)

Fog is also used as a substitute for mist systems in cutting propagation greenhouses. The object here is to stop water loss through transpiration by holding 100 percent relative humidity. In this case, fog is turned on just as the visible appearance of the previous fog pulse begins to disappear. Since fog cooling does not wet the foliage, less disease has been reported in greenhouses using this system.

Fog is used in a similar manner in seed germination greenhouses. The goal here is to greatly reduce evaporation and transpiration to the point where water is needed only at the frequency that liquid fertilizer needs to be applied. In this way, the application of water between fertilizations is eliminated. The problem with watering, whether it occurs through mist or larger droplets, is the film of water that forms in the root medium. This water film adversely reduces oxygen supply to the seeds and roots. A relative humidity setting slightly lower than the 100 percent level used for cutting propagation is used in seed germination.

It is possible to fertilize seedlings and also cuttings being propagated by injecting nutrients into the water supplying the fog system. The system is then controlled to hold the air saturated so that moisture condenses on plant surfaces. Fog very effectively penetrates the plant canopy, depositing a nutrient film on all upper as well as lower leaf surfaces for foliar uptake.

Advantages cited by greenhouse firms that have installed fog cooling include the following:

1. There is less electrical consumption since the sum of the wattage of the fog pump plus exhaust fans is less than the exhaust fans and pad water pumps in the fan-and-pad system.
2. Heat rise across the greenhouse is controlled.
3. Cooler average temperatures can be achieved across the greenhouse.
4. The system is a good substitute for the mist system in cutting propagation greenhouses, where it uses less water and causes less disease.

GREENHOUSE WINTER COOLING SYSTEM

Description of Fan–Tube Ventilation

The temperature at which winter ventilation is desired is set on a thermostat, which, in turn, activates three events simultaneously (Figures 4–8 and 4–9). An exhaust fan, located anywhere in the greenhouse, is turned on to create a vacuum. A louver is opened in a gable through which cold air enters in response to the vacuum. A pressurizing fan in the end of the clear polyethylene distribution tube turns on to pick up the cool air entering the louver since the end of the distribu-

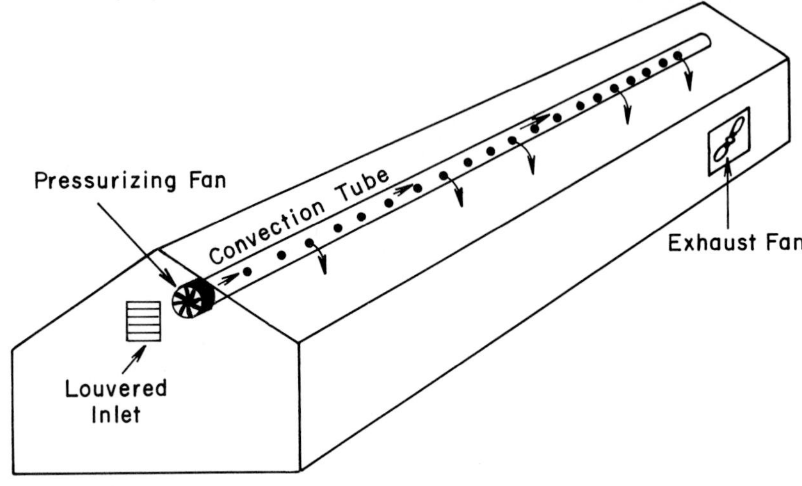

Figure 4–8

Diagram of a greenhouse showing the components of a fan–tube winter cooling system. When cooling is required, a thermostat activates an exhaust fan, opens the louvered inlet, and turns on the pressurizing fan. Cold air enters the louver and is directed down a transparent polyethylene convection tube by a pressurizing fan. Jets of cold air leave the tube through holes along both sides of the tube and thoroughly mix with warm greenhouse air before reaching the plants.

tion tube is separated from the louvered inlet by 1–2 feet (0.3–0.6 m). Cold air under pressure in the distribution tube shoots out of holes on either side of the distribution tube in turbulent jets. The cold air mixes with the warm greenhouse air well above plant height. The cooled mixture of air, being heavier, gently falls to the floor, cooling the plant area.

The pressurizing fan directing incoming cold air into the distribution tube must be at least equal to the exhaust fan. If it is smaller, excess incoming cold air will drop to the ground at the point of entry and cause a cold spot. When cooling is not required, the inlet louver closes, and the pressurizing fan continues circulating air within the greenhouse. This step replaces the horizontal airflow (HAF) circulation system but requires more power.

Specifications

Under standard conditions, a volume of 2 cfm of air should be removed from the greenhouse for each square foot of floor area (0.61 cmm/m^2 of floor). (Remember that 8 cfm of air for each square foot of floor is required for summer cooling.) The volume obtained by multiplying the floor area by 2 would therefore define the capacity of the exhaust fan in terms of cubic feet of air movement per minute.

Various published specifications call for as little as 1.5 cfm and as much as 4 cfm of air to be exhausted for each square foot of floor area (0.46 and 1.22 cmm/

Figure 4–9

Air inlet components of a winter cooling system including the louvered inlet, a polyethylene distributing tube a short distance from the louvered inlet, and a pressurizing fan to direct air into the tube under pressure.

m^2 of floor). The high-capacity system costs more to set up but can be operated earlier in the fall and later in the spring to extend the winter cooling season. This can have an advantage since frosts usually occur during these extension periods. A high-capacity fan–tube system eliminates the necessity of switching back and forth between the summer fan-and-pad and the winter fan–tube systems at these times.

When fan–tube ventilation is used, standard conditions specify a maximum inside temperature of 15°F (8°C) above the outside temperature. The temperature inside the greenhouse can become adversely high on a winter day when the sun is shining, even though the outside temperature is below the desired level. The fan–tube cooling system is designed to reduce the internal temperature to within 15°F (8°C) of the outside temperature.

If a lower inside temperature is desired, cold air must be introduced into the greenhouse at a greater rate. The compensating factors to be used in this case are given in Table 4–6. As in the case of the summer cooling system, standard conditions also specify an elevation under 1,000 feet (305 m) and a maximum interior light intensity of 5,000 fc (53.8 klux). If other elevation or light intensity specifications are desired, factors must be selected from Tables 4–1 and 4–2 and used to correct the rate of air entry.

Table 4–6

Factors (F_{winter}) for Adjusting Standard Rate of Air Removal in a Winter Greenhouse Cooling System for the Temperature Difference between the Inside and Outside of the Greenhouse*

	Greenhouse Temperature above Outdoor Temperature									
°F	18	17	16	15	14	13	12	11	10	9
°C	10.0	9.4	8.9	8.3	7.8	7.2	6.7	6.1	5.6	5.0
F_{winter}	0.83	0.88	0.94	1.00	1.07	1.15	1.25	1.37	1.50	1.67

*From National Greenhouse Manufacturers' Assoc. (1971).

Distribution tubes are conventionally oriented from end to end in the greenhouse. Each distribution tube can be used to cool up to 30 feet (9.1 m) of greenhouse width, although it is desirable to use two tubes for greenhouses 30 feet (9.1 m) wide. One tube placed down the center of the house will cool houses up to 30 feet (9.1 m) in width. Houses 30–60 feet (9.1–18.3 m) in width are cooled by two tubes placed equidistant across the house. Holes along the tube exist in pairs on the opposite vertical sides. The holes vary in size according to the volume of greenhouse to be cooled. The number and diameter of tubes needed to cool a greenhouse can be determined from Table 4–7. If two or more tubes are needed, they should be of equal size and should be spaced evenly across the greenhouse. Recommendations in Table 4–7 are based on an airflow rate of approximately 1,700 cfm/ft^2 (518 cmm/m^2) of cross-sectional area in the tube. When the greenhouse is large and the required number of 30 inch (76 cm) diameter tubes becomes cumbersome, tubes may be installed with air inlets in both ends. These inlets double the amount of cool air that can be brought in through a single tube.

The winter cooling system requirements should be taken into consideration when fans are ordered for the summer cooling system. In this way, one or more of the summer fans could be used for the winter exhaust fan requirement. Fans used for the summer system should all be of equal size or at least nearly equal. However, one fan could be purchased with a two-speed motor that provides half its capacity at the lower speed.

Example Problem

Determine the winter cooling specifications for a greenhouse measuring 50 feet wide by 100 feet long (15 m by 30 m) and situated at 3,000 feet (914 m) elevation. The maximum interior light intensity anticipated is 5,000 fc (53.8 klux), and the desired interior-to-exterior temperature difference is 15°F (8.3°C).

Table 4–7

Number (N) and Diameter (D) of Air Distribution Tubes Required for Winter Cooling of Greenhouses of Various Widths and Lengths

Greenhouse Width		Greenhouse Length																							
		50 ft (15 m)			*100 ft (30 m)*			*150ft (46 m)*			*200 ft (61 m)*						*250 ft (76 m)*								
														IBE						IBE					
			D			D			D			D			D			D			D				
ft	*m*	N	*in.*	*cm*	N	*in.*	*cm*	N	*in.*	*cm*	N	*in.*	*cm*	N	*in.*	*cm*	N	*in.*	*cm*	N	*in.*	*cm*			
15	4.6	1	18	46	1	18	46	1	24	61	1	30	76		—	—	1	30	76	1	24	61			
20	6.1	1	18	46	1	24	61	1	30	76	1	30	76		—	—	2	24	61	1	24	61			
25	7.6	1	18	46	1	24	61	1	30	76	2	24	61	1	24	61	2	30	76	1	30	76			
30	9.1	2	18	46	2	18	46	2	24	61	2	30	76		—	—	2	30	76		—	—			
35	10.7	2	18	46	2	24	61	2	24	61	2	30	76		—	—	3	30	76	2	24	61			
40	12.2	2	18	46	2	24	61	2	30	76	2	30	76		—	—	3	30	76	2	24	61			
50	15.2	2	18	46	2	24	61	2	30	76	3	30	76	2	24	61	3	30	76	2	30	76			

Tubes run the length of the greenhouse and are spaced equidistant across the greenhouse. Tubes derive cold air from a louvered air inlet on one end only, unless otherwise specified. Those open to louvered inlets on both ends are identified as *IBE*.

1. The capacity of the exhaust fan is equal to 2 cfm (0.61 cmm) times the greenhouse floor area under standard conditions:

$$\begin{aligned} cfm_{standard} &= 2 \times \text{length} \times \text{width} \\ &= 2 \times 100 \times 50 = 10{,}000 \text{ cfm} \end{aligned}$$

or

$$cmm_{standard} = 0.61 \times 30 \times 15 = 275 \text{ cmm}$$

2. Correct the exhaust fan capacity just calculated for deviations from standard conditions. The only deviation in the sample problem is the elevation of 3,000 feet (914 m), which has an F_{elev} value of 1.12 from Table 4–1. An exhaust fan with a capacity of 11,200 cfm (308 cmm) at a static water pressure of 0.1 inch (30 Pa) is needed:

$$\begin{aligned} cfm_{adjusted} &= cfm_{standard} \times F_{winter} \times F_{elev} \times F_{light} \\ &= 10{,}000 \times 1.0 \times 1.12 \times 1.0 = 11{,}200 \text{ cfm} \end{aligned}$$

or

$$cmm_{adjusted} = 275 \times 1.0 \times 1.12 \times 1.0 = 308 \text{ cmm}$$

3. The number of air distribution tubes can be determined from Table 4–7. Two 24 inch (61 cm) tubes are needed for this greenhouse with its 50 foot width and 100 foot length (15 m by 30 m).

4. The diameter of individual holes along the side of distribution tubes and the distance between them must next be decided. Tables are presented in the catalog of greenhouse supply companies specifying the model of tube required for given tube diameters and greenhouse lengths. The model identification, unfortunately, does not indicate the size or distance between holes in these tubes.

   The hole specifications can be calculated if you wish to purchase unpunched tubing or purchase tubing from a company that punches holes to your specifications. Work in England by G. A. Carpenter specifies that the total area of all holes in a single tube should be 1.5–2 times the cross-sectional area of the tube. The cross-sectional area of a 24 inch (61 cm) tube is 3.14 ft^2 (890 cm^2). Thus, the combined area of all holes in a tube should be between 4.71 and 6.28 ft^2 (1,334 and 1,778 cm^2). As the required tube length increases, the distance between holes should increase to maintain a reasonable diameter hole. Distances of 2–4 feet (60–120 cm) are common.

5. The pressurizing fan in the inlet end of the distribution tube should be equal to the exhaust fan in capacity. If this is not possible, then the pressurizing fan should be larger. The two pressurizing fans needed in the example greenhouse should have a combined capacity of 11,200 cfm (308 cmm), which is equal to the exhaust fan capacity. Each pressurizing fan thus has half the capacity or 5,600 cfm (154 cmm) at a static water pressure of 0.1 inch (30 Pa).

INTEGRATION OF COOLING AND HEATING SYSTEMS

Cooling and heating are often required during the winter when days are bright and evenings are cold. In either case, the same polyethylene tubes are used to distribute the cold air from the outside or the warm air from the heater. Unit heaters are placed near the open end of the tube so that the warm air emitted from them is directed into the tube. One design calls for the unit heater to be attached to the inlet end of the tube, as illustrated in Figure 4–10. During the cooling phase, louver A is open and B is closed. External cold air enters as a result of an exhaust fan located elsewhere and is directed into the polyethylene tube under pressure by the fan in the unit heater. When the greenhouse is sufficiently cool, louver A closes and B opens. The unit heater fan continues to circulate air within the greenhouse. If the temperature drops, the same louver arrangement is maintained and the unit heater turns on. Then, air from inside the greenhouse is heated and distributed through the tube.

A second integrated heating–cooling design calls for a pressurizing fan in the tube inlet and placement of the unit heaters away from and perpendicular to the inlet of the tube, as shown in Figure 4–11. The pressurizing fan runs continuously. A motorized louver in the greenhouse end wall opens only during cooling. An exhaust fan located elsewhere causes air to enter through the louvered inlet. This air is, in turn, directed into the tube for uniform distribution by the pressurizing fan. In the interim between cooling and heating, the pressurizing fan continues to circulate air within the greenhouse. When heat is required, the unit heaters turn on and blow warm air toward the tube inlet. When the air is in close proximity to the inlet, the pressurizing fan picks it up and directs it into the tube.

The integrated winter cooling–heating systems just discussed are adequate for winter conditions but do not adequately cope with the changeable weather situation in the fall and spring. During these periods, it is possible to require evaporative cooling one day, winter convection-tube cooling the next day, and heat the following night. All three systems can be integrated under the control of a single multistage thermostat or microprocessor. This system is illustrated in Figure 4–12 and can be visualized to occur in the following sequence of steps. Suppose that the evaporative cooling system is operating on a hot autumn afternoon. As the af-

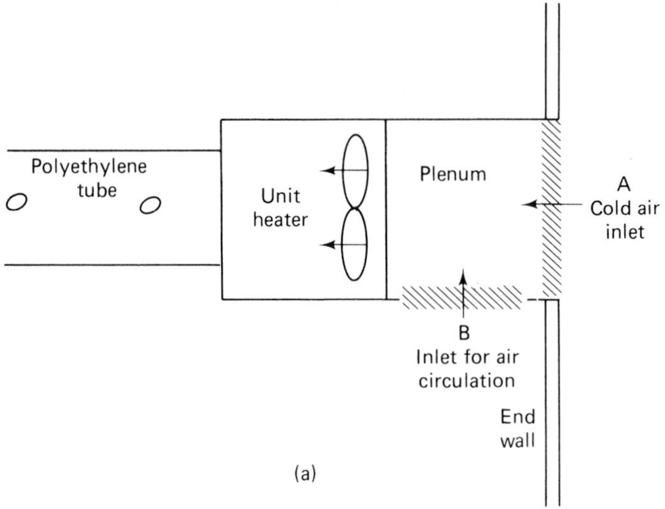

Figure 4–10

(a) An integrated winter cooling and heating system. The unit heater fan operates continuously, serving as a pressurizing fan for the tube. Only louver A is open during cooling; louver B is open and A is closed during the heating stage. When neither cooling nor heating is required, air is continually circulated within the greenhouse. (b) A commercial installation of such a system.

Figure 4–11

General view of an alternative winter cooling–heating system with unit heaters mounted apart from the tube inlet. Warm air is expelled from the heaters toward the tube inlet, where it is picked up by the pressurizing fan.

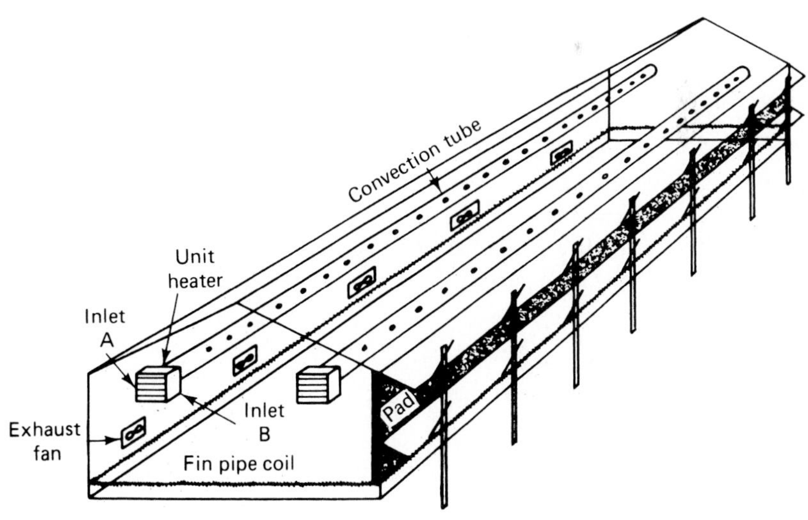

Figure 4–12

A completely integrated system for evaporative cooling, fan–tube cooling, and heating.

ternoon wears on and outside temperatures drop, the cooling requirement diminishes. A reduction in the inside temperature activates a thermostat switch that turns off the water-circulating pump in the evaporative pad. The exhaust fans continue to operate, drawing air in through the dry pads. As the need for cooling diminishes, all the exhaust fans turn off except those needed for the winter fan–tube cooling system. The ventilators adjacent to the pads close. The winter cooling system is now in operation with the pressurizing fan in the tube running and the louvered inlet in the end wall open. As evening approaches, no cooling is necessary. The exterior louvered inlet (A) closes, and the interior inlet (B) opens. Air is now circulated within the greenhouse. (An alternative to the fan–tube circulation of air that is sometimes preferred at this point is the HAF system, in which case the tube-pressurizing fans would turn off and the HAF fans would turn on in their place to circulate air.) Temperatures continue to drop during the night. Heat is first supplied through the perimeter pipe coil. When this cannot hold the desired temperature, half of the overhead unit heaters are activated and later, if necessary, the remaining half. In the morning, the reverse sequence of events occurs.

COOLING HOBBY GREENHOUSES

The principles are basically the same for cooling hobby greenhouses. A fan-and-pad system is used during the summer. To ensure proper vertical distribution of cool air, the pad should not be under 2 feet (60 cm) in height. Cooling problems inherent in these small greenhouses demand a higher-capacity system. A minimum of 12 cfm/ft^2 (3.66 cmm/m^2) of floor area should be exhausted from the greenhouse. If the greenhouse is attached to the east, west, or especially the south side of another building, then considerable solar heat will be collected inside the greenhouse by this wall. Half the area of the wall should be added to the floor area in calculating the ventilator requirement.

Package evaporative coolers are practical for small greenhouses. A package cooler, as pictured in Figure 4–13, consists of a cubical structure with evaporative pads on three sides. Water conduction and collection lines, as well as a pump, are built into the package. A fan is located inside the package to draw air in through the pads and expel the cool air to the greenhouse interior. A ventilator must be open at the opposite end of the greenhouse to serve as an air exit. The package coolers can be less expensive for a small greenhouse. They are easier to install and are more aesthetically pleasing than the conventional fan-and-pad systems.

The winter cooling system for a hobby greenhouse again follows the principles of a larger greenhouse. Fan–tube ventilation works well except that 3 cfm/ft^2 (0.9 cmm/m^2) of floor area should be exhausted under standard conditions. The force with which air is expelled from these heaters is sufficient to cause uniform circulation throughout a hobby-size greenhouse. If this is the case, the fan–tube system can be simplified with resulting economy. For winter cooling, the polyethylene tube may be connected directly to a stovepipe elbow mounted in the wall of

Figure 4–13

An Arctic Air® package evaporative cooler for a small or hobby-type greenhouse. Water is circulated through pads on three sides of the package. A fan is located within the unit to draw air in through the pads. (*Photo courtesy of* J. W. *Love, Department of Horticultural Science, North Carolina State University, Raleigh,* NC 27695–7609)

the greenhouse with the end outside pointing down. The elbow serves as an air inlet. When this system is off, the polyethylene tube hanging from attachments along its upper side collapses and seals itself off from the outside. The tube inflates when an exhaust fan in the greenhouse turns on. An elbow inlet should be used rather than a straight pipe to prevent wind from blowing into the system and bringing about cooling at times when it could not be tolerated. To further prevent wind entry, it is best to place the inlet for this type of cooling system on the leeward side of the greenhouse.

Very small greenhouses do not require a distribution tube for winter cooling. Air entering high in the gable will mix sufficiently well with existing air along the short length of the greenhouse. When neither cooling nor heating is required, it is well to use an 8–12 inch (20–30 cm) fan for air circulation to prevent hot or cold spots and to decrease the incidence of disease.

SUMMARY

1. Summer cooling requires that large volumes of air be cooled and brought into the greenhouse. The cool air must pass in a smooth pattern throughout the

entire plant zone. A fan-and-pad system is one evaporative cooling alternative used for this purpose. It consists of pads on one wall, through which water is circulated, and exhaust fans on the opposite wall. Air entering through the pads is cooled and then drawn across the greenhouse to the exhaust fans. Air is drawn through the greenhouse at the rate of 8 cfm/ft^2 (2.5 cmm/m^2) of floor area under standard conditions of an elevation under 1,000 feet (300 m), a maximum interior light intensity of 5,000 fc (53.8 klux), an air temperature rise of 7°F (4°C) between the pads and the exhaust fans, and a distance of 100 feet (30 m) or more between pad and fans.

2. Fog cooling is an alternative evaporative cooling system to the fan-and-pad system. Water droplets of 40 microns or smaller (0.016 in.) are generated under high pressure (1,000 psi, 6.9 MPa). Fog introduced into the incoming air, just inside the intake ventilators along one wall, cools the air as it evaporates. A second set of fog nozzles across the greenhouse counteracts any temperature rise as cooled air moves toward the exhaust fans opposite the intake ventilators. An air exhaust rate of 4–5 cfm/ft^2 (1.2–1.5 cmm/m^2) of floor is used.
3. Winter cooling calls for the introduction of a small volume of already cold air from the outside. It must be introduced in a turbulent flow up high in the greenhouse gable so that it thoroughly mixes with the interior air before reaching the plant zone; otherwise, cold spots occur. A fan–tube cooling system is used. The system consists of an exhaust fan used to develop a negative pressure in the greenhouse, a louvered air inlet in the gable, a polyethylene distribution tube with holes along opposite sides for turbulent air emission that runs from a short distance inside the inlet along the length of the greenhouse, and a pressurizing fan in the inlet end of the distribution tube. A flow rate of 2 cfm of air for each square foot of floor area (0.61 cmm/m^2 of floor) is satisfactory for standard conditions, which include elevation under 1,000 feet (300 m), a maximum interior light intensity of 5,000 fc (53.8 klux), and a capacity to bring the inside temperature down to within 15°F (8.3°C) of the colder outside temperature.
4. Present-day winter cooling and heating systems make use of the same polyethylene tube for distribution of the cool or the warm air. When neither cooling nor heating is required, air is circulated through the tube to bring warm air down from the gable and to provide uniform temperatures in the plant zone. A single controller is used to integrate the summer cooling, winter cooling, air circulation, and heating systems.
5. The horizontal airflow (HAF) system is an energy-efficient alternative to the fan–tube system for moving air during air circulation and during heating. It is not used for winter cooling. Small fans are placed above the plant height at 50 foot (15 m) intervals down one half of the greenhouse and back up the other half. The fans are designed to set up a horizontal circular flow of air that will

conserve fuel by bringing hot air down from the gable and also minimize temperature gradients at plant height.

6. The principles are the same for cooling hobby greenhouses. Somewhat simpler systems can be utilized. When the greenhouse is attached to an existing building on any side but the north, half of the attachment wall area is added to the floor area in calculating summer ventilation rates. For summer cooling, a minimum airflow of 12 cfm/ft^2 (3.66 cmm/m^2) of floor area is necessary. For winter cooling, an exhaust rate of 3 cfm/ft^2 (0.9 cmm/m^2) of floor area is used.

REFERENCES

Various manufacturers of cooling and ventilation equipment offer valuable literature covering products, price, and technical information.

1. Aldrich, R. A., W. A. Bailey, J. W. Bartok, Jr., W. J. Roberts, and D. S. Ross. 1976. *Hobby Greenhouses and Other Gardening Structures*. Pub. NRAES–2. Northeast Reg. Agr. Eng. Ser., Cornell Univ., 152 Riley-Robb Hall, Ithaca, NY 14853.
2. Aldrich, R. A., and J. W. Bartok, Jr. 1989. *Greenhouse Engineering*. Pub. NRAES–33. Northeast Reg. Agr. Eng. Ser., Cornell Univ., 152 Riley-Robb Hall, Ithaca, NY 14853.
3. American Society of Agricultural Engineers. 1983. Heating, ventilating, and cooling greenhouses. In Baxter, J. F., and R. H. Hahn, Jr., eds. *Agricultural Engineers Yearbook of Standards*, pp. 387–389. Amer. Soc. Agr. Engineers, St. Joseph, MI 49085.
4. Anon. 1974. Glasshouse ventilation. Ministry of Agriculture, Fisheries and Food. Mechanization Leaflet 5. Her Majesty's Stationery Office, London.
5. Bartok, J. W., Jr. 1970. Fan tube greenhouse ventilation. *Connecticut Greenhouse Newsletter* 32:9–12.
6. Bohanon, H. R., C. E. Rahilly, J. Stout, and P. E. Bush. 1988. The greenhouse climate control handbook. Form C7S. Acme Engineering and Manufacturing Corp., Muskogee, OK.
7. Gray, H. E. 1956. *Greenhouse Heating and Construction*. Florists' Publishing Co., 343 S. Dearborn St., Chicago, IL.
8. Koths, J. S., and J. W. Bartok, Jr. 1986. Horizontal air flow. Dept. of Nat. Res. Mgn. and Eng. Leaflet 85–14. Univ. of Connecticut, 1376 Storrs Rd., Storrs, CT 06268.
9. Laurie, A., D. C. Kiplinger, and K. S. Nelson. 1979. *Commercial Flower-Forcing*, 8th ed. New York: McGraw-Hill.
10. National Greenhouse Manufacturers' Association. 1971. Standards for ventilating and cooling greenhouses—1971 revision. Natl. Greenhouse Mfg. Assoc., P.O. Box 128, Pleasantville, NY 10570.
11. The Electricity Council. 1975. *Ventilation for Greenhouses*. Farm-electric Centre, National Agr. Centre, Stoneleigh, Kenilworth, Warwickshire CV82LS, England.
12. Walker, J. N., and G. A. Duncan. 1973. Estimating greenhouse ventilation requirements. AEN–9. Univ. of Kentucky, Dept. of Agr. Eng., Lexington, KY.

13. ______1973. Air circulation in greenhouses. AEN–18. Univ. of Kentucky, Dept. of Agr. Eng., Lexington, KY.

14. ______1973. Greenhouse humidity control. AEN–19. Univ. of Kentucky, Dept. of Agr. Eng., Lexington, KY.

15. ______1974. Cooling greenhouses. AEN–28. Univ. of Kentucky, Dept. of Agr. Eng., Lexington, KY.

16. ______1974. Greenhouse ventilation systems. AEN–30. Univ. of Kentucky, Dept. of Agr. Eng., Lexington, KY.

17. ______1975. An automatic sidewall system for greenhouse environmental control. AEN–37. Univ. of Kentucky, Dept. of Agr. Eng., Lexington, KY.

CHAPTER 5

Root Media

Once greenhouses are constructed and the heating and cooling systems are set into operation, it is time for the first cultural consideration—that of selecting a root medium. Taken at face value, this appears to be a monumental task. Some fifteen or more components including field soil, sand, perlite, polystyrene, peats of many types, barks of various origins, sawdust, and rock wool are to be found in a myriad of formulations used by growers, sold as commercial preparations, or recommended by research institutions. Many are well proven, while others are ineffective. There is a magical lure about concocting one's own root medium, which often leads to poor combinations of components and to the use of more components than are needed or can be justified economically. Selection of a root medium, however, should be an easy matter once some fundamentals are understood.

FUNCTIONS OF ROOT MEDIA

There are four functions that a root medium must serve in order to support good plant growth:

1. It must serve as a reservoir for plant nutrients.
2. It must hold water in a way that it is available to the plant.

3. At the same time, it must provide for the exchange of gases between roots and the atmosphere above the root medium.
4. It must also provide an anchorage or support for the plant.

Some individual materials can provide all four functions but not at the required level of each. Sand, for instance, provides excellent support and gas exchange but has insufficient water- and nutrient-supplying capacity. The coarse particles of sand have little surface area per unit of volume compared to the finer particles of soil or peat moss. Since water is held on the surfaces of particles, sand has a small water reserve. Plants grown in sand would need to be watered 3 or more times per day in the summer. Since most nutrients in a sand medium are held in the water films, there is likewise little nutrient reserve.

Clay, however, has a high nutrient- and water-holding capacity and provides excellent plant support, but the small particles of clay are close to one another. The water films of adjacent particles come into close contact, leaving little open space for gas exchange. Carbon dioxide produced by the roots and by microorganisms cannot adequately leave the clay. In high concentration, carbon dioxide suppresses respiration, which, in turn, slows growth. Oxygen, also needed to keep the processes of respiration going, cannot adequately diffuse into the clay. Consequently, clay is a poor medium for plant growth.

Water is sometimes used as a root medium. It provides water and nutrients but lacks the ability for gas exchange and plant support. When plants are grown in water, air must be bubbled into it and the plants must be supported in some sort of frame. This cultural procedure is known as *hydroponics.* Aside from hydroponics, greenhouse root media contain two or more components to ensure that all four functions are met.

ADAPTATION OF FIELD SOIL TO CONTAINERS

You might ask, why not use only field soil in greenhouse containers? Greenhouse crops often can be grown in the field without significant alteration of the soil, but when this soil is transferred to containers and the same crop is grown, failure ensues. While all four functions are provided by soil in the field, the function of aeration is usually not adequately provided by this soil in containers. Water retention and aeration go hand in hand.

Drainage is proportional to the depth of the soil above the water table (free water). The bottom of any container is equivalent to a water table. Most cut flower beds contain a 7 inch (18 cm) depth of soil, while potted plants range from 7 inches down to 0.75 inch (1.9 cm) in various pots, flats, and plug seedling trays. The water content in a bedding-plant container shortly after watering would be similar to that in a soil situated 2 inches above freestanding watering—in other words, a swamp situation. The soil pores would be filled mostly with water, and little room would remain for gas exchange.

One dimension by which soil is classified is *texture.* Texture is the size distribution of particles in a soil. Field soil is composed of three mineral components (Figure 5–1). The finest particles, clay, extend up to a maximum diameter of 0.002 mm. Silt is composed of particles from 0.002 mm up to 0.05 mm, and the third component, sand, is everything larger. Clay feels sticky to the touch, silt is floury, and sand is gritty. Texture terms include *sandy loam, silt loam,* and *clay loam* for soils that are predominately composed of sand, silt, and clay, respectively. *Loam* refers to a reasonable balance of all three materials.

Texture relates to water retention for a very simple reason. Water will remain in soil because it is attracted to the surface of soil particles. Water exists as a film or layer coating each soil particle. The thickness of the water layer depends upon the gravitational force attempting to pull the water out of the soil and down to the water table. The greater the distance from a given soil particle to the water table, the stronger the gravitational force. Within the water layer, water that is farthest from the soil particle surface is held the least tightly. This water will be pulled away first by the gravitational force. Thus, as the gravitational force, or the depth of the soil, increases, the thickness of the water layer on the soil particle surfaces decreases (Figure 5–2), and the air-filled center of the pore gets larger, permitting better gas exchange.

The logical solution to the shallow-container problem would appear to be a change toward coarser texture to increase the diameter of the pores. This does solve the problem of aeration, but it creates a new problem by reducing the water-

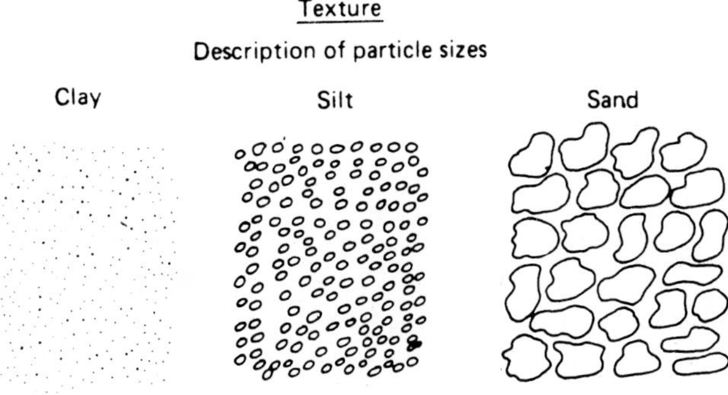

Figure 5–1

Soil is composed of three mineral components, the relative sizes of which are shown above. Clay particles are the smallest and have a maximum diameter of 0.002 mm. Silt particles have a diameter extending from 0.002 mm to 0.05 mm. The largest particles are sand. The texture classification of a soil gives an indication of the proportion of these three mineral particles contained in it.

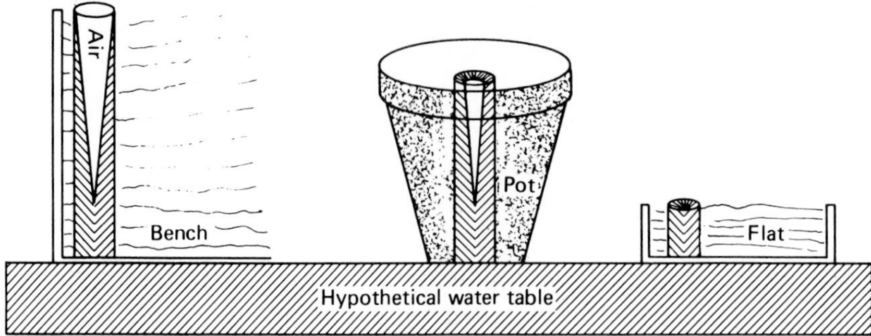

Figure 5–2

A greatly magnified soil pore is shown in various greenhouse containers filled with soil. All are shown to be perched on a water table, or reservoir of freestanding water, which is effectively the situation existing in the greenhouse shortly after watering. The pore depicts the moisture situation that exists within each container. Water is attracted to the walls of the pore, and at the base the entire pore fills. Higher in the pore, the downward gravitational pull on the water becomes greater, and the water farthest away from the pore wall is removed. The layer of water in the pore becomes thinner with increasing height. Spaces between soil particles in the container are interconnected and form pores running the depth of the soil. Pores in the bench are filled with water at the bottom and are mostly open at the top. Shortly after watering, roots can grow in the upper layers of soil in this bench but not in the lower layer, where there are no open pores for gas exchange. Pores in the pot do not rise as high above the water table; thus, in the upper layer of soil there is more water and less aeration than in the upper layer of the bench soil. The poorest situation for growth exists in the flat, where the pores are so short as to be completely filled with water.

holding capacity of the soil. When the diameter of particles making up a soil is increased, the total surface area of these particles in a given volume decreases. Since water is held on the surface of these particles, the total amount of water in the soil decreases as the particle diameter increases (texture becomes coarser).

There is another dimension of soil that can be altered to increase aeration without decreasing the water-holding capacity. *Structure* is the degree of combining of particles into aggregates. A soil with good structure is said to be *friable* (loose). The product of organic-matter degradation is humus, which, along with microbial secretions and hyphae, acts as a cement to bind particles together into aggregates. This is the greatest importance of organic matter in field soils. Through the development of structure, a dimension is given to soil that cannot be achieved through alterations in texture. High water retention of fine-textured soil can be combined with excellent drainage of coarse-textured soil. This is accomplished by extensive retention of water in the small-diameter pores within each aggregate and rapid percolation of water out of—and conversely good gas exchange into—the large pores between the aggregates (Figure 5–3).

It should now be apparent that field soil must be prepared for use in containers by altering it to a coarser texture and by increasing its structure prior to planting. There is no luxury of time to permit structure to form as a consequence

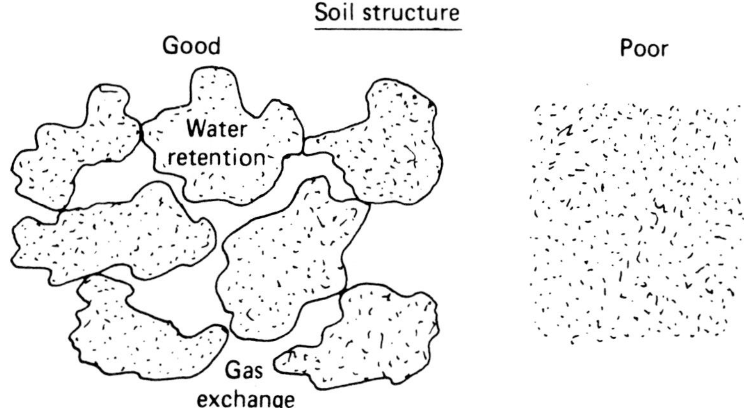

Figure 5–3

An important property of soil is structure. The soil on the left has good structure because the particles comprising it are cemented together into larger aggregate particles. Small-diameter pores still exist within the large aggregates, and because of the large surface area of these pores a large volume of water is held in each aggregate. Between the aggregates are very large pores that do not fill with water, thus providing a channel for gas exchange. The soil on the right has very little structure. Only small pores exist. While water retention is good, aeration is poor.

of decomposing organic matter. A coarser texture can be achieved by mixing coarse sand into the soil. Structure can be improved instantly by incorporating large aggregate particles such as sphagnum peat moss and bark into the soil. Numerous materials can be added to soil, but before a selection can be made, one more set of properties should be understood. These properties pertain to greenhouse root media specifically.

DESIRABLE PROPERTIES OF A ROOT MEDIUM

Stability of Organic Matter

Greenhouse plants are generally sold after a growth period of one to four months. Good structure must exist when seed is sown or plants are potted. It is important that decomposition of organic matter in the root medium to be used in pots be minimal. Decomposition of the organic aggregates will lead to finer texture and, consequently, poorer aeration. Also, since the volume of the root medium available within the pot for root growth is small, any significant reduction in the volume during growth of the plant is detrimental. Straw and sawdust, except redwood sawdust, decompose rapidly and therefore are not desirable in a root medium used for pot crops.

The situation is somewhat different for fresh flower and vegetable crops in benches where the volume of the root medium is sufficiently great to permit shrinkage. Soil is used indefinitely for fresh flower crops. With time, organic matter deteriorates and requires replacement, which is generally done on an annual basis. Direct addition of materials such as sphagnum peat moss or coarse composted bark are made in quantities sufficient to compensate for the lost volume.

Carbon:Nitrogen Ratio

The amount of nitrogen (N) relative to carbon (C) in a root-medium amendment is important. Decomposition of organic matter occurs largely through the action of living microorganisms. The largest component of organic matter (50 percent or more) is C, which is utilized by the microorganisms. N in the organic matter must be available to the microorganisms in the quantity of at least 1 pound for every 30 pounds of C; otherwise, decomposition slows down. Whenever this ratio of 30 C:1N is exceeded (when more than 30 pounds of C exist for each pound of N), N already present in the root medium or N added as fertilizer will be utilized by the microorganisms rather than by the crop plants. The crop will become deficient in N. If this situation occurred slowly and continuously, a grower could easily compensate for it by increasing the N fertilizer application. The decomposition of materials such as straw and sawdust occurs rapidly, however, and thereby creates a peak of N demand followed by a quickly diminishing demand for N as organic matter available to the microorganisms runs out. Only the most experienced growers can compensate for this process.

The C:N ratio for sawdust is about 1,000:1. It has been reported that, in addition to the small amount of N already present in the sawdust, 24 pounds of N must be added to facilitate the decomposition of 1 ton of sawdust by microorganisms (12 kg N/ton). Bark has a C:N ratio of about 300:1 and requires an addition of 7 pounds of N to facilitate the decomposition of 1 ton (3.5 kg N/ton). It is not only the C:N ratio that determines the suitability of a root-media component but also the rate of decomposition. While the bark has an undesirably wide C:N ratio of 300:1, its rate of decomposition is slow and steady, requiring as long as three years to decompose. The drain of 7 pounds of N per ton of bark carried out over three years presents a negligible N tax at each fertilization date. Bark is therefore a desirable root-media component in spite of its wide C:N ratio. Sawdust, however, will decompose in a few months and has a wider C:N ratio of 1,000:1. The N tax in this case is great, and this material should be avoided by the inexperienced grower. Redwood sawdust is an exception since the waxes and similar compounds in it slow down its rate of decomposition. It is frequently used in greenhouses in the western United States.

Bulk Density

The bulk density of a root medium relates to support of the plant. Nearly any solid medium will provide for anchorage of the plant roots, but it is also important that the medium be sufficiently heavy to prevent a potted plant from falling over due to the weight of the plant. A mixture of sphagnum peat moss and perlite is sufficiently heavy just after watering, but when its available water had been taken up by the plant, large plants in this medium easily topple over when handled in any way. However, a high bulk density can be uneconomical when extensive handling of the root medium or of the potted plants, particularly during shipping, is required. An acceptable range for bulk density of potting media is 40–75 pounds/ft^3 (640–1,200 g/dm^3) just after watering at *container capacity* (CC), which is the maximum amount of water that the root medium in a container can hold against gravity.

As mentioned earlier, soil must be amended with coarse particles such as sand to provide aeration. Wet soil and sand at container capacity can weigh 100 pounds or more per cubic foot (1,600 g/dm^3) (see Table 5–1). Therefore, perlite with a wet density of 32 pounds/ft^3 (500 g/dm^3) and polystyrene with a wet density of 7.5 pounds/ft^3 (120 g/m^3) are often used as substitutes for sand in spite of their higher cost. The problems of bulk density are not nearly as important for media used in greenhouse benches.

Moisture Retention and Aeration

A wet root medium is composed of (1) the solid particles of the medium, (2) the liquid water coating the surfaces of the particles, and (3) the air occupying the center of the pores. To ensure a suitably long interval between watering and to provide adequate aeration at all times, the balance of water and air in the root-medium pores must be controlled through selection of the particles comprising the medium. After watering, 10–20 percent of the volume of the root medium should be occupied by air in a 6½ inch (17 cm) azalea-type pot. The available water content should be as high as possible, providing air porosity and density of the total root medium are adequate. A survey of Table 5–1 indicates that the property of aeration can be provided by components such as vermiculite, pine bark, perlite, polystyrene, and rock wool. The coarse concrete-grade sand (rather than the fine sand) listed in the table would also be an excellent additive for aeration. Excellent components for providing a high available water content are sphagnum peat moss and rock wool.

When all three properties—sufficient density, adequate available water, and aeration—cannot be met by one component, a mixture is required. Four common mixes are listed at the bottom of Table 5–1. A heavy clay soil in the soil-based mix results in a high available water content (40.2 percent) at the expense of aeration (5.9 percent air at CC). A larger proportion of sand is needed in this mix. The

Table 5–1

Percent of Total Volume in a 6.5 Inch (17 cm) Azalea-Type Pot Occupied by Solids and by Water and Air at Moisture Tensions of Container Capacity and 15 Bar for Various Root-Media Components and Formulas[1]

Material/Mix	Solid (%)	Water (%) CC[2]	Water (%) 15 bar[3]	Air (%) CC	Air (%) 15 bar	Available Water[4] (%)	Bulk Density CC lb/ft³	Bulk Density CC g/dm³	Bulk Density 15 bar lb/ft³	Bulk Density 15 bar g/dm³
Soil (sandy clay)	53.3	39.8	6.4	6.9	40.3	33.4	106.0	1698	85.3	1364
Sand (concrete-grade)	59.3	35.4	4.4	5.3	36.3	31.0	107.1	1714	87.8	1404
Sphagnum peat moss[5]	15.4	76.5	25.8	8.1	58.8	50.7	53.7	859	22.0	352
Vermiculite (Progro No. 2)[5]	17.3	53.2	29.1	19.5	43.6	24.1	46.1	738	31.1	497
Pine bark (aged, <⅜ in., <10mm)[5]	20.7	58.9	30.3	20.4	49.0	28.6	50.6	809	32.7	523
Perlite (Krum, hort.-grade)[5]	36.9	38.3	20.2	24.8	42.9	18.1	32.1	514	20.8	333
Polystyrene beads[5]	64.6	10.5	1.0	24.9	34.4	9.5	7.5	120	1.6	25
Rock wool (Pargro®, medium, granular)	8.9	65.0	4.4	26.1	86.7	60.6	54.4	870	16.5	264
1 soil:1 peat moss:1 sand	45.4	48.7	8.5	5.9	46.1	40.2	99.7	1595	74.6	1193
1 peat moss:1 vermiculite	13.1	70.3	24.1	16.6	62.8	46.2	53.3	853	24.4	391
3 pine bark:1 sand:1 peat moss	29.5	53.4	21.5	17.0	49.0	31.9	58.9	942	38.9	623
1 rock wool:1 peat moss	8.3	70.9	11.3	20.8	80.4	59.6	51.8	829	14.6	233

[1]Data provided by William C. Fonteno, Department of Horticultural Science, North Carolina State University, Raleigh, NC 27695–7609. Components used in the formulas include: heavy clay soil, sphagnum peat moss, concrete-grade sand, and aged < ⅜ in. pine bark.

[2]Container capacity—the amount of water a root medium can hold against gravity just after watering.

[3]15 bar—the permanent wilting point where the plant has essentially taken up all available water.

[4]Available water is calculated as the amount of water released between container capacity and 15 bar tension, unless otherwise stated, and is expressed as a percent of the total pot volume.

[5]Computation of percent of water, percent of air, and percent of available water is based on a soil moisture tension of 300 cm rather than the stated 15 bar. Since water content for these five components differs very little between 300 cm and 15 bar tension, only small differences occur as a result.

sphagnum peat moss and vermiculite mix is excellent, with a bulk density of 53.3 pounds/ft^3, an air content of 16.6 percent at container capacity, and an available water content of 46.2 percent of the volume of the pot. The pine bark mix has good bulk density and aeration but is relatively lower in available water content. The water content is acceptable to most growers. But, to those faced with long periods of shipping or poor maintenance in the marketplace, a mix with a higher available water content would be better. The rock wool and sphagnum peat moss mix is excellent on all counts.

It should be recalled that water retention is related to the depth of the root medium. As seen in Table 5–2, the water content of root media just after watering increases with decreasing size and depth of the container. The capillary force holding water to the surfaces of the root medium is equal in each pot, but the gravitational force pulling water out of the pot becomes greater as the pot increases in depth. With increasing water content comes a decreasing air content. Fortunately, the range in acceptable air and water content values is wide. Well-formulated root media with high air- and water-retention values are suitable for a wide range of pot sizes. Two cases for which special mixes are frequently formulated are the shallow plug flats and the larger (deep) green plant containers.

Table 5–2

Percentages of Total Container Volume Occupied by Water and by Air at Container Capacity for Three Root Media in Five Different Size Containers*

	Standard Pots			*Flats*	
	8 in. (20 cm)	*6 in. (15 cm)*	*4 in. (10 cm)*	*48 cells*	*512 plugs*
			1 soil:1 sand:1 peat moss		
Water (%)	45.0	47.2	51.2	52.9	54.3
Air (%)	9.5	7.4	3.4	1.7	0.3
			1 peat moss:1 vermiculite		
Water (%)	64.4	67.9	75.2	79.5	84.8
Air (%)	22.5	19.0	11.7	7.4	2.1
			3 pine bark:1 sand:1 peat moss		
Water (%)	48.7	51.5	57.6	61.4	66.9
Air (%)	21.8	18.9	12.9	9.1	3.6

*Data provided by William C. Fonteno, Department of Horticultural Science, North Carolina State University, Raleigh, NC 27695–7609. Components used in the formulas include: heavy clay soil, sphagnum peat moss, concrete-grade sand, and aged $<$ ⅜ in. pine bark.

Cation Exchange Capacity

Root-media components such as clay, silt, organic matter, and vermiculite have fixed negative electrical charges. These charges will attract and hold positive electrical charges (cations). Most fertilizers have electrical charges, some negative and others positive. Positively charged fertilizer components are ammonium nitrogen, potassium, calcium, magnesium, iron, manganese, zinc, and copper. Field soil and greenhouse media electrically attract and hold these nutrients so that they are not washed away during a rain or heavy watering. At the same time, these electrically held nutrients are available to the plant. *Cation exchange capacity* (CEC) is a measure of the magnitude of fixed negative electrical charge and is generally expressed as milliequivalents per 100 cubic centimeters (me/100 cc) of dry root-media component. A level of 6–15 me/100 cc is considered desirable for greenhouse root media. Higher levels are not common but are very desirable. With lower levels, the medium will not act as a suitable reservoir for nutrients, and frequent fertilizing will become necessary. Clay, peat moss, vermiculite, and most composted organic matter have a high CEC; sand, perlite, polystyrene, and noncomposted materials such as rice hulls and peanut hulls have an insignificant CEC. In preparing a root medium, it is desirable to include a component with a high CEC.

pH

The importance of root-media pH level will be further developed in Chapter 8. It is sufficient to say here that the pH level controls the availability of nutrients to the plant. Greenhouse crops fall into two categories. Most grow best in a slightly acid pH range of 6.2–6.8 in soil-based media and 5.4–6.0 in soil-less media. A small number of crops are termed "acid-loving" since they grow best in a strongly acid pH range of 4.5–5.8. Sphagnum peat moss, pine bark, and many composts are acid. Peat moss can have a pH level below 4.0. Sand and perlite are neutral (pH 7.0). Vermiculite and some hardwood barks are alkaline (pH above 7.0). Field soil can range from acid (pH 3.5) to alkaline (pH 8.5). Rock wool can range from neutral to mildly alkaline. It is important to check the pH level of the medium one has formulated and to adjust it to the proper level prior to planting. (Instructions are given in Chapter 8.) Commercial root media are usually adjusted to the proper pH level by the manufacturer.

COMPONENTS OF ROOT MEDIA

Numerous materials exist from which the components of a root medium can be selected. Listed in Table 5–3 are the more common components, the functions that each performs, and the cost of each. Alternative components exist for each

Table 5–3

Root-Media Components, Their Functions, and Cost Including Delivery

Component	*Water Retention*	*Nutrient Retention*	*Aeration*	*Light Weight*	*$/ft^3*	*$/m^3*
Field soil	X	X			0.40	14.12
Sphagnum peat moss	X	X			0.95	33.52
Bark (0–3⁄8 in.)	X	X			0.56	19.76
Sawdust (rotted)	X	X			0.56	19.76
Manure	X	X			0.56	19.76
Vermiculite	X	X		X	1.45	51.18
Calcined clay	X	X	X			
Bark (3⁄8–3⁄4 in.)	X	X	X		0.56	19.76
Sand (concrete-grade)			X		0.56	19.76
Perlite			X	X	1.50	52.94
Polystyrene			X	X	—	—

of the four needed functions of a root medium. Selection of components is based on the required function, cost, and availability.

Field Soil

Prior to the practice of soil pasteurization, which took hold in the early 1950s, it was customary to replace greenhouse media annually, usually during the summer. Much attention was paid to the type of field soil used. Soil with a high degree of structure and a loam texture proved to be the most desirable.

Texture was ensured by locating the greenhouse range in a region of proper soil type. Structure was developed in the field soil by growing a mixed crop of grasses and clover in the soil for one to three years. These crops continually renew their root systems, leaving behind vast quantities of roots that decompose into humus and lead to good structure development. Crops commonly used were Kentucky bluegrass, timothy, red-top, red clover, alsike clover, and ladino clover. The crop was mowed twice per year and allowed to lie on the ground. During the fall prior to the summer when the soil was to be moved into the greenhouse, the crop was disked and the soil was placed in piles, where decomposition of the crop took place.

Since fresh flower and vegetable growers no longer replace their root media, it is important only at the time of establishing the greenhouse range that a proper field soil be developed. Pot plant growers, however, must have a continuous supply of proper field soil if they utilize soil-based media. Many established greenhouse areas have been inundated by residential and commercial development, and newer ranges have located in regions of poor soil to take advantage of the availability of other factors such as transportation, labor supply, and utilities. Such businesses, lacking suitable field soil, have purchased soil with only sporadic success because of the cost or variation from one lot to another. These growers have found it expedient to use soil-less media.

Peat Moss and Peats

There are different types of peat. *Peat moss* is light tan to brown in color, is the least decomposed, and is formed from sphagnum or hypnum moss (mostly the former). It has a nitrogen content of 0.6–1.4 percent and decomposes slowly; thus, nitrogen tie-up is not a problem. It has the highest water-holding capacity of all the peats, holding up to 60 percent of its volume in water. Sphagnum peat moss is the most acid of the peats with a pH level of 3.0–4.0 and requires 14–35 pounds of finely ground limestone per cubic yard (8–20 kg/m^3) to bring the pH up to the level that is best for most crops. In areas with hard water containing calcium, the lower rate may be suitable.

The fine structure of the moss can still be seen in peat moss. Large quantities of water are held on the extensive surface area of the moss, while good gas exchange occurs in the large pores between the aggregates (chunks) of peat moss. For this latter reason, peat moss should not be finely ground down to the level of fibers prior to use. Hypnum peat moss has a pH level in the range of 5.2–5.5. When it is used with vermiculite, no limestone is needed since vermiculite is mildly alkaline. One successful greenhouse pot crop mixture calls for 50 parts hypnum peat moss to 40 parts perlite to 10 parts vermiculite.

Reed–sedge peat is brown to reddish brown in color and is formed from swamp plants, including reeds, sedges, marsh grasses, and cattails. It occurs in varying degrees of decomposition but is generally more highly decomposed than peat moss. As a result, more fine particles are present, giving a poorer structure than that of peat moss. Also, the water-holding capacity of reed–sedge peat is lower than that of peat moss. Depending on the source, the pH level of reed–sedge peat can vary from 4.0 to 7.5. Although sphagnum peat moss is preferred for the general range of greenhouse applications, reed–sedge peat can be used in root media for pot and bench crops if the pH is properly adjusted.

Peat humus is dark brown to black in color and is the most highly decomposed of the peats. It is usually derived from hypnum peat moss or reed–sedge peat. Original plant remains are not distinguishable, and water-holding capacity is less than that of other peats. The pH level can range from 5.0 to 7.5. Peat humus has a moderately high nitrogen content, which makes it undesirable in seed-flat media or media used for salt-sensitive plants. Ammonium nitrogen released from the peat humus can build up to levels that are toxic to the more sensitive plants, such as young seedlings, African violet, snapdragon, and azalea. Ammonium nitrogen is released during microbial decomposition of peat humus because more than 1 pound of nitrogen is available per 30 pounds of carbon. Peat humus is rarely used in the greenhouse.

Bark

Redwood bark and fir bark have been used on the west coast of America for many years as a component of nursery and greenhouse root media. Coarse fir bark provides an excellent medium for orchids. Pine bark (Figure 5–4) is extensively used throughout America. Hardwood barks are used in many of the interior states. All are highly satisfactory.

Bark is inexpensive compared to some materials it replaces in root media (mainly sphagnum peat moss and soil). Because of the need to compost bark prior to use in root media, several companies are now processing bark for this purpose. This processing, of course, adds to the price; however, the price advantage over materials replaced by bark is still great.

When bark is removed from logs, varying quantities of cambium and young wood are included. These materials decompose faster than bark and accentuate

Figure 5–4

Barks of various origins are widely accepted throughout America today as a substitute for peat moss. Pine bark is pictured here. Typical processing calls for composting in a pile for three months or longer and then screening into different sizes for various markets. Particles passing through a ⅜ inch mesh screen are used in pot plant media (*left*); those between ⅜ inch and ¾ inch are used for fresh flower media amendment (*right*); and larger particles are used for landscape mulches (*center*).

the nitrogen tie-up problem. The wood content tends to be highest in the spring when growth is more active. A period of composting rids bark of these components and brings it to a stage where the rate of decomposition is slow and steady; nitrogen tie-up is then not a problem.

Accounts have been given of fresh hardwood and softwood barks causing growth suppression and injury to plants. Unknown compounds are apparently destroyed during composting for a period of 30 days. One explanation is that the toxic material is acetic acid that is given off in the initial stages of composting and then quickly destroyed in subsequent stages of composting (Hoitink, H., personal communications). Composting has an additional beneficial effect for bark and for sawdust as well. Fresh bark and sawdust do not hold fertilizer nutrients very well because of a low CEC of about 8 me/100 g (about 1.6 me/100 cc). After composting takes place, the CEC rises to a level of 60 me/100 g (about 12 me/100 cc) or higher, which imparts a strong nutrient-retention capacity to the bark and sawdust.

Composting is accomplished in two ways. Nitrogen is mixed in at the rate of 3 pounds of actual nitrogen per cubic yard (1.8 kg N/m^3), and the bark is set in piles in the field. Ammonium nitrate is a good source of nitrogen and is used at the rate of 9 pounds per cubic yard (5.3 kg/m^3) since it contains 33 percent nitrogen. A period of four to six weeks is sufficient to complete the rapid phase of decomposition. In the second system, no nitrogen is used and a period of three months to a year is required. While the first system guarantees a more satisfactory end-product, composting in either case results in destruction of inhibitory compounds, degradation of wood, and fragmentation of larger particles into smaller ones.

Compost piles must not be over 12 feet (3.7 m) deep because during the process of composting heat is given off that, if permitted to become too intense, can set the pile on fire. The surface layer should be turned into the pile after one to two weeks of composting to ensure that all the bark has been processed. The heat given off by fermentation is sufficient to pasteurize the bark. Harmful disease organisms, insects, nematodes, and weed seeds are thus eliminated. It is important that subsequent handling be carried out in a way to maintain this cleanliness. The bark should not be piled where crops have been grown or where the runoff from crop lands has accumulated. Equipment used for moving bark should be sterilized first if it has been used on crops. If the bark is bagged, clean handling is almost ensured. Larger growers find economy in purchasing bark in bulk (unpackaged). Prior to sale, bark is screened for various purposes. Particles ⅛ inch (3 mm) and under are used as soil conditioners in applications such as golf course greens. Particles ⅜ inch (10 mm) and under are preferred for greenhouse pot plant media; those from ⅜ inch to ¾ inch (10–19 mm), for organic-matter amendment of greenhouse fresh flower media. Larger pieces are used for landscape mulching.

Since the largest part of the cost of bark often lies in the shipping expense—costing $2 or more per mile for a 60 cubic yard (46 m^3) truckload—it is beneficial to obtain bark from local sources. Consequently, numerous types of bark are used throughout America. In general, processed bark will cost from one-fourth to two-thirds the price of imported sphagnum peat moss.

Sawdust

Sawdust in many respects is similar to bark. It should be partially composted because in the fresh state its rate of decomposition and nitrogen tie-up is excessive and it may contain toxic substances such as resins, tannins, or turpentine. Even after composting, sawdust decomposes at a faster rate than bark, and, because of its wider C:N ratio (1,000:1), a greater amount of nitrogen is tied up in the root medium. Whereas the problem is insignificant with bark, it must be taken into account in fertilizing a medium containing composted sawdust.

Abandoned piles of sawdust are often available for the cost of transportation in forested areas. If a pile has existed for a year or more, the sawdust below the surface layer should be well composted. Care should be taken to avoid unleached areas deep in the pile, which are strongly acid and injurious to plants. These areas did not receive sufficient oxygen during fermentation, and, as a result, volatile organic acids were formed and trapped here. These problem areas can be identified by the exceptionally dark color of the sawdust and its pungent, acrid odor. This sawdust can be reclaimed by exposing it to the air and to leaching rains for a season, but it still will be more acid than the properly composted sawdust.

Sawdust composted with additional nitrogen for one month to the stage appropriate for use in root media is itself acid and requires limestone to neutralize it. In this stage, it is granular and is medium dark brown in color. It continues to decompose during use in the pot or greenhouse bench. Various types of pine and some types of hardwood sawdust require further additions of limestone as time passes. Sawdust, like other plant materials, ends up close to neutral in pH when thoroughly composted; however, this is well beyond the stage at which it is initially used in greenhouse root media.

Manure

Annual addition of manure, generally rotted cow manure, was a standard practice in fresh flower beds and quite frequently was used in bedding and potted plant media until the middle of this century. When soil pasteurization became popular, ammonium toxicity problems arose as a result and discouraged the further use of manure. (Ways around this problem will be discussed in Chapter 6 on root-media pasteurization.) A few growers use manure today and realize good benefits from it.

Manure has a high CEC and thus serves as a good reservoir for nutrients. In addition, it is a good source of nutrients, and thus micronutrient deficiencies rarely occur when manure is used. As a matter of fact, micronutrient deficiencies were rare in the days when manure was used routinely. Today, such deficiencies present a serious problem. Manure also contains low levels of nitrogen, phosphorus, and potassium (see Table 5–4). Because large quantities of manure are used in root media, a significant part of the total requirement of these three nutrients is met. Manure has a high water-holding capacity, a basic requirement of greenhouse media. Peat moss perhaps comes the closest to manure in the functions that it serves in root media and, indeed, has been the component substituted for manure since the 1950s.

Rotted cow manure is the best type to use in the greenhouse. Other types are stronger and must be used cautiously and in smaller quantities. Often, as in the case of poultry manure, the ammonia content is too high and causes root and foliage injury. Cow manure is incorporated into a root medium at the volume rate of 10–15 percent. The medium is then pasteurized with steam or chemicals in order to get rid of harmful disease organisms, insects, nematodes, and weed seed. (Manure contains a sizable quantity of weed seed, which would otherwise become troublesome.) Following pasteurization, it is very important that each time water is required, a sufficient quantity be applied to ensure leaching so that a buildup of ammonium nitrogen originating from the manure does not occur. Even if a crop is not planted in the medium, it must be leached periodically. A buildup of ammonium nitrogen contributes to the total soluble-salt content of the root medium and can be detected readily by a soluble-salt test. This test can easily be performed by growers. (It will be discussed in Chapter 8.)

Manure has traditionally been used in a moist state, which renders it a difficult material to introduce into a mechanized system of root-media preparation. Its after-pasteurization problems preclude its use in media to be stockpiled for later use. Its messy physical condition and heavy weight prevent its being shipped more than a few miles from its origin. Until a process is devised for drying, grinding, and getting around the problem of ammonium nitrogen buildup, the use of manure will be limited to a few growers who have a local supply and the technical knowledge to handle it.

Table 5–4

Primary Nutrient Content of Some Types of Fresh Animal Manure

	Nutrient Content (% of fresh wt)		
Type of Manure	*Nitrogen (N)*	*Phosphorus (P_2O_5)*	*Potassium (K_2O)*
Cattle (cow)	0.5	0.3	0.5
Chicken	1.0	0.5	0.8
Horse	0.6	0.3	0.6
Sheep	0.9	0.5	0.8
Swine	0.6	0.5	1.0

Crop By-Products

Straw is occasionally used as a root-media amendment but must be chopped into pieces 3 inches (8 cm) or less in length to permit uniform incorporation into the soil. The labor input is expensive. Since straw decomposes rapidly, it must be added 2–3 times per year, which is also an expensive proposition. A variety of other organic amendments is occasionally used, including peanut hulls, bagasse (sugar cane fiber), and rice hulls. All of these can be used successfully but require knowledge and careful handling. Materials such as straw, peanut hulls, bagasse, and rice hulls have a wide C:N ratio that causes nitrogen tie-up. If this is gauged and extra nitrogen is added, no problem arises.

Flower crop stubble—the foliage, stems, and roots left in the benches after the harvesting of fresh flower crops—has logically been looked upon as a source of organic matter. Growers have chopped the stubble into small pieces and rototilled it into the root medium. Because this organic material is the very crop being grown, it is an excellent host for carrying diseases over from one crop to another. It should be pasteurized with the root medium. Since many growers do not pasteurize after each crop, crop remains are generally removed from the greenhouse. Crop remains thoroughly composted outside the greenhouse can be used successfully as a root-media amendment.

Composted Garbage

Many municipalities combine the collection and disposal of kitchen wastes and solid household trash. When a compost is produced from this waste, most metals, rags, and large items are first reclaimed, and then the remaining refuse is ground and set out in heaps to compost. The action of microorganisms breaking down the organic matter in these heaps generates heat, which destroys harmful organisms and results in a dark brown, somewhat granular product. Glass is ground fine enough to prevent its becoming a safety hazard. The pH level is about 8.5, and the salt content is moderately high but subject to removal by leaching. Processed garbage has worked well as a mulch in landscaping but has not been as satisfactory as a root-media component. The problem stems from the variation in refuse ingredients. When a high proportion of kitchen waste is present, a product rich in humus is produced that makes a good peat moss substitute in the traditional soil-based media. When high proportions of wood, paper, plastic, or other such materials are present, a product is produced that can tie up nitrogen in root media or simply act as an inert component that would be a better sand replacement. This variability within single batches of product has led to variable results within trials, ranging from excellent to poor. More work is needed before this product can be fully accepted as a component of greenhouse root media.

Vermiculite

Vermiculite ore is mined principally in the United States (primarily in Montana and South Carolina) and in Africa as a mica-like, silicate mineral. The ore itself has a dry bulk density of 55–65 pounds/ft^3 (880–1,040 g/dm^3), but when expanded to the state used in root media, the density drops to 7–10 pounds/ft^3 (110–160 g/dm^3) (Figure 5–5). This lightweight property makes it very desirable in pot plant media. Each particle of vermiculite ore contains numerous thin plates lying parallel to one another. Between the plates is moisture that expands when heated to high temperatures, causing the plates to move apart into an open accordion-like structure. The expanded volume can be as much as 16 times the volume of the original ore. The water-holding capacity of expanded vermiculite is high because of the extensive surface area within each particle. Aeration and drainage properties are also good because of the large pores between particles. The common size is 6–10 mesh (USS).

Numerous negative electrical charges on the surface of each vermiculite platelet give rise to a CEC of 19–22.5 me/100 g (1.9–2.7 me/100 cc). The predominant fertilizer nutrients in vermiculite are potassium, magnesium, and calcium. The potassium content of U.S. vermiculite will provide part, but certainly

Figure 5–5

Expanded vermiculite as it is used in greenhouse root media. The exceptional water- and nutrient-holding capacities of vermiculite make it an excellent component of soil-less media. (*Photo courtesy Grace-Sierra Horticultural Products Co.*, P.O. Box 4003, *Milpitas*, CA 95035-2003)

not all, of the total needs of a crop. The magnesium content of African vermiculite is high and has been known to provide the total needs of a greenhouse crop. Vermiculite varies in pH level. U.S. vermiculite is slightly alkaline, while African vermiculite tends to be very alkaline with pH levels approaching 9 in some cases. The alkaline African vermiculite constitutes no problem when combined with an acidic media component such as peat moss or pine bark. If this vermiculite is used alone, in a propagation bed or in a hydroponic operation, its pH level should be adjusted down. U.S. vermiculite can be used without alteration.

Vermiculite is a very desirable component of soil-less root media because of its high nutrient and water retention, good aeration, and low bulk density. It is commonly included in soil-less media. Expanded vermiculite can be compressed easily between the fingers. Under the weight of soil-based media, expanded vermiculite tends to compress, which greatly reduces aeration. Vermiculite is generally not used with soil.

Calcined Clay

Aggregates of clay particles are heated to high temperatures (calcined) to form hardened particles that resist breakdown in root media. These aggregates are large (mostly 8–45 mesh) and irregularly shaped. As a result, they fit together loosely in a root medium, creating large pores for drainage and aeration. Within each calcined clay aggregate are numerous clay particles forming a myriad of small water-holding pores. One pound of calcined clay can contain over 13 acres of surface area within its structure. Calcined clay brings the property of structure to root media in the form of a hardened, buff-colored aggregate weighing about 30–40 pounds/ft^3 (480–640 g/dm^3). The pH levels of different calcined clay products range from acid to alkaline (4.5–9.0), but they have only a small influence on the pH level of root media. Calcined clays have a sizable CEC, 6–21 me/100 g (3.4–11.8 me/100 cc), which gives them the property of good nutrient retention. The variation in properties of calcined clays stems back to the type of clay used. Examples are *montmorillonite* clay from the Mississippi Valley and *attapulgite* clay from Florida and Georgia. Lusoil®, made from attapulgite clay, has a pH of 7.5–9.0 and a CEC of 21 me/100 g (11.8 me/100 cc). Terragreen® and Turface® are derived from montmorillonite clay.

Calcined clays should be used in a quantity equal to 10–15 percent of the volume of fresh flower media. For pot plant media, they should constitute 25–33 percent of the total volume, the remainder being composed of either soil, peat moss, or a combination of the two.

Sand

Sand is used in root media for adding the coarser texture needed to induce proper drainage and aeration. For this reason, concrete-grade sand (a sharp, coarse sand) is used. Concrete-grade sand has the specifications listed in Table 5–5. Washed sand should be purchased since it is nearly free of clay, silt, and organic matter. In regions where there are snowfalls, caution should be exercised during the winter to avoid purchasing sand containing road salt (sodium chloride or calcium chloride). Road salt is added to batches of sand to be sold to highway departments because it melts road ice. The level used in sand is injurious to greenhouse crops.

Perlite

Perlite is a good substitute for sand for providing aeration in root media. Its main advantage over sand is its light weight of about 6 pounds/ft^3 (95 g/dm^3), as compared to 100–120 pounds/ft^3 (1,600–1,920 g/dm^3) for sand. Perlite is a siliceous volcanic rock that, when crushed and heated to 1,800°F (982°C), expands to form white particles with numerous closed, air-filled cells. Water will adhere to the surface of perlite, but it is not absorbed into the perlite aggregates. Perlite is sterile, chemically inert, has a negligible CEC (0.15 me/100 cc), and is nearly neutral with a pH value of 7.5. It does not appreciably affect the pH level of root media. Perlite costs considerably more than sand. As a result, it is used when low root-media density constitutes an economic advantage.

Polystyrene Foam

This material is known more commonly as Styrofoam®, Styropor®, and Styromull®. Like perlite, it constitutes a good substitute for sand, bringing improved aeration and light weight to root media. It is a white synthetic product

Table 5–5

ASTM (American Society for Testing and Materials) Specifications for Concrete-Grade Sand

Percent of Total Passing the Screen	*Screen Size*	*Particle Size (mm)*
100	⅜ in.	9.5
95–100	No. 4*	6.4
80–100	No. 8	3.2
50–85	No. 16	1.6
25–60	No. 30	0.85
10–30	No. 50	0.51
2–10	No. 100	0.25

*These figures refer to the number of holes per inch. A No. 4 screen has holes slightly smaller than ¼ inch due to the width of the wire between each hole.

containing numerous closed cells that are filled with air. It is extremely light, weighing less than 1.5 pounds/ft^3 (24 g/dm^3). Like sand, it does not absorb water and has no appreciable CEC. It is neutral and thus does not affect root-media pH levels.

Polystyrene can be obtained in beads or in flakes. Beads from ⅛ inch to $^3/_{16}$ inch (3–10 mm) diameter and flakes from ⅛ inch to ½ inch (3–13 mm) diameter are satisfactory for pot plant media. Larger particles may be used in bench media and for epiphytic plants such as orchids (Figure 5–6). Depending upon the source, the price of polystyrene can vary considerably. The edges cut from large blocks prior to cutting into sheets or the leftover pieces from shapes stamped from sheets can be ground to form an excellent media component. Polystyrene has been banned in some coastal regions due to its movement in wind and surface water to beaches where it becomes an aesthetic problem. In other localities, it has been banned from landfills. The future of polystyrene as a root-media component is questionable at this time.

Rock Wool

A description of rock wool propagation cubes and slabs for growing fresh flowers and vegetables as well as the method of manufacture are presented in Chapter 9. Rock wool is also available in granular form for use as a component in formulating

Figure 5–6

Equal parts of polystyrene foam (Styromull®) and sphagnum moss make a good root medium for the orchid plant shown here. Polystyrene is an excellent lightweight substitute for sand in root media. (*Photo courtesy of* BASF-*Wyandotte Corporation, Wyandotte*, MI 48192)

root media. As seen in Table 5–1, the granular form has very high available water and aeration properties. Although slightly alkaline, it is not buffered. Mixing with an acid component such as pine bark or peat moss will immediately lower the pH level. Rock wool has a negligible CEC. It neither contributes nor holds nutrients to any extent. This property should be provided by other components such as sphagnum peat moss in the mix. Granular rock wool may be purchased by itself or in commercially formulated mixes. A blend of equal volume parts of rock wool and sphagnum peat moss makes an excellent mix.

Other Coarse-Textured Components

In the future, numerous substitutes for sand will appear—some derived from minerals and some perhaps by-products of industry. Their usefulness will be determined by their bulk density, size, shape, and cost. A few interesting and effective products have appeared on the market in recent years. One product consists of short lengths of plastic wire-coating stripped from the ends of electrical wire during the process of making electrical components. It serves as a lightweight sand substitute. A second product, Polytrol, consists of pellets and flakes from ⅛ inch to ¼ inch (3–6 mm) in size made from plastics. Reject plastic materials that cannot be used in prime products are combined with recycled municipal solid-waste plastics to make this product. Many other substitutes can be found for sand if one bears in mind the function of sand.

SOIL-BASED MEDIA

The largest division in root-media types falls between those containing soil and the soil-less types. One type is not necessarily superior to the other. Plants of equal quality can be grown in each if cultural adjustments are made. Selection of a root-media type is made on the basis of economics and the physical situation in which it must serve. During the 1960s, a discussion of soil-less media would have been included in this book more as a curiosity or a prediction of things to come. Today, when one looks around the pot plant industry, it seems conceivable that a discussion of soil-based media for container crops will be obsolete in a few years. This should not be the case, however, when a grower has an abundant source of good, uniform soil and has developed an efficient mixing procedure.

Formulation

A minor percentage of the pot plants in America are grown in soil-based media. By contrast, virtually all of the fresh flower crops are grown in such media. Traditionally, a soil-based medium has been composed of equal parts by volume of loam field soil, concrete-grade sand, and sphagnum peat moss amended with phosphorus and adjusted to the proper pH level. Sandy field soil is compensated by an increase in the proportion of peat moss and field soil and a decrease in sand, while clay soil calls for more sand.

Sand is used in soil-based media to develop large-diameter pores for good aeration. Two materials, perlite and polystyrene, have proven to be good substitutes. Like sand, both materials resist compaction and absorption of water. Unlike sand, they are very light in weight. A moist mixture of equal parts of soil, sand, and peat moss weighs about 100 pounds/ft^3 (1,600 g/dm^3), which is suitable for use in greenhouse benches but not for pot plants that must be handled frequently or moved great distances. Perlite can cost as much as 3 times the price of sand. Polystyrene, while more expensive than sand, is more reasonably priced than perlite.

Field soil provides reasonable nutrient- (CEC) and water-holding capacities. When one-third of the soil is replaced by sand, these two properties are significantly reduced. To restore them, sphagnum peat moss, an amendment with a high CEC and water-holding capacity, has traditionally been added into the medium at the expense of an additional one-third of the field soil. Coarse peat moss should be obtained when possible. Some peat moss is hydraulically mined, and the particles are so small that much of the effect of structure is lost. The large pieces of sphagnum peat moss fit together loosely to form wide pores for aeration. The intimately fine leaf structure of the sphagnum moss comprising the peat moss forms copious narrow pores for holding water. Sphagnum peat moss has one of the greatest available water capacities of any root-media amendment—about 60 percent by volume. Thus, sphagnum peat moss provides good water-holding capacity and a fair amount of aeration if it is coarse. Sand provides the balance of aeration.

Sphagnum peat moss is compressed into bales for shipment and sales purposes. If large pieces appear when a bale is opened, they should be broken with a hoe or, if necessary, passed through a soil-shredding machine. If passed through the machine more than once, however, the pieces are nearly broken down to individual moss filaments, and much of the desirable aeration property is lost.

Soil-based media generally require three nutrient amendments during formulation. First, the pH level should be adjusted into the range of 6.2–6.8 with agricultural dolomite limestone. When neutral to alkaline soils are used, no upward adjustment is required. Acid soils may require as much as 10 pounds of limestone per cubic yard (6 kg/m^3). The second amendment should consist of 3.0 pounds of 0–20–0 superphosphate (1.8 kg/m^3) or 1.5 pounds of 0–45–0 superphosphate (0.9 kg/m^3) per cubic yard to provide phosphorus for up to one year. The third amendment is a complete micronutrient mixture for which a number of commercial preparations are available. (For further details on fertilizer amendments, see Chapter 8.)

Maintenance

The structure of root media is sufficiently stable to persist until the time when the final purchaser of potted plants would ordinarily report them. At that time, one to two years, some of the old root medium can be removed and a new medium prepared to fill the larger pot, thus restoring the original level of structure. In any event, loss of structure is not a problem for the grower of potted plants. It is a problem for fresh flower growers since they maintain soil permanently in their ground beds and benches.

The action of decomposition results in loss of organic matter and the periodic need to add more. This is customarily done once each year at the time when the root medium is pasteurized. The standard additive has been coarse sphagnum peat moss rototilled into the bench in a quantity equal to about 10 percent of the volume of the root medium in the bench.

Coarse bark from 3/8 inch to 3/4 inch (10–19 mm) has proven to be a good alternative to peat moss in bench media. The decomposition rate of bark is slow, requiring up to three years for complete breakdown. In the first year, a quantity equal to 10 percent of the bench volume should be incorporated into satisfactor-

Figure 5–7

A fresh flower medium containing too much clay. Note the cracks that occur upon drying. This medium has inadequate gas exchange, as witnessed by symptoms of oxygen deficiency in the chrysanthemum plants. Growth is stunted, leaves are light green in color with veins lighter than the rest of the leaf blade, and the plants wilt on bright days.

ily drained media and 15 percent into poorly drained media. As a rule of thumb, each year thereafter a quantity equal to 5 percent of the bench volume is added. In any event, organic matter should be added in sufficient quantity to make up the volume loss in the bench.

Sometimes, the organic-matter level is adequate but the clay content is too high. Poor drainage and excessive cracking of the root medium upon drying (Figure 5–7) are symptoms of this condition. This is particularly prevalent when clay soil is used. The problem is remedied by a single addition of concrete-grade sand to the medium. Perlite is generally not used since weight is not a problem in benches. Calcined clay is sometimes used because, in addition to providing macropores for drainage and aeration, it contains numerous micropores within each particle to improve water-holding capacity and it has a high CEC that improves nutrient retention. A quantity equal to 10–15 percent of the bench volume is incorporated into the medium. It is expensive but need be applied only once since it is resistant to breakdown.

SOIL-LESS MEDIA

Growers who do not have field soil of their own have found it difficult to purchase soil of consistent texture from load to load. This demands considerable attention on the part of managers to compensate for soil changes in root-media formulations. When such changes are overlooked, poor crops and loss of profits ensue. Soil-less media are attractive to these growers.

Other growers are involved in shipment of potted plants long distances by truck and must have a finished plant as light as possible. Soil-less media can be formulated in lighter densities than soil-based media.

Still other growers look on soil-less media as a form of automation since they can be purchased ready for use, thus eliminating the need for any labor input or mixing facilities. Such growers may be in a labor market of high wages or in a situation of limited labor availability.

Components of Soil-Less Media

So many materials are available for soil-less media that growers make the mistake of mixing too many or the wrong types together. The four functions of root media—plant support, aeration, nutrient retention, and moisture retention—should be considered in developing a formulation. Organic matter or clay is needed to provide CEC for nutrient retention. Unless the organic matter or clay is in coarse aggregates to facilitate aeration, coarse-textured particles such as sand, perlite, or polystyrene will be required. If the organic matter or clay selected has a high water-holding capacity, as does peat moss, no further components are necessary. However, if organic matter of insufficient water-holding capacity is used, such as coarse bark, it will be necessary to include a second organic material or clay component (such as peat moss or calcined clay) to increase the water-holding capacity. The desired density of the medium can be attained by avoiding heavy coarse particles or clay components.

Good root media need not contain more than one to three components. The selection of components will generally depend upon their availability and cost. A grower who markets peat moss and thus can obtain it at wholesale cost, or who is located close to the point where it is dug so that transportation costs are minimal, should use peat moss for its superior water-holding capacity and CEC. If media weight is not a problem, the grower should mix it with the cheapest coarse-textured component, which is sand. If light weight is required, the considerably more expensive components perlite or vermiculite may have to be used. If light weight is required and the grower is fortunate enough to be located near a source of polystyrene flakes or beads, the lighter density can be achieved with less cost than perlite. A grower located in a timber area will probably find bark to be economical. Sand is added to bark because it nests between the bark particles, thus adding more surface area, and as a consequence, more water retention to a given volume of medium. Remember that sand is added to soil for the opposite purpose, that of pushing soil particles apart to open up large pores for aeration. Often, sphagnum peat moss is also added to bark to further increase water-holding capacity as well as nutrient retention.

Formulations

Peat-Moss-Based Formulations One of the earliest commercially prepared soil-less media developed was Einheitserde (standardized soil), a mixture of half peat moss and half well-aggregated subsoil clay amended with nitrogen, phosphorus, and potassium and limed to a pH level between 5 and 6. It was introduced by Dr. A. Fruhstorfer in Hamburg, Germany, in 1948. Einheitserde is marketed by several companies in Europe and is used for a wide range of crops and applications from seed germination to plant finishing.

The U.C. (University of California) mixes were some of the earliest soil-less media adopted in America during the 1950s. These are a series of five media ranging from 100 percent sphagnum or hypnum peat moss to 100 percent fine sand with intermediate combinations of the two. These media are formulated by individual growers. The more popular greenhouse pot plant medium of this series is the half peat moss, half fine sand mixture. The designation of fine sand indicates sand between 0.5 and 0.05 mm in diameter, which is equivalent to 1/50 to 1/100 of an inch, or to sand that passes a 30 mesh screen but is retained on a 270 mesh screen.

The Peat-Lite mixes were introduced by Drs. J. W. Boodley and R. Sheldrake at Cornell University in the early 1960s. Mix A is composed of half sphagnum peat moss and half horticultural-grade vermiculite. Mix B contains horticultural perlite in the place of vermiculite. While some growers formulate Peat-Lite mixes, there are a number of commercial preparations of soil-less media on the market similar to Peat-Lite Mix A. Some of these are Ball Germinating Mix®, Fafard Peat-Lite Mix®, Heco Plug Mix®, Jiffy Mix®, Mr. Mulch Mark III®–seed starter, Ogilvie Professional Mixes 2® and 5®, Premier Germinating Mix®, ProMix A®, PV®, and Redi-earth Peat Lite Mix®.

It is significant that the media thus far discussed have been composed of only two components. This is possible because one is peat moss, which has the highest water-holding capacity of any of the components discussed, a significant CEC, and a modest degree of aeration if not too finely shredded. In cases where sand, perlite, or clay aggregates are used, increased aeration is provided. Clay and vermiculite additions increase the CEC along with aeration. Peat moss comes very close to an ideal medium by itself if it contains coarse aggregates. European growers have learned to grow top-quality crops in it alone. If this system is used, it is important to guard against overwatering (watering too frequently). Because peat moss effectively retains nutrients, it is important that overdoses of fertilizer not be applied and that the medium is thoroughly watered each time water is needed to ensure that excess nutrient salts are leached from the medium.

Formulators of soil-less media must remain competitive. A significant part of the expense of these media to the grower is the shipping cost. For this reason, media are in a rather dry state when shipped. Dry peat moss, particularly when it is finely ground, can be exceedingly difficult to wet because it repels water. Therefore, wetting agents are incorporated into peat-moss-based soil-less media. See Table 5–6 for a partial list of wetting agents suitable for this purpose.

The wetting agent, however, does not completely correct the problem. The peat-moss–vermiculite media pose no problem when used for seed germination because newly seeded flats are usually placed under a mist irrigation system that gently and thoroughly moistens these media without permitting drying of the surface during the process. When some of these media are used for pot plant or fresh flower culture in beds, they require a prohibitively long initial wetting period. Upon flooding the surface of the medium, a period of time must be allotted for the water to penetrate. Then the surface is flooded again, and the procedure is repeated several times until water finally penetrates to the bottom.

This tedious procedure can be partially avoided by adding coarse-textured particles such as sand or perlite to the media. These components provide large pores that allow quicker penetration of water throughout the media. Lateral as well as vertical movement of water occurs in the initial soaking of smaller peat moss pores, resulting in a saving of time. Some commercially available media that contain sand and/or perlite in addition to peat moss and vermiculite are Ball Growing Mix II®, Fafard Mix No. 2®, Grower's Choice®, Metro Mixes 200® and 220®, Mr. Mulch Mark III®–regular, Ogilvie Professional Mix I®, ProMix C®, Sunshine Mix #1® and Mix #2®, VJ #2 Mix® and #3 Mix®, and VSP®.

Table 5–6

Some Wetting Agents, Sources, and Rates That Can Be Used for the Initial Wetting of Dry Peat-Moss-Based Soil-Less Media[1]

Chemical[2]	*Source*	*Percent Active*	*Rate*[3]	
			oz/yd^3	*g/m*^{3}
Aqua Gro®	Aquatrols Corp. of America 1432 Union Ave. Pennsauhen, NJ 08110	100	3	110
Ethomid 0/15	Armak Co. 8401 West 41st Street McCook, IL 60525	100	3	110
Hydro-Wet (L 237)	Colloidal Products P.O. Box 621 Petaluma, CA 94952	87.5	3	110
Surf Side	Monto Products Corp. P.O. Box 404 Ambler, PA 19002	100	3	110
Tetronic 908	Wyandotte Chemical Co. Wyandotte, MI 48192	100	3	110
Triton B–1956®	Rohm & Haas Co. Independence Mall W. Philadelphia, PA 19106	77	3	110

[1]From Boodley and Sheldrake (1982).

[2]No endorsement of products is intended, nor is criticism of unnamed products implied.

[3]The simplest way to add wetting agents is in the granular formulation. If used as a liquid, dilute the 3 ounces in 5–10 gallons of water and add to the mix. To wet dry mixes after preparation, use a drench of 1 pint per 100 gallons. This is equivalent to about 1 teaspoonful per gallon for small amounts.

Bark-Based Formulations As previously discussed, the use of bark is economically expedient in many areas. Water- and nutrient-holding capacities of bark are generally not as good as those of peat moss. As a result, vermiculite or peat moss is commonly used in commercial preparations of bark media. In addition to these two ingredients, perlite and/or sand is also often used. Commercial mixes based on bark include Ball Growing Mixes I® and II®; Choice Container Mix®; Fafard Mix No. 3® and No. 4®; Metro Mixes 300®, 350®, and 500®; Pro-Mix Peat-Bark Mix®; Strong-Lite Bark Mix®; and VJ #1 Mix® and #3 Mix®.

Pine bark up to 3/8 inch (10 mm) diameter, hardwood bark, as well as redwood bark and redwood sawdust, are commonly mixed with sand. Often, about 30 percent sand is used in these mixtures. Most often, peat moss is added to these mixtures to increase water- and nutrient-holding capacity. A ratio of 3 parts bark to 1 part sand to 1 part peat moss is favored.

Formulation Summary Ten root-media formulas are presented in Table 5–7. These are the more common mixes produced by growers themselves and are representative of many of the commercially prepared mixes. The first mix is the classical soil-based mix containing equal volumes of loam soil, sphagnum peat moss, and concrete-grade sand. If one considers vermiculite as a substitute for soil, then the remaining soil-less mixes in the table emerge. This is reasonable since vermiculite has high nutrient- and water-retention properties. Note that the peat moss of the classical mix can be retained or can be partially or completely replaced by bark. The formulas and components used with pine bark and hardwood bark are the same. When peat moss is combined with bark, it is not necessary to use vermiculite. Other organic matter including the various composted plant materials should be looked upon as a partial or complete replacement for peat moss. Perlite, polystyrene, or any other coarse particle capable of imparting drainage and aeration properties to the medium can be substituted for the sand of the classical soil-based mix. Firms producing large quantities of root media often avoid sand because it rapidly wears out the mixing equipment and can increase shipping costs.

Future Formulations Media discussed thus far include the more common components. Numerous other components exist, and many new ones will be developed as the trend away from soil-based media continues. You should now be able to determine with only a minimum of testing whether these components are use-

Table 5–7

Several Currently Popular Greenhouse Root-Media Formulas and Their Functions

Media Components			*Function*
1 soil	1 peat moss	1 sand	Pot and bench mix
1 vermiculite	1 peat moss		Germination mix
2 vermiculite	2 peat moss	1 perlite	Pot plant mix
1 vermiculite	1 pine bark		Pot plant mix
2 vermiculite	2 pine bark	1 perlite	Pot plant mix
2 vermiculite	1 peat moss, 1 pine bark	1 perlite	Pot plant mix
	1 peat moss, 3 pine bark	1 sand	Pot plant mix
	1 peat moss, 3 hardwood bark	1 sand	Pot plant mix
1 rock wool	1 peat moss		Pot plant mix
3 rock wool	7 peat moss		Pot plant mix

ful to you and how they should be used. First select a component that provides adequate moisture and nutrient retention. If one component does not provide both functions adequately, two components may be required. Seek components that have aggregate structure so that optimum aeration is provided. If this is not possible, a coarse-textured component will be needed to provide aeration. The fewer components the better because of the cost of mixing. Be sure that none of the components provides an excessive quantity of nutrients or salt, such as excessive ammonium released by rapidly decomposing peats or from chicken manure.

Fertilizer Amendments As in the case of soil-based root media, soil-less root media require three nutrient amendments. If needed, dolomitic limestone should be added to bring the pH level into the range of 5.4–6.0. Most often, 10 pounds of agricultural dolomitic limestone per cubic yard (6 kg/m^3) is used for this purpose. Phosphorus is added either as regular superphosphate (0–20–0) at the rate of 4.5 pounds per cubic yard (2.7 kg/m^3) or as triple superphosphate (0–45–0) at the rate of 2.25 pounds per cubic yard (1.3 kg/m^3). The third nutrient additive is a micronutrient mix in a quantity sufficient to last at least one crop time (three to four months). In addition to these three amendments, a wetting agent is almost always included. Quite often, but not always, nitrogen and potassium sufficient to last two to four weeks is likewise included. (Specific instructions for nutrient amendment of soil-based and soil-less media are presented in Chapter 8 under "Preplant Fertilization.") Most commercial formulations contain all of the above-mentioned amendments.

ECONOMICS OF MEDIA

The greenhouse grower who elects to use a soil-less medium must decide whether to purchase it ready-for-use or to formulate it. This decision must be made individually and is based on economics. The grower should calculate the cost of the medium he or she formulates and compare it with the price of commercial media including shipment. In calculating the formulation cost, be sure to include management time, office expenses, depreciation cost of the mixer, any conveyor belts and front-end loaders used to fill the mixer, buildings used for holding components of the medium, cost of pasteurization if this is necessary, and all labor costs. Whether you formulate a soil-based or a soil-less medium, you may be startled by the true cost.

Commercial media, while expensive at face value, are not very different in cost from media individually formulated and can actually be cheaper if a steady source of relatively inexpensive components is not available for mixing your own media. Several of the widely available brands of commercial media cost \$2.00–\$2.50/ft^3 (\$71–\$88/m^3) when purchased in bags or bales. Some brands are available in bulk at lower prices. Many local formulators sell at even lower prices. The

Table 5–8

Number of Pots That Can Be Filled from 1 Cubic Foot of Root Medium

Pot Size (in.)	*Number/ft³*
Standard Type	
2¼	296
2½	176
3	120
4	44
5	24
6	14
7	9
8	5.6
12	1.6
Azalea Type	
4	64
5	32
6	18
6½	15
Low Pan	
5	40
6	31
7	14

figure of \$2.50/ft³ appears to be high but is not necessarily intolerable. Fifteen 6½ inch (17 cm) azalea-type pots used for pot mum culture can be filled from 1 ft³ of medium (485 pots/m³) (Table 5–8) at a cost of \$0.17 per pot. If each finished pot wholesales for \$4.50, the medium cost will be less than 4 percent of the total costs of production.

PREPARATION AND HANDLING OF MEDIA

You have now made several important decisions. First, you have decided whether to use a soil-based medium or a soil-less one. Next, you have decided whether to purchase or prepare your own medium. If you have decided to formulate your own medium, you have determined the minimum number of components necessary to ensure reasonable nutrient and moisture retention without sacrificing aeration.

You have further studied all possible component substitutes to reduce costs by investigating materials ranging from bark, sawdust, and sewage to polystyrene and reprocessed plastic beads. Now, you have worked out a formulation that is tailored to your conditions and needs. It meets the required functions of a root medium, has the proper weight for your format of handling and shipping, and incorporates the most economical combination of various components available in your locality. You must complement this plan with an efficient system for mixing and handling.

Small-Batch Handling

Very small batches of a medium (up to 5 or 6 ft^3) may be mixed by hand shovel on a potting bench or on any hard surface (Figure 5–8a). Components are piled on one another and the nutrient amendments, including limestone, superphosphate, and micronutrient mix, are broadcast over the pile. The pile is thoroughly mixed in three or four shifts. The pile is methodically removed by shovel from its base in the front. As material is removed, other material higher up tumbles downward, mixing as it falls. The new pile is built in front of the original pile by continually dropping material on the top point of this conically shaped pile. As material is added, it tumbles down all sides of the pile, mixing as it goes. This procedure is repeated 2–3 times more by moving the pile to the side and then to the back.

Intermediate-Volume Handling

Preparation of larger batches requires motorized equipment. The simplest system calls for a concrete pad and a tractor with a bucket. Components are piled on the pad and then are mixed by tractor in a similar fashion as that described for hand mixing. Although this is the most common mixing system, one questions the uniformity of the product. A more sophisticated system makes use of a mixer 2–10 cubic yards in capacity (1.50–7.5 m^3) (Figure 5–8b and c). Growers often purchase old concrete trucks. The mixer is removed, reconditioned, and set up for greenhouse operation. The mixer is located near piles of the root-medium components, which are fed into it either by a conveyor belt or a tractor-mounted front-end loader. Upon mixing, the medium is automatically discharged from the mixer into a potting trailer. The bed of one commercial design trailer has a perforated plate with a chamber below it. For homemade trailers, a series of 1¼ inch (3 cm) pipes spaced 1 foot (30 cm) apart are fixed to the bottom of the trailer. The pipes are connected to a manifold pipe that has a single steam inlet. The other ends of all pipes are capped. Holes from ⅛ inch to ¼ inch (3–6 mm) in diameter are drilled in pairs every 6 inches (15 cm) on opposite sides of each pipe to permit the escape of steam.

When the trailer is filled with the medium, a tarp is fastened over it and steam is injected into the chamber below the false bottom or into the pipe distri-

(a)

(b)

(c)

Figure 5–8

(a) A hand-shovel procedure for mixing small batches of a root medium. (b) A small-scale root-medium mixing operation. The soil shredder on the left is used to break up clods in field soil and sphagnum peat moss. Components of the medium including fertilizer amendments are mixed in the 2 cubic foot cement mixers. The freshly prepared medium is placed in the pasteurizing wagons in the background and is pasteurized. (c) An intermediate-size root-medium mixing operation making use of the mixer from a concrete truck.

bution system. Steam rises through the perforations and percolates up through the root medium, thereby destroying harmful disease organisms, insects, and weed seeds. This pasteurization process requires about two hours. The tarp is then removed, and the soil is permitted to cool. Then, the trailer is moved to a convenient location for potting plants, and the sides are lowered to a horizontal position to serve as a potting bench (Figure 5–9).

Large, Fully Automated Systems

Large growers are in the best position to automate. Soil-handling systems of two general types can be purchased ready-built or can be designed and assembled by the grower. Where an automated system is justified, it is generally in daily use and therefore is placed under a roof to permit its use regardless of weather.

The first system (Figure 5–10) begins with storage bins for the root-medium components, which can be filled directly by trucks. Components are then moved by tractor to a hopper mounted over a conveyor belt that feeds them into a mixer. Chemical amendments are added directly to the mixer. Upon mixing, steam is injected into the mixer to pasteurize the root medium. The medium is then expelled into a storage bin by reversing the mixer. Later, it can be moved from the storage bin to an automatic pot- or flat-filling machine by conveyor belt.

The second system is a continuous-belt mixing system. Each of the root-medium components is loaded by tractor into a hopper mounted over a belt. A gate at the bottom of each hopper can be adjusted to control the ratio of components in the mix. Nutrient amendments are placed in a smaller hopper that meters these out over the other components, such as peat moss, already on the belt.

Figure 5–9

A potting trailer with sides lowered to the horizontal position to serve as a potting bench.

(a)

(b)

(c)

Figure 5–10

A root-medium mixing system for large operations: (a) Components of the medium are placed in the hopper, through which they drop into a grinder and then pass up an elevator into a mixer. Perlite and chemical amendments are added directly into the mixer from above. The root medium is steam-pasteurized in the mixer with steam produced in the portable steam generator at the right. After pasteurization, the rotation of the mixer is reversed to expel the medium into the 6 cubic yard storage hopper on the left. The duct over the elevator is used to blow cool air into the mixer when it is emptying in order to reduce the time before the root medium can be handled. (b) Further along the system, the root medium is automatically brought by conveyor belt to a pot-filling machine as needed. In the scene above, 157 three-inch pots are being filled per minute. Pots leave the filling machine on a belt and can be planted directly or can be removed and planted elsewhere. (c) A close view of the pot-filling machine. Excess soil is recycled back to the hopper on the filling machine. This machine can fill flats or pots of any size, including three-gallon cans. (*Photos courtesy of Soil Systems, Inc., Apopka,* FL 32703)

Further along, the belt passes through a box in which spinning tines are located for mixing the various medium components and nutrient amendments together. The mixed root medium continues along the belt to either a storage bin or the hopper on a flat- or pot-filling machine. When the root medium runs low in the hopper of the potting machine, a button is pushed to turn on the belt mixing system, which results in the hopper being refilled. All that is necessary is to keep the raw-ingredient hoppers in the belt system supplied.

SUMMARY

1. Root media must serve four functions: to provide water, to supply nutrients, to permit gas exchange to and from roots, and to provide support for plants.
2. Desirable properties of greenhouse root media include the following:
   a. For pot plant media, a stable organic-matter content that will not diminish significantly in volume during growth of a crop.
   b. Organic matter with a reasonable carbon:nitrogen ratio and rate of decomposition so that nitrogen tie-up is not troublesome.
   c. For pot plant media, a bulk density light enough to enhance handling and shipping but sufficiently heavy to prevent toppling of plants—40–75 pounds/ft^3 (640–1,200 g/dm^3) when wet at container capacity.
   d. At least 10–20 percent air by volume at container capacity in a 6½ inch (17 cm) azalea-type pot with as high an available water content as possible without sacrificing bulk density or aeration needs.
   e. A high cation exchange capacity for nutrient reserve (6–15 me/100 cc).
   f. A pH level of 6.2–6.8 in soil-based media and 5.4–6.0 in soil-less media for crops in general but lower for acid-requiring plants.
   g. Sufficient level of all nutrients other than nitrogen and potassium to prevent a deficiency for the duration of at least one crop.
3. A long list of potential components exists for use in greenhouse media. One should select root-media components on the basis of meeting the four functions of root media and of economics, steady availability, and use of a minimal number of components.
4. Soil-based media have traditionally been used in greenhouses. Soil provides water and nutrient retention. Concrete-grade sand is added to increase aeration, and peat moss is used to restore moisture and nutrient retention lost by the addition of sand. A standard formulation of 1 part loam soil to 1 part sand to 1 part peat moss can be altered to accommodate various soil textures.
5. Soil-less media are an asset where soil procurement or weight is a problem. Peat moss alone or combined in equal volume amounts with vermiculite or

sand constitutes an effective root medium. Composted bark of species ranging from pine to hardwoods also provides a good base for soil-less media. Two successful formulations include either equal volumes of bark and vermiculite or 3 parts bark to 1 part peat moss to 1 part concrete-grade sand.

6. It is desirable to amend root media with three nutrient packages: agricultural dolomitic limestone to achieve desired pH levels, superphosphate, and a micronutrient mixture. In addition, soil-less media should be amended with a wetting agent. Although not necessary, some growers and most producers of commercial formulations include sufficient nitrogen and potassium to last two to four weeks. (Specific recommendations are given in Chapter 8.)
7. The preparation and handling of root media pose an important economic consideration for growers. A root medium may be purchased already mixed and chemically amended and pasteurized, thus circumventing considerable labor, or it may be formulated by the grower. Various degrees of automation are available for formulating and handling media and should be considered.

REFERENCES

1. Anon. 1983. Tracking down the proper growing media. *Greenhouse Manager* 2(7):55–57, 60–65, 68–69.
2. Baker, K. F., ed. 1957. The U.C. system for producing healthy container-grown plants. Univ. of California Agr. Exp. Sta. and Ext. Ser. Manual 23. Berkeley, CA.
3. Blom, T. J. 1983. Working with soilless mixes. *Florists' Review* 173 (4480):29–34.
4. Boodley, J. W., and R. Sheldrake, Jr. 1982. Cornell peat-lite mixes for commercial plant growing. New York State College of Agr. and Life Sci. Ext. Info. Bul. 43.
5. Bunt, A. C. 1976. *Modern Potting Composts*. University Park, PA; and London: The Pennsylvania State Univ. Press.
6. Coker, E. G. 1971. *Horticultural Science and Soils*. Vol. 2. *Soils and Fertilizers*. London: Macdonald and Co., Ltd.
7. DeBoodt, M., ed. 1974. First symposium on artificial media in horticulture. *Acta Hort.* No. 37.
8. Johnson, P. 1968. *Horticultural and Agricultural Uses of Sawdust and Soil Amendments*. P. Johnson, 3106 Simbar Rd., Bonita, CA 92002.
9. Kelly, J. C., ed. 1978. Symposium on production of protected crops in peat and other media. *Acta Hort.* No. 82.
10. Lemaire, F., ed. 1982. Symposium on substrates in horticulture other than soils in situ. *Acta Hort.* No. 126.
11. Penningsfeld, F., chairman. 1972. Third symposium on peat in horticulture. *Acta Hort.* No. 26.
12. Poincelot, R. P. 1975. The biochemistry and methodology of composting. Connecticut Agr. Exp. Sta. Bul. 754.

13. Potter, C. H. 1971. Bedding plants 6: Choosing a soil: The real thing or a mix? *Florists' Review* 147 (3819):32–33, 71–74.

14. Robinson, D. W., and J. G. D. Lamb, eds. 1975. *Peat in Horticulture.* New York: Academic Press.

15. Van der Borg, H. H., ed. 1975. Symposium on peat in horticulture. *Acta Hort.* No. 50.

16. White, J. W. 1974. Criteria for selection of growing media for greenhouse crops. *Florists' Review* 155 (4009):28–30,. 73–74.

17. ———. 1976. Growing media. In Mastalerz, J. W., ed. *Bedding Plants,* 2d ed., pp. 113–133. Pennsylvania Flower Growers' Assoc., 103 Tyson Bldg., University Park, PA 16802.

18. Wilson, G. C. S., ed. 1980. Symposium on substrates in horticulture other than soils in situ. *Acta Hort.* No. 99.

CHAPTER 6

Root-Media Pasteurization

Subtropical conditions exist in the greenhouse that are conducive to the development of plant disease organisms. The environment never freezes, the atmosphere is continually moist, and temperatures are always warm. The continuous culture of one or, at best, a few crops accentuates the disease problem by providing a continuous host on which disease organisms can build.

Before 1950, in order to combat the soilborne disease problem, root media were removed from greenhouses annually and replaced with root media that had been carefully prepared by a proper succession of crops in the field and by composting, as described in Chapter 5. During the 1950s, this cumbersome labor-consuming system became less prevalent as root-media pasteurization was adopted.

Root-media pasteurization is a standard practice for virtually all greenhouse ranges today. It generally is done on an annual basis, although a number of growers are pasteurizing their root media between every crop. The need for such an increase in frequency is occasionally dictated by the buildup of disease in the greenhouse. For a relatively short crop such as chrysanthemums, media pasteurization could be required every 12–16 weeks. The summer is a preferred time for pasteurization because crop production is usually at a low point, student labor is more available, root media are warmer, and, in the case of steam pasteurization, all or much of the boiler capacity is available at this time.

Root-media pasteurization, in addition to eliminating disease organisms, is used to control nematodes, insects, and weeds. Field operators have been known to pasteurize soil for the single benefit of weed control.

Pasteurization may be accomplished by injecting steam into the soil or by injecting one of several chemicals such as methyl bromide and chloropicrin. These two methods will be discussed separately next.

STEAM PASTEURIZATION

Temperature Requirements

A number of organisms are injurious to plants, and each organism has its own condition under which it is destroyed, as set forth in Figure 6–1. It has been customary to apply steam for 30 minutes beyond the time when the coldest spot in the batch of root medium being pasteurized reaches 160°F (71°C). While this

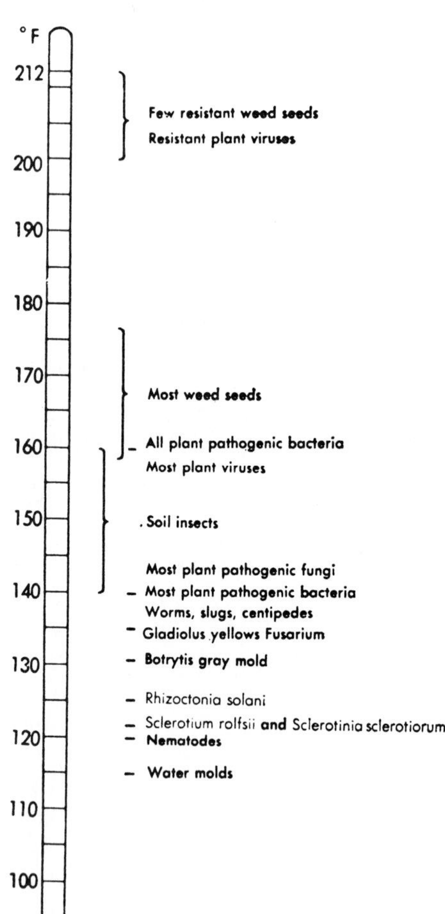

Figure 6–1

Temperature necessary to kill pathogens and other organisms harmful to plants. Most of the temperatures indicated here are for exposures of 30 minutes under moist conditions. (From *Baker*, 1957)

practice guarantees 30 minutes at a minimum temperature of 160°F, the root medium temperature usually rises to 212°F (100°C), the temperature of steam.

This chapter refers to *pasteurization* rather than to *sterilization* because sterilization would imply destruction of all organisms in root media, whereas pasteurization indicates that only selected organisms are killed. Root media contain, in addition to the harmful disease organisms, many beneficial organisms. A root medium heavily occupied by beneficial organisms is not readily infected by disease organisms. By virtue of their strong foothold, the beneficial organisms compete successfully for oxygen, space, and nutrients and present resistance to the establishment of disease organisms. Pasteurization at a temperature of 212°F (100°C) results in considerable destruction of beneficial organisms. This situation is not harmful if beneficial organisms are the first ones to reinoculate a root medium. However, if disease organisms are first, they will develop rapidly without resistance or competition.

Equipment is available today that will mix air with steam (Figure 6–2). The temperature of the mixture can be adjusted to a desired level below 212°F

Figure 6–2

A steam aerator that permits pasteurization of root media at a temperature of 140–160°F (60–71°C) rather than at 212°F (100°C), the temperature of steam. Steam from a boiler enters the aerator at the right while a blower introduces air. The two gases mix in the tank at the top and are then conducted through the hose on the left to a covered potting wagon containing the root medium to be pasteurized. A hand valve is used to regulate the amount of air introduced, which, in turn, controls the temperature of the mixture. The temperature is indicated on the temperature gauge shown.

(100°C) and injected into the root medium. The root medium will rise to this desired temperature and no higher. This system is known as *aerated steam pasteurization*. Several recommendations call for a temperature of 140°F (60°C) for 30 minutes, although many growers pasteurize at a temperature of 160°F (71°C) for 30 minutes. Most harmful organisms are destroyed, while only a minimum of beneficial organisms are killed.

Root-Media Preparation

The root medium should be loosened before pasteurizing. If it is in a bench, it should be rototilled. Heat moves more rapidly within the root medium by convection through the pores than it does by conduction from particle to particle. The large pores in loose root media facilitate the movement of steam and thereby cut down the length of time required to pasteurize bench or container root media.

The root medium should not be dry. Dry root media acts very much as an insulator, resisting the conduction of heat and causing the medium to warm up slowly. The addition of water speeds up the rate of pasteurization, but there is an optimum level of water beyond which further additions again slow down the speed of pasteurization. Water requires 5 times as much heat to raise its temperature as does an equal weight of soil. Since all the excess water in the root medium must also be raised to the desired temperature of pasteurization, the process becomes very slow and consequently expensive. As a general rule, the root medium should be at the moisture level one would desire at the time of planting a crop.

A few types of weed seed can survive temperatures approaching 212°F (100°C). Some of these are morning glory, buttonweed, bur clover, shepard's purse, and Klamath weed. This problem can be circumvented by moistening the root medium a week or two prior to pasteurization. As soon as seed begins the germination process of taking up moisture, it is easily killed at lower temperatures typically used for pasteurization.

Since root media must be mixed prior to pasteurization, it is desirable to add the various chemical and physical amendments at that time. Superphosphate, limestone, fritted micronutrients, inorganic complete fertilizers, and the slow-release fertilizer MagAmp® can undergo the process of pasteurization without adverse effect. The slow-release fertilizer Osmocote® requires further consideration. It can withstand temperatures up to 200°F (94°C) without damage to the coating; however, the rate of release may increase. It is unadvisable to pasteurize root media containing Osmocote® since high soluble-salt levels may ensue.

Bench media require periodic additions of organic matter such as peat moss or bark, which are most easily incorporated at the time a root medium is rototilled prior to pasteurization. It is also a good practice to carry these amendments through the pasteurization process to destroy any harmful organisms that might be in them.

Steam Sources

The temperature of 1 cubic foot of a greenhouse root medium on the average can be raised 1°F by the addition of 24 Btu of heat. (One cubic meter of a root medium can be raised 1°C by the addition of 1.6 MJ or 381 kcal of heat.) The lower the initial temperature of the medium, the greater the quantity of heat that must be applied to pasteurize it. Table 6–1 lists the heat required to raise soil-based media to 180°F (82°C) from various starting temperatures.

Steam pasteurization efficiency may be as low as 50 percent. Half of the heat generated in the boiler may be lost from the boiler itself, the lines leading to the root medium, the walls of the bench, and the cover over it. It is therefore necessary to double the figures in Table 6–1 for determining the size of boiler needed. Since 1 boiler horsepower (hp) is equal to 33,475 Btu per hour, a total of about 6 cubic feet of medium at 65°F (18°C) can be pasteurized in 1 hour with 1 boiler hp of heat at 50 percent efficiency. This would be equivalent to about 12 square feet of bench area. (One cubic meter of a root medium requires 208 MJ or 50,000 kcal during pasteurization.)

Boilers can also be rated in terms of pounds of steam generated. In this case, we are referring to 1 pound of water heated to the state of steam. When 1 pound of steam at 212°F changes state to 1 pound of water at 212°F, it releases 970 Btu of heat. One more Btu is released for each degree the water drops below this point. If the root medium is pasteurized at 180°F, the water will drop 32°F releasing an additional 32 Btu beyond the 970 Btu released when it changed states. Thus, 1 pound of steam contributes 1,002 Btu to the job of pasteurization. About 6 pounds of steam are required to pasteurize 1 cubic foot of a root medium (96 kg steam/m^3 of root medium).

Table 6–1

Heat Required to Raise 1 Cubic Foot or 1 Cubic Meter of Greenhouse Root Media Containing 15 Percent Moisture from Various Starting Temperatures to 180°F (82°C)*

Start, °F	*Heat,* *Btu/ft^3*	*Start,* °C	*Heat,* *kcal/m^3*
70	2,640	20	21,824
60	2,880	15	23,584
50	3,120	10	25,344
40	3,340	5	27,104
30	3,600	0	28,864

*Adapted from Gray (1960).

A steam boiler used for heating a greenhouse can be used for pasteurization. A tee and valve should be installed in the main steam line at a convenient point in each greenhouse from which steam can be obtained.

Steam does not have to be generated under high pressure for pasteurization purposes. Once it is released in the root medium, it is under very low pressure—considerably less than 1 pound per square inch (psi) (6.9 kPa). Pressure at the boiler serves the purpose of driving the steam through the lines to the root medium. For this purpose, a pressure at the boiler of 10–15 psi (70–100 kPa) is practical. It is true that the heat content of steam rises as it is put under pressure. However, the increase in heat content is small, and a high-pressure system must be justified on other grounds, such as heat distribution in a large greenhouse range. When steam pressure is increased to 50 psi (345 kPa), the temperature rises to about 297°F (147°C), and the additional heat content of 1 pound of water increases by only 29 Btu over steam at zero pressure (the heat content of 1 kg water increases by 67 kJ or 16 kcal).

Steam Distribution

Steam should be conducted from the portable steam generator or main steam line in the greenhouse through a low-pressure steam hose of at least 1.25 inch (32

Figure 6–3

When steam is provided by a central boiler for root-media pasteurization, it is best to have a permanent steam line in each greenhouse from which steam can be obtained for this purpose. A subsurface steam line with periodic risers is used in the situation here to minimize the length of steam hose and the amount of labor required.

mm) diameter. Couplings on the hose should be full flow. If steam is provided from a central boiler, there should be a valve in each greenhouse section from which steam can be obtained (Figure 6–3).

Steam is distributed in fresh flower ground beds through buried perforated pipes. For beds 3 feet (0.9 m) wide, one row is buried; for 4 foot (1.2 m) beds, two rows are used. Used rain gutters, used boiler flue tubes, irrigation pipe, and other materials can be used for this purpose. A pair of holes from ⅛ to ¼ inch (3–6 mm) in diameter should be drilled on opposite sides every 6 inches (15 cm) to distribute steam. The end of each pipe is plugged with a cap. A simple pipe manifold can be assembled to distribute steam from the inlet hose to each pipe (Figure 6–4).

Many older ground beds, particularly in rose ranges, were constructed with a concrete V-shaped bottom. At the lowest point in the V, a drainage tile was installed along the length of the bed. Steam can be very effectively applied through this tile, minimizing the equipment and labor of setup needed. Ground beds without bottoms can present another problem. Disease organisms and nematodes can exist below the point to which the soil has been loosened. Steam does not penetrate rapidly into this hard area. Harmful organisms below this point can return after pasteurization to the upper levels where roots grow. It is best to bury the steam conduction pipes at the bottom of the rototilled root medium. This results

Figure 6–4

An easily constructed steam line manifold. The 4 foot wide (1.2 m) bench pictured here is best pasteurized with two perforated steam conduction pipes buried in the root medium.

in deeper penetration of steam and also prevents nematodes and symphillids from escaping by burrowing deeper ahead of the steam.

Raised benches filled with a root medium may be pasteurized with or without buried steam conduction pipes. If pipes are used, they are buried at half the depth of the soil. This is the best system. Some growers inject steam between the cover and the root medium through 5 inch (13 cm) diameter canvas hoses. Once the cover is inflated, steam readily penetrates the loosened root medium. Although this system is easier to set up than the buried steam pipe system, it can require a longer time for steam to penetrate the root medium.

Empty raised benches also can be pasteurized with steam distributed through a 5 inch (13 cm) diameter canvas hose, which costs about $1.30 per linear foot. The hose is slipped over the end of the steam hose and tied in place. It is then placed on the root medium, and the distant end is tied closed with a piece of wire. The hose should be wet before pasteurizing to speed up the initial release of steam.

Potting media are best pasteurized in a wagon equipped with perforated steam pipes at the bottom or a perforated false bottom with steam chamber below. Such wagons have already been described in Chapter 5. Ideally, the sides of such wagons can be lowered to a horizontal position to serve as potting benches.

Fields of soil also can be steam pasteurized, which is commonly done in chrysanthemum production areas such as Florida and California. It would be quicker to inject methyl bromide into the soil by tractor, but this practice would not completely kill *Verticillium* wilt—a very devastating and prevalent disease of chrysanthemums in production fields. Steam is effective against this disease. The boiler may be in a fixed central location or may be mounted on a truck so that it may be moved from field to field. Steam is conducted from the boiler by a steam hose across the field to a steam rake (Figure 6–5). The rake consists of a 4 inch (10 cm) pipe header 12 feet (3.65 m) long, drawn perpendicular to a cable that pulls it across the field. Projecting down into the soil from the header are 16–18 inch (40–46 cm) blades spaced 9 inches (23 cm) apart. Behind each blade is a 1/2 inch (1.3 cm) pipe carrying steam from the header to the soil at the lower rear side of each blade. A winch is often used to draw the rake across the field at a rate of 10–20 inches (25–50 cm) per minute. One acre (0.4 ha) of soil can be pasteurized by a single rake in 40–70 hours of operating time. A sterilizing cover is attached to the back side of the header and is thus dragged across the field. The cover should be sufficiently long to require 30 minutes to pass over any given point in the field. The cover should be 50 feet (15 m) long for a rake moving at 20 inches per minute. The cover serves to hold the steam in the soil so that the soil temperature will be maintained at or above 160°F (71°C) for 30 minutes.

The coldest spot during pasteurization is at the end of the bench or trailer where the steam enters and usually near the outer wall at this end. A thermometer should be placed in the coldest spot. Pasteurization should not be stopped until the coldest spot reaches the temperature and time conditions desired. If the ther-

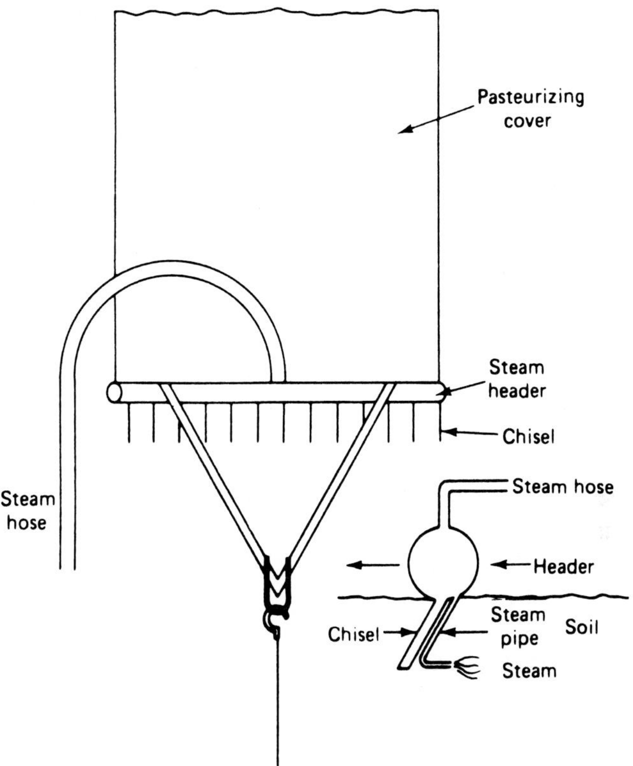

Figure 6–5

A steam rake used for pasteurizing soil in the field. Steam is conducted via hose to a 12 foot long (3.65 m) header. Chisels about 9 inches (23 cm) apart project into the soil at a distance of 16–18 inches (40–46 cm). Small pipes behind each chisel carry steam into the soil to the depth of the chisels. A pasteurizing cover is drawn behind the rake to maintain a high soil temperature for 30 minutes. The rake itself often is drawn across the field by a cable and winch.

mometer were placed in a warm spot, pasteurization would stop before harmful organisms were killed in the colder areas. These areas would become a source of inoculation for the remainder of the soil. Because of the lack of competition, the harmful organisms would spread rapidly. It would be better not to pasteurize the soil than to do an incomplete job such as this.

The cold spot in a greenhouse bench can be corrected by applying an extra quantity of steam at that point. Figure 6–6 shows a system for doing this. A short piece of pipe is connected to and run parallel to the steam conduction pipe at the point where it enters the root medium being pasteurized. The extra piece of pipe runs about a third of the length of the bed and has numerous perforations on opposite sides spaced about 2 inches (5 cm) apart.

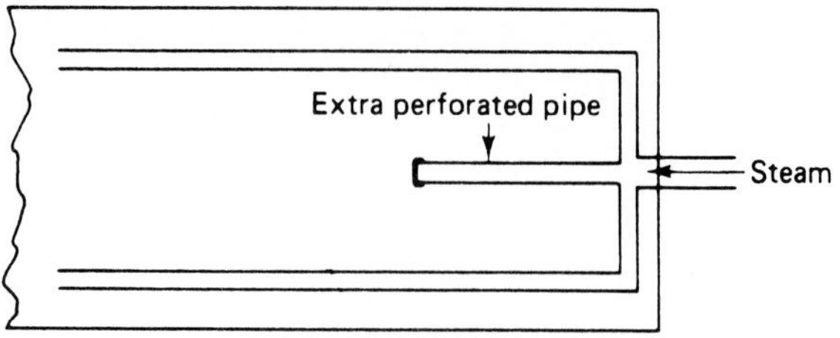

Figure 6–6

An extra perforated steam conduction pipe (center of bed) used to deliver additional steam to the cold end of a bed to prevent excessive pasteurization time.

Covers

Without a cover, steam will quickly rise through the root medium and be lost, further reducing the efficiency of an already inefficient use of steam. A cover is placed over the root medium during pasteurization to catch and hold steam in close contact with the root medium so it can be of further value in raising the temperature.

Basically, there are three types of covers: polyethylene, vinyl, and neoprene-coated nylon fabric. Polyethylene film has the shortest life expectancy but is the cheapest. An inexpensive grade costs about 3¢/ft^2. It may be used several times during one season of pasteurization but cannot be stored from season to season. Vinyl covers are the most popular and are usually purchased in 8 mil thicknesses. They are advertised to last for up to 25 uses. Actually, these covers last much longer with proper handling and storage away from sunlight. Ultraviolet light breaks down vinyl plastic. These vinyl covers cost about 20¢/ft^2. The longest-lasting covers are the neoprene-coated nylon fabric ones, which are claimed to last up to 100 uses but will actually last well beyond 200 uses if they are dried each time they are stored. These covers cost about 36¢/ft^2.

Covers used on benches with smooth outer side walls do not have to be fastened to benches. They should overhang each side by 1 foot (30 cm) or more. As steam contacts the inner side of the cover, it condenses and moistens that side. The film of water that forms between the outer side of the bench and the inner side of the cover causes the two to stick together, preventing the cover from blowing off as steam builds up under it. Covers used on benches with outside posts or rough side boards must be fastened to the bench. The simplest method is to lay a chain or other heavy object over the cover against the inner side wall of the bench (Figure 6–7). A reusable plastic tube is commercially available that can be inflated with water for this same purpose. Some growers squeeze the cover between the top of the bench side and a lath strip with a clamp. Other growers with wooden benches place a lath strip over the cover at the top outer sides of the bench and nail the lath to the bench. This puts holes in the cover, which is unde-

Figure 6–7

When the outer side of a bed or bench wall is uneven, rough, or short, the pasteurizing cover must be fastened to prevent lifting by steam beneath. The simplest method is to weight it down with heavy objects such as chain or pipe.

sirable, particularly in the case of a higher-quality cover that must be used many times.

Thirty minutes after 160°F (71°C) has been achieved, the steam should be shut off. The cover will fall back to the root medium in a few minutes, and then it can be cautiously removed. When the medium has cooled to a comfortable working temperature, seeds and young plants may be planted. This cooling can require from four to eight hours, depending upon depth and moisture content. Media pasteurized with aerated steam can be cooled much faster by using the aerator to pass cool air through the root medium for 30 minutes after the cover has been removed.

After-Steaming Problems

Two toxicity problems can occur as a result of steam pasteurization. One is manganese toxicity, and the other is ammonium toxicity. Large quantities of manganese exist in many soils. Fortunately, a small but adequate amount is available for plant use while the majority is in an unavailable form. Steam pasteurization results in further conversion of unavailable to available manganese. The longer the soil is steamed, the greater is the buildup of available manganese and, hence, the greater the risk of manganese toxicity. It is important that media containing field soil be pasteurized at the recommended temperature for only the length of time necessary—30 minutes. Soil-less media usually present no problems since the components contain little or no manganese.

A high level of manganese in the plant is toxic in itself, causing tip burn of older leaves. A high level of manganese in the root medium also interferes with root uptake of iron. In fact, iron deficiency is commonly caused by high available-manganese levels.

Root media that contain organic matter rich in nitrogen can release ammonium nitrogen during pasteurization and may continue to release it for a few weeks. Manure, highly decomposed peats, leaf mold, and composts are examples of such materials. Microorganisms feed upon the organic matter for the carbon, nitrogen, and other elements contained in it. When an overabundance of nitrogen is contained in it, much will be released for plant use. As illustrated in Figure 6–8, ammonifying microorganisms convert nitrogen in organic matter to ammonium nitrogen, and then nitrifying bacteria convert the ammonium nitrogen to nitrate nitrogen.

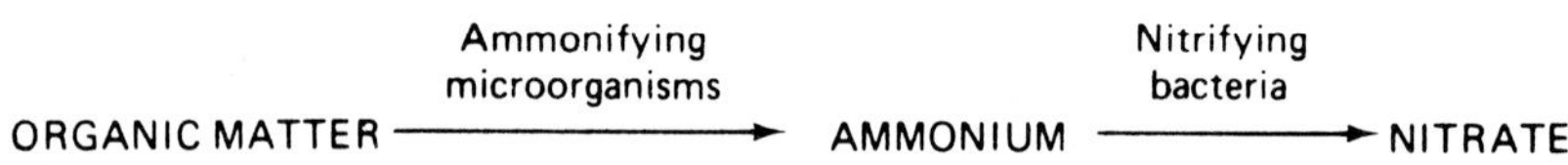

Figure 6–8

Ammonium toxicity can be a problem when organic materials rich in nitrogen are pasteurized with either steam or chemicals. Nitrogen contained in organic matter is released as ammonium when ammonifying microorganisms, including bacteria, fungi, and actinomycetes, break down the organic matter in order to utilize its carbon content. Nitrifying bacteria, in turn, convert ammonium to nitrate nitrogen. During pasteurization, both populations of microorganisms are reduced to low levels. The ammonifying organisms build back to an effective level before the nitrifying organisms. During the interim period, plants are prone to ammonium injury.

Most plants grow best in a mixture of ammonium and nitrate forms of nitrogen. Many may be injured by ammonium nitrogen alone—for example, poinsettia and rose—or will grow less vigorously. Normally, ammonium nitrogen is continuously converted to nitrate nitrogen by soil bacteria, so there is always a mixture. During pasteurization, ammonifying and nitrifying bacteria are nearly eliminated. In a few weeks, the ammonifying bacterial population builds back to an effective level, and sizable quantities of ammonium nitrogen are released from organic matter. It is not until three to six weeks after pasteurization that nitrifying bacteria generally build back to a population size where they can cope with the ammonium nitrogen being released. In the meantime, two to six weeks after pasteurization, toxic quantities of ammonium nitrogen may develop. This may burn the roots of plants and cause stunting of the entire plant as well as wilting of the tops. Then, any type of nutrient deficiency can ensue as a result of the root injury. Once the nitrifying population becomes large, the high levels of ammonium nitrogen are converted to nitrate nitrogen, which is less toxic to plants and is more readily leached from the root medium during watering. Because of these lower levels and the fact that many plants can tolerate higher levels of nitrate than ammonium nitrogen, the problem usually ends at this time. It is mainly for this reason that the use of manure gave way to peat moss during the 1950s when pasteurization became popular. Peat moss, because of its low nitrogen content and slow rate of decomposition, does not support a toxic buildup of ammonium nitrogen.

A third event that can occur from oversteaming of media attracts considerable attention but is not harmful. The fungus *Pezziza ostrachoderma* will build into a large conspicuous population when competition from other microorganisms is reduced by overpasteurization (too high a temperature or excessive time). The fungus forms spores at the medium surface that are at first white, then yellow, and finally brown. The fungus *Pyronema* sp. forms pink spores. These fungi do not attack plants, but their common occurrence serves to illustrate the ease with which a disease organism can get a foothold in overpasteurized media where competition has been suppressed.

CHEMICAL PASTEURIZATION

Chemicals offer an alternative to steam for growers who do not heat with a steam boiler and who are not in a position to afford a portable steam generator. The field grower of crops other than chrysanthemum would also see a value in chemical pasteurization because it can be set up for less cost and applied much more rapidly than steam.

Counterbalancing these advantages of chemicals are three disadvantages. Chemically treated media cannot be used for young plants for 10 days after treatment. For fresh flower crops, costly overhead continues during this time. Chemicals are injurious to humans, and stringent safety precautions must be taken. While steam and methyl bromide may be used in a greenhouse containing plants, chloropicrin may not. Basamid® (also Mylone®, Microfume®, and Crag®), known by the common name DMTT or dasomet, while commonly used in several countries, is not used to any extent in America because of the long (three- to four-week) period between application and planting.

Methyl Bromide

Methyl bromide is available under various trade names and in different combinations with chloropicrin. Methyl bromide is extremely hazardous to humans, and for this reason a small quantity, usually 2 percent, of tear gas (chloropicrin) is added as an irritant to warn against exposure. It is available in 1 and 1½ pound (454–680 g) cans or larger cylinders for tractor mounting. It is a liquid under pressure and turns to gas when released. Methyl bromide is effective against disease organisms, insects, nematodes, and weed seeds.

Root media should be worked up to a loose state for rapid penetration of the gas and should be at a moisture content desired for planting. Root media at 40°F (4°C) or lower should not be treated. It is best if the media are at 50°F (10°C) or higher. A potting medium should be placed in a container or on a hard, flat surface preferably not over 1 foot (30 cm) deep. Then, cans of methyl bromide are placed adjacent to the pile or to the bench and are used at the rate of 1 pound per cubic yard (0.6 kg/m^3) of root medium. Each can is placed in an applicator, as pictured in Figure 6–9. A tube extends from the applicator to the top of the root medium where it is placed in an open saucer or can to collect any liquid that might come out with the gas. From here, the liquid can quickly evaporate. If it were to enter the root medium as a liquid, it might take several days longer to evaporate than anticipated and in the meantime would be injurious to plants. A polyethylene cover is placed over the bench or pile. The bench cover can be weighted down by chain along the edges, and the pile cover can be weighted down along the edges with sand. Clay pots or wooden blocks should be placed on the root medium to hold the cover up so that the gas can contact all of the surface.

When the medium is ready for pasteurization, the handle on the applicator is closed. As this is done, a hollow spike is driven into the can, allowing methyl bromide to escape through the tube to the space between the medium and the cover. An alternative method of release consists of a plastic tray with hollow spikes in the bottom. Cans are placed over the spikes. Then, the tray is placed on the root medium and a plastic sheet is placed over the medium and the tray. Cans are released by pushing down on them from outside the plastic sheet.

The medium should be exposed to the gas with the cover on for at least 24 hours at temperatures of 60°F (15°C) and higher. At the cooler temperature of 50°F (10°C), the exposure time should be 48 hours. The cover is then removed, and the root medium is left undisturbed to aerate for 24 hours (48 hours at 50°F).

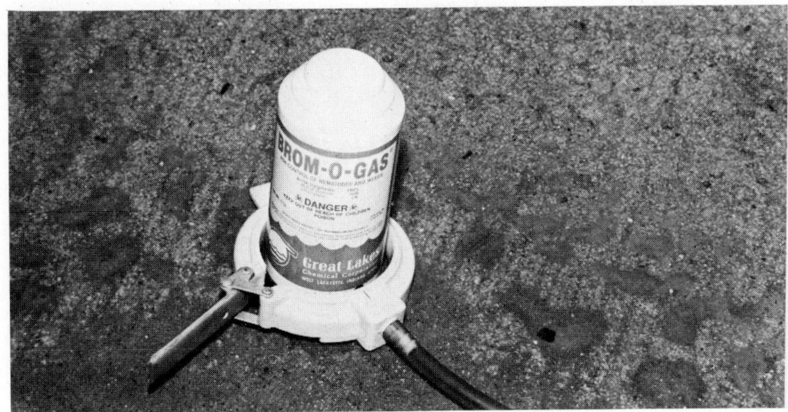

Figure 6–9

An applicator for small cans of methyl bromide. The can is placed in a ring. As the ring is clamped tight, a hollow spike punctures the can. Methyl bromide liquid under pressure expands to gas as it exits from the spike into a plastic tube that conducts it to the root-medium pile. It is used at the rate of 1 pound per cubic yard of medium.

After this time, the medium may be handled. Seeds can be safely planted after three days of aeration, but plants including cuttings and seedlings should not be planted for seven to ten days.

Methyl bromide should not be used in a greenhouse where there are other plants unless full ventilation can be provided during the process. Carnations are susceptible to even slight concentrations of methyl bromide, so this chemical should not be used for this crop. Cauliflower, salvia, and snapdragon may sustain a moderate degree of distorted growth from media not thoroughly aerated.

Methyl bromide can be applied by tractor in the field. Gas from a pressurized cylinder of methyl bromide is conducted through plastic tubes to a row of chisels mounted behind the tractor 6–8 inches (15–20 cm) apart (Figure 6–10). The gas is released at the bottom of the chisels 4–6 inches (10–15 cm) deep. Also mounted to the back of the tractor is a roll of polyethylene film. The end is buried at the beginning of the row to anchor it. As the tractor moves across the field, the plastic sheet is unrolled. The leading edge of the first sheet is buried with soil by a disk mounted on the tractor. Subsequent sheets are glued to the preceding sheet to form one continuous covering over the field. A rig such as the one described sells for about $3,500 and can be depreciated over 10 years. Three men with one tractor rig can treat up to 5 acres (2 ha) in one day.

A less expensive rig buries both sides of the plastic sheet. No gluing is involved. A 9 foot (2.75 m) strip of the field is treated; the next 9 foot strip is skipped. This procedure is repeated across the field. In a few days, when sufficient exposure time has lapsed, the plastic is removed and the untreated strips are treated. This rig sells for about $2,100.

Figure 6–10

Tractor-mounted rig for injecting gaseous chemicals into field soil for pasteurization: (a) Chisels extend into the soil. Behind each is a tube that delivers the gas into the soil. A rake follows to seal the holes made by the chisels. (b) A roll of polyethylene film is located behind the rake. At the beginning of the row, the end of the polyethylene is anchored by burying it in the soil. As the tractor moves across the field, the film unrolls. (c) One side of the film is buried by a disk while the other side is glued to the previous sheet of plastic. Up to 5 acres of field can be treated by three people in one day with a single tractor. (*Photos courtesy of* W. A. *Skroch, Department of* Horticultural *Science,* North *Carolina* State *University,* Raleigh, NC 27695–7609)

Other materials for field fumigation include 1.7 rolls of 10.5 foot by 3,000 foot (3.2 m by 914 m), 1 mil (0.025 mm) polyethylene ($204) and 325 pounds (150 kg) of actual methyl bromide ($300). If the glue system is used, 6–7 gallons of glue are required per acre at a total cost of $78. Custom applicators can be contracted for a 3–5 acre plot at the rate of about $1,200 per acre ($3,000/ha) by those who are not set up to apply the chemical themselves. Everything is included in the custom applicator price except two laborers to bury the ends of each plastic strip applied and the labor of removing the plastic after a few days of exposure.

Methyl bromide, like steam, greatly reduces the populations of ammonifying and nitrifying bacteria. The same toxic buildup of ammoniacal nitrogen can occur if organic matter rich in nitrogen and capable of rapid breakdown is used.

Chloropicrin

This fumigant, also known as "tear gas," is a popular choice for carnation crops because of their sensitivity to methyl bromide. Chloropicrin, however, cannot be used in a greenhouse where there are plants. Another disadvantage of chloropicrin is its poor penetration into plant tissue in root media.

Chloropicrin is used at the rate of 3 cc/ft^3 (32 cc/m^2) of bench or field surface and at the rate of 3–5 cc/ft^3 for bulk media. Chloropicrin is injected into media in the greenhouse by a hand injector. A spike at the base of the injector is pushed by foot into the medium. As this occurs, 3 cc of liquid chloropicrin is released from the end of the spike. The injector is inserted on 12 inch (30 cm) centers. After application, the bench or pile of medium is covered with a polyethylene cover. Chloropicrin may be injected through tractor-drawn chisels in the field. The treated field is covered with polyethylene film as in the case of methyl bromide.

Chloropicrin should not be used at media temperatures below 60°F (15°C); 70°F (21°C) is best. An exposure time of one to three days is needed, the longer time being needed at 60°F. Media should be aerated for seven to ten days before planting in it.

Residue Test

Wet, heavy, or cold media are slow to release chemical fumigants upon aeration. A grower must be certain that the residue is below an injurious level before planting a crop. A simple lettuce test can determine this. The procedure is as follows:

1. Fill a few jars three-quarters full with treated medium. The medium should be at a moisture content for planting. Wet it if necessary.
2. Place wet, 1 inch (2.5 cm) squares of absorbent cotton on the medium and on each square of cotton place 10–15 lettuce seeds that were presoaked in water for 30 minutes.

3. Seal the jars tightly as soon as possible and place at room temperature in an area where they receive daylight. (Some lettuce seed will not germinate in the dark.)
4. Prepare some other jars in the same manner, using untreated medium as a control.

After two days, the seeds in the control should have germinated as well as those in the treated-medium jars if the residue is down to a safe level. If the seeds fail to germinate in the treated-medium jars, aerate the medium longer. It will help to mix or rototill the medium.

REINOCULATION

Root-media pasteurization serves the purpose of eradicating biological pests. It does not provide a resistance to these pests. Growers must think through all of the operations in which they might introduce contaminated media to clean media.

Pots and flats are of first concern. If they have been used before, they contain media and possibly plant tissue that could be contaminated. They should be cleaned. Clay and wooden containers can be steamed along with root media. Because plastic pots will distort at high temperature, they (as well as clay and wooden containers) can be treated with chemical fumigants.

Tools are another source of disease inoculum. They should be periodically disinfected to prevent the spread of any disease that might be present in the range and certainly before using a recently pasteurized medium. Many florist supply firms sell a hospital-type disinfectant that can be maintained in a bucket conveniently located in the headhouse and in the greenhouses so that tools can be easily dipped in it. Household bleach diluted 1:9 with water serves well also, but it will break down in sunlight in a day or so. These disinfectants work well for plastic pots as well.

Another common source of contamination is the soil on the soles and heels of shoes. Placing one's foot on the side of a bench in the greenhouse is an efficient way to transfer inoculum. Visitors with an interest in plants have probably been in another greenhouse range or a garden, and the probability of their carrying contaminated soil is great. It should be a standard rule around the greenhouse that feet are to be kept off the benches. Some growers place a fiber mat in a shallow tray of a disinfectant solution at the entry to their range so that everyone steps through it, disinfecting his or her shoes before entering. This is a particularly wise practice for a propagation greenhouse, where disease prevention is an even more serious matter.

Plastic watering systems become distorted when left under the cover during steam pasteurization. They are customarily removed or raised above the bench during pasteurization. They should be syringed with household bleach diluted 1:9 with water or with a disinfectant before they are placed back on the root medium.

In a small operation, these pipes may be wiped with a rag saturated with disinfectant. The thin tubes and weights used in automatic pot-watering systems should be dipped in a container of disinfectant. Wire and string supports for fresh flowers should likewise be sterilized before they are reused on a recently pasteurized bench.

For pasteurization to be effective, the grower must think through all operations to identify and correct those that can cause reinoculation of the growing media. Means exist to ensure a clean range. Where failure occurs, it is due to a lack of foresight.

ECONOMICS

Steam pasteurization is particularly desirable when the steam can be obtained from an already existent heating system. An average of 5,600 Btu of boiler capacity is required to supply the 2,800 Btu needed to pasteurize 1 ft^3 of root medium. One gallon of oil with an approximate heat content of 135,000 Btu and a burning efficiency of 75 percent provides sufficient heat to pasteurize 18 ft^3 of root medium. The fuel cost per cubic foot is therefore $0.039/$ft^3$ ($1.38/$m^3$) based on a price of $0.70 per gallon.

Methyl bromide in 1 pound cans can be purchased for $1.43 and is sufficient to treat 27 ft^3 of soil. The unit price here is $0.053/$ft^3$ (1.58/m^3).

There are other economic considerations. A large operator without a central steam source could easily depreciate the cost of a steam generator and still end up pasteurizing root media for an acceptable cost. A small grower, or one who operates only during one season per year, often finds the cost of steam pasteurization unacceptable if he or she must purchase a steam generator.

For the purpose of illustration, a 1 acre greenhouse range could be expected to have 29,000 ft^2 of bench area containing 16,900 ft^3 of root media. A $4,000 steam generator financed for 10 years at 12 percent interest would add $0.041 to each cubic foot of media for a total oil-plus-equipment cost of $0.080 ($2.82/m^3).

One last factor must be considered, and that is the cost of labor required to carry out each method of pasteurization. Preparation of media is the same in each alternative, calling for a loose, moderately moist condition. Covers are needed for each alternative also. The differences lie principally in the steam conduction hose or pipes to and in the bench. This is a very small consideration and would not likely influence the decision as to which system to use.

SUMMARY

1. Greenhouse root media should be pasteurized at least once per year, and more often as required, to rid them of harmful disease organisms, nematodes, insects, and weed seed.

2. Numerous microorganisms develop in root media that are not harmful. These can be beneficial by providing competition for harmful microorganisms, which might otherwise proliferate. For this reason, root media are pasteurized and not sterilized; that is, only some organisms are killed.
3. A root medium may be pasteurized with steam by raising it to a temperature of 160°F (71°C) for 30 minutes.
4. Volatile chemicals also are used for pasteurizing root media. Methyl bromide is most popular, although chloropicrin is used as well, especially for carnation crops, which are injured by methyl bromide residues for a few months after application. Chemical pasteurization precludes the need for a steam boiler—an advantage for field and small-greenhouse growers.
5. Both steam and chemical pasteurization require that the root medium be loose and of a moisture content suitable for planting. Amendments such as peat moss, manure, and bark should be incorporated prior to pasteurization to prevent introduction of diseases or pests.
6. Pasteurization can result in ammonium and manganese toxicities in certain situations. If the root medium contains organic matter rich in nitrogen, such as manure, steam and chemical pasteurization can result in an excessive release of ammonium, particularly in the period of two to six weeks after pasteurization. Either these materials should be avoided, or an adjustment should be made in the watering practice to ensure adequate leaching of ammonium. Many soils contain large levels of manganese, most of which is unavailable. Steam pasteurization causes a conversion of unavailable manganese to an available form. A toxic level is sometimes reached. This is another reason for pasteurizing root media at a low temperature (160°F, 71°C) and for only the necessary length of time (30 minutes).
7. Pasteurization of root media is designed to eliminate harmful organisms. It does not protect against future infestation. Good sanitation practices must be employed to maintain clean conditions. Some considerations include disease-free seeds and plants, sterilization of containers and tools, a pesticide program, foot baths, a clean working area, sanitation outside the greenhouse, and proper control of temperature and humidity.

REFERENCES

1. Baker, K. F., ed. 1957. The U.C. system for producing healthy container-grown plants. Univ. of California Agr. Exp. Sta. and Ext. Ser. Manual 23. Berkeley, CA.
2. Ball, V. 1975. Soil sterilizing—steam. In Ball, V., ed. *The Ball Red Book,* 13th ed., pp. 91–107. West Chicago, IL: Geo. J. Ball, Inc.
3. Bunt, A. C. 1976. *Modern Potting Composts,* pp. 229–251. University Park, PA: The Pennsylvania State Univ. Press.

4. Gray, H. E. 1960. Steam sterilization. *Florists' Review* 127 (3292):13–14, 77–79.

5. Griffin, R., R. Maire, and W. Humphrey. 1965. Sterilizing nursery soils with steam—a new method. Univ. of California Agr. Ext. Ser. Pub. AXT–177.

6. Horst, K. 1985. Chemicals for sterilizing. In Ball, V., ed. *The Ball Red Book,* 14th ed., pp. 133–145. Englewood Cliffs, NJ: Reston Publishing (a Prentice-Hall Co.).

CHAPTER 7

Watering

Watering is the greenhouse operation that most frequently accounts for loss in crop quality. Taken at face value, it would appear to be the simplest operation. When performed correctly, it is simple and perhaps a bit boring. For this reason, the task is often mistakenly assigned to a less experienced employee. If this employee waters at the wrong times or uses an incorrect amount of water, the crop will be injured. The original quality cannot be regained.

The decision of when to water should be made by the greenhouse manager. He or she should inspect every bench of plants daily and should supervise the watering operation when it is carried out by another employee. Actually, with the wide variety of inexpensive automatic watering systems available today, the range should be equipped with a system simple enough to permit the manager to do the actual watering while inspecting the range. The few minutes it takes for each section to be watered affords the manager a chance to further inspect plants in each section for insects, disease, nutritional disorders, and any other problems. Success or failure is due not so much to the quantity of labor expended as to the correct timing of the various labor operations. It is of utmost importance that the greenhouse range be inspected daily by the most knowledgeable person and that work plans be altered by his or her findings.

EFFECTS OF WATERING ON PLANTS

Underwatering

When water is not applied frequently enough, plants wilt, thus retarding photosynthesis and slowing growth. The elongation of young developing cells is reduced, resulting in smaller leaves, shorter stem internodes (the length of stem between leaves), and, in general, a hardened appearance to the plants. In more extreme cases, burns may begin on the margins of leaves and spread inward, affecting whole leaves. On plant species capable of leaf abscission, the leaves will drop off. Before the days of chemical height retardants, it was customary to control height of some crops by allowing plants to wilt between waterings. Today, this practice is restricted primarily to bedding plants. The availability of chemical height retardants and the risk of foliar injury from drying has brought about this change.

Overwatering

When water is applied a little too frequently, new growth may become large but soft as a result of high water content, and, as a whole, plants tend to be taller. This situation is undesirable because some of these plants wilt easily under bright light or dry conditions and do not ship or last well. If water is supplied even more frequently, the oxygen content of the root medium is reduced by the higher average content of water in the pores, resulting in damage to the roots. A damaged root system cannot readily take up water or nutrients. This condition causes wilting, hardened growth, an overall stunting of the plants, and several nutrient-deficiency symptoms.

RULES OF WATERING

Rule 1: Use a Well-Drained Medium

The importance of texture and structure was brought out in Chapter 5. If the root medium is not well drained and aerated, then proper watering cannot be done. Either you will underwater to achieve aeration, or you will provide the required water at the expense of aeration. In either case, poor plant quality will result. A well-drained medium of high water-holding capacity is required for use in containers. This calls for coarse texture and a high degree of stable structure—in short, a formulated medium and not field soil alone.

Rule 2: Water Thoroughly Each Time

Because media cannot be partially wetted, it is important to water all of the medium in a container each time water is applied (Figure 7–1). Water applied to the root surface of the medium enters the pores at the top and adheres to the particle surfaces making up the pore walls. Additional water causes the layer on the particle surfaces to become thicker. Eventually, the layer of water becomes thick enough that any additional water is too far away from the particle surface to be held, and gravity pulls this additional water down to the next particle below. There, it is attracted to the particle surface, and as more water enters, the water layer on this particle grows thicker. This process keeps repeating itself until water finally reaches the particles at the bottom of the container. Additional water then flows through the medium and out the bottom of the container.

If 6 ounces of water are required to water the root medium in one pot and only 3 ounces of water are applied, the medium in the top half of the pot will be thoroughly wetted while the medium in the lower half will remain dry. Late in the afternoon or on Saturdays, there is always a temptation to water a crop partially to carry it over until more time is available for watering. From the preceding discussion, one can readily see the fallacy of doing this. The root medium in the lower part of the pot or bench will not receive water, and, as it continues to dry, roots will die.

It is important to apply, besides the amount of water needed for wetting all of the medium, an additional amount. Some 10–15 percent of the water applied

Figure 7–1

Only half of the amount of water the soil in the beaker is capable of holding was applied. Instead of all the particles being partially wetted, those at the top are thoroughly wetted, while those at the bottom remain completely dry. This points out the fallacy of trying to partially water a root medium.

to a pot or bench should run out of the bottom. This is done to leach excessive fertilizers and nonfertilizer elements that might otherwise build up to toxic levels. Some fertilizers contain elements that are not used in large quantity by plants. As fertilizer is repeatedly applied to provide the elements needed in large quantity, these other elements accumulate.

As a general rule of thumb for soil-based media, 1/15 gallon of water should be applied to each square foot of bench for each inch of root-medium depth. A typical bench 8 inches deep containing 7 inches of medium should receive 7/15 gallon of water, or in practical terms, ½ gallon of water per square foot. (Apply 1.1 l per square meter per centimeter depth or 20 l per square meter to an 18 cm deep bed.) A 6 inch (15 cm) azalea pot requires about 10–12 ounces (300–350 ml) of water. This rule applies to the application of nutrient solution as well as to water. These quantities of water should be checked out for each individual situation since media vary in water-holding capacity. Large or smaller quantities may be justified for various soil-less media.

Rule 3: Water Just Before Moisture Stress Occurs

It is apparent from rule 2 that overwatering does not refer to the amount of water applied during a single application. Overwatering indicates that water is applied too frequently. When this is done, too much of the lifetime of the root is spent under conditions of minimum aeration, and as a result root development is suppressed.

Water should be applied just before the plant enters into the early symptoms of water stress. For each plant, these signs are different. Some plants, such as chrysanthemum, take on a darker leaf color; others, such as begonia, exhibit a gray-green leaf color. By observing a crop, one can quickly learn the early warning signs of moisture stress. It is important that the color and feel of the root medium associated with early moisture stress also be learned. Some crops, such as azalea, do not show signs of moisture stress until permanent damage occurs to the roots. Judgment of when to water rests in this case entirely on media appearance, feel, and weight.

WATER QUALITY

It is very important to know the chemical content of water to be used in the greenhouse. A common problem is that of *salinity* (a high salt content). This problem occurs frequently along coastal areas, where seawater may infiltrate the groundwater. Quantities of sodium bicarbonate or sodium chloride can become high enough to be injurious to plants. Groundwater in the southwestern United States can contain excessive quantities of sodium and boron. A total-soluble-salt reading gives a good assessment of this problem.

Listed in Table 7–1 are several problems that can occur in irrigation water. This water may also have a high salt content. If so, the water should be analyzed and those specific elements making up the salts should be avoided or at least reduced in the fertilizer program. When high salt levels exist, the root medium should not be allowed to dry excessively since that would concentrate the salts. Removal of salts is expensive. Reverse-osmosis systems have been used successfully by a few greenhouse firms, but the added cost of these systems renders a firm less competitive.

High boron is a problem in many arid, coastal regions. Boron availability to plants can be reduced by precipitating it in the root medium with calcium. Adding calcium or raising the pH to the upper end of the safe range for a crop will lessen a boron toxicity.

Table 7–1

Water-Quality Guidelines[1]

	Degree of Problem		
Type of Problem	*None*	*Increasing*	*Very Severe*
Salinity			
EC (mmho/cm)[2] *or*	Less than 0.75	0.75–3.0	More than 3.0
Total dissolved solids (mg/l)[3]	Less than 480	480–1,920	More than 1,920
Toxicity of specific ions to sensitive crops			
Related to soil:			
Chloride (me/l)	Less than 2	2–10	More than 10
(mg/l)	Less than 70	70–345	More than 345
Boron (mg/l)	1.0	1.0–2.0	2.0–10.0
Related to foliar adsorption (sprinkler irrigated):			
Sodium (me/l)	Less than 3.0	More than 3	—
(mg/l)	Less than 70	70	—
Chloride (me/l)	Less than 3.0	More than 3	—
(mg/l)	Less than 100	100	—
Miscellaneous			
Bicarbonate (me/l)	Less than 1.5	1.5–8.5	More than 8.5
(mg/l)	Less than 40	40–520	More than 520

[1]From Farnham, Ayers, and Hasek (1977). Interpretation is related to type of problem and its severity but modified by circumstances of soil, crop, and local experience.

[2]mmho/cm = 100 mho × 10^{-5}/cm.

[3]mg/l = ppm.

Bicarbonate is particularly damaging to plants. It causes variable chlorosis over plants, burning of leaf margins, and generally poor growth. Besides by reverse osmosis, bicarbonate can be removed by acidifying the water with acids such as sulfuric acid, nitric acid, or phosphoric acid. Phosphoric acid is the safest of the three to handle. These acids may be injected into the water source (Matkin and Petersen 1971). At the lower pH level desired for plant growth, much of the bicarbonate converts to carbon dioxide gas and water. A pH level of 6.0 is often used.

To determine the amount of 75 percent phosphoric acid to use, one multiplies the milliequivalents (me) of carbonate hardness per liter, which is given in a water test report, by 7. The resulting answer is the number of fluid ounces of phosphoric acid to inject into 1,000 gallons of water (1 fl oz/1,000 gal = 7.8 ml/1,000 l). If hardness is reported in terms of ppm of calcium carbonate hardness instead of me, one divides the ppm figure by 50 to convert to the me number. Realizing that phosphoric acid is a phosphorus source, one must reduce the amount of phosphorus in the fertilizer program accordingly. For each fluid ounce of phosphoric acid that is injected into 1,000 gallons of water, a phosphorus (P_2O_5) concentration of 6.6 ppm is achieved. Food-grade phosphoric acid should be used because it is free of heavy-metal contaminants.

Either sulfuric acid or nitric acid may be used in the place of phosphoric acid. If sulfuric acid is used instead of phosphoric acid, one multiplies the me of carbonate hardness in the water supply by 3.2. The resulting figure is the number of fluid ounces of 66° Baumé-grade (98 percent) sulfuric acid to use in 1,000 gallons of water. To determine the amount of 42° Baumé-grade (67 percent) nitric acid to inject into 1,000 gallons of water, one multiplies the me of carbonate hardness by 10.5. A concentration of 1.7 ppm nitrogen (N) will result from the addition of each fluid ounce of nitric acid to 1,000 gallons of water.

When one encounters poor water quality, it is worth consulting an area hydrologist or perhaps a well-drilling firm for advice. Drilling into a different stratum has solved many problems.

City water is not free of problems. Chlorination of water normally does not affect greenhouse crops unless they are grown hydroponically. A chlorine concentration of 0.4 ppm can cause root-tip injury to some crops, including chrysanthemum and rose grown in nutrient solutions. Municipalities may inject 0.7 ppm chlorine into the water; however, much of it will volatilize from the water or change to the safe chloride form by the time it gets to the greenhouse bench. It does not appear that chlorinated water is injurious to plants in any solid root medium.

Fluoridation does cause injury to some crops. The 0.5–1 ppm concentration of fluoride that is added to many water supplies to reduce the incidence of tooth decay is injurious to some green plants. Plants that are highly sensitive to fluoride are as follows: *Chlorophytum* (spider plant), *Cordyline terminalis* (mainly the cultivar 'Baby Doll'), and *Dracaena deremensis* (mainly the cultivars 'Janet Craig' and "Warneckii'). Sensitive plants include: *Dracaena fragens* (corn plant), *Maranta leuconeura erythroneura* (red nerve plant), *Maranta leuconeura kerchoviana* (prayer plant), *Spathiphyllum* (most species), *Yucca elephantipes* (spineless yucca), *Ctenanthe oppenheimiana, Ctenanthe amabilis* and *Chamaedorea elegans*. Plants that are probably sensitive are *Chamaedorea sigfritzii, Aspidistra eleatior, Calathea insignis, Calathea makoyana, Dracaena marginata, Dracaena sanderana*, and *Pleomele thalioides*. It is interesting to note that most of the plants belong to the families Liliaceae and Marantaceae. For these crops, it is best to avoid fluoridated water. The pH level of their root media can also be raised to tie up fluoride.

WATERING SYSTEMS

Hand Watering

Hand watering today is uneconomical. A grower can afford hand watering only where a crop is still at a high density, such as in seed flats, or when he or she is "spot watering"—that is, watering a few select pots or areas that have dried sooner than others. We will first consider the price of handwatering a bench 4 feet wide by 100 feet long (1.22 m by 30 m) and then compare this price to those of automatic systems for watering a bench of equal size. The price of materials in each system is based on minimum order rates, which maximizes the cost. The water main to each bench is not calculated into the cost of each system. The labor of installation is not included either but is quite minimal. A fair estimation of time required to install an automatic system on one bench would be four hours. Thus, the labor bill would be only about $40.00 at an hourly rate of $8.00 plus all benefits. (Benefits include two 15-minute coffee breaks per day, six holidays, five vacation days, five sick leave days, unemployment insurance, workmen's compensation, and social security for a total of 23.5 percent of the hourly rate.) In all cases, the labor saved will pay for the automatic system in less than one year.

A bench area of 400 ft^2 (37 m^2) with a fresh flower crop requires 200 gallons (750 l) of water at each watering. The frequency of watering can range from once a week in the dark part of the winter to more than 3 times a week during the summer. Taking a conservative average of 2 times per week, the bench is watered 104 times in a year. At a water flow rate of 8 gpm (30 l/min), which is not uncommon for a ¾ inch (19 mm) hose, 25 minutes are required to apply 200 gallons (750 l). For the whole year, 43.3 hours are spent watering one 4 foot by 100 foot (1.22 m by 30 m) bench. At an hourly rate of $6.00 plus 23 percent in benefits, the cost is $320.85.

It soon will become apparent that this cost is too high. In addition to this deterrent to hand watering, there is a great risk of applying too little water or of waiting too long between waterings. Hand watering requires considerable time and is very boring. It is usually performed by inexperienced (lower-paid) employees who may be tempted to speed up the job or put it off to another time. Automatic watering is rapid and easy and is performed by a manager, who is less tempted to submit to error. Where hand watering is practiced, a water breaker should be used on the end of the hose (Figure 7–2). Such a device breaks the force of the water, permitting a higher flow rate without washing the root medium out of the bench or pot. It also lessens the risk of disrupting the structure of the root-medium surface.

Perimeter Watering System for Fresh Flowers

A perimeter watering system consists of a plastic pipe around the perimeter of a bench with nozzles that spray water over the root-medium surface below the foliage (Figure 7–3). Either polyethylene or PVC pipe can be used. While PVC pipe has the advantage of being very stationary, polyethylene pipe tends to roll if it is not anchored firmly to the side of the bench. This causes nozzles to rise or fall from proper orientation with the root-medium surface.

Nozzles are made of nylon or a hard plastic and are available to put out a spray arc of 180°, 90°, or 45°. For fresh flowers other than roses in benches up to 42 inches (107 cm) wide and for rose benches up to 48 inches (122 cm) wide, the 180° nozzles are used and are spaced 30 inches (76 cm) apart. For fresh flowers other than roses in benches 48 inches (122 cm) wide, 180° and 90° or 45° nozzles are alternated 20 inches (51 cm) apart. The 90° and 45° nozzles project water far-

Figure 7–2

The device on the end of the hose is a water breaker. It reduces the force of water striking the root medium by increasing the cross-sectional area through which it flows. Reduced water pressure minimizes the breakdown of the root-medium structure and the loss of medium from containers.

Figure 7–3

A perimeter watering system for fresh flower production in benches or beds. A polyethylene or PVC pipe carries water around the perimeter of the bed. Plastic or nylon nozzles screwed into the perimeter pipe spray water into the bed below the foliage.

ther into a bed than the 180° nozzles do. Regardless of the types of nozzles used, they are staggered across the benches so that each nozzle projects out between two other nozzles on the opposite side. A hole is punched in the polyethylene pipe or drilled in the PVC pipe, and the threaded nozzle is then turned in with a wrench.

Perimeter watering systems with 180° nozzles require one water valve for benches up to 100 feet in length. For benches over 100 feet (30 m) and up to 200 feet (61 m), a water main should be brought to the middle of a bench and ¾ inch (19 mm) water valves should be installed on either side, one to service each half of the bench. This system applies 1/10 gpm of water per foot of pipe (1.25 l/min/of pipe). Where 180° and 90° or 45° nozzles are alternated, the length of a bench serviced by one water valve should not exceed 75 feet (23 m).

The cost of this perimeter watering system for a 4 foot by 100 foot (1.22 m by 30 m) bench with alternating 180° and 90° nozzles is $76.86. This includes PVC pipe and two water valves. The cost breakdown is as follows:

2	¾ in. valves	$15.00
15	¾ in. PVC pipe fittings	4.96
210 ft	¾ in. PVC pipe	39.90
120	nozzles	12.00
		$76.86

Dew-Hose® System for Fresh Flowers

The Dew-Hose® system utilizes 1¼ inch (32 mm) wide (when flat) polyethylene tubes that run along the length of a bench at 8 inch (20 cm) intervals. The Dew-Hose® is connected to a ¾ inch (19 mm) polyethylene pipe that runs across the ends of benches up to 60 feet (18 m) long or crosses benches at their midpoint if the benches are up to 120 feet (37 m) long (Figure 7–4a). Individual Dew-Hose® lengths must not exceed 60 feet (18 m). A single ¾ inch (19 mm) water supply can handle up to 1,200 ft² (111 m²) of level bench.

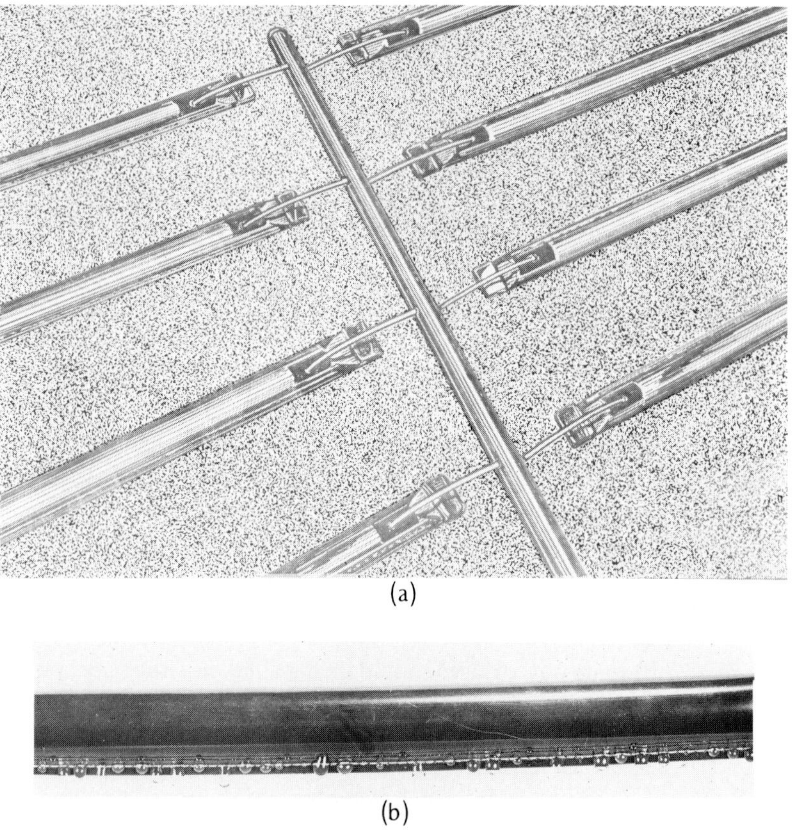

(a)

(b)

Figure 7–4

A Dew-Hose® system of automatic watering for fresh flower production: (a) A supply-tube connection for a Dew-Hose® or a Turbulent Twin Wall® watering system. Hoses run the length of the bench and are spaced 8 inches (20 cm) apart. (b) Water seeps out of the stitching along one side of the hose. The same method of release occurs in the Ooze-Header® and Jumbo Header® systems. (*Photos courtesy of Chapin Watermatics, Inc., Watertown,* NY 13601)

The Dew-Hose® is manufactured from a flat piece of black, 8 mil (0.2 mm) polyethylene that is sewn into a tube with plastic thread. Under pressure, water oozes from the stitching (Figure 7–4b). A water pressure of 4–9 psi (28–62 kPa) within the Dew-Hose® is applied. To prevent plugging, a 150 mesh strainer should be installed in the water supply.

The cost for this Dew-Hose® system for a 4 foot by 100 foot (1.22 m by 30 m) bench is $42.21. This includes a ¾ inch (19 mm) valve and a header at the midpoint of the bench. The cost breakdown is as follows:

600 ft	Dew-Hose®	$27.60
1	header kit	5.75
5	¾ in. plastic pipe fittings	1.36
1	¾ in. valve	7.50
		$42.21

Ooze-Header® System for Fresh Flowers

The Ooze-Header® system is similar to the Dew-Hose® system except that the tubes run across benches at 8 inch (20 cm) intervals from a ½ inch (13 mm) polyethylene header pipe that runs along the length of one side of each bench (Figure 7–5). The ooze tubes are of the same construction as Dew-Hose®, but they are ⅝ inch (16 m) wide. They are used in lengths 2 inches (5 cm) shorter than the width of the bench they service in order to accommodate the header pipe. Each ooze tube is sealed at both ends, but extending from one is a thin polyethylene supply tube that is inserted into a hole in the ½ inch (13 mm) polyethylene header pipe. Brass inserts may be installed in the header pipe, and holes can be made in the header pipe with a hand punch fashioned after an ice pick or with a commercially available Quik-Punch® tool. Squeezing the handle of this tool drives a punch through one wall of the pipe. The supply tube is immediately pushed into the hole. The flexible wall of the header pipe expands toward the center of the hole, thus squeezing the supply tube to make a watertight seal. A water pressure of 4–9 psi (28–62 kPa) is used in this system. As much as 1,200–1,600 ft^2 (110–150 m^2) of bench can be handled by a ¾ inch (19 mm) water supply system.

The Ooze-Header® system drips water slowly onto the root-medium surface and depends upon lateral movement of water a distance of 4 inches (10 cm) from either side of each tube. Some media that are unusually porous may undergo channeling of the water downward without sufficient lateral movement to wet all areas, particularly those at the upper surface. In this case, puddling from a more rapid application is needed. Jumbo Oozers® are used for this purpose. They are

Figure 7–5

An Ooze-Header® system of automatic watering for fresh flower production. Ooze-Headers® run across the bed at 8 inch (20 cm) intervals and are supplied water through a thin polyethylene tube connected to a ½ inch (13 mm) plastic water line along one side of the bed. (*Photo courtesy of Chapin Watermatics, Inc., Watertown,* NY 13601)

the same as Ooze-Headers® except that they are 1¼ inches (32 mm) wide and are attached to a ¾ inch (19 mm) polyethylene pipe along the length of the bench. One ¾ inch (19 mm) water supply system will handle 600–800 ft² (55–75 m²) of bench.

The Ooze-Header® system for a 4 foot by 100 foot (1.22 m by 30 m) bench costs $69.86. This includes a ¾ inch (19 mm) valve and a ½ inch (13 mm) polyethylene header pipe with ⅝ inch (16 mm) Ooze-Header® tubes at 8 inch (20 cm) intervals across the bench. The cost breakdown is as follows:

100 ft	½ in. polyethylene pipe	$ 8.00
150	46 in. Ooze-Headers®	52.50
7	plastic pipe fittings	1.86
1	¾ in. valve	7.50
		$69.86

Turbulent Twin-Wall® Hose System for Fresh Flowers

The Turbulent Twin-Wall® hose system (Figure 7–6) is considerably more popular than the Dew-Hose® or Ooze-Header® systems because longer lengths of bench can be handled from a single header (over 200 feet, 61 m) and because this hose better equalizes water pressure along the length of sloping benches (slopes up to 2 percent).

Turbulent Twin-Wall® hose, when flat in the roll, is 1 inch wide (2.5 cm) and is constructed from 10 or 15 mil (0.025 or 0.038 mm) black polyethylene. While the 10 mil hose is most popular for cut flower application, the 15 mil hose will last longer. Water outlet spacings are available at 2 or 4 inch (5 or 10 cm) intervals. Water flow rates for the 2 and 4 inch spacing tubes are 1.5 and 1.0 gpm per 100 feet of tube (5.7 and 3.8 l per min per 30 m), respectively. The recommended pressure for this system is 10 psi (70 kPa).

Turbulent Twin-Wall® tubes are placed on the surface of the medium from end to end in the bench. Individual hoses are spaced 8 inches (20 cm) across the bench. Each end of each hose is folded over double and clamped with an end closer supplied by the manufacturer. A small hole is made through the wall of the hose near the inlet end with a piercing tool. One end of a supply tube is inserted through the hole, and the other end of the supply tube is connected to a ¾ inch (19 mm) polyethylene header running across the end or midpoint of the bench (Figure 7–4a).

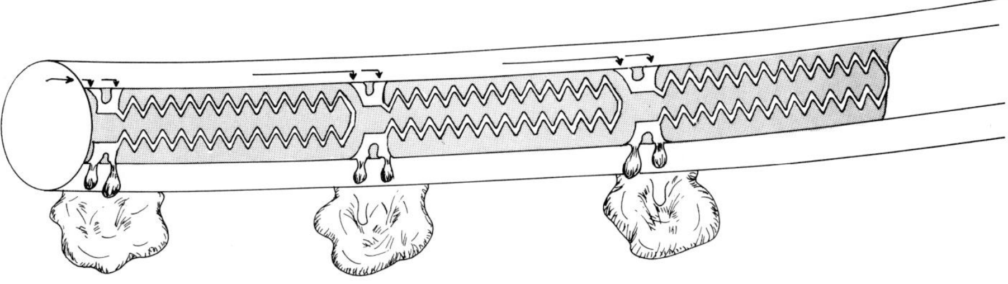

Figure 7–6

A cutaway view of a Turbulent Twin-Wall® hose. Water enters the large tube and quickly runs the length of the bed. Water then moves through pores in the upper wall of the large tube into the small turbulent channel. Water in the turbulent channel moves along a serrated path that produces a turbulent flow. After flowing a short distance, water turns 180° and flows back to a point opposite to where it entered the turbulent channel. At this point, water drips out onto the root medium. The turbulent flow helps prevent blockage from debris.

A Turbulent Twin-Wall® hose system for a 4 foot by 100 foot (1.22 m by 30 m) bench making use of six lengths of 10 mil hose with outlets every 1.5 inches (3.8 cm) and a ¾ inch (19 mm) polyethylene header with a valve costs $30.98. The cost breakdown is as follows:

600 ft	10 mil Turbulent Twin-Wall® hose	$18.60
6	supply tubes	0.66
12	end closers	0.96
5	¾ in. PVC pipe fittings	1.36
10 ft	¾ in. PVC pipe	1.90
1	¾ in. valve	7.50
		$30.98

Tube Watering System for Potted Plants

Tube watering has been the standard for automatic watering of potted plants. Water is carried to each pot by a thin polyethylene microtube (Figure 7–7). The tube is available in various inside diameters from different sources including 0.036, 0.045, 0.050, 0.060, 0.075, and 0.076 inch (0.9, 1.1, 1.3, 1.5, 1.9, and 1.9 mm). The number of pots that can be watered from a single ¾ inch (19 mm) water main depends upon this inside diameter. The 0.036, 0.050, 0.060, and 0.076 inch microtubes can handle 1,600, 900, 700, and 400 pots, respectively. The narrower-diameter microtubes are used for small pots, where the density is high in the bench and the water requirement per pot is low. This minimizes the expense of laying larger water lines. The 0.060 inch (1.5 mm) size is popular for 6 inch (15 cm) pots, and the 0.075 or 0.076 inch (1.9 mm) size is used for 2–5 gallon (7.5 18 l) containers for such items as poinsettia stock plants.

The microtube must have a weight at the end in the pot to prevent it from being thrown from the pot when the water is turned on. The weight further serves the purpose of breaking the force of water so that it does not dig a hole in the root medium. Usually, there is a baffle in the weight opposite the outlet end of the microtube that breaks the flow of water and permits it to trickle out either side. The weight also prevents light root-media components from being drawn into the microtube and plugging it. When the water is turned off, a suction often occurs, which can draw particles into the microtube. Various types of weights are sold. One weight consists of a plastic cylinder with the tube entering through the side (Figure 7–7). Drop-in weights are conical in shape and are made of noncorrosive metal. On–Off® tubes are available in the 0.076 inch (1.9 mm) size and are also made of noncorrosive metal. When a pot is removed, the microtube can be sealed by pushing the On–Off® weight. A quick pull on it turns it on again.

Figure 7–7

The "tube system" is used for automatic watering of potted plants. Water is carried the length of the bench in a plastic pipe generally located down the center. Each pot is connected to the central pipe by a separate small polyethylene tube. A weight is attached to the end of the tube in each pot to anchor the tube and to break the force of the water before it reaches the root medium.

Generally, water is provided along the bench by a ¾ inch (19 mm) polyethylene or PVC pipe. The latter lies straighter. Microtubes to each pot may be connected directly into holes punched or drilled into the water pipe, which is usually run down the center of the bench from end to end. The microtube can be pushed into the hole directly, or a brass insert can be pressed into the hole first and the microtube inserted into it. The brass insert facilitates subsequent removal and replacement of microtubes. Plugs are available to fill holes left by removed microtubes.

Each microtube must be the same length because the flow rate depends upon the length of the microtube. To cut down on the quantity of tubing, particularly in benches with numerous small pots, Long-Header® and Add-A-Header® systems are used. In each case, a number of microtubes run from a plastic header; the header, in turn, is connected to the water main by a single larger tube.

Microtube watering can be used for hanging baskets as well (Figure 7–8). A plastic water line is run along the length of a row of baskets. A separate thin polyethylene microtube connects each pot to the water line. Some growers install a galvanized water pipe and hang pots directly from it.

Figure 7–8

An automatic tube watering system for hanging baskets. Each pot is connected to the plastic water line above by a thin polyethylene tube.

When a coarse root medium is used in large pots, it becomes difficult to wet all of the medium in the pot. Water slowly flowing from a tube tends to channel down through the root medium in a conical shape. In such situations, a Spray Tube® water distributor can be used (Figure 7–9). Water is delivered at a greater flow rate and is sprayed out over the surface of the pot. This works well for plants that have little foliage at the base and that are in 6 inch (15 cm) or larger pots.

A microtube system of pot plant watering for a 4 foot by 100 foot (1.22 m by 30 m) bench costs $111.10. This includes a manual valve, a ¾ inch (19 mm) PVC water main along the length of the bench in the center, and 400 24 inch (61 cm) tubes with weights and brass inserts where each is connected directly to the water main. The cost breakdown is as follows:

100 ft	¾ in. PVC pipe	$ 19.00
400	24 in. 0.060 ID microtubes with weights	80.00
400	brass inserts	3.00
1	¾ in. valve	7.50
6	¾ in. PVC pipe fittings	1.60
		$111.10

Mat Watering System for Potted Plants

Mat (capillary) watering offers a very good alternative for the pot plant grower who has different pot sizes in a given bench during the year (Figure 7–10). The tube system would require a constant removal and addition of tubes to suit the changing pot density. Mat watering is also beneficial to the grower of small potted

Figure 7–9

A Spray Tube® water distributor. This method of water distribution is used in larger pots and in root media that is very porous, such as that used for orchids. Broad distribution of water over the surface of the pot reduces the problem of water channeling down through the root medium.

plants where it is best not to wet the foliage. The number of tubes in such a system would be cumbersome. The mat watering system uses a mat from 3/16 to 1/2 inch (5–13 mm) thick that is kept constantly moist. Pots are set on the mat and take up water by capillarity through holes in the bottom of the pots. Pots of any size can be placed on the mat at one time. No adjustment is needed for shifting pot sizes.

Mat watering is an old system based on subirrigation. Years ago, sand was placed in a bench and kept moist. Pots were set in the sand, and water continuously rose by capillarity into the root medium in the pots. This system maintains a constant moisture content in the pot and greatly reduces the labor of watering.

A number of mats are available, but to use them, benches should be level. A polyethylene sheet is placed on the level bottom of each bench. It is preferable, but not necessary, that it be black to reduce light in the mat and, thus, algal growth. A sheet of 2 mil (0.05 mm) thickness is sufficient since its only role is to serve as a water barrier. The mat is placed on the polyethylene sheet. Care should be taken to keep the edges of the mat level with the plane of the mat. If they are lower, they act as a wick, drawing water from the mat and dripping it to the ground. Mats can be cut with a scissors, and more than one piece can be used to line a bench by butting the edges together. Various types of mats are used. One

Figure 7–10

A mat (capillary) watering system for pot plant crops. Water is applied to the mat several times a day through tubes such as Turbulent Twin Wall® or Dew-Hose® that are spaced 2 feet apart. Water moves by capillarity from the mat into the root medium in the pot and maintains a constant moisture content in the pot at all times. Various types of mats are available.

branch makes use of reprocessed cloth, while others are composed of virgin synthetic fiber.

Watering tubes including Turbulent Twin-Wall® and Dew-Hose® are used to deliver water to the mat. These tubes run the length of the bench and are placed 2 feet (61 cm) apart. The mat should be kept moist at all times. Often, water application is required several times per day. A time clock can be set to activate a solenoid water valve. Overwatering is not a problem because excess water simply drips from the edge of the mat.

Algae is a problem in that it is very unsightly on the mat and on pots, it harbors insects, and it emits a foul odor upon drying. Much of the algae can be washed off periodically under a strong stream of water from a hose. Caution should be exercised here since some mats may not stand up to the pressure. Disinfectants such as bleach may also be used but should be washed from the mat after use. Disease organisms can build up on mats. Following any crop in which disease appears, the mat should be sterilized with a material such as bleach. A 1:9 bleach-to-water solution can be sprinkled on, allowed to sit for 5–10 minutes, and then hosed off. Some mats will withstand steaming, which kills algae.

Nutrient solutions can be applied to the mat on a continuous basis as a sole source of fertilizer for crops. Generally, 200 ppm each of nitrogen (N) and potassium (K_2O) and 100 ppm of phosphorus (P_2O_5) provide a good starting concentration. The more common problem encountered is a buildup of salts in the root medium. Water utilization generally exceeds nutrient uptake; thus, fertilizer salts concentrate, particularly at the top of the pot. This situation should be monitored through periodic soluble-salt tests (Chapter 8). When it occurs, pots should be watered one time heavily from the top to leach the root medium.

Algal buildup is a problem on mats supplied with fertilizer solution. Black perforated polyethylene (up to 150,000 perforations per square meter) is available alone or in combination with mats. The perforated polyethylene lies on the mat, and the pots rest on the plastic. This film restricts light from the mat, which blocks algal growth, and is easy to wash. Roots do not penetrate the polyethylene film.

The cost of materials in a mat watering system can range from about $92 to $162. The variation is due to the type of mat used. The example system includes a ¾ inch (19 mm) manual valve, ¾ inch (19 mm) header system, two lengths of Turbulent Twin Wall® hose for water distribution, and a 4 mil (0.05 mm) black polyethylene underliner. The cost breakdown is as follows:

400 sq ft	Mat	$66.80–$136.00
200 ft	Turbulent Twin Wall® tube plus connectors	6.74
400 sq ft	black, 4 mil polyethylene	10.00
1	¾ in. valve	7.50
5	¾ in. plastic header fittings	1.36
		$92.40–$161.60

Overhead Spray for Potted Plants

While the foliage on the majority of crops should be kept dry for disease-control purposes, a few crops do tolerate wet foliage. These crops can most easily and cheaply be irrigated from overhead. Bedding plants, field-grown fresh flowers, some green plants, and azalea liners are crops commonly watered from overhead.

A pipe is installed along the middle of a bed. Riser pipes are installed periodically to a height well above the final height of the crop. Usually 2 feet (0.6 m) is sufficient for bedding plant flats and 6 feet (1.8 m) for fresh flowers. A nozzle is installed at the top of each riser. Nozzles vary from those that throw a 360° pattern continuously to types that rotate around a 360° circle. Nozzles with a 180° arc can be obtained for the ends of beds. The spray diameter of various nozzles can range up to 36 feet (11 m) or more. Dripless overhead sprinkler systems are also available.

GREENHOUSE WATER LINES

A greenhouse area of 20,000 ft^2 (1,860 m^2) requires a 2 inch (51 mm) water main that can accommodate a 50 gpm (190 l/min) flow rate. An area of 50,000 ft^2 (4,645 m^2) needs 3 inch (76 mm) mains for a flow rate of 125 gpm (473 l/min). Plastic (PVC) pipes are commonly used because they are cheaper and have less pressure drop due to friction than iron pipes. Mains can be installed underground or overhead. More commonly they are overhead, which greatly reduces the cost of the system and facilitates subsequent repairs and alterations. Water mains are used for delivering fertilizer solutions to the crop as well as water. It will occasionally be necessary to switch from one fluid to the other.

Consider a greenhouse firm of 20,000 ft^2 (1,860 m^2) laid out in one block measuring 144 feet wide and 139 feet long (44 m by 42 m). A roadway runs through the middle along the length of the greenhouse. Benches 6 feet wide by 68 feet long (1.8 m by 21 m) run out from either side of the roadway. Pot mums are grown in 6.5 inch (16.5 cm) azalea-type pots at a bench space allotment of 1.25 ft^2 each (13.5 pots/m^2). There are 326 pots on each bench. Each requires 12 fluid ounces (350 ml) of water at each watering. Benches are grouped in sets of three, and each set is supplied water through a single valve and manifold. Water or fertilizer is applied to 1,008 plants simultaneously. The best arrangement of water mains calls for 2 inch (51 mm) mains running the length of the greenhouse, each perpendicular to the benches and running over the midpoint of each bench, for a total of about 350 feet (107 m) of 2 inch (51 mm) main pipe. Each linear foot of pipe holds 17.4 ounces of water (1,686 ml/m of pipe). The total main system holds 47.6 gallons (180 l). Assume that one day after a watering, an application of fertilizer must be applied. The fertilizer proportioner is turned on at the beginning of the water main. At the opposite end of the water main, the valve on a three-bench station is opened. Before fertilizer reaches plants in that station, 47.6 gallons (180 l) of water must be flushed from the lines onto the 1,008 pots. This provides 4.8 fluid ounces (142 ml) of water to each pot. Also, 1 fluid ounce (30 ml) of water is pushed out into each pot from the 0.75 inch (19 mm) supply pipes (2.44 fl oz/ft of pipe or 236 ml/m of pipe) located on the bench, for a total of 5.8 ounces (171 ml). Of the 12 ounces (354 ml) of fluid supplied, only 6.2 ounces (183 ml) are fertilizer solution. After this station is fertilized, another station will be opened. This time 12 ounces (354 ml) of fertilizer solution are applied.

A much worse situation occurs in a greenhouse area of 50,000 ft^2 (4,645 m^2) where 800 feet (244 m) of 3 inch (76 mm) main pipe are required. Each linear foot of pipe holds 39.1 fluid ounces (1,155 ml) for a total of 244.4 gallons (924 l) in the whole system. The combined water in the main system and in the 0.75 inch (19 mm) pipes on the bench provide 12 ounces (354 ml) of water to the first 2,840 pots supposedly fertilized. Ten percent of the plants in the firm therefore receive water rather than fertilizer.

The problem can be rectified by installing double mains, one for water and the adjacent for fertilizer (Figure 7–11a). The appropriate valve is opened at each station, depending upon the need for water or fertilizer. A second solution calls for installing a solenoid water valve at the end of a single main system. In order to change from water to fertilizer, a fertilizer proportioner is turned on at the beginning of the water main, and the solenoid at the other end of the main is opened by a switch in the fertilizer room. When the fertilizer solution reaches the end of the greenhouse main, the solenoid is closed. The time required to reach this point is predetermined.

The number of benches in one water station is determined by the size of a single planting of one crop species. It can be safely assumed that all plants in this

(a)

(b)

Figure 7–11

(a) A dual main system suspended overhead at the midpoint and perpendicular to benches. One pipe carries water while the other carries fertilizer solution. Each main is connected to the water distribution system on the bench below through a manual valve. The manual valves could be replaced with solenoid valves, and these, in turn, could be controlled by two stations on a sequential timer. (b) A sequential timer capable of watering 23 separate zones in a greenhouse individually.

unit will be watered and fertilized on a single schedule. Generally, from one to three of the earlier described benches would constitute a station.

Water is distributed along the bench from a microtube watering system through two 0.75 inch (19 mm) plastic pipes running the length of the bench. Water is supplied to the midpoint of each 0.75 inch (19 mm) pipe, rather than to the end, to minimize the pressure drop along the bench. A 0.75 inch (19 mm) pipe 70 feet (21 m) long supplied with water at one end can distribute water to 70 pots. The same length of pipe supplied with water at its midpoint can distribute water to 280 pots without an adverse differential in the amount of water delivered to each pot. These figures are based on 0.06 inch (1.5 mm) inside diameter microtubes 2 feet (61 cm) long. For further details on greenhouse water main systems, see Brumfield et al. (1981).

FURTHER CONSIDERATIONS

Life Expectancy

It is difficult to assess a life expectancy for each watering system, and yet this must be done in order to give proper economic consideration to this form of automation. In general, it can be assumed that the more delicate parts of these systems, such as 8 mil (0.2 mm) polyethylene tubes and plastic nozzles, will last five to six years if properly maintained. The pipes, valves, and overhead metal nozzles can last considerably longer, at least ten years, particularly if PVC is used.

Problems arise when particles are not strained from well or pond water. These particles accumulate in the smaller tubes and nozzles. A 150 mesh strainer should be used in all systems, even when city water is used. Metal fittings should be avoided after the filter to prevent clogging from rust. When river water is used, it is best to strain the water through a sand filter prior to the 150 mesh filter.

Sufficient light enters white thin-wall PVC pipe to permit algal growth, which can cause plugging of tubes and nozzles. To prevent this problem, pipes can be painted. The best color is aluminum since it restricts light and at the same time keeps the pipe cool. Water in black pipes that are not used continuously on summer days can become sufficiently hot to burn plants.

Sterilization

The plastic components of automatic watering systems should not be steam-sterilized. This process tends to reduce the life expectancy of the polyethylene components and to distort PVC pipe and plastic nozzles. Prior to steaming, the flexible tubes should be rolled up, and the plastic pipe mains should be lifted above the bench and secured to the superstructure above.

Once these components are removed, the watering system must be sterilized; otherwise, there is the risk of recontaminating the bench medium with particles adhering to the watering system. A sponge or rag dipped in a pail of disinfectant such as bleach can be used to wipe pipes and nozzles. Disinfectants could also be proportioned into the water line and applied by hose. The flexible water tubes can be removed and soaked in a barrel of disinfectant.

The problem is not as great for pot plant benches because there is no medium to be pasteurized. These benches and the watering system may be hosed with a disinfectant.

Automation

It is perhaps best for small growers to use manual valves on the watering system. In this way, the owner or manager can check each bench daily, and the expense of further automation is avoided. Larger firms tend to have a heavier investment in management, which better guarantees careful daily monitoring of all growing areas. Because of the extensive area to be watered, these firms should install automatic valves.

A fixed interval cannot be set between waterings. Bright and warm conditions increase the frequency of drying, while cold or overcast conditions reduce it. Commonly in Europe and occasionally in America, a solar control switch is used to determine the time to water. This instrument has a remote light-sensing mechanism that measures solar energy at the point in the greenhouse where the sensor is installed. A given level can be set on the instrument, and when it is reached, any electrical system plugged into it, such as a solenoid switch on the watering system, can be turned on.

Invariably, a firm investing in automatic water valves will have numerous water zones, each with a solenoid valve. To cut down on the size of the water main and pump, one area is watered at a time. A sequential control instrument is used to coordinate the watering of a number of areas (Figure 7–11b). The sequential control instrument may be turned on manually, or it may be activated by a solar control instrument. Once activated, it will open and close any number of solenoid valves, one at a time, for any preset time from 15 seconds to 30 minutes. The price of sequential controllers begins at $100 for six-station systems and increases according to features included and number of stations activated. Up to 40 stations can be handled by one controller.

Sequential timers can result in considerable labor savings in large firms. Consider the time required for a manager to open valves, wait for water to be applied, and close valves on each of 40 water zones. With a sequential timer, the manager walks through the 40 zones, making a list of those that need watering. Then, he or she programs the sequential timer to apply water to those zones and is thus free to perform other tasks. The cost savings are considerable since the person capable of making watering decisions should be one of the more experienced (higher-paid) employees.

Economics

As one manufacturer states, "Automatic watering doesn't cost, it pays." This statement applies more to automatic watering than to most other systems of automation in the greenhouse. The automatic systems discussed range in materials plus installation costs from $77 to $162 as compared to a labor cost of $321 for hand watering a 4 foot by 100 foot (1.22 m by 30 m) bench for one year. The labor of operation throughout the year is very negligible since it simply entails opening and closing valves or programming a timer. It can be done by the manager during the rounds he or she would ordinarily make. In a large range, a sequential timer could ensure that this time is minimized. Taking all materials and labor into consideration, the automatic systems cost less the first year than hand watering does.

Other factors make automatic watering a necessity for greenhouse operators. First, as already mentioned, the ease of watering better ensures that water will be applied when needed and in the quantity required. Second, automatic watering provides a means of applying water without wetting the foliage, which is very important for the control of disease, particularly in such crops as African violet, gloxinia, Rieger begonia, primula, cyclamen, and the lower foliage of fresh flower crops. Third, automatic watering systems provide the means through which liquid fertilizer can be automatically applied.

SUMMARY

1. Watering would appear at face value to be a boring, unimportant operation, but it is probably the most common cause of poor greenhouse crops. Underwatering can have as deleterious an effect on crops as overwatering.
2. Proper watering depends upon three rules:
   a. Use a well-drained medium having good structure. This will allow for ample moisture retention along with good aeration, even immediately after application of water.
   b. Water thoroughly each time. Root media cannot be partially wetted. Water should be applied until it flows from the bottom of the container. As a rule, a 10–15 percent excess of water is applied. In general, for soil-based media, water is applied at the rate of 2 quarts per square foot (20 l/m) of bench, or 10–12 ounces (300–350 ml) per 6.5 inch (16.5 cm) azalea-type pot.

c. Water just before initial moisture stress occurs. This can be determined in most crops by the occurrence of subtle foliar symptoms such as texture, color, and turgidity changes. Some crops, such as azalea, do not show symptoms until root damage has occurred. Color, feel, and weight of the root medium are the cues for these crops.

3. Water quality is very important and is often overlooked. Levels of the total salt content, of individual ions such as sodium and boron, and of pH can all have a serious bearing on crop success. There are corrections for some quality problems but not for others. The water source should be tested before a greenhouse is established. See Table 7–1 for water-quality guidelines.

4. Hand watering is too expensive in today's labor market. Numerous automatic watering systems exist for both fresh flower and pot plant production. These systems can pay for themselves within a year. In addition to having an economic advantage over hand watering, automatic watering systems better guarantee that sufficient water will be applied on time because of the ease of application they offer. Automatic watering systems help to foster disease control by keeping foliage drier. These systems are also used for the automated application of fertilizers.

REFERENCES

Florist supply company catalogs are available annually to greenhouse growers and are a primary source of information. The manufacturers themselves are another good source of literature.

1. Ball, V., ed. 1985. *The Ball Red Book*, 14th ed. Reston, VA: Reston Publishing Co.
2. Brumfield, R. G., P. V. Nelson, A. J. Coutu, D. H. Willits, and R. S. Sowell. 1981. Overhead costs of greenhouse firms differentiated by size of firm and market channel. North Carolina Agr. Res. Ser. Tech. Bul. 269.
3. Farnham, D. S., R. S. Ayers, and R. F. Hasek. 1977. Water quality affects ornamental plant production. Univ. of California Div. of Agr. Sci. Leaflet 2995.
4. Matkin, O. A., and F. H. Petersen. 1971. Why and how to acidify irrigation water. *Amer. Nurseryman* 133:14, 73.
5. Waters, W. E., J. NeSmith, C. M. Geraldson, and S. S. Woltz. 1972. The interpretation of soluble-salt tests and soil analysis by different procedures. *Florida Flower Grower* 9 (4):1–10.
6. Wilcox, L. V. 1948. The quality of water for irrigation use. USDA Tech. Bul. 962.

CHAPTER 8

Fertilization

Greenhouse fertilization has no equal in agriculture. Heavy plant growth is forced year round under subtropical conditions. Root-media volume is minimal by field standards. As a result, nitrogen applications of 4,000 pounds (1,800 kg) are commonly applied to an acre of chrysanthemums in a year. Excessive levels and imbalances of fertilizer nutrients frequently account for the difficulties encountered. Micronutrient deficiencies are a constant threat because soils are held in continuous production under conditions of heavy leaching.

A typical plant is composed of about 90 percent water. The solid materials in the plant, commonly referred to as *dry weight*, are comprised of seventeen essential nutrient elements (Table 8–1) plus any of a number of nonessential elements that happen to be available in the root environment. Nearly 90 percent of the dry weight can be attributed to carbon, hydrogen, and oxygen—three essential elements that are not provided in a fertilization program but that are obtained pursuant to other cultural procedures.

Carbon and oxygen are derived from carbon dioxide (CO_2) in the air, while oxygen and hydrogen are derived from water. Carbon deficiency is common in the greenhouse and is covered in Chapter 9. Oxygen and hydrogen deficiencies are essentially nonexistent. Since only a small quantity of water is needed to provide these requirements, water stress injuries are usually related to other factors, such as reduction in photosynthesis caused by closing of stomates or by desiccation of cells.

The remaining 10 percent of the dry weight includes fourteen essential elements. Two of these, sodium and chloride, are available in sufficient quantities in

Table 8–1

Essential Plant Nutrients, Related Chemical Symbols, Classification, and Typical Foliage Composition for Greenhouse Crops Expressed as a Percentage of the Leaf Dry Weight

Nutrient Element	*Chemical symbol*	*Classification*	*Typical Plant Content (% of dry wt)*
Carbon	C	Nonfertilizer	89.0
Hydrogen	H	Nonfertilizer	
Oxygen	O	Nonfertilizer	
Nitrogen	N	Macronutrient, primary	4.0
Phosphorus	P	Macronutrient, primary	0.5
Potassium	K	Macronutrient, primary	4.0
Calcium	Ca	Macronutrient, secondary	1.0
Magnesium	Mg	Macronutrient, secondary	0.5
Sulfur	S	Macronutrient, secondary	0.5
Iron	Fe	Micronutrient	0.02
Manganese	Mn	Micronutrient	0.02
Zinc	Zn	Micronutrient	0.003
Copper	Cu	Micronutrient	0.001
Boron	B	Micronutrient	0.006
Molybdenum	Mo	Micronutrient	0.0002
Sodium	Na	Micronutrient	0.03
Chloride	Cl	Micronutrient	0.1

root-media components or as contaminants in fertilizers. Thus, twelve elements must be applied in a fertilization program. These elements fall into two categories: (1) the six macronutrients, which are present in the plant in large (macro) quantities and (2) the six micronutrients, which are present in small (micro) quantities.

FERTILIZATION PROGRAM

A new chapter in greenhouse fertilization began about the middle of this century when the practice of soil pasteurization eliminated the need for periodic replacement of soil. Prior to that time, nutrients were available from the humus in the rich soils used to replace the greenhouse soils every year or two. Annual applications of manure provided additional nutrients, including most, and often all, of the required micronutrients. Further nutritional needs were satisfied as dictated by soil testing, which was usually done once a month. Dry fertilizer carriers were used including organic sources such as dried blood, cottonseed meal, and tankage, while inorganic sources included nitrate of soda, muriate of potash, superphosphate, and ammonium sulfate. This system of fertilization worked quite well, but in time it had to shift in order to come into line with changes in other cultural procedures aimed at reducing labor input.

The perpetual use of soil made possible by soil pasteurization and dictated by economics, as well as the virtual elimination of manure necessitated by after-pasteurization problems, greatly increased dependency on a continuous system of fertilization. Heavy watering practices further aggravated the problem through leaching of nutrients, including micronutrients. The advent of automated watering provided an easy and economical means of applying nutrients periodically but has since necessitated the use of highly soluble fertilizers.

Today, the standard practice is to dissolve high-analysis fertilizer carriers into concentrated solutions. The concentrate is then proportioned by means of a fertilizer injector into the water line of the greenhouse at the final concentration desired for crop application. Automatic watering systems connected to this line deliver the fertilizer solution to individual pots or to the soil surface in cut flower beds. Fertilizer is most commonly applied either with each watering (this practice is known as *fertigation*) or on a seven-day basis.

Preplant Fertilization

It would be a very difficult task to provide all of the twelve essential fertilizer elements on a continuous basis. Fortunately, several elements may be applied prior to planting without further application. The results of a soil test provide the basis for preplant nutrient additions. Only four categories need to be considered.

Limestone The generally desired pH ranges for most crops are, for soil-based media, 6.2–6.8 and, for soil-less media, 5.4–6.0. Some crops do well at lower levels, such as azalea and rhododendron, but very few prefer higher levels. Nutrient availability is controlled by the root-medium pH level, as illustrated in Figure 8–1. Low pH levels result in high proportions of soluble (available) iron, manganese, and aluminum—all of which react with phosphorus to render it insoluble (unavailable). Also, at a low pH level, the available levels of calcium, magnesium, sulfur, and molybdenum decrease. High pH levels, on the other hand, result in the tie-up of phosphorus, iron, manganese, zinc, copper, and boron. It is readily apparent in Figure 8–1 that the best compromise of nutrient availability lies, for soil-based media, in the pH range of 6.2–6.8 and, for soil-less media, in the range of 5.4–6.0. A lower pH range is allowed in organic (soil-less) media for two reasons. First, in organic media, there is less native iron, manganese, and aluminum

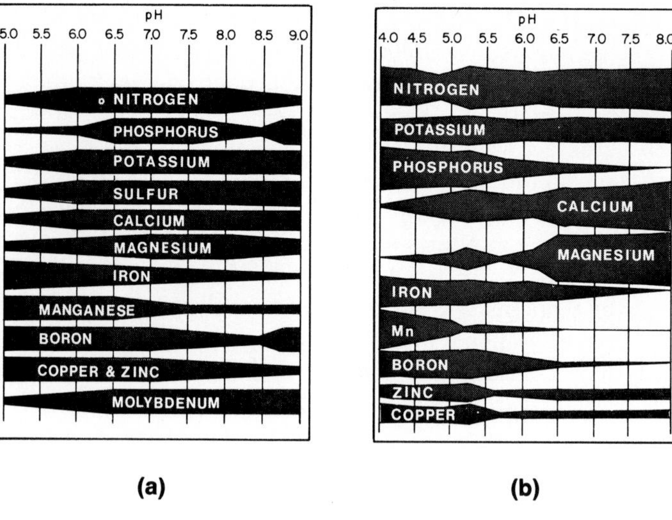

Figure 8–1

The influence of pH level on the availability of essential nutrients in (a) a mineral soil (*from* Truog, 1948) and (b) a soil-less root medium containing sphagnum peat moss, composted pine bark, vermiculite, perlite, and sand (*from* Peterson, 1982)

to convert to a soluble form and thus become toxic or cause a phosphorus tie-up. Second, higher quantities of calcium and/or magnesium are required in organic media to attain a given pH level; thus, a sufficient level of calcium and magnesium can be attained at a lower pH level.

Most greenhouse root media are of an acid (low) pH from the use of acidic amendments such as peat moss and pine bark. Agricultural limestone is used to raise the pH level. Unless the soil test indicates a high magnesium level, which is rare, dolomitic limestone should be used. This material contains magnesium, an essential nutrient, in addition to calcium. Regular limestone contains primarily one essential nutrient, calcium. Rates of addition vary for each type of root medium and are presented in Table 8–2. Depending on the initial pH level and the clay content, soil-based media can require from 0 to 10 pounds of dolomitic limestone per cubic yard (0–6 kg/m^3), while soil-less media typically require 10 pounds per cubic yard. This is sufficient to provide the required calcium and magnesium for up to one year or for as long as the pH level remains in the desired range—whichever comes sooner.

Pulverized limestone should not be used at the rates just given because it has a finer particle size than agricultural limestone. When it is used at rates given for agricultural limestone, pulverized limestone can raise the pH to levels of 7.5 and higher. Lower rates must be used for pulverized limestone. Unfortunately, no national standard exists for the particle size of limestone. Each state sets its own definition of agricultural limestone. North Carolina defines agricultural limestone by indicating that 90 percent will pass through a 20 mesh screen ($^1/_{20}$ inch,

Table 8–2

Nutrient Sources Commonly Added into Root Media during Formulation

Nutrient Source	*Rate per Cubic Yard (per m³)*	
	Soil-Based Media	*Soil-Less Media*
To Provide Calcium and Magnesium		
Dolomitic Limestone	0–10 lb (0–6 kg)	10 lb (6 kg)
To Provide Phosphorus and Sulfur		
Superphosphate (0–20–0)	3.0 lb (1.8 kg)	4.5 lb (2.7 kg)
or		
Superphosphate (0–45–0)	1.5 lb (0.9 kg)	2.25 lb (1.3 kg)
+ gypsum (calcium sulfate)	1.5 lb (0.9 kg)	1.5 lb (0.9 kg)
To Provide Micronutrients: Iron, Manganese, Zinc, Copper, Boron, Molybdenum		
F-555HF	3 oz (112 g)	3 oz (112 g)
or		
F-111HF	1 lb (0.6 kg)	1 lb (0.6 kg)
or		
Esmigram®	5 lb (3 kg)	5 lb (3 kg)
or		
Micromax®	1–1.5 lb (0.6–0.9 kg)	1–1.5 lb (0.6–0.9 kg)
To Provide Nitrogen and Potassium (optional)		
Calcium nitrate	1 lb (0.6 kg)	1 lb (0.6 kg)
Potassium nitrate	1 lb (0.6 kg)	1 lb (0.6 kg)

1.27 mm) and 35 percent will pass through a 100 mesh screen (0.01 inch, 0.25 mm). Particles larger than 20 mesh dissolve slowly and are of little value during a typical greenhouse crop length. If 90 percent of the limestone particles were smaller than 100 mesh, they would dissolve too rapidly and result in an adversely high pH level. Each bag should have the screen size indicated on it.

Where root media are of neutral pH and do not require limestone additions, 5 pounds of gypsum (calcium sulfate) should be incorporated into each cubic yard (3 kg/m^3). This will provide sufficient calcium for one year. However, it will be important to check the magnesium status of the crop (perhaps through foliar analyses) to determine when an occasional application of this nutrient is required. A good application, when called for, consists of 0.5 pound of Epsom salts (magnesium sulfate) dissolved in sufficient water to treat each cubic yard of medium (0.3 kg/m^3).

Superphosphate A second very important reading in the soil test is that of phosphorus. Unless it is high due to application to a previous crop, an application of 3 pounds of superphosphate (0–20–0) per cubic yard (1.8 kg/m^3) should be made to soil-based media and 4.5 pounds (2.7 kg/m^3) to soil-less media. Virtually all newly formulated media require the rates of superphosphate just given. Higher rates are required in soil-less media because phosphorus is not extensively fixed (held) and is readily leached out. One application will provide the necessary phosphorus for a year. It also provides the necessary sulfur and a sizable amount of calcium since 20 percent superphosphate is approximately half gypsum (calcium sulfate). Because of the gypsum content, 20 percent superphosphate (0–20–0) is more desirable than the high-analysis treble superphosphate (0–45–0) as a preplant amendment. If 0–20–0 superphosphate is not available, equal parts of 0–45–0 superphosphate and gypsum should be used, and a combined weight of the two equal to the weight recommended for 0–20–0 superphosphate should be applied. Generally, regular superphosphate (0–20–0) is available as a powder while treble superphosphate is a coarse prill. The former is more desirable for small containers such as plug seedling trays because there is a better chance that uniform amounts will be distributed into each tiny planting cell.

Micronutrients The preceding two amendments, limestone and superphosphate, provide four of the twelve essential fertilizer nutrients. Six more, the micronutrients iron, manganese, zinc, copper, boron, and molybdenum, can be applied in a single application. Several commercial preplant micronutrient mixtures are available for incorporation during root-media formulation. Some are simply a mixture of the micronutrient salts. Esmigran® consists of micronutrients impregnated into clay granules, which increases the particle size and total volume for ease of blending during root-media formulation. Frit-F-555HF®-trace element mix (formerly FTE-555®) (Pro·Sol® Division, Frit Industries, Inc., Ozark, AL 36361) is a mixture of slowly soluble nutrients in the fritted and oxide forms. This product is also available on a clay filler as Frit-F-111HF® to increase its particle size and the amount added to a volume of root media for ease and accuracy of blending. While these two formulations are generally used for floricultural purposes, other Frit formulations are available for specialty purposes. There are other products in which micronutrients have been incorporated into a mix containing superphosphate as well as some nitrogen and potassium, leaving only the possible need for limestone during formulation. Barring adversely high pH levels, all of the above-mentioned micronutrient applications can last up to one year.

Liquid application of micronutrients after planting provides an alternative to dry preplant application. Some products are designed to be applied once, shortly after planting, in a thorough watering. They generally provide micronutrients for three to four months. Other soluble products are applied at dilute rates along with macronutrient fertilizers throughout crop production. Most complete (N–P–K) greenhouse fertilizers contain a full complement of micronutrients. Those sold for use on soil-less media generally have higher micronutrient contents since micronutrient deficiencies are more prevalent in soil-less than in soil-based media. When micronutrients are not used in a continuous fertilization program, the crop should be carefully monitored through foliar analyses to determine if or when the preplant application runs out.

Both the preplant and the liquid micronutrient systems work well. That they may or may not provide sodium and chloride is of no concern. These two nutrients occur as contaminants in root media, water, and fertilizers. Except in the case of carnations, where a small amount of sodium is recommended, they are disregarded.

Nitrogen and Potassium Incorporation of nitrogen and potassium into root media is optional. A two- to three-week supply can be provided by 1 pound each of calcium nitrate and potassium nitrate in 1 cubic yard of medium (0.6 kg each/m^3). The advantage to incorporating these nutrients when a root medium is used for seed germination is that the need for fertilization is eliminated until after the seedlings are transplanted. Thus, the possibility of a fertilizer burn is reduced. Where nitrogen and potassium are left out of the root medium, seedlings or cuttings can be fertilized with a complete fertilizer on the day of planting. This practice will immediately establish sufficient levels of these nutrients. The problem of uniform mixing of potentially damaging fertilizers during root-media formulation is thereby eliminated.

Continual Fertilization

All twelve fertilizer nutrients except nitrogen and potassium have been applied at this point. These two nutrients are not retained long enough in the root media to warrant preplant application exclusively unless a slow-release fertilizer is used. They are most commonly applied as a solution continually throughout crop production.

Two programs of application are most common. The first program is fertigation, whereby nitrogen and potassium are supplied at a dilute concentration between 90 and 250 ppm of each in the irrigation water every time the crop is watered (6–17 ounces of a 20 percent nitrogen fertilizer per 100 gallons, 5–1.3 g/l). Surprisingly, one rate of 200 ppm works for many crops. The second program calls for a more concentrated application of liquid fertilizer at weekly intervals. Concentrations range from 240 ppm nitrogen and potassium (K_2O) for sensitive crops such as bedding plants and Elatior begonias to 720 ppm of each for poinsettias (1–3 pounds of a 20 percent nitrogen fertilizer per 100 gallons, 1.2–3.6 g/l).

Concentration Expression and Conversions Fertilizer recommendations are expressed in terms of either ppm or pounds and ounces per 100 gallons of water (g/l). One must be able to convert from one expression to the other in order to utilize the available literature. If we could purchase nitrogen or potassium by itself, these conversions would be straightforward; however, this is not the case. Fertilizer carriers usually contain two or more elements. Some of the elements are essential plant nutrients while others may not be. Complete fertilizers always contain the three primary macronutrients, nitrogen, phosphorus, and potassium, and are labeled with a numerical grade such as 10–5–10. The first number indicates the percentage of elemental nitrogen (N), the second indicates the percentage of phosphorus in the oxide form (P_2O_5), and the third indicates the percentage of potassium also in the oxide form (K_2O). A very common fertilizer grade used in the greenhouse is 20–10–20.

Fertilizer recommendations expressed in terms of pounds or ounces per 100 gallons pose no problems since they generally refer to the fertilizer carrier rather than to the specific essential nutrient—for example, 3 pounds of 20–10–20-grade fertilizer dissolved in 100 gallons of water or 1 pound of potassium nitrate per 100 gallons. Recommendations expressed as ppm are a problem because they do not indicate the ounces or pounds of fertilizer carrier to weigh out or the volume of water to dissolve it in. Such ppm recommendations can be converted by either of two methods to ounces or pounds per 100 gallons.

The first method calls for determining the amount of fertilizer carrier needed by using Equation 8–1:

$$\frac{\text{desired ppm}/75}{\text{decimal fraction of desired nutrient in fertilizer carrier}} = \text{oz of fertilizer carrier per 100 gal} \qquad (8\text{–}1)$$

Let us assume that a recommendation calls for 200 ppm of nitrogen and that we have a 20–10–20-grade fertilizer available. Using Equation 8–1, we divide 200 ppm by 75, which results in a value of 2.66. Then, we divide this number by 0.20, which is the decimal fraction of nitrogen in the 20–10–20 fertilizer, to obtain a final answer of 13.33 ounces of 20–10–20 fertilizer per 100 gallons of water:

$$\frac{200/75}{0.20} = 13.33 \text{ oz/100 gal}$$

Since this fertilizer also contains 10 percent phosphorus and 20 percent potassium, we end up with a final solution containing 200 ppm N + 100 ppm P_2O_5 + 200 ppm K_2O.

Assume now that we have potassium nitrate available and want 200 ppm of potassium. This fertilizer carrier contains 13 percent nitrogen and 44 percent potassium (K_2O). Applying Equation 8–1, we find that 6.1 ounces must be dissolved into each 100 gallons of water to yield a final concentration of 200 ppm of potassium (K_2O):

$$\frac{200/75}{0.44} = 6.1 \text{ oz/100 gal}$$

We also obtain nitrogen from this fertilizer carrier, and it is important to know what quantity. Equation 8–2 is used to generate this information:

$$\text{oz of fertilizer carrier per 100 gal} \times 75 \times \text{decimal fraction of desired nutrient in fertilizer carrier} = \text{ppm of desired nutrient} \quad (8\text{–}2)$$

Applying this equation to our problem, we find that the concentration of nitrogen in the final solution is 59.5 ppm:

$$6.1 \times 75 \times 0.13 = 59.5 \text{ ppm}$$

These equations can be cumbersome to use in the field. A simplified second alternative is to use Table 8–3. Consider again the situation where we desire to know how much potassium nitrate carrier to use in 100 gallons of water to supply a concentration of 200 ppm of potassium (K_2O). To use Table 8–3, we proceed as follows:

1. Locate the percentage of the desired nutrient (K_2O) in the fertilizer carrier (potassium nitrate) in the upper row of Table 8–3. In this case, the value is 44.
2. Read down the column under 44 until you arrive at the desired ppm. It is 200 in this case, but 197.6 is close enough.
3. Read to the left across the row in which 197.6 is located to locate the figure in the extreme left column, which is the number of ounces of fertilizer carrier (potassium nitrate) to dissolve in 100 gallons of water. This answer of 6 corresponds to that which was obtained by using Equation 8–1.

Realizing that potassium nitrate also supplies nitrogen, we would like to know the concentration of nitrogen. Using Table 8–3, we take the following steps:

1. Locate the ounces of potassium nitrate needed per 100 gallons in the extreme left column. The value is 6 in this problem.
2. Read to the right across the row in which 6 is located until you locate a value (58.4) in the column headed by 13, the percentage of nitrogen in potassium nitrate. The value 58.4 is the concentration of nitrogen in ppm provided by 6 ounces of potassium nitrate in 100 gallons of water and is nearly equivalent to the answer that was obtained by using Equation 8–2. Occasionally, values will be sought in the table that are not printed. In these cases, it becomes necessary to estimate their position.

Table 8–3

Conversion Table for ppm of Desired Nutrient to Ounces of Fertilizer Carrier in 100 Gallons of Water (or Grams in 1 Liter) and Vice Versa*

Ounces of Fertilizer Carrier in 100 Gallons	Percentage of Desired Nutrient in Fertilizer Carrier													
	12	*13*	*14*	*15.5*	*16*	*20*	*20.5*	*21*	*33*	*44*	*45*	*53*	*60*	*62*
							ppm							
1	9	9.7	10.5	11.6	12.0	15.0	15.3	15.7	24.7	32.9	33.7	39.7	44.9	46.4
2	18	19.5	21.0	23.2	24.0	29.9	30.7	31.4	49.4	65.9	67.4	79.3	89.8	92.0
3	27	29.3	31.4	35.0	35.9	44.9	46.0	47.2	74.1	98.8	101.0	117.0	134.7	139.2
4	36	38.9	41.9	46.4	47.9	59.9	61.4	62.9	98.8	131.7	134.7	158.7	179.6	185.6
6	54	58.4	62.9	70.0	71.9	89.8	92.1	94.3	148.2	197.6	202.1	238.0	269.4	278.4
8	72	77.8	83.8	92.8	95.8	119.7	122.7	125.7	197.6	263.4	269.4	317.3	359.2	371.2
16	144	155.7	167.7	185.6	191.7	239.5	245.5	251.5	395.2	526.9	538.9	634.6	718.5	742.4
24	216	233.5	251.5	278.4	287.5	359.2	368.2	377.2	592.7	790.3	808.3	952.0	1,077.7	1,113.6
32	288	311.4	335.4	371.3	383.4	479.0	490.9	502.9	790.3	1,053.7	1,077.7	1,269.3	1,436.9	1,484.8
40	359	389.2	419.2	464.0	479.2	598.7	613.7	628.6	987.9	1,317.2	1,347.1	1,586.6	1,796.2	1,856.1
48	431	467.0	503.0	556.8	575.0	718.5	736.4	754.4	1,185.5	1,580.6	1,616.5	1,903.9	2,155.4	2,227.2
56	503	544.9	586.9	649.7	670.9	838.2	859.2	880.1	1,383.0	1,844.0	1,886.0	2,221.2	2,514.6	2,598.4
64	575	622.7	670.7	742.4	766.7	958.0	981.9	1,005.8	1,580.6	2,107.5	2,155.4	2,538.6	2,873.9	2,969.7
Grams of Fertilizer Carrier in 1 Liter														
							ppm							
0.1	12	13	14	16	16	20	20.5	21	33	44	45	53	60	62
0.2	24	26	28	31	32	40	41.0	42	66	88	90	106	120	124
0.3	36	39	42	47	48	60	61.5	63	99	132	135	159	180	186
0.4	48	52	56	62	64	80	82.0	84	132	176	180	212	240	248
0.6	72	78	84	93	96	120	123.0	126	198	264	270	318	360	372
0.8	96	104	112	124	128	160	164.0	168	264	352	360	424	480	496
1.0	120	130	140	155	160	200	205.0	210	330	440	450	530	600	620
1.5	180	195	210	233	240	300	307.5	315	495	660	675	795	900	930
2.0	240	260	280	310	320	400	410.0	420	660	880	900	1,060	1,200	1,240
2.5	300	325	350	388	400	500	512.5	525	825	1,100	1,125	1,325	1,500	1,550
3.0	360	390	420	465	480	600	615.0	630	990	1,320	1,350	1,590	1,800	1,860
3.5	420	455	490	543	560	700	717.5	735	1,155	1,540	1,575	1,855	2,100	2,170
4.0	480	520	560	620	640	800	820.0	840	1,320	1,760	1,800	2,120	2,400	2,480

*Adapted from J. W. Love, Department of Horticultural Science, North Carolina State University, Raleigh, NC 27695–7609.

Specific Crop Recommendations The most commonly used fertilizer in the greenhouse in past years was 20–20–20. Because of occasional injuries from high ammoniacal nitrogen content in 20–20–20, a 20–10–20 fertilizer is more commonly used today. Several companies formulate this grade and include in it the essential micronutrients as well as a dye that is used for tracing the fertilizer in the water lines. If the preplant recommendations for phosphorus are followed, the phosphorus content of this fertilizer is superfluous, and thus it would be better to use a 20–0–20 grade.

Recommended concentrations of fertilizer vary widely from crop to crop. Listed in Table 8–4 for several crops are concentrations of a 20 percent nitrogen fertilizer to be used for weekly fertilization and for fertigation (with every watering) programs. Both programs work equally well. Labor inputs determine which to use. In a greenhouse where one brings a fertilizer proportioner to the end of each bench, connects it, and waits for application to be made before moving to the next bench, it is best to apply only once per week. In a larger firm where fertilizer is injected into the main water lines, it is easiest to apply fertilizer with every watering. To do otherwise, one would constantly have to turn the proportioner on and off and flush water lines.

Table 8–4

Standard Concentration Requirements of Fertilizers Containing 20 Percent Nitrogen for Several Greenhouse Crops

		Concentration[1]			
		Weekly		*Constant*	
Crop	*Concentration Category*	*oz/100 gal*	*g/l*	*oz/100 gal*	*g/l*
Daffodil	None	—	—	—	—
Iris	None	—	—	—	—
Hyacinth	None	—	—	—	—
Tulip[2]	Very light	—	—	—	—
Snapdragon	Very light	16	1.2	6	0.5
Bedding plants	Very light	16	1.2	13.5	1.0
Elatior begonia	Very light	17	1.3	8.5	0.6
Azalea	Light	20	1.5	—	—
Gloxinia	Light	24	1.8	13.5	1.0
Rose	Moderate	32	2.4	10	0.8
Carnation	Moderate	32	2.4	13.5	1.0
Geranium	Moderate	32	2.4	13.5	1.0
Easter lily	Moderate	32	2.4	13.5	1.0
Chrysanthemum	Heavy	40	3.0	13.5	1.0
Poinsettia	Heavy	48	3.6	17	1.3

[1]13.5 oz of 20 percent nitrogen fertilizer/100 gal (1 g/l) = 200 ppm nitrogen.

[2]As an insurance against nitrogen and calcium deficiencies, calcium nitrate should be applied at the rate of 32 oz/100 gal (2.4 g/l) at the start and at the midpoint of the growth-room stages and at the start of greenhouse forcing.

It is not necessary to use a fertilizer containing 20 percent nitrogen. Fertilizer ratios of 1–0–1 and 1–1–1 are available in grades such as 15–0–15, 15–15–15, and 25–0–25. If the fertilizer contains 15 percent nitrogen, one-third more is used; if it contains 25 percent nitrogen, one-fifth less is used in each 100 gallons of water than would be used if it contained 20 percent nitrogen.

Most crops develop best on a fertilizer equally balanced in nitrogen and potassium. There are a few exceptions. The Elatior begonia grows faster and develops more side shoots when it is fertilized with a ratio of 2 parts nitrogen to 1 part potassium. The azalea requirement is similar in that a 3:1 ratio is best. The carnation requirement is quite different since a ratio of 2 parts nitrogen to 3 parts potassium is favored.

As time passes, the concentration and balance of nitrogen and potassium in the root medium usually change, necessitating adjustments in the concentration and ratio of fertilizer applied. Many fertilizer ratios and grades are commercially available to serve these needs.

Formulating Fertilizers Complete fertilizers (those containing nitrogen, phosphorus, and potassium) are commercially available in a number of grades. Many florists formulate their own fertilizers, thus saving a significant part of their fertilizer bill and making possible an even wider range of grades. Most fertilizers are formulated from combinations of two or more of nine fertilizer carriers. For example, 1 pound of potassium nitrate added to 1 pound of ammonium nitrate yields 2 pounds of 23–0–22-grade fertilizer.

Several formulations that a grower can easily make are presented in Table 8–5. The first nine fertilizer entries are the fertilizer carriers from which all of the subsequent fertilizer formulas are derived. For example, an 18–0–22 formula fertilizer can be formulated by blending 1 pound of ammonium nitrate plus 2 pounds of potassium nitrate plus 1 pound of ammonium sulfate together. This formulation was determined by locating the 18–0–22 formula in the "Analysis" column. Then, the three numbers 1, 2, and 1 were located in the row after this formula. Each of these three numbers was traced to the "X" above it and then to the fertilizer carrier to the left of the "X."

Additional formulations can be found in Table 8–6. Three common complete fertilizers are listed first followed by three "make-your-own" formulations. The percentage of total nitrogen in ammonium plus urea form (NH_4) in each is given. Quantities to dissolve in 100 gallons of water to yield concentrations of 50–600 ppm each of nitrogen and potassium are also given.

While the make-your-own fertilizers do not contain micronutrients or dye, commercial preparations are available. They include Compound 111 (Grace-Sierra Horticultural Products Co., Milpitas, CA), which is added at the rate of 1 pound per 40 pounds of macronutrient formulation, and Mitrel M (Miller Chemical and Fertilizer Corp., Hanover, PA), which is added at the rate of 8 ounces per 100 pounds of macronutrient formulation and will provide a dye and micronutrients in chelated form. The complete set of micronutrients without

Table 8–5

Amounts of Fertilizer Carrier Sources To Combine in Making Various Fertilizer Formulas[1]

Fertilizer		*Nutrient Sources*[2]											
Name	*Analysis*	*33–0–0*	*13–0–44*	*15.5–0–0*	*16–0–0*	*21–0–0*	*45–0–0*	*0–0–60*	*12–62–0*	*21–53–0*	*% of N as* NO_3	*Cost per Pound*[4]	*Reaction in Soil*[5]
Ammonium nitrate	33–0–0	x									50	12	A
Potassium nitrate	13–0–44		x								100	26	N
Calcium nitrate	15.5–0–0			x							94	10	B
Sodium nitrate	16–0–0				x						100	10	B
Ammonium sulfate	21–0–0					x					0	5	A
Urea	45–0–0						x				0	14	SA
Potassium chloride	0–0–60							x			—	8	N
Monoammonium phosphate	12–62–0								x		0	34	A
Diammonium phosphate[3]	21–53–0									x	0	16	SA
Chrysanthemum green	18–0–22	1	2			1					53	17	A
General summer	20–10–24	1					1	2		1	17	12	A
General low phosphate	21–4–20	7						4		1	45	12	A
General summer	21–17–20	1					2	3		3	10	12	A
General	17–6–27							4		1	43	11	A
UConn Mix	19–5–24		6	2			2		1		51	22	N
Editor's favorite	20–5–30		13				4			2	43	22	SA
20–20–20 substitute	20–20–22		4				1			3	33	21	SA
Starter and pink hydrangea	12–41–15		1						2		35	31	SA
Starter and pink hydrangea	17–35–16						1	4		10	0	14	SA
N–K only	16–0–24	2			1			2			60	10	SA
N–K only	20–0–30	1	2								72	21	SA
Blue hydrangea	13-0–22					2		1			0	6	VA
Blue hydrangea	15-0–15					3		1			0	6	VA
Acid	21–9–9	3	1			7		1		2	21	10	VA
Spring carnation	11–0–17				5			2			100	10	B
Winter nitrate	15–0–15		1	2							95	15	B
Winter potash	15–0–22		1	1							96	18	B
Lily substitute	16–4–12	1	4	6						1	78	16	N
High K	15–10–30		7	1						2	72	22	N

[1]Adapted from Koths et al. (1980).

[2]For names of fertilizer carrier sources, see the first nine entries in the fertilizer "Name" column.

[3]Diammonium phosphate may be pelletized and coated. To dissolve, use very hot water and stir vigorously. Do not worry about sediment. Use crystalline potassium chloride if possible.

[4]Based on lowest available prices published by greenhouse supply firms.

[5]B = basic, N = neutral, SA = slightly acid, A = acid, VA = very acid.

Table 8–6

Quantities of Fertilizers or Fertilizer Carriers To Dissolve in 100 Gallons of Water To Make Solutions Containing Concentrations of 50–600 ppm Each of Nitrogen (N) and Potassium (K_2O)

Fertilizer	*% NH_4 + urea*	*Concentration of N and K_2O* 50	100	200	300	400	500	600
					oz/100 gal			
20–20–20*	70	3.3	6.7	13.3	20.0	26.7	33.4	40.0
15–15–15*	52	4.5	8.9	17.8	26.7	35.6	44.5	53.4
20–10–20*	40	3.3	6.7	13.3	20.0	26.7	33.4	40.0
Ammonium nitrate	36	1.4	2.9	5.7	8.6	11.4	14.3	17.1
+ potassium nitrate		1.5	3.0	6.1	9.1	12.1	15.2	18.2
(23–0–23)								
Calcium nitrate	0	3.0	6.0	12.0	18.0	24.0	30.0	36.0
+ potassium nitrate		1.5	3.0	6.0	9.0	12.0	15.0	18.0
(15–0–15)								
Ammonium nitrate	40	1.2	2.5	4.9	7.4	9.9	12.3	14.8
+ potassium nitrate		1.5	3.0	6.0	9.0	12.0	15.0	18.0
+ monoammonium phosphate		0.5	1.1	2.2	3.2	4.3	5.4	6.5
(20–10–20)*								

*These formulations also contain phosphorus (P_2O_5) at equal or half the concentration of nitrogen.

dye may be added as STEM (Grace-Sierra Horticultural Products Co., Milpitas, CA 95035) at the rate of 8 ounces per 100 pounds of fertilizer formulation; as Masterblend® Formula 222 Micronutrient Additive (Vaughan Products, Inc., Masterblend Fertilizer Division, Chicago, IL) at 1.25 pounds per 100 pounds of fertilizer; as Olympic Minor Element Soluble (Olympic Chemical Co., Mainland, PA) at 8 ounces per 100 pounds of fertilizer; or as CHL-MIN (Pro·Sol® Division, Frit Industries, Inc., Ozark, AL) at the rate of 1 pound per 50 pounds of fertilizer.

None of the formulations listed in Table 8–5 containing sulfate or phosphate in combination with calcium can be concentrated for application through a fertilizer injector. These formulations are permissible if they are formulated at the strength desired for direct application to the crop. This is not the usual case. To take advantage of automated application, fertilizer solutions are first made in concentrated form and are then diluted as they are metered into the greenhouse water system through mechanical fertilizer proportioners (fertilizer injectors). Calcium and/or magnesium will precipitate (settle out as a solid) with sulfate or phosphate when it is formulated into a concentrated fertilizer solution. Therefore, these combinations are avoided unless appropriate dual (two-stage) fertilizer injectors are used.

Care should be taken in the selection of fertilizer carriers to bring about the proper soil reaction (pH). Ammonium nitrate, ammonium sulfate, and diammonium phosphate are acidic (they lower the soil pH), while calcium nitrate, sodium nitrate, and potassium nitrate are basic (they raise the soil pH). Potassium chloride is neutral. Moderate changes in root-media pH can be brought about by proper selection of the fertilizer formulation. In general, the proportion of ammonium nitrogen is raised when a lower pH is desired and nitrate nitrogen is raised when a higher pH is desired.

Three forms of nitrogen are generally used for fertilization: nitrate (NO_{3-}), ammonium (or ammoniacal) (NH_{4+}), and urea. Plants vary in response to these forms. The response to ammonium and urea is generally identical in plants since urea must be converted to ammoniacal nitrogen to be assimilated in plants. Plants, such as azalea and rhododendron, that grow well in highly acid root media develop best on a high proportion of ammonium nitrogen. It is interesting to note that when acid-tolerant plants such as azalea are grown at an adversely low pH for them, nitrate becomes the preferred nitrogen form. This is fortuitous since the use of nitrate raises the pH. Other crops, however, may be injured when more than 50 percent of the total nitrogen is provided as ammonium plus urea. Best growth is obtained when a mixture of nitrate plus ammonium and/or urea is supplied.

The standard greenhouse fertilizer used until this past decade was 20–20–20. This fertilizer contains approximately 70 percent of its nitrogen in the ammonium plus urea forms. Ammonium toxicity was not attributed to 20–20–20 fertilizer until soil-less root media became popular. Soil-less media tend to be lower in pH level than soil-based media. The optimum pH for bacteria that convert ammonium to nitrate nitrogen in the soil is slightly above 7.0. In the pH range of 6.0–7.0 used for soil-based media, adequate populations of bacteria develop to reduce the high level of ammonium plus urea supplied by 20–20–20 fertilizer. This is not true for soil-less media, where pH values below 6.0 are established. A popular fertilizer today is 20–10–20, which contains 40 percent ammoniacal nitrogen.

Ammonium toxicity is a greater problem in the winter than in the summer. Root-media temperatures are cooler in the winter. As a consequence, the nitrifying bacteria responsible for conversion of ammonium to nitrate are less active. Years ago, switching from a 20–20–20 to a 15–15–15 formulation in the winter was known to give better results. It is now known that the drop in ammonium plus nitrate nitrogen from 70 percent in 20–20–20 to about 50 percent in 15–15–15 was probably the reason.

Different fertilizers are recommended in Table 8–5 for blue and pink hydrangea crops. Aluminum serves to regulate flower color in hydrangea. Copious quantities of aluminum exist in most soils. When the pH is low, much of the aluminum is available to the plant and flowers are blue. When the pH is high, alumi-

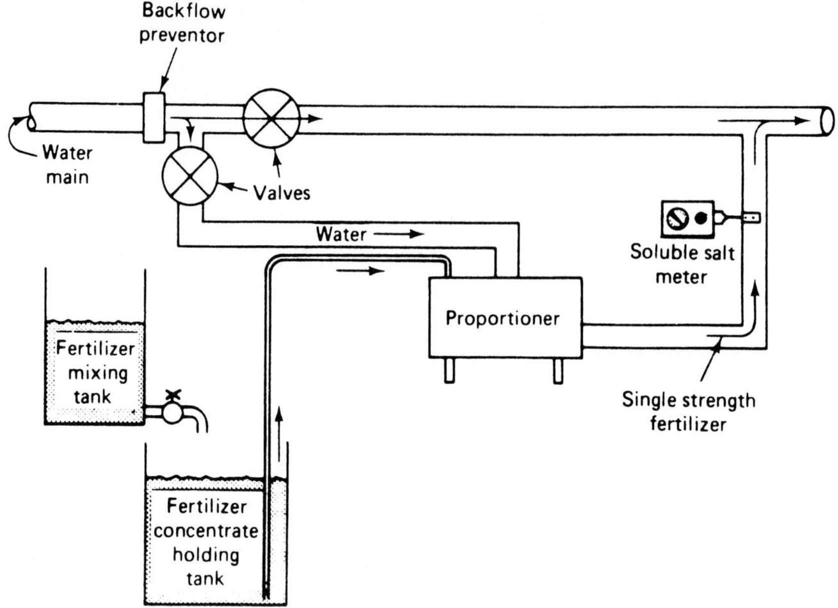

Figure 8–2

A typical arrangement of fertilizer mixing tank, holding tank, proportioner, and soluble-salt meter along the main water line in a greenhouse range.

num is rendered unavailable and flowers are pink. High levels of phosphorus also render aluminum unavailable. You will note that fertilizer formulations used for blue flowers are devoid of phosphorus and are very acid, while those used for pink flowers contain large quantities of phosphorus and are not very acid.

Automated Fertilizer Application The most expedient method for applying fertilizer is the automatic watering system present in most greenhouses. The fertilizer must be dissolved into a concentrated solution in order to conserve space in the mixing and holding tanks. This necessitates the use of a fertilizer injector (also known as a proportioner). This device mixes precise volumes of concentrated fertilizer solution and water together. By plumbing the proportioner into the main water line that serves the greenhouse range, all lines will carry a single-strength fertilizer solution. The proportioner is located on a bypass line so that either water or fertilizer solution can be obtained from the lines (Figure 8–2).

It is advisable, and in most states mandatory, that in a potable water system a backflow preventor be installed on any water supply fixture that has an outlet that may be submerged (Figure 8–3). Such fixtures include fertilizer proportioners and hoses used to fill spray tanks or equipment washtubs. The backflow preventor stops back-siphoning of contaminated water into the water system in the event that a negative pressure (suction) develops. Nitrate, commonly supplied

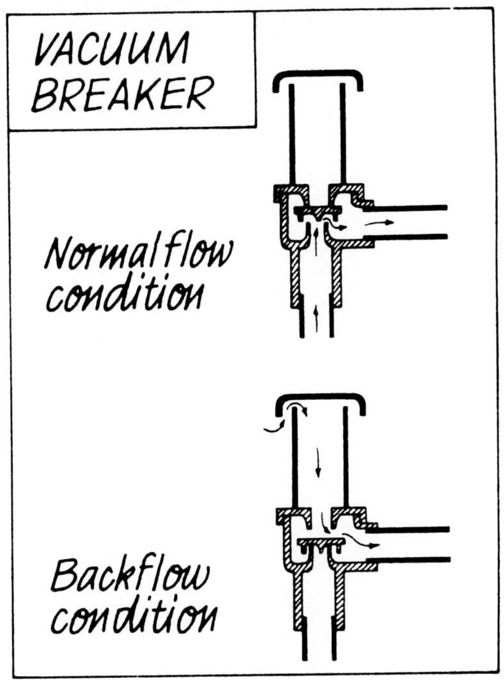

Figure 8–3

A backflow preventor in the open position permitting normal flow of water (*top*). When water pressure drops to a predetermined level, the check valve closes and shuts off the flow of water (*bottom*). At this point, air can enter the device, thus eliminating the negative pressure and any backflow of water. (*From* J. W. *Bartok*, Jr., 1973)

in fertilizers, is harmful to humans. Babies are particularly susceptible to low levels of nitrate. The World Health Organization standards for drinking water set the maximum acceptable concentration of nitrate nitrogen at 23 ppm in Europe and at 45 ppm in the United States. Backflow preventors are not required when there is a gap equal to twice the diameter of the supply line between the water supply line and the highest possible level of water in a mixing tank receiving the water. In such a setup, it is not possible for contaminated water to enter the water supply line.

Most greenhouse fertilizer is purchased in solid form. It is dissolved in a mixing tank (Figure 8–2) where it is allowed to stand for the better part of a day to permit settling of solids, which occasionally occurs. A tap is located an inch or two from the bottom of the mixing tank for transferring the clear liquid to a holding tank. The proportioner draws fertilizer concentrate from the holding tank. This sequence of tanks prevents unwanted solids from getting into and plugging the proportioner and automatic watering system.

Several types of proportioners (Figure 8–4) are used, depending upon the application. The five criteria to use in selecting the proportioner best suited for a given greenhouse application are as follows.

1. The ratio of fertilizer concentrate to water should be sufficiently wide to keep the concentrate tank volume needed for one complete fertilizer application down to a manageable size. For a small firm, 1:16 ratio would be sufficient but

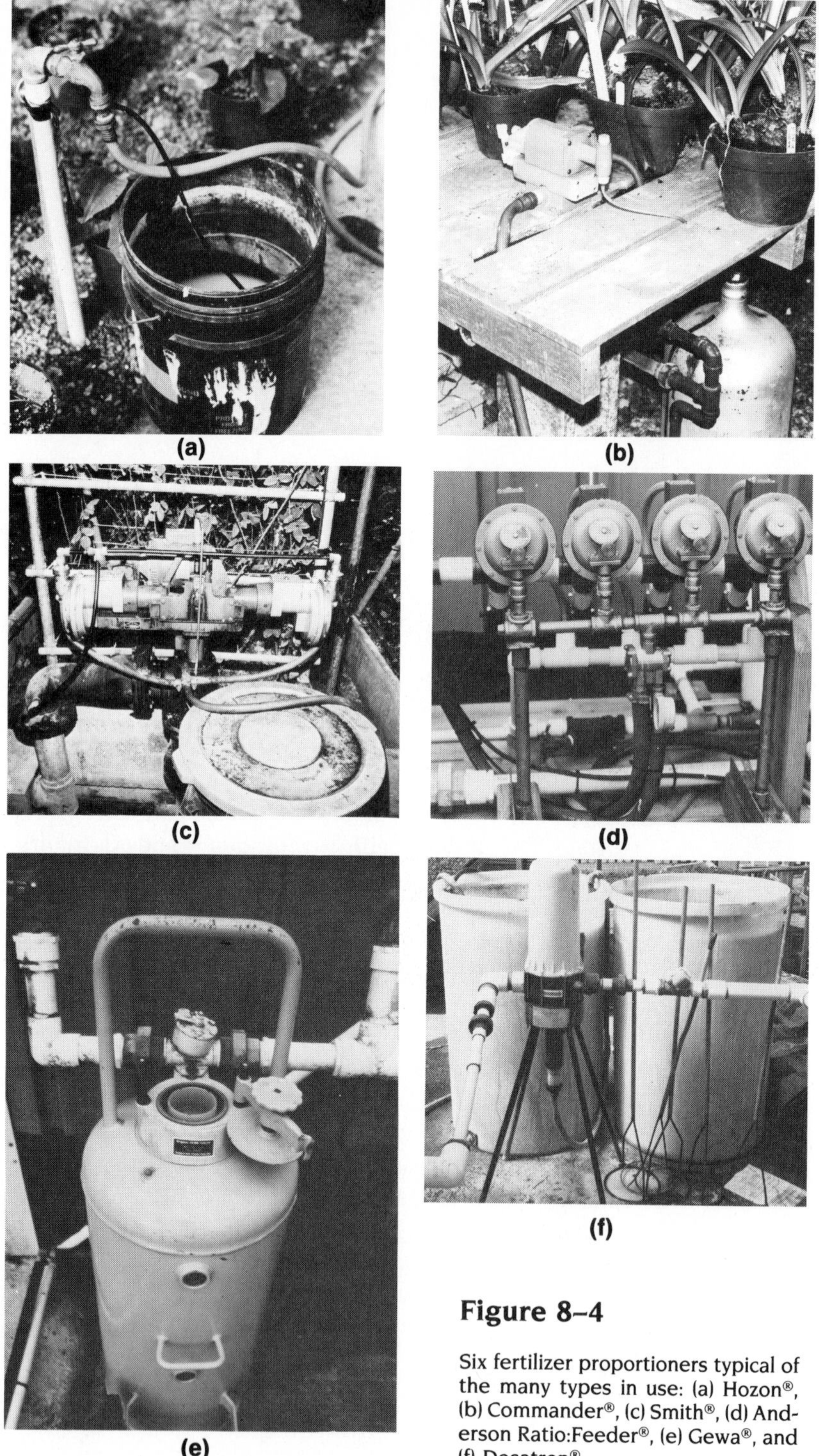

Figure 8–4

Six fertilizer proportioners typical of the many types in use: (a) Hozon®, (b) Commander®, (c) Smith®, (d) Anderson Ratio:Feeder®, (e) Gewa®, and (f) Dosatron®.

would not be for a large firm. The solubility of greenhouse fertilizers allows them to be concentrated up to about 200-fold. Ratios higher than 1:200 are rarely used.

2. An adjustable ratio is highly desirable. In this way, a single fertilizer concentrate can be applied at different strengths to several plant species.

3. The flow rate of the proportioner determines the area of plants that can be fertilized at one time. An 8 gpm flow rate will service only one ¾ inch pipe and, thus, only one bench of plants at a time. In a very large firm, it may be necessary to fertilize five to ten benches at a time in order to finish the task in half a day.

4. The concentrate tank should have sufficient volume to allow the entire fertilization job to be completed with one batch of fertilizer concentrate. Larger firms purchase proportioners without a built-in concentrate tank. In this way, they provide their own tank of required size.

5. As soon as a firm is large enough to afford a dual-head proportioner, it should obtain one. Such a proportioner siphons simultaneously from two separate fertilizer concentrates. Calcium or magnesium can be supplied in one concentrate, while sulfate or phosphate may be supplied in the other. These nutrients are compatible in this case because they do not mix until after they are diluted to single strength.

Proportioners such as the Hozon® and the Syfonex® operate on the venturi principle, whereby water passing at a high velocity through an orifice sets up a suction in a line entering from the side. Fertilizer concentrate is drawn in through the side line. This type of proportioner is inexpensive and serves well in a small greenhouse but is limited in application because of its fixed, narrow proportioning ratio of approximately 1:16. Where large volumes of fertilizer solution are needed, the concentrate tank would become prohibitively large. The ¾ inch (1.9 cm) thread size and 3 gpm (8 l/min) flow rate limit the area that can be fertilized at one time.

The Commander® proportioner draws in fertilizer concentrate by means of a pump that is driven by water passing through it. It requires a much smaller concentrate volume with its fixed ratio of 1:128 (1 fl oz/gal), but it is limited to a ¾ inch thread size and 6.6 gpm (25 l/min) flow rate.

Fert-O-Ject® and Smith Measuremix® proportioners have factory-fixed ratios including 1:100 or 1:200 for the Fert-O-Ject and 1:20 to greatly in excess of 1:200 for the Smith. They can be purchased to fit pipe sizes up to 6 inches (15 cm). Their flow rates, which go up to 560 gpm (2,100 l/min) at a ratio of 1:200, permit simultaneous fertilization of many benches. These proportioners use the water-pumping principle to pick up fertilizer concentrate and do not have built in concentrate tanks.

The Gewa® proportioner adds versatility since its ratio is adjustable on site from 1:15 to 1:350. This proportioner includes a concentrate tank available in 4, 6, 15, and 26 gallon (15, 20, 57, and 100 l) sizes and fits up to a 2 inch water line (5 cm). The concentrate is contained in a rubber bag positioned inside an iron tank. Entering water builds up pressure between the rubber bag and the iron tank wall, thereby pressing concentrate out into the line. The ratio is set by moving a lever to the appropriate numbered setting. The number is determined by dividing 300 by the dilution factor desired. For a ratio of 1:100, 300 would be divided by 100 to achieve a setting of 3.

Anderson Ratio:Feeder® proportioners are available in several models, each with on-site adjustable step ratios ranging from 1:80 to greater than 1:200. A flow rate of 450 gpm (1,700 lpm) is possible at a ratio of 1:200. Separate concentrate tanks are supplied by the grower.

Dosatron® proportioners may be adjusted on site from a ratio of 1:50 to greater than 1:200. Flow rates extend up to 100 gpm (380 1/min) in pipe sizes up to 2 inches (5 cm). The concentrate tank is not a part of these proportioners.

A soluble-salt meter should be installed in the plumbing downstream from the proportioner. The same meter used for testing root media can be used, but the probe containing the electrodes is different in that it is inserted permanently into the water line. Each time the proportioner is turned on, the soluble-salt level of the solution coming from the proportioner should be checked. If the special probe is not available, then a conventional meter may be used. A sample of fertilizer solution should be drawn from the bench and tested. The salt reading should always be the same for a given fertilizer at a given concentration. Listed in Table 8–7 are the conductivity values that should be obtained for various greenhouse fertilizers.

SLOW-RELEASE FERTILIZERS

Many of the nutrient sources used in the early days of greenhouse culture were in effect slow-release fertilizers. They were mainly organic materials of plant and animal origin, which, upon degradation, slowly gave up their nutrient content to the soil. Today, synthetically produced slow-release fertilizers have slow, sustained release patterns ranging from three months to several years. For greenhouse culture, the three-month release period is most popular. There are five common categories of these fertilizers. Some, when incorporated into the soil prior to planting, will provide all the necessary nitrogen, phosphorus, and potassium for the entire crop period, thus eliminating the need for a continual fertilization program. Others provide micronutrients in an equally effective manner. The five common categories are as follows:

1. Plastic-encapsulated fertilizers.
2. Slowly soluble fertilizers.

Table 8–7

Soluble-Salt Conductivity Values in Millimhos per Centimeter for Various Fertilizers*

Nitrogen (ppm)	*Fertilizer* 20–20–20 20–19–18	20–10–20	20–2–20	20–5–30	25–5–20	15–16–17 15–11–29 15–20–25	15–15–15	15–0–15	21–7–7 (Acid)	21–7–7 (Neutral)
50	.23	.33	.31	.22	.12	.32	.30	.36	.28	.21
100	.45	.65	.62	.44	.24	.65	.62	.74	.56	.42
150	.68	.98	.93	.69	.36	1.00	.96	1.15	.84	.63
200	.90	1.30	1.24	.94	.51	1.40	1.30	1.55	1.12	.84
250	1.13	1.63	1.55	1.20	.62	1.72	1.65	1.90	1.40	1.05
300	1.35	1.95	1.86	1.43	.80	2.10	1.98	2.28	1.68	1.26
350	1.58	2.28	2.17	1.66	.92	2.45	2.31	2.64	1.96	1.47
400	1.80	2.60	2.48	1.90	1.04	2.80	2.65	3.00	2.24	1.68
450	2.03	2.93	2.79	2.15	1.18	3.15	2.98	3.34	2.52	1.89
500	2.25	3.25	3.10	2.40	1.32	3.50	3.25	3.68	2.80	2.10
550	2.48	3.58	3.41	2.61	1.45	3.84	3.55	3.98	3.08	2.31
600	2.70	3.90	3.72	2.82	1.58	4.18	3.85	4.28	3.36	2.52
650	2.93	4.23	4.03	3.03	1.71	4.52	4.15	4.58	3.64	2.73
700	3.15	4.55	4.34	3.24	1.84	4.80	4.45	4.88	3.92	2.94
800	3.60	5.20	4.96	3.66	2.11	5.54	5.05	5.50	4.48	3.36
900	4.05	5.85	5.58	4.08	2.37	6.22	5.65	6.10	5.04	3.78
1000	4.50	6.50	6.20	4.50	2.63	6.90	6.25	6.70	5.60	4.20

*Values are for Peters fertilizers from Grace-Sierra Horticultural Products Co., Milpitas, CA 95035.

3. Urea formaldehyde.
4. Sulfur-coated fertilizers.
5. Chelated micronutrients.

Slow-release fertilizers are in one sense a form of automation since they eliminate the need for a continual input of labor into fertilization. These fertilizers are more efficient than water-soluble fertilizers in that a greater percentage of applied nutrients is utilized by the plant. Conversely, less nutrients leach from the root zone into the water table. This factor is important today as pollution guidelines and regulations are being developed by government agencies. Traditionally, little emphasis has been placed on researching the keeping quality of potted plants after purchase by the final consumer. Proper use of slow-release fertilizers by the grower can ensure adequate nutrition during the postmarket period. Although crops can be fertilized exclusively with slow-release fertilizers, currently many growers use these fertilizers in conjunction with a continual fertilization program merely as an insurance program against nutrient shortage.

Plastic-Encapsulated Fertilizers

Notable examples of the plastic-encapsulated slow-release fertilizers are the products under the trade names Osmocote® and Sierra®. They consist of plastic-coated spheres of dry, water-soluble fertilizers formulated from such carriers as potassium nitrate and ammonium sulfate. Particle diameters are about ⅛ inch (3 mm) or less.

These fertilizers are mixed into root media prior to planting. Water vapor in the soil atmosphere penetrates the capsule wall. Once inside, the water vapor condenses on the fertilizer surface because the fertilizer lowers the vapor pressure. This reduces the moisture content of the atmosphere inside the capsule to a level lower than that in the moist soil atmosphere outside. As a result, water vapor continues to diffuse into the capsule in an attempt to equalize the moisture content of the atmosphere on both sides of the plastic film. Soon, sufficient water has condensed inside to dissolve the fertilizer. As water continues to enter and pressure builds up inside, the walls of the capsule enlarge forming fissures through which the fertilizer solution passes to the soil solution, where it can be taken up by plant roots. The longevity of this process is controlled by the composition and thickness of the plastic coating.

Osmocote® is available for greenhouse fertilization in 14–14–14 and 19–6–12 grades, which have a 3- to 4-month release period; in 13–13–13 and 18–6–12 grades, which have an 8- to 9-month release period; and in a 17–7–12 grade, which has a 12- to 14-month release period at 70°F (21°C) root-medium temperature. The former grades of fertilizers are well suited to most greenhouse crops having a 12- to 14-week cultural requirement. The latter grade of fertilizer is bet-

Table 8–8

Osmocote® and Sierra® Controlled-Release Fertilizers and Their Release Periods[1]

Analysis	*Longevity (months)*	*Product Name*[2]
14–14–14	3–4	Osmocote®
19–6–12	3–4	Osmocote®
13–13–13	8–9	Osmocote®
18–6–12	8–9	Osmocote®
17–7–12	12–14	Osmocote®
15–10–12	3–4	Sierra® General-Purpose
15–10–10	5–6	Sierra® General-Purpose
17–6–12	3–4	Sierra® Plus Minors
17–6–10	8–9	Sierra® Plus Minors
16–6–10	12–14	Sierra® Plus Minors
12–10–17	3	Sierra® Chrysanthemum Mix
13–12–11	5	Sierra® Geranium Mix
12–12–15	3	Sierra® Poinsettia Mix
16–8–12	8–9	Sierra® Tablets

[1]From Grace-Sierra Horticultural Products Co., Milpitas, CA 95035.

[2]The Sierra® products contain a complete complement of micronutrients while the Osmocote® products do not.

ter suited to long-term crops such as azalea, carnation, and rose. Note that these fertilizers have approximately two ratios, 1:1:1 and 3:1:2. Listed in Table 8–8 are the various Osmocote® Controlled-Release Fertilizers and Sierra® Controlled-Release Fertilizers.

Another product on the market with a similar release mechanism to Osmote® is Nutricote®. Again, it consists of a variety of solid, soluble fertilizers coated with resin. The resin can vary in composition to yield products with release periods of 40, 70, 100, 140, 180, 270, or 360 days at a root-medium temperature of 77°F (25°C). Analyses available include 14–14–14, 16–10–10, and 20–7–10. Recommended rates for incorporation into root media are given in Table 8–9. An important precaution for Osmocote® and Nutricote® is that neither should be steam sterilized. This could result in excessive nutrient release and an ensuing plant injury. The ammonium and nitrate forms of nitrogen in Osmocote®, Sierra®, and Nutricote® are well balanced.

Slowly Soluble Fertilizers

Gypsum and limestone are examples of fertilizers with limited solubility. When they are applied to the soil, a small percentage becomes available. As the initially

Table 8–9

Rates in Pounds per Cubic Yard (kg/m^3) for Incorporation of Nutricote® into Root Media[1]

Release Type (days)	*Sensitive[2] Crops*		*Medium-Feeding[3] Crops*		*Heavy-Feeding[4] Crops*	
	14–14–14 and 16–10–10					
40	1.75	(1.0)	3.5	(2.0)	5	(3.0)
70	2.5	(1.5)	5	(3.0)	8.5	(5.0)
100	3.5	(2.0)	7.5	(4.4)	12	(7.1)
140	5	(3.0)	9	(5.3)	13	(7.7)
180	7	(4.1)	12	(7.1)	15	(8.9)
270	9	(5.3)	14	(8.3)	17	(10.1)
360	12	(7.1)	17	(10.1)	20	(11.9)
	20–7–10					
40	1	(0.6)	2.5	(1.5)	4	(2.4)
70	2	(1.2)	4	(2.4)	6	(3.6)
100	3	(1.8)	6	(3.6)	8	(4.7)
140	4	(2.4)	7	(4.1)	10	(5.9)
180	5	(3.0)	8	(4.7)	11	(6.5)
270	7	(4.1)	10	(5.9)	13	(7.7)
360	9	(5.3)	12	(7.1)	15	(8.9)

[1]For soil or root media that is sandy or loose with good drainage (low CEC), a higher rate should be used; for heavier, clay-type soils (high CEC), a lower rate should be used.

[2]African violets, azaleas, ferns, orchids, greenhouse vegetables.

[3]bedding plants, cut flower crops.

[4]most pot and green (foliage) crops.

available quantity is depleted through plant utilization or leaching, more is released to replace it.

A good example of a complete fertilizer in this category is MagAmp®. It is a coprecipitate of magnesium ammonium phosphate and magnesium potassium phosphate. MagAmp® has the grade 7–40–6 and is an effective source of nitrogen, phosphorus, and potassium for three to four months. It is designed to be mixed into the root medium. Recommended crops and rates of application appear in Table 8–10. The unusually high level of phosphorus in MagAmp® can result in the reduced availability of iron, manganese, copper, and zinc in the root medium. Careful attention should be paid to the micronutrient fertilizer program as a result. This fertilizer also contains 12 percent magnesium (Mg), which is high enough to antagonize the uptake of calcium in some plants. Special care should be exercised to maintain calcium at a moderately high level in the root medium to

Table 8–10

Recommended Uses and Rates of Application for MagAmp®
Slow-Release Fertilizer

Crop	*Rate*	*MagAmp® Grade*
Bedding plants	8–10 lb/cu yd (5–6 kg/m^3)	Medium
Cut flowers	15 lb/100 sq ft (0.75 kg/m^2)	Medium
Geranium	10–12 lb/cu yd (6–7 kg/m^3)	Medium
Pot mums, Easter lily, poinsettia	15–20 lb/cu yd (9–12 kg/m^3)	Medium

avert a deficiency. This problem is particularly important in areas where the water supply has a low calcium content. MagAmp® at one-third the normally recommended rate supplemented with periodic liquid fertilizer is suggested in New England. The supplemental liquid fertilizer should contain nitrogen in the nitrate form to compensate for nitrogen in MagAmp®, which is all ammoniacal plus urea.

Urea Formaldehyde

This slow-release nitrogen-containing fertilizer is sold under several trade names including Borden's 38®, Ureaform®, and Uramite®. It contains 36 percent nitrogen and is slowly available, with about two-thirds released the first year and successively smaller amounts in succeeding years. This fertilizer has gained considerable prominence as a source of nitrogen for home lawns and golf courses. Much of the urea formaldehyde exists in long chemical chains that cannot be taken up by plant roots. Once it is in the soil, microorganisms feed upon these chains, breaking them down into smaller pieces, some of which are urea. Urea is a form of nitrogen readily utilized by the plant. This breakdown process occurs slowly over a long period of time.

Urea formaldehyde has not been used extensively in greenhouse culture, except in mixed formulations, for two reasons. First, it provides only the nutrient nitrogen, leaving the need for a potassium source. Second, it provides nitrogen in the form of urea, which is ultimately converted to ammonium either in the soil or in the plant. As discussed earlier, most greenhouse plants do not respond well to ammonium nitrogen exclusively. Urea formaldehyde is used by some azalea growers as a top dressing to guarantee against nitrogen deficiency because of the high requirement of this crop for nitrogen relative to potassium. It is used at the rate of 1 rounded teaspoon (5 g) per 6 inch (15 cm) pot at two-month intervals during periods of heavy growth. A continual fertilization program is used in addition to this application (see Table 8–4).

Sulfur-Coated Fertilizers

Prills of various fertilizers including urea, ammonium polyphosphate, triple superphosphate, potassium sulfate, and potassium chloride are coated individually with a combination of sulfur, a wax-like sealant, and possibly a conditioner such as diatomaceous earth. Various combinations of these sulfur-coated materials are blended to yield a multitude of grades such as 13–13–13, 21–6–12, and 7–34–0. Release of nutrients is dependent upon soil microorganisms, which convert the insoluble elemental sulfur to soluble sulfate. When this happens, water enters the capsule and dissolves the fertilizer contained in it. The release period is typically three to four months, but coating alterations can extend the release period to one year. The sulfur-coated products have gained wide acceptance outdoors for turf, nursery, and landscape uses. They are not used to any extent in greenhouses because all of the nitrogen is ammonium and/or urea. While nitrates could theoretically be coated, they have not been because of the danger of explosion when the molten sulfur is sprayed on the prills of nitrate.

Chelated Micronutrients

The word *chelate* is derived from a Greek word meaning claw. It is appropriate because chelates are large, organic chemical structures that encircle and tightly hold the micronutrients iron, manganese, zinc, and copper. Plant roots can absorb the micronutrient–chelate combination. The micronutrient is then released inside the plant. Alternatively, plants can absorb micronutrients alone as they are slowly released into the soil solution by chelates. When the soil pH is higher than that desired for a specific crop, it contains high levels of hydroxide and possibly carbonates that will precipitate iron, manganese, zinc, and copper. Precipitate nutrients are insoluble and unavailable to plants. Chelated micronutrients are protected from precipitation. However, micronutrients are slowly released from chelates, after which they can be precipitated. The value of chelates stems in great measure from their long release period.

Roses were traditionally grown in a moderately acid media of pH 5.5–6.0. With time, it was learned that the benefit of the low pH level was the heavy release of available iron, a feature necessary for this poor accumulator of iron. Actually, the rose grows better at a higher pH level, providing sufficient iron is available. Today, iron is routinely applied in the chelated form at the rate of 1 pound per 1,000 ft^2 (4.9 g/m^2) of bed at a frequency of about every three months. Although the alternative source of iron, iron sulfate, is much cheaper pound for pound, under adversely high pH conditions, it can be more expensive because it needs to be applied at a greater frequency than chelated iron. Iron sulfate rapidly releases iron into the soil solution where it precipitates.

The chelated forms of iron, manganese, zinc, and copper are the most common forms used in the premium greenhouse fertilizers. Their high solubility compared to alternative forms makes them very desirable to fertilizer formulators. In correcting individual micronutrient deficiencies, there is usually an advantage to using chelated iron when the pH level is adversely high for the given crop. If the pH level is normal, the cheaper iron sulfate (ferrous) form serves well. Chelated manganese, zinc, and copper, however, do not show as great an advantage. Unless the soil pH is extremely high, the extra expense of the chelated forms of manganese, zinc, and copper is not usually warranted. The sulfate form works well for reasons of economics and effectiveness.

NUTRITIONAL MONITORING

Nutritional problems will develop even in the best of fertilization programs. The careful grower makes use of three systems for monitoring nutrient status and is thus able to forecast problems as well as develop remedies. These systems are (1) visual diagnosis, (2) soil testing, and (3) foliar (leaf) analysis. Each test provides some information that is not provided by the others.

Visual Diagnosis

Visual diagnosis can be employed only after damage has occurred. Often, the damage is only partially reversible. Therefore, one should not rely on visual diagnosis as a routine measure of nutrient status. Each nutrient deficiency has several symptoms that are common to many crops. These symptoms are listed in Table 8–11 and are shown in Figures 8–5 through 8–16. It should be noted that some crops will not develop these symptoms and many crops, in addition to these symptoms, will develop others. Only the more typical symptoms are presented here.

A few definitions will be of help in reading Table 8–11. *Chlorosis* refers to a process whereby green chlorophyll is lost. The leaf tissue turns progressively lighter green and finally yellow. *Necrosis* refers to the death of cells and is manifested as various shades of brown. *Interveinal chlorosis* is chlorosis occurring between the veins (vascular tissue) of the leaf. The veins remain green in color. A *witch's broom* is a typical boron deficiency symptom because more boron is required for flower-bud formation than for vegetative-shoot development. When the plant reaches the stage of flower-bud formation, it aborts, giving rise to lateral vegetable shoots. These develop but, in turn, abort as flower buds are initiated. This process continues until a proliferation of developing shoots gives the appearance of a broom. *Strap leaves*, typical of calcium deficiency, are long, thin leaves having the appearance of a strap.

Soil Testing

Analyses of greenhouse soils will generally include a measurement of the pH and soluble-salt levels in the soil. Neither of these levels is determined by visual diagnosis or foliar analysis procedures. Only a portion of most nutrients in the soil is

Table 8–11

Key to the Classical Symptoms of Various Nutrient Deficiencies

Deficiency Symptoms	*Deficient Nutrient*	*Reference*
a. The dominant symptom is chlorotic foliage.		
b. Entire leaf blades are chlorotic.		
c. Only the lower leaves are chlorotic followed by necrosis and leaf drop.	Nitrogen	Figure 8–5
cc. Leaves on all parts of plant are affected and sometimes have a beige cast.	Sulfur	Figure 8–10
bb. Yellowing of leaves takes form of interveinal chlorosis.		
c. Only recently mature or older leaves exhibit interveinal chlorosis.	Magnesium	Figure 8–9
cc. Only younger leaves exhibit interveinal chlorosis. This is the only symptom.	Iron	Figure 8–11
d. In addition to interveinal chlorosis on young leaves, gray or tan necrotic spots develop in chlorotic areas.	Manganese	Figure 8–12
dd. While younger leaves have interveinal chlorosis, the tips and lobes of leaves remain green followed by veinal chlorosis and rapid, extensive necrosis of leaf blade.	Copper	Figure 8–14
ddd. Young leaves are very small, sometimes missing leaf blades altogether, and internodes are short, giving a rosette appearance.	Zinc	Figure 8–13
aa. Leaf chlorosis is not the dominant symptom.		
b. Symptoms appear at base of plant.		
c. At first all leaves are dark green, and then growth is stunted. Purple pigment often develops in leaves, particularly older leaves.	Phosphorus	Figure 8–6
cc. Margins of older leaves become chlorotic and then burn, or small chlorotic spots progressing to necrosis appear scattered on old leaf blades.	Potassium	Figure 8–7
bb. Symptoms appear at top of plant.		
c. Terminal buds die, giving rise to a witch's broom. Young leaves become very thick, leathery, and chlorotic. Rust-colored cracks and corking occur on young stems, petioles, and flower stalks. Young leaves are crinkled.	Boron	Figure 8–15
cc. Margins of young leaves fail to form, sometimes yielding strap-leaves. Growing point ceases to develop, leaving a blunt end. Light green color or uneven chlorosis of young tissue develops. Root growth is poor in that roots are short and thickened.	Calcium	Figure 8–8

(a)

(b)

Figure 8–5

Nitrogen deficiency and toxicity: Nitrogen deficiency appears first on the lower foliage and then progresses up the plant. Leaves turn light green, then yellow, and finally necrotic. If the plant is one that forms an abscission layer, those leaves will drop off. The overall plant is stunted. (a) A series of Rieger begonia plants fertilized with increasing levels of nitrogen from deficient on the left to toxic on the right. Deficient plants are stunted, have poor secondary shoot development, and have chlorotic foliage. Toxic plants are stunted, have poor secondary shoot development, and are deep green in color. In addition to these symptoms of nitrogen toxicity, there are typical symptoms of soluble-salt injury, such as wilting during the bright part of the day, necrosis of foliage, and root death. Nitrogen and potassium toxicities are often complicated by high-soluble-salt injuries because of the high levels of these nutrients required in the root medium to get a toxicity. (b) Nitrogen deficiency of carnation exhibits itself in a very distinctive symptom known as "curly tip." The tips of leaf pairs tend to hook together, so that subsequent leaves do not have adequate growing room and as a result become folded as they develop. Nitrogen deficiency also results in narrow, stiff leaf formation in carnation, often referred to as "grassiness," as seen in the plant on the left.

(a) (b)

Figure 8–6

Phosphorus deficiency: (a) Foliage appears very healthy as it becomes darker green than normal. The deficient plant is well proportioned but is generally smaller than normal, as seen in the contrast with a normal Rieger begonia plant to the right of the deficient plant. (b) Foliage eventually turns chlorotic, as seen in this tomato plant, and later, leaves become necrotic. Some plants develop purple pigmentation, as in the case of this particular plant. (*Photograph b by Woolley and Broyer and courtesy of The Fertilizer Institute, Washington,* D.C. 20036)

(a) (b)

Figure 8–7

Potassium deficiency: This deficiency occurs first on older foliage as chlorosis, which quickly progresses to necrosis. Symptoms may start at the leaf margin in some plant species such as begonia or may be scattered across the leaf in other species such as carnation (a). The necrotic spots spread and eventually destroy the entire leaf, as seen in the tomato leaves in (b). The overall plant shows a progression of injury from the base of the plant upward. (*Photograph b by Woolley and Broyer and courtesy of The Fertilizer Institute, Washington,* D.C. 20036)

(a) (b)

(c)

Figure 8–8

Calcium deficiency: This deficiency is generally expressed at the top of the plant as a rather irregular chlorosis of foliage and incomplete formation of tissue. (a) Leaves of the chrysanthemum plant are incompletely formed, giving the appearance of long, narrow "strap" leaves. (b) Often, the growing point (*meristem*) stops developing and takes on a blunt appearance, as seen in this rose plant. Note the incompletely formed leaves on the lower left side of the rose shoot. (c) Flower tissue may also be incompletely formed, as in the case of this petunia plant. Collapse of tissue in the petal lobes and corolla tube is evident.

Figure 8–9

Magnesium deficiency: Symptoms of magnesium deficiency, like those of nitrogen and potassium deficiencies, begin at the base of the plant and progress upward. Interveinal chlorosis of foliage is the predominant symptom, as seen in this petunia plant.

immediately available to a plant. Soil-testing procedures must give an estimate of the proportion of each nutrient that is available. Soil testing is commonly practiced during crop growth but is equally valuable when it is done prior to planting. The pH level of greenhouse media is best adjusted prior to planting because of the need to thoroughly mix into it the limestone or sulfur used to adjust pH. A soil test prior to planting will also support the decision of which nutrients can be provided in a single application at that time.

Most soil testing is performed by institutional and commercial laboratories. Growers can purchase equipment to test their own root media. Inexpensive test kits generally purchased for nutrient tests are only moderately accurate, giving just an approximate indication of nutrient level. Very accurate equipment, however, can be purchased by growers for testing pH and soluble-salt levels. Every greenhouse business should own a pH meter (usually priced at $150 and up) and a soluble-salt meter (priced at about $200). The two tests can be run in 30 minutes time and are extremely valuable in root-media preparation, monitoring of general nutrient status, and diagnosing nutritional problems.

An important decision in soil testing is that of the number of samples to be drawn. No set area can be assigned to a sample. To determine the boundaries of

Figure 8–10

Sulfur deficiency: The plant as a whole is affected. Foliage becomes uniformly lighter green in color. Chrysanthemum leaves here show symptoms increasing in intensity from left to right. Some plants develop a beige cast in addition to chlorosis. (*Photograph courtesy of* A. M. *Kofranek, University of California, Davis,* CA)

(a) (b)

Figure 8–11

Iron deficiency: Symptoms of iron deficiency are similar to those of magnesium deficiency in that interveinal chlorosis is the principal symptom, but they differ in that iron deficiency appears at the top of the plant first. (a) A close-up of interveinal chlorosis on a young Rieger begonia leaf. (b) An iron-deficient petunia plant.

Figure 8–12

Manganese deficiency: Symptoms of manganese deficiency start out the same as iron deficiency with interveinal chlorosis of young foliage. In the later stages of manganese deficiency, however, tan to gray spots develop in the chlorotic areas, as seen in these chrysanthemum leaves. (*Photograph courtesy of* A. M. *Kofranek, University of California, Davis,* CA)

the area included in one sample, one should consider the origin of the medium and its fertilization history. The wide variety of components in greenhouse media react differently with plant nutrients. Clays tend to tie up potassium (some more than others), while pine bark and peat-moss-based soil-less media are often associated with micronutrient deficiencies, particularly iron. Although two media might be handled under the same fertilization program, in time the available levels of nutrients will vary so much that separate soil tests will be needed. On the other hand, a single medium might be subjected to two fertilization programs, perhaps dictated by two different crops. Even though only one crop might be growing in these areas, it will be necessary to take two soil samples because residual nutrients such as phosphorus might have been applied in greater quantity to one area than to the other.

Other more subtle factors to consider in soil testing will become more recognizable as one becomes familiar with a greenhouse range. For example, a chrysanthemum grower experienced root injury, necrosis of leaf margins, and overall stunting of plants in specific sections of outdoor ground beds during rainy seasons. The problem was due to poor drainage in the low spots of the beds. Under this condition of low soil-oxygen content, an excessive proportion of the large manganese reserve of the soil was converted to an available form and, in turn, resulted in manganese toxicity. The higher areas of the beds were sufficiently drained and aerated to prevent an excessive conversion of unavailable to available

(a)

(b)

Figure 8–13

Zinc deficiency: Reduced leaf size is very typical of zinc deficiency; in fact, zinc deficiency is frequently called "little leaf disease" in field crops. Shortened internodes and irregular chlorosis of young foliage are also typical. (a) Zinc-deficient carnation shoots on either side of a normal shoot. Symptoms include small leaves and very short internodes. (b) *Kalanchoe* are more prone to zinc deficiency than most other greenhouse crops. Prolific branching from a broad, flattened stem is indicative of this deficiency in *Kalanchoe*. This condition is termed *fasciation*. The stem on the left is normal, while that on the right is deficient in zinc.

(a) (b) (c) (d)

Figure 8–14

Copper deficiency: The early symptom is interveinal chlorosis of young foliage. It is different from that caused by iron deficiency because lobes and points at the leaf margin tend to be deeper green than the inner portion of the leaf blade, as seen in the chrysanthemum leaves in (a). When copper deficiency progresses in chrysanthemum, the first fully expanded leaves suddenly turn necrotic (b) as the upper leaves partially regain a green color. With time, the chlorosis of the plant tip intensifies and necrosis occurs again. Some crops exhibit veinal chlorosis as a late stage of copper deficiency, as seen in the chrysanthemum plant in (c). Copper deficiency in rose (d) is seen as irregular interveinal chlorosis of young leaves. When leaves are forming, necrosis occurs on the leaf blade, resulting in the development of very small leaves. This pattern of small leaves may be cyclic, giving an hourglass effect.

Figure 8–15

Boron deficiency: Leaves become thickened and leathery in some plant species, and irregular chlorosis develops as in the case of the petunia in (a). Other plant species develop crinkled leaves with irregular chlorosis of young leaves as in the Rieger begonia plant in (b). Rust-colored cracks are common on stems, petioles, flower stalks, and sometimes on the leaf blades of many plants. Cork develops over the cracks (b). A cross section of tissues of many boron-deficient plants would show rust coloration and a breakdown of vascular tissue. The boron requirement of reproductive (floral) growth is greater than that for vegetative growth; thus, abortion of the meristem often occurs when the flower bud begins to form. Side shoots develop and in turn abort, only to give rise to more and more side shoots. Eventually, a "witch's broom" forms as in the carnation shoots in (c). If flowers should form, they are usually incomplete. Carnation flowers frequently have split calyx and a low petal count. The gladiolus flower on the left in (d) shows incompletely formed petals as a result of boron deficiency.

Figure 8–16

Molybdenum deficiency: This deficiency is rare in greenhouse crops except for poinsettia, where it is common. As pictured here, median poinsettia leaves develop a chlorotic margin that turns yellow and later necrotic. These symptoms spread inward, eventually killing the entire leaf.

manganese. To identify this problem, it was necessary to recognize and sample the problem section only.

State soil-testing laboratories in most states offer services for no fee or for a nominal cost. Many commercial laboratories also offer soil-testing, foliar analysis, and consulting services. The customary volume of soil submitted is 1 pint (500 cc). It is important that this sample be collected properly so that it is truly representative of the several thousand square feet of greenhouse benches it may represent. A soil-sampling tool should be used such as the one shown in Figure 8–17. The top ½ inch (1 cm) of soil is scraped aside, and the soil-sampling tube is then pressed into the soil until it makes contact with the bottom of the pot or bench. In this way, the entire root zone is sampled. The top 1/2 inch is avoided because abnormal levels of fertilizer salts build up there as a result of water evaporation and also because roots rarely grow where there is rapid drying. At least ten soil cores should be taken for one sample. Some should be taken from the edge of the bench, and others from the center since drying conditions, which affect salt accumulation, differ in these locations. The ten cores should be collected from all sectors of the sample area.

The soil sample should be mailed to the testing laboratory without delay. If the soil is wet enough to cause a breakdown of the package during shipment, it should be partially dried in the sun or on a warm surface, such as a boiler, prior to

Figure 8–17

A sampling tool used for obtaining cores of soil from pots or beds in greenhouses for soil-testing purposes. The side of the tube is cut away to permit removal of the soil core.

shipping. It is very important that information sheets supplied by the testing laboratory be completed and sent with the sample. This information aids in identifying problems and developing recommendations.

pH The soil-testing laboratories will interpret most of the results and make recommendations. However, it is still important for the grower to be able to interpret the test results. The soil pH level has far-reaching effects. The soil is neutral at pH 7.0, alkaline if above, and acidic if below (Figure 8–18). The soil pH level controls the availability of all essential plant nutrients to one degree or another, as was illustrated in Figure 8–1. The greatest average level of availability for all essential plant nutrients exists in the pH range of 6.2–6.8 for soil-based media and 5.4–6.0 for soil-less media. It is possible to grow successful crops at much higher and lower levels, but the further one strays from the recommended range, the greater are the odds against success.

Most greenhouse media require an upward adjustment of pH. This can be accomplished at the time of mixing by incorporating finely ground dolomitic limestone into the media. Rates vary for each media type, with clay, peat moss, and pine bark requiring the heaviest rates. In general, 3 pounds of limestone per cubic yard (1.75 kg/m^3) of a soil-based medium will raise the pH about 0.3–0.5 unit. Soil-testing reports will indicate more precise amounts.

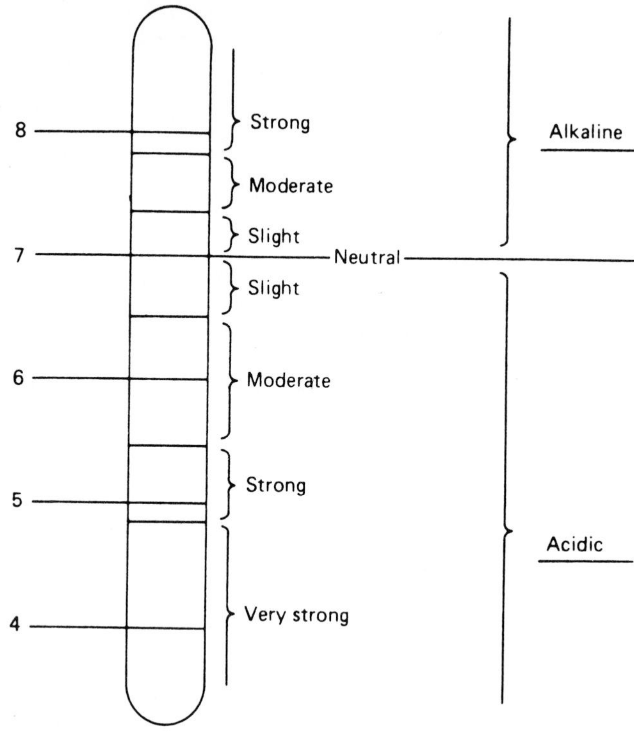

Figure 8–18

Classification of soil pH levels according to plant response.

Ground limestone dissolves very slowly; thus, it is important that it be thoroughly mixed into the root medium to speed up the process of release. Dissolution occurs too slowly for effective application of limestone after the crop is planted. Two procedures can be used for raising the pH level after planting. When a small upward adjustment is needed (0.5 pH unit or less), one can switch to alkaline fertilizers in the continuous liquid program. Table 8–12 indicates the acidity and alkalinity of several common fertilizer carriers. To adjust the pH level up, sodium, potassium, or calcium nitrates can be used. A good fertilizer formulation for finishing crops calls for 2 pounds (2.4 g/l) of calcium nitrate in combination with 1 pound (1.2 g/l) of potassium nitrate in 100 gallons of water applied weekly. If one carries out the appropriate mathematics, one finds that this program is equivalent to applying 3.4 ounces of ground limestone per cubic yard (125 g/m^3) of root media each week. This is a small addition, but in time it has an effect. Fertilizer adjustment of soil pH works for the grower who through periodic testing of the soil sees pH change before it becomes injurious. The grower who permits a severe drop in pH level to occur during culture of the crop must use more drastic measures that can entail an element of risk. It may be necessary to apply hydrated lime (calcium hydroxide), referred to as "builder's lime." This material can be injurious to green tissue and in large quantities can damage roots. A rate of 1.5

Table 8–12

Effect of Various Fertilizers on the pH Level of Root Media*

Fertilizer	*Alkaline (lb of limestone equal to 10 lb of fertilizer)*	*Acidic (lb of limestone needed to neutralize 10 lb of fertilizer)*
Sodium nitrate	2.9	—
Potassium nitrate	2.6	—
Calcium nitrate	2.0	—
Ammonium sulfate	—	11.0
Urea	—	8.4
Diammonium phosphate	—	7.4
Ammonium phosphate	—	6.5
Ammonium nitrate	—	5.9
Superphosphate	Neutral	
Potassium chloride	Neutral	
Potassium sulfate	Neutral	

*From Anon. (1980).

pounds per 100 ft^2 (75 g/m^3) is recommended. The hydrated lime can be applied dry to the soil surface and then immediately syringed with water to remove any from the plant surfaces as well as to begin dissolving and moving the lime into the soil. Hydrated lime can also be applied by mixing 1 pound of it into 5 gallons of water (24 g/l) and applying the dissolved portion to 20 ft^2 (10 l/m^2) of root medium. Hydrated lime is more soluble than ground limestone but not completely water soluble. It reacts much faster than ground limestone yet has a shorter residual effect in the root medium. If one application does not solve the problem, a second one can be made after a few weeks.

The high pH level of hydrated lime can cause a conversion of ammonium nitrogen to ammonia gas. This gas is injurious to roots and foliage. Hydrated lime should not be used when ammonium-containing slow-release fertilizer such as MagAmp® or Osmocote® is in the root medium or when a high proportion (over 50 percent) of ammonium is used in a liquid fertilizer program.

It may be necessary to lower the pH level of root media. This can be accomplished by the use of sulfur, aluminum sulfate, or iron sulfate with a crop absent or present. All of these sources react in the soil to ultimately form sulfuric acid. Rates of application are listed in Table 8–13. These recommendations are designed to lower the pH level to 5.0, a level required for producing a crop of blue-flowered hydrangeas. The table is useful for determining other changes. To lower the pH level from 6.5 to 6.0, one would use 0.5 pound of sulfur per cubic yard (the difference between 2.0 and 1.5 pounds listed in column 2)or 1.5 pounds of aluminum sulfate (the difference between 5.25 and 3.75 pounds listed in column 4).

Table 8–13

Quantities of Sulfur or Aluminum Sulfate Necessary To Lower the pH Level of Greenhouse Root Media from Various Levels to 5.0*

	Sulfur		*Aluminum Sulfate*	
pH Change	*lb/yd*^{3}	*kg/m*^{3}	*lb/yd*^{3}	*kg/m*^{3}
8.0 to 5.0	3.5	2.1	8.75	5.2
7.5 to 5.0	3.25	1.9	7.75	4.6
7.0 to 5.0	2.5	1.5	6.5	3.9
6.5 to 5.0	2.0	1.2	5.25	3.1
6.0 to 5.0	1.5	0.9	3.75	2.2
5.5 to 5.0	0.75	0.5	2.0	1.2

*From Tayama (1966).

Iron sulfate is used at the same rates as those listed for aluminum sulfate. All three materials can be mixed into the soil dry. They also may be added to water and applied to the soil during mixing or to the surface of the soil of an existing crop. Aluminum and iron sulfates are water soluble, whereas sulfur is not and, therefore, must be held in suspension. The sulfates react very rapidly, while sulfur must be oxidized by soil microbes, a process requiring several weeks or more if the medium has been pasteurized.

Soluble Salts Another valuable test provided only through soil testing is the measure of the soluble-salt level. Salt concentrations in the soil solution and in the root cells determine to a large extent the flow of water between the two. Water flows in the direction of the higher salt concentration, which generally exists in the root cells. For various reasons, salt levels in the soil solution can build up so that water no longer moves into the root. Following transpirational loss of water from the foliage, cells begin to desiccate (lose adverse amounts of water).

An excessive level of soluble salts in the root medium is first seen as wilting of plants during bright times of the day even though the root medium is moist. Overall growth slows down. Roots die from the tips back, particularly in the dryer zones of the root medium. Leaves become necrotic, in some cases along the margin and in others as circular spots scattered across the leaf blade. Ultimately, deficiency symptoms of many nutrients will occur as a result of acutely impaired nutrient uptake by the injured root system.

Soluble salts come from various sources. Soluble fertilizers are soluble salts. Initially insoluble, slow-release fertilizers dissolve with time, releasing nutrients into the root medium that are in themselves soluble salts. Thus, some soluble salt must be present to ensure a proper level of fertilizer, but the level must not be too high. Other sources may not be desirable. Occasionally, a well is drilled that yields water of low quality (it contains quantities of impurities). The impurities may be sulfate in areas of old coal-mine shafts, sodium chloride (table salt) or sodium bicarbonate (baking soda) along coastal areas, calcium bicarbonate in areas of limestone deposits, and sodium in the alkaline areas found in arid parts of the world.

Organic matter of high nitrogen content that undergoes rapid decomposition constitutes another source of soluble salts. Manure and highly decomposed peats may have sizable nitrogen contents that are rapidly released through degradation in the root medium as ammonium nitrogen. Ammonium nitrogen can quickly build up to a toxic level because its positive electrical charge causes it to be held in the root medium.

Fertilizers vary in the manner in which they affect the soluble-salt level. Table 8–14 lists the relative salt effect of several fertilizers. Sodium nitrate was arbitrarily set at 100. Potassium chloride is shown to have 16 percent greater effect on raising the soluble-salt level of root media than sodium nitrate, while urea has only three-fourths of the effect of sodium nitrate. The nutritive value of these fertilizers should be taken into account along with their salt index. As the fertilizer is utilized by the plants, the influence upon the soluble-salt level is reduced. Ammonium nitrate has a high salt index of 105 but is comprised of ammonium nitrogen and nitrate nitrogen only. These nutrients in combination are readily utilized by

Table 8–14

Relative Salt Index for Several Fertilizers[1]

Fertilizer	*Salt Index*
Sodium nitrate (nitrate of soda)[2]	100
Potassium chloride (muriate of potash—60% K_2O)	116
Ammonium nitrate	105
Urea	75
Potassium nitrate	74
Ammonium sulfate	69
Calcium nitrate	53
Potassium sulfate	46
Magnesium sulfate	44
Diammonium phosphate	34
Monoammonium phosphate	30
Concentrated superphosphate	10
48% superphosphate	10
20% superphosphate	8
Gypsum	8
Limestone	5

[1]From Rader, White, and Whittaker (1943).

[2]Sodium nitrate was arbitrarily set at 100. The lower the index value, the smaller the contribution that the fertilizer makes to the soluble-salt level of the root medium.

the plant; thus, the salt effect of this fertilizer is quickly reduced to an insignificant level. Although sodium nitrate has a lower salt index of 100, it is comprised of sodium and nitrate nitrogen. The nitrate nitrogen is readily utilized, but the sodium is not. Repeated applications of this fertilizer will lead to a buildup of sodium and ultimately a high soluble-salt level. Chloride has an effect similar to that of sodium. Therefore, sodium- and chloride-containing fertilizers are generally avoided in the greenhouse. The presence of excessive levels of soluble salts is a rare problem for field crops, but in the greenhouse where unusually high levels of fertilizer are applied, it is a very common problem.

Soil-testing laboratories vary in the manner in which they conduct their testing. The amount of water used to remove the salts from the root medium is the variable in the salt test. Basically, there are three tests:

1. The saturated-paste extract test in which the intent is to add only enough water to the root-medium sample to saturate it to a level typical of watering.
2. A 1:2 dilution test in which 2 volumes of water are added to 1 volume of dry medium.
3. A 1:5 dilution test in which 5 volumes of water are added to 1 volume of dry medium.

In each of the last two tests, the root medium is left in contact with the water for at least 30 minutes to permit movement of the salt into the water. The electrical conductivity of the water is then measured by placing two electrodes in the water and measuring the flow of current between them. The higher the salt content, the greater the flow of electrical current through the water. The electrical conductivity (EC) is measured in terms of mho/cm (the opposite to ohms of electrical resistance). Since the conductivity is very low, it is recorded in fractions of a mho—thousandths of a mho in the case of the saturated-paste extract (mho $\times 10^{-3}$/cm), also called a millimho, and hundred-thousandths of a mho for the other two tests (mho $\times 10^{-5}$/cm). These terms will be of little concern to the grower. Each laboratory will use one test only and will make available an interpretation chart. Interpretation charts are presented in Table 8–15 for the three test procedures.

Seedlings are more sensitive to high soluble-salt levels than are established plants. Established plants vary in their resistance to high soluble-salt levels. African violets and azalea are particularly sensitive and should not be grown in media with a level exceeding 80 on the 1:2 dilution test. Snapdragon is moderately sensitive and should be grown at levels below 125 on the 1:2 dilution test. Several of the houseplant crops are sensitive as well. Little research has been conducted on each of these many crops, and soluble-salt interpretations are missing for most. The exact level at which injury occurs depends to a large degree on watering practices. If the root medium is not permitted to dry, then a high salt content may be

Table 8–15

Interpretation of Soluble-Salt Levels

Dilution[1] 1:2 Soil	Dilution[1] 1:2 Soil-less	Dilution[1] 1:5 Soil	Saturated[2] Paste Extract, Soil and Soil-less	Interpretation
0–25	0–?	0–10	0–.075	Insufficient nutrition
26–50	?–100	11–25	0.75–2	Low fertility unless applied with every watering
100		50	—	Maximum for planting seedlings or rooted cuttings
51–125	100–175	26–60	2–4	Good for most crops
126–175	176–225	61–80	—	Good for established crops
176–200	225–350	81–100	4–8	Danger area
Over 200	Over 350	Over 100	Over 8	Usually injurious

[1]mho × 10^{-5}/cm.
[2]mmho/cm.

tolerated. When the medium dries, the salts become more concentrated than indicated by the test, and injuries may ensue. Ordinarily, it is not wise to maintain root media at a high moisture content, but between the time that a high salt level is identified and the cure is administered, it is expedient to do so.

Fortunately, soluble salts, as the name implies, are water soluble and can be leached from root media. The standard corrective recommendation calls for application of 1 gallon of water per square foot (40 l/m^2) of root medium for bench crops or per half cubic foot (200 l/m^3) of root medium for pot crops, a waiting period of a few hours, and then a second application of water at the rate of 2 quarts per square foot (20 l/m^2) of root-medium surface. The waiting period gives the more slowly soluble salts time to dissolve.

Often, a root medium with a soil base is adversely affected by the second application of water. The soil structure breaks down. This is particularly harmful in carnation and rose root media, where the crop is maintained for one, two, or five years without an opportunity to amend the root media. Researchers at the University of Connecticut have developed a more desirable procedure for leaching in these cases. Up to 5 gallons of water are supplied to each square foot (200 l/m^2) of root medium in one application, preferably with a trickle-type irrigation system. This procedure utilizes more water but eliminates the destructive second application of water when the soil is excessively wet and subject to breakdown of structure.

Soil testing is quite well justified by the benefits derived from the pH and soluble-salt tests alone, yet a major portion of the analysis is given over to determination of the available levels of essential nutrients including nitrate nitrogen, phosphorus, potassium, calcium, magnesium, manganese, and sometimes ammonium nitrogen, iron, copper, and zinc. It is important to remember that soil tests are designed to estimate the available fraction of each nutrient tested rather than the total quantity of that nutrient present in the root medium.

This point is exemplified in the situation of iron. The crust of the earth contains about 4 percent iron, which amounts to 80,000 pounds in the upper 6 inches of a 1 acre field (90,000 kg/ha). Iron (Fe) deficiency often develops in such fields. When it does, it can be corrected with an application of as little as 5 pounds of iron (5.5 kg/ha). It would appear that the addition is insignificant, but in relation to the pool of plant-available iron in the field, the 5 pound addition is large. Somewhat less than 0.1 percent of the total iron is available.

An extracting solution must be used in a soil test that will draw out the available but not the unavailable iron in the same fashion that the root does. Since the nutrient-holding power of soils and the extracting power of roots vary, it is difficult, if not impossible, to develop a perfect extracting solution. Several have been developed over the years that are in use today. Not one is perfect, and each yields different numerical values. Within each testing system, the numerical levels of individual nutrients are related to crop response. A phosphorus level of 50 in one test is indicative of an adequate level for growth, while a level of 6 may be adequate in another. In either case, the grower uses the standards provided by the testing laboratory.

About five tests are in use for greenhouse soils in America, but the most widely used is the Spurway test. Interpretative tables have been well developed for this test. Table 8–16 lists the recommended levels of various nutrients included in the test for greenhouse crops in general. There are other tests—for example, the double-acid test, for which interpretative tables have not been developed in the floriculture field. Growers who use tests for which there are no standards should record and relate over the years their crop responses to fertilizer applications and soil-test results. This procedure ultimately indicates to the grower the levels of each nutrient that should be maintained for best growth. Whether interpretive tables exist or not, one should take monthly soil samples and should keep a log book in which are recorded crop responses; soil-testing, and foliar analysis results; application dates of water, fertilizer, and pesticides; and any other factors affecting growth. Quite often, it is necessary to adapt values in the interpretive table to individual situations. This can be accomplished through the logging procedure.

After an individualized interpretative table is developed, monthly soil sampling should be continued. This practice permits identification of faulty samples, which might infrequently occur as a result of poor sampling procedure or an error in testing. Note in Figure 8–19 the March value for sample A, which is abnormally high. This value is an indication of a faulty sample. It also indicates the direction in which nutrient levels are changing in the root medium. Note again in Figure 8–19 that the potassium levels in root media represented by samples A and B in May are equal. If this level was desirable and May was the only month that a sample was taken, no action would be taken. Yet, from the series of sample results,

Table 8–16

Interpretative Values for the Spurway[1] and the Saturated-Media Extract[2] (Saturated-Paste) Tests[3]

Nutrient	Spurway				
	Low	*Medium*	*High*	*Very High*	*Toxic*
Ammonium (N)	Below 2	2	5	10	Over 15
Nitrate (N)	Below 5	10–20	25–50	50	Over 60
Phosphorus	Below 12	5	5–10	10–15	Over 15
Potassium	Below 10	—	30–50	50	Over 60
Calcium	Below 40	60–120	150	Over 200	—
Nutrient	*Saturated-Media Extract*				
	Low	*Acceptable*	*Optimum*	*High*	*Very High*
Nitrate (N)	0–39	40–99	100–199	200–299	300+
Phosphorus	0–2	3–5	6–9	11–18	19+
Potassium	0–59	60–149	150–249	250–349	350+
Calcium	0–79	80–199	200+	—	—
Magnesium	0–29	30–69	70+	—	—

[1]From University of Connecticut, Plant Science Department, Greenhouse Soil Report Form. Medium levels are suggested for establishing seedlings and rooted cuttings, while high levels are generally appropriate for established plants.

[2]From Warncke and Krauskopf (1983).

[3]Values are listed in parts per million (ppm).

it can be seen that in one medium the level of potassium application should be diminished at this time, while in the other it should be increased so that imbalances do not occur the following month. Only sequential sampling will bear out these facts.

Foliar Analysis

Foliar analysis constitutes a third system for determining the nutrient status of crops. Like soil testing, it is valuable because it can be used to assess a problem before damage occurs. Foliar analysis is an analysis of representative leaves from a crop to determine the quantities of essential as well as potentially hazardous nonessential elements that the crop has taken up. The laboratory conducting the analysis compares the results to standards developed at many research institutions around the world and draws the necessary conclusions for the grower.

Foliar analysis works well because of the strong relationship between leaf composition and plant response, which is illustrated in Figure 8–20. Except in the zone of *luxury consumption*, where changes in leaf composition have no effect

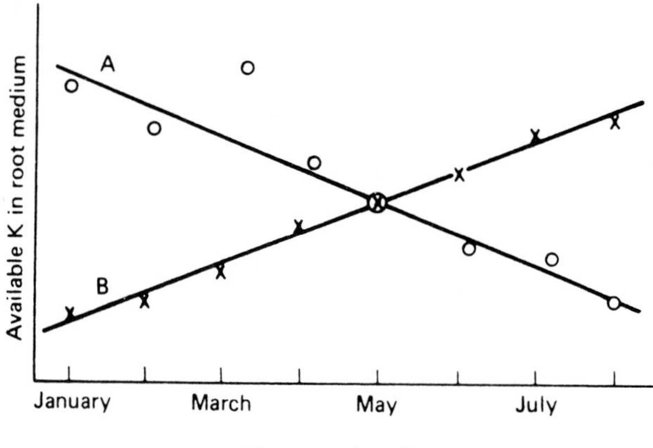

Figure 8–19

An illustration of the value of monthly soil sampling as opposed to a single sample date. Samples A and B drawn in May would indicate similar nutrient situations. This is erroneous since the root medium represented by sample A is decreasing in K level while that represented by sample B is increasing. These facts are borne out only by sequential sampling.

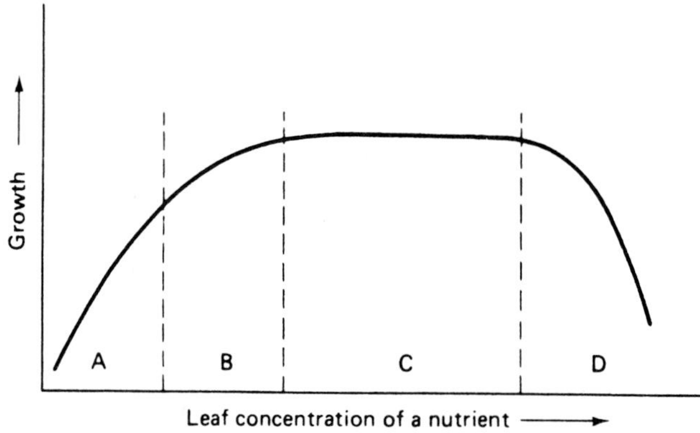

Figure 8–20

When all other factors are adequate, the leaf content of an essential nutrient strongly affects growth. Little growth occurs at low concentrations of the nutrient, but with small additions of the deficient nutrient large increases in growth occur (zone A). When the rate of growth comes closer to the optimum level, increases in the leaf content of the deficient nutrient bring about continually diminishing growth responses (zone B), until a point is reached beyond which no growth response is effected by increases in leaf concentration of the nutrient (zone C). This is the zone of *luxury consumption*. Eventually, nutrient increases in the leaf reach a toxic level, resulting in decreases in growth and eventually in death (zone D).

upon growth, the nutrient content of the leaf can be used to predict the growth of the plant. It is fortunate that the zone of luxury consumption exists because it lessens the chance of injury from overapplication of fertilizer.

Foliar analysis is not a substitute for soil testing. Although both it and soil testing are intended for the same purpose of assessing nutrient status, each provides some information that the other does not. Where both do yield an assessment of the same factor, it is derived in a different manner, which strengthens the conclusions. Foliar analysis does not give a measure of root-media pH or soluble-salt levels, but, unlike soil tests, it does give an analysis of all essential nutrients. Soil tests give information about the present and future by indicating levels of nutrients available for uptake. Foliar analysis gives information about the levels of nutrients already accumulated by the plants; thus, it is directed from the past to the present. Just as one would not enter a serious medical operation without two independent assessments of the situation, one should not base the nutritional future of crops on one system of assessment.

The strength of soil testing in combination with foliar analysis is seen in a situation that occurred in a carnation range some years ago in New York. The crop was growing slowly and showing symptoms of potassium deficiency. Contrary to this observation, a soil test indicated that levels of nitrogen and potassium were high. Foliar analysis indicated that potassium was very deficient, while nitrogen was only moderate to high. The combination of information led to the conclusion that potassium uptake was blocked by a high soil-nitrogen level. This relationship is an antagonism that frequently occurs. The conclusion was verified when four weeks after reducing the rate of 20–20–20 fertilizer application to half of the previous level, the grower observed a twofold increase in the foliar level of potassium and the disappearance of potassium-deficiency symptoms.

Foliar analysis samples should be taken every four to six weeks and the results logged. The optimum level of nutrients in the foliage of each crop is different, necessitating the taking of a different sample for each crop. If one crop is growing in two dissimilar media or has been fertilized in two different manners, two samples must be taken for this crop. It is important that the correct leaves be sampled since the nutrient level in each is different from the rest. The age of the crop is also important because the nutrient levels in each leaf change with time. The laboratory conducting the foliar analysis tests will provide a mailing envelope for the leaves and a set of instructions for collecting the proper leaves.

Rose plants are sampled by picking the two uppermost five-leaflet leaves on a stem whose flower calyx is cracking and whose color is just beginning to show. Thirty leaves with petioles attached should be collected.

Carnation plants that have not yet been pinched are sampled by collecting the fourth and fifth leaf pairs up from the base of the stem (area A in Figure 8–21). Sampling continues in area A after pinching and until the resulting lateral shoots develop seven pairs of leaves. Then, the fifth or sixth leaf pairs are sampled on the new shoots (area B), counting the first pair of leaves to be separated for

Figure 8–21

Leaf-sampling instructions for foliar analysis of florists' crops as used at North Carolina State University.

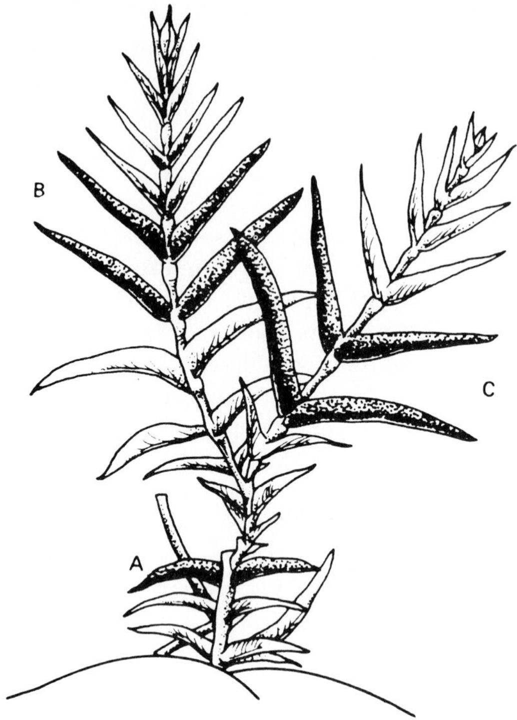

one-half the length of the leaves as the first leaf pair. Sampling continues in area B until a flower bud appears on this shoot. Then, sampling should be shifted to secondary lateral shoots, again using the fifth or sixth leaf pairs from the terminal end of the shoot (area C). When secondary lateral shoots develop flower buds, sampling is shifted to tertiary lateral shoots, and so on.

Chrysanthemums are typical of plants in general in that the youngest fully expanded leaves are sampled. These leaves are usually found on chrysanthemum plants about one-third of the distance down the stem from the top. Chrysanthemums are generally sampled five to six weeks after planting for a single-stem crop or five to six weeks after pinching for a pinched crop.

Foliar analysis kits contain an information form similar to the one shown in Figure 8–22. This form permits laboratory personnel to gather the information necessary to enable them to draw conclusions and make nutritional recommendations. Ordinarily, leaves are placed in the mailing envelope as collected and mailed immediately to the testing laboratory. If it is apparent that nutrient residues are on the leaf surfaces from, for example, foliar fertilization or nutrient-containing pesticides, the leaves should be soaked in water for 1 minute, blotted

MAILING ADDRESS: PLANT ANALYSIS LABORATORY — DEPARTMENT OF HORTICULTURAL SCIENCE
N. C. STATE UNIVERSITY, RALEIGH, N. C. 27607

SAMPLE INFORMATION FOR FLORICULTURE CROPS		LAB USE ONLY
Name of Grower	County	Date Sample Received
Street, Route	Date Sampled	Condition of Sample
City, State, Zip Code	Grower Sample No	Grower #
Telephone No	Name of Crop	County #
Identification of Field Sampled	Description of Sample Site (which field)	Sample #
		Date Analysis Received

SAMPLE INFORMATION

1. Name of crop ________ 2. Variety ________ 3. Date planted ________

4. Date pinched (if applicable) ________

5. This sample represents (a) an average condition ____ (b) a problem area ______

(c) a spotty or sporadic situation ____

6. Appearance or condition of plant and/or leaves ________________

7. Location of sample on plant ________________

8. Previous crop ________ 9. What is your fertilization program for the crop represented by this sample?

(List fertilizers used, rates, and frequency of application).

10. What ammendments did you use during preparation of the soil mix in which this crop is growing (List such materials as dolomitic limestone, superphosphate, fritted trace elements and the rates used).

North Carolina State University Agricultural Experiment Station
and North Carolina Agricultural Extension Service, Cooperating

FARMER OR GROWER COPY

Figure 8–22

A typical information form to be completed by the grower and submitted to the foliar analysis laboratory as an aid in the interpretation of results.

Table 8–17

Minimum Critical Foliar Levels of Nutrients for Florists' Crops in General and for a Few Specific Crops

Nutrient	*General Crops*	*Rose*	*Carnation*	*Chrysanthemum*	*Poinsettia*	*Geranium*	*Rieger Begonia*
N %	—	3.0	3.0	4.5	3.5	2.4	4.7
P %	0.3	0.2	0.45	0.3	0.2	0.3	0.2
K %	—	1.8	3.0	3.5	1.0	0.6	0.95
Ca %	—	1.0	1.0	1.0	0.5	0.8	0.5
Mg %	0.3	0.25	0.3	0.3	0.2	0.14	0.25
Fe ppm	50–60	—	—	—	—	—	—
Mn ppm	30	—	—	—	—	—	—
Zn ppm	20	—	—	—	—	—	—
Cu ppm	5	—	—	7	—	—	—
B ppm	25	—	—	—	—	—	14

Concentrations above these are sufficient, while those below are associated with deficiency. Macronutrient standards are specific to each crop. Few micronutrient standards have been developed for specific crops. Fortunately, micronutrient standards do not vary much among crops.

dry, and then mailed. Deionized or distilled water is preferred, but if unavailable, clear tap water will do. The charge for foliar analysis is considerably more than that for soil testing, ranging from $6 to $30 per sample. This charge is nominal, however, when one considers the total investment in a crop.

Considerable research has been conducted to determine the optimum levels of nutrients in foliage. Carefully developed standards exist for many florists' crops, and for other crops good estimates have been developed from years of observation. Table 8–17 lists the minimum critical levels for several nutrients for some of the major crops. Concentrations below these levels are associated with deficiency. Macronutrient standards vary sharply with each crop, whereas micronutrient standards remain rather constant for most crops. There are few crop variations for the general micronutrient standards listed in Table 8–17.

Listed in Table 8–18 are acceptable ranges of macronutrients for 26 tropical foliage plants. Macronutrients are expressed as a percentage of the dry weight of the leaf tissue analyzed. This would not be convenient for micronutrients since they constitute only a small fraction of 1 percent. A smaller term, parts per million (ppm), is used. The conversion from percent to ppm is simple since 1 percent equals 10,000 ppm.

The testing laboratories report their results on a form more or less similar to that reproduced in Figure 8–23. Generally, the numerical level of each nutrient is reported along with an indication of which of five categories each of the nutrient levels fits:

1. Deficient—showing deficiency symptoms.
2. Low—hidden hunger.
3. Sufficient.
4. High—hidden toxicity.
5. Very high—showing toxicity symptoms.

Also included are recommended fertilization changes to correct any existent nutrient problems.

Table 8–18

Acceptable Ranges of Nitrogen, Phosphorus, Potassium, Calcium, and Magnesium in 26 Tropical Green Plants*

	Percent of Dry Weight				
Botanical Name	*N*	*P*	*K*	*Ca*	*Mg*
Adiantum raddianum	1.5–2.5	0.40–0.80	2.0–3.0	0.2–0.3	0.2–0.4
Aechmea fasciata	1.5–2.0	0.40–0.70	1.5–2.5	0.5–1.0	0.4–0.8
Aglaonema commutatum 'Franscher'	2.5–3.5	0.20–0.35	2.5–3.5	1.0–1.5	0.3–0.6
Aphelandra squarrosa	2.0–3.0	0.20–0.40	1.0–2.0	0.2–0.4	0.5–1.0
Asparagus myriocladus	1.5–2.5	0.30–0.50	2.0–3.0	0.1–0.3	0.1–0.3
Brassaia actinophylla	2.5–3.5	0.20–0.35	2.5–3.5	1.0–1.5	0.3–0.6
Chamaedorea elegans	2.5–3.0	0.20–0.30	1.0–2.0	0.4–1.0	0.3–0.4
Chlorophytum comosum	1.5–2.5	0.10–0.20	3.5–5.0	1.0–2.0	0.5–1.5
Chrysalidocarpus lutescens	1.5–2.5	0.10–0.20	1.0–2.0	1.0–1.5	0.3–0.6
Coffea arabica	2.5–3.5	0.15–0.25	2.0–3.0	0.5–1.0	0.3–0.5
Dieffenbachia exotica	2.5–3.5	0.20–0.35	3.0–4.5	1.0–1.5	0.3–0.8
Dizygotheca elegantissima	2.0–2.5	0.40–0.60	1.5–2.5	0.5–1.0	0.2–0.3
Dracaena deremensis 'Janet Craig'	2.0–3.0	0.20–0.30	3.0–4.0	1.5–2.0	0.3–0.6
Dracaena deremensis 'Warneckii'	2.5–3.5	0.15–0.30	3.0–4.5	1.0–2.0	0.5–1.0
Dracaena fragrans 'Massangeana'	2.0–3.0	0.15–0.25	1.0–2.0	1.0–2.0	0.5–1.0
Dracaena sanderana	2.5–3.5	0.20–0.30	2.0–3.0	1.5–2.5	0.3–0.6
Dracaena surculosa	1.5–2.5	0.20–0.30	1.0–2.0	1.0–1.5	0.3–0.5
Epipremnum aureum	2.5–3.5	0.20–0.35	3.0–4.5	1.0–1.5	0.3–0.6
Ficus benjamina	1.8–2.5	0.10–0.20	1.0–1.5	2.0–3.0	0.4–0.8
Ficus elastica	1.3–1.6	0.10–0.20	0.6–1.0	0.3–0.5	0.2–0.4
Maranta leuconeura kerchoveana	2.0–3.0	0.20–0.30	3.0–4.5	0.5–1.5	0.5–1.0
Monstera deliciosa	2.5–3.5	0.20–0.35	3.0–4.5	0.4–1.0	0.3–0.6
Philodendron scandens oxycardium	2.0–3.0	0.15–0.25	3.0–4.5	0.5–1.5	0.3–0.6
Sansevieria trifasciata 'Laruentii'	1.7–3.0	0.15–0.30	2.0–3.0	1.0–1.5	0.3–0.6
Stromanthe amabilis	2.5–3.0	0.20–0.50	3.0–4.0	0.1–0.2	0.3–0.5
Syngonium podophyllum	2.5–3.5	0.20–0.30	3.0–4.5	0.4–1.0	0.3–0.6

*From Poole, Connover, and Joiner (1976).

PLANT ANALYSIS REPORT

Name of Grower: Paul Nelson	County: Wake	Date Sample Received: 3-19-85
Street, Route: 29 Main St.	Date Sampled: 3-17-85	Condition of Sample: Good
City, State, Zip: Raleigh, N. C. 27607	Grower Sample #: 2	Grower #: 27
Telephone No.: 737-3132	Name of Crop: Cut Chrysanthemum	County #: 13
Identification of Field Sampled: III	Description of Sample Site (Within The Field):	Lab Sample #: 1971 Date Analysis Received: 3-26-85

COUNTY SAMPLE NUMBER	FARMER OR GROWER SAMPLE NUMBER	N %	P %	K %	Na %	Ca %	Mg %	Mn ppm	Fe ppm	B ppm	Cu ppm	Mo ppm	Zn ppm	Al ppm
	2	4.50	0.85	2.10	0.02	1.2	0.38	125	150	23	9	1	44	
RANGE														
DEFICIENT				X										
LOW										X				
SUFFICIENT		X			X	X	X	X	X		X	X	X	
HIGH			X											
EXCESS														

COMMENTS AND RECOMMENDATIONS.

1. Potassium is low. Apply potassium nitrate (13-0-44) for the next two weekly applications at the rate of 2 lbs. per 100 gal.

2. Phosphorus is too high. After correcting the potassium problem use a 1-0-1 ratio fertilizer rather than the 1-1-1 you have been using.

3. Boron is approaching the deficiency level. Apply one ounce of borax per 100 sq. ft. of bench space once.

Mailing Address: Plant Analysis Laboratory, Department of Horticultural Science, N. C. State University, Raleigh, N. C. 27607
North Carolina State University Agricultural Experiment Station and North Carolina Agricultural Extension Service, Cooperating.

FARMER OR GROWER COPY

Figure 8–23

A typical foliar analysis report as it is received by the grower.

CORRECTIVE PROCEDURES

Recommendations

Fertilization systems were recommended in the earlier part of this chapter. Under ideal conditions, these systems will work well, but conditions are not always ideal. The optimum rate of fertilizer application relates to the rate of plant growth, which, in turn, can be adversely affected by inclement weather, a poor root medium that does not drain well, over- or underwatering, a dirty greenhouse covering, nutrient tie-up by constituents of the root medium, antagonisms by other nutrients, and many other factors. Some nutrients are affected more than others; thus, it is important not only to adjust the rate of fertilization but also to change the ratio of nutrients in the fertilizer. Occasionally, a single nutrient will go far enough out of balance that it alone must be applied. Nitrogen and potassium ratio adjustments can be accomplished through alterations in the continual fertilizer formula (refer to Table 8–5). Corrective procedures for ten other nutrient deficiencies are listed in Table 8–19.

Phosphorus deficiency is uncommon but not altogether nonexistent. Its occurrence would indicate failure to incorporate sufficient phosphorus into the root medium prior to planting and could easily be corrected by switching to a complete, phosphorus-containing fertilizer such as 20–10–20 in the continual fertilization program. Calcium and magnesium deficiencies do not often occur where the root-medium pH level has been properly adjusted with dolomitic limestone. Poinsettia was traditionally, and in many cases still is, grown in an acid medium to minimize the development of root-rot organisms. Calcium and magnesium deficiencies often occur under these conditions. The new varieties of poinsettia are prone to magnesium deficiency even when the root-medium pH level is adjusted to the recommended range. Easter lilies are very susceptible to calcium deficiency. The use of calcium nitrate as a nitrogen source in the complete fertilizer can solve these calcium problems. An application of 2 pounds of Epsom salts (magnesium sulfate) per 100 gallons (2.4 g/l) is used to solve either a magnesium or a sulfur deficiency. Sulfur deficiencies have become more prevalent in recent years in soilless media that do not contain single superphosphate or gypsum.

It is generally safe to apply a micronutrient mixture when symptoms of a single micronutrient deficiency occur and there is evidence that no other micronutrients are present in high quantity. If this information is not known, the status of all micronutrients should be determined by a foliar analysis test. If all micronutrients are present in moderate or low concentrations, then a micronutrient mix can be applied. Otherwise, only the deficient nutrient or nutrients should be applied. In the event that a foliar analysis is not possible, small plots may be tested with the suspected deficient nutrient. Then, the deficient nutrient alone should be applied. Micronutrient excesses can be far more troublesome than deficiencies

Table 8–19

Fertilizer Sources and Rates for Correction of Various Nutrient Deficiencies

Deficient Nutrient	*Fertilizer Source*	*Rate of Application*[1]	
		oz/100 gal	*g/l*
P	Switch to a complete fertilizer containing N–P–K for the continual program		
	or one application of diammonium phosphate or monopotassium phosphate	32	2.4
Ca	Switch part or all of the N source to calcium nitrate for a few weeks		
Mg	Magnesium sulfate (Epsom salts)	32	2.4
S	Magnesium sulfate	32	2.4
	or switch N or K source to ammonium or potassium sulfate for a few weeks		
Fe	Iron chelate (Sequestrene® 330) or ferrous sulfate	4	0.300
	or foliar spray ferrous sulfate or Sequestrene® 330 iron chelate	4	0.300
Mn	Manganese sulfate	2	0.150
	or foliar spray manganese sulfate or manganese chelate	8	0.600
Zn	Zinc sulfate	2	0.150
	or zinc chelate	1	0.075
	or switch to the fungicide Zineb and spray at the recommended rate monthly		
Cu	Copper sulfate	2	0.150
	or copper chelate	1	0.075
	or foliar spray tri-base copper sulfate	4	0.300
B	Borax	0.5	0.038
	or Solubor	0.25	0.019
Mo	For soil-based media, drench once with sodium or ammonium molybdate	0.027[2]	0.002
	For soil-less media, drench once with sodium or ammonium molybdate	2.67	0.200
	or foliar spray sodium or ammonium molybdate with a spreader-sticker	2	0.150

[1]These corrective procedures are to be applied once. Subsequent applications should be made only after soil and foliar analysis tests indicate the need. All fertilizers are to be applied to the root medium unless foliar spray is specified.

[2]Dissolve 1 ounce sodium or ammonium molybdate in 40 fluid ounces of water. Use 1 fluid ounce of this stock solution in each 100 gallons of final-strength fertilizer solution.

because micronutrients are difficult and sometimes impossible to remove from root media.

Iron deficiency is common in gloxinia, rose, hydrangea, and azalea. It also readily occurs in crops grown in soil-less media if iron has not been incorporated into the media. The symptoms of manganese deficiency are similar to those of iron deficiency. Fortunately, manganese deficiency is fairly rare in the greenhouse. Zinc deficiency is rare in greenhouse crops except in the case of the *Kalanchoe* (Figure 8–13).

Copper deficiency occurs in specific soil types and thus follows geographical patterns. Soils of the southeastern United States are very prone to copper deficiency. The rose crop is an exception, in that the deficiency occurs almost universally. Certain cultivars, such as 'Golden Wave', 'White Butterfly', and 'Mary DeVor', are most sensitive. The cultivar 'Forever Yours' is moderately sensitive. Copper deficiency is most prevalent in old, established rose soils that are high in humus.

Boron deficiency is a problem with carnation and snapdragon crops. The requirement for boron is similar in these and other crops, but the ability of these crops to take up boron is lower. Boron is readily taken up by chrysanthemum. When carnation or snapdragon crops follow a chrysanthemum crop, boron deficiency often occurs. The pink varieties of carnation are most prone.

Molybdenum deficiency often occurs in poinsettia but is practically nonexistent in other greenhouse crops. The symptoms for poinsettia are chlorosis along the margin of leaves of intermediate age. Chlorosis is rapidly followed by necrosis along the margin of these leaves. Affected leaves may be twisted or half-moon-shaped. These symptoms spread to other leaves above and below on the plant.

Interactions

Before attempting to correct a nutrient deficiency, one should always be certain which nutrient is the cause of the problem. The carnation problem previously cited, in which potassium deficiency was induced by an excessive soil-nitrogen level, is a good example. What first appeared to be a reasonable solution—to apply potassium fertilizer—would not have solved the problem; it might have led to an excessive soluble-salt level. The potassium deficiency was caused by an excessive level of nitrogen, and only a reduction of nitrogen in the soil would correct the deficiency. Such a relationship is known as an *antagonism*. Once the basic antagonisms are known, it is a simple matter to identify them in soil and foliar analysis reports.

The more common antagonisms are listed in Table 8–20. When a deficiency of one of the nutrients in the right column of Table 8–20 is identified, it should be determined if an abnormally high level of the nutrient in the left column exists. If so, corrective action should involve reduction of the concentration of the nutrient in the left column. Note that some, but not all, of the nutrient antagonisms are reciprocal. For example, a high level of iron will reduce manganese uptake, and reciprocally a high level of manganese will reduce iron uptake.

Table 8–20

Common Antagonisms Occurring in Crops in General

Nutrient in Excess	*Induced Deficiency*
N	K
K	N, Ca, Mg
Na	K, Ca, Mg
Ca	Mg
Mg	Ca
Ca	B
Fe	Mn
Mn	Fe

High root-media levels of nutrients in the left column bring about deficiencies of the nutrients in the right column.

SUMMARY

1. It is expedient to supply all essential nutrients, except possibly nitrogen and potassium, in sufficient quantity to last the full term of the crop at the time of preparing the root medium. A pH adjustment with dolomitic limestone provides calcium and magnesium. An application of 20 percent superphosphate supplies phosphorus, sulfur, and more calcium. The six fertilizer micronutrients can be incorporated into the medium as a solid during mixing or immediately after planting as a single application of a liquid mixture.
2. Nitrogen and potassium are commonly applied as a liquid formulation with every watering or once per week. The rate and ratio of these two nutrients vary according to the crop.
3. The nitrogen and potassium formulation is prepared as a concentrate to conserve space and reduce the labor of mixing and then is diluted and metered into the greenhouse water line by mechanical fertilizer proportioners. It is delivered to the bench or pots through the automatic watering system.
4. Nitrogen and potassium can be alternatively applied in a single application of a dry slow-release fertilizer that, depending on formulation, can provide N–P–K for 3–14 months. Different formulations and types of slow-release fertilizers are available, eliminating the need for any regular fertilization during the crop schedule.
5. Identification of nutritional disorders is as important as the fertilization program itself. Visual diagnosis of disorders can be effective, but unfortunately it depends upon the presence of an injury that may not be completely reversible.

6. Soil testing is a valuable diagnostic tool in that it gives a measure of the root-medium pH and soluble-salt levels as well as a determination of the available levels of many, but not all, nutrients. It is inexpensive.
7. Foliar analysis is an excellent diagnostic tool to be used with soil testing. It provides a different view of the status of all the essential nutrients, some of which are not included in soil testing.
8. The pH level of a root medium is important because it regulates the availability of all essential nutrients to one degree or another.
9. The problem of excessive soluble salts is prevalent in greenhouse culture because of heavy fertilization procedures. High soluble-salt concentrations result in reduced water availability to plants, which leads to desiccation and death of roots.
10. Soil-less root media differ from soil-based root media in that a lower pH level is desirable, micronutrients are readily tied up, ammonium toxicity is more prevalent, and greater quantities of preplant phosphorus are necessary.

REFERENCES

1. Anon. 1980. Dictionary of plant foods. In *Farm Chemicals Handbook.* Willoughby, OH: Meister Publishing Co.
2. Bartok, J. W., Jr. 1973. Preventing backflow from your fertilizer injector. Univ. of Connecticut. Coop. Ext. Ser. *Connecticut Greenhouse Newsletter* No. 52. pp. 1–3.
3. Bould, C., E. J. Hewitt, and P. Needham. 1984. *Diagnosis of Mineral Disorders in Plants.* Vol. 1. *Principles.* New York: Chemical Publishing.
4. Bunt, A. C. 1976. *Modern Potting Composts.* University Park, PA; and London: The Pennsylvania State Univ. Press.
5. Chapman, H. D., ed. 1966. *Diagnostic Criteria for Plants and Soils.* H. D. Chapman, 830 S. Univ. Dr., Riverside, CA 92507.
6. Criley, R. A., and W. H. Carlson. 1970. Tissue analysis standards for various floricultural crops. *Florists' Review* 146:19–20, 70–73.
7. Farnham, D. S., R. S. Ayers, and R. F. Hasek. 1977. Water quality affects ornamental plant production. Univ. of California Div. of Agr. Sci. Leaflet 2995.
8. Jones, J. B., Jr. 1974. Plant analysis handbook for Georgia. Georgia Coop. Ext. Ser. Bul. 735.
9. Koths, J. S., R. W. Judd, Jr., J. J. Maisano, G. F. Griffin, J. W. Bartok, Jr., and R. A. Ashley. 1980. Nutrition of greenhouse crops. Coop. Ext. Ser. of the Northeast States. NE 220.
10. Peterson, J. C. 1982. Effects of pH upon nutrient availability in a commercial soilless root medium utilized for floral crop production. Ohio Agr. Res. and Devel. Center Res. Cir. 268, pp. 16–19.

11. ______. 1982. Monitoring and managing fertility—part I: Monitoring the fertilizer content of irrigation water. *Ohio Florists' Assoc. Bul.* 629:4–7.

12. Poole, R. T., C. A. Connover, and J. N. Joiner. 1976. Chemical composition of quality tropical foliage plants. *Proc. Fla. State Hort. Soc.* 89:307–308.

13. Rader, L. F., Jr., L. M. White, and C. W. Whittaker. 1943. A measure of the effect of fertilizers on the concentration of the soil solution. *Soil Sci.* 55:201–208.

14. Robinson, J. B. D., ed. 1984. *Diagnosis of Mineral Disorders in Plants.* Vol. 1. *Principles.* New York: Chemical Publishing.

15. Roorda van Eysinga, J. P. N. L., and K. W. Smilde. 1980. *Nutritional Disorders in Chrysanthemum.* Center for Agricultural Publishing and Documentation, Wageningen, The Netherlands.

16. Scaife, A., and M. Turner. 1984. *Diagnosis of Mineral Disorders in Plants.* Vol. 2. *Vegetables.* New York: Chemical Publishing.

17. Smilde, K. W., and J. P. N. L. Roorda van Eysinga. 1968. *Nutritional Diseases in Glass House Tomatoes.* Center for Agricultural Publishing and Documentation, Wageningen, The Netherlands.

18. Sprague, H. B. 1964. *Hunger Signs in Crops*, 3d ed. New York: David McKay Co.

19. Tayama, H. K. 1966. Extension slants—production pointers. *Ohio Florists' Assoc. Bul.* 442:9.

20. Truog, E. 1948. Lime in relation to availability of plant nutrients. *Soil Sci.* 65:1–7.

21. Walsh, L. M., and J. D. Beaton. 1973. *Soil Testing and Plant Analysis*, rev. ed. Madison, WI: Soil Sci. Soc. of Amer.

22. Warncke, D. D., and D. M. Krauskopf. 1983. Greenhouse growth media: Testing and nutrition guidelines. Michigan State Univ. Agr. Ext. Bul. E–1736.

23. Waters, W. E., J. NeSmith, C. M. Geraldson, and S. S. Woltz. 1972. The interpretation of soluble-salt tests and soil analysis by different procedures. *Florida Flower Grower* 9 (4):1–10.

24. White, J. W. 1976. Fertilization. In Mastalerz, J. W., ed. *Bedding Plants*, 2d ed., pp. 146–165. Pennsylvania Flower Growers' Assoc., 103 Tyson Bldg., University Park, PA 16802.

CHAPTER 9

Alternative Cropping Systems

Since the beginning of commercial greenhouse crop production, our intrigue with futuristic technology, desire to direct nature, and aspiration for achievement have led to the trial of many innovative cultural systems. Recently, two separate powerful forces have come together to enhance the quest for these systems. First, internationalization of greenhouse production has given birth to a level of competition that demands reduced costs of production and marketing. Solutions are being sought through automation and subsequent computerized control of these emerging high-technology cropping systems. Second, antipollution regulations demand that cropping systems be developed that reduce nutrients and pesticides in greenhouse effluent. Most attention is being given to *closed cultural systems* in which water, with its contained nutrients and pesticides, is captured, treated, and reused. *Open cultural systems*, where excess water from the bottom of pots or beds is allowed to flow into the ground, are being modified to reduce the volume of effluent.

Solutions for both of the current needs of production efficiency and pollution abatement are found simultaneously in a number of new systems. Two systems commercialized in the early 1970s employ the principles of *nutriculture* (hydroponics) and are used for fresh flower and vegetable production. These systems are the *nutrient film technique* (NFT) and *rock wool culture*. Remaining alternatives include the *ebb-and-flow system* for potted plants and bedding plants, *trough culture* for potted plants, and *whole-firm recirculation* for all crop types. These latter systems are not forms of nutriculture since conventional root media and pots or flats are used. However, the methods for delivering nutrient solution in these systems make use of the principles of nutriculture.

Nutriculture involves the culture of plants in an inert substrate such as water (hydroponics), gravel (gravelculture), sand (sandculture), rock wool, or air (aeroponics). An inert substrate is one that neither contributes nor alters the form of plant nutrients. Soil, peat moss, and bark are examples of non-inert substrates that are both biologically and chemically active. These substrates contribute nutrients that are held on their negative exchange sites and others that are released during substrate weathering and decomposition. In addition, these substrates are handled in a manner in which large populations of microorganisms develop in them, which can change the form of applied nutrients (for example, convert ammonium to nitrate). Inert media, such as rock wool or water in the NFT system, afford much greater control over plant nutrition than is possible in today's non-inert substrates. Before the fore-mentioned cultural systems are described, it will be useful to explore their origin and the subsequent developments that led to the present situation.

HISTORICAL BACKGROUND

Setting the Stage (1860–1928)

The origin of the current commercialization of nutriculture is better identified with the period around 1860 than with any other time during the 290-year history of nutriculture research. While the six essential macronutrients and iron had been identified by 1844, it was not until 1860 that Sachs introduced in Germany a complete nutrient formula for growing plants hydroponically. In 1861, Knop described an improved formula that is used to this day. Through the late 1800s and the first three decades of the present century, considerable effort was directed at improving hydroponic cultural systems and nutrient formulas and at discovering most of the remaining micronutrients. The importance of solution aeration and periodic replacement of the nutrient solution was yet to be realized. Throughout this period, nutriculture remained a technique for research purposes.

Early Commercial Attempts (1928–1970)

The first published attempt to develop the commercial potential of hydroponics occurred in the United States in 1929. Gericke (1929) built an experimental nutrient-solution tank covered with wire netting, canvas, and 0.5 inch (1.3 cm) of sand. Plants were anchored in the sand. A 2 acre (1 ha) commercial planting followed.

Sandculture dates back to studies of Count Salm-Horstmar (1849), who introduced the idea of using sand as well as other inert media. Commercial impetus goes back to McCall (1916) in America, who saw an advantage in the nutritional control that hydroponics offers and the physical properties of support and aeration provided by sand. Robbins (1928) worked out a method for growing a number of crops in sand in the greenhouse environment. Laurie (1931) indicated the commercial potential for sandculture. In 1935, a procedure for growing carnations in sandculture was developed at the New Jersey Agricultural Experiment Station (Bickart and Connors 1935). Refinements in the physical system for sandculture and gravelculture followed (Eaton 1936; Withrow and Biebel 1936; Shive and Robbins 1937; Chapman and Liebig 1938). The American technology was duplicated and advanced in England by Templeman and Watson (1938). They did not find superior growth in nutriculture.

The next notable application of nutriculture came during World War II when both Japan and the United States used sandculture and gravelculture to produce fresh vegetables for the war effort (Ticquet 1952). The first American installation was in early 1945 on Ascension Island, an island nearly devoid of soil. Twenty-five 3 foot by 400 foot (0.9 m by 122 m) sandculture beds produced 94,000 pounds (43,000 kg) of salad vegetables the first year. Additional installations occurred at Atkinson Field in British Guiana and on Iwo Jima later that year. At the same time, Japan constructed 5 acres (2 ha) under glass and 50 acres (20 ha) outside at Chofu and 25 acres (10 ha) outside at Otsu. These installations later were used by American troops during the war in Korea.

Hoagland and Arnon (1950) developed the famous Hoagland's solution, which is commonly used to this day in research and commerce (Table 9–1). They found that tomato growth was equal in soil, sand, and water culture and stated that the use of hydroponics would be dictated by economic considerations.

The most common commercial nutriculture systems used until the early 1970s were sandculture and gravelculture (Kiplinger 1956; Weinard and Fosler 1962; Epstein and Krantz 1965; Hewitt 1966; Marvel 1966; Maynard and Barker 1970; Maas and Adamson 1971; Sowell 1972). Watertight beds or benches, often constructed from concrete, served to hold gravel. Nutrient solution, generally similar to Hoagland's solution, was flushed through the gravel 1–4 times per day and less often in sand, depending on season and size of crop. Between flushes, the nutrient solution was stored in tanks. Periodic analysis and adjustment of the solution for volume, pH level, and nutrient concentration permitted continuous use for many weeks before replacement. Aeration presented no problem since the aggregate pores were filled with nutrient solution for only brief periods. The primary problems that emerged were nutrient imbalances, particularly micronutrients, and disease. Firms with access to rapid solution analyses and with a staff member well-versed in nutritional chemistry did not find nutrition to be a problem. Rapid spread of diseases was a constant threat for everyone. Many firms maintained diazoben in the nutrient solution to suppress development of pathogens.

Table 9–1

Chemical Composition of Hoagland's All-Nitrate Nutrient Solution[1]

Chemical	*Formula*	*Weight*	
		mg/l	*oz/100 gal*
Potassium dihydrogen phosphate	KH_2PO_4	136.0	1.81
Potassium nitrate	KNO_3	505.0	6.73
Calcium nitrate	$Ca(NO_3)_2 \cdot 4H_2O$	1,180.0	15.73
Magnesium sulfate	$MgSO_4 \cdot 7H_2O$	492.0	6.55
Iron tartarate[2]	$FeC_4H_6O_6$	5.0	0.067
Manganous chloride	$MgCl_2 \cdot 4H_2O$	1.81	0.024
Zinc sulfate	$ZnSO_4 \cdot 7H_2O$	0.22	0.003
Copper sulfate	$CuSO_4 \cdot 5H_2O$	0.08	0.001
Boric acid	H_3BO_3	2.86	0.038
Molybdic acid	$H_2MoO_4 \cdot H_2O$	0.02	0.0003

[1]From Hoagland and Arnon (1950). The following ppm concentrations are achieved in this formulation: N—210, P—31, K—234, Ca—200, Mg—48, S—64, Fe—1.4, Mn—0.5, Zn—0.05, Cu—0.02, B—0.5, and Mo—0.01.

[2]Today, iron chelates are substituted for iron tartarate. Iron DTPA is commonly used at rates from 2 to 4 ppm iron (20 to 40 mg iron DTPA/l).

A modest number of firms around the world substituted coarse (0.5 inch, 1.3 cm) Palabora vermiculite from Africa for gravel (Bentley 1955, 1959). Its light weight made it attractive for use in movable benches. The high water- and nutrient-holding capacity allowed operators to reduce nutrient-solution application to 3–4 times per week. This cultural system became known as vermiculaponics.

Throughout this period, there was no major commercial adoption of a nutriculture system. Major deterring factors were the absence of plastics for inert, watertight construction; insufficient equipment for automated monitoring and control of nutrient solutions; and the lack of computers for overall control. However, considerable technology was developed in this period to fuel the large-scale adoption of nutriculture about to come.

Large-Scale Successes (1970–Present)

The first nutriculture system to gain wide acceptance in greenhouse culture and to prove itself economically efficient was the nutrient film technique (NFT). Its background is interesting. DeStigter (1961, 1969), at the Plant Physiological Research Center in The Netherlands, developed the prototype for this system. For research purposes, he developed a method of growing roots in a thin, retrievable layer to facilitate making autoradiographs of them. Cooper (1973), in England, through communications with DeStigter, saw the commercial potential in this procedure and developed the NFT system from it.

NFT is a form of hydroponics in which plants are grown in narrow, sloped channels (Figure 9–1). A thin film of recirculating nutrient solution flows through the roots in the channels. With NFT, unlike the classical hydroponic systems, aeration is not a problem because the nutrient solution is confined to a depth of ⅛ inch (3 mm). Commercial installations of NFT began in the early 1970s. In 1982, there were approximately 125 acres (50 ha) in England and considerably more area in Holland. Although the area in the United States is unknown, several hundred small firms are producing vegetables by the NFT system in greenhouses.

The most extensive development of NFT occurred in The Netherlands partly because of pasteurization problems. Most greenhouses there heat with hot water, which is inappropriate for pasteurization; thus, methyl bromide is very popular. In the sandy soils of the concentrated greenhouse region known as the Westland, methyl bromide readily permeates the soil as well as the plastic walls of water pipes lying within these soils. Contaminated drinking water prompted a restriction in the dosage rate of methyl bromide and threatens its future use altogether. Without steam to fall back on, NFT became very attractive.

NFT production in northern Europe appears to have peaked out in the early 1980s. A strong reason for the change was disease buildup in the closed recirculating solution. Contamination from one plant soon reached all other plants. The high initial cost of an NFT system and its continual consumption of electrical energy might also have contributed to this shift (Dungey 1983).

Open cultural systems, in which nutrient solution makes a single pass by the roots and then on to waste, were sought next to get around the disease problem while still accommodating the need for automation. The system of rock wool slab culture had reached a sufficient stage of development by the early 1980s to take over as the predominant alternative cropping method. Rock wool consists of fibers formed from melted rock that, in final form, resemble fiberglass insulation. These fibers are formed into cubes for propagating plants and into slabs for growing plants on to maturity.

Rock wool culture was pioneered in Denmark during the late 1950s. By the early 1970s, horticultural rock wool was in production in Denmark. Today, nearly all greenhouse cucumbers and many cultivars of tomato are produced in rock wool in Denmark. Greenhouse area in rock wool production has grown in The Netherlands from an estimated 450 acres (180 ha) in 1980 to 2,500 acres (1,000 ha) in 1983 and to 5,000 acres (2,000 ha) in 1988. In England, while there were only 15 acres (6 ha) in 1978, there were 63 acres (25 ha) in 1982 (Hanger 1982). The areas of rock wool production in Belgium and West Germany in 1988 were 1500 acres (600 ha) and 125 acres (50 ha), respectively (Molitor 1990). Rock wool appeared in the American market in the early 1980s. The first crops grown in rock wool were the full range of greenhouse vegetables. More recently, chrysanthemum, carnation, gerbera, and rose have been grown in it.

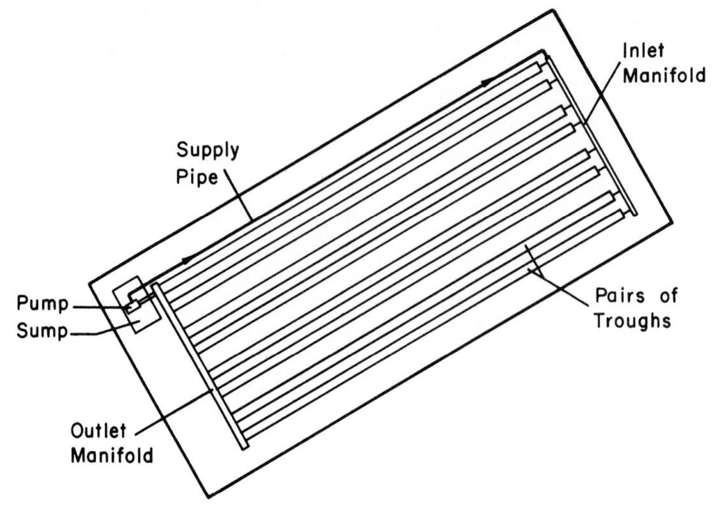

(a)

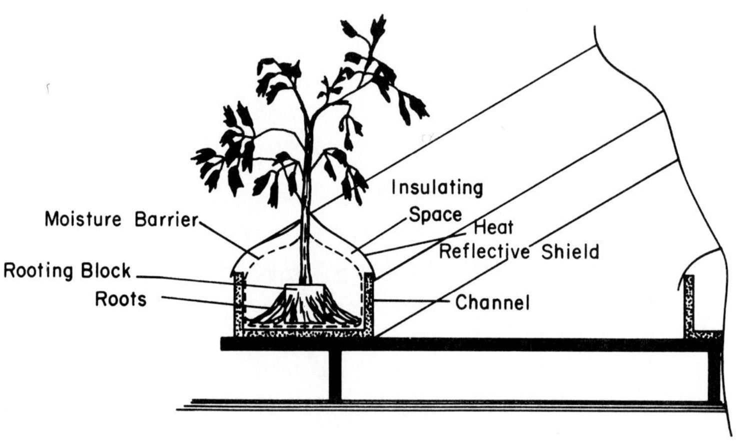

(b)

Figure 9–1

(a) The floor plan of one possible NFT system. Nutrient solution is pumped from the sump tank to an inlet manifold at the upper end of the NFT troughs. From there, the solution flows by gravity to an outlet manifold at the lower end of the troughs and finally back to the sump. (b) A cross-sectional view of a trough showing plant placement and the arrangement of the film plastic moisture barrier and thermal barrier. The outer thermal barrier is optional.

Antipollution Legislation

The history of pesticide regulation is a short one. The first legislation in the United States included the Insecticide Act of 1910 and the Federal Insecticide, Fungicide, and Rodenticide Act (FIFRA) of 1947. Both were intended to protect the purchaser against fraud relative to the effectiveness of the pesticide purchased. This direction is understandable when one realizes that the importance of synthetic organic pesticides began around 1940 with the worldwide use of the insecticide DDT for purposes such as controlling mosquito-carrying malaria. However, by 1984, there were about 600 basic pesticide chemicals on the market in 45,000 to 50,000 formulations (Johnson 1984).

The legislative shift to protection of public health and the environment came in 1952 with an amendment to the Federal Food, Drug, and Cosmetic Act. The amendment established a procedure for setting tolerance levels for pesticides in food, feed, and fiber. Social sensitivities were piqued in their early stages by Rachael Carson's book *Silent Spring* (1962), which dramatically pointed out the dangers of pesticides to people and to the environment. This was augmented by the worldwide "environmental" movement of the 1960s. In 1964, FIFRA was amended to encompass safety considerations in the labeling of pesticides. The year 1970 was a milestone in that the first Earth Day was held and the Environmental Protection Agency (EPA) was established. FIFRA was again amended to include a mandate for the protection of public health and the environment as a guiding principle for the use of pesticides. The mandate allowed for a reasonable balance between economic, social, and environmental costs and the benefits of the use of any pesticide. Such a balance of risk and benefit was important, given the estimate of a 30 percent loss in crop productivity from pests if pesticides were not used (Wilkinson 1987). In today's world, with its high rate of death from malnutrition and its rapid rise in population, such a crop reduction would be devastating.

Current initiatives to clean up water drew strength in the late 1970s when the following pesticides were found in groundwater supplies: aldicarb in Long Island, New York, and in Wisconsin; atrazine in Iowa; and ethylene dibromide in California. EPA subsequently formulated plans to assess groundwater contamination and in 1984, 1986, and 1988 released plans and updates. The last update, "Proposed Pesticide Strategy," indicated the need to evaluate each pesticide independently and set a standard of acceptable risk for it. Other legislation, including the Water Quality Act of 1987, the Federal Insecticide, Fungicide, and Rodenticide Act, and the Safe Drinking Water Act, provide mandates and authority to federal, state, and local agencies to assess, monitor, and regulate contamination in water supplies. These responsibilities have not been placed on any one level of government. Agencies at federal, state, and municipal levels are involved in all three functions at the present. While national standards will continue to emerge from federal agencies such as the EPA, state and municipal agencies are empowered to issue stricter standards for their jurisdictions.

Nutrient pollution can take several forms including nitrate nitrogen, phosphate, total salt level, or heavy metals such as copper or zinc. A national limit has been set for nitrate in effluent waters at 10 ppm of nitrate nitrogen, which equates to 44.3 ppm of nitrate. Similar limits have been set in many western European countries. While a strict national limit has not been set for phosphate, regional measures have been taken to reduce use. Bans on phosphate detergents are one example of initiatives being taken. Phosphates in surface water foster algal growth, which, in turn, robs water of oxygen and leads ultimately to fish death. Limits on phosphate in greenhouse effluent will undoubtedly occur. Likewise, limits on total salt level and individual heavy-metal micronutrients are not universally set but probably will be one day.

NFT SYSTEM

Cultural Procedures

Cooper (1979) has thoroughly outlined the NFT system in his book. The system begins with a channel, free of valleys and peaks, laid out on a 1 percent slope. The channel must be level across its width to ensure that the whole floor will be covered with nutrient solution. Such channels may be molded into a concrete floor or may be situated on raised platforms. For crops such as tomato and cucumber, a channel is typically about 9 inches (23 cm) wide and 2 inches high (5 cm). It may be constructed from wood, plastic, metal, or concrete. Lettuce, chrysanthemums, snapdragons, and other fresh flowers are more often grown in a bed fashioned from several closely spaced parallel channels (see Figure 9–1).

The channel needs to be watertight. Channels constructed from leaky materials are lined with a film plastic sufficiently large to cover the top of each channel, including the plant-propagation blocks. The film plastic should be 5 mils (0.127 mm) or thicker; otherwise, the plastic will adhere to roots, which will cause it to ripple along the bottom of the channel. This, in turn, will force solution to puddle in spots and to flow around roots in other places. Watertight channels, while not requiring a lining, do need a covering. This may be formed from a solid material or a film plastic.

Channel coverings serve to (1) prevent water loss through evaporation; (2) restrict light entry to prevent algal growth, which would remove nutrients and plug the system; and (3) help control root temperature. The outer surface of the covering should be white or silver to reduce heat absorption and to reflect light to the plants for better growth. Air inside a black channel would become hot enough to burn roots on warm, bright days. White plastic does not sufficiently restrict light; therefore, film plastic is sold with one (inner) surface black and the other surface white. In regions of temperature extremes, an insulated channel covering may be constructed by using two film plastic coverings with a dead-air space between them.

The nutrient solution is handled in a closed recirculating system (see Figure 9–1 again). A tank, usually built into the floor, collects solution by gravity flow from the ends of the channels. Solution is pumped from the tank to a header pipe that runs perpendicular to the upper ends of the channels. Small tubes running from the header pipe supply each channel. The flow rate should be sufficient to maintain a nutrient film thickness of not more than ⅛ inch (3 mm) over the entire bottom surface of the channel. Greater depth will exclude oxygen from the roots. A flow rate of about 0.5 gpm (2 l/min) per channel is required. In some systems, the solution is constantly recirculated. More commonly in America, the solution is circulated for 10 minutes out of every 15 minutes to increase aeration of the roots. A considerable volume of water will be lost through transpiration, necessitating continual additions to the holding tank. This can be automatically handled by installing a float valve on a water inlet line in the tank.

Cooper (1979) suggests the nutrient concentrations listed in Table 9–2 as being ideal for NFT culture. He has grown over 50 species of ornamental, fruit, and vegetable plants in this solution for three continuous years without problems. Sources of nutrients and required weights are presented in Table 9–3. It is not necessary for a firm to formulate its own nutrient solution. Various companies sell NFT fertilizers. Generally, they come in two or three packages that must be added separately to the tank to prevent precipitation.

Table 9–2

Theoretically Ideal Concentrations of Elements in Nutrient Solution for NFT Cropping*

Element	*Symbol*	*Concentration (ppm)*
Nitrogen	N	200
Phosphorus	P	60
Potassium	K	300
Calcium	Ca	170
Magnesium	Mg	50
Iron	Fe	12
Manganese	Mn	2
Boron	B	0.3
Copper	Cu	0.1
Molybdenum	Mo	0.2
Zinc	Zn	0.1

*From Cooper (1979).

Table 9–3

Weights of Chemical Compounds Required To Give Theoretically Ideal NFT Cropping Concentrations*

Chemical	Formula	Weight	
		g/1,000 l	*oz/100 gal*
Potassium dihydrogen phosphate	KH_2PO_4	263	3.51
Potassium nitrate	KNO_3	583	7.77
Calcium nitrate	$Ca(NO_3)_2 \cdot 4H_2O$	1,003	13.37
Magnesium sulphate	$MgSO_4 \cdot 7H_2O$	513	6.84
EDTA iron	$[CH_2 \cdot N(CH_2 \cdot COO)_2]_2FeNa$	79	1.05
Manganous sulphate	$MnSO_4 \cdot H_2O$	6.1	0.081
Boric acid	H_3BO_3	1.7	0.023
Copper sulphate	$CuSO_4 \cdot 5H_2O$	0.39	0.005
Ammonium molybdate	$(NH_4)_6Mo_7O_{24} \cdot 4H_2O$	0.37	0.005
Zinc sulphate	$ZnSO_4 \cdot 7H_2O$	0.44	0.006

*From Cooper (1979).

The solution is used in most European systems for many months before replacement. In several American systems, it has been replaced at two-week intervals. This latter practice is inconsistent with present needs to comply with antipollution rules. In either case, it is necessary to test the solution for pH level and electrical conductivity (soluble-salt) level at least daily. The pH level should remain in the range of 5.8–6.5. When it decreases, potassium hydroxide is added; when it increases, sulfuric acid (battery acid) is added. Different fertilizer formulations will have different electrical conductivity levels. For Cooper's solution, the level should start at 3 millimhos. When it drops to 2 millimhos, all nutrients should be added in sufficient quantity to restore the level to 3 millimhos.

Equipment is available that will automatically sample nutrient solution from the holding tank, analyze it for pH and electrical conductivity, and make the appropriate additions of acid, base, or fertilizer. Even more sophisticated equipment automatically tests for individual nutrients. One or more nutrients are held in each of four or more concentrate tanks. Concentrate from any individual tank or combination of tanks can be added to the single-strength nutrient tank in order to hold all nutrients in balance. Such a system permits the use of a nutrient solution for a considerably longer time before it is discarded. The automated system also allows the pH and nutrient concentrations of the solution to be maintained more precisely than by merely analyzing solutions once per day.

Plants to be set in an NFT system are propagated in containers such as blocks of rock wool, foam cubes, or in netlike pots containing soil-less media. It is important that the propagation unit not contribute peat moss or other loose substances that will plug the system. A propagation area is set up for establishing plants under conditions more ideal to this stage. It also permits growing at high plant densities to cut overhead costs. Young plants are often grown in channels in the propagation area; however, plants within the channels as well as the channels themselves are placed much closer than they are in the finishing greenhouse. When established plants are then moved to channels in the finishing greenhouse (Figure 9–2), there can be a problem of nutrient solution meandering along the plastic and missing some root blocks. This problem can be solved by placing sticks beneath the plastic just below each plant to form a dam for puddling water around each block. In a week or two, when roots develop across the channel, the sticks can be removed.

Advantages

The growth in popularity of NFT can be attributed to several factors.

1. NFT is a system that eliminates the materials and labor costs for steam or methyl bromide pasteurization between crops as well as the period of 10–14 days required for methyl bromide application and aeration. If the channel in which plants are grown is formed from film plastic, the plastic is gathered up with the crop and discarded, and the new plastic is laid out. Permanent channels not lined with film plastic are rinsed with a sterilant such as bleach between crops.

Figure 9–2

Carnations growing in an NFT system. Note header pipes running across the upper end of the troughs for delivering nutrient solution.

2. NFT has the potential for conserving water and nutrients. The nutrient solution is recirculated in a mostly closed system where little evaporation occurs and excess water and nutrients are reused. In addition to reducing the costs of water and fertilizers, this recirculation of solution also provides an excellent method for reducing nutrient and pesticide effluent from greenhouses.

3. NFT has the very attractive advantage of the potential for automation. Formulation, testing, and adjustment of nutrient solutions can be handled at a central point, and even this can be done automatically. The solutions are mechanically delivered to the crop. Some of the heat may likewise be delivered in the nutrient solution. Heavy root media and the handling of them are eliminated.

In-Line Pasteurization

Closed-system NFT lost ground to open-system rock wool culture in the 1980s because economically acceptable means of pasteurization of the nutrient solution were not available. Six options for pasteurization are receiving current attention. Their adoption not only will clear the way for further development of NFT but also will permit operation of the rock wool system in a closed fashion rather than in the open system that is most common today. These pasteurization systems will also have application in all other types of recirculating crop systems.

Equipment is available for one method of pasteurization that heats nutrient solution while it is recirculating between crop and sump tank. Solution is heated into the range of 203–221°F (95–105°C) (depending upon the equipment purchased) in 30 seconds and held at this temperature range for 10–30 seconds, after which it is cooled at an equally rapid pace.

Other pasteurization systems are available that are installed in the recirculation system in a similar position. One system produces ozone to destroy microorganisms. An additional benefit from the ozone is that it replenishes oxygen in the solution. Another system is an ionization device in which microorganisms are killed by copper and silver ions. In yet another system, chlorine or bromine is injected as a microbicide. When chlorine is used, it is important to filter organic matter out of the solution since chlorine will bind to it and thus become ineffective.

Ultraviolet (UV) light is used to destroy microorganisms in a fifth system. UV lamps are contained inside a stainless steel tube. The recirculating nutrient solution flows through the tube, over the lamps. A 2.5 kW lamp can treat 2,640 gallons per hour (10 m^3/hr) and has a life expectancy of 8,000 hours.

Filtration is a sixth method for excluding disease organisms from the solution. Membrane filters, fine enough to trap bacteria, are contained in cartridges. One cartridge can treat nearly 3,200 gallons per day (12 m^3/day). A 5 acre (2 ha) greenhouse could be serviced by six cartridges. Filters must be cleaned periodically with chemicals or high-pressure flushing, depending on water quality. The life expectancy of filter cartridges is three to four years.

ROCK WOOL CULTURE

Manufacture

Rock wool is produced by burning a mixture of coke, basalt, limestone, and possibly slag from iron production. At a 2,900°F (1,600°C) temperature in the furnace, the rock minerals melt. This liquid is tapped from the base of the furnace. A stream flows onto a high-speed rotor. Droplets thrown from the rotor lengthen into fibers. The fibers are sprayed with a binding agent in an air stream, which cools and carries them to a conveyor, where they are deposited onto a belt. The pad of fibers is then compressed between rollers to a specified density. Finally, it is cut into desired dimensions.

Product Description

Insulation- and acoustical-grade rock wool is not suitable for plant growth. Horticultural-grade rock wool is formulated to a prescribed density to provide the air- and water-holding requirements of plants. Rock wool used in cubes for propagation and in slabs for finishing crops is, unlike industrial rock wool, treated with surfactants to improve water absorbance. It contains about 3 percent solid and 97 percent pore space.

Rock wool is not biodegradable, but it does slowly weather. Slabs are often used for two years of cropping before disposal. Initially, rock wool contains no significant quantity of soluble materials. However, fibers can contain calcium, magnesium, iron, manganese, copper, and zinc, and there is evidence that these can slowly be released for plant uptake (Rupp and Dudley 1988). Since the cation exchange capacity is negligible, applied nutrients are not adsorbed. Nutrient availability is dictated by the nutrient solution applied. The pH of rock wool is between 7.0 and 8.5 (often 8.0) but is not buffered. It is important that the nutrient solution applied have a pH level in the range of 5.5–6.0. The pH level of the rock wool will adjust to the nutrient solution pH level after one application.

Horticultural rock wool is available in 0.7–4 inch (18–100 mm) cubes with or without predrilled holes for propagation of seed or cuttings (Figure 9–3). The smaller cubes can be obtained unwrapped in blocks suitable for use in trays. Larger cubes are often wrapped on the vertical sides with polyethylene to prevent evaporation and spread of roots into adjacent cubes and are sold in single-row strips. The 3 inch and 4 inch (76 mm and 100 mm) cubes can be obtained with a depression in the top of suitable size to insert smaller cubes into them for trans-

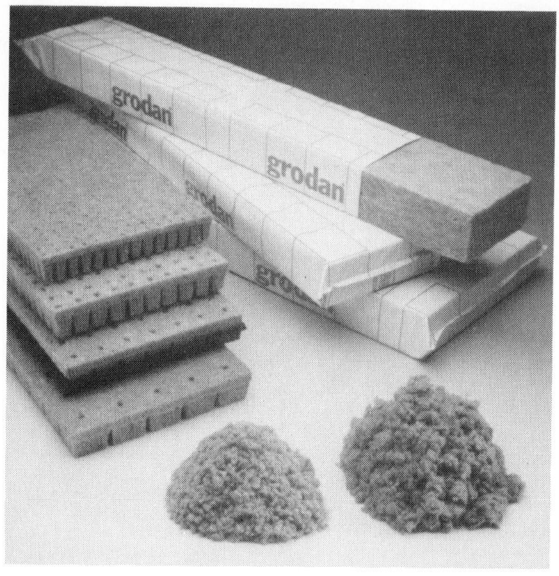

(a) (b)

Figure 9–3

Various rock wool products used in the greenhouse. (a) Blocks of cells of various dimensions for propagation of seeds and cuttings, polyethylene wrapped slabs of rock wool for supporting vegetable and fresh flower crops, and loose rock wool to be used as a component in root media for pots. (b) An individual propagation cell in which a seed or cutting would be propagated, a block with pre-drilled hole to accommodate the propagation cell, and a slab on which the block will ultimately be placed after plants have been grown for an interim period of time at close spacing in the block. (*Photos courtesy of Grodania A/S, Hovedgaden 483, 2640 Hedehusene, Denmark; distributed in North America by Agro Dynamics, 12 Elkins Rd., E. Brunswick, NJ 08816.*)

planting purposes. For purposes of finishing crops, slabs of rock wool are available. These can be obtained unwrapped or wrapped in white polyethylene. Slab widths can be 6, 8, 12, or 18 inches (150, 200, 300, or 450 mm), lengths can be 30 or 39 inches (750 or 1,000 mm), and the height is usually 3 inches (75 mm). Granulated rock wool is also available for potting media (as previously described in Chapter 5).

Cultural Procedures

As in the case of NFT, plants can be propagated at a high density in small cubes in a specially regulated environment. They may then be transplanted into larger blocks and spaced out into a moderately high-density nursery area to cut down overhead costs. The large cubes are finally set on top of slabs for final production (Figure 9–4).

Figure 9–4

Pictured here is a tomato crop growing in a rock wool system. The 3 inch (75 mm) rock wool propagation cubes are sitting on 6 inch (150 mm) wide by 3 inch (75 mm) deep rock wool slabs. The slabs are wrapped in white polyethylene film. Nutrients and water are provided to the propagation cubes through plastic microtubes fed from PVC pipe running along the side of the slabs.

Evenness of the floor is not as important for rock wool culture as it is for NFT. Where there is a slope along the length of the bed, solution in individually wrapped slabs cannot drain from the high end to the low end of the bed. Narrow slabs are placed end to end in a double row for cucumbers, tomatoes, and roses (Figure 9–5) to form a bed. A space is generally left between the two rows for vegetables. For fresh flowers, the wider slabs are used to line a bench. Ideally, for double-row culture, the floor should be level from end to end but sloped at a 2° angle to a drain between the two rows of the bed.

Cubes with individual plants are placed on top of the slabs at the desired final spacing for the crop involved. Roots penetrate into the slabs below the cubes in two to four days. During this period of adaptation, it is necessary to water plants frequently. The additional height of the cube plus slab causes the cube to drain excessively and remain too dry. In temperate climates, slabs are covered with polyethylene. The cover may be omitted in tropical climates to allow for evaporative cooling of the root zone. When wrapped slabs are used, three drain holes must be cut along one side—the low side if the floor is sloped to a drain between double rows. A 1.5 inch (4 cm) slit is made starting at the bottom of the side and extending upward at a 45° angle from the floor.

Figure 9–5

Pictured here are roses growing in slabs of rock wool that are individually wrapped in polyethylene film and placed end to end. Nutrient solution is delivered from the black plastic pipes above the slabs through microtubes to individual plants.

Nutrient solution is applied with each watering. Solutions used for NFT and other nutriculture systems are appropriate. Crops can require 3–10 applications per day. This frequency will vary with plant size and weather conditions. When only two or three plants are grown on a slab, as in the case of tomatoes or cucumbers, nutrient solution is delivered to each cube through a microtube supplied from a plastic pipe running along the bed. This is not feasible when large numbers of cubes are grown on a slab. In this instance, three or four fertilizer emitters are placed directly on top of the slab. Traditional fertilizer injectors and water mains can be used to supply the plastic pipes.

Rock wool in a 6 inch (150 mm) deep configuration can hold water in about 50 percent of its pore space. The distribution of water is unequal, with pores in the lower inch (25 mm) holding nearly 100 percent water and those in the top inch holding less than 10 percent. A 3 inch (75 mm) deep slab will hold enough water to fill 77 percent of its pore space, leaving 23 percent of the pores open for aeration. It follows that the small cubes will have even less aeration. When seeds or cuttings of plants sensitive to oxygen stress are propagated in these cubes, it is advisable to place the cubes on a well-drained substance such as sand or perlite. This increases the effective depth of the cube and consequently its drainage and aeration.

Just as the nutrient solution in NFT systems is sometimes heated to keep the root zone warm, heat may be applied under rock wool slabs. A sheet of polystyrene is placed on the ground. It has a notch at the middle of its top side running along its length. A plastic hot water pipe is placed in this notch. Rock wool is placed directly on the pipe. By warming the root zone, cooler air temperatures can be maintained in the greenhouse, which results in a fuel savings.

The salt content of rock wool can be lowered for the next crop by applying only water during the last days of the previous crop. Old crops can be removed by twisting the cubes off the slab. Rock wool may be used for one year for cucumbers and two years for tomatoes and floral crops less sensitive to oxygen stress. If the rock wool is to be used for a second year, it is advisable to pasteurize it. Most of the water can be removed prior to pasteurization by cutting off the water supply during the last days of the final crop. The slabs are then stacked and covered with a pasteurization cover, and steam is applied for 30 minutes. Methyl bromide may be used as well. It can be readily washed out of the rock wool after fumigation. Repeated use of rock wool results in collapse of its structure and a buildup of organic matter from roots with a resultant loss of aeration. Cucumbers are very sensitive to this problem.

Advantages

Rock wool offers several advantages.

1. Elimination of pasteurization: As in the case of NFT, pasteurization can be eliminated in rock wool culture, unless it is used for a second year.

2. Production efficiency: Rock wool is an excellent inert substrate for open-system nutriculture. This greatly reduces the chances for the spread of disease since the nutrients are not recirculated. It is, however, possible to recirculate nutrient solution in a rock wool system. In this case, slabs are placed on a sloped, paved floor. Nutrient solution is collected at the low point and is handled in the same way as in NFT.

3. Reduced production space: Rock wool is lightweight and self-contained, which allows movement of plants into different environments and densities in different stages for faster crop production and lower overhead cost. The light weight further permits growth of crops on movable benches. Both of these factors reduce overhead costs of the crop by reducing average growing space.

EBB-AND-FLOW SYSTEM

The ebb-and-flow system is basically a subirrigation system for potted plants and bedding plants (Figure 9–6). Pots or flats are grown in a level, watertight bench.

Figure 9–6

An ebb-and-flow bench for pot and bedding plant production. Nutrient solution enters through the plastic pipe in the foreground. Channels molded into the bottom of the water tight bench ensure rapid and even delivery of nutrient solution to the base of each pot. Solution is held at a depth of 0.75–1 inch (2–3 cm) for 10 to 15 minutes to allow time for it to move up through the root medium by capillarity. Then the dark colored valve in the right bottom of the picture is opened and the solution drains back to a holding tank to be used again the next time plants require water.

Nutrient solution is pumped into the bench to a depth of about 0.75–1 inch (2–3 cm) and is held there for 10–15 minutes, or long enough for solution to rise to the top of the root medium in each pot by capillarity. The solution is then allowed to drain back to a storage tank where it is held until the next bench requires watering. Fertilizer is applied at each watering. The nutrient solution is tested, altered as required, and recycled for months. This closed system is for container-grown plants, and it eliminates nearly all effluent from the greenhouse. It is not a nutriculture system in that conventional root media and containers are used. Also, it is not necessary to provide all of the essential nutrients in the fertilizer solution as in the case of the NFT and rock wool systems. Calcium and magnesium can be provided as dolomitic limestone, phosphorus as superphosphate, and micronutrients as a commercial mixture—all of which are mixed into the root medium prior to planting. Estimates indicate that about 80 percent of Dutch and Danish pot and bedding plant crops are produced in ebb-and-flow systems. Adoption of this system has been slower in America but should gain momentum as the need to meet antipollution standards intensifies.

System Description and Operation

Benches are prefabricated primarily from plastic or fiberglass components in various widths of 4–6.5 feet (1.2–2 m) and a customary length of 39 inches (1 m). Bench components are glued together to form the desired bench length. Ebb-and-flow benches can work well as movable (rolling) benches. The floor of the bench has channels molded into it to conduct nutrient solution to all parts of the bench before reaching the bottom of the pots and also to aid in drainage from the bench. The bench must be absolutely level for uniformity of watering and for complete emptying of the bench after watering. Many designs have leveling screws on the bench legs. Below the bench is located a solution holding tank. The tank is covered to exclude dust and light and thus prevent algal growth. During watering, nutrient solution is pumped from this tank into the bench through a hole in the floor of the bench. After watering, solution returns to the tank through the same hole by way of a pressure-sensitive tee valve. A filter is built into the return line to remove debris such as plant tissue and root media.

The area of bench(es) to be watered at one time and the size of the pump should be matched to ensure filling of the bench to the prescribed depth in about 10 minutes or less. The solution is allowed to remain at this level for 10–15 minutes for wetting of the root medium to occur. Drainage should occur in 10 minutes or less. Pots with holes that extend up the sides work well. Pots with holes on the bottom only work best if there is a ridge on the bottom of the pot to elevate it off the bench floor. Situation of the drainage hole off the floor of the bench permits thorough drainage of water from the pot when the bench is emptied. It also gives a separation of the root medium in pots from slight puddles that could remain in the bottom of the bench after emptying.

Precise fertilizer concentrations to use for ebb-and-flow systems are not well established. Generally, they will be lower than concentrations used in the procedure of applying fertilizer to the top of pots at each watering. Where nitrogen concentrations of 200–400 ppm are used for top watering of heavy to very heavily fertilized crops, such as chrysanthemum and poinsettia, a concentration of 100–250 ppm should be trialed for ebb-and-flow fertilization. Bedding plant concentrations for ebb-and-flow fertilization can be in the range of 25–75 ppm of nitrogen. When a root medium is used that does not fully absorb water during subirrigation, the higher concentrations of fertilizer are needed to compensate. Incomplete water absorption can be caused by using a medium that is too coarse or by allowing it to dry too much between watering such that it repels water. The use of a fine-textured root medium reduces the former problem, while the use of a wetting agent in the root medium reduces the latter problem. Root media currently used are selected from among the mix-your-own formulas and commercial products traditionally used.

During subirrigation, water and fertilizer move up through the pot to the top of the root medium, where water evaporates and leaves fertilizer behind to accumulate as salt. The accumulating salt levels are generally not a problem when the proper root medium is selected and thus permits the use of low fertilizer concentrations. Where higher fertilizer concentrations have been used, firms have gone to periodic leaching at four- to six-week intervals. Leaching is accomplished by a single application of clear water to the top of the pots. The resulting effluent is not collected in the holding tank but is discarded.

Solution Monitoring and Adjustment

Several zones of ebb-and flow benches will often be fertilized in succession with the same solution. After a series of zones are fertilized, or at least once per week, the nutrient solution should be tested for pH and salt (EC) levels. If these levels have deviated, adjustments should be made. Generally, the fertilizer solution does not change. After entering pots by capillarity, little, if any, fertilizer solution returns to the bench; thus, changes usually do not occur. Losses in volume of fertilizer solution returning to the holding tank are generally made up by adding more of the original fertilizer formulation through a fertilizer proportioner system. Some evaporation of water can occur from the fertilizer solution when it is in the benches. This will raise the salt concentration that is determined by the EC meter. When this happens, additional water is added to lower the concentration to the desired level.

In the more sophisticated systems, the solution is automatically tested in the holding tank after each zone is watered. Equipment commercially available to growers will automatically make additions including an acid if the pH is too high, a base such as potassium hydroxide if the pH is too low, fertilizer concentrates if the salt level is too low, water if the salt level is too high, and, finally, more fertilizer solution to restore the original level in the holding tank.

Disease Control

Disease pathogens would appear to be a very formidable threat to an ebb-and-flow system, where solution contacting one pot will ultimately contact all other pots over and over for weeks to come. Years of experience have demonstrated that disease is not a problem with this system. However, one would be well advised to take preventive measures. Benches should be cleaned and sterilized between crops. Chlorine bleaches, bromine from Agribrom®, or hospital disinfectants work well. The disinfectant should be rinsed from the bench, plumbing, and tank after use. Care should be taken to use disease-free plants. During the crop production time, plant debris and any diseased plants should be removed from benches.

Fungicidal drenches can be applied to the top of pots in ebb-and-flow benches in the conventional manner. Growers will generally not allow the drench effluent from the bottom of the pots to return to the fertilizer holding tank but rather will reroute it to waste. A problem stemming from the application of water or drench to the top of a pot is the washing of the root medium out of the pot and onto the bench. This root medium may harbor disease organisms and creates a cleanup problem.

Although the feasibility of applying drench fungicides through subirrigation in the fertilizer solution has been demonstrated, this practice does not have label clearance. For this reason, it cannot be done. More research should be directed toward this objective because it would appear that lesser amounts of fungicide could ultimately be used. Also, this would be an excellent way of nearly eliminating the flow of fungicide to the environment. It would be contained in a closed system where extensive degradation could occur. Should disease become a problem in an ebb-and-flow system, a grower could use one of the six in-line pasteurization systems described for the NFT system earlier in this chapter.

Advantages and Disadvantages

The ebb-and-flow system is expensive, costing about \$4.00/ft^2 of bench. This cost includes the holding tank, pump, and plumbing. Nevertheless, growers who have adopted this system find that it pays for itself. Advantages include the following:

1. Fertilizer effluent can nearly be eliminated since the ebb-and-flow system is closed.

2. Less water and fertilizer are used. The exact amount saved depends on the amount that would normally be lost through leaching. For most greenhouses, this would probably be 30–40 percent.

3. The labor input is reduced because watering is automatically handled, and there is no need to install or remove microtubes before and after each crop.

4. It is easy to change from one pot size to another between crops. In a tube watering system, it would be necessary to change the density of tubes. However, it is important that all pots in a zone require the same watering frequency. Thus, the same species of plant, age of plant, and pot size are situated in a zone at the same time.

The disadvantage that goes along with an ebb-and-flow system is the high relative humidity that can build up in the canopy of plants. This situation can lead to condensation and ultimately to foliar diseases. Humidity rises because air is unable to circulate through the floor of the bench. To combat this problem, growers frequently place heating beneath their benches, which helps to dry the air in the plant canopy and sets up air currents during the heating season. It is likewise important to have an effective air movement system that will replace the moist air in the plant canopy resulting from plant transpiration with drier air. A final measure that can be taken is to apply fertilizer solution early in the day when drying can occur long before the cooler hours of the evening.

Floor Ebb-and-Flow System

Bedding plants are commonly grown on the greenhouse floor. Some other potted crops that have a low labor input once they are placed in the greenhouse are also occasionally grown on floors. These crops require a modification of the ebb-and-flow recirculating system. The floor is paved with a lip around the edge and a drain in the center so that it can be flooded and drained in the same fashion as an ebb-and-flow bench. The advantage of the floor recirculating system is the considerably cheaper cost of setting it up. Expensive benches are not needed. This is not a complete savings since the floor must be very precisely laid out using a laser beam. The disadvantage of this system is the difficulty laborers have bending over to work on crops. But, this disadvantage would exist regardless of whether the recirculation system or some other watering system was used.

Since the floor is much larger than a bench and it is difficult to construct an intricate pattern of channels in the floor for drainage, the floor is usually sloped from either side to a drain channel in the center. Slopes of 0.25–0.75 inch per 10 feet (2–6 mm/m) have been used. Individual zones should not be made larger than can be flooded in 10 minutes, or preferably in 5 minutes. Without channels in the floor, the pots at the highest point of the floor are the last to begin taking up fertilizer solution and the first to lose contact with the solution. Dutch greenhouses commonly have bays 21 feet (6.4 m) wide. The width of the bay constitutes the width of the ebb-and-flow zone. The drain is at the centerpoint of the bay and runs along the length of the greenhouse.

Hot water heat pipes are installed in the floor of many ebb-and-flow systems to dry the floor rapidly after watering and to prevent condensation in the foliage. Some precautions must be taken for bedding plants. A heated concrete floor is slow to cool. Heat application in the concrete may have to be restricted after the first few weeks of growth to ensure that the floor cools before the heat of day occurs. If not, plants will grow too tall.

TROUGH CULTURE

Trough culture is a variation of ebb-and-flow culture that is used for growing potted plants (Figure 9–7). Single rows of plants are grown in watertight troughs. Several troughs parallel to one another with a space between each trough constitute the equivalent to a bench. Troughs are sloped from end to end at a decline of 0.25–0.5 inch per 10 feet (2–4 mm/m). Nutrient solution is pumped to the high end, where it slowly trickles down by gravity to supply each pot along the way. At the low end of each trough, solution drops into a single gutter, perpendicular to the troughs, which returns it to the holding tank. The length of time the solution is left recirculating is determined by how long it takes the solution to rise by capillarity to the top of the root medium in the pot. The same fertilizer solutions and methods of handling are used in trough culture as are used in ebb-and-flow systems.

The advantage of the trough over the ebb-and-flow system is the air circulation which occurs through the plant canopy. The space between troughs allows

Figure 9–7

A trough culture system for pot plant production. Each trough is inclined so that nutrient solution pumped to the top flows down around the base of each pot in the trough and finally spills from the lower end into a collection gutter. The gutter returns the solution to a holding tank. The nutrient solution is recirculated sufficiently long to allow some of it to move throughout the root medium in each pot by capillarity. The unused solution is stored in the holding tank to be used the next time plants require water. (*Photo courtesy of* D. A. *Bailey, Dept. Horticultural Science, North Carolina State University, Raleigh, North Carolina* 27695-7609)

natural convection currents to move up through the bench platform and the plants. This results in drier plants and consequently less foliar disease.

WHOLE-FIRM RECIRCULATION

Some firms, like those in California, are faced with a zero tolerance of nitrate in the effluent water from their property. This, in effect, means there can be no runoff. One way of achieving this is to recirculate all water from the firm (Figure 9–8). Whole-firm recirculation is being done commercially (Skimina 1986).

Plants in the greenhouse or field are grown on a plastic-lined or paved surface. Water or nutrient solution is applied in the conventional manner to the top of the pot, flat, or bench if it is a fresh flower crop. Leachate passing out of the bottom of the container is caught on the greenhouse floor and flows to a lined ditch. A network of ditches from each growing area carries water to a set of settling ponds. Much of the sediment in the leachate settles out in these ponds.

Figure 9–8

An effluent water treatment system at Monrovia Nursery Co. in Azusa, Calif. Effluent from plant pots during watering or fertilization is channeled throughout the entire firm to a settling pond where large particles settle to the bottom. A coagulant is added to aggregate fine particles and these are filtered. Chlorine is added to eliminate disease organisms. After testing, appropriate nutrients and/or water are added to the effluent to restore the desired fertilizer concentration and balance for subsequent application.

From these ponds, water is pumped to an equalization pond to better establish an average level of fertilizer in the leachate coming from the previous applications of water or fertilizer to the crops. A flocculent, such as alum, is added to cause remaining, suspended solids to flocculate (gather together) so that they can settle out. Clear leachate is drawn from this pond above the sediment and then is injected with chlorine. Chlorine pasteurizes it to ensure that disease pathogens are not returned to the crop. Chlorine can also cause iron and manganese to precipitate. The leachate is filtered to remove any remaining solids that might otherwise have clogged small orifices in the watering system. The cleaned leachate is tested for pH level and individual nutrient concentrations. Acid or base is added to adjust the pH level, and water or individual nutrient concentrates are added as indicated by the tests. Since much of the water and some of the nutrients were used by the crop in the previous applications, new nutrient solution is made and is added to restore the volume of the recycled leachate. This solution is held in a reservoir from which it will be drawn when needed for the crop again. If only water is next required on the crop, clean water is used and the leachate from it is captured in the same system as just described.

PULSE WATERING

The construction of closed systems can be very costly. Modification of open systems is an attractive alternative because many components of the traditional system can be retained. Pulse watering is a modification of an open system designed to reduce consumption and effluent of water and nutrients. A major innovator in this system is El Moderno Gardens in Irvine, California. Although this firm is a nursery operation, the principles can carry over well to a greenhouse firm. Nitrates in the runoff water from this and other nurseries in the area originally made their way to the Newport Beach yacht harbor and a nearby wildlife preserve. The resulting algae bloom turned the water to "green soup." El Moderno Gardens was not only able to solve the problem, but in doing so, they developed a system with considerable savings in production costs. Their benefits include reductions of nitrate and water runoff of 90 percent and 77 percent, respectively; a 50 percent reduction in fertilizer usage; a 30 percent drop in water consumption; significantly reduced labor input for irrigation; and compliance with EPA and the regional water-quality control board.

There are a few reasons why excesses of fertilizer and water are applied in greenhouses. First, customary recommendations for greenhouse watering and fertilization call for the addition of 10–15 percent excess fluid at each application. Since water is not controlled in many greenhouses by time clock, an extra minute of watering can easily occur. This minute can result in the doubling or tripling of the amount of excess water desired. It is probably more common to see 40–50 percent excess fluid and, consequently, fertilizer applied in greenhouses. The second reason for excess application relates to the porosity of the root medium used. If there are excessively large drainage pores in the medium, water will quickly pass through and out the bottom without moving laterally to the dry, fine-textured medium. To compensate, growers leave the water or fertilizer solution running longer to allow sufficient time for lateral movement of fluid to occur. Excess fertilizer solution is lost during this time. Of course, partial solutions to these problems are to precisely time the application of water or fertilizer solution and to avoid root media with too high a percolation rate.

Pulse watering goes a step further in reducing water or fertilizer application. In the El Moderno Gardens program, fertilizer solution is applied 5–6 times a day rather than once. However, less solution is applied each time so that close to zero leaching occurs. Since water is generally consumed faster than fertilizer in a pot, fertilizer salts build up with time. The purpose of the 10–15 percent excess fluid application in the conventional watering system is to remove this buildup. In the pulse watering system, the fertilizer salt buildup is allowed to proceed for four days. Then, for three days, clear water is applied 5–6 times per day with nearly zero leaching. During these three days, the excess fertilizer is used by the plants.

This concept is new to floriculture. There should be numerous ways of applying it in part or in full. As a start, firms should consider several short pulses of water or fertilizer solution spaced perhaps 15–30 minutes apart rather than a single application. This practice would allow for total wetting of the root medium without excess fluid draining from the container.

SUMMARY

1. Current antipollution legislation regarding nutrients and pesticides in greenhouse effluent water and the need to reduce production costs to meet intense international competition are resulting in the development of several alternative crop production systems for greenhouses.
2. NFT (nutrient film technique) is a closed production system in that leachate from root media is recycled and does not go to the environment. It is used for vegetable and fresh flower production. Plants are grown with bare roots in covered, sloped channels. Nutrient solution, containing all essential fertilizer nutrients, is recirculated through the roots in a thin layer about ⅛ inch (3 mm) deep. The nutrient solution must be tested repeatedly and altered for pH level and nutrient concentrations.
3. Rock wool culture can be used for growing vegetables or fresh flowers in either a closed or an open production system. In the open production system, nutrient solution passes over the roots and then is released to the environment for disposal. Rock wool, which bears a resemblance to glass wool, is made by melting various forms of rock and spinning it into fibers. The fibers are formed into cubes for propagating plants and into slabs for growing plants on to ma-

turity. Nutrient solution, containing all essential fertilizer nutrients, is passed frequently through the rock wool from top to bottom.

4. Ebb-and-flow culture is a closed cultural system for potted flowering plants, green plants, or bedding plant flats. Conventional containers and root media are used. Special watertight benches or greenhouse floors are used that have drainage built into them. Nutrient solution, which needs to contain only nitrogen and potassium, is pumped into the bench or floor to a depth of 0.75–1 inch (2–3 cm) for about 10–15 minutes. The solution rises into the container by capillarity. Solution not used is returned to a holding tank until the next watering. Although the nutrient solution must be tested periodically, minimal alteration is necessary.
5. Trough culture is a closed system for producing potted flowering and green plants that is nearly identical to ebb-and-flow culture. Rather than growing plants in benches, pots are placed in narrow, sloped troughs. Nutrient solution, similar to that used in ebb-and-flow culture, is passed through the troughs each time watering is required for a sufficient period of time to permit thorough wetting of the root medium by capillarity. An advantage of this system over ebb-and-flow culture is the opening in the bench between each row of plants. This opening allows air to pass between plants, thus keeping the foliage drier for better disease control.
6. Whole-firm recirculation is a closed production system for all greenhouse crops. Plants can be grown in conventional containers and root media. Conventional fertilizer solutions are applied to the surface of the root medium. Effluent from the bottom of the pots or beds throughout the entire firm is captured and directed to a single holding pond. The effluent is pasteurized, tested, altered to correct the pH level and fertilizer concentrations, and then reused.
7. Pulse watering is a procedural alteration that can be used in any conventional open production system for reducing the amount of effluent. The object is to apply only enough water or fertilizer solution to thoroughly wet the root medium at each application. This is done by applying liquid in several short applications instead of one. In this way, time is provided for lateral movement of water into difficult-to-reach areas before much has leaked from the bottom of the container. Selection of root media with a relatively low percolation rate is important for this system to work. To avoid salt buildup, several days of fertilizer application are alternated with a few days of plain water application.

REFERENCES

1. Anon. 1976. A new twist for hydroponics. *Amer. Vegetable Grower* (November): 21–23.

2. Bentley, M. 1955. *Growing Plants without Soil.* Johannesburg: Hydro Chemical Industries Ltd.
3. ______. 1959. *Commercial Hydroponics.* Orange Grove, Johannesburg: Bendon Books (Pty.) Ltd.
4. Bickart, H. M., and C. H. Connors. 1935. The greenhouse culture of carnations in sand. New Jersey Agr. Exp. Sta. Bul. 588.
5. Biggs, T. 1982. Rockwool in horticulture—European experiences. *Australian Hort.* (July):18–21.
6. Carson, R. 1962. *Silent Spring.* Boston: Houghton Mifflin.
7. Chapman, H. D., and G. F. Liebig. 1938. Adaptation and use of automatically operated sand-culture equipment. *J. Agr. Res.* 56:73–80.
8. Cooper, A. J. 1973. Rapid crop turn-round is possible with experimental nutrient film technique. *Grower* 79:1048–1052.
9. ______. 1979. *The ABC of NFT.* London: Grower Books.
10. DeStigter, H. C. M. 1961. Translocation of C^{14} photosynthates in the graft muskmelon, *Cucurbita ficifolia. Acta Botanica Neerlandica* 10:466–473.
11. ______. 1969. A versatile irrigation-type water-culture for root-growth studies. *Zeitschrift für Pflanzenphysiologie* 60:289–295.
12. Dungey, N. O. 1983. Assessing the future of NFT and rockwool. *Hort. Now* 12:17–18.
13. Eaton, F. M. 1936. Automatically operated sand-culture equipment. *J. Agr. Res.* 53:433–444.
14. Epstein, E., and B. A. Krantz. 1965. Growing plants in solution culture. Univ. of California Agr. Ext. Ser. Bul. 196.
15. Gericke, W. F. 1929. Aquaculture, a means of crop production. *Amer. J. Bot.* 16:862.
16. Hanger, B. 1982. Rockwool in horticulture: A review. *Australian Hort.* (May):7–16.
17. Hewitt, E. J. 1966. *Sand and Water Culture Methods Used in the Study for Plant Nutrition.* London: The Eastern Press, Ltd.
18. Hoagland, D. R., and D. I. Arnon. 1950. The water-culture method for growing plants without soil. Univ. of California Agr. Exp. Sta. Cir. 347, rev. ed.
19. Hurd, R. G., ed. 1980. Symposium on research on recirculating water culture. *Acta Hort.* No. 98.
20. Johnson, E. 1984. *Environmental Protection Agency J.* p. 4.
21. Kiplinger, D. C. 1956. Growing ornamental greenhouse crops in gravel culture. Ohio Agr. Exp. Sta. Cir. 92.
22. Knop, W. 1860. Über die Ernährung der Pflanzen durch Wässerige Lösungen bei Ausschluss des Bodens. Landw. Vers.-Stat. 2:65.
23. Krause, W. 1983. Rockwool development. *Grower* 99 (16):43–44.
24. Laurie, A. 1931. The use of washed sand as a substitute for soil in greenhouse culture. *Proc. Amer. Soc. Hort. Sci.* 28:427–431.
25. Maas, E. F., and R. M. Adamson. 1971. Soilless culture and commercial greenhouse tomatoes. Canada Dept. of Agr. Pub. 1460.

26. Marvel, M. E. 1966. Hydroponic culture of vegetable crops. Florida Agr. Ext. Ser. Cir. 192–B.

27. Maynard, D. N., and A. V. Barker. 1970. Nutriculture: A guide to the soilless culture of plants. Massachusetts Coop. Ext. Ser. with USDA Pub. 41.

28. McCall, A. G. 1916. The physiological balance of nutrient solutions for plants in water culture. *Soil Sci.* 2:207–253.

29. Molitor, H. 1990. Irrigation, nutrition, and growth media: The European perspective with emphasis on subirrigation and recirculation of water and nutrients. *Acta Hort.* No. 272.

30. Robbins, W. R. 1928. The possibilities of sand culture for research and commercial work in horticulture. *Proc. Amer. Soc. Hort. Sci.* 25:368–370.

31. Rober, R., ed. 1983. Nutrient film technique and substrates. *Acta Hort.* No. 133.

32. Rupp, L. A., and L. M. Dudley. 1988. Rockwool: How inert is it? *Greenhouse Grower* 6 (11):17–18, 20.

33. Sachs, J. von. 1887. *Lectures on the Physiology of Plants.* Oxford: Clarendon Press.

34. Salm-Horstmar, F. 1849. Versuche uber die Nothwendigen Aschenbestandtheile einer Pflanzen-Species. *J. Prakt. Chem.* 1.

35. Shive, J. W., and W. R. Robbins. 1937. Methods of growing plants in solution and sand cultures. New Jersey Agr. Exp. Sta. Bul. 636.

36. Skimina, C. A. 1986. Recycling irrigation runoff on container ornamentals. *HortScience* 21 (1):32–34.

37. Sowell, W. F. 1972. Hydroponics: Growing plants without soil. Auburn Univ. Coop. Ext. Ser. Cir. P–1.

38. Templeman, W. G., and F. J. Watson. 1938. Growing plants without soil by nutrient solution methods. *J. Ministry of Agr.* 45:771–781.

39. Ticquet, C. E. 1952. *Successful Gardening without Soil.* London: Arthur Peterson Ltd.

40. Weinard, F. F., and G. M. Fosler. 1962. Hydroponics as a hobby. Univ. of Illinois Agr. Ext. Ser. Cir. 844.

41. Wilkinson, C. F. 1987. The science and politics of pesticides. In Marco, G. C., R. M. Hollingworth, and W. Durham, eds. *Silent Spring Revisited,* pp. 25–46. Washington, D.C.: Amer. Chem. Soc.

42. Withrow, R. B., and J. B. Biebel. 1936. A sub-irrigation method of supplying nutrient solutions to plants growing under commercial and experimental conditions. *J. Agr. Res.* 53:693–701.

43. Withrow, R. B., and A. P. Withrow. 1948. Nutriculture. Purdue Univ. Agr. Exp. Sta. Sp. Cir. 328.

CHAPTER 10

Carbon Dioxide Fertilization

ROLE OF CARBON

Carbon is an essential plant nutrient and is present in the plant in greater quantity than any other nutrient. About 40 percent of the dry matter of plants is composed of carbon. Plants obtain carbon from carbon dioxide gas (CO_2) in the air. For the most part, CO_2 gas diffuses through the stomatal openings in leaves when they are open. Once inside the leaf, carbon from CO_2 gas moves into the cells, where, in the presence of energy from the sun, it is used to make carbohydrates (sugars). The carbohydrates are translocated to various parts of the plant and transformed into other compounds needed for growth or maintenance of the plant. The process whereby CO_2 is utilized by the plant is known as *photosynthesis* and occurs in the green chloroplasts within cells. The process is summarized in the following equation:

$$CO_2 + \text{water} + \text{energy from sunlight} \longrightarrow \text{carbohydrate} + \text{oxygen}$$

Air, on the average, contains slightly more than 0.03 percent CO_2. The average level at the present time is 345 ppm—in each 1 million pounds of air are 345 pounds of CO_2. The level of CO_2 in air outdoors can vary from 200 to 400 ppm. Levels of 400 ppm are common in industrial areas where fuels are combusted. The carbon in fuels is converted to CO_2 during the process of combustion. Due to combustion and deforestation, the level of CO_2 has been increasing since around 1880 when the level was about 294 ppm. The present rate of increase is 1–2 ppm per year. The CO_2 level will also be higher in areas such as swamps and riverbeds, where large quantities of plant material are decomposing. Microorganisms feeding upon plant or animal remains respire CO_2 gas, much as we humans do when we utilize plant- and animal-derived foods. This CO_2 gas is evolved through a process called *respiration*, which is summarized as follows for carbohydrates:

$$\text{carbohydrate} + \text{oxygen} \longrightarrow CO_2 + \text{energy} + \text{water}$$

Respiration is the opposite of photosynthesis. It is a process that releases energy originally captured from sunlight in the process of photosynthesis. The energy released is used by the plant for various functions of growth, such as nutrient uptake.

A CO_2 level of 300 ppm is sufficient to support plant growth as we know it in the world today. Most plants, however, have the capacity to utilize greater concentrations of CO_2 and, in turn, attain more rapid growth. This genetic capability apparently stems back to primordial times, when plants adapted to CO_2 levels 10–100 times the level that currently exists.

CARBON DEFICIENCY

In the winter, greenhouses may be closed during the day to consume heat. This situation may occur for several consecutive days during periods of inclement weather in the northern production areas. During the daylight hours, CO_2 is removed from the air by plants through the process of photosynthesis. The level continually drops in a closed greenhouse, and the rate of photosynthesis decreases until a point is reached at which growth stops.

It has been reported that an active sunflower leaf can consume the CO_2 in a column of air 8 feet (2.4 m) above it in an hour. Not all crops utilize CO_2 at this rate. However, in a matter of a few hours, the CO_2 level in a closed greenhouse can drop to the compensation point where growth stops. The actual level where this happens varies for different greenhouse crops, but, in general, it occurs at levels of 50–125 ppm CO_2. Carbon deficiency can occur for several days at a time, prolonging, the culture time of the crop by the same number of days or reducing the quality of the crop. Deficiency of CO_2 can be even more pronounced inside the plant canopy. Circulation of air in the greenhouse can help to alleviate this problem.

CARBON DIOXIDE INJECTION

Effects on Plants

Researchers were surprised to find that plant responses continued to increase as CO_2 levels were raised above the 300 ppm level present in the atmosphere. Levels of 2,000 ppm continued to evoke growth responses in some crops. Apparently, as previously stated, this stems back to the earlier adaptation of plants to higher CO_2 levels in primordial times.

For most greenhouse crops tested over a wide range of geographical latitudes, a response has been reported for increased CO_2 levels up to the range of 1,000–1,500 ppm. At levels of 1,500 ppm and greater, the results vary from a positive to a negative response. This is not surprising since the level of CO_2 required for maximum photosynthesis is related to the other factors that can control photosynthesis. Lettuce growing in the winter in England or Holland at 50°N latitude will have a lower potential photosynthetic rate because of lower available sunlight than a crop in Spain or in the southern United States. A higher level of CO_2 will be required to support the higher photosynthetic rate in the brighter region. Negative responses appear to be caused by a CO_2 toxicity, which is manifested in lower yield, leaf chlorosis (sometimes interveinal), and necrosis. Upper threshold levels of CO_2 are crop specific—for example, 2,200 ppm for tomato, 1,500 for cucumber, and 1,200 for gerbera and chrysanthemum. The commonly injected levels of CO_2 in greenhouses around the world today are 1,000–1,500 ppm. This level is not generally considered harmful to people, although much higher levels can have adverse effects. The maximum level tolerated in submarines is 5,000 ppm.

Weight increases in lettuce of 31 percent have been reported from the use of 1,600 ppm CO_2. In other studies, this has translated into a 20 percent earlier harvest. A 48 percent increase in tomato production has been reported as a result of injection of 1,000 ppm CO_2. Injection of 1,000 ppm CO_2 in England has resulted in a 23 percent increase in cucumber fruit weight.

Specific effects from CO_2 injection on rose crops include a decrease in the number of blind shoots, increased stem length and weight, greater number of petals, and a shorter cropping time in the winter. A test in Massachusetts (42°N latitude) showed a 53 percent increase in weight of roses cut when 1,000 ppm CO_2 was injected.

Chrysanthemum yields increase in the form of thicker stems and greater height when CO_2 is injected (Figure 10–1). Excess stem lengths reduce the value of pot mums and, in the case of cut mums, are left behind in the bench when the flowers are cut. The increased height, however, can be translated into a reduction in the length of time required to flower the crop. Because the flower date is controlled by manipulating the length of day, it is possible to program chrysanthemums to flower up to two weeks earlier without a reduction in height when CO_2 is injected. This represents a considerable savings in production time, considering a normal crop time of 12–16 weeks.

Carnation yields have been increased up to 38 percent by CO_2 injection. The weight of flowers and strength of stems have been increased, and the time required for shoots to reach flowering has been reduced by as much as two weeks. Equally beneficial effects have been obtained for carnation stock plants. Cuttings of greater quality and number have been produced, and the useful life of the stock plant has been increased as well.

Figure 10–1

Dramatic increases in growth can be achieved by enriching the CO_2 level of the greenhouse atmosphere, as seen in the pot mums here. (*Photo courtesy of* R. A. *Larson, Department of Horticultural Science, North Carolina State University, Raleigh,* NC 27695–7609)

CO_2 injection has caused a variety of beneficial effects on a number of other crops. Fall crops of snapdragons were of better quality, while spring crops were reported to have flowered 13 days early in Connecticut. Rooting of geranium cuttings was improved and the height, as well as number of branches on subsequent plants, was increased. Blindness was decreased in Dutch iris. The number, quality, and size of blooms on orchid plants were increased, as were poinsettia bract diameters. Other crops reported to benefit from CO_2 injection include African violet, *Campanula isophylla, Kalanchoe,* and poinsettia.

Crop responses vary according to the extent to which elevated levels of CO_2 can be maintained. CO_2 levels drop appreciably when ventilators are open more than 2 inches (5 cm) and even more so when cooling fans are on. Our own studies, where CO_2 was injected only when the ventilators were open less than 2 inches (5 cm), demonstrated that it was uneconomical for a number of crops in climatic zone 8 (Raleigh, North Carolina, at 35°N latitude) and points farther south (Nelson and Larson, 1969). There were too few hours when elevated CO_2 levels could be maintained.

More recent studies in England and Holland are investigating summer injection of CO_2. When ventilators are open more than 5 percent of their capacity or fans are on, the atmosphere is enriched to the ambient level of 330 ppm. When ventilators are open less than 5 percent, levels up to 1,000 ppm are set. Initial results indicate an economic advantage in both situations. These procedures might work well for cooler locations above 40°N latitude where greenhouses are frequently opened and closed during the summer months. In warmer climates where fans are used for cooling continuously throughout the summer, closed-loop heating and cooling systems (as described in Chapter 3) may in the future afford an opportunity to inject CO_2 for a greater portion of the summer.

Increased growth stimulated by CO_2 injection has necessitated other changes in the cultural programs of some crops. Growers often fertilize lightly in the winter because slow growth is expected. Enrichment of the atmosphere with CO_2 leads to heavier rates of growth and ultimately a nutrient shortage. If a heavier rate of fertilizer is applied, the growth rate continues to increase in response to applied CO_2. Fertilization should probably be increased by an amount equal to the increase in the rate of growth.

Light is often another limiting factor. When light intensity is low, the rate of photosynthesis is slowed down. Once sufficient CO_2 is added to achieve the maximum rate of photosynthesis at the low light intensity, further additions of CO_2 have no effect. If light intensity is increased by cleaning the glass on the greenhouse or by using supplemental lights during the daytime, higher levels of CO_2 will stimulate further increases in growth. CO_2 can be injected when the light intensity is above 500 fc (5,500 lux) but is not economically feasible at lower intensities.

Heat is another limiting factor. Temperatures established before the era of CO_2 injection are not always adequate, now that the limiting factor of CO_2 has been eliminated. Raising daytime temperatures for crops fertilized with CO_2 has been generally beneficial, while raising nighttime temperatures has not. An increase of as much as 10°F (6°C) has been recommended for roses. Geranium, snapdragon, and chrysanthemum respond well to a 5–10°F (3–6°C) increase. The increase for carnation should be 5°F or less since this is a cool-temperature crop having a maximum beneficial daytime temperature as found by Holley, Goldsberry, and Juengling (1964) to be 69°F (20°C). Temperatures for vegetables, including tomato, cucumber, lettuce, and pepper, can be raised 5–9°F (3–5°C).

Today's grower, in injecting CO_2, should be certain that the greenhouse covering is clean enough to ensure the maximum light intensity possible that can be tolerated by the crop. The grower should experiment with raising the daytime temperature 5–10°, as well as increasing the fertilization rate, and, in general, should ensure that all cultural procedures are practiced in a manner that promotes optimal growth.

Method of CO_2 Injection

Since CO_2 injection is only effective during the daylight hours when photosynthesis occurs, it should be injected from sunrise until 1 hour before sunset. It should be injected only when the ventilation fans are off or, in the case of greenhouses cooled by ventilators, when the roof ventilators are open less than 2 inches (5 cm). CO_2 cannot be injected during the warm seasons because cooling generally coincides with the daylight hours. Depending on the latitude where the greenhouse is located, the season for CO_2 injection will begin between late September and early November and extend to April or early May.

A few brands of CO_2 generators are popular today (Figure 10–2). One unit sells for close to $450 with a gas pressure gauge and a 24-volt solenoid valve. This unit provides 1,500 ppm CO_2 in a typical greenhouse of 5,000 ft^2 (465 m^2) floor area. It burns LP or natural gas. This generator has a burner range up to 60,000

Figure 10–2

A CO_2 generator used for enriching the greenhouse atmosphere with CO_2 for the purpose of increasing photosynthesis and growth. (*Photo courtesy of Johnson Gas Appliance Co., Cedar Rapids,* IA 52405)

Btu/hr (15,120 kcal/hr or 17,580 W); thus, it can consume 60 ft^3 (1.7 m^3) of natural gas per hour. A control package that automatically turns up to three units on at sunrise and off at sunset is available for \$100. Another popular brand can be obtained in various models that burn either natural gas, propane, or kerosene. The larger model with a natural gas burner can provide up to 1,200 ppm CO_2 in a typical greenhouse of 25,000 ft^2 floor area and sells for about \$1,900.

CO_2 generators are hung above head height along the center of the greenhouse. Within each is a precisely calibrated burner with an open flame. Under conditions of complete combustion, gas is converted to water and CO_2. CO_2 produced in some units rises out of the burner into the greenhouse atmosphere, where convection currents move the gas about the greenhouse. In other products, the CO_2 is positively displaced from the burner by a fan.

Gas consumed in the CO_2 generator must be of a high purity level since sulfur contained in it is converted to sulfur dioxide gas. When sulfur dioxide comes in contact with moisture on plant surfaces, it is converted to sulfurous and eventually to sulfuric acid. This burns the plant (see Figure 3–5). The sulfur content of natural gas and propane should not exceed 0.02 percent by weight (Blom et al. 1984), while the sulfur content of kerosene should not exceed 0.06 percent (Hand 1971).

Incomplete combustion will cause the formation of ethylene and carbon monoxide gases, which are injurious to a plant (see Figure 3–4). Internodes on the plant become shortened, branching increases, and flowers become distorted and injured from ethylene. The upper limit for ethylene is 0.05 ppm. Carbon monoxide is harmful to humans. The upper average limit for carbon monoxide is 50 ppm (Anon. 1986). Therefore, only a burner designed for CO_2 production should be used inside a greenhouse, and it should be periodically calibrated. The burner should be kept clean and adjusted to a clear blue flame. The plumbing should be checked for gas leaks since unburned fuel may be injurious to plants. Manufactured gases, and to a degree natural gas, can contain propylene and butylene, which are injurious to plants, causing symptoms similar to ethylene. The threshold for propylene, above which injury occurs, is 10 ppm (Hicklenton 1988).

It is equally important to provide sufficient oxygen to support complete combustion of the fuel. In a film plastic greenhouse or a glass greenhouse located in an area where it is prone to ice formation on the surface, an air inlet must be provided. The rule for heating systems applies here, where 1 square inch of opening is provided per 2,500 Btu of burner capacity per hour (1 cm^2 per 100 kcal or per 733 W).

Considerable progress has been made since injection of CO_2 was commercialized in the early 1960s. The concept actually dates back to the earlier part of this century, but it was not until commercial methods of application were available that extensive efforts were put forth to develop a system. Early research by Professor Holley at Colorado State University in the late 1950s, as well as work in

Holland and England, led to commercial systems using liquid CO_2 or dry ice, which is solid (frozen) CO_2. (See Hicklenton 1988 for historical details.)

CO_2 gas under pressure becomes liquid. At a low temperature, it can be solidified into dry ice. In the early 1960s, liquid CO_2 tanks were installed at a greenhouse range and were serviced by CO_2 distributors. CO_2 gas formed above the liquid in these tanks and was carried by a metal tubing to the greenhouses. A set of pressure-regulating valves reduced the pressure to a low level. Once in the greenhouse, the gas was distributed the length of the greenhouse in a plastic tube from ⅛ to ¼ inch (3–6 mm) in diameter with needle holes each foot (30 cm) along the length.

Liquid and solid CO_2 proved a more expensive source of CO_2 in the 1960s than the combustion of fuels. Burners were developed. Some early equipment was large and had to be located outside the greenhouse. The exhaust, essentially pure CO_2, was brought into the greenhouse through a duct and distributed along the length of the greenhouse through the conventional winter tube ventilation system (as described in Chapter 4).

With time, smaller generators were developed that were installed overhead in the greenhouse. These produced CO_2 in open-flame burners using kerosene, propane, or natural gas. Being simpler systems, they cost less to purchase. Depending upon the equipment purchased, they could handle greenhouse areas of 5,000–15,000 ft^2 (365–1,400 m^2). This generation of CO_2 generators is in common use today in America.

Partly because of recent shifts in fuel costs, larger greenhouse firms find the cost of CO_2 from liquid CO_2 comparable to that of CO_2 generated from the combustion of fuel. A large consumption volume is necessary in order to negotiate an economical, steady source of liquid CO_2 from the supplier. Liquid CO_2 has the advantage of purity. Unlike CO_2 generation in burners, the use of liquid CO_2 releases no heat, which can be a disadvantage during the winter and an advantage at the beginning and end of the CO_2 injection season.

Measurement and Control of CO_2 Level

Various CO_2 control systems can be used. The CO_2 generator can be turned on in the morning and off in the evening by either a time clock or a light sensor. During the day, the CO_2 generator would be automatically turned off when the ventilating fans come on. In the event of roof ventilation, mechanical switches can be installed on the ventilators to allow the CO_2 generator to operate only when the vents are open less than 2 inches (5 cm).

CO_2 generators will not have the same net effect in all greenhouses. The CO_2 level will be lower in glass greenhouses, where air leaks exist, than in film plastic greenhouses. In order to adjust the fuel pressure on some generators, it is important to know what level is being maintained in the greenhouse atmosphere.

Simple CO_2 testers can be purchased for about $300. These consist of a small hand pump that is stroked a given number of times to pass air through a tube. The tube contains a CO_2-sensitive chemical that changes color as CO_2 is absorbed. The length of the tube that changes color is measured on a scale that directly indicates the level of CO_2 in the air passed through the tube. The tubes are disposable and sell for about $37 for a box of 10. (Testers are available from Fisher Scientific Co., 711 Forbes Ave., Pittsburgh, PA 15219, and from Hydro Gardens, Inc., P.O. Box 9707, Colorado Springs, CO 80932).

More sophisticated CO_2 sensors are available for automatically monitoring the CO_2 level in the greenhouse and controlling the CO_2 generator. These sensors are priced in the range of $750–$1,500. A sensor can be connected to several greenhouses by sampling tubes through which air is drawn by a pump. Typically, air is sampled and tested for 1 minute from each greenhouse. Information from the single sensor is received by a computer, which, in turn, controls CO_2 generators in each greenhouse.

Computer systems are available for setting a few different levels of CO_2 in accordance with the light intensity sensed. These programs will also raise the day temperature in accordance with the level of CO_2 being injected and will turn off CO_2 injection when ventilation is in progress. Future growers will have computer equipment and programs that will continually adjust to numerous CO_2 levels and temperatures in the greenhouse to balance the changing light levels. This technology will bring crops closer to their photosynthetic potential than is possible today. It will also result in considerable savings in energy since heat and CO_2 will be applied only as needed.

ECONOMICS OF CO_2 INJECTION

In the northern United States, it would be common to inject CO_2 for an average of 5 hours per day over a six-month period (900 hours). At an output of 60,000 Btu/hr, this amounts to 54 million Btu or 540 therms (100,000 Btu/therm) of natural gas per burner. Since one burner handles about 5,000 ft^2 of greenhouse, the natural gas consumption is 0.108 therm/ft^2 (29,300 kcal or 11.4 MJ/m^2) of greenhouse area per year. At $0.60 per therm, this carries a fuel cost of $.065/$ft^2$ ($0.70/$m^2$) of greenhouse area per year. Depreciation on the equipment adds very little to the cost of injecting CO_2. The higher yields and shorter production time of crops more than justify the costs.

Professor Koths at the University of Connecticut points out an additional benefit from CO_2 injection. Many crops are grown at a 5°F (3°C) warmer daytime temperature when CO_2 is injected. The greenhouse acts as a solar collector. Heat is stored in the greenhouse structure, soil, plants, and benches. At night, the extra heat resulting from the higher day temperature is released. This conserves heating fuel and thereby pays part of the cost of CO_2 injection. Additional heating fuel is consumed during the daytime when the CO_2 generators are on and releasing heat. Professor Koths indicates that these two benefits of supplemental heat could pay from half to all of the fuel consumed by the CO_2 generators.

SUMMARY

1. Carbon is an essential plant nutrient and is supplied as CO_2 gas in the atmosphere. A concentration of about 0.03 percent (345 ppm) is present in the atmosphere.
2. CO_2 is used during daylight hours in the process of photosynthesis. When the greenhouse is closed on cold winter days, the CO_2 concentration in the air inside the greenhouse can be lowered in a few hours to a level where the rate of carbohydrate manufactured in photosynthesis equals the rate of carbohydrate breakdown through respiration. Net growth ceases at this point, delaying the crop or reducing quality.
3. CO_2 is often added to the greenhouse atmosphere during daylight hours of months when greenhouses are not continuously ventilated. The common method of addition is through the burning of kerosene, LP gas, or natural gas in special burners inside the greenhouse.
4. Reestablishment of a normal level of CO_2 (about 300 ppm) results in dramatic growth responses. Interestingly, further increases in CO_2 concentration up to 2,000 ppm or above induce even greater growth responses. Concentrations of 1,000–1,500 ppm are the levels generally established in the greenhouse.

REFERENCES

1. Anon. 1986. Carbon dioxide: Documentation of the threshold limit values and biological exposure indices. *Amer. Conf. Govt. Industrial Hygenists*, pp. 102–103. Cincinnati, OH.
2. Bauerle, W. L., and T. H. Short. 1984. Carbon dioxide depletion effects in energy efficient greenhouses. In Short, T. H., ed. Energy in protected cultivation. III. *Acta Hort.* No. 148.
3. Blom, T., W. Straver, and F. J. Ingratta. 1984. Using carbon dioxide in greenhouses. Ontario Ministry of Agr. and Food. Factsheet 290–27.
4. Gaastra, P. 1966. Some physiological aspects of CO_2 application in glasshouse culture. In Hardh, J. E., ed. Symposium on vegetable growing under glass. *Acta Hort.* 4:111–116.
5. Hand, D. W. 1971. CO_2 and hydrocarbon fuels. *ADAS Qtr. Review* 1:18–23.
6. Hicklenton, P. R. 1988. *Grower Handbook Series.* Vol. 2. *CO_2 Enrichment in the Greenhouse.* Portland, OR: Timber Press.

7. Hicklenton, P. R., and P. A. Jolliffe. 1978. Effects of greenhouse CO_2 enrichment on the yield and photosynthetic physiology of tomato plants. *Can. J. Plant Sci.* 58:801–817.

8. Holley, W. D. 1975. The CO_2 story. In Ball, V., ed. *The Ball Red Book,* 13th ed., pp. 156–159. West Chicago, IL: George J. Ball, Inc.

9. Holley, W. D., K. L. Goldsberry, and C. Juengling. 1964. Effects of CO_2 concentration and temperature on carnations. Colorado Flower Growers Assoc. Bul 174:1–5.

10. Mastalerz, J. W. 1969. Environmental factors: Light, temperature, carbon dioxide. In Mastalerz, J. W., and R. W. Langhans, eds. *Roses: A Manual on the Culture, Management, Diseases, Insects, Economics and Breeding of Greenhouse Roses,* pp. 95–108. Pennsylvania Flower Growers' Assoc., New York State Flower Growers' Assoc., Inc., and Roses, Inc.

11. Nelson, P. V., and R. A. Larson. 1969. The effects of increased CO_2 concentration on chrysanthemum and snapdragon. North Carolina Agr. Exp. Sta. Tech. Bul. 194.

12. Shaw, R. J., and M. N. Rogers. 1964. Interaction between elevated carbon dioxide levels and greenhouse temperatures on the growth of roses, chrysanthemums, carnations, geraniums, snapdragons, and African violets. *Florists' Review* 135 (3486):23–24, 88–89; (3487):21–22, 82; (3488):73–74, 95–96; (3499):21, 59–60; (3491):19, 37–39.

13. Wittwer, S. H. 1966. Carbon dioxide and its role in plant growth. *Proc. 17th Intl. Hort. Cong.* 3:311–322.

14. Wittwer, S. H., and W. M. Robb. 1964. Carbon dioxide enrichment of greenhouse atmospheres for food crop production. *Economic Bot.* 18:34–56.

CHAPTER 11

Light and Temperature

LIGHT INTENSITY FOR PHOTOSYNTHESIS

Photosynthesis

Visible light constitutes a source of energy for plants. Light energy, carbon dioxide (CO_2), and water all enter into the process of photosynthesis through which carbohydrates are formed:

$$CO_2 + \text{water} + \text{light energy} \rightarrow \text{carbohydrate} + \text{oxygen}$$

Considerable energy is required to reduce carbon that is combined with oxygen in CO_2 gas to the state in which it exists in carbohydrate. The light energy thus utilized is trapped in the carbohydrate. Later, the carbohydrate can be translocated (moved) from the green stem and leaf cells where photosynthesis occurs to all other parts of the plant. The carbohydrate can be converted into all other compounds needed in the plant. Amino acids may be formed and then combined into protein chains. Fats may be formed from carbohydrates. From all these compounds, yet other compounds arise such as cellulose for cell walls, pectin to cement the walls together, hormones to regulate growth, and DNA to constitute chromosomes. Energy of the sun is passed along in all of these compounds. These processes result in growth of the plant, which can be detected as an increase in dry matter.

Energy must be liberated at times to power other processes in the plant. The uptake of nutrients, formation of proteins, division of cells, maintenance of membranes, and several other processes require an input of energy. This energy is obtained when compounds formed as a direct or indirect result of photosynthesis are broken down in very much the reverse process of photosynthesis. This is the process of respiration:

$$\text{carbohydrate} + \text{oxygen} \longrightarrow CO_2 + \text{water} + \text{energy}$$

Respiration occurs in all living organisms at all times. It is temperature dependent, increasing with increases in temperature. When animals eat plants, they obtain energy from the compounds they ingest. This energy was originally derived from light through photosynthesis. It can be released from these compounds by the animals through respiration. The same holds true for humans when we eat animal or plant tissue. Thus, we see that most living organisms are ultimately dependent upon light energy.

When all factors such as CO_2 level, temperature, and water are optimized for photosynthesis, an optimum light intensity can be determined. If the light intensity is diminished, photosynthesis (and growth) slows down. If higher than optimal light intensities are provided, growth again slows down because the chloroplasts are injured. Chloroplasts are the organelles within green cells in which photosynthesis occurs.

Greenhouse crops are subjected to light intensities as high as 12,000 fc (129 klux) on clear summer days to below 300 fc (3.2 klux) on cloudy winter days. For most crops, neither condition is ideal. Many crops become light-saturated (photosynthesis does not increase at higher light intensities) at about 3,000 fc (32.3 klux). Of course, this is assuming that all leaves are exposed to an intensity of 3,000 fc (32.3 klux), which is rarely the case. Upper leaves cast shadows on lower leaves, thus reducing the light intensity at the lower leaves. As illustrated in Figure 11–1, an individual leaf at the top of the plant may saturate at 3,000 fc (32.3 klux), while the plant as a whole may not reach light saturation until 10,000 fc (108 klux).

Rose and carnation plants will grow well under full summer light intensities. Poinsettia foliage is deeper green if the greenhouse is shaded to the extent of about 40 percent from mid-spring to mid-fall. This is typical of most crops. In addition to shading crops to prevent chloroplast suppression, crops such as chrysanthemum and geranium are shaded to prevent petal burn. The high light intensity is believed to raise the temperature of the petal tissue to an injurious level. Other crops require even more shading. Foliage plants are burned at light intensities over 2,000–3,000 fc (21.5–32.3 klux), and African violets lose chlorophyll at intensities of 1,500 fc (16.1 klux) and higher. The optimum light intensity for African violets is near 1,000 fc (10.8 klux). As will be seen later in this chapter, many foliage plants, gloxinia, African violets, and annual seedlings can be grown quite satisfactorily in growth rooms at a light intensity of 600 fc (6.5 klux). Thus, it is

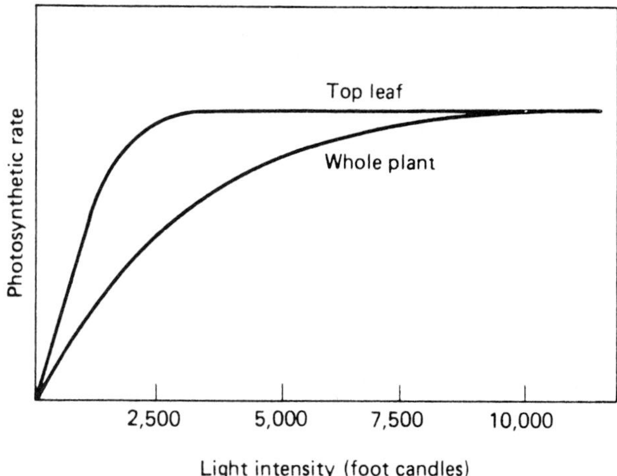

Figure 11–1

The effect of light intensity on the rate of photosynthesis of a single leaf at the top of a plant and of the whole plant. While the single leaf reaches its maximum rate of photosynthesis at 3,000 fc (32.3 klux), an intensity of 10,000 fc (108 klux) might be required for the whole plant in order to raise the light intensity within the leaf canopy to 3,000 fc (32.3 klux).

apparent that light intensity requirements of photosynthesis vary considerably from crop to crop.

Light Quality

Not all light is useful in photosynthesis. Light is classified according to wavelength (nm). This classification is referred to as *quality.* Ultraviolet (UV) light has short wavelengths below 400 nm (Figure 11–2). For the most part, UV light

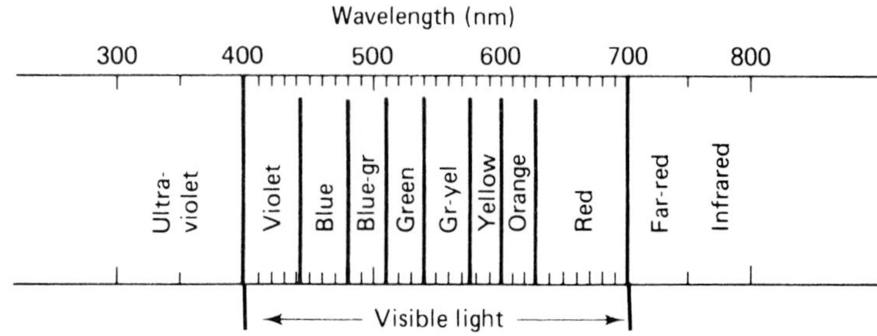

Figure 11–2

Types of radiant energy having wavelengths of 300–800 nm. Visible light is in the range of 400–700 nm.

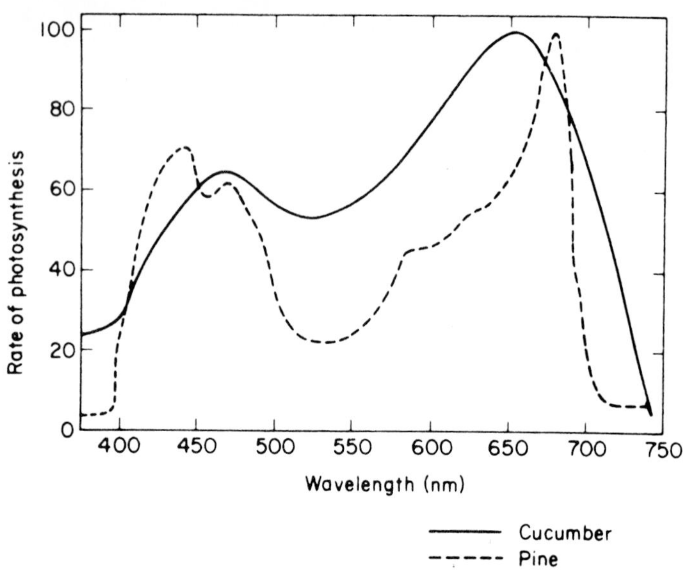

Figure 11–3

Rates of photosynthetic activity occurring under different qualities of light between the ultraviolet wavelength of 350 nm and the far-red wavelength of 750 nm. (*From The Electricity Council,* 1972)

cannot be seen by the human eye. In large quantities, it is harmful to plants. Glass screens out most UV light and all light below a wavelength of 325 nm. Visible, or *white,* light occurs between the wavelengths of 400–700 nm. At the shortest wavelength, visible light appears violet. Blue, green, yellow, orange, and red light occur around wavelengths of 460, 510, 570, 610, and 650 nm, respectively. Far-red light (700–750 nm) occurs at the limit of our visual perception and has an influence on plants other than through photosynthesis. Infrared energy occurs at longer wavelengths and is not involved in plant processes.

It is primarily the visible spectrum of light that is used in photosynthesis (Figure 11–3). There are peaks in the blue and red bands where photosynthetic activity is higher. When blue light alone is supplied to plants, growth is shortened, hard, and dark in color. When plants are grown in red light, growth is soft and internodes are long, resulting in tall plants. Figure 11–3 clearly shows that all visible light qualities (wavelengths) are readily utilized in photosynthesis.

Maximizing Light Intensity

It is important to ensure the highest light intensity possible during the dark portion of the year from mid-fall through early spring for all crops except the low-light group already mentioned. In this way, growth is maximized.

Range Design Maximization of light begins in the planning stage of the greenhouse range. The simpler the frame and the farther apart the sash bars, the greater the light intensity inside. A very significant stride forward was made when all-metal greenhouses were popularized in the 1950s. Because of the strength of the metal members of these greenhouses, fewer sash bars were required to support the heavy weight of the glass. Glass widths increased from 16 to 24 inches (41 to 61 cm), reducing the number of sash bars by one-third. Fewer shadows in the greenhouse meant more light.

Frame simplicity is particularly important in film plastic greenhouses. The wooden-frame plastic greenhouses (which have almost entirely passed out of the picture now) required very massive frames that greatly reduced interior light intensity. It is very important to keep the wood of such structures painted white so that it reflects light into the greenhouse rather than absorbing it. The same is true of wooden sash bars on glass greenhouses. They should be painted every other year on the outside and about every five years (or as needed) on the inside. The pipe-frame Quonset and all-metal gutter-connected plastic greenhouses, with their minimal frames, are very good in terms of maximizing light intensity.

The importance of the greenhouse design can be seen in light-transmission figures presented by Professor W. D. Holley of Colorado State University. The frame blocks 10 percent of the sunlight, the sash bars another 5 percent, and the glass another 7 percent. Actually, the 78 percent light-transmission figure for this overall greenhouse is unusually high. Figures near 65 percent would not be uncommon. Other factors that further decrease the transmission level are (1) overhead equipment such as automatic shading, heating and cooling systems, plumbing, and plant supports and (2) the geographical orientation of the greenhouse. (Orientation was discussed in Chapter 2.)

The covering material is another consideration. Glass transmits about 89 percent of light impinging on it. FRP has a slightly lower (86 percent) transmission value under high light intensities but a superior value under low light intensities. If light transmission remained constant over the years for fiberglass, it would be a superior covering. With time, however, the surface erodes, light transmission diminishes, and resurfacing becomes necessary. The guaranteed life expectancy of FRP (up to 20 years) is much shorter than the life expectancy of glass. Resurfacing and replacement costs must be weighed against the value of increased light during the early life of the FRP. It is difficult to quantify these factors, but it can be said that FRP is declining in this industry at the present.

A double layer of polyethylene transmits less light (84 percent) than a single layer of glass (89 percent). The lower light-transmission value might be completely compensated by the absence of sash bars in the film plastic greenhouse.

Clean Glass Many greenhouses are shaded during the summer to reduce light intensity. A residue of shade may still remain in winter. In addition, dust will usually accumulate on the glass. These deposits reduce light intensity—20 percent reductions commonly occur. Dirty glass should be washed as the dark season approaches (usually in October or November). Commercial glass-cleaning products are available through greenhouse supply companies. Some can be used on glass, rigid plastic, and film plastic. One make-your-own formula calls for dissolving 11 pounds of oxalic acid in 33 gallons of water. The greenhouse is sprayed with this solution when the greenhouse is damp. A good time to spray is in the morning after a heavy dew or after a light shower. If the weather is dry, the greenhouse should be hosed down first. The solution should remain on the glass for three days, after which it can be rinsed off or the rain can be allowed to remove it.

FRP greenhouses need cleaning as well. A household detergent can be applied with a sponge or rag at the end of a pole. Commercial materials are also available. Sometimes, the inside of glass becomes dirty as well. The formulation given above can be sprayed inside the glass greenhouse and hosed off, providing it

Figure 11–4

A winter planting arrangement for chrysanthemums that allows for a space along the center of the bench to increase light intensity at that point with the resultant effect of improved quality.

does not contact plants. Benches containing plants should be covered with polyethylene during cleaning.

Plant Spacing Plants tend to proliferate within a bench until the available light energy is fully utilized. In other words, an equal amount of dry matter will be produced in a bench whether plants such as chrysanthemum are spaced on 5 or 7 inch (13 or 18 cm) centers. In the former case, smaller stems and blooms are produced. The size and quality of product desired will dictate the proper plant spacing.

Generally, a greater amount of space per plant is provided in the winter than in the summer because of less available light. Catalogs provided by suppliers of plant material will indicate the proper spacing for various seasons of the year. It is best to follow their recommendations.

Some growers of fresh flowers have found it best to leave an open space along the center of the bench from end to end as pictured in Figure 11–4. This permits light to enter the center of the bench where it would normally be darkest. There is a resultant increase in overall quality. The same number of plants are used in a bench in this system. They are simply spaced closer to compensate for the open space in the center.

Reducing Light Intensity

The need for reducing light intensity during mid-spring to early fall has already been pointed out. This may be accomplished in two ways: (1) by spraying a shading compound on the greenhouse or (2) by installing a screen fabric over the greenhouse or in the greenhouse above head height.

When the entire greenhouse range needs shading, some growers use the spray method because it is less expensive. Commercial shading compounds can be purchased from florist supply companies or can be made on the premises by mixing white latex paint with water. One part paint in 10 parts water provides a very heavy shade, while one part paint in 15–20 parts water provides a standard shade. The shading compound can be sprayed on from the ground by means of a pesticide sprayer. In some large operations, it is sprayed on from the air by a helicopter. Most of the shading compound will wear off by early fall. If it does not, it needs to be washed off.

When shade is desired only to protect flowers, sheets of screening are sometimes used just where needed. Chrysanthemums and geraniums may be grown at full light intensity in northern areas, but the flowers must be protected from sunburn. Cheesecloth was commonly used years ago and is still used when it affords a price advantage. Longer-lasting synthetic fabrics are more popular today including such materials as polypropylene, polyester, saran, and aluminum-coated polyester. The former three can be purchased in different densities of weave providing many shade values from 20 to 90 percent, although 50 percent is commonly used. Aluminized polyester sheets are constructed from thin strips of clear polyester and aluminum-coated polyester sewn together. The ratio of the clear to coated strips determines the degree of shading. Clear polyester plastic does a good job keeping radiant heat out during a bright summer day as well as heat in during a cold winter night. The aluminum coating reflects this form of heat and thus substantially improves this barrier.

The problem with spraying shading on the outside of the greenhouse or installing a fixed sunscreen in the greenhouse is that the barrier is still in place when the light intensity is low on cloudy days and early in the morning or late in the afternoon on all days. Thus, periods of inadequate light intensity occur and thus reduce growth and delay crops.

Modern greenhouses have automated equipment to draw sunscreens across the greenhouse in response to photo cells. In this way, screening is only applied during the hours when needed. If the sunscreens are judiciously selected, they can also serve as the thermal blankets used for retaining heat on winter nights. The same apparatus used for drawing the screens in the daytime during the bright months can be used for drawing them during the nights in the winter. Manual operation of sunscreens would require constant vigilance seven days a week, which is out of the question. Photo cells can perform this task just as time clocks can perform the task of drawing thermal blankets on winter nights. Computers make the job even easier. They can be preprogrammed long in advance and for a large number of different crop zones, each with its own separate events and dates.

Supplemental Lighting

During the dark seasons of the year, light intensity is below optimum for most crops in most greenhouse production areas of the world. While the previously discussed methods for maximizing light intensity help, they do not completely solve the problem. Growth of crops affected is erratically slow because of day-to-day variations in weather conditions, and final quality is reduced. There is an increase in blindness (failure of shoots to develop) on crops such as rose and orchid. Size (grade) of fresh flowers is smaller, stems are thinner, and plants can be adversely tall. This situation can be rectified by using supplemental lighting in the greenhouse to increase the rate of photosynthesis.

Lamp Types Many types of lamps have been used in the greenhouse. Basically, they fall into three groups: (1) incandescent, (2) fluorescent, and (3) high-intensity-discharge (high-pressure mercury, metal-halide, low-pressure sodium, and high-pressure sodium). Light emissions typical of each type can be seen in Figure 11–5.

Incandescent (tungsten-filament) lamps (Figure 11–5a) are generally not used for supplemental lighting because of excessive heat, poor light quality, and low efficiency. In order to avoid excess heat, the light intensity must be kept too low. For most plants, the high proportion of red and far-red light emitted causes

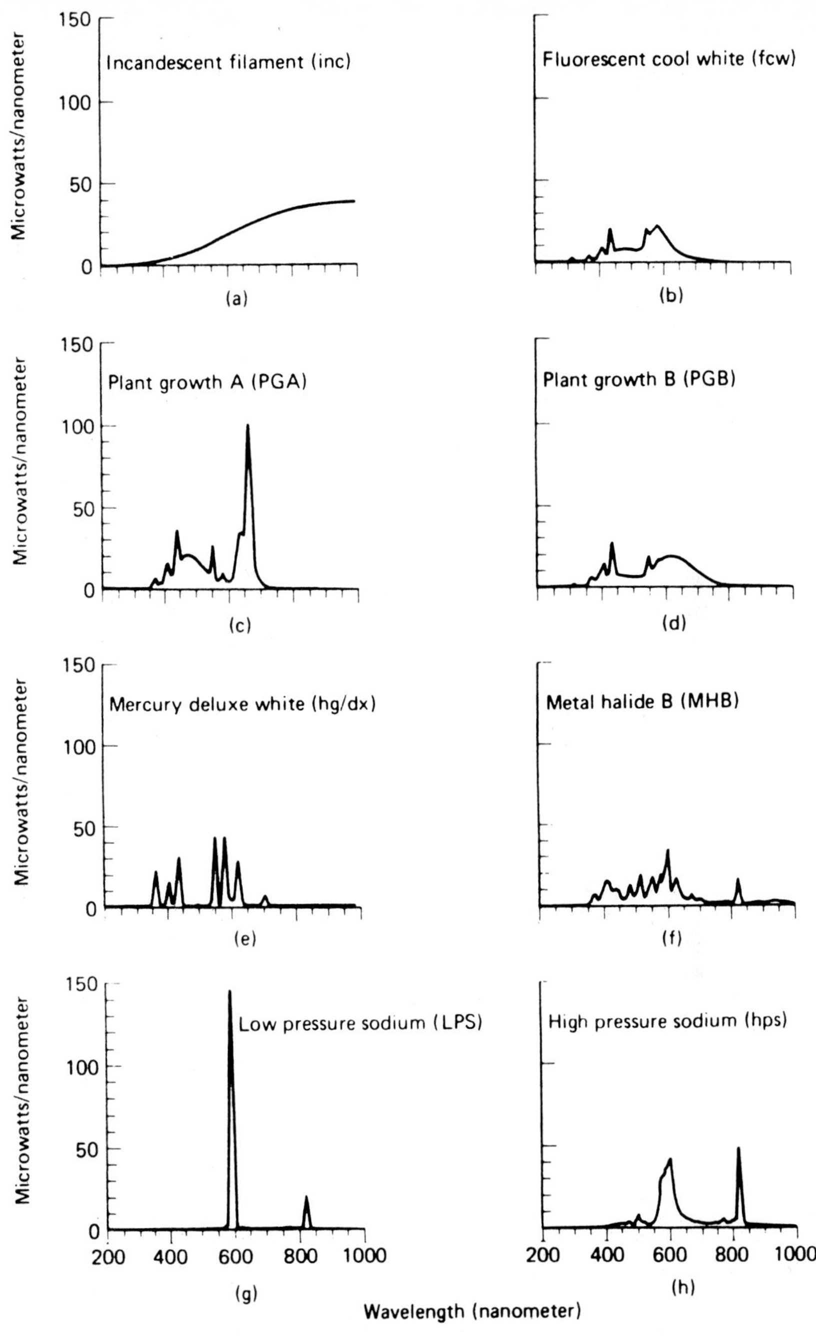

Figure 11–5

The spectrum of light emissions measured as radiant power per lumen from eight types of lamps considered for use in greenhouses. (*From Campbell, Thimijan, and Cathey*, 1975)

tall, soft growth and other changes in plant form. These lamps are also very inefficient, converting only 7 percent of the electrical energy consumed into light energy. Much of the energy is converted into heat, which at times is of value and at other times is a detriment. While incandescent lamps are of little value for supplemental lighting, they are the lamp of choice for photoperiodic lighting (as will be discussed in a following section of this chapter). For this application, a low intensity (10 fc, 108 lux) is applied for a short duration during the middle of the night in the winter.

Fluorescent lamps are the most common lamps used in growing rooms and over small germination areas in the greenhouse. (This application will be discussed in the next section on growth rooms.) They are rarely used for finishing crops. In separate trials, E. D. Bickford (1972) and J. W. Mastalerz (1969) increased the yield of roses using Gro-Lux® (plant growth A) fluorescent lamps. Best results were obtained by placing lamps without reflectors between the plants. These and other commercial trials have shown positive results on the crops, but the economics are questionable because of the large number of lamps required. The low power (wattage) of the lamps increases the number needed and, consequently, the total cost of fixtures and wiring required to do the job. The larger number of fixtures increases the area of shadows cast on the crop.

Among the more efficient of the fluorescent lamps are the cool white and warm white tube types. These lamps convert 20 percent of electrical energy consumed by them and the ballast to visible light energy and have similar spectral light emissions. Cool white (Figure 11–5b) is perhaps the most commonly used fluorescent lamp for plant growth. Light emitted tends to predominate in the blue region. There are a number of other fluorescent lamps with special phosphors for emitting a spectrum of wavelengths more in line with the requirements of photosynthesis. These are categorized into two groups: Plant growth A (Figure 11–5c) includes the earlier lamps with enhanced radiation in the red range, while plant growth B (Figure 11–5d) includes the later generation of lamps with extended spectral emission beyond 700 nm.

High-intensity-discharge (HID) lamps are the preferred lamps for finishing crops in greenhouses today (Figure 11–6). High-pressure mercury type HID lamps were more common in Europe than in America. These lamps were mostly replaced by metal-halide lamps and, more recently, are being replaced by high-pressure sodium type HID lamps. Light emissions from high-pressure mercury lamps are somewhat similar to those from fluorescent tubes. Model MBFR/U (formerly popular in Europe) has fluorescent powder on the inner surface of the glass bulb, which converts much UV light to visible wavelengths, particularly red. This feature makes the lamp more desirable for plant growth and increases its efficiency to 13 percent of the electrical energy input into the lamp and ballast. Similar American lamps are the Mercury Clear and Mercury Deluxe White models (Figure 11–5e), which are often seen along roadways. These lamps are available in

Figure 11–6

High-pressure mercury and high-pressure sodium type HID lamps under test to supplement the natural winter daylight for the purpose of increased photosynthesis.

sizes up to 1,000 W. They have been used for up to 10,000 hours, at which point they still had 70 percent of their original output.

High-pressure metal-halide-type HID lamps (Figure 11–5f) were also more commonly used in Europe than in America. These lamps are available in sizes up to 2,000 W and can convert 20 percent of total electrical input energy into light in the 400–700 nm band. These lamps cost more than the high-pressure mercury lamps, have a shorter life, and lose their output level faster, but they more efficiently utilize electricity.

Low-pressure sodium-(LPS-)type HID lamps (Figure 11–5g), available in 35, 55, 135, and 180 W sizes, were popular for awhile. As refinements came along in the metal-halide and high-pressure sodium lamps, the former lamps lost popularity in the greenhouse. LPS lamps are the most efficient with 27 percent of the electrical input into lamp and ballast being converted to visible radiation. These lamps have a life expectancy of 18,000 hours.

LPS lamps emit most of the light in a narrow band around 589 nm. Because little light is emitted in the 700–850 nm range, there are adverse effects on some crops when these lamps are the only source of light. In tests, African violet, petunia, and lettuce plants grown under LPS lamps only, developed pale green foliage. Lettuce plants were smaller in comparison to plants under LPS plus incandescent lamps. If 10 percent of the total light is supplied from incandescent lights or from natural daylight, the problem is averted. Lettuce plants grown under LPS lamps in northern Europe developed strap leaves. This problem does not occur in the United States, where winter light intensities are higher and days are longer. The problem is believed to be caused by low levels of blue light. The fore-mentioned problems are not encountered with HPS lamps because of the broader spectrum of light emitted. Reasons given in the greenhouse industry for not using LPS lamps include their bulky reflectors, which cast shadows, and the higher cost of purchasing and installing the large number of LPS lamps required relative to HPS lamps.

High-pressure sodium-(HPS-) type HID lamps (Figure 11–5h) gained more popularity in America than the high-pressure mercury lamps because they are cheaper to purchase and to operate. The majority of lamps being installed in greenhouses today worldwide are HPS lamps. The light-emission spectrum predominates more in the higher wavelengths with a peak at 589 nm (yellow). The light-emission spectrum extends beyond the visible range (400–700 nm) into the 700–850 nm range. Radiation in this latter range is required for stem elongation, increased fresh weight, and early flowering of most plants. HPS lamps are very efficient, converting 25 percent of the electrical input into the lamp and ballast into visible radiation. Suitable models of HPS lamps for greenhouse use are available in 250, 400, and 1,000 W sizes. The life expectancy of HPS lamps can be as much as 24,000 hours.

Commercial Application While supplemental lighting is common in the northern latitudes above 40°N in North America and 50°N in Europe, it is also gaining popularity in more southern latitudes. Although little has been done academically to evaluate the economics of supplemental lighting, years of commercial success indicate that it is profitable, particularly with decreasing winter light. It costs about \$2.25/ft^2 (\$24/m^2) of greenhouse floor to purchase and install an HPS system. The price of a 400 W lamp plus fixture including ballast is \$150. The price of wire and installation is about \$50–\$75 per lamp. One lamp will provide a light intensity of 400 fc (4,300 lux) over a plant area of 100 ft^2 (9.3 m^2). A second cost to consider is the consumption of electricity. A 400 W fixture consumes 465 W of energy per hour.

Supplemental lighting is used for most crops but is particularly popular for chrysanthemum and geranium stock plants, Elatior begonias, roses, and plug seedlings. Light intensities of 300–600 fc (3,200–6,500 lux) at plant height are generally used, with 500 fc (5,400 lux) being a more common maximum. The average intensity being used today is about 400 fc (4,300 lux). The various manufacturers of lamps determine for growers the height and spacing of lamps according to the desired light intensity and configuration of greenhouse. The 400 W lamps are used almost exclusively because of the better uniformity in light intensity across plants that can be achieved with this size of lamp within the confines of the greenhouse. The 1,000 W lamps can be used only in the taller greenhouses.

Equally important to the lamp is the fixture that holds it and reflects the light to the plant area. Special horticultural fixtures are used. They are designed to spread the light in a square pattern as broadly and as uniformly as possible and with a minimum size of fixture to reduce shading. Specialty designs include a reflector for lamps hung over an aisle to minimize the light in the aisle and direct it toward the two adjacent beds instead. Likewise, reflectors are available for use along the sides and ends of greenhouses to direct light into the greenhouse that would otherwise strike the wall.

Crops receiving supplemental lighting are generally given a light period of 16–18 hours. This includes the time when lamps are on as well as part of the day when it is bright enough to turn lamps off. Generally, lamps are turned off when the natural light intensity exceeds a set point, often twice the intensity provided by the supplemental lamps. The yield benefit of extending the 18 hours of light to 24 hours is small for many crops. The postproduction life of some crops is reduced when they are grown under 24 hours of light. In the case of cut roses, many growers see a disadvantage to applying 24 hours of light because blooms develop during the night beyond the desired stage for cutting in the morning when the work crew arrives. Lighting roses for 18 hours speeds up flower development to the point where successive harvests can be made for the four dates of maximum profit: Christmas, Valentine's Day, Easter (if it falls on the right date), and Mother's Day. In addition, a 50 percent or better increase in yield can be obtained.

Plant response to supplemental light is greatest in the young-plant stage, beginning with the first true leaves, and diminishes with time. This is fortuitous because plants can be grown at a higher density when they are young, and thus it is possible to light a relatively small area of the greenhouse. A good example would be bedding plants, which are often lighted when they are in plug flats, where there can be as many as 648 seedlings, but which are not lighted as often in the finish-flats stage.

Tomato seedlings in flats or soil blocks are often lighted starting at the time of germination for a period of two to three weeks at an intensity of 465 fc (5,000 lux). In some cases, light is applied for 12 hours per day, enabling the lighting arrangement to be drawn on tracks to a second batch of seedlings each day. The switching of lights occurs at midnight and at noon. In this way, each batch of seedlings can be exposed to a 16-hour daylength since an additional 4 hours of daylight will be obtained when they are not under the lights. Daylengths of more than 16 hours are avoided since they retard growth and flowering. "Five-week-old" plants can be produced in less than half the time with this method.

Cucumber seedlings for greenhouse fruit production are started under supplemental light intensities of 280–465 fc (3,000–5,000 lux) from November to February. Lettuce seedlings produced for growing in the greenhouse can require from two weeks in the summer to eight weeks in the winter to produce under natural light in England. If they are lighted at 700 fc (7,500 lux), they can be produced in 11 days in the winter.

Some pot chrysanthemum growers set up two zones for producing this crop. In the first zone, plants are spaced tightly and are provided a warmer temperature, elevated CO_2, and supplemental lighting. The plant is most responsive to all of these environmental factors in the early stages. Thus, the higher costs of providing this environment can be confined to a short period when the crop occupies minimal space.

Growth Rooms

Growth rooms are used for producing seedlings (Figure 11–7). They may be constructed in the headhouse, in a barn, or in the greenhouse. Many materials can be used for construction including waterproof plywood. The chamber should be well insulated with a material such as polyurethane board and have a moisture-tight barrier on the inside.

Figure 11–7

A growth room for starting seedlings. Plants are grown on tiered shelves to conserve space. Light is supplied entirely by fluorescent lamps above each shelf. (*Photo courtesy of George J. Ball, Inc., W. Chicago, IL 60185*)

Shelves may be built inside in tiers, up to 2 feet (60 cm) apart, although they can be as close as 9 inches (23 cm). Space between shelves should be sufficient to permit a minimum space of 6 inches (15 cm) between the lamps and the top of the plants when low-energy, 40–75 W lamps are used. If 8 foot long high-energy, 215 W lamps are used, the shelves should be 2 feet apart. Attached to the bottom of the shelf above are the lamps. Fluorescent lamps are best for growth rooms because of the uniform light intensity they emit over a wide area and the low heat level they emit. High-intensity lamps would be difficult to use in such close proximity to the plants, although they are used in some chambers. Cool white fluorescent lamps are commonly used.

A light intensity of 500–1,400 fc (5,400–15,000 lux) is used, depending on the crop. Light intensities of 500, 750, and 1,400 fc can be provided by 8 foot long (244 cm), 125 W lamps installed 2 feet (60 cm) above the shelf at spacings of 8.9, 6.0, and 3.2 inches (22.6, 15.2, and 8.1 cm), respectively. A sheet of aluminum foil or a coat of aluminum paint should be provided above the tubes to maximize light intensity below, even when reflectorized tubes are used.

Light is generally applied for 16 hours per day; however, some crops, such as many of the bedding plants and lettuce, will respond to 24 hours of illumination. During the illumination period, the temperature is held between 70° and 80°F (21–27°C) depending on the type of seed being germinated.

The lamps will provide most of the heat needed. Only during exceptionally cold periods is it necessary to provide supplemental heat. A thermostatically controlled heater can be installed for this purpose. The greatest requirement regard-

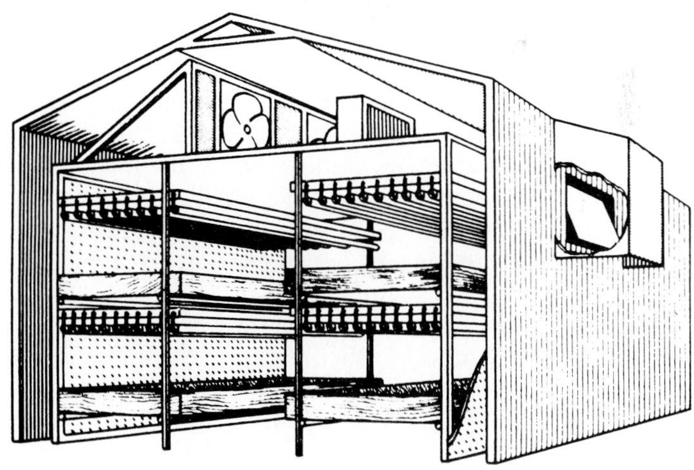

Figure 11–8

Arrangement of benches, fluorescent tubes, air circulation system, heater, and ventilator in a six-bench growing room. (*From The Electricity Council*, 1972)

ing temperature is that of maintaining a uniform temperature. Hot and cold spots will form if the air within the room is not circulated. The two walls running the length of the room should be constructed of perforated material such as pegboard. The pegboard should be set 6–8 inches (15–20 cm) in from the outer wall of the room to provide a chamber for air movement behind the pegboard (Figure 11–8). A false ceiling provides a chamber overhead that is connected to the wall chambers. A fan is placed overhead that will cause air to be drawn in one wall and expelled through the other, thus setting up an airflow pattern across the growth room. The heater can be installed in the space over the ceiling in front of the fan. Should the room become too hot, a thermostatically activated motorized ventilator is used in the air duct behind the wall or over the ceiling. For very fine details for a number of growth room designs, see The Electricity Council (1972) and Mastalerz (1985).

LIGHT DURATION FOR PHOTOPERIODISM

What is Photoperiodism?

We have just taken a look at one dimension of light, its intensity. Now we focus on a second dimension, its duration. Living organisms are innately aware of rhythmic forces in their environment. Fiddler crabs at Cape Cod, Massachusetts, like any other of their species in the world, will feed when the tide is low. It is then that food is trapped in small pools in which they can maneuver. When the tide comes in, it is time to sleep. If these crabs are placed in a tank of seawater in the darkness on Cape Cod, they will continue to feed when the tide goes out and sleep when it comes in on the beaches outside the tank. Upon being moved to Chicago, they eventually change their feeding time to the time when the tide would be low if there were an ocean in Chicago. Clearly, the crab is responding to the gravitational forces of the moon, which regulate the tides.

Plants and animals respond to many such rhythmic forces. The rate of metabolism of an earthworm has predictable peaks and valleys in accordance with the lunar month and the 24-hour solar day. Japanese industries have gone so far as to plot efficient and inefficient days in the lives of some of their key employees. What emerges from these data is a recognizable rhythm, such that one can be assured that on certain days an individual will perform at peak potential while on other days it might be better that he or she is not at work.

There is a mechanism in plants that tracks time. It is highly precise and can discern a five-minute difference within a 24-hour cycle. It is called *photoperiodism* because it is locked into the 24-hour solar day and is based upon the light–dark cycle. Photoperiodism is the response of a plant to the day–night cycle. Response can mean many things, including rosette growth of lettuce versus bolting, bulb formation in onion versus leaf and stem formation, tuber formation in dahlia, flowering of chrysanthemum, downward flagging of leaves of bean, a change in the shape of newly forming leaves, red pigmentation in bracts (leaves) of poinsettia, the formation of plantlets along the margins of bryophyllum leaves *Kalanchoe daigremontiana*, and so on.

Plants are customarily classified in regard to photoperiodism as long-day plants, short-day plants, and day-neutral plants. In this book, the long-day plant is called a short-night plant and the short-day plant is called a long-night plant because the mechanism that permits plants to track time actually measures the dark period. This change of terminology avoids the need for reciprocal thinking and corrects two long-standing misnomers.

Long-night plants are ones that undergo a response such as flowering only when the night length becomes longer than a critical length. Poinsettias require about 12 hours of darkness to flower. This length of night occurs in the latter part of September. Prior to September 15, since the nights are too short to afford a 12-hour dark period, plants grow vegetatively. In the latter part of September and on later dates, the nights are long enough to permit at least 12 hours of darkness; thus, the poinsettia buds change from vegetative buds that form leaves and stems to reproductive buds that form flower parts. Of course, several weeks must pass before these flower parts become large enough to be seen. Chrysanthemum, *Kalanchoe,* azalea, and Rieger and Lorraine begonias are all long-night plants in terms of the flowering response. Tuber formation in dahlia and tuberous begonia is a long-night response.

Short-night plants undergo a response when the nights are shorter than a critical length. Asters form a rosette type of growth when nights are longer than a critical length and develop tall stems and initiate flower buds under shorter nights. Short-night conditions prevent tuber formation in dahlia and tuberous begonia and thereby encourage flowering. *Calceolaria* and *cineraria* initiate flower buds at low temperatures. After this point, short nights hasten flowering. Short nights increase the height of Easter lily. Plantlets form along the margins of some bryophyllum leaves under short-night conditions.

Day-neutral plants, such as the rose, do not respond to the relative length of the light and dark periods. Other forces determine when a response will occur in these plants. Some require a certain level of maturity before they flower, while others must accumulate a specific quantity of solar energy. Some varieties of chrysanthemums as well as stock, *Calceolaria,* and *cineraria* initiate flower buds when a sufficient length of time at a cool temperature has passed. *Calceolaria* and *cineraria* require four to six weeks at 50°F (10°C) for flower initiation. In terms of the length of the night and these particular responses, these are all day-neutral plants.

Some plants will flower at any night length but do so faster at a particular night length. Carnations flower at any night length but flower fastest under short-

Table 11–1

Critical Night Length for the Chrysanthemum Cultivar Encore at Each of Three Night Temperatures

Night Temperature (°F)	*Critical Night Length (hr)*
50	10.25
60	9.5
80	8.75

night conditions. Rieger begonias will flower at any night length but flower fastest under long-night conditions. These are called *facultative short-night* and *facultative long-night* plants, respectively.

The critical night length is not any set figure. It is different for each plant species and can be different for cultivars within a species. Take as an example the single species of chrysanthemum classified as *Chrysanthemum morifolium* Ramat. The hardy garden varieties can have a critical night length of 8 hours, while many greenhouse-forcing varieties have a critical night length of 9.5 hours. Since a night length of 9 hours is below the critical length for the greenhouse varieties, they remain vegetative. Since 9 hours is more than the critical length for the garden varieties, they initiate flower buds and proceed to flower. *Kalanchoe* have a critical night length of about 11.5 hours; poinsettia, about 12 hours. Flowering occurs in each case at night lengths greater than these critical lengths.

The critical night length is also dependent upon temperature. The night temperature is more important than the day temperature. Table 11–1 shows the effect of night temperature on the critical night length of the chrysanthemum cultivar Encore. As the night temperature goes up, the critical night length gets shorter. Thus, it is clear that a garden chrysanthemum will initiate flower buds sooner during a hot summer than during a cold summer.

The Mechanism of Photoperiodism

The pigment in photoperiodic plants known as *phytochrome* serves as the light receptor. When the plant is in daylight or artificial light, phytochrome exists in a form known as Pfr, which is sensitive to light in the far-red region with a peak response at 735 nm. If the plant is exposed to far-red light, Pfr phytochrome will quickly change to Pr phytochrome, which is sensitive to red light with a peak response at 660 nm. This same response will occur when the plant is placed in darkness, but it occurs very slowly under this condition. The Pr form developed in darkness or under far-red light rapidly returns to the Pfr form when the plant is exposed to daylight again. Levels of Pfr might look like those proposed in Figure 11–9 during summer and winter daily cycles.

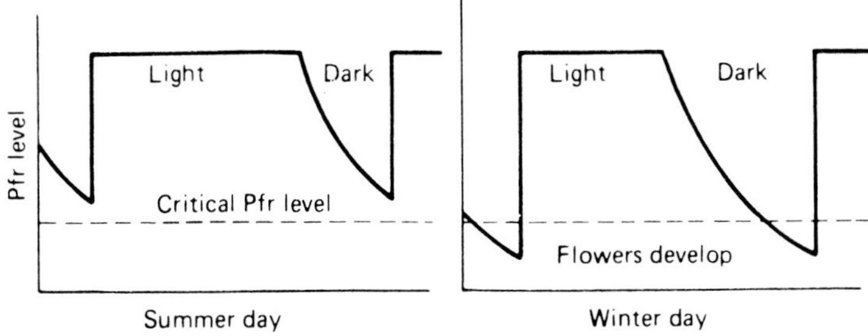

Figure 11–9

The effects of a summer and winter day–night cycle on the Pfr phytochrome level in a plant. Pfr quickly builds up in the light period and slowly diminishes in the dark period. A long-night plant will flower only when the Pfr level falls below the critical level, as shown, for the long winter night. (*Adopted from The Electricity Council*, 1973)

The important point is that the Pfr form is rapidly produced in the light, and the Pr form is slowly produced in the dark. The Pfr form is the active form that controls the photoperiodic response. It inhibits flowering in long-night plants and promotes flowering in short-night plants. During the summer when nights are short, the level of Pfr in a long-night plant such as chrysanthemum does not get low enough to permit flowering. During a long winter night, the level of Pfr does become low enough to permit flowering.

Methods of Photoperiodic Control

Daylength control for the greenhouse chrysanthemum is typical of the long-night crops as a whole. Chrysanthemums are grown for an initial period under short-night conditions to develop a plant of suitable size that will support large blooms and tall stems. Then, the plants are grown under long-night conditions to induce flower-bud initiation and subsequent development.

Short-Night Treatment Depending on the season of the year and the variety of chrysanthemum, the short-night treatment can last from two to eight weeks. If this stage occurs during the summer, there is no need to do anything but grow the plants under the natural short nights. However, if the crop is planted during the winter when nights are long, it will then be necessary to shorten the dark period by turning lights on during the night. Lights may be turned on in the late afternoon to extend the day into the evening, or they may be turned on during the middle of the night to break the dark period. Fewer hours of lighting are required if the dark period is interrupted in the middle of the night, and this procedure is commonly used. The light break in the middle of the night restores the Pfr

Table 11–2

Duration of Light To Apply during Night for Different Months to Ensure Short-Night Conditions at a Latitude of 40°N

Month	*Hours of Light*
June–July	0
May–August	2
March–April and September–October	3
November–February	4

phytochrome level, and, since neither of the two dark periods before or after the light break is very long, the Pfr level does not diminish sufficiently to permit flowering.

Since the dark period becomes longer as December 21 approaches, the number of hours of supplemental light required increases. The number of hours of light to apply for any given month at 40°N latitude is presented in Table 11–2. A word of caution is needed here: The night length and, consequently, the amount of light to apply depend upon the latitude at which one is located on the earth. The shortest night of the year for the Northern Hemisphere occurs on June 21. On this day, the dark period is 12 hours long near the equator, while no darkness occurs at the North Pole. Thus, the farther north one is located, the shorter the night is. The longest night of the year occurs on December 21. There are 24 hours of darkness at the North Pole on this day and 12 hours of darkness near the equator. In this case, the farther north one goes, the longer the night is. Northern latitudes have shorter summer nights and longer winter nights than points farther south. The light period near the equator is always 12 hours long. All places in the world reach a midway point on March 21 and September 21 when the light period is 12 hours everywhere. These relationships can be seen in Figure 11–10.

From this discussion, it should be apparent that the period of the year in which light must be applied and the duration needed on any given night will depend upon the latitude where one is located. Some companies providing chrysanthemum cuttings make available excellent catalogs presenting cultural techniques as well as lighting and shading schedules for this crop. The schedules are given according to the zone in which one lives.

Incandescent lamps work best for extending the day or reducing the night length because a large percentage of the light emitted is in the red zone, which is required by Pr phytochrome. The required light intensity is very low, and most plants respond to 1–2 fc (11–22 lux). A minimum intensity of 10 fc (108 lux) should be provided, however, to avoid any failure. The most important parts of the plant to illuminate are the recently mature leaves.

To provide the required intensity of light for a 4 foot (1.2 m) wide bed, one string of 60 W bulbs 4 feet (1.2 m) apart should be installed not more than 5 feet

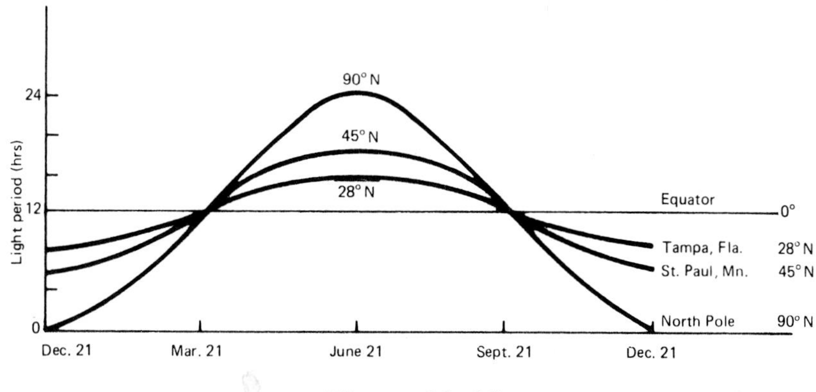

Figure 11–10

The length of the light period throughout the year at different latitudes of the Northern Hemisphere.

(1.5 m) above the soil along the middle of the bed. Two beds can be lighted by installing a row of 100 W bulbs 6 feet (1.8 m) apart and not more than 6 feet (1.8 m) above the soil between the beds. Larger incandescent floodlight bulbs can be installed along the center ridge of the greenhouse to light the entire width. A minimum of 1½ W is required for each square foot of ground lighted (16 W/m^2). Occasionally, the larger lights are installed in clusters to reduce the cost of wiring.

The cost of lighting a crop can be reduced by *flash-lighting* or *cyclic lighting*. As little as 1 second of light at 10 fc (108 lux) intensity every 5 seconds will keep phytochrome in the Pfr form and cause some chrysanthemum cultivars to remain vegetative. This frequency requires heavy-duty switches; thus, longer light periods are generally used.

If the standard program calls for four hours of light in the middle of the night, from perhaps 10 P.M. to 2 A.M., one can divide this duration into 30-minute periods and apply light for 20 percent of each period. In this way, one would apply for 6 minutes out of each 30 minutes between 10 P.M. and 2 A.M. Shorter periods will work as well as long as light is applied 20 percent of the time. It is essential that a minimum light intensity of 10 fc (108 lux) be applied in this system.

A greenhouse range using cyclic lighting could be divided into five zones and all could receive their light requirement during one four-hour period. This would reduce the consumption of electricity by 70–75 percent and would permit the use of lighter main wiring, which would reduce the initial wiring cost. Time clocks are available that can control such a system.

Long-Night Treatment After a period of short nights has been provided to establish the plant, a period of long nights must be provided to bring about flower-bud initiation and development. During the winter, since the nights are naturally long enough, nothing is done. When this stage of growth occurs in the summer, however, it is necessary to pull an opaque screen over the plants in late afternoon and off again in the morning. The screen should be applied from 7 P.M. to 7 A.M. Some growers apply it at 5 P.M. before their work force leaves, which can have harmful effects during the summer if heat builds up underneath. Flowering will be delayed, and, at higher temperatures, flower buds will abort. If the screen must be pulled at 5 P.M., the sides should be left up for air circulation and someone should return at 7 P.M. to lower them. It is necessary to continue pulling the screen until color shows in the buds. Beyond that time, it need not be applied. The screen should be applied every day of the week. For each day that is skipped every week, the crop will flower a day or so later.

A good grade of sateen (cotton) cloth works well. More recently, polyester cloth has been used for light screening. It carries the advantage of resisting rot. Cloth should be dense enough to reduce the light intensity beneath to 2 fc (22 lux) when the intensity outside is 5,000 fc (54,000 lux). Cloth should be sufficiently porous to permit water to penetrate if it is used in a leaky greenhouse or in the field. Black polyethylene also may be used as long as water is not a problem. Tears in the cover should be immediately repaired to prevent light leaks. Wherever light leaks in, plants will develop with incomplete or hollow flower buds called *crown buds*. Commercial opaque screens are made of a number of materials. Some have an aluminized outer side to reflect heat and keep plants cooler under it. In

Figure 11–11

Manual pulling of black cloth in the early evening during the summer to establish long-night conditions for photoperiodic control of flowering. The light bulbs are used during the middle of winter nights to give a short-night effect. (*Photo courtesy of* J. W. Love, *Department of* Horticultural *Science, North Carolina State University, Raleigh,* NC 27695–7609)

the summer, heat can build up under the screen since it has to be pulled before sunset and removed after sunrise. Such heat buildup can lead to delayed flowering and even bud abortion.

The expenditure in labor to manually pull black cloth over frames as pictured in Figure 11–11 is considerable. Larger growers use power-operated shading (Figure 11–12). Some make this apparatus themselves. An electric motor turns a pipe shaft along one side of the greenhouse. Cables attached to the shaft run across the greenhouse to a shaft on the other side and back again. Cloth is attached to the cables, enabling it to be drawn across the greenhouse and back again.

A number of commercial systems are available for automatically pulling photoperiodic shade fabric as well as thermal blankets (see the "Heat Conservation" section in Chapter 3) and sunscreens (see "Reducing Light Intensity" earlier in this chapter). The same fabric used for heat retention during winter nights may be used for photoperiodic shading in the summer. Fabric with an aluminized or reflective outer surface is desirable.

The cost might seem high, but the advantages that go with it easily sell these systems. One person at the flip of a switch can cover an acre (0.4 ha) of greenhouse in a few minutes, alleviating perhaps as much as two to three hours of

Figure 11–12

A commercially available, power-operated system for shading plants to create long-night conditions for photoperiodic control of flowering. (*Photo courtesy of* Simtrac, Inc., 8243 N. *Christiana Avenue, Skokie*, IL 60076)

manual labor. The system can be further controlled by an automatic time clock, which eliminates the need for any person. This savings occurs twice a day. Because a single sheet of fabric is suspended overhead, it is possible to operate the fan-and-pad cooling system, pulling the cool air beneath the cover. This prevents excess buildup of heat, which can occur even at 7 P.M. in the summer, and, in turn, prevents reduction in plant quality and delays in flowering.

TEMPERATURE

We have already taken a long look at heat in terms of providing it in the greenhouse, removing it from the greenhouse, and controlling it at the desired level. Now we look briefly at its influence on crops. Temperature is a measure of the level of heat present. All crops have a temperature range in which they can grow. Below this range, processes necessary for life stop, ice forms within the tissue, tying up water necessary for life processes, and cells are possibly punctured by ice crystals. At the upper extreme, enzymes become inactive, and again processes essential to life stop.

All biochemical reactions in the plant are controlled by enzymes. Enzymes are heat sensitive. The rate of reactions controlled by them will often double or triple each time the temperature is increased by 18°F (10°C) until an optimum temperature is reached. Further increases in temperature begin to suppress the reaction until it stops.

Numerous biochemical reactions are involved in the process of photosynthesis. These all have the net effect of building carbohydrate and storing energy. Photosynthesis occurs during the daylight hours because of its dependence on light. Another extensive set of biochemical reactions is involved in the overall process of respiration. The net effect here is a breakdown of carbohydrate and a release of energy. Respiration occurs in all living cells at all times.

When photosynthesis exceeds respiration, net growth occurs. When they equal each other, net growth stops. If respiration exceeds photosynthesis, the plant declines in vigor and will eventually die. To ensure that photosynthesis exceeds respiration, plants are grown cool to night to keep the respiration rate down and warm by day to enhance photosynthesis.

As a general rule, greenhouse crops are grown at a day temperature 5–10°F (3–6°C) higher than the night temperature on cloudy days and 15°F (8°C) higher on clear days. With CO_2 enrichment, the day temperatures may be an additional 5°F (3°C) higher. The night temperature of greenhouse crops is generally in the range of 45–70°F (4–21°C). Primula, stock, and *Calceolaria* grow best at 45°F (7°C); carnation and *cineraria*, at 50°F (10°C); rose, at 60°F (16°C); chrysanthemum and poinsettia, at 62–64°F (17–18°C); and African violet at 70–72°F (21–22°C).

Temperature Interrelationships

A rule by F. F. Blackman, in essence, states that the rate of any process that is governed by two or more factors will be limited by the factor in least supply. Photosynthesis is a good case in point. It is dependent upon heat, light, CO_2, and other factors. On cloudy days, it is futile to raise the temperature more than 5–10°F (3–6°C) above the night temperature because the low light intensity will limit the rate of photosynthesis and any additional heat applied will be without beneficial effect. On bright days, light does not limit photosynthesis; thus, if the temperature is not raised, heat may become the limiting factor for photosynthesis. Even on dark days, the rate of photosynthesis will increase with CO_2 enrichment of the greenhouse atmosphere.

Light intensity is higher in the summer than in the winter, and photosynthetic rates can be expected to be higher in the summer. This is very fortunate since it calls for higher daytime temperatures in the summer than in the winter to prevent heat from becoming the limiting factor. Cooling fans can be set at a

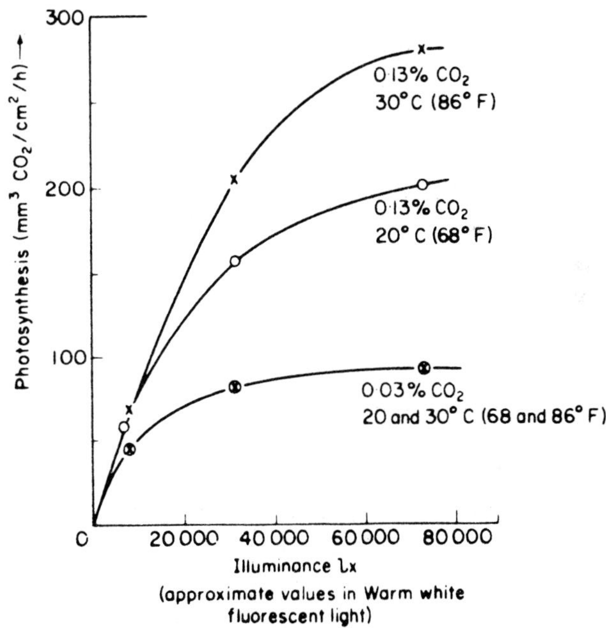

Figure 11–13

Effects of CO_2 concentration, light intensity, and leaf temperature on photosynthesis in cucumber. (*From Gaastra,* 1962)

higher temperature in the summer—as high as 80–85°F (27–29°C)—which saves considerable electrical energy.

Blackman's Law is well illustrated in the curves of Figure 11–13, which were developed by Gaastra (1962). In the lowest curve, the rate of photosynthesis began to plateau at about 3,800 fc (40,000 lux) of light intensity regardless of whether the temperature was at 68°F or 86°F. The 300 ppm level of CO_2 became a limiting factor at that point. When the temperature was held at 68°F and the CO_2 level was increased to 1,300 ppm, the rate of photosynthesis increased. Then the 68°F temperature became the limiting factor because increase in temperature to 86°F at the same 1,300 ppm CO_2 level brought about another increase in photosynthesis.

This interaction of CO_2, light intensity, and temperature is reminiscent of observations in Chapter 10. It was stated there that increases in the CO_2 level in the greenhouse brought about beneficial effects from raising the daytime temperature above that normally maintained for many crops. When CO_2 is eliminated as a limiting factor for photosynthesis, a daytime temperature increase of 5°F (3°C) can often be profitable.

One must be careful when determining how high to raise the temperature because it affects processes in addition to photosynthesis. Generally, higher temperature results in faster growth but with it a reduction in quality can occur. Longer stems, thinner stems, and smaller flowers may occur. Quality and quantity must always be weighed in making such a decision. In the former discussion about raising the temperature 5°F (3°C) along with an increase in the CO_2 level, no adverse loss in quality is to be expected.

DIF—Day to Night Temperature Relationship

Effects of temperature during the day versus the night on growth and flowering of floral crops have been reported for some time (Cathey 1954; Parups 1978; Cockshull et al. 1981; Parups and Butler 1982). Recently, scientists at Michigan State University, including Drs. Heins, Karlsson, Erwin, and Berghage, uncovered a practical relationship between plant height and the day to night temperature differential. They gave the abbreviation *DIF* to this temperature differential. DIF refers to the differential obtained when one subtracts the night temperature from the day temperature:

$$\text{DIF} = \text{day temperature} - \text{night temperature}$$

The DIF values are +10, 0, and −10 for day and night temperature combinations of 70°F and 60°F, 65°F and 65°F, and 60°F and 70°F, respectively. The information that follows is drawn from the work of this Michigan State University team.

Height Control by DIF Plant height can be controlled by DIF. A shift from a positive DIF toward a zero DIF results in a large reduction in height (Figure 11–14). While height continues to decline as the DIF value is shifted from zero to negative values, it is of smaller magnitude. Two underlying relationships are involved. Plant height can be decreased by decreasing the day temperature and also by increasing the night temperature. Conversely, plant height is increased by increases in day temperature as well as by decreases in night temperature. The effect is upon the length of stem internodes rather than the number of leaves. Controlling plant height by altering DIF is being used commercially on a wide range of crops. Large responses have been achieved in Asiatic lilies, celosia, chrysanthemum, dianthus, Easter lily, fuchsia, geranium, gerbera, hypoestes, impatiens, Oriental lilies, petunia, poinsettia, portulaca, rose, salvia, snap bean, snapdragon, sweet corn, tomato, and watermelon. Small or no response has been obtained in aster, French marigold, hyacinth, narcissus, platycodon, squash, and tulip. DIF provides an effective means for controlling height because a shift in growth can be seen within one to two days of a shift in DIF.

Controlling plant height through environmental modification rather than by chemical height retardants is particularly attractive in this day when all synthetic chemicals are under scrutiny. A second plus is the cost savings realized by reducing and, in many cases, dropping the use of chemical height retardants.

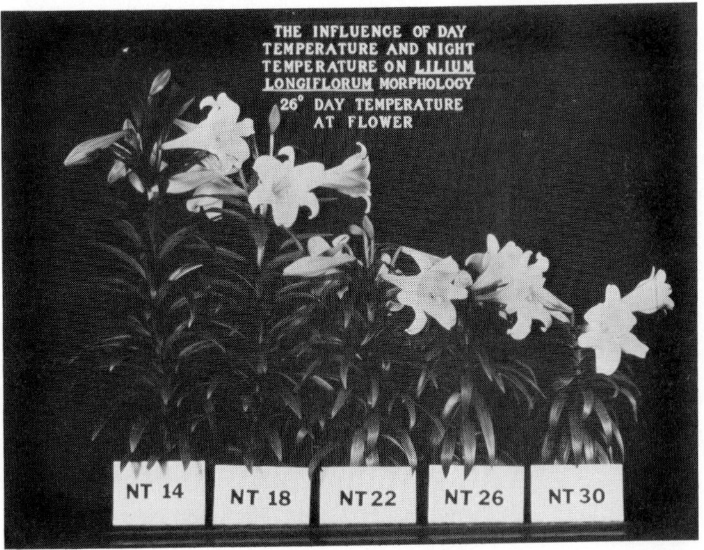

Figure 11–14

The effect of decreasing DIF values from left to right on decreasing final Easter lily height. For all five plants, the day temperature was 26°C, but the night temperatures were 14, 18, 22, 26, or 30°C (57, 64, 72, 79, or 86°F). From left to right, the DIF values were 29, 22, 16, 7, and 0°F. (*From Heins and Erwin,* 1990)

Flowering Time The rate of growth and maturation of plants is generally temperature dependent. Fortunately, it is the 24-hour temperature average and not just the day or the night temperature alone that usually controls the rate of development. Because of this, tall, intermediate, or short plants may be produced for the same flowering date by reducing the DIF values in a way that the daily average temperature remains constant. The +10, 0, and −10 DIF values referred to earlier all have the same average daily temperature of 65°F if the day and night lengths are taken to be the same length. The day–night temperature combinations were 70°F/60°F, 65°F/65°F, and 60°F/70°F. Each combination has an average of 65°F; thus, these three DIF values offer a choice of three heights of plants for the same market date.

Two factors limit the range of temperatures that can be selected for developing a value of DIF. Each crop plant has a unique temperature to growth relationship, as shown in Figure 11–15. Temperatures may be selected within the linear range of the curve (the straight dashed line) and up to the optimum temperature (50–80°F in this curve). Higher and lower temperatures should not be selected because unacceptably low growth rates occur at these temperatures. Both timing and quality of the crop could be jeopardized. The temperature range for "warm" crops, including hibiscus and poinsettia, is 50–80°F (10–27°C). The range for crops tolerant of cool temperatures, such as Easter lily, chrysanthemum, and petunia, is 40–80°F (4–27°C).

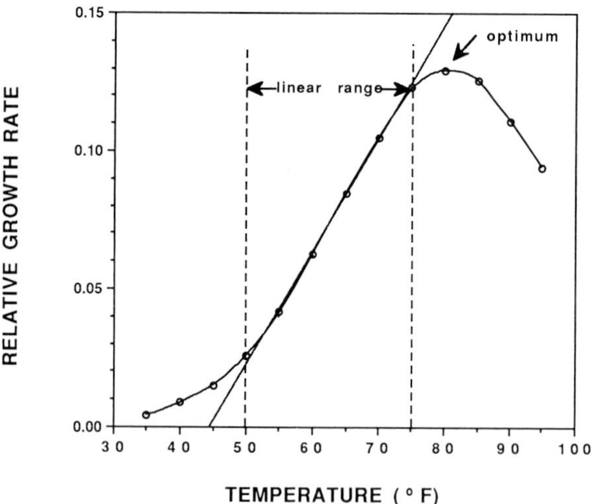

Figure 11–15

Hypothetical effect of temperature on relative growth rate. A straight line has been superimposed on the curve to show the range of linear response which lies between 50–75°F. Most processes in the plant have a similar relationship with temperature.

The second limit to the range of temperatures available for selection is the temperature requirement for flower initiation and development. At a night temperature of 73°F (23°C), poinsettia flower development is inhibited. While day temperatures may be higher, night temperatures may not exceed this level. Night temperatures above 72–75°F (22–24°C) can cause heat delay in flowering of chrysanthemums. It may be necessary to raise night temperatures to 75°F (24°C) to slow height development in Easter lily, but one pays a price in increased flower abortion at temperatures above 70°F (21°C). Such temperature sensitivities are greatest at the time of flower initiation and the early stages of flower-bud development. Once flower buds are visible, the plant is much less sensitive to heat delay. Higher night temperatures can be attempted at these times to achieve large negative DIF values when plants are excessively tall.

Side Effects The lower the DIF value, particularly in the negative range, the greater the chance of chlorosis of leaves. Chlorosis occurs on young immature leaves. If the low DIF treatment is applied correctly, normal green color will return as these affected leaves mature. Chlorosis becomes a permanent problem when the plant is treated at too early an age. Plug seedlings treated during the first week have only immature leaves; thus, the whole plant turns completely chlorotic. Growth of the plant is severely reduced. Such stunting is not later corrected. Depending on species, a DIF value lower than −2 to −3 should not be applied to plug seedlings during the first one to three weeks.

A second side effect of very low DIF treatments is downward curling of leaves. This problem is particularly pronounced on Easter lilies. If the curled leaves are not mature, they will uncurl when returned to a normal positive DIF value.

Implementation of DIF in Warm Seasons There is little difficulty in lowering the day temperature in northern locations during the winter. Later in the spring and even in the winter in warm climates, it may appear impossible to do so. Low DIF effects can still be produced by lowering the day temperature for the first two hours of the day immediately after sunrise. This is based on the fact that the greatest rate of internode elongation occurs during the night with a maximum peak at sunrise. Greater height suppression of Easter lily was achieved by applying a negative DIF only during the two hours after sunrise than by applying negative DIF for seven hours beginning two hours after sunrise and ending at sunset.

It is important that the temperature be at the lower setting as soon as the shift from dark to light occurs. For a hot water heating system, this means that the thermostat should be set lower perhaps 45 minutes before sunrise to allow sufficient time for the system to cool. The thermostat could be set lower 15 minutes before sunrise for faster reacting heating systems such as unit heaters.

Graphical Tracking The day-to-day implementation of DIF to control height is best handled through *graphical tracking* (Heins and Erwin 1989; Carlson and

Heins 1990). A good example of such a graph for Easter lily can be seen in Figure 11–16. In this case, lilies were grown in a 6 inch standard pot having a height of 6 inches. The final plant plus pot height desired was in the range of 22–24 inches. Based on previous experience, the plant was expected to double in height after the point of visible bud. Thus, for the date of emergence the height was plotted as 6 inches (the height of the pot), and at market stage it was plotted as 22–24 inches. Typically, the Easter lily is at half final height at the first point of visible flower bud. For the date of visible flower bud, minimum and maximum heights were plotted as 14 inches and 15 inches (half the final plant height plus the 6 inch pot height). Growth between each of these pairs of dates proceeds in a straight line; thus, points were connected by straight lines to form the minimum and the maximum height curves. Twice a week the grower measured the height of the plants and plotted the results on the graph. On January 27, plants were too tall and a −10°F DIF treatment was applied (53°F day–63°F night). By February 10, plant height gain had been suppressed to where it was at the minimum acceptable level. DIF was increased to +8°F and resulted in an increase in the rate of

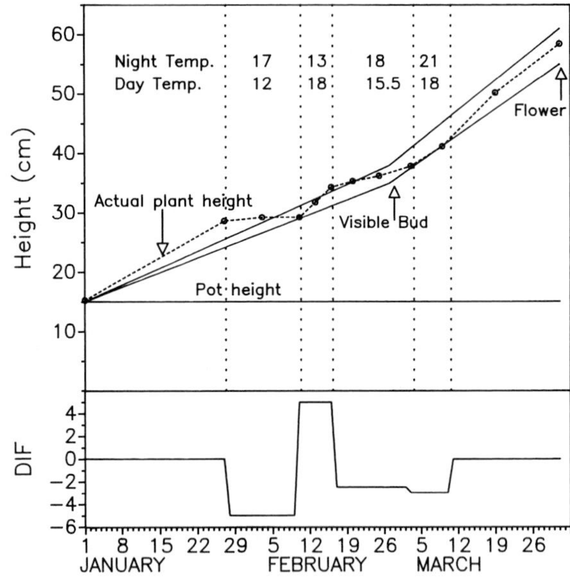

Figure 11–16

Graphical tracking plot for Easter lily. Solid curves depict the range of desired heights for various dates (the tracking window). The dashed line shows the actual measured heights of a commercial crop in which DIF was used to control height. Day and night temperatures applied to the commercial crop are shown in °C. Temperature conversions for 12, 13, 15.5, 17, 18, and 21°C are 54, 55, 60, 63, 64, and 70°F, respectively. The actual DIF values applied are given in °C in the curve at the bottom of the figure. (*From Heins and Erwin,* 1989)

height rise. On three subsequent dates, further adjustments in DIF were made. In the end, the crop reached a desired height without the use of chemical growth regulators.

Unlike Easter lily, growth of chrysanthemum and poinsettia proceeds in a sigmoidal curve fashion, as shown by Figure 11–17 (Carlson and Heins 1990). In this curve, the percent of final plant height (not including the pot height) is plotted on the vertical axis against the relative time to flower on the horizontal axis. Relative time to flower is used since different cultivars of mums and poinsettias can require a different number of weeks to flower. If the crop requires 10 weeks to flower, its relative time to flower after 5 weeks of growth will be 0.5 (50 percent). The relative time to flower begins at the date of pinch. To develop a theoretical tracking curve for chrysanthemum or poinsettia, the final plant height desired is selected. Based on the percentages in Figure 11–17, the height the crop should be at each week is determined, and these heights are plotted on the vertical axis of a graph against weeks of growth on the horizontal axis. Then, the actual height of the crop is measured twice a week and plotted on the same graph as the theoretically computed height curve. When actual crop height differs from the theoretical height, the DIF value is altered to bring the crop back into line.

Computer Control Each year the need for an environmental computer to monitor and control the greenhouse environment becomes more critical to making a profit. Implementation of height control through DIF is a good example. DIF plans can be handled through thermostats and manual settings. However, increases in the number of crop zones requiring different DIF values and complications brought on by warm weather restriction of low day temperatures to the first two hours of the day can make the computer the most efficient way to go. In the future, growth curves will probably be available in computer software for all crops. Such programs will take over temperature control of the greenhouse. The crop

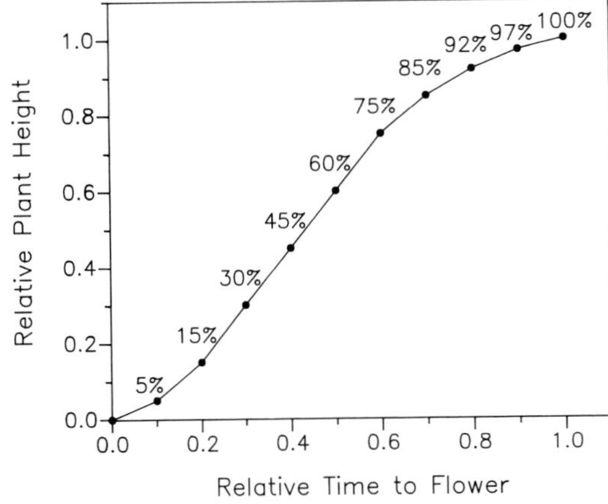

Figure 11–17

Growth curve for chrysanthemum and poinsettia beginning at the date of pinch and ending at market date. (*From Carlson and Heins*, 1990)

manager will simply enter into the program the dates of planting, pinching, and harvesting; the final desired height; and biweekly height measurements. The computer will do the rest, and with less labor input as well as greater conservation of heating and cooling energy.

SUMMARY

1. Light plays two general roles in the growth and development of plants. Light is a source of energy for the process of photosynthesis in which carbon is fixed into carbohydrates and ultimately all organic compounds of the plant. A relatively high intensity of light in the energy spectrum of 400–700 nm is required. Light also regulates the developmental forms of plants—for example, vegetative versus reproductive growth. It is the duration of light and not so much its intensity that is important in this process.
2. Light is often a limiting factor to photosynthesis and growth during the winter at northern latitudes. In order to maximize interior light intensity, single greenhouses can be oriented with the ridge east to west and ridge-and-furrow greenhouses with the ridge north to south. The glass or FRP covering can be washed. Plants should be spaced farther apart in the winter to increase the amount of light per plant.
3. Supplemental lighting during the daylight hours to enhance photosynthesis is highly effective. The economics, however, bear scrutiny. There are situations of high-density plantings such as rooting and seedling beds and the production of young plants where it is most profitable. High-pressure sodium lamps are most commonly used today. Continued research is needed to reduce the electrical costs through lamps of increased efficiency and to minimize the size of the fixture for reasons of shading.
4. A number of seedling producers construct growth rooms. Plants are grown on tiered shelves with a bank of fluorescent lights above each shelf. This is the sole source of light for photosynthesis. A growth room can be better insulated than a greenhouse. Often, the heat from the lamps is sufficient to meet the heat requirement of the room.
5. Light plays its second role in photoperiodism, which is the response of an organism to the day–night cycle. The relative length of the light and dark periods governs a number of responses including flowering, leaf shape, stem elongation, bulb formation, and pigmentation. In terms of flowering, long-night plants are those that initiate and develop flower buds when the night is longer than a critical length. Conversely, short-night plants are those that initiate and develop flower buds when the night is shorter than a critical length. The critical night length varies among plant species and even among cultivars

within a species. Not all plants are photoperiodic. Those that do not respond to the day–night cycle are day-neutral plants.

6. Long nights are established in the greenhouse during the summer by covering the plants with a plastic or cloth fabric in the early evening (about 7 P.M.) and removing it in the morning (7–8 A.M.). The cover should be capable of reducing the light intensity beneath to 2 fc (22 lux) when the outside intensity is 5,000 fc (54,000 lux). Automatic equipment is available for this operation. Short-night conditions can be established in the winter by providing 10 fc (108 lux) of illumination for a period of one to four hours during the middle of the night. Incandescent lights serve this purpose best.
7. Phytochrome is the receptor pigment in young tissue that responds to the light–dark cycle. The Pfr form of phytochrome rapidly builds up during the light period and is slowly converted to the Pr form during the dark period. The Pfr form is the active form that inhibits flowering in long-night plants and promotes flowering in short-night plants. A long night is required to lower the level of Pfr phytochrome to the point where flowering can occur in a long-night plant.
8. Heat is a form of energy and a factor essential to growth. Deleterious effects occur from levels too high or too low. Heat is just one factor governing growth. The rate of growth is limited by the factor in shortest supply. It is not always economically feasible to optimize all factors affecting growth in a greenhouse; thus, the best temperature for a crop will depend upon the following factors:
    a. Light is often limiting in the winter. On low light intensity days (cloudy), a day temperature 5–10°F (3–6°C) above the night temperature is maintained; on brighter winter days, a 15°F (8°C) higher day temperature is beneficial to growth. Although even higher temperatures would not be beneficial to growth in the winter, they are beneficial in the summer when light intensity is higher and not limiting to growth.
    b. The CO_2 level inside greenhouses often limits growth. When it is raised, growth increases to a point where previously adequate temperatures become the limiting factor. A 5°F (3°C) rise in day temperature is often beneficial when the greenhouse atmosphere is enriched with CO_2.
9. Plant height can be controlled by adjusting the day to night temperature ratio. DIF is a term that refers to the temperature difference obtained by subtracting the night from the day temperature. The rate of stem internode elongation is increased by increases in day temperatures and by decreases in night temperatures. Therefore, when DIF is highly positive (day temperatures are much higher than night temperatures), plants become tall. Large reductions in plant height are achieved by reducing DIF from positive to zero values; further, but more modest, growth reductions are obtained by continuing to reduce DIF to negative values. The concept of DIF works best when plants are young and their rate of growth is rapid.

REFERENCES

1. Anon. 1960. *Fundamentals of Light and Lighting.* General Electric Co., Large Lamps Dept., Nela Park, Cleveland, OH 44112.
2. ______. 1964. *Plant Growth and Lighting.* General Electric Co., Large Lamps Dept., Nela Park, Cleveland, OH 44112.
3. ______. 1980. *Horticultural Lighting.* Engineering Bul. 0–351. GTE Products Corp., Sylvania Lighting Center, Danvers, MA.
4. ______. 1982. *Artificial Lighting in Horticulture.* Phillips Gloeilampenfabrieken, Lighting Design and Engineering Center, Lighting Division, Eindhoven, The Netherlands.
5. Bickford, E. D., and S. Dunn. 1972. *Lighting for Plant Growth.* Kent, OH: The Kent State Univ. Press.
6. Campbell, L. E., R. W. Thimijan, and H. M. Cathey. 1975. Spectral radiant power of lamps used in horticulture. *Trans. Amer. Soc. Agr. Engineers* 18 (5):952–956.
7. ______. 1977. Lighting systems for growing plants—A new look. Amer. Soc. Agr. Engineers. Paper No. NA77–304. P.O. Box 410, St. Joseph, MO 49085.
8. Carlson, W. H., and R. Heins. 1990. Get the plant height you want with graphical tracking. *Grower Talks* 53 (9):62–63, 65, 67–68.
9. Cathey, H. M. 1954. Chrysanthemum temperature study. C. The effect of night, day, and mean temperature upon the flowering of *Chrysanthemum morifolium. Proc. Amer. Soc. Hort. Sci.* 64:499–502.
10. Cathey, H. M., and L. E. Campbell. 1975. Plant productivity: New approaches to efficient light sources and environmental control. Amer. Soc. Agr. Engineers. Paper No. 75–7501. P.O. Box 410, St. Joseph, MO 49085.
11. ______. 1979. Relative efficiency of high- and low-pressure sodium and incandescent filament lamps used to supplement natural winter light in greenhouses. *J. Amer. Soc. Hort. Sci.* 104:812–825.
12. Cockshull, K. E., D. W. Hand, and F. A. Langton. 1981. The effects of day and night temperature on flower initiation and development in chrysanthemum. *Acta Hort.* 25:101–110.
13. Downs, R. J. 1975. *Controlled Environments for Plant Research.* New York: Columbia University Press.
14. Gaastra, P. 1962. Photosynthesis of leaves and field crops. *Netherlands J. Agr. Sci.* 10 (5):311–324.
15. Garner, W. W., and H. A. Allard. 1920. Effect of the relative length of day and night and other factors of the environment on growth and reproduction in plants. *J. Agr. Res.* 18:553–607.
16. Heins, R. D. 1990. Choosing the best temperature for growth and flowering. *Greenhouse Grower* 8 (4):57–64.
17. Heins, R., and J. Erwin. 1989. Tracking Easter lily height with graphs: Easter lily response to temperature during forcing. Part 2. *Grower Talks* 53:64, 66, 68.

18. ______. 1990. Understanding and applying DIF. *Greenhouse Grower* 8 (2):73–78.

19. Illuminating Engineering Society. 1972. *IES Lighting Handbook,* 5th ed. Illuminating Engineering Soc., 345 E. 47th St., New York.

20. Mastalerz, J. W. 1969. Environmental factors: Light, temperature, carbon dioxide. In Mastalerz, J. W., and R. W. Langhans, eds. *Roses,* pp. 95–108. Pennsylvania Flower Growers' Assoc., New York State Flower Growers' Assoc., Inc., and Roses, Inc. (Available from R. W. Langhans, Dept. of Flor. and Orn. Hort., Cornell Univ., Ithaca, NY 14853.)

21. ______. 1985. Growth rooms. In Mastalerz, J. W., and E. J. Holcomb, eds. *Bedding Plants.* III, pp. 141–150. Pennsylvania Flower Growers' Assoc. (Available from E. J. Holcomb, Dept. of Hort., The Pennsylvania State Univ., University Park, PA.)

22. Parups, E. V. 1978. Chrysanthemum growth at cool night temperatures. *J. Amer. Soc. Hort. Sci.* 103:839–842.

23. Parups, E. V., and G. Butler. 1982. Comparative growth of chrysanthemum at different night temperatures. *J. Amer. Soc. Hort. Sci.* 107:600–604.

24. Stolze, J. A. B., J. Meulenbelt, and J. Poot, eds. 1984. *Application of Grow Light in Greenhouses.* Poot Lichtenergie B. V., Box 2444 Station B, St. Catherines, Ontario L2M7M8, Canada.

25. Templing, B. C., and M. A. Verbruggen, eds. 1977. *Lighting Technology in Horticulture,* 2d ed. Phillips Gloeilampenfabrieken, Lighting Design and Engineering Center, Lighting Division, Eindhoven, The Netherlands.

26. The Electricity Council. 1972. *Growelectric Handbook No. 1: Growing Rooms.* The Electricity Council, 30 Millbank, London SW1P4RD.

27. ______. 1973. *Growelectric Handbook No. 2: Lighting in Greenhouses.* The Electricity Council, 30 Millbank, London SW1P4RD.

28. Van der Veen, R., and G. Meijer. 1959. *Light and Plant Growth.* New York: The Macmillan Co.

CHAPTER 12

Chemical Growth Regulation

Floriculture is unlike other areas of agriculture in that an entire plant, or at least a major portion of the plant, is appraised according to its aesthetic value. While minor insect damage, leaf blemishes, or unusually tall height may not affect the yield or value of a bean crop, it does reduce the value of a potted plant. Several chemicals are used by greenhouse growers to control growth in one or another of its many forms to give the desired aesthetic effect. For example, final plant height can be made shorter than the natural height, terminal buds can be pinched (destroyed), the cold requirement of crops such as azalea can be chemically substituted, and rooting can be promoted. Hopefully, lateral shoots will soon be chemically disbudded (removed).

CLASSIFICATION

Chemicals used to control growth are either naturally occurring plant hormones or synthetically produced compounds. *Hormones* are compounds produced in the plant at one site and then transported to a different part of the plant where they affect growth. There are five categories of plant hormones: (1) auxins, (2) gibberellins, (3) cytokinins, (4) ethylene, and (5) inhibitors.

Auxins promote growth primarily through cell enlargement. The major auxin produced in plants is indole-3-acetic acid (IAA). Synthetic auxins include indole-3-butyric acid (IBA), indolepropionic acid (IPA), and naphthalene acetic acid (NAA). Auxins play an important commercial role in plant propagation.

Gibberellic acid (GA) likewise promotes growth through cell enlargement. Various gibberellins have been isolated from species of the fungus *Gibberellic.* This fungus attacks rice plants and causes them to grow tall and threadlike. Gibberellins promote growth, but unlike that produced by auxins, the growth is uniform throughout the plant tissue. The commercial roles of gibberellins are varied.

Cytokinins are associated with rapidly growing tissue. They might be thought of as the juvenility or antisenescence hormone. Cytokinins enhance growth mainly through cell division. These hormones are used in tissue culture preparations to stimulate callus cell growth. Otherwise, they do not play a commercial role in greenhouse crop production.

Ethylene is naturally produced in fruits, seeds, flowers, stems, leaves, and roots and controls a multitude of processes. Ethylene lends itself to numerous commercial applications. In some cases, ethylene gas or a synthetic ethylene-producing chemical, ethephon, is applied to enhance ethylene levels for purposes such as height retardation, prevention of stem topple, flower promotion, color formation in fruit, and fruit ripening. In other situations, ethylene levels are reduced through the application of silver thiosulfate (STS) to prolong flowering and prevent petal or floret abscission.

The best-known hormonal inhibitor is *abscisic acid* (ABA). ABA promotes abscission of leaves and petals as well as a number of other processes. It is not a major hormone in the vegetative stages of growth but comes into play in the later stages of maturity and senescence. ABA is not commercially important in greenhouse crop production.

A number of synthetic compounds also exist for control of greenhouse plant growth. These include the height-retarding chemicals A-Rest®, B-Nine®, Bonzi®, Cycocel®, and Sumagic®; the chemical pinching agents Atrimmec® and Off-Shoot-O®; and the ethylene producer Florel®.

GROWTH-REGULATING COMPOUNDS

Only the commercially important hormones and synthetic plant-growth-regulating compounds will be covered in this section. Headings follow compound names rather than roles because of the overlapping roles of these materials. Recommendations for the use of these and other growth regulators appear in Tables 12–1 through 12–12 (Tayama and Carver 1989). Recommendations exceed the registered uses of growth regulators. The grower, however, must be careful to follow the label instructions.

Auxins

Auxins are involved in *tropistic* growth movements. Such movements include the downward growth of roots, the upward growth of shoots, and the growth of shoots

Table 12–1

Growth Regulator Recommendations[1] for Floricultural Crops[2]

Material	*Crop*	*Purpose*	*Concentration and Method*	*Application*	*Remarks*
Accel® N-(phenylmethyl)-9-(tetra-hydro-2H-pyran-2-yl)-9H purin-6-amine *See Table 12–2*	Carnation (standard and miniature)	Lateral branching.	500 ppm SPRAY	On young plants, spray the entire plant following a pinch. On older plants, spray a 12–18 in. zone of the plants where branching is desired following harvesting.	Use wetting agent. Apply only to cultivars listed on the label. The material is not translocated.
	Rose	Lateral branching.	200 ppm SPRAY	Spray portion of plants where branching is desired. Best results achieved when application made following pruning or harvesting.	Use wetting agent. Apply only to cultivars listed on the label. The material is not translocated.
A-Rest® (ancymidol) *See Tables 12–3, 12–4*	Bedding plants (see label list)	Height control.	33–132 ppm SPRAY	Apply 2–4 weeks after transplanting when roots are well established.	Wide variation in sensitivity of species.
	Chrysanthemum (pot)	Height control.	33–66 ppm SPRAY	When shoots or new growth is 2–2½ in. long. Approximately 14 days after pinch. Repeat if necessary 1–2 weeks later.	Some cultivars are more sensitive than others.
			0.25–0.50 mg per 6 in. pot DRENCH	When shoots or new growth is 2–2½ in. long. Approximately 14 days after pinch. Second application should not be necessary unless split application is used.	Some cultivars are more sensitive than others. Very important that entire soil mass is uniformly drenched.

Table 12–1 *(continued)*

Material	*Crop*	*Purpose*	*Concentration and Method*	*Application*	*Remarks*
	Dahlia (pot)	Height control.	0.5–2 mg per 6 in. pot DRENCH	Apply no later than 2 weeks after planting. Shoots approximately ¼ in.	Some cultivars may not require treatment. Others vary in sensitivity.
	Easter lilies 'Ace' 'Nellie White'	Height control.	33–66 ppm SPRAY	When plants are 6–8 in. tall. If split application is used, then apply second dose 1–2 weeks later.	Do not spray if buds are visible. Bud injury may occur. "Palm tree" appearance may also occur.
			0.25 mg per 6 in. pot DRENCH	When plants are 6–8 in. tall. If split application is used, then apply second dose 1–2 weeks later.	Split application is generally recommended. Very important that soil mass is uniformly drenched.
	Foliage plants (see label list)	Height control.	33–132 ppm SPRAY	Apply 2–4 weeks after transplanting when roots are well established.	Wide variation in sensitivity of species. Labeled in Florida for certain species.
	Geranium (seedings)	Height control, early flowering.	200 ppm SPRAY	Apply when plants have 2–4 true leaves. About 2–3 weeks after transplanting.	Promotes branching also.
	Gerbera (pot)	Height control.	0.125–0.25 mg per 6 in. pot SPRAY or DRENCH	Apply 2–4 weeks after transplanting when roots are well established. No repeat.	Application may not be needed. Response by cultivars does vary. Trial small group first.
	Poinsettia	Height control.	33–66 ppm SPRAY	Apply when shoots or new growth is 2–2½ in. long. Approximately 14 days after pinch. Repeat if necessary 1–2 weeks later.	Some cultivars are more sensitive than others. Last application should be made Oct. 7 for cool, dark fall or Oct. 23 for bright, warm fall.

Table 12–1 *(continued)*

Material	*Crop*	*Purpose*	*Concentration and Method*	*Application*	*Remarks*
			0.25–0.50 mg per 6 in. pot DRENCH	Apply when shoots or new growth is 2–2½ in. long. Approximately 14 days after pinch. Second application should not be necessary unless split application is used.	Some cultivars are more sensitive than others. Very important that entire soil mass is uniformly drenched. Last application on Oct. 7 for cool, dark fall or Oct. 23 for bright, warm fall.
	Tulip (pot)	Height control.	0.125–0.500 mg per 6 in. pot DRENCH	Apply 1–2 days after bringing into greenhouse for forcing. Effect greatly reduced if applied after 2 days.	Response varies with cultivars and flowering period. Proper cooling must have been done.
Atrimmec® (dikegulac sodium) *See Table 12–5*	Azalea	Lateral branching, reduced shoot elongation.	3,120–6,240 ppm SPRAY	Apply to either unpinched shoots 1–3 in. long or to pinched shoots within 3 days after pinching. Repeat applications can be made following same guidelines. Last application should be 2 weeks before last pinch would normally be made.	Variation among cultivars. May delay flowering if applied too late. Yellowing and growth stoppage can be expected. See notes in product information.
	15 other floral crops on label	Lateral branching, reduced shoot elongation.	460–4,680 ppm SPRAY	Generally apply within 3 days after trimming or hand pinching.	Yellow leaves can be expected. Specific use directions given with product. Translocated to shoot tips of sprayed branches only.
Benzyladenine (BA) (N-6, benzylaminopurine) *See Table 12–6*	Holiday cactus	Increased branching under vegetative conditions.	100 ppm SPRAY	Apply after planting when new growth begins under vegetative conditions. No repeat under vegetative conditions.	Results vary with cultivars. Trial small group first. Use wetting agent with spray.

Table 12–1 *(continued)*

Material	*Crop*	*Purpose*	*Concentration and Method*	*Application*	*Remarks*
		Increased number of buds under reproductive conditions.	100 ppm SPRAY	Apply 10–14 days after start of short days or when buds just become visible.	Results vary with cultivars. Trial small group first. Use wetting agent with spray.
B-Nine SP® Alar 85® (daminozide) *See Table 12–7*	Azalea	Early and enhanced flower formation.	1,500–2,500 ppm SPRAY	Apply 4–6 weeks after last pinch.	Encourages short-day response and early bud formation.
	Bedding plants (see label list)	Height control.	2,500–5,000 ppm SPRAY	Apply 2–4 weeks after transplanting. May be repeated at 3–4 week intervals.	Petunias should have 1½–2 in. diameters.
	Chrysanthemum (pot)	Height control.	2,500–5,000 ppm SPRAY	When shoots or new growth is 1–1½ in. long. Approximately 10–14 days after pinch. Repeat if necessary 1–2 weeks later.	Some cultivars are more sensitive than others.
	Chrysanthemum (cut)	Control of neck elongation.	2,500–5,000 ppm SPRAY	Apply 4–6 weeks prior to bloom and no later than disbud.	Predominantly for flowering plants to reduce stretching of flower neck and to strengthen the neck.
	Foliage plants	Height control, coloration intensity.	2,500 ppm SPRAY	When new growth begins to elongate. Two or more applications may be necessary.	Recommended for the Sun Belt.

Table 12–1 *(continued)*

Material	*Crop*	*Purpose*	*Concentration and Method*	*Application*	*Remarks*
	Gardenia	Height control.	5,000 ppm SPRAY	Apply when plants are two-thirds of finished size.	
	Gloxinia	Height control.	750 ppm SPRAY	Apply 1–2 weeks after transplanting and before plants start to stretch.	Needed under low-light conditions conducive to stretch.
	Hydrangea (summer)	Height control.	5,000–7,500 ppm SPRAY	Apply 4 weeks after pinch. Repeat if necessary, but not after early August.	
	Hydrangea (forcing)	Height control.	5,000 ppm SPRAY	Apply 2–3 weeks after forcing begins (4–5 leaf stage). Repeat application 1 week later.	Can apply after flower buds are visible if necessary. Stop treatment at least 6 weeks before sale (nickel sized) to avoid reduction in bloom size.
	Kalanchoe	Vegetative height control.	5,000 ppm SPRAY	First apply approximately 2 weeks after pinching. Use other applications at 2-week intervals if necessary while under long days.	May delay flowering 7–10 days compared to nonuse.
	Kalanchoe	Flowering stems height control.	5,000 ppm SPRAY	First apply 2–3 weeks after start of short days. Repeat 2–3 weeks later.	Shortens main flowering stem as well as axillary flowering stems.
	Poinsettia	Height control.	2,500 ppm SPRAY	When shoots or new growth is 1½–2 in. long. Subsequent application may be made at 1–2 week intervals if needed.	If combined with Cycocel®, do not apply after September 30; make only one application; and use B-Nine SP® at 2,500 ppm and Cycocel® at 1,500 ppm.

Table 12–1 *(continued)*

Material	*Crop*	*Purpose*	*Concentration and Method*	*Application*	*Remarks*
Bonzi® (paclobutrazol) *See Tables 12–8, 12–9*	Poinsettia	Height control.	8–63 ppm SPRAY	When shoots or new growth is 1½–2 in. long.	Thorough and uniform coverage essential when spraying. Rate is night-temperature dependent.
			0.125–0.25 mg per 6 in. pot DRENCH	Apply 4 ounces per 6 in. pot when shoots or new growth is 1½–2 in. long.	
Cycocel® (chlormequat, CCC) *See Table 12–10*	Azalea	Early flower formation.	2,500 ppm SPRAY	First application 4–6 weeks after last pinch. Reapply once, 1 week later.	Some cultivars are more sensitive than others. May give chlorosis and flower delay if misapplied.
	Calceolaria	To keep compact appearance (see remarks).	1,000 ppm SPRAY	Apply when buds are visible. Split application can be made ½ rate, 2-week interval.	Useful when artificial daylength extension is used or at high forcing temperatures.
	Geranium (cutting)	Height control.	1,500–2,000 ppm SPRAY	When shoots or new growth is 1½–2 in. long. Second application may be made 2 weeks later.	Heavy dosage may cause leaf chlorosis on leaf margins.
	Geranium (seedling)	Height control, early flowering.	1,500 ppm SPRAY	Apply when plants have 2–4 true leaves. About 2–3 weeks after transplanting. Repeat at 1- to 2-week intervals if needed. Do not apply if bud visible.	Promotes branching and early flowering. May cause chlorosis on leaf margins.
			3,000–4,000 ppm DRENCH	Apply when plants have 2–4 true leaves. Do not repeat.	

Table 12–1 *(continued)*

Material	*Crop*	*Purpose*	*Concentration and Method*	*Application*	*Remarks*
	Poinsettia	Height control.	1,500–3,000 ppm SPRAY	When shoots or new growth is 1½–2 in. long. Subsequent applications may be made at 1- to 2-week intervals if needed.	May cause chlorosis on leaf margins, which will disappear. Last application should be made Oct. 15 for dark, cool fall or Oct. 30 for warm, bright fall.
			3,000 ppm DRENCH	When shoots or new growth is 1½–2 in. long. Second application should not be necessary.	Last application on October 15.
Florel® (ethephon) *See Table 12–11*	Bromeliads	Flower induction.	2,500 ppm SPRAY	Apply when plants are 1½–2 years old to induce flowering.	Plants should flower in 2–3 months.
	Daffodil (pot)	Height control.	2,000 ppm SPRAY	Apply when leaves or floral stalk is 4–5 in. long. Foliage should be dry. If required, use a second application 2–3 days later. Do not apply if flower bud is visible!	Concentration and number of applications vary with cultivar and flowering period. Bulbs should have received proper cold treatment for given flowering period. Do not wet foliage for 12 hours after treatment. Florel® should be applied in a well-ventilated 60–65°F greenhouse.
	Geranium (cutting)	Increased branching of stock plants.	500 ppm SPRAY	Apply 4 weeks apart after establishment of stock plants (only 2 applications). Start 4–6 weeks prior to major harvest of cuttings.	Encourages development of laterals, reduces leaf size, reduces stem elongation, hastens rooting, and aborts flower spikes.
		Increased branching of pot plants.	500 ppm SPRAY	First application when breaks or new growth is 1½–2 in. long. Maximum of 2 applications. Discontinue 6 weeks prior to sale.	Encourages development of laterals, reduces leaf size, reduces stem elongation, and aborts flower buds.

Table 12–1 *(continued)*

Material	*Crop*	*Purpose*	*Concentration and Method*	*Application*	*Remarks*
	Hyacinth	Height control, reduced stem topple.	1,000 ppm SPRAY	Apply when leaves or floral stalk is 3–4 in. long. Foliage should be dry. No florets should be in color. If required, use a second application 2 days later.	Concentration and number of applications vary with cultivar and flowering period. Bulbs should have received proper cold treatment for given flowering period. Do not wet foliage for 12 hours after treatment. Florel® should be applied in a well-ventilated 60–65°F greenhouse.
Off-Shoot-O®	Azalea	Lateral branching.	2–5 oz/qt (63–155 ml/l) SPRAY	Apply any time the plant is actively growing to chemically pinch. Use a very fine mist to be most effective.	Apply only when there is good air movement.
Pro-Gibb® (gibberellic acid, GA_3) *See Table 12–12*	Azalea	Substitution for cold treatment.	250 ppm SPRAY	After 3 weeks of cold treatment, apply 3 weekly sprays at beginning of forcing period.	Used to substitute or replace 3 weeks of cold treatment. Use wetting agent in solution.
	Chrysanthemum (pompon)	Flower stems elongation.	20 ppm SPRAY	About 4 weeks after start of short days. Buds should be visible but apply before laterals start to elongate away from the stem.	Use wetting agent in solution.
	Chrysanthemum (standard)	Stem elongation.	10 ppm SPRAY	Apply 2 weeks after planting. Apply again 2 weeks later.	Overtreatment may result in very weak stems. Use wetting agent in solution.
	Cyclamen	Hastened flowering.	10–25 ppm SPRAY	Apply when buds are size of pinhead in leaf axils. Approximately 10–12 leaf stage. Spray crown below leaves. Use 10 ppm on F1 cultivars.	Hastens flowering approximately 1 month over normal schedule. Weak flower stems formed if applied later than directed.

Table 12–1 *(continued)*

Material	*Crop*	*Purpose*	*Concentration and Method*	*Application*	*Remarks*
	Fuchsia	Stem elongation.	250 ppm SPRAY	Apply 4 sprays at weekly intervals to induce tree forms.	Treated stems will require staking for upright growth. Use wetting agent in solution.
	Geranium	Stem elongation.	250 ppm SPRAY	Apply 4 sprays at weekly intervals to induce tree forms.	Treated stems will require staking for upright growth. Use wetting agent in solution.
	Hydrangea	Substitution for cold treatment.	5 ppm SPRAY	Apply up to 4 weekly sprays at the start of forcing to overcome insufficient cooling.	Use with caution. Plants may become leggy. Use wetting agent in solution.

[1]This list is presented for information only. No endorsement is intended for products mentioned, nor is criticism meant for products not mentioned. Before purchasing and using any growth regulator, you must check all labels for registered use, rates, and application frequency. Typical application rates consist of: For sprays, 1 gallon per 200 ft^2 of growing area (1 l/m^2); for drenches, 1 oz per 2¼ in., 3 oz per 4 in., 4 oz per 5 in., 6 oz per 6 in., and 8 oz per 10 in. pot.

[2]Tables 12–1 through 12–12 from Tayama and Carver (1989).

Table 12–2

Accel® Concentrations and Dilutions—Foliar Spray
(1.3% a.i.; 13.1 mg a.i. per milliliter)

Concentration (ppm)	Dilution	
	oz/gallon of solution	*ml/liter of solution*
50	0.66	3.8
100	1.33	7.7
200	2.64	15.4
500	6.66	38.5

Table 12–3

A-Rest® Dosages, Concentrations, and Dilutions—Growing Medium Drench*
(0.0264% a.i.; 0.264 mg a.i. per milliliter)

	Dosage (mg per pot at given volume)									*Dilution*	
Drench Volume (oz):	*1*	*2*	*3*	*4*	*5*	*6*	*8*	*10*	*Concentration (ppm)*	*oz/gallon of solution*	*ml/liter of solution*
	0.02	0.04	0.063	0.08	0.11	0.125	0.17	0.21	0.7	0.35	2.7
	0.04	0.08	0.126	0.17	0.21	0.25	0.34	0.42	1.4	0.68	5.3
	0.075	0.15	0.225	0.30	0.375	0.45	0.60	0.75	2.5	1.3	9.5
	0.15	0.30	0.450	0.60	0.750	0.90	1.2	1.50	5.0	2.5	19.0

*Locate the desired dosage in the column under the appropriate drench volume. Find the corresponding dilution in the dilution columns.

Table 12–4

A-Rest® Concentrations and Dilutions—Foliar Spray
(0.0264% a.i.; 0.264 mg a.i. per milliliter)

	Dilution	
Concentration (ppm)	*oz/gallon of solution*	*ml/liter of solution*
10	4.9	38
25	12.1	95
33	16.0	125
50	24.2	190
66	32.0	250
100	48.5	380
132	64.0	500
200	97.0	760

Table 12–5

Atrimmec® Concentrations and Dilutions—Foliar Spray
(18.5% a.i.; 200 mg a.i. per milliliter)

	Dilution*	
Concentration (ppm)	*oz/gallon of solution*	*ml/liter of solution*
460	0.3	2.3
780	0.5	3.9
940	0.6	4.7
1,180	0.75	5.9
1,560	1.0	7.8
2,040	1.3	10.2
2,340	1.5	11.7
2,500	1.6	12.5
3,120	2.0	15.6
4,680	3.0	23.4
6,240	4.0	31.2

*Recommendation for crops on label is given in oz/gallon.

Table 12–6

Benzyladenine (BA) Dilutions To Provide a 100 ppm Foliar Spray

*Dilution for 100 ppm**
100 mg in 1 l water
500 mg in 5 l water (1.3 gal)
1 g in 10 l water (2.6 gal)
5 g in 50 l water (13.2 gal)
25 g in 250 l water (66.1 gal)

*Dilute first in smaller volume of grain alcohol to dissolve BA; then use distilled water to provide the rest of volume needed.

Table 12–7

B-Nine SP® or Alar 85® Concentrations and Dilutions—Foliar Spray (85% a.i.; 850 mg a.i. per gram)

	Dilution		
Concentration (ppm)	*Level scoops*/ gallon of solution*	*oz/gallon of solution*	*grams/liter of solution*
750	1 small	0.11	0.88
1,500	1 large	0.23	1.76
2,500	2 large	0.40	2.94
5,000	4 large	0.80	5.88
7,500	6 large	1.20	8.82

*Approximate dosage only. Measuring scoop provided with product has a large and small end. Use weight measurements wherever possible.

Table 12–8

Bonzi® Concentrations and Dilutions—Foliar Spray (0.4% a.i.; 4.0 mg a.i. per milliliter)

	Dilution	
Concentration (ppm)	*oz/gallon of solution*	*ml/liter of solution*
10.00	0.32	2.5
25.00	0.80	6.3
31.25	1.00	7.8
46.90	1.50	11.7
50.00	1.60	12.5
62.50	2.00	15.5
75.00	2.40	18.8
93.75	3.00	23.4
100.00	3.20	25.0

Table 12–9

Bonzi® Concentrations and Dilutions—Growing Medium Drench
(0.4% a.i.; 4.0 mg a.i. per milliliter)

	Dilution	
Concentration (mg per 6 in. pot)	*oz/gallon of solution*	*ml/liter of solution*
0.125	0.03	0.26
0.188	0.05	0.39
0.250	0.07	0.52

Table 12–10

Cycocel® Concentrations and Dilutions—Foliar Spray
or Growing Medium Drench
(11.8% a.i.; 118 mg a.i. per milliliter)

	Dilution	
Concentration (ppm)	*oz/gallon of solution*	*ml/liter of solution*
1,000	1.1	8.5
1,500[1]	1.6	12.7
2,000	2.2	17.0
2,500	2.7	21.2
3,000[2]	3.3	25.4
4,000	4.4	34.0
5,000	5.4	42.4

[1]Also referred to as 1 to 80.
[2]Also referred to as 1 to 40.

Table 12–11

Florel® Concentrations and Dilutions—Foliar Spray*
(3.9% a.i.; 39 mg a.i. per milliliter)

	Dilution	
Concentration (ppm)	*oz/gallon of solution*	*ml/liter of solution*
500	1.6	13
1,000	3.2	26
1,500	4.8	39
2,000	6.4	52
2,500	8.0	65
3,000	9.6	77

*Use distilled water if results with tap water are questionable. Water buffered above pH 7 reduces Florel® effectiveness.

Table 12–12

Pro-Gibb® Concentrations and Dilutions—Foliar Spray
(3.91% a.i.; 39.1 mg a.i. per milliliter)

Concentration (ppm)	Dilution	
	oz/10 gallons of solution	*ml/10 liters of solution*
10	0.32	2.6
25	0.80	6.5
50	1.60	13.0
100	3.20	26.0
250	8.00	65.0
500	16.00	130.0
1,000	32.00	260.0

and leaves toward the light. It is believed that shoots grow toward the light source because auxin is inactivated by light. This occurs more on the bright side of the stem; thus, there is greater promotion of growth on the darker side.

Auxins also inhibit lateral shoot development. When the top of the main shoot of a plant is removed, the source of auxin is lost from that shoot, and lateral shoots are free to develop. This is why pinching (the removal of shoot tips) is practiced on some floral crops; multiple lateral shoots are promoted. A plant is said to display *apical dominance* when only one shoot predominates. When apical dominance is lost, several lateral shoots usually develop simultaneously.

Auxins are effectively used for promoting root formation on cuttings. Materials commercially used include IBA, IPA, and NAA. IBA and NAA are often found in combination. Many types of cuttings benefit from the use of rooting substances. Root formation occurs faster, and in the end the root system is usually more extensive. The benefit is least on plant species that normally root fast, and there are a few species where no benefit is seen.

Rooting compounds are very concentrated and so are always diluted. Talc powder is a customary diluent. Active-ingredient concentrations of 0.1–1.0 percent are used—the lower concentrations for easy-to-root soft cuttings and the higher concentrations for slower-to-root woody cuttings. The base of the cutting is dipped into the powder and then tapped to remove all but a thin film of powder. To reduce the possibility of disease transfer, a duster is often used.

Rooting compounds can be diluted by another method for use on woody cuttings where penetration is difficult. A concentrated stock solution of the rooting compound is made by dissolving it in alcohol. The stock solution is further diluted with water to a final concentration in the range of 500–5,000 ppm (0.05–0.5 percent). The cut end of cuttings is dipped in this solution for a short time and then "stuck" into propagation media in a propagation bed. The concentration of the solution and the length of dipping time (five seconds to a few minutes) are determined by the ease of rooting and the penetrability into the woody stem of the cutting.

Rooting compounds are a very common and valuable aid to the propagators of greenhouse crops since so many crops are propagated by cuttings. Chrysanthemum, carnation, African violet, azalea, begonia, geranium, hydrangea, *Kalanchoe,* poinsettia, and many green plants are examples of plants that benefit from rooting compounds.

Gibberellins

GA inhibits root formation on leaves and stems; thus, it is not found in root-promoting products. It is used by gardeners for enlarging the size of camellia blooms. GA sprayed on geranium flowers at the time of first color appearance (at a concentration of 5 ppm) stimulates a 25–50 percent increase in flower size. The number of petals remains constant, but each is larger. When greater concentrations are applied, however, increased responses carry an adverse effect. Stems and flower stalks elongate and become thinner. Stems may become adversely weak; flowers that are normally flat may become undesirably spike-like.

Flowering of cyclamen can be accelerated by four to five weeks with a single spray of 50 ppm GA 60–75 days prior to the anticipated flower date (Widmer et al. 1974). Higher concentrations result in adversely tall and weak flower stems. A recent report (Lyons and Widmer 1983) suggests applying 0.25 ounce (8 ml) of 15 ppm GA_3 solution 150 days after seed is sown to the crown of the plant below the leaves.

Researchers have used the gibberellins to replace the cold treatment of azalea. In the cold treatment, when the plant has reached sufficient size, it is pinched for the last time. New shoots are allowed to develop for about six weeks,

Figure 12–1

A cooler is required for the growth of certain crops that need a cold period for flower-bud development. Such crops include azalea, flowering bulbs, hydrangea, and Easter lily.

and then flower-bud initiation is induced by about six weeks of long-night treatment. Once flower buds are established, a period of six weeks at a temperature of 45°F (7°C) or lower is required for development of flower buds. After this treatment, the plants are moved to the greenhouse and are forced into bloom in four to six weeks.

The cold treatment is expensive, requiring costly moving of plants and also cooler facilities (Figure 12–1). Considerable efforts have been made to reduce or eliminate the cold treatment (Boodley and Mastalerz 1959). Five weekly sprays of GA_{4+7} or GA_3 at a concentration of 1,000 ppm have proven effective (Figure 12–2) (Larson and Sydnor 1971; Nell and Larson 1974). The five consecutive weekly sprays begin when flower buds are well developed after the short-day treatment. Plants treated in this manner usually flower earlier and have larger blossoms than plants given the cold treatment. Most cultivars respond well; however, there can be some variation. For instance, flower pedicels may become too long, causing flowers to droop.

There have also been studies on the partial replacement of the cold treatment. In one such study, after three weeks of cold treatment, plants were moved to the greenhouse for forcing, and three weekly sprays of GA_3 at 250 ppm were made. Half of the cold treatment was eliminated, thereby permitting twice the volume of plants to be moved through the cooler facilities.

Figure 12–2

Azalea 'Dogwood' plants during greenhouse forcing. The plant on the left received the standard cold treatment for flower-bud development. It is fully budded and will bloom in a few weeks. The plant on the right, rather than being placed in a cooler, was left in the greenhouse and sprayed 6 times at weekly intervals with gibberellic acid at a concentration of 1,000 ppm. In addition to replacing the cold treatment, this chemical hastened flowering and resulted in larger flowers. (*Photo courtesy of* R. A. *Larson, Department of Horticultural Science, North Carolina State University, Raleigh,* NC 27695–7609)

Hydrangeas are also subjected to a period of cold storage. On occasion, they are removed prematurely, and slow development, small flowers, and short stems ensue. Research studies show promise of eliminating this situation by a spray of GA at a concentration of 5–50 ppm.

A 250 ppm GA spray applied to fuchsia four times at weekly intervals temporarily prevents flowering and stimulates rapid growth (Heins et al. 1979). This could lend itself well to production of tree-type fuchsia. Tree-type geraniums can likewise be produced (Carlson 1982) by applying GA_3 as a spray to plants two weeks after potting. A total of five weekly applications of 250 ppm must be applied. A tolerable delay in flowering occurs. Excessive GA application results in distorted growth and poor plant quality.

Florel®

Ethephon is the common name for the commercial product Florel®. (It is produced by Union Carbide Agricultural Products Co., Research Triangle Park, NC 27709.) It is a 3.9 percent liquid concentrate of the chemical](2-chloroethyl) phosphonic acid[. Ethephon undergoes a chemical conversion that releases ethylene to the plant.

Commercial appeal of bromeliads is enhanced by the presence of a flower stalk. Flowering can be induced in two months time by pouring 1/3 ounce (10 ml) of a diluted solution of ethephon (12 ml ethephon/l water) into the vase of plants at least 18–24 months old (Heins et al. 1979). Flowering of Dutch iris bulbs is likewise affected by ethephon. A number of bulbs, particularly smaller bulbs, fail to bloom when they are greenhouse forced. A spray of 156 ppm (4 ml ethephon/l water) applied to green plants in the Dutch bulb-production fields just prior to bulb harvest led to earlier flowering, less bud abortion, and fewer leaves during greenhouse forcing (Kamerbeek et al. 1980). British work showed that the reduction in leaf number permitted increased plant density from 14 to 30 bulbs/ft^2 (150 to 320/m^2) (Krause 1984). Many Dutch iris bulbs are now treated by the producer in the storage area after harvest with 500 ppm ethylene gas for 24 hours to promote earlier and more extensive flowering on higher-quality plants.

As might be expected, ethylene plays a role in fruit maturation. Ethylene gas, or the ethylene-producing compound ethephon, is used to ripen apples, bananas, coffee, grapefruit, oranges, peppers, tobacco, and other fruit. Ethephon spray is applied to about 30 percent of processing tomatoes in the field to hasten maturity. About 60 percent of the fresh-use field tomato crop in America is treated after harvest in the mature-green stage with 200 ppm ethylene gas. This enhances color formation and hastens ripening by about two days (Lutz and Hardenburg 1968).

Leaf abscission, like flower and fruit formation, is part of the maturation process. It likewise is enhanced by ethephon. This has a commercial advantage in hydrangea production, where it is desirable to remove the leaves for the six-week cold treatment that occurs after flower-bud initiation and just prior to greenhouse forcing. An application of 1,000–5,000 ppm ethephon two weeks prior to the start of cold treatment has been shown to result in the defoliation of the cultivars 'Merville' and 'Rose Supreme' (Tjia and Buxton 1976).

Light intensity at the crown of rose bushes diminishes as the canopy grows larger over the years. This discourages the development of new canes from the base of the plant. Renewal of the plant is dependent in great part on the large, floweriferous shoots that come from these basal breaks. The best hope for encouraging such breaks has come from scoring lower canes with a saw blade dipped in 7,500 ppm ethephon (Zeislin et al. 1972). Ethephon sprays have, in fact, been used commercially in Israel to stimulate basal branching of 'Baccara' rose.

Surprisingly, ethephon is used as a height retardant as well. Drenches or sprays serve well to control the height of narcissus (Briggs 1975; DeHertogh 1989; Moe 1980). Ethephon sprays prior to floret color result in shorter hyacinths and prevent stem topple, which is a problem with some cultivars (DeHertogh 1989).

Cycocel®

Potted plants must be grown to a height compatible with the environment in which they will be used. Many plants grow too tall if not checked. In past years, water and nutrients were withheld to reduce height, resulting in negative side effects in the appearance of the foliage and size of the bloom. Poinsettia stems were sometimes folded (Figure 12–3) to reduce height, which was an effective but time-consuming process. Cycocel® is used today.

Height retardants, in general, result in shorter stem internodes but do not affect the number of leaves formed. Stems are thicker and leaves are deeper green because chlorophyll is more dense in the smaller cells. As a result, plants have a very pleasing appearance.

Cycocel® [(2-chloroethyl) trimethylammonium chloride] is available in a liquid formulation containing 11.8 percent active ingredient. The common name of the chemical is *chlormequat.* (It is produced by American Cyanamid Company, P.O. Box 400, Princeton, NJ 08540.)

Cycocel® is applied as a spray to azaleas six to eight weeks after the plants have been pinched for the last time. This checks growth and prompts early flower-bud initiation. Quite often, a larger number of flower buds develop. The retardant helps further by reducing the formation of vegetative shoots at the time of flower-bud development. These undesirable side shoots give the plant an unbalanced appearance.

Cycocel® is recommended only as a drench for poinsettia height retardation. Sprays can result in blotchy yellowing of foliage about 24 hours after application. This is a temporary situation and is not noticed at flowering time. Cycocel® is also labeled for height control of geranium and hibiscus.

Figure 12–3

Years ago, poinsettia stems were often folded to reduce their height, as shown here. This time-consuming process has been replaced by the use of the chemical Cycocel®. Chemically treated plants have the same number of leaves on shorter, thicker stems with deeper green foliage. (*Photo courtesy of* J. W. *Love, Department of Horticultural Science, North Carolina State University, Raleigh,* NC 27695–7609)

B-Nine SP®

B-Nine SP® (N-dimethylaminosuccinamic acid) is known under the common name *daminozide.* (It is produced by Uniroyal Chemical Co., World Headquarters, Middlebury, CT 06749.) It is an effective height retardant labeled for use on azalea, potted chrysanthemum, cut chrysanthemum, foliage plants (except in California), gardenia, hydrangea, poinsettia, and bedding plants including ageratum, aster, begonia, cosmos, dahlia, dusty miller, marigold, petunia, phlox, salvia, verbena, and zinnia. B-Nine SP® is sold as a soluble powder containing 85 percent active ingredient plus a wetting agent and is applied as a foliar spray to the upper leaf surfaces.

Azaleas are treated with B-Nine SP® for the same reason that Cycocel® is used—to promote early and more extensive flower-bud set and to retard vegetative shoot development. Some cultivars of standard chrysanthemum develop a long pedicel (flower stem) that is unattractive. A compact flower with a short pedicel can be produced by spraying the upper third of the foliage to the point of runoff two days after disbudding with a 0.25 percent concentration of B-Nine

SP®. Pot mums are sprayed when new shoots are 1½ inches (4 cm) long, about two weeks after the pinch. No delay in flowering occurs. B-Nine SP® is particularly useful in producing compact bedding plants but is not effective on celosia, coleus, French-type marigold, pansy, or snapdragon.

A-Rest®

The chemical A-Rest® [α-cylopropyl-α-(p-methoxyphenyl)-5-pyrimidinemethanol] (produced by Elanco Products Company, Division of Eli Lilly and Company, Indianapolis, IN 46285) takes the common name of *ancymidol.* A-Rest® effectively controls the height of and is labeled for chrysanthemum (Figure 12–4), dahlia, lilies including Easter lily, poinsettia, and tulip. Certain bedding and foliage plants are labeled for Florida only. It is purchased as a solution containing 250 mg of active ingredients per quart (264 ppm). A-Rest® can be applied as a spray or as a drench depending on the crop.

A-Rest® loses activity at low pH levels. Consequently, effectiveness of A-Rest® drenches in pine bark substrates has been found to be poor (Larson et al.

Figure 12–4

Chrysanthemum 'Nob Hill' treated with the chemical height retardant A-Rest® at increasing concentrations from left to right. The plant on the extreme left received no chemical treatment. Those to the right have the same number of leaves but shorter internodes, thicker stems, and deeper green foliage. (*Photo courtesy of* V. P. *Bonaminio, Department of Horticultural Science, North Carolina State University, Raleigh,* NC 27695–7609)

1974; Tschabold et al. 1975). A solution to the problem was found by Simmonds and Cumming (1977) by dipping hybrid lily bulbs in A-Rest® solution. This procedure worked well for Easter lilies as a dip prior to cold-storage treatment (Lewis and Lewis 1982). Larson (1985) refined the procedure, calling for a dip in 24 ppm A-Rest® for 30 minutes after cold-storage treatment.

Another interesting function of A-Rest® has been seen in research, where it was used to induce flowering of clerodendron (Koranski et al. 1978). Retardation of vegetative growth prompts flowering in this plant. Cycocel® has a similar effect in clerodendron (Hildrum 1973).

Bonzi®

Bonzi® is the most recent height retardant to be introduced. This product contains 0.4 percent of the active ingredient [(±)-(R*,R*)-β((4-chlorophenyl) methyl)-α-(1,1,-dimethylethyl)-1 *H*-1,2,4-triazole-1-ethanol]. This ingredient is a member of the triazine group of compounds from which some notable herbicides have originated. The common name is *paclobutrazol.* (It is distributed by Sandoz Crop Protection Corp., Des Plaines, IL.)

Bonzi® can be absorbed by the roots from a soil drench or through the shoots from a spray. In either event, it is translocated to the upper portion of each shoot where it reduces internode elongation. If a spray is used, it is very important that the spray coats all the stems of the plant; otherwise, some shoots will grow longer than others. As in the case of A-Rest®, this material is less effective in pine-bark-based root media. Higher rates must be used if it is applied as a drench to these root media. Higher rates are also needed when it is applied to very vigorous growing varieties compared to those that are naturally shorter and when it is applied during high-temperature periods.

Bonzi® is labeled for spray application on bedding plants including ageratum, celosia, coleus, dianthus, impatiens, marigold, New Guinea impatiens, pansy, periwinkle, petunia, and snapdragon; for spray or drench application on pot chrysanthemum; for bulb dip application on pot freesia; for spray application on geranium; for spray application on hibiscus in Florida only; and for spray application on poinsettia.

Sumagic®

Sumagic®, not yet on the market, is a new chemical height retardant. (It is being developed by Valent USA Corp., P.O. Box 8025, Walnut Creek, CA 94596.) It has chemical properties closer to Bonzi® than to the other height retardants and is also a member of the triazine chemical group. The common name for this chemical is *uniconazole.* Proposed uses at this time are for several bedding plant species, chrysanthemum, Easter lily, and poinsettia. Like Bonzi®, it will be effective at very low rates.

Off-Shoot-O®

Off-Shoot-O® is primarily composed of methyl octanoate and methyl decanoate in combination with an emulsifying agent. (It is produced by The Buckeye Cellulose Corp., a subsidiary of Procter and Gamble, P.O. Box 8307, Memphis, TN 38108.) It is termed a chemical pinching agent because it causes death of the terminal bud on shoots, which, in turn, results in the development of side shoots (Figure 12–5). Often, more side shoots are produced from a chemical pinch than from a manual pinch. Off-Shoot-O® is applied in a very fine spray to wet the shoot tips. The remainder of the plant need not be treated, and spraying is stopped before the point of runoff. Runoff increases the possibility of injury to lateral buds and leaves.

Azaleas are effectively pinched with this chemical. Considerable labor is saved since azaleas must be pinched many times in order to produce a large plant with numerous shoots. Concentrations of 2–5 ounces of product per quart (63–155 ml/l) are used depending upon the cultivar. A concentration of 3.2 ounces per quart (100 ml/l) is common. Chrysanthemums can be chemically pinched, but there is an element of risk. Solution running down the stem often causes gir-

Figure 12–5

A greenhouse-forcing azalea plant sprayed with the chemical pinching agent Off-Shoot-O®. Note the dead terminal buds and the resulting side shoots. This process is repeated several times over a period of 12–18 months to develop a highly branched plant of suitable size for forcing into bloom. (*Photo courtesy of* J. W. Love, *Department of Horticultural Science, North Carolina State University, Raleigh,* NC 27695–7609)

dling of the stem at the soil level and ultimately death of the plant. Cultivars vary in their susceptibility. The spray must be applied in a very fine mist to avoid runoff. Growers generally do not use chemical pinching for chrysanthemums. Several species of woody ornamentals can also be chemically pinched, including *Cotoneaster, Juniper, Ligustrum, Rhamnus,* and *Taxus.*

Atrimmec®

Atrimmec® [sodium salt of 2,3,:4,6-bis-O-(1-methylethylidene)-*a*-L-xylo-2-hexulofuranosonic acid] is known by the common name *dikegulac.* (It is distributed by PBI/Gordon Corp., P.O. Box 4090, Kansas City, MO 64101.) The predecessor to this product was Atrinal®. Atrimmec® temporarily stops shoot elongation, thereby promoting lateral branching. It is thus a pinching agent for greenhouse crops, including azalea, Elatior begonia, clerodendron, fuchsia, gardenia, grape ivy, ivy geranium, *Kalanchoe, Pachystachys lutea* (shrimp plant),

Figure 12–6

Various chemicals are under study to find a safe disbudding agent. Buds in each leaf axil of the 'Wildfire' chrysanthemum stem on the right were removed by hand. Buds were removed from the stem on the left by spraying it with an experimental disbudding agent. (*Photo courtesy of* R. A. *Larson, Department of Horticultural Science, North Carolina State University, Raleigh,* NC 27695–7609)

Schefflera arboricola, and verbena. Branching can also be enhanced in 41 species of landscape ornamentals. Atrimmec® is used to prevent flowering and ultimately fruiting in glossy privet, Japanese holly, multiflora rose, and ornamental olive.

Disbudding Agents

Growth suppressants that are under study today and that show promise of commercial application are the chemical disbudding agents (Figure 12–6). Standard chrysanthemums and most potted chrysanthemum cultivars require disbudding. This process is very time-consuming in that all buds except the terminal flower bud are removed from each main stem. Some chemicals are now being tested that, when sprayed on the plant, will inhibit lateral bud development and leave the terminal bud unharmed. They are not yet ready for commercial use since there is still too close a margin of safety in timing and too much variation within cultivars. If they are applied too early, the terminal bud is injured; if they are applied too late, the effectiveness is reduced.

COST OF MATERIALS

It is difficult to make cost comparisons for height retardants and pinching agents. All are not effective on each crop. Some are applied as a drench, while others are

Table12–13

Costs of Various Height Retardants and Pinching Agents for Treating a Single Plant in a 6 Inch (15 cm) Pot

Regulant	*Cost of Product*	*Method of Application*	*Rate of Product Dilution*	*Rate of Application*	*Cost per 6 Inch Pot*
A-Rest®	$38.00/qt (liquid)	Drench	0.68 oz/gal	6 oz/pot (0.25 mg/pot)	3.8¢
		Spray	16 oz/gal	0.33 oz/pot (0.33 mg/pot)	5.0¢
B-Nine SP®	$50.00/lb (powder)	Spray	0.4 oz/gal (0.25%)	0.67 oz/pot	0.7¢
Bonzi®	$68.00/qt (liquid)	Drench	0.05 oz/gal	4 oz/pot (0.188 mg/pot)	0.3¢
		Spray	1 oz/gal	0.33 oz/pot	0.5¢
Cycocel®	$133.00/gal (liquid)	Drench	1 qt/10 gal (0.3%)	6 oz/pot	15.6¢
		Spray	1 qt/10 gal (0.3%)	0.67 oz/pot	1.7¢
Off-Shoot-O®	$53.00/gal (liquid)	Spray	3.2 oz/qt	0.67 oz/pot	2.8¢
Atrimmec®	$204.00/gal (liquid)	Spray	3 oz/gal	0.67 oz/pot	2.5¢

applied as a spray. The number of pots that can be sprayed with a gallon depends upon the density of pots in the bench and the spray equipment; a high-pressure, fine-droplet spray covers more area. The concentration of growth regulator required varies according to the crop, its stage of growth, and the weather conditions. Calculations presented in Table 12–13 are intended to give a rough idea of the cost of using these materials. You will have to correct these values for the concentrations and amounts applied in your operation. The resulting figures indicate that chemical height control and pinching is inexpensive, considering the improved quality of the crop that is achieved.

SUMMARY

1. The five categories of plant hormones are auxins, gibberellins, cytokinins, ethylene, and inhibitors such as abscisic acid. Auxins, gibberellins, and ethylene are used in greenhouses as growth regulators. The other greenhouse plant-growth regulators (height retardants and pinching agents) are of synthetic origin.
2. The speed and extent of root formation of cuttings can be enhanced by the auxin IAA (indole-3-acetic acid). Related compounds IBA (indolebutyric acid), IPA (indolepropionic acid), and NAA (naphthalene acetic acid) are used alone and in combination in commercial rooting products.
3. Gibberellic acid (GA) can play a variety of roles in the greenhouse. It may be used to substitute totally for the cold treatment of azalea or partially for hydrangea. Cyclamen flowering can be hastened, while flower size of geranium can be enlarged. GA can also be used to enhance growth and retard flowering of fuchsia and geranium for the purpose of developing tree-type forms.
4. The roles of ethylene are likewise varied. Flowering is induced in bromeliads by the application of ethylene or Florel®, an ethylene-releasing compound. Treatment of Dutch iris bulbs with ethylene gas induces earlier and more extensive flowering. Both ethylene gas and Florel® are used to hasten ripening of many fruits. Hydrangea leaf abscission can be accomplished by spraying with Florel®. Florel® has been used to stimulate basal shoot formation in rose. Finally, height of narcissus and hyacinth can be retarded with Florel®.
5. Many greenhouse potted plants grow taller than desired. Plants with short internodes can be produced by treatment with chemical height retardants. Products and their labeled uses include the following:
   a. A-Rest® for chrysanthemum, dahlia, Easter lily, lilies, poinsettia, and tulip as well as specific bedding and foliage plants in Florida.
   b. B-Nine® for azalea, several bedding plants, chrysanthemum, foliage plants (except in California), gardenia, hydrangea, and poinsettia.

c. Bonzi® for bedding plants (including ageratum, celosia, coleus, dianthus, impatiens, marigold, New Guinea impatiens, pansy, periwinkle, petunia, and snapdragon), pot chrysanthemum, pot freesia, geranium, hibiscus, and poinsettia.

d. Cycocel® for azalea, geranium, hibiscus, and poinsettia.

e. Florel® for narcissus and hyacinth.
Height retardation in azalea and clerodendron fosters more rapid flower-bud initiation and sometimes a greater number of flower buds.

6. It is necessary to stimulate branching in some greenhouse crops. This has been done in the past by manually pruning shoots. Off-Shoot-O® sprays accomplish this in azalea by killing the growing points. Atrimmec® suppresses growth of the growing points, thereby fostering branching of azalea, Elatior begonia, clerodendron, fuchsia, gardenia, grape ivy, ivy geranium, *Kalanchoe*, *Schefflera arboricola*, shrimp plant, and verbena. Florel® stimulates branching in azalea and geranium.

7. There are several other uses for which the commercial growth regulants have been proven effective in research studies. However, they have not been labeled through EPA for these uses, and, as a result, it is illegal to use them for these purposes. It is the intent of this book to recommend only those chemicals and uses that are cleared by EPA.

REFERENCES

The manufacturers of growth regulators have technical literature available covering crop responses, methods of application, modes of action, and other background information. References with an asterisk before them lend themselves well to a general overview of the subject of chemical growth regulation.

1. Boodley, J. W., and J. W. Mastalerz. 1959. The use of gibberellic acid to force azaleas without a cold temperature treatment. *Proc. Amer. Soc. Hort. Sci.* 74:681–685.

2. Briggs, J. R. 1975. The effects on growth and flowering of the chemical growth regulator ethephon on narcissus and ancymidol on tulip. *Acta Hort.* 47:287–296.

3. Carlson, W. H. 1982. Tree geraniums. In Mastalerz, J. W., and E. J. Holcomb, eds. *Geraniums*. III, pp. 158–160. Pennsylvania Flower Growers' Assoc., University Park, PA.

* 4. Cathey, H. M. 1975. Comparative plant growth-retarding activities of ancymidol with ACPC, phosphon, chlormequat, and SADH on ornamental plant species. *HortScience* 10:204–216.

5. DeHertogh, A. A. 1989. *Holland Bulb Forcers Guide*, 4th ed. The International Flower-Bulb Center, Hillegom, The Netherlands. (Available from The Netherlands Flower-Bulb Info. Center, 250 West 57th St., Suite 629, New York, NY 10019.)

* 6. Dicks, J. W. 1976. Chemical restriction of stem growth in ornamentals, cereals and tobacco. *Outlook on Agriculture* 9 (2):69–75.

7. Heins, R. D., R. E. Widmer, and H. F. Wilkins. 1979. Growth regulators effective on floricultural crops. Mimeo. Dept. of Hort. and Land Architecture, Univ. of Minnesota, St. Paul, MN.

8. Hildrum, H. 1973. The effect of daylength, source of light, and growth regulators on growth and flowering of *Clerodendron thomsonae* Ball. *Scientia Hort.* 1:1–11.

9. Kamerbeek, G. A., A. J. B. Durieux, and J. A. Schipper. 1980. An analysis of the influence of Ethrel® on flowering of iris 'Ideal': An associated morphogenic physiological approach. *Acta Hort.* 109:235–241.

10. Koranski, D. S., B. E. Struckmeyer, and G. E. Beck. 1978. The role of ancymidol in *Clerodendron* flower initiation and development. *J. Amer. Soc. Hort. Sci.* 103:813–815.

11. Krause, W. 1984. Experiments in early forcing show dramatic results. *Grower* 101 (3):27–31.

*12. Larson, R. A. 1985. Growth regulators in floriculture. *Hort. Review* 7:399–481.

13. Larson, R. A., J. W. Love, and V. P. Bonaminio. 1974. Relationship of potting mediums and growth regulators in height control. *Florists' Review* 155 (4017):21, 59, 62.

14. Larson, R. A., and T. D. Sydnor. 1971. Azalea flower bud development and dormancy as influenced by temperature and gibberellic acid. *J. Amer. Soc. Hort. Sci.* 96:786–788.

15. Leopold, A. C., and P. E. Kriedemann. 1975. *Plant Growth and Development*, 2d ed. New York: McGraw-Hill.

16. Lewis, A. J., and J. S. Lewis. 1982. Height control of *Lilium longiflorum* Thunb. 'Ace' using ancymidol bulb dips. *HortScience* 17:336–337.

*17. Luckwill, L. C. 1981. *Growth Regulators in Crop Production.* Studies in Biology 129. London: Edward Arnold Pub., Ltd.

18. Lutz, J. M., and R. E. Hardenburg. 1968. The commercial storage of fruits, vegetables, and florist and nursery stocks. USDA Agr. Handbook 66.

19. Lyons, R. E., and R. E. Widmer. 1983. Effects of GA_3 and NAA on leaf lamina unfolding and flowering of *Cyclamen persicum*. *J. Amer. Soc. Hort. Sci.* 108:759–763.

20. Mitchell, J. W., and G. A. Livingston. 1968. Methods of studying plant hormones and growth-regulating substances. USDA ARS Agr. Handbook 336.

21. Moe, R. 1980. The use of ethephon for control of plant height in daffodils and tulips. *Acta Hort.* 109:197–204.

22. Nell, T. A., and R. A. Larson. 1974. The influence of foliar applications of GA_3, GA_{4+7}, and PBA on breaking flower bud dormancy on azalea cultivars 'Redwing' and 'Dogwood'. *J. Hort. Sci.* 49:323–328.

*23. Nickell, L. G. 1982. *Plant Growth Regulating Chemicals.* Berlin: Springer-Verlag.

*24. Nickell, L. G., ed. 1984. *Plant Growth Regulating Chemicals.* Vols. I and II. Boca Raton, FL: CRC Press.

*25. Sachs, R. M., and W. P. Hackett. 1977. Chemical control of flowering. *Acta Hort.* 68:29–49.

*26. Seeley, J. G. 1979. Interpretation of growth regulator research with floriculture crops. *Acta Hort.* 91:83–92.

*27. Shanks, J. B. 1970. Chemical growth regulation for floricultural crops. *Florists' Review* 147:34–35, 50–58.

*28. ———. 1982. Growth regulating chemicals. In Mastalerz, J. W., and E. J. Holcomb, eds. *Geraniums*. III, pp. 106–113. Pennsylvania Flower Growers' Assoc., University Park, PA.

29. Simmonds, J. A., and B. G. Cumming. 1977. Bulb-dip application of growth regulating chemicals for inhibiting stem elongation of 'Enchantment' and 'Harmony' lilies. *Scientia Hort.* 6:71–81.

30. Tayama, H. K., and S. A. Carver. 1989. Growth regulator chart. In Tayama, H. K., ed. *Floriculture Crops Insect and Mite Control, Disease Control, Growth Regulator, and Herbicide Booklet*, pp. 26–32. Ohio Florists' Assoc. Bul. 711. (Available from Ohio Florists' Assoc., 700 Ackerman Rd., Suite 230, Columbus, OH 43202.)

*31. Thomas, T. H. 1976. Growth regulation in vegetable crops. *Outlook on Agriculture* 9 (2):62–68.

32. Tjia, B., and J. Buxton. 1976. Influence of ethephon spray on defoliation and subsequent growth on *Hydrangea macrophylla* Thunb. *HortScience* 11:487–488.

33. Tschabold, E. E., W. C. Meredith, L. R. Guse, and E. V. Krumkalns. 1975. Ancymidol performance as altered by potting media composition. *J. Amer. Soc. Hort. Sci.* 100:142–144.

*34. Weaver, R. J. 1972. *Plant Growth Substances in Agriculture*. San Francisco: W. H. Freeman and Co.

35. Widmer, R. E., L. C. Stephens, and M. V. Angell. 1974. Gibberellin accelerates flowering of *Cyclamen persicum* Mill. *HortScience* 9:476–477.

*36. Wilkins, H. F., W. E. Healy, and R. D. Heins. 1979. Past, present, future plant growth regulators. *Acta Hort.* 91:23–32.

37. Zeislin, H., A. N. Halevy, V. Mor, A. Brachrach, and I. Sapir. 1972. Promotion of renewal canes in roses by ethephon. *Hort. Sci.* 7:75–76.

CHAPTER 13

Insect Control

Insects, mites, and other pests constitute an ever-present threat to the quality of greenhouse crops. Aside from the damage done to the crop, the presence of insects on the final product is disconcerting to the consumer. Most greenhouse crops are sold for aesthetic value. Yet, regulations limiting the presence of pesticides in greenhouse effluent, the banning of specific pesticides, and the declining rate of new pesticide introductions for the greenhouse are challenging the grower's ability to control pests. A careful plan of prevention and control of insects must be developed for any greenhouse range.

INTEGRATED PEST MANAGEMENT (IPM)

IPM is what its name implies—a pest control system in which preventive, surveillance, and corrective measures are integrated into a holistic program. The principal goals are to attain an acceptable level of pest control while reducing the use of pesticides and minimizing the impact of the overall program on the environment. IPM addresses all categories of pests including insects, mites, animal pests, pathogenic diseases, and weeds. Steps in the process, in the order in which they would likely be enacted, are as follows:

1. Weed control in and around the greenhouse.
2. Sanitation including cleaning and pasteurization prior to crop establishment.

3. Inspection and cleanup of newly acquired plants.
4. Screening of greenhouse entrances.
5. Routine surveillance for identification of and quantification of pest appearances in the greenhouses as well as accurate recording of the same.
6. Adjustment of environmental conditions to render them suppressive to the pests at hand but not to the crop.
7. Pest eradication methods of either biological control or pesticide application.

Each method of pest eradication will be discussed after the section "Insects and Other Pests in the Greenhouse."

Weed Control

Insects abound in our world. During the warm seasons, they live in the soil and on vegetation outside the greenhouse. They crawl or fly into the greenhouse, or they may be carried in on clothing. Smaller insects such as thrips are carried in the airstream entering the greenhouse through the pads of the cooling system. Weeds harbor insects and diseases. They give the greenhouse establishment an unsightly appearance, which discourages customers and weakens the morale of employees. You can be sure that weeds reduce profitability. Weeds should be cleared away from the area surrounding the greenhouse and should also be eliminated in the greenhouse because they provide a hiding place and a source of food for insects. It does no good to spray crop plants in the bench if weeds under the bench are not sprayed; yet, to spray these weeds is a waste of time and money. Some growers keep the area bare around their greenhouses, while others maintain mowed grass. Thrips develop in grass flowers; hence, mowing is important. Mowing greatly reduces the types and numbers of insects invading the greenhouse.

Be very careful in selecting a herbicide (weed killer) for use adjacent to a greenhouse. Any herbicide that volatizes is potentially dangerous. Only three herbicides have federal (Environmental Protection Agency) registration for use inside greenhouses.

1. Diquat® can be used in aisles and under benches as a contact killer for all weeds.
2. Roundup® is a contact killer labeled for eliminating the broad spectrum of weeds in greenhouses providing there is no crop inside.
3. Safer Sharpshooter® Weed and Grass Killer can be used for contact weed control under benches.

Sanitation

The best hope for pest control is prevention. There is no better time to take preventive measures than before the crop is planted. Measures can be taken then that are not possible later. Prior presence of disease may indicate the need to pasteurize root media. Pot plant benches, watering systems, plant support systems, tools, and used plant containers should be sterilized. (All of these measures were covered in Chapter 6 and will be covered again in Chapter 14.) Unmarketable plants, portions of plants remaining after fresh flowers are removed, and leaves on the floor should all be cleaned out. They are the perfect hosts for insects and disease and become the vehicle for carry-over to the next crop.

Algae should be killed in benches and on the floor. This is easily and safely accomplished with the bromine in products such as Dibrom® and Agribrom®. Algae, in addition to being a safety hazard by virtue of its slippery nature, harbors fungus gnats. Root media should be hosed off pot plant benches and off walks so that it does not provide a habitat for insects or disease. Improperly functioning floor drains should be cleared so that wet conditions do not occur, which, in addition to providing an environment for insects and disease, also provide high-humidity conditions conducive to foliar disease development.

Plant Entry

Insects can be brought into the greenhouse on plants. Purchased seedlings and cuttings should be inspected carefully for insects and disease. If they are present, these plants should be isolated and treated with pesticides or rejected. Common sources of insect and disease problems are established plants brought to the greenhouse by customers. You will often be approached by friends and customers who want you to rejuvenate a plant for them, which often leads to more trouble than the plant is worth. Do not allow the entry of such plants into your production area.

Insect Screens

Insect screens are currently under test in commercial and research installations. Early reports show that they are effective in preventing entry into the greenhouse of all individuals among the larger size insect species and nearly all individuals in the smaller insects, such as thrips and spider mites. Polyethylene screens with 400 mesh size holes are available commercially. Such screens are installed over the cooling pads to filter insects that would otherwise be drawn in. The screens impede the flow of air—some by as much as fivefold. To maintain the cooling capacity of the system, it is therefore necessary to install a screen with 5 times as much surface area as the pad. It is important to hose off such screens periodically to prevent plugging with dust. While such a screen is expensive and space consuming, it could result in considerable downsizing in the pest control program within the greenhouse. A strong impetus at the moment for using insect screens is the devastating effect of the tomato spotted wilt virus disease spread by the western flower thrips. Control can be accomplished only through exclusion of the western flower thrips. This insect–disease interrelationship is discussed later in this chapter under "Thrips."

Pest Surveillance

It is inevitable that insects and disease are going to get into the greenhouse. If they can be detected early, control measures can be taken before any significant damage is done and before any drastic pesticide applications are required. For one reason or another, insects will often establish themselves in a particular location in the greenhouse. It may be a warmer temperature zone or an air current that carries them there, or perhaps it is an area that is difficult to spray and thus not well protected. The grower should identify such spots and check them regularly. Insects often exhibit plant preferences. Some varieties of a crop are more attractive to them than others. These varieties should be watched carefully. Most insects seek the undersides of leaves. An inspection of plants from above may not reveal their presence. Plants should be picked up and turned on their side to reveal the underside of the pot and the leaves. Other pests, such as slugs, hide beneath pots or pieces of bark or leaves on the surface of the root medium during the day and come out to feed at night. You must be aware of these habits and look in the proper place for the pest or for the signs of the pest, such as slime trails.

The entire greenhouse should be inspected at least twice per week. It is recommended that three plants be examined on each bench. If insects are found, these plants are flagged for future observations to determine the speed of development of the insects. Unless a plant has been flagged, different plants should be inspected each time because insects are very erratic in their points of initial appearance. Yellow sticky cards should be installed on sticks such that they can be raised as the crop grows to keep them just above the height of the plants. For small greenhouses, one card per 1,000 ft^2 (93 m^2) is sufficient. For large greenhouse blocks, one card might suffice for 10,000 ft^2 (930 m^2). Plants and cards should be inspected at the same time. It will help to have a 10X lens for identifying the insects. The type and number of insects should be determined and recorded. Cards need to be replaced weekly so that newer insect entries are not confused with older entries. It is important to inspect both plants and cards because flying stages of insects including aphids, fungus gnats, leaf miners, thrips, and whiteflies can be found on sticky cards but might leave plants when they are picked up. Conversely, spider mites, slugs, and immature stages of some insects would not be found on cards.

Records of types of insects present, their numbers, stage of development, and rate of development are necessary for several reasons.

1. *Biological control:* As will be discussed later, this information is absolutely necessary if biological control is to be used.

2. *Pesticide selection:* Many pesticides are selective for certain insect species. Lannate®, for instance, is effective on worms, aphids, and thrips but is ineffective on leaf miners and spider mites.

3. *Pesticide formulation:* Thrips located deep in flowers are often beyond the penetration of sprays. It would be necessary to use an aerosol or fog to penetrate the flowers.

4. *Application zone:* Surveillance makes it possible to distinguish the areas that need treatment from those that do not. Far less pesticide is used in this way.

5. *Pesticide timing:* Whiteflies are most vulnerable to sprays in the crawler through the second enstar stages. By the time they are in the fourth enstar stage, they have an outer exoskeleton that protects them from pesticide sprays. The systemic insecticide Oxamyl® takes five days to get into the plant and then is active for about two weeks. It only kills insects that are feeding on the plant. This includes whiteflies in the crawler or second and third enstar stages but not in the egg, pupa, or adult stages.

Environmental Adjustments

Many pathogenic diseases require periods of high humidity and/or free water on foliage. When surveillance identifies the initial occupancy of such pests, the greenhouse environment should be adjusted to avoid such conditions. (The techniques are discussed in Chapter 14.) Insects likewise have specific requirements for rapid spread. Spider mites require high temperatures and low humidity. Frequent syringing of plants and an effective cooling system help to diminish a spider mite infestation.

Pest Eradication

Two schools of thought have existed concerning pest control. Historically, the preventive spray program has been most popular. In this program, the crop is sprayed weekly with a combination of a fungicide, insecticide, and miticide. The strategy is to keep the plant covered with a residue so that pests cannot infect it. Recent problems with this program include the large amount of pesticides that make their way to the environment, the increased risk of litigation from accidental handling of pesticides, and the development of resistance in pests that are continually exposed to the same pesticides. The resistance problem becomes more acute as a result of the recent reduction in the number of pesticides approved for greenhouse use.

The alternative IPM approach serves the current situation much better. The intent of IPM is not to eliminate the use of pesticides, but rather to restrict their use to strategic situations. IPM calls for heavy investment of time into pest prevention and surveillance. However, the payoff is to be found in reduced pesticide cost and less risks of pesticide resistance, crop injury, and litigation.

INSECTS AND OTHER PESTS IN THE GREENHOUSE

There are numerous insects and related pests that attack plants in the greenhouse. In order to effectively control these pests, their life cycles must be understood. The majority of infestations are due to ten types of pests. Before any control measures can be planned, the pest must be identified. While a few pesticides kill pests in general, most are made to kill one specific pest or a few particular pests. Spider mites, for instance, are controlled by a specific group of pesticides (miticides).

Feeding habits are very important. A pest such as the cyclamen mite, which feeds in the small scales of buds, is likely to escape injury unless a surfactant is added to the spray to ensure penetration into the bud. Whiteflies, which feed on the lower sides of leaves, point out the importance of spraying from beneath as well as from above. Knowledge of feeding habits also serves to tell the manager where to check for early detection of a problem.

The method of feeding by a pest will permit detection of those that are too small to be seen with the unaided eye or those that hide beneath clods of soil or under pots during the day. Slime trails are indicative of slugs and snails, distorted growth of new leaves can indicate cyclamen mites, light brown tracks in a leaf signify the presence of leaf miners, and patches of sandy colored pinpoint spots on leaves are the result of a pest with piercing–sucking mouth parts, such as aphids and spider mites.

Many pesticides do not kill eggs; thus, the life cycle of a pest must be known. An insect such as the aphid, which can reproduce at seven to ten days of age, requires a more frequent spray program than one such as the mealybug, which takes six to eight weeks to mature. Some of the more important greenhouse pests are described in this section. Pertinent features about their identity and habits are presented to aid in an understanding of their control.

Aphids

Aphids attack a wide variety of greenhouse crops. The several types of aphids may be differentiated by color. The most prevalent greenhouse species is the green peach aphid (*Myzus persicae* Sulzer) (Figure 13–1). The wingless forms of green peach aphid are yellowish green in summer and pink to red in the fall and spring. The winged forms are brown. Aphids are 1/8 inch (3 mm) or less in length. They feed by inserting a tube-like piercing mouth part into the leaf and sucking out the sap. Feeding usually occurs in buds and undersides of leaves. Feeding on young bud leaves results in distorted leaves as they continue to grow. Older leaves may display patches of chlorotic pinpoint spots where cell contents have been drawn out.

Aphids excrete honeydew, which is rich in sugar. A black sooty mold often grows on the honeydew, marring the appearance of the plant. Ants collect the honeydew and sometimes go as far as to farm aphids by moving them to suitable host plants and protecting them.

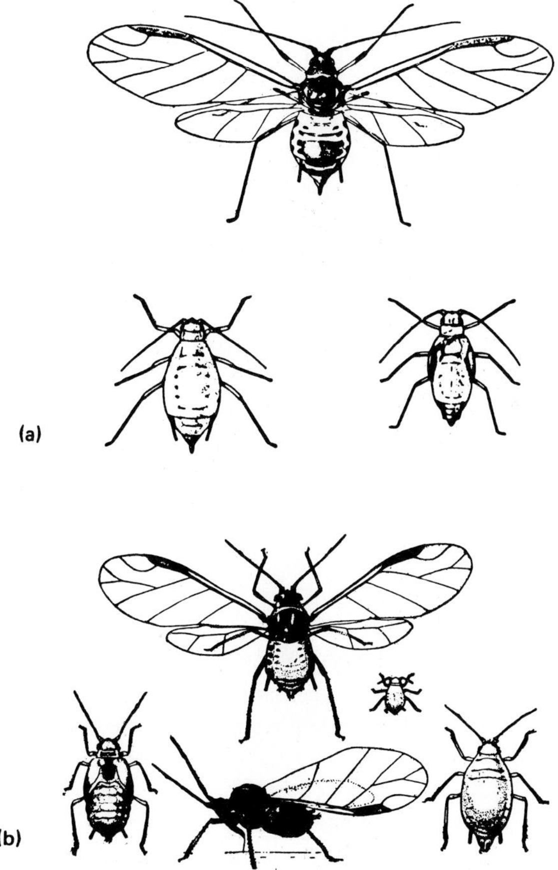

Figure 13–1

Winged and wingless forms of aphids: (a) green peach aphids and (b) melon aphids. (USDA *sketch*)

Aphids usually give birth to living female nymphs. The nymphs give birth to successive generations of female nymphs in as short a time as seven to ten days. Each aphid reproduces for a period of 20–30 days. One aphid can give birth to 60–100 nymphs. The entire process takes place without mating. When the food supply becomes short or the colony becomes overcrowded, winged females appear and migrate. Male and female forms appear outdoors with advancing winter in the northern but not in the southern United States. These mate and lay eggs, which constitute an overwintering stage.

Fungus Gnats

Fungus gnats (*Bradysia* sp. and *Sciara* sp.) are thin, gray-colored flies with long legs and antennae (Figure 13–2). They reside mainly on soil and will fly short distances when disturbed. The adult is about 1/8 inch (3 mm) long and has one pair of clear wings. The body ranges in color from a black head to brownish yellow legs and abdomen.

Damage is caused by the larvae, which are legless white worms with a black head and which grow up to 3/16 inch (5 mm) in length. These larvae normally feed on soil fungi and decaying organic matter. When population densities increase, fleshy storage organs such as bulbs and roots may be attacked. Delicate seedlings may be killed. A wide variety of crops are injured by these larvae. Infected plants may turn yellow, lack vigor, or wilt.

The female lays clusters of 20–30 eggs on moist soil surfaces. Soil rich in organic matter is preferred. As many as 300 eggs are laid during the ten-day life span of the adult. The egg hatches in about six days into a larva. The larva feeds for 12–14 days and then changes into a pupa in the soil. After five to six days, an adult fly emerges from the pupal stage. The life cycle from egg to adult requires about four weeks.

Leaf Miners

Leaf miners, in their larval (worm) stage, tunnel within leaves making unsightly tunnels (Figure 13–3). A heavy infestation renders the plant useless for sale. In recent years, leaf miner resistance to pesticides has led to devastating population buildups, particularly on chrysanthemum. This insect has been the focal point of a major research effort to understand and control it. A recent pesticide introduction effective for its control has been abamectin (Avid®).

The adult female is a stocky fly about 1/12 inch (2 mm) long. It punctures the leaf surface with a tube-like appendage on the abdomen known as an *ovipositor* and inserts eggs through it. This activity leaves small white spots on the leaf. A larger number of punctures are made than the number of eggs deposited. Males and females feed on the sap that oozes from the punctures. Each female lays

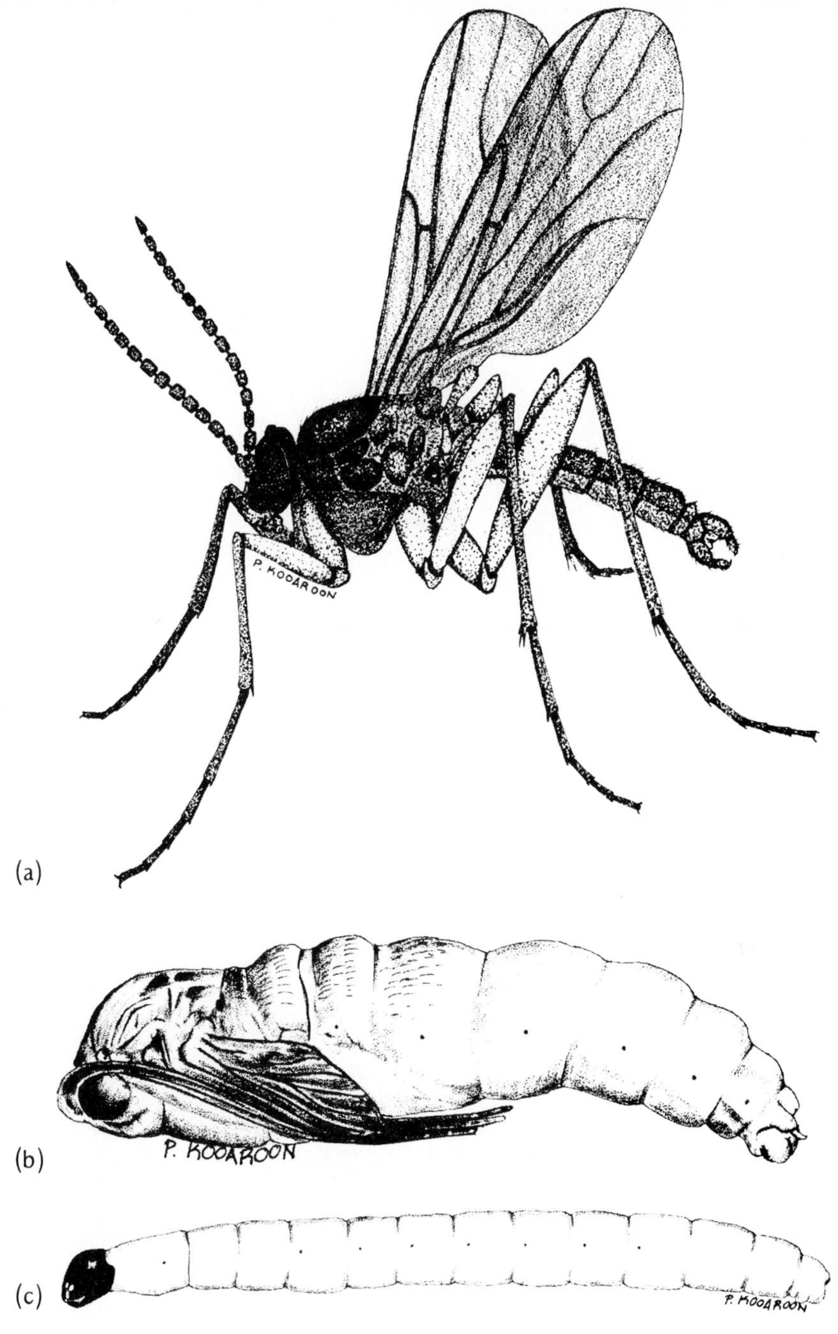

Figure 13–2

Stages of a fungus gnat: (a) adult fly, ⅛ inch (3 mm) long; (b) pupa, ⅛ inch (3 mm) long; and (c) larva, up to $^{3}/_{16}$ inch (5 mm) long. (*Sketch courtesy of* J. R. *Baker and* P. *Kooaroon, North Carolina Agricultural Extension Service, Raleigh,* NC 27695–7613)

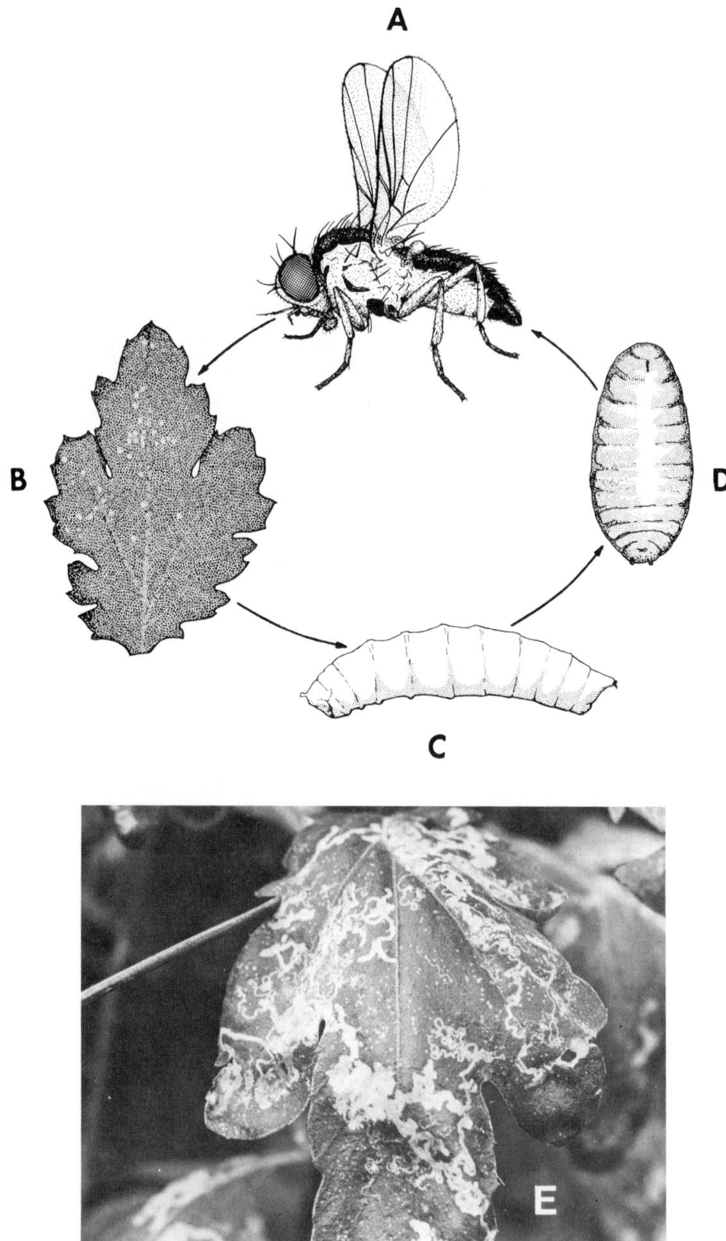

Figure 13–3

Stages of the leaf miner fly: (a) adult; (b) egg and feeding punctures; (c) larva; (d) pupa; (e) damage to chrysanthemum in a commercial greenhouse. (*Sketch courtesy of J. R. Baker, North Carolina Agricultural Extension Service, Raleigh, NC 27695–7613*)

about 100 eggs in its two- to three-week life span. The egg hatches in five to six days into a soft white maggot, which reaches 1/10 inch (3 mm) long when mature. The maggot can tunnel for up to two weeks, at which time it drops out of the leaf into the bench or soil and turns into a pupa. After about two weeks, an adult fly emerges from the pupa, flies to a new leaf, and the life cycle begins again. About five weeks is required for the life cycle from egg to adult.

There are numerous species of leaf miners, but two are most prevalent in the greenhouse. A serpentine leaf miner adult (*Liriomyzia trifolii* Burgess) has a blackish body with yellow markings, a yellow head, and brown eyes. It makes serpentine mines. The chrysanthemum leaf miner adult (*Phytomyza atricornis* Meigen) is larger and black in color. Blotchy as well as serpentine mines are formed by these maggots.

Mealybugs

Mealybugs (*Pseudococcus*) are oval-shaped insects that appear white because of a waxlike powder that covers their bodies (Figure 13–4). The waxy deposit on their bodies includes filaments extending out around the periphery as well as some longer filaments up to 1/2 inch (13 mm) long extending from the back to give the appearance of a tail in the long-tailed mealybug. The actual insect is 1/5 to 1/3 inch (5–8 mm) long.

Mealybugs feed by means of a piercing–sucking mouth part. During feeding, citrus mealybugs inject a toxic substance into the plant. The plant becomes chlorotic and malformed. Like aphids, these insects also excrete honeydew, which provides a substrate for a black sooty mold to grow upon and further disfigure the plant. Ants sometimes farm these insects as they do aphids.

Long-tailed mealybugs give birth to living nymphs. Citrus mealybugs lay eggs that are deposited in a cottony sac. Several hundred yellowish or orange eggs are contained in a sac. The eggs can hatch in five to ten days into nymphs. The nymphs move about feeding for six to eight weeks, at which time they finally become adults. The life cycle from egg to adult takes seven to ten weeks under favorable conditions.

Their waxy protective layer makes it difficult to control mealybugs. Surfactants help wettable powder formulations of pesticides stick better. Aerosols play a useful role here as well. The nymphs, having a thinner protective coating, are easier to kill than the adults.

Mites

Mites are not insects. They belong to the class *Arachnida,* which includes spiders and scorpions. In the adult form, they have four pairs of legs. There are many species of mites, including several that attack crops.

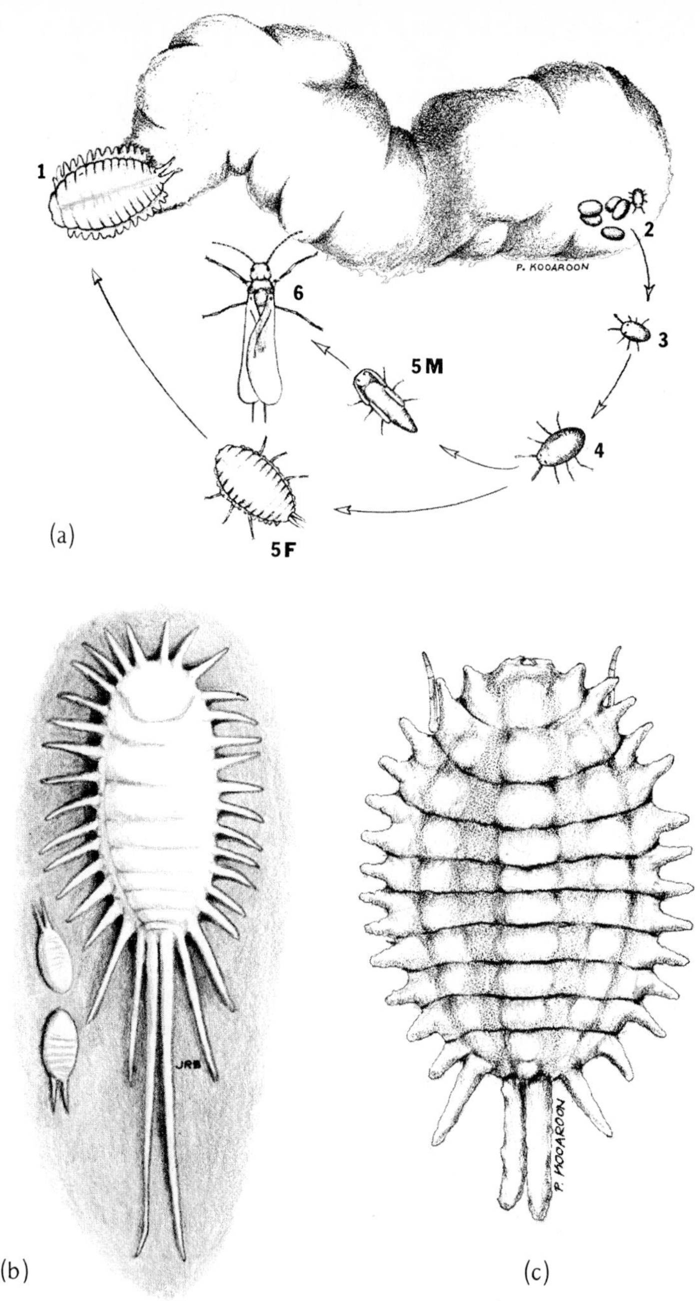

Figure 13–4

Various stages of mealybugs: (a) citrus mealybugs in all stages; (b) adult long-tailed mealybug; and (c) Mexican mealybug. (*Sketch courtesy of* J. R. *Baker and* P. *Kooaroon, North Carolina Agricultural Extension Service, Raleigh,* NC 27695–7613)

Cyclamen mites (*Steneotarsonemus pallidus* Banks) are very small—about 1/100 inch (0.25 mm) long when full grown. They cannot be seen with the unaided eye. These mites (Figure 13–5) are semitransparent with a brownish tinge. Their development is favored by a high humidity (80 percent or more) and a low temperature (60°F, 16°C). The life cycle from egg to adult can occur in two weeks, but the adult female lives on for three to four weeks and lays up to 100 eggs.

Cyclamen mites affect a broad range of plants, many of which are green plants. The mite lives and feeds in the bud and small adjacent leaves. It feeds by way of a piercing–sucking mouth part. Symptoms of infestation are curling of leaflets from outside inward and distortion of young leaves such that small depressions are formed. Flowers may also be distorted or fail to open altogether.

Two-spotted mites, or red spiders (*Tetranychus urticae* Koch), are perhaps the most troublesome of all greenhouse pests (Figure 13–6). These mites may be greenish, yellowish, or red in color and have two dark spots on their bodies. They are about 1/50 inch (0.5 mm) in length.

Two-spotted mites cause chlorotic stippling of leaves, as though a very fine tan to yellow sand had been sprinkled on them, when populations increase. However, on mums and other plants with thick leaves, chlorotic stippling may not be noticed. The spiders spin a silk strand that forms a web over leaves and flowers.

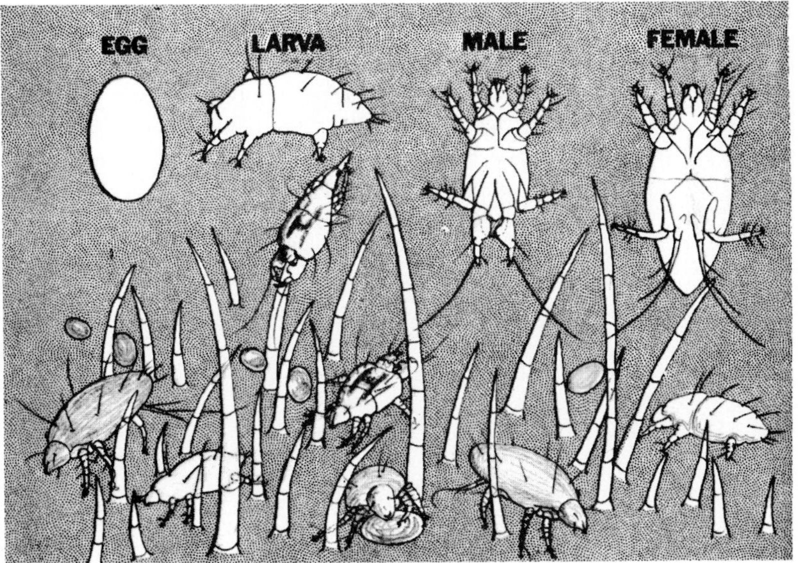

Figure 13–5

All stages of the cyclamen mite shown to scale with the trichomes (leaf hairs) on a gloxinia leaf. (*Sketch courtesy of* J. R. *Baker, North Carolina Agricultural Extension Service, Raleigh,* NC 27695–7613)

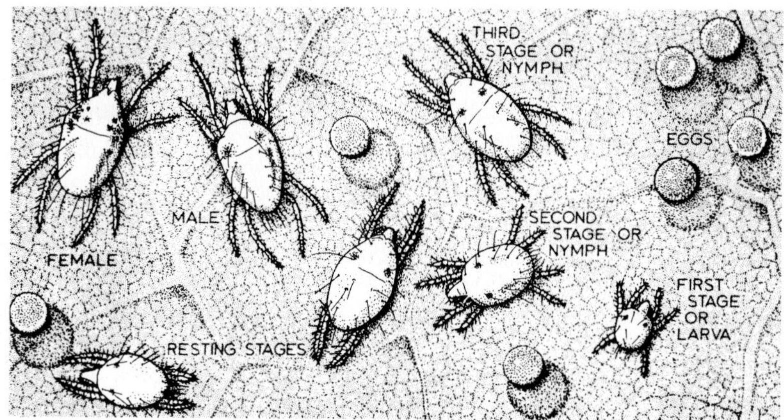

Figure 13–6

All stages of the two-spotted spider mite. (*Sketch courtesy of* J. R. *Baker, North Carolina Agricultural Extension Service, Raleigh,* NC 27695–7613)

Leaves and flowers soon begin to desiccate and consequently turn brown. These mites are most prevalent on the undersides of leaves and in flowers. They are difficult to control in flowers.

The time span from egg to adult is 10 days at 80°F (27°C), or 20 days at 70°F (21°C), or several months at lower temperatures. Low relative humidity favors development of this mite. Eggs hatch in four to five days into six-legged nymphs, which feed for a short time. Next comes an inactive resting stage, a nympho-chrysalis, that lasts about 1½ days. This sequence is repeated for a total of three resting stages. The eight-legged adult emerges from the last resting stage.

During the egg stage and the resting stages, most miticides are ineffective, whether applied as an aerosol, smoke, or nonresidual spray. Since all stages are usually present simultaneously, several miticide applications are necessary. At high temperatures, it may be necessary to make applications as often as two days apart.

Scale Insects

There are several genera of scale insects, all of which belong to the superfamily Coccoidea (Figure 13–7). They vary in overall shell size up to ¼ inch (6 mm). Scale insects are similar to mealybugs and are included in the same superfamily. The unarmored types of scale insects (coccids) have a rubbery outer coating that cannot be detached. Some secrete wax. They may be flat, oval, or globular. Other unarmored scale insects secrete honeydew, which encourages development of a black sooty mold.

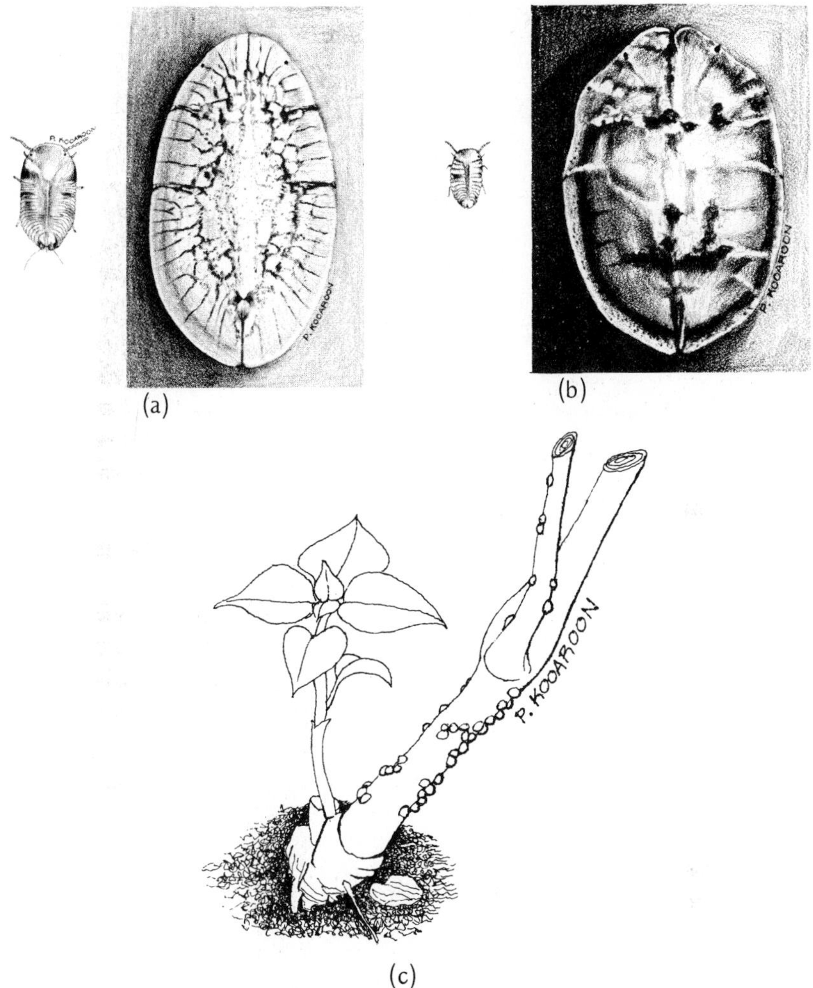

Figure 13–7

Scale insect pests of ornamental plants: (a) brown soft scale (*right*) with its crawler; (b) hemispherical scale (*right*) with its crawler; and (c) bloodleaf plant infested with hemispherical scale. (*Sketch courtesy of* J. R. *Baker and* P. *Kooaroon, North Carolina Agricultural Extension Service, Raleigh,* NC 27695–7613)

The many other types of scale insects (diaspidids) are armored. The scale is not attached to the body and is composed of a wax secretion and castoff skins of the immature stages of the insect. The scale covering can take on several configurations from round to oyster-shell-shaped, can be several colors, and can be smooth or rough. Armored scale insects do not secrete honeydew.

The female armored scale insect does not move about as does the mealybug. It is saclike, wingless, usually legless, and feeds through a piercing–sucking mouth part that injects toxic saliva. Some scale insect species give birth to living young, while others lay eggs. The male has legs and one pair of wings, but no mouth parts (it does not feed). In some species, males are rare or absent, and virgin females give birth to young or lay eggs.

The first nymph (crawler) has legs and can travel about for two days in search of a suitable feeding area. It then inserts its mouth parts into the leaf and begins forming a shell. It remains here through several molts, losing its legs on the first molt. Eggs or young are produced under the body of the female and under the armor of the scales. Three to seven generations can develop in a year.

Slugs and Snails

Slugs and snails (Figure 13–8) are not insects. They are mollusks (a group of animals including snails, sea snails, clams, oysters, and octopuses). The slug lacks a shell, whereas the snail has a hard shell similar to those of some of its counterparts in the sea. Slugs range in size from ½ to 4 inches (1.3–10 cm) in length.

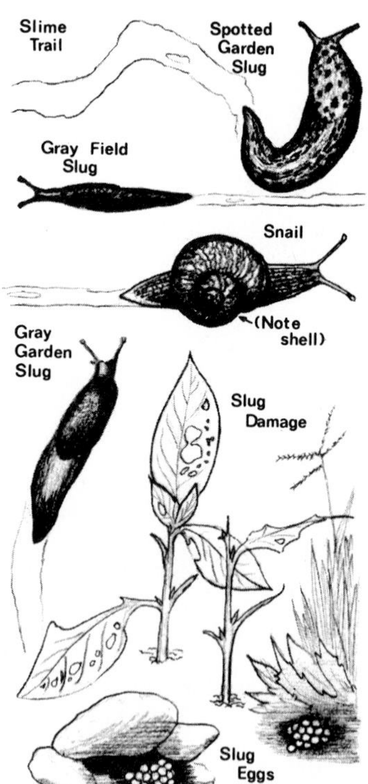

Figure 13–8

Various slugs and a snail. (*Sketch courtesy of* J. R. *Baker, North Carolina Agricultural Extension Service, Raleigh,* NC 27695–7613)

Slugs and snails have chewing mouth parts that allow them to eat seedlings and leaves. They feed by night and hide beneath pots, benches, or litter on the bench surface by day. Dark, moist hiding places are preferred. Slugs exude a slippery liquid as they move along. When it dries, shiny trails can be seen, which easily identifies their presence.

Slugs and snails may crawl into the greenhouse from vegetation or debris immediately outside the greenhouse. Thus, it is important to keep the greenhouse surroundings clear or mowed. They are also easily transported in on pots, flats, soil, or plants.

Slugs and snails lay clusters of 20–100 eggs in moist crevices along the soil or containers. Eggs can hatch in ten days or less at temperatures above 50°F (10°C). Maturity occurs in three months to a year. Slugs and snails are usually killed with one of the two available baits, metaldehyde or methiocarb.

Thrips

Thrips (Figure 13–9) are small—1/25 inch (1 mm) long—and have two pairs of fringed wings. They build up in large numbers outdoors and swarm into green-

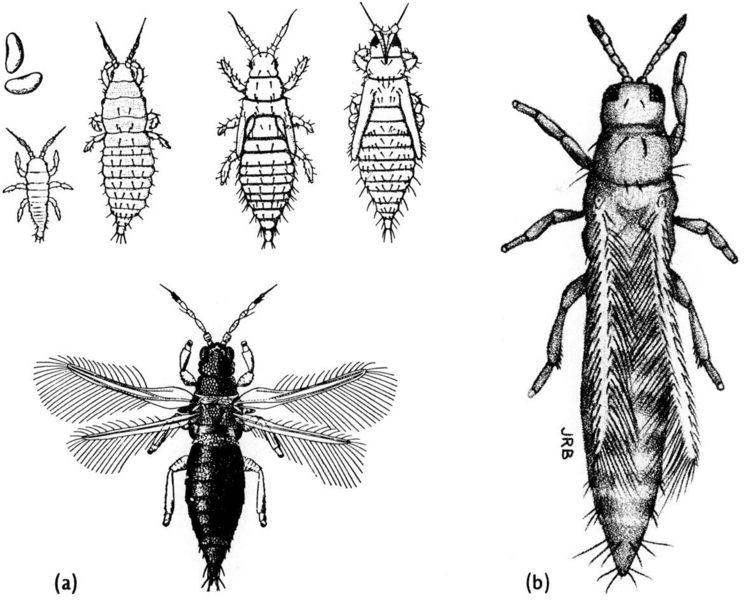

Figure 13–9

Thrips (both species about 1/16 inch maximum): (a) stages of the greenhouse thrips and (b) an adult flower thrips. (*Sketch courtesy of* J. R. *Baker, North Carolina Agricultural* Extension Service, *Raleigh*, NC 27695–7613)

houses during the warm months. Many are carried in air currents. Thrips feed on a broad range of crops. They are commonly found in buds, on flower petals, in axils of leaves, and between the scales of some bulbs. The adults are visible to the unaided eye but are usually hidden in buds or flowers. They can be detected by tapping buds or flowers over a sheet of white paper. Thrips will fall onto the paper and can be seen. The adults can be yellow, tan, brown, or black, depending on the species encountered.

Until recent years, the western flower thrips (*Frankliniella occidentalis*) was confined to areas west of the Rocky Mountains. Today, it is widespread across America and in Europe. It is a partner in what is probably the most serious pest problem of greenhouses today. Western flower thrips transmit tomato spotted wilt virus (TSWV). This virus infects a large number of greenhouse crops, destroys them, and has no cure. The only control is through elimination of the western flower thrips in the greenhouse. This has been exceedingly difficult to do because of the wide range of alternate hosts both inside and outside the greenhouse. A main driving force for the development of insect screens for greenhouses is the need to control TSWV.

The adult female thrips cuts holes in leaves with a sawlike ovipositor on its abdomen and inserts eggs in them. Eggs hatch into nymphs in two to seven days and begin feeding. They have a rasping mouth part that is used to scrape the tender leaf or petal surface. They then suck the exuding plant sap, which causes a white (sometimes silver) discoloration. The injury occurs in streaks rather than in a stippling pattern as is the case with mites or aphids. Later, the whitish areas turn tan or brown as the cells dry. The entire life cycle can occur in two weeks. Longer times are required at lower temperatures. The feeding nymphs and adults excrete brown droplets that turn black and can then be detected on petals and leaves.

Whiteflies

Two types of whiteflies constitute serious pests in the greenhouse: (1) the greenhouse whitefly (*Trialeurodes vaporariorum* Westwood) and (2) the sweet-potato whitefly (*Bemisia tabaci*). The sweet-potato whitefly appeared in recent years as a major pest. It is highly prone to developing pesticide resistance, has a wide range of host plants, and is particularly adept at transmitting viruses.

Whiteflies are small insects—about $^{1}/_{16}$ inch (2 mm) long—and have four wings (Figure 13–10). They are covered with a white waxy powder and resemble miniature moths. Whiteflies fly short distances when plant foliage is disturbed. They are found mainly on the undersides of young leaves. Crops on which whiteflies are particularly troublesome are ageratum, chrysanthemum, fuchsia, lantana, petunia, poinsettia, salvia, and tomato.

With the aid of a hand lens, it is possible to distinguish between the two types of whiteflies. The greenhouse whitefly adult is larger and holds its wings flat over its abdomen, somewhat parallel to the leaf surface. The sweet-potato

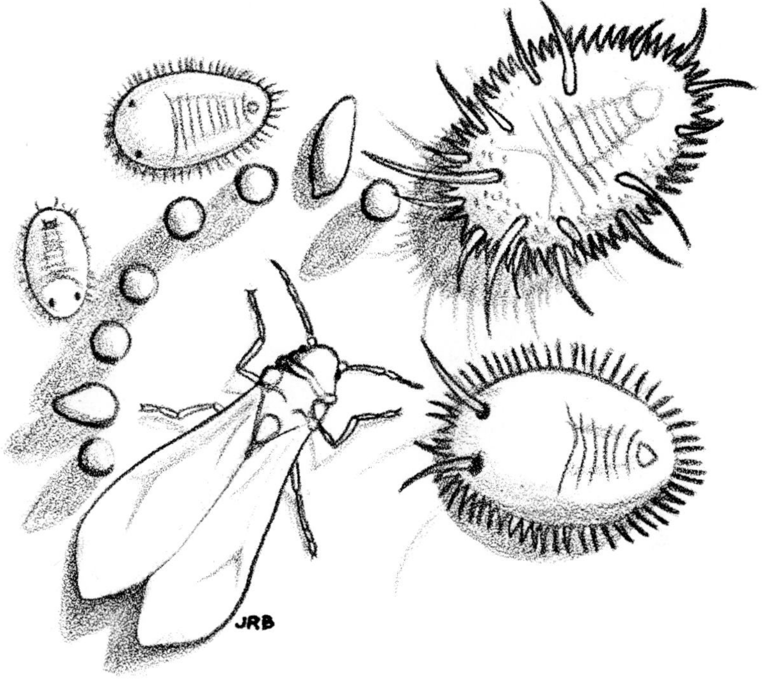

Figure 13–10

The greenhouse whitefly: eggs, nymphs, pupa, and adult all found on lower leaf surface. (*Sketch courtesy of* J. R. *Baker*, *North Carolina Agricultural* *Extension Service*, *Raleigh*, NC 27695–7613)

whitefly holds its wings at a 45° angle with the leaf surface so that they form an A-frame roof over the abdomen.

Although whiteflies are tropical insects, they are always present in one greenhouse or another during the winter. This is a testimony to their ability to tolerate pesticides. During the summer, they fly into the greenhouse from numerous host plants outside; in the winter, they spread from one greenhouse range to another on plant material or on the clothing of workers. Yellow clothing is especially attractive to whiteflies.

Whiteflies feed through a piercing–sucking mouth part. They sometimes cause yellow stippling of leaves. They excrete honeydew, which supports growth of a black sooty mold.

The life cycles of the greenhouse and sweet-potato whiteflies are fairly similar. The adult whitefly lays from just a few eggs to 20 eggs, often in a circle. Up to 250 eggs are laid by each female. Each is attached to the leaf in an upright fashion by a thin stalk. The eggs are creamy at first but eventually become dark. Newly hatched crawlers emerge from eggs in five to ten days and seek a feeding place.

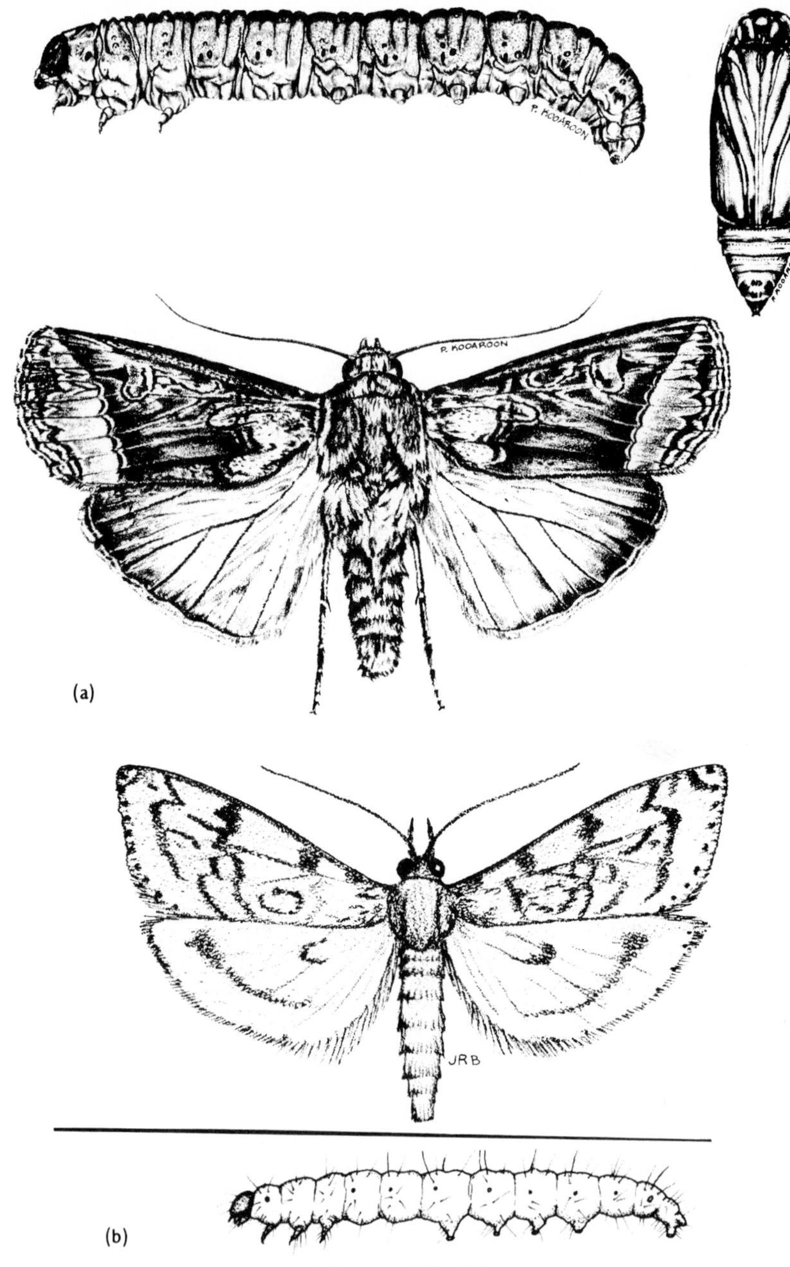

Figure 13–11

Various caterpillar pests in the greenhouse: (a) larva (*top*), pupa, and adult of the black cutworm; (b) larva and adult of the greenhouse leaf tier; (c) beet armyworm; and (d) corn earworm adult, eggs, larva, and pupa. (*Sketch courtesy of* J. R. *Baker and* P. Kooaroon, *North Carolina Agricultural* Extension *Service, Raleigh,* NC 27695–7613)

(c)

Pupa

Eggs

Larva

(d)

Figure 13–11 (*Continued*)

They insert their mouth into the leaf tissue and remain stationary for three weeks or so while they undergo three molts. During these stages, they are flat, scale-like insects and are transparent to greenish yellow in color. At the end of this period, they transform into a nonfeeding yellowish green pupa with two conspicuous eyes. A week later, the winged adult emerges. Females begin laying eggs two to seven days later. Depending upon temperature, the whole life cycle can take four to five weeks.

Eggs, pupae, and to a degree the scale-like larvae in the stage prior to the pupal stage are not susceptible to pesticides. The adults are readily killed. Aerosols and smokes do a good job of knocking down adults, but a day later new adults may emerge. At warm temperatures, pesticides may need to be applied as often as 3 times per week. Sprays, because of their residual activity, are much more effective, but a continual program with spray applications possibly as often as every five days must be maintained through the period of one life cycle. If one application is missed such that adults are afforded an opportunity to lay eggs, the whole program must be started again.

Worms

Worms, the immature stages of several types of moths, attack crops in a variety of ways (Figure 13–11). Worms are a problem, particularly during the warm months when moths abound outdoors. They randomly fly into the greenhouse or are attracted by lights. Once inside, moths lay eggs from which worms hatch.

Beet armyworms eat leaves of carnation, chrysanthemum, cyclamen, geranium, snapdragon, and other crops. Corn earworms eat succulent plant parts (preferably the buds) of chrysanthemums, gladioli, and roses. European corn borers tunnel into the stems of plants, particularly chrysanthemums. Cutworms feed on aerial plant parts. Leaf tiers and leaf rollers tie young leaves together or into a nest and feed on them from within.

Many other kinds of worms are occasionally encountered, but the control for all worms is similar. Stomach poisons with long residual lives are most effective, such as Mavrik® and Lannate®. Biological control is available through sprays of *Bacillus thuringiensis* Berliner (Biotrol BTB®, Dipel®, or Thuricide®). This is a bacterium that attacks worms. Plants must be sprayed as new growth occurs to keep all surfaces protected. Once worms are inside the stem, bud, or nest of webbed leaves, control of these insects is almost impossible.

BIOLOGICAL CONTROL

Biological control is a system of reducing pest populations through the action of living organisms that are encouraged and released by humans. The living organisms used to reduce pest populations can fall into three categories: *Predators* are insects that attack more than one host individual. Examples are ladybugs and predatory mites. *Parasites* attack a single host individual and complete their development in or on this individual. An example is the nematode *Steinernema feltiae*, which enters a leaf miner larva and develops within at the cost of life to the leaf miner. Predator and parasites are collectively termed *beneficial insects. Pathogens* are microorganisms that bring about disease in their host. *Bacillus thuringiensis* Berliner, which infects worm larvae, is a good example.

For biological control to work, it is necessary that a strict protocol be followed. The pest population must be at a relatively low level for effective control. If

Table 13–1

Pesticides That Are Safe To Use in a Biological Control Program with Beneficial Organisms*

Pesticide	*Concentration (ppm a.i.)*	*Comments*
Acaracides		
Cyhexatin (Plictran®)	250	Conflicting results not always safe.
Dicofol (Kelthane®, Mitigan®)	278	Harmful to *Encarsia* and *Phytoseiulus*.
Fenbutatin-oxide (Vendex®)	—	
Tetradifon	96	Very safe.
Aphidicides		
Diazinon (soil drench)	—	
Diflubenzuron (Dimilin®)	—	
Hostaquick (Heptenophos®)	340	Harmful to *Encarsia* and *Phytoseiulus*.
Larvicides		
Abamectin (Avid®)	—	Can also be used as an acaricide.
Bacillus thuringiensis	—	
Broad spectrum insecticides		
Soap (Safer® insecticidal soap)	—	Most are compatible. However, benomyl, bupirimate (Nimrod®), imazalil, and pyrazophos (Afugan®) are harmful to some natural enemies.
Fungicides	—	

*From Heinz and Parrella (1990).

a high population is present, it is necessary to decrease it with a safe pesticide such as insecticidal soap. The number of beneficial insects applied must be in a specified proportion to the number of pest individuals present. A surveillance program is necessary to determine the density of pests to meet both of these requirements. Pesticides toxic to the beneficial insects or pathogens must not be used during treatment, and residues of these cannot be present from previous applications. It is best that such pesticides not be applied for one month prior to application of beneficial organisms. Some reasonably safe pesticides that can be used under specific conditions include insecticidal soap, sulfur, and several others (see Table 13–1). Finally, environmental conditions may need to be altered in the greenhouse to favor the beneficial organisms and at the same time suppress the pests.

Most beneficial organisms are difficult to maintain and need to be ordered as required. Upon arrival, they are directly released in the crop. Again, this treatment dictates the need for constant surveillance in order to have the few days advance notice required for shipping time. Several insectaries produce beneficial organisms. (A list can be obtained from the California Department of Food and Agriculture, Biological Control Services Program, 3288 Meadowview Rd., Sacramento, CA 95832.)

The beneficial organisms described next are some of those that are commercially available. Considerable private and governmental research is underway. New introductions are occurring and will undoubtedly increase in the near future. Such biological control offers an excellent potential for coping with diminishing pesticides and with governmental pollution regulations.

Aphid Predator

The midge *Aphidoletes aphidimyza* feeds on several aphid species including the green peach aphid. Larvae of this predator inject a toxin into the knee of aphids that paralyzes them. The predator then sucks out the body fluids through the thorax of its prey. One larva can kill 4–65 aphids per day. *Aphidoletes* are released at the rate of one pupa per ten aphids or one pupa per square yard (1.2 pupa/m^2). The predator should be reintroduced 3–4 times every week or two. Optimum conditions include a temperature between 73°F and 77°F (23°C and 25°C) and a relative humidity of 80–90 percent.

Leaf Miner Parasites

Diglyphus isaea is a black wasp about 2 mm long with short antennae. This parasite enters the leaf miner's tunnel, kills the pest, and lays an egg beside it. The developing predator feeds on the dead leaf miner. The parasite leaves the tunnel and then kills other small leaf miner larvae for food and eventually lays an egg in a tunnel to start the cycle over again.

Another black wasp, *Dacnusa sibirica*, slightly larger (3 mm) with long antennae, lays an egg in a leaf miner larva. The larva continues to live, while the parasite develops within. Only the parasite emerges from the leaf miner pupa.

A nematode parasite is also used for killing leaf miners. *Steinernema feltiae* enters the leaf miner larva through body openings such as the mouth. Inside, the nematode penetrates the gut wall and releases a bacterium *Xenorhadbis nematophilus* that kills the host. The nematode is sprayed on plants at night because it is killed by UV light during the day. The temperature should be about 70°F (21°C), and the drying time must be at least several hours to give the nematode time to swim to the host.

Mealybug Predator and Parasite

Larvae of the Australian lady beetle *Cryptolaemus montrouzieri* kill mealybugs and will also kill aphids and scale insects if food is in short supply. The adult beetle lays eggs among the mealybugs. When the beetle larva emerges, it sucks the body contents out of mealybug eggs and young nymphs. This predator requires a large supply of food; thus, the pest population does not have to be reduced to a low level before its introduction. Optimum conditions for egg laying and larval development are a temperature of 72–77°F (22–25°C) and a relative humidity of 70–80 percent. As in the case of aphid predators, ants have to be controlled since they will protect these pests from predators. A boric acid bait can be used for controlling ants. The predator is released at the rate of two predators per square yard (1.2 predators/m^2).

There is also a parasite of mealybugs. The wasp *Leptomastix dactylopii* attacks only citrus mealybugs by laying an egg in either the third-stage nymph or the adult mealybug. The wasp develops inside the mealybug.

Mite Predators

Several species of mites have been employed to kill damaging spider mites, primarily two-spotted spider mites. The predator mites draw out the body fluid of host mites. The predatory mites are released when the pest population is light and at the rate of 20 predators per square yard (24 predators/m^2). Reintroductions are made at two- to four-week intervals until control is achieved. Sometimes, two or more predatory mite species are introduced simultaneously to increase their surviving power and effectiveness. Each predatory mite species has a different set of optimum conditions. *Phytoseiulus persimilis* develops best at 69–81°F (20–27°C) and a relative humidity of 60–90 percent. *Phytoseiulus longipes* handles temperatures up to 100°F (38°C) and somewhat lower humidity levels. *Amblyseius californicus* develops best at more intermediate temperatures up to 90°F (32°C) but at relative humidity levels above 60 percent. Predatory mites are shipped in drinking straws, capsules, or shaker bottles.

Thrips Predator

The mite *Amblyseius cucumeris* attacks mites, including spider mites, as well as western flower thrips. The predatory mite feeds on young thrips larvae. Each predator can destroy one mite per day during its 30-day life. Favorable conditions for the predator include moderate temperatures with an optimum at 86°F (30°C) and a high humidity. Fortunately, in the case of spider mite pests, this is the opposite of the conditions favorable to the pest. When thrips are first detected, predator mites are released at the rate of 30 per plant. The predator is sold in cereal bran.

Whitefly Parasite

The chalcidoid wasp *Encarsia formosa* is sold for parasitizing greenhouse whitefly pupae. The female adult lays eggs in 50–100 pupae. Most adult wasps are female. The egg hatches inside the pupa, and the parasite remains there until it has finished its development to the adult stage. The adult emerges from the dead, black pupa and immediately seeks other pupae to begin the life cycle over again.

Encarsia populations develop best when the temperature is at 73–81°F (23–27°C), the relative humidity is 50–70 percent, and the light intensity is 650 fc (7,000 lux) or higher. At 81°F, *Encarsia* produces twice as many eggs as the whitefly; below 70°F, the whitefly produces 10 times as many eggs. Under lower light intensities, *Encarsia* is not fully reproductive. This parasite is often available on paper tags containing parasitized whitefly pupae. The tags are hung on plants to be treated.

General Insect Pathogen

The bacterium *Bacillus thuringiensis* Berliner is available commercially under several trade names. This bacterium is non-infectious to plants and humans but does kill the caterpillars (larva) of many species of moths. The caterpillar ingests the bacterial spores. Inside the insect, the spore germinates and the bacteria enter the blood system. Shortly after, the insect stops feeding; after several days, it dies.

METHODS OF PESTICIDE APPLICATION

Eight methods for bringing pesticides into contact with insects on plants are widely used. For a given pest problem, generally two or more methods of control are available. Existing equipment, weather conditions, the type and stage of development of a crop or pest, susceptibility of a particular crop to injury, and economics will dictate which method to use.

Sprays, dusts, and mists require more effort to apply but leave a residue on the plant that continues to kill after the application. Aerosols, fogs, and smokes propel fine droplets of the pesticide into the air so that any existing insects, whether they are on the crop, beneath the bench, or elsewhere, are killed. An effective residue is not left by these methods of applications. Repeated application is necessary; otherwise, these systems must be used in conjunction with spraying or dusting. While aerosols, fogs, and smokes are simple to apply, the materials tend to be expensive and only a limited number of insecticides are available in such forms. Systemic insecticides in granules are not the easiest to apply, but they offer a long residual period. A rather broad spectrum of insects and nematodes can be killed with a material such as oxamyl (Vydate®) for a period of several weeks. On some crops, systemic pesticides eliminate the need for a tedious spray program.

Spray Application of Pesticide

Spraying is the most common method of pesticide application in the greenhouse. Numerous pesticides are formulated for mixing with water and spraying on the plant. Emulsifiable concentrates (EC) are pesticides in an oily preparation with an emulsifying agent that renders the oil miscible in water. Without the emulsifying agent, the oil (which dissolves the pesticide) would not mix with water.

Wettable powder (WP) pesticides are solid particles, usually clays, that are dispersed in water. The spray tank should have an agitator in it to prevent the particles from settling out. WP formulations tend to be less toxic to plants than EC formulations of the same pesticide.

Leaf and stem surfaces have a waxy cuticle covering them. This surface has a tendency to repel water to varying degrees depending upon the plant species. When spray droplets bead up on the leaf surface, a considerable area is left unprotected and small insects are able to continue feeding. The problem can be remedied by the addition of a surfactant to the spray. Surfactants are also known as spreaders, wetters, or spreader-stickers. The surfactant lowers the surface tension, which increases the ability of the spray to spread out over the plant surface. A number of surfactants are on the market for this purpose, and among them are materials such as Du Pont Spreader-Sticker®, Triton B-1956®, Bio-Film®, and Ortho R-77®. The recommended rate should be used because too much surfactant can cause plant distortion. Mild liquid household detergents can also be used at the rate of 1 pint per 100 gallons (½ teaspoon per gallon) (1.25 ml/l). Incomplete wetting is mainly a problem of wettable powders, since EC formulations already contain an emulsifying agent that is itself a surfactant.

WP formulations should be first mixed in a bucket and then poured into the sprayer tank. This is done to avoid solid deposits plugging the nozzle or an error in the concentration. Sprayers can range from 1–4 gallon (4–15 l) hand-pumped units to electric or gasoline motor-powered sprayers of 10–200 gallon (40–750 l)

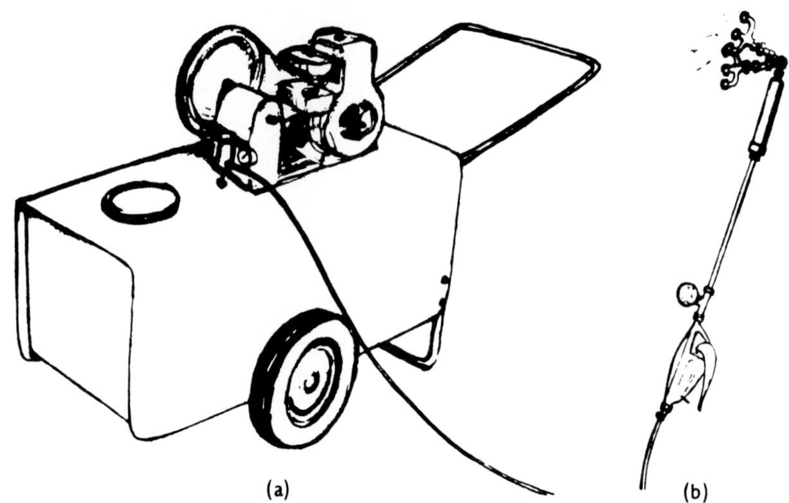

Figure 13–12

(a) A gasoline motor-powered pesticide sprayer with a 30 gallon (110 l) tank capacity typical of many used for greenhouse pest control. Such sprayers commonly operate at 200 psi (1,380 kPa). (b) A Cornell nozzle used for spraying greenhouse crops. Six nozzles spray at a variety of angles to ensure complete coverage of upper and lower leaf surfaces. A gauge indicates spray pressure, and a lever gives the operator on–off control of the spray. (*Sketch courtesy of* J. R. *Baker, North Carolina Agricultural Extension Service, Raleigh,* NC 27695–7613)

capacity (Figure 13–12a). Sprayers up to 30 gallons (110 l) are on wheels and are brought into the end or main aisles of the greenhouse. A hose attached to the sprayer is dragged along each aisle to permit spraying of the entire bench. A nozzle at the end of the hose is used to break the spray into fine droplets and direct the spray in a full pattern for maximum coverage of plants sprayed. Pressures up to several hundred pounds per square inch (psi) are used to ensure small droplets. A pressure of 200 psi (1,380 kPa) is very common. A pressure gauge should be installed at the sprayer or near the nozzle to assure the correct pressure for even coverage.

To ensure that the undersides of leaves are sprayed, the nozzle should be at a 45–90° angle to the axis of the nozzle handle, or a sprayer with several nozzles, such as the Cornell nozzle (Figure 13–12b), at different angles should be used. The nozzle should be handled in a sweeping action to ensure that all of the plant is covered. Particular attention should be paid to reach plants in the interior of a bench; otherwise, a point of reinfestation is left.

Some larger greenhouse ranges make use of a permanently installed plumbing system that brings spray from the mixing tank to any given section in the range. A single spray hose is attached at the point where spraying is desired. Consideration must be given to disposing of the pesticide in the line after each use.

Many sprays are corrosive to the spray equipment. They can be dangerous to workers if left in the hose or sprayer. With time, solid deposits can occur in the tank, lines, or nozzles. Some pesticides, upon standing for some time in the lines, break down to a form injurious to plants. For these reasons, the sprayer should be emptied after use and rinsed out. Clear water then should be pumped through the entire system to clean it.

Dust Application of Pesticide

A few pesticides can be obtained in a dust form. The active pesticide is mixed with talc, clay, diatomaceous earth, or similar filler. Dusters are used to apply dusts. These range from hand-cranked units for small greenhouse uses to large motorized dusters. Dusts, being lightweight, remain in the air for a period of time. Respirators or gas masks, depending on the toxicity of the pesticide, should be used to avoid inhaling them. Dusting is not a common method of pest control because of the visible residue left on the plants.

Ultralow-Volume (ULV) Applicators

Several types of ULV pesticide equipment are in various stages of development and use (Beasley and Skroch 1984; Weekman 1983). These use pesticides at 10–20 times the concentration encountered in hydraulic sprayers. One type seen around greenhouses since the early 1970s is the "mist blower." Application volumes of 5–10 gallons per acre (45–90 l/ha) are common for mist blowers. Concentrated pesticide is passed down a tube or plate such that at the bottom edge the liquid covers a large area in a very thin film. A high-velocity airstream passing perpendicular to the bottom edge shears off small droplets of pesticide and delivers them to the plant.

Droplet size is very important in terms of the volume of pesticide formulation needed and the pattern of leaf coverage. Hydraulic sprayers produce a wide range of droplet sizes. The large droplets, several hundred microns, are propelled in a fairly straight line, impacting on the outer leaves. Smaller droplets reach inner foliage as they are carried around the outer leaves by turbulence and eddy effects in the airstream. Ultrasmall droplets, less than 50 microns, are a problem because they drift in the air for considerable time and may even leave the greenhouse.

Droplet size dictates the volume of spray liquid required for effective coverage of foliage. If the droplet size is cut in half from 400 microns to 200 microns, only one-eighth of the volume is required for effective foliar coverage. Halving droplet size again to 100 microns reduces the required volume again by one-eighth, for a total reduction to one-sixty-fourth of the original volume. Uniformity of droplet sizes is important so that they distribute uniformly over the foliage. Small droplets will not cover all of a given leaf. This is permissible because there is a zone of protection extending out from each droplet. One large droplet in a nonuniform spray will contain the same volume of liquid as a high number of small droplets, but the large droplet greatly reduces the leaf area contacted. The volume of pesticide required, thus, goes up. Ideally, ULV applicators should deliver small (50–100 micron), uniform droplets.

Advantages of ULV pesticide application include (1) the use of less pesticide, (2) a reduction in time required for application, and (3) the possibility of highly uniform coverage. Disadvantages are found in the possibilities of applying too little or too much pesticide in local areas. It is difficult to see the pesticide emitted from a mist blower and almost impossible for other lower-volume equipment. The applicator must predetermine the volume of pesticide and length of time for application and then adhere strictly to this schedule.

A second type of ULV equipment is the spinning-disk applicator (Beasley and Skroch 1984; Weekman 1983). Spinning disks offer an advantage over mist blowers in that a higher percentage of droplets can be produced in the 50–100 micron range. This lowers the required volume to about 1 gallon per acre (10 l/ha). A concentrated pesticide is delivered to a spinning disk either by gravity flow or under low pressure. The liquid moves by centrifugal force to the outer perimeter of the disk, where small droplets shear off into the air. In some equipment, the centrifugal force continues to move the droplets out to the plant. In this case, a high proportion will land on the upper leaf surfaces unless the applicator is careful to direct the mist toward all surfaces. Other equipment has a fan to generate an airstream that picks up the droplets leaving the spinning disk and directs them at the plant. Both leaf surfaces are easily contacted. Droplet size can be controlled by the pesticide flow rate to the disk or by the speed of rotation of the disk. Large droplets are avoided in order to permit use of lower volumes of water with the pesticide, while ultrasmall droplets are avoided to prevent pesticide drift.

Perhaps the most recent addition to the ULV applicator list is the electrostatic applicator (Anon. 1979; Lindquist 1983). This applicator produces small droplets and develops a positive electrical charge in them. The positive droplets are attracted to plants since plants always carry a negative electrical charge. Because the droplets are of similar charge, they repel one another, thereby distributing themselves uniformly over the plant surfaces. There are problems yet to be worked out, including the need for proper grounding of the plant. Plastic sheets under the plants or plastic trays, such as those used for bedding plants, can impede grounding.

Aerosol Application of Pesticide

A few insecticides (no fungicides) can be obtained in cylinders under pressure (Figure 13–13, Table 13–2). Propellants used in these cylinders include hydrocarbons such as isobutane and isopropane, fluorocarbon (Freon), and compressed carbon dioxide gas. The former propellants are under pressure in liquid form.

Figure 13–13

Application of an aerosol insecticide, resmethrin, to plants in a greenhouse. (*Photo courtesy of Whitmire Research Laboratories, Inc.*, St. Louis, MO)

Table 13–2

Pesticides Available in Aerosol, Fog, and Smoke Formulations

	Formulation		
Pesticide	*Aerosol*	*Fog*	*Smoke*
DDVP (Vapona®)		×	×
Dithio (sulfotepp)		×	×
Endosulfan (Thiodan®)		×	×
Lindane		×	×
Nicotine		×	×
Acephate (Orthene®)	×	×	
Parathion			×
Resmethrin	×	×	
Tedion			×
Tedion-dithio			×

When released into the lower pressure of the atmosphere, they expand into a gas and move at a high velocity, carrying small droplets (15–20 microns) of insecticide with them. The carbon dioxide gas likewise expands when released.

The small liquid pesticide droplets are small enough to drift on the air currents, quickly dispersing throughout the entire greenhouse atmosphere. With time, they settle out, mostly onto the upper surfaces of plants. Since little residue accumulates on lower leaves and under surfaces, this form of pesticide application is used for immediate killing of existing insects and is very often used in combination with a spray, dust, or mist application that leaves a residue.

The quantity of insecticide to be applied is in some cases related to the volume of the greenhouse. For other products, including resmethrin (SBP 1382®) and acephate (Orthene®), it is applied at the rate of 1 pound product per 3,000–6,000 ft^2 of greenhouse floor area (0.8–1.6 g/m^2). It is usually sufficient to make one pass through the center aisle of narrow greenhouses—those up to 35 feet (11 m) wide—and two or more passes through wider greenhouses.

There are some very critical temperature requirements for the use of aerosol bombs. The temperature should be preferably 70–80°F (21–27°C). Below 60°F (16°C), improper distribution and reduced pest kill occur. At temperatures above 85°F (29°C), injury can occur to the plants. One temperature should be selected and maintained as closely as possible since dosage rate is dependent upon it. This temperature range is best held during the evening in the summer or late afternoon in the winter. Pyrethroid materials such as resmethrin break down in sunlight. It would be best to apply these in the evening.

It is also important that the aerosol be applied on a calm day so that it is not drawn out of the greenhouse or caused to distribute unevenly. The greenhouse must remain closed for at least two hours. It is usually left closed overnight. Furthermore, moisture on the foliage during application can lead to injury. The plants should be well watered and the foliage dry at the time of application.

Fog Application of Pesticide

A limited number of insecticides and fungicides are available in oil-base carrier preparations for use in fogging equipment (see Table 13–2). Most are prepared at 10 percent insecticidal strength. In addition, carriers are available for mixing with most EC and WP insecticides and fungicides to permit their use in fog equipment. This method of application is very similar to that of aerosols. The same precautions must be followed. The pesticide is heated by a device to form small droplets (10–60 microns), which are then propelled into the greenhouse atmosphere. Unlike the aerosol, which cannot be seen, a white fog forms in this case and makes it easier to know whether all areas have been treated equally.

Various foggers may have gasoline motors or propane burners and may be carried on the back or pulled through the greenhouse on wheels. The pesticide formulation is injected into either a hot pipe, or the exhaust, or a hot airstream to cause vaporization. For narrow greenhouses, one pass through the center aisle is sufficient; in wide greenhouses, the fogger should be moved through two or more aisles. Protective clothing and masks should be worn in accordance with the toxicity of the pesticide since it is very difficult to avoid contact in this method of application.

The fog should not be directed toward the plants because heavy deposits as well as hot exhaust scales can be injurious to the plant. The oils used are injurious to some plant species. Flowers tend to be more susceptible than foliage. The fog should be aimed into the aisles.

Air leaks in the greenhouse and windy conditions outside make it difficult to do a uniform job with fogging. Carbon buildup in the machine may also impair the effectiveness. The fogger should be cleaned periodically with wood alcohol or with a cleaner provided by the manufacturer.

Smoke Application of Pesticide

Smokes are the simplest forms of pesticides to use. No special equipment is needed. Small containers of a combustible formulation containing the pesticide are placed along the center aisle of the greenhouse and ignited, usually with a sparkler. The pesticide is carried in the smoke throughout the greenhouse. Pesticides that can be used in smoke are limited to those few that can withstand the intense heat (see Table 13–2).

Smokes are generally less phytotoxic to plant foliage and flowers than aerosols and fogs, but the dose rate is as important. The volume of the greenhouse must be calculated and divided by the volume one can will treat to determine how many cans to use.

Further precautions are the same for smokes as they are for aerosols and fogs:

1. Do not use at temperatures above 85°F (29°C) or below 60°F (16°C).
2. Close ventilators on the greenhouse and turn off fans.
3. Avoid using these methods on a windy day.
4. Be sure the plants are well watered and the foliage is dry.
5. Once the pesticide is applied, place warning signs on all doors indicating that the greenhouse is under fumigation.

Volatilization of Pesticides

According to the current pesticide law, it is permissible for a grower to apply pesticides in a manner not stated on the label as long as it is not forbidden on the label. However, advisory personnel may not recommend to a grower a method of application not specifically on the label. Volatilization is one such method currently gaining acceptance among growers.

In this method, household frying pans are situated throughout the greenhouse above plant height. Pesticides, such as the fungicide Bayleton®, the insecticide resmethrin, and the miticide Pentac®, are added to the pan in the quantity labeled for spraying the crop in the area affected by the pan. The pan is wired to a time clock, which turns the system on during the night for a period of six to eight hours. A few hours before employees arrive in the morning, the system shuts off. Final dissipation of the pesticide is accomplished by turning on the exhaust fans. This system has been highly effective in controlling powdery mildew on roses. It has advantages of labor simplicity and very low residual levels for employee contact.

Root-Media Applications

Soil-inhabiting insects can be killed by drenching root media with insecticides such as resmethrin and insecticidal soap. Apart from these, the systemic insecticide oxamyl (Vydate®) warrants special mention. It is available as a 10 percent granular formulation that is applied to the root-medium surface. When moistened, the insecticide is released into the root medium, killing insects in it. From there, the insecticide is taken up by plants, rendering them toxic to insects feeding on them. Oxamyl is very effective on fungus gnats as well as a broad range of other insects. It has not been too effective recently for resistant strains of spider mites, thrips, or whiteflies.

Application to individual pots can be made with a small spoon or to large numbers of pots through applicator equipment such as the Perfect-A-Feed® and the EZ Feeder Measure Master®, which have been modified for metering out small quantities. One-eighth of a teaspoon (0.6 cc) is used for spaced 6 inch (15 cm) pots. These insecticides must be applied uniformly over the surface of the pot to ensure even uptake in all parts of the plants. Broadcast application can be made to pots from rim to rim or to fresh flower beds. Holes are punched in the cap of plastic or metal cans with an ice pick. The insecticide is placed in the can and is shaken from it over the plants. The plants should be dry so that the granules settle on the root medium.

Oxamyl in the granular formulation is moderately toxic to humans. The applicant should wear protective clothing and a respirator. Care should be taken to avoid spilling granules on nongrowing areas. Equipment that grinds granules should be avoided since safety rests in the entrapment of these insecticides in the granules. Once applied, they should be watered in well to begin the release process. For a period of one week, the root medium should not be handled.

Systemic granular insecticides should not be used in root media prior to planting because this will bring the workers into needless contact with them. Granules should not be applied prior to steam pasteurization since this can cause a hazardous release.

Table 13–3

Greenhouse Ornamental and House Plant Insect Control*

NOTE: Always follow label directions when handling or applying pesticides. *Aldicarb* is extremely toxic. Apply after plants are established and as pests appear. Abamectin B_1 may injure ferns. Repeat in 6 to 8 weeks if necessary. *Demeton* is extremely toxic and also may damage roots of chrysanthemum. *Dichlorvos* may damage chrysanthemum varieties Shasta, Pink Champagne and Nightingale. *Dimethoate* will damage chrysanthemums and Easter lily. Use on trial basis on each variety of azalea, fern, gloxinia, hydrangea, schefflera, and Saintpaulia. *Endosulfan* will damage some geraniums and chrysanthemum varieties Bottafon Deluxe and others. *Malathion* may injure begonia, crassula, fern, petunia, orchids, violet, Saintpaulia, gloxinia, some red carnations and some rose varieties. *Metaldehyde* will injure Cattleya and Phalaenopsis orchids. *Naled* may damage chrysanthemum variety Pink Champagne, dutchman's pipe, wandering jew, poinsettias and rose varieties White Butterfly and Golden Rapture. *Nicotina sulfate* will damage young chrysanthemum and lily. *Plictran* may injure poinsettia bracts and chrysanthemum blossoms; do not add surfactant when applied to roses; will injure crassula. *TEPP* is extremely toxic. *Tetradifon* may injure roses, especially White Butterfly and Cinderelia.

Smoke generators are available containing combinations of many of the above materials. Be sure to follow manufacturers' recommendations as to rates of use and precautions for the operator. Treated houses should be ventiliated for one hour before re-entering. As a rule, aerosols are used at a rate of 1 lb per 50,000 cu ft of house. For best results, bomb temperature should be 80° to 90° F. and greenhouse air temperature 70° to 75° F. May bleach open mums or cause leaf drop on roses (if sulfur present).

Some of the insecticides above are extremely toxic. All instructions on the label regarding handling, protective clothing, etc. should be followed. They are recommended for use by experienced operators. Learn symptoms of poisoning. If symptoms develop, call a doctor. Take the label or pesticide container to the hospital with the victim.

Flower	Insect or Mite	Insecticide and Formulation	Amount of Formulation per Gallon of Spray	Amount Per 100 Gallons of Water	Minimum Interval Between Application and Reentry	Precautions and Remarks
ANY	Aphids	acephate (Orthene) 75 SP	2/3 to 1 2/3 tsp	1/3 to 2/3 lb	When dry	
		bifenthrin (Talstar) 10 WP	1 to 5 tsp	6.4 to 32 oz	When dry	
		cyfluthrin (Tempo 2) 24.3 EC	3/32 tsp	1½ oz		
		endosulfan (Thiodan) 24.2 EC	2 tsp	2 pt	24 hours	Apply as needed. Repeated application usually necessary.
		50 WP	1 tbsp	1 lb	24 hours	
		diazinon (Knox-Out) 23 EC	1 to 2 tbsp	1 to 2 lb	When dry	
		†1 A			After house ventilated for 1 hour	5 to 10 seconds per 100 sq ft.
		fluvalinate (Mavrik) 22.3 F	⅛ to ⅝ tsp	2 to 10 oz	When dry	Also labeled as a dip.
		†horticultural oil (Ultra Fine, Sun Spray) 98.8 EC	2½ to 5 tbsp	1 to 2 gal	When dry	
		†soap (Insecticidal) 50.5 EC	4 oz	3½ gal	When dry	
		lindane 25 WP	1 tbsp	1 lb	When dry	
		†malathion 57 EC	2 tsp	2 pt	When dry	
		nicotine sulfate 40 EC	1½ tsp	1½ pt		

*From Baker (1990). In *North Carolina Agricultural Chemicals Manual.* College of Agr. Life Sci., North Carolina State Univ., Raleigh, NC 27695–7603.

†Suitable for home use

Table 13–3 *(continued)*

Flower	Insect or Mite	Insecticide and Formulation	Amount of Formulation per Gallon of Spray	Amount Per 100 Gallons of Water	Minimum Interval Between Application and Reentry	Precautions and Remarks
		oxamyl (Vydate L) 24 L	2 to 4 tsp	2 to 4 pt		
		10 G			After granules worked into topsoil or watered in.	22 to 30 oz per 1000 sq ft.
		resmethrin 24.3 EC	1 tsp	1 pt	When dry	
		sumithrin 25 EC 0.5 A	1 tsp	1 pt	When dry	5 to 10 seconds per 100 sq ft.
		dichlorvos (Vapona) endosulfan (Thiodan) sulfotepp (Dithiono, Plantfume 103) parathion			After house ventilated for 1 hour.	Smoke generators.
		acephate (PT 1300) 3 A			After house ventilated for 1 hour.	1 lb/3000 sq ft. Treat as late in day as possible. Ventilate the next morning.
		naled (Dibrom) 60 EC			After house ventilated for 1 hour.	Apply on steam pipes at rate of 1 oz per 10,000 cu ft. Have pipes at 160°F. Will corrode pipes with continued use.
		†pyrethrins (X-clude) 0.3 A			After house ventilated for 1 hour	5 to 10 seconds per 100 sq ft.
	Armyworms	bifenthrin (Talstar) 10 WP cyfluthrin (Tempo 2) 24.3 EC	1 to 5 tsp 1/16 tsp	6.4 to 32 oz 1 oz	When dry	
		fluvalinate (Mavrik) 22.3 F	⅛ to ⅝ tsp	2 to 10 oz	When dry	
	Broad mite	bifenthrin (Talstar) 10 WP dienochlor (Pentac) 50 WP 38 F	1 to 5 tsp 1 tsp ½ tsp	6.4 to 32 oz 8 oz ½ pt	When dry	Repeat in 5 to 14 days.
	Brown soft scale	bifenthrin (Talstar) 10 WP sulfotepp (Dithiono) 5 A	1 to 5 tsp	6.4 to 32 oz	After house ventilated for 1 hour	
		bendiocarb (Dycarb, Ficam, Turcam) 76 WP	¾ tsp	5½ oz	When dry	

Cabbage looper	cyfluthrin (Tempo 2) 24.3 EC	1/16 tsp	1 oz		
	fluvalinate (Mavrik) 22.3 F	⅛ to ⅝ tsp	2 to 10 oz	When dry	
	naled (Dibrom) 60 EC	1½ tsp	1½ pt		Treat as needed.
	dichlorvos (Vapona) smoke generator			After house ventilated for 1 hour	
	acephate (PT 1300) 3 A				
	pyrethrins (X-clude) 0.3 A			After house ventilated for 1 hour	5 to 10 seconds per 100 sq ft.
Crickets	cyfluthrin (Tempo 2) 24.3 EC	1/16 tsp	1 oz		Apply as for aphids.
	†soap (Insecticidal soap) 50.5 EC	4 oz	3⅛ gal	When dry	
	pyrethrins (X-clude) 0.3 A			After house ventilated for 1 hour	5 to 10 seconds per 100 sq ft.
Cucumber beetle	bifenthrin (Talstar) 10 WP	1 to 5 tsp	6.4 to 32 oz		
	fluvalinate (Mavrik) 22.3F	⅛ to ⅝ tsp	2 to 10 oz	When dry	
	pyrethrins (X-clude) 0.3 A			After house ventilated for 1 hour	5 to 10 seconds per 100 sq ft.
	†resmethin (SBP 1382) A			After house ventilated for 1 hour	1 lb/3000 sq ft. Treat as late in day as possible. Ventilate late the next morning.
Cutworms	bifenthrin (Talstar) 10 WP	1 to 5 tsp	6.4 to 32 oz		Apply to soil beneath plants.
	cyfluthrin (Tempo 2) 24.3 EC	1/16 tsp	1 oz		
	†carbaryl (Sevin) 50 WP	2 tbsp	2 lb	When dry	
	fluvalinate (Mavrik) 22.3 F	1/6 to 1/3 tsp	2 to 5 oz	When dry	
Earwigs	†soap (Insecticidal) 50.5 EC	4 oz	3⅛ gal	When dry	
Fungus gnats	*Bacillus thuringiensis* H-14 (Gnatrol AS)	1 to 8 tsp	1 to 8 pt	When dry	
	(Gnatrol 12 AS)	½ to 4 tsp	½ to 4 pt	When dry	
	pyrethrins (X-clude) 0.3 A			After house ventilated for 1 hour	5 to 10 seconds per 100 sq ft.
	†resmethrin (SBP 1382) A			After house ventilated for 1 hour	1 lb/3000 sq ft. Treat as late in day as possible. Ventilate late the next morning.
	24.3 EC	1 tsp	1 pt	When dry	

†Suitable for home use

Table 13–3 *(continued)*

Flower	Insect or Mite	Insecticide and Formulation	Amount of Formulation per Gallon of Spray	Amount Per 100 Gallons of Water	Minimum Interval Between Application and Reentry	Precautions and Remarks
ANY (continued)		oxamyl (Vydate L) 24 L	2 to 4 tsp	2 to 4 pt		
		10 G			After granules worked into top-soil or watered in.	22 to 30 oz per 1000 sq ft.
		diazinon (Knox-Out) 23 EC	1 to 2 tbsp	3 to 6 pt	When dry	
	Hemispherical scale	bendiocarb (Dycarb, Ficam, Turcam) 76 WP	3/8 tsp	2½ to 20 oz	When dry	Avoid excessive runoff.
	Leafminers	abamectin B_1 (Avid) 2 EC	½ tsp	8 oz	When dry	Do not use on ferns or conifers.
		bifenthrin (Talstar) 10 WP	1 to 5 tsp	6.4 to 32 oz		
		dichlorvos (Vapona) smoke generator acephate (PT 1300) A			After house ventilated for 1 hour	
		†malathion 57 EC	2 tsp	2 pt	When dry	
		permethrin (Pramex) 13.3 EC	1 to 3 tsp	1 to 3 pt	When dry	
		oxamyl (Vydate) 24 L	2 to 4 tsp	2 to 4		
		10 G			After granules worked into soil or watered in thoroughly.	22 to 30 oz per 1000 sq ft.
		diazinon (Knox-Out) 23 EC	1 to 2 tbsp	3 to 6 pt	When dry	
	Leafrollers	naled (Dibrom) 60 EC acephate (PT 1300) 3A			After house ventilated for 1 hour	Apply as for aphids.
	Mealybugs	acephate (PT 1300) 3A dichlorvos (Vapona) sulfotepp (Dithiono, Plantfume 103) naled (Dibrom) 60 EC			After house ventilated for 1 hour	
		†pyrethrins (X-clude) 0.3 A			After house ventilated for 1 hour	5 to 10 seconds per 100 sq ft.

Mealybugs (cont.)	acephate (Orthene) 75 SP	1 1/3 tsp	2/3 lb	When dry	
	bifenthrin (Talstar) 10 WP	1 to 5 tsp	6.4 to 32 oz		
	bendiocarb (Dycarb, Ficam, Turcam) 76 WP	¾tsp	6 to 20 oz	When dry	
	cyfluthrin (Tempo 2) 24.3 EC	3/32 tsp	1½ oz		
	diazinon (Knox-Out) 23 EC	1 to 2 tbsp	3 to 6 pt	When dry	
	fluvalinate (Mavrik) 22.3 F	⅛ to ⅝ tsp	2 to 10 oz	When dry	Labeled as a dip.
	†horticultural oil (Ultra Fine, Sun Spary) 98.8 EC	2½ to 5 tbsp	1 to 2 gal	When dry	
	†malathion 57 EC	2 tsp	2 pt	When dry	
	†soap (Insecticidal) 50.5 EC	4 oz	3⅛ gal	When dry	
	sumithrin 25 EC 0.5 A	2 tsp	2 pt	When dry	5 to 10 seconds per 100 sq ft.
	oxamyl (Vydate L) 24 L	2 to 4 tsp	2 to 4 pt		
	10 G			After granules worked into soil or watered in thoroughly.	22 to 30 oz per 1000 sq ft.
Millipedes	ethion 81.9 EC	5 oz	4 gal	When dry	75 gal per 2500 sq ft bench space.
	†malathion 57 EC	1 tsp	1 pt	When dry	150 sq ft per gal each 7 to 10 days.
Mites	diazinon (Knox-Out) 23 EC	1 to 2 tbsp	3 to 6 pt	When dry	
	fluvalinate (Mavrik) 22.3 F	⅛ to ⅝ tsp	2 to 10 oz	When dry	
Omnivorous leafroller	bifenthrin (Talstar) 10 WP	1 2/3 to 4 tsp	10 to 24 oz	When dry	
Plant bugs	bifenthrin (Talstar) 10 WP	1 to 5 tsp	6.4 to 32 oz		
	cyfluthrin (Tempo 2) 24.3 EC	1/16 to 1/8 tsp	1 to 2 oz		
	†resmethrin 24.3 EC	1 tsp	1 pt	When dry	
	fluvalinate (Mavrik) 22.3 F	⅛ to ⅝ tsp	2 to 10 oz	When dry	
Rose chafer	endosulfan (Thiodan) 24.2 EC	2 tsp	2 pt		
	50 WP	2 tsp	2/3 lb		
Scales	acephate (Orthene) 75 SP	—	2/3 lb	When dry	

†Suitable for home use

Table 13–3 *(continued)*

Flower	Insect or Mite	Insecticide and Formulation	Amount of Formulation per Gallon of Spray	Amount Per 100 Gallons of Water	Minimum Interval Between Application and Reentry	Precautions and Remarks
ANY (continued)		diazinon (Knox-Out) 23 EC	1 to 2 tbsp	3 to 6 pt	When dry	
		†pyrethrins (X-clude) 0.3 A			After house ventilated for 1 hour	5 to 10 seconds per 100 sq ft.
		oxamyl (Vydate L) 23.4 EC	2 to 4 tsp	2 to 4 pt		
		10 G			After granules worked into soil or watered in thoroughly.	22 to 30 oz per 1000 sq ft.
		acephate (PT 1300) 3 A				Apply as for aphids.
		†soap (Insecticidal) 50.5 EC	4 oz	3⅛ gal	When dry	
	Slugs and snails	†metaldehyde B 15 D				More than one application usually necessary. Follow label directions.
	Sowbugs	lindane 25 WP †malathion 4 D	1 tbsp	1 lb		1 gal/150 sq ft each 7 to 10 days.
	Spider mites	abamectin B_1 (Avid) 2 EC	¼ tsp	4 oz	When dry	Do not use on ferns or conifers.
		bifenthrin (Talstar) 10 WP	1 to 5 tsp	6.4 to 32 oz	When dry	
		dichlorvos (Vapona) sulfotepp (Dithiono)			After house ventilated for 1 hour.	Smoke generators.
		†horticultural oil (Ultra Fine, Sun Spray) 98.8 EC	2½ to 5 tbsp	1 to 2 gal	When dry	
		naled (Dibrom) 60 EC †dienochlor (Pentac) 50 WP tetradifon (Tedion) 90 P				Apply naled as for aphids. Apply Pentac as slurry on steam pipes at a rate of one lb active per 450,000 cu ft every 5 days until control obtained. Apply Tedion as slurry on steam pipes at a rate of 1 lb active per 200,000 cu ft.
		†pyrethrins (X-clude) 0.3 A			After house ventilated for 1 hour	5 to 10 seconds per 100 sq ft.
		fluvalinate (Mavrik) 22.3 F	5/16 to 5/8 tsp	5 to 10 oz	When dry.	

Spider mites (cont.)	oxamyl (Vydate L) 24 L	2 to 4 tsp	2 to 4 pt		
	10 G			After granules worked into soil or watered in thoroughly.	22 to 30 oz per 1,000 sq ft
	diazinon (Knox-Out) 23 EC †1 A	1 to 2 tbsp	3 to 6 pt	When dry After house ventilated for 1 hour	5 to 10 seconds per 100 sq ft.
	dienochlor (Pentac) 38 F 50 WP	½ tsp 1 tsp	½ pt 8 oz	When dry When dry	
	sumithrin 25 EC 0.5 A	2 tsp	2 pt	When dry	5 to 10 seconds per 100 sq ft.
	†soap (Insecticidal) 50.5 EC	4 oz	3⅛ gal	When dry	
	tetradifon (Tedion) 25 WP	1 tbsp	1 lb		
Spittlebugs	cyfluthrin (Tempo 2) 24.3 EC	3/32 tsp	1½ oz		
	resmethrin 24.3 EC	1 tsp	1 pt	When dry	
	†soap (Insecticidal) 50.5 EC	4 oz	3⅛ gal	When dry	
Thrips	resmethrin 24.3 EC	1 tsp	1 pt	When dry	
	bifenthrin (Talstar) 10 WP	1½ to 5 tsp	9.6 to 32 oz		
	acephate (Orthene) 75 SP	1 1/3 tsp	2/3 lb	When dry	
	diazinon (Knox-Out) 23 EC †1 A	1 to 2 tbsp	3 to 6 pt	When dry After house ventilated for 1 hour.	5 to 10 seconds per 100 sq ft.
	cyfluthrin (Tempo 2) 24.3 EC	3/32 tsp	1½ oz		
	†resmethrin (SBP 1382) A acephate (PT 1300) 3 A			After house ventilated for 1 hour	1 lb/3,000 sq ft. Treat as late in day as possible. Ventilate next morning.
	oxamyl (Vydate L) 24 L	2 to 4 tsp	2 to 4 pt		
	10 G			After granules worked into soil or watered in thoroughly.	22 to 30 oz per 1000 sq ft.

†Suitable for home use

Table 13–3 *(continued)*

Flower	Insect or Mite	Insecticide and Formulation	Amount of Formulation per Gallon of Spray	Amount Per 100 Gallons of Water	Minimum Interval Between Application and Reentry	Precautions and Remarks
ANY (continued)		bendiocarb (Dycarb, Ficam Turcam) 76 WP	1½ tsp	12 to 20 oz	When dry	Avoid excessive runoff.
		lindane 25 WP †malathion 25 WP	1 tbsp 2 tbsp	1 lb 2 lb	When dry	
	Twospotted spider mite	fenbutatin oxide (Vendex) 50 WP 42 L	 1½ to 3 tsp ½ to 1 tsp	 ½ to 1 lb ½ to 1 pt	When dry	
		fluvalinate (Mavrik) 22.3 F	5/16 tsp	5 oz	When dry	Labeled as a dip.
		propargite (Ornamite) 30 WP	1 tsp	1 lb		Check phytotoxicity list on label before treating.
	Whiteflies	dichlorvos (Vapona) endosulfan (Thiodan) sulfotepp (Dithiono, Plantfume 103)			After house ventilated for 1 hour	Smoke generators.
		acephate (PT 1300) 3 A †resmethrin (SBP 1382) 1 A			After house ventilated for 1 hour	1 lb/3,000 sq ft or 5 to 10 seconds per 100 sq ft. Apply in late evening or at night. Ventilate next morning.
		sumithrin 0.5 A			After house ventilated for 1 hour	5 to 10 seconds per 100 sq ft. Apply in late evening. Ventilate next morning.
		†pyrethrins (X-clude) 0.3 A			After house ventilated for 1 hour	5 to 10 seconds per 100 sq ft.
		naled (Dibrom) 60 EC			After house ventilated for 1 hour	Vapor: Apply as for aphids.
		oxamyl (Vydate L) 24 L	2 to 4 tsp	2 to 4 pt		
		10 G			After granules worked into soil or watered in thoroughly.	22 to 30 oz per 1000 sq ft.
		acephate (Orthene) 75 SP	1 1/3 tsp	2/3 lb	When dry	
		bendiocarb (Dycarb, Ficam, Turcam) 76 WP	2½ tsp	1 lb 5 oz	When dry	Avoid excessive runoff.
		bifenthrin (Talstar) 10 WP cyfluthrin (Tempo 2) 24.3 EC diazinon (Knox-Out) †1 A	1 to 5 tsp 3/32 tsp	6.4 to 32 oz 1½ oz	When dry After house ventilated for 1 hour	 5 to 10 seconds per 100 sq ft.

	Whiteflies (cont.)	endosulfan (Thiodan) 24.2 EC 50 WP fluvalinate (Mavrik) 23.3 F †horticultural oil (Ultra Fine, Sun Spray) 98.8 EC resmethrin (SPB 1382) 24.3 EC †soap (Insecticidal) 50.5 EC	 2 tsp 1 tbsp 5/16 to 5/8 tsp 2½ to 5 tbsp 2 tsp 4 oz	 2 pt 1 lb 5 to 10 oz 1 to 2 gal 2 pt 3⅛ gal	 24 hours 24 hours When dry When dry When dry When dry	
		sumithrin 25 EC	1 tsp	1 pt	When dry	
AFRICAN VIOLET	Cyclamen mite	Hot water (110° F)				Submerge for 15 minutes.
		endosulfan (Thiodan) 24.2 EC 25 WP smoke generator	 2 tsp 2 tbsp	 2 pt 2 lb	 24 hours 24 hours After house ventilated for 1 hour	
	Mealybugs	malathion 57 EC	2 tsp	2 pt	When dry	
		dichlorvos (Vapona) 81 EC			After house ventilated for 1 hour.	Vaporize 1 ft oz per 10,000 cu ft. Ventilate after 2 hours.
ASTER	Aphid	endosulfan (Thiodan) 24.2 EC 25 WP †malathion 25 WP	 2 tsp 2 tbsp 2 tbsp	 2 pt 2 lb 2 lb	 24 hours 24 hours When dry	
	Cyclamen mite	endosulfan—as for aphid on aster				
	Leafhopper	†malathion 25 WP	2 tbsp	2 lb	When dry	Spray every 10 days.
	Mealybug	†malathion 25 WP	2 tbsp	2 lb	When dry	Several applications may be necessary.
	Plant bug	Same as for mealybug on aster.				
	Spider mite	Same as for mealybug on aster.				
	Thrips	Same as for mealybug on aster.				
AZALEA	Aphid	SPRAY endosulfan (Thiodan) 24.2 EC 50 WP †malathion 57 EC	 2 tsp 1 tbsp 2 tsp	 2 pt 1 lb 2 pt	 24 hours 24 hours When dry	

†Suitable for home use

Table 13–3 *(continued)*

Flower	Insect or Mite	Insecticide and Formulation	Amount of Formulation per Gallon of Spray	Amount Per 100 Gallons of Water	Minimum Interval Between Application and Reentry	Precautions and Remarks
AZALEA (continued)	Cyclamen mite	endosulfan (Thiodan) 24.3 EC 50 WP	 1 tbsp 1 tbsp	 3 pt 1 lb	 24 hours 24 hours	
	Leaf miner	bendiocarb (Dycarb, Ficam, Turcam) 76 WP	7 tsp	2 lb, 10 oz	When dry	Avoid excessive runoff.
		†malathion 57 EC 25 WP	 1½ tbsp 2 tbsp	 1½ pt 2 lb	 When dry When dry	
		dichlorvos (Vapona) 81 EC			After house ventilated thoroughly 1 hour	Apply dichlorvos as vapor at 1 fl oz 81 EC per 10,000 cu ft. Ventilate after 2 hours.
	Spider mite	†malathion 57 EC 25 WP tetradifon (Tedion) 25 WP	 1½ tsp 2 tbsp 1 tbsp	 1½ pt 2 lb 1 lb	 When dry When dry When dry	
BEGONIA	Aphid	Same as for aphid on azalea.				
	Cyclamen mite	Same as for cyclamen mite on azaleas.				
	Mealybug	Same as for mealybug on African violet and aster.				
		bendiocarb (Dycarb, Ficam, Turcam) 76 WP	¾ tsp	6 to 20 oz	When dry	Avoid excessive runoff.
	Spider mite	Same as for spider mite on aster.				
	Thrips	†malathion 50 EC 25 WP	 1½ tsp 2 tbsp	 1½ pt 2 lb	 When dry When dry	
	Whitefly	Same as for whitefly on azalea.				
BULB CROPS	Aphid	endosulfan (Thiodan) 24.2 EC 50 WP	 2 tsp 1 tbsp	 2 pt 1 lb	 24 hours 24 hours	
CALCEOLARIA	Aphid	endosulfan (Thiodan) 24.2 EC 50 WP	 2 tsp 1 tbsp	 2 pt 1 lb	 24 hours 24 hours	
	Thrips	†malathion 50 EC 25 WP	 2 tsp 2 tbsp	 2 pt 2 lb	 When dry When dry	

CALLA	Spider mite	†malathion 57 EC 25 WP	 2 tsp 2 tbsp	 2 pt 2 lb	 When dry When dry	
	Thrips	Same as thrips on calceolaria.				
CARNATION	Aphid	acephate (Orthene) 75 WP endosulfan (Thiodan) 24.2 EC 50 WP †malathion 57 EC 25 WP	 2 tsp 2 tsp 1 tbsp 1½ tsp 2 tbsp	 2/3 lb 2 pt 1 lb 1½ pt 2 lb	 When dry 24 hours 24 hours When dry When dry	
	Bud mites					Sanitation important; cut and destroy infested buds.
	Spider mite	demeton (Systox) 66 EC			After watered in thoroughly	Applied week after benching; gives 4 to 6 weeks protection.
		propargite (Ornamite) 30 WP	1 to 2 tsp	1 to 1½ lb		
	Thrips	malathion 15 A 25 WP	 2 tbsp	 2 lb	 When dry	
CHRYSAN—THEMUM	Aphid	acephate (Orthene) 75 WP	2 tsp	2/3 lb	When dry	Phytotoxic to Show Off, Iceberg, Albatross, Bonnie Jean and Statesman. Try on a few plants first. Wait 28 days between applications.
		bendiocarb (Dycarb, Ficam, Turcam) 76 WP	1 tbsp	12 to 20 oz	When dry	Avoid excessive runoff.
	Cabbage looper	†*Bacillus thruringiensis* (Dipel) 3.2	1 to 2 tsp	1 to 2 pt	When dry	Cover thoroughly.
	Chrysanthemum gall midge	lindane 25 WP	1 tbsp	1 lb		Weekly applications as needed.
	Corn earworm	†carbaryl (Sevin) 50 WP	2 tbsp	2 lb	When dry	Repeat as needed. Dusts also effective.
	Spider mite	propargite (Ornamite) 30 WP	1 to 2 tsp	1 to 1½ lb		
CYCLAMEN	Cyclamen mite	†hot water				Soak entire plant in 110° F water for 15 minutes.
	Cyclamen mite (cont.)	endosulfan (Thiodan) 24.2 EC 25 EC	 2 tsp 1 tbsp	 2 pt 1 lb	 24 hours 24 hours	
ROSE	Aphid	acephate (Orthene) 75 WP	2 tsp	2/3 to 1 lb	When dry	
	Rose chafer	endosulfan (Thiodan) 24.2 EC 50 WP	 1 tbsp 1 tbsp	 3 pt 1 lb		

†Suitable for home use

PESTICIDE RECOMMENDATIONS

Pesticide recommendations can be obtained from a number of sources, and some are listed at the end of this chapter. All recommend the pest and crop for which they are registered with the federal Environmental Protection Agency (EPA). The use of a pesticide for another crop constitutes a violation of the law, even though it may be safe to the crop. The pesticide may be applied against pests not named on the label unless the label specifically states that the pesticide must be used only for the pests named on the label.

Some materials are designated "Restricted Use Pesticide" because of their toxicity to humans or their danger to the environment. These pesticides may be found in each toxicity category. In all states, they can only be sold to and applied by a certified applicator. This is a person who has passed a course on pesticide handling and safety and who has been certified by the state. (Check with your Cooperative Extension Service for further information in this regard.)

Pest Control Tables

Table 13–3 was developed by J. R. Baker for greenhouse flower crops and Table 13–4 by K. A. Sorensen and G. G. Kennedy for greenhouse vegetable crops. These tables have been reproduced from the 1990 *North Carolina Agricultural Chemicals Manual.*

Pest Resistance

A number of greenhouse pests have developed levels of resistance to pesticides that seriously challenge their control. These pests include spider mites, aphids, whiteflies, leaf miners, and thrips. Any given population of an insect is a rather heterogeneous mixture. Often, there will be a few individuals in the population that are resistant to whichever miticide is used. The others will be killed while these resistant strains will survive and multiply. Fortunately, these strains are less prolific than the susceptible strains, but occasionally they can build up to a serious level.

When the possibility of resistance is a problem, one pesticide should be selected for the program against an insect. This pesticide should be used for at least one generation. Since it is difficult to determine when a generation ends, it is safest to use the pesticide for the length of time of two or three generations. For western flower thrips during high temperatures, this time frame would be two to three weeks. Then, a pesticide from a different chemical class should be selected for the next time period (see Table 13–6 for chemical classes). In this way, insects that developed resistance to the first pesticide will likely be eradicated by the second pesticide. The third pesticide should be from yet another chemical class. By this

Table 13–4

Greenhouse Vegetable Insect Control*

NOTE: Sound cultural practices, such as sanitation and insect-free transplants, help prevent insect establishment and subsequent damage. Be sure that the insecticide used is registered specifically for use on greenhouse vegetables. Separate plant production houses, use of yellow sticky traps, and timely sprays early will help prevent whitefly buildup. Use of *Encarsia* parasites for whitefly in conjunction with wise use of pesticides is encouraged.

Commodity	Insect	Insecticide and Formulation	Amount of Formulation	Minimum Interval (Days) Between Last Application and Harvest	Precautions Precautions and Remarks
CUCUMBER	Aphid	dichlorvos (DDVP) 10 A	Follow Label Directions	1 day	
		malathion (various) 10 A 57 EC 25 WP	 1 lb/50,000 cu ft 1 qt/100 gal water 4 lb/100 gal water	 1 day 1 day 1 day	Apply as needed in the closed greenhouse in air above the plants. Spray when the temperature is 70° to 85° F. Keep ventilator closed for 2 hours or overnight. Ventilate before re-entry. Hazardous to honey bees.
		naled (Dibrom) 60 EC	5 fl oz/50,000 cu ft	1 day	When plants are dry, apply undiluted to pipes by means of a plastic squeeze bottle or other dispenser. Apply continuously or to intermittent sections of pipe on each side and on one or more of the pipes through center of each range depending on the width. Heat pipes to 160° F. Keep house closed over night. Ventilate thoroughly before re-entry. Repeat as necessary. For aphids, treat when they first appear. Avoid overtreatment and direct application to plants, as injury may result. Hazardous to honey bees.
		nicotine sulfate (various)	4.5 oz/50,000 cu ft	1 day	Foliage sprays may be used.
		parathion (various) 10 A	1 lb/50,000 cu ft	15 days	Highly toxic. Ventilate before re-entry.
		soap (insecticidal) 49 EC	2 tbsp/gal water	0	
	Cabbage looper	*Bacillus thuringiensis* (various)	½ to 1 lb/100 gal water	—	
	Cucumber beetles	methoxychlor (Marlate) 10 A 50 WP 25 EC	 1 lb/50,000 cu ft 2 tbsp/gal water 2 tsp/gal water	 7 days 7 days 7 days	
	Leafminers	naled (Dibrom) 60 EC	5 fl oz/50,000 cu ft	1 day	See remarks under aphids above.
		parathion (various) 10 A	1 lb/50,000 cu ft	15 days	Highly toxic—use with caution. Hazardous to honey bees. Ventilate before re-entry.

Table 13–4 *(continued)*

	Spider mite	naled (Dibrom) 60 EC	5 fl oz/50,000 cu ft	1 day	For details see: Cucumber—Aphid. Make 4 treatments at 4-day intervals.
		parathion (various) 10 A	1 lb/50,000 cu ft	15 days	Highly toxic—Ventilate *before* re-entry.
		tetradifon (Tedion) 25 WP	1 lb/100 gal water	—	Not more than 3 applications during the fruiting season. Effective against mite eggs.
		soap (insecticidal) 49 EC	2 tbsp/gal water	0	
	Whitefly	malathion (various) 10 A	1 lb/50,000 cu ft	1 day	For details see Cucumber—Aphid.
		57 EC	1 qt/100 gal water	1 day	
		25 WP	4 lb/100 gal water	1 day	
		naled (Dibrom) 60 EC	5 fl oz/50,000 cu ft	1 day	For details see Cucumber—Aphid. Make treatments at 2-day intervals.
		soap (insecticidal) 49 EC	2 tbsp/gal water	0	
LETTUCE	Aphid, leafminer, whitefly	parathion (various) 10 A	1 lb/50,000 cu ft	21 days	See remarks under tomato.
		malathion (various) 10 A 57 EC 25 WP	1 lb/50,000 cu ft 1 qt/100 gal water 4 lb/100 gal water	10 days 14 days 14 days	Do not use endosulfan or naled on lettuce.
		dichlorvos (Vapona, DDVP) 10 A	1 oz/3,000 cu ft	1 day	
		soap (insecticidal) 49 EC	2 tbsp/gal water	0	
	Cabbage looper, fruitworm, armyworm	parathion (various) 10 A	1 lb/50,000 cu ft	21 days	
		malathion (various) 10 A 57 EC 25 WP	1 lb/50,000 cu ft 1 qt/100 gal water 4 lb/100 gal water	10 days 14 days 14 days	
		Javelin WG	½ to 1¼ lb per 100 gallons of water	0	
	Spider mite	parathion (various) 10 A	1 lb/50,000 cu ft	21 days	
		dichlorvos (Vapona, DDVP) 10 A	1 oz/3,000 cu ft	1 day	
		soap (insecticidal) 49 EC	2 tbsp/gal water	0	

Crop	Pest	Insecticide / Formulation	Amount	Days to harvest	Remarks
TOMATO	Aphid	dichlorvos (DDVP) 10 A	Follow Label Directions	1 day	
		endosulfan (Thiodan) 10 A	1 lb/50,000 cu ft	15 hr	Make sure the greenhouse is tightly closed, then apply in the air above the plants. The optimum temperature for application is 70° to 80° F. Keep greenhouse closed for at least 2 hours. Highly toxic—use with caution. Ventilate before re-entry.
		50 WP	1 lb/100 gal water	1 day	
		2 EC	1 qt/100 gal water	1 day	
		malathion (various) 10 A	1 lb/50,000 cu ft	15 hr	Apply as needed in the closed greenhouse in the air above the plants. Spray when the temperature is 70° to 85° F. Keep ventilator closed for 2 hours. Hazardous to honey bees.
		57 EC	1 qt/100 gal water	1 day	
		25 WP	4 lb/100 gal water	1 day	
		naled (Dibrom) 60 EC	5 fl oz/50,000 cu ft	1 day	When plants are dry, apply undiluted to pipes by means of a plastic squeeze bottle or other dispenser. Apply continuously or to intermittent sections of pipe on each side and on one or more of the pipes through center of each range. Heat pipes to 160° F. Close house over night. Ventilate before re-entry. May also use on hot plates.
		nicotine sulfate (various)	4.5 oz/50,000 cu ft	1 day	Foliage sprays may be used.
		parathion (various) 10 A	1 lb/50,000 cu ft	10 days	Highly toxic—Ventilate *before* re-entry.
		soap (insecticidal) 49 EC	2 tbsp/gal water	0	
	Armyworm	endosulfan (Thiodan) 10 A 50 WP 2 EC	 1 lb/50,000 cu ft 1 lb/50,000 cu ft 1 qt/100 gal water	 15 hr. 1 day 1 day	See remarks under aphids.
		malathion (various) 10 A 57 EC 25 WP	 1 lb/50,000 cu ft 1 qt/100 gal water 4 lb/100 gal water	 15 hr. 1 day 1 day	See instructions for aphids (above). Hazardous to honey bees.
		Javelin WG	½ to 1¼ lb per 100 gallons of water	0	
	Cabbage looper	*Bacillus thuringiensis* (various)	½ to 1 lb/100 gal water		
		Javelin WG	½ to 1¼ lb per 100 gallons of water	0	
	Climbing cutworm	See armyworm.			
	Leafminer	malathion (various) 10 A	1 lb/50,000 cu ft	15 hr	See remarks—Tomato—Aphid.
		naled (Dibrom) 60 EC 60 EC	 5 fl oz/50,000 cu ft 1 pt/100 gal water	 1 day 1 day	See Remarks—Tomato—Aphid.

Table 13–4 *(continued)*

Commodity	Insect	Insecticide and Formulation	Amount of Formulation	Minimum Interval (Days) Between Last Application and Harvest	Precautions Precautions and Remarks
TOMATO (continued)		diazinon (Diazinon, Spectracide) AG 500 50 WP	 4 to 8 oz/100 gal water 4 to 8 oz/100 gal water	 3 days 3 days	Keep ventilators closed for 2 hours or overnight. Plant injury may result if labeling directions are not followed. For use by members of N. C. Greenhouse Vegetable Growers Association, Inc., only.
	Millipedes and crickets	malathion (various) 5 D	Follow Label		Apply to soil at base of plants. Do not contaminate fruit.
	Slug	metaldehyde (Metason) bait	Follow Label Directions		Apply to soil surface around plants. Do not contaminate edible parts.
	Spider mite	naled (Dibrom) 60 EC 60 EC	 5 fl oz/50,000 cu ft 1 pt/100 gal water	 1 day 1 day	See—Tomato—Aphid.
		parathion (various) 10 A	1 lb/50,000 cu ft	10 days	Highly toxic. Ventilate *before* re-entry.
		soap (insecticidal) 49 EC	2 tbsp/gal water	0	
	Thrips	methoxychlor (Marlate) 10 A	0.5 lb/50,000 cu ft	7 days	
		parathion (various 10 A	1 lb/50,000 cu ft	10 days	Highly toxic—ventilate *before* re-entry.
	Tomato fruitworm	See armyworm.			
	Whitefly	dichlorvos (DDVP, Vapona)	Follow Label Directions	24 hr	Sanitation, use of yellow sticky traps, and *Encarsia* parasites are encouraged.
		malathion (various) 10 A	1 lb/50,000 cu ft	15 hr	Apply as needed in the closed greenhouse in the air above the plants. Spray when the temperature is 70° to 80° F. Sprays every second day may be needed. Keep ventilator closed for 2 hours. Hazardous to honey bees.
		57 EC	1 qt/100 gal water	1 day	
		25 WP	4 lb/100 gal water	1 day	
		naled (Dibrom) 50 EC	5 fl oz/50,000 cu ft	1 day	For adult whiteflies make applications at 2-day intervals. Repeat as necessary. Avoid over-treatment and direct application to plants, as injury may result. Hazardous to honey bees. See—Tomato—Aphid.
		methomyl (Lannate, Nudrin) 90 SP	0.5 to 1 lb	7 to 14 days	Apply at 5- to 7-day intervals to maintain control. Methomyl will not control leafminers. More frequent applications may be needed as only adult whiteflies are controlled.
		soap (insecticidal) 49 EC	2 tbsp/gal water	0	

*From Sorensen and Kennedy (1990). In *North Carolina Agricultural Chemicals Manual.* College of Agr. Life Sci., North Carolina State Univ., Raleigh, NC 27695-7603.

point, it should be possible to safely return to the first pesticide. Care should be taken not to mix or alternate pesticides since simultaneous resistance to a number of pesticides can occur, thus reducing one's ability to control the pest.

One further point that helps to avoid resistance is to use pesticides with nonspecific modes of action. Many pesticides adversely affect a single process in the insect. It is possible for a mutant to occur with an alternative to that process such that it is not affected by that pesticide. Insecticidal soap is thought to kill in part by suffocation. Many processes in the insect would have to be altered to impart resistance to this mode of action. Thus, it is not likely that resistance would soon appear for this pesticide.

FURTHER PESTICIDE CONSIDERATIONS

Timing

The length of time between pesticide applications is very important. It depends upon (1) the residual life of the pesticide, (2) the life cycle of the pest, and (3) the method of kill of the pesticide.

In killing insects with a seven-day life cycle by aerosol or smoke insecticides that kill adults but not eggs, it is necessary to treat at six-day intervals until the insect is eliminated. Usually, three treatments are sufficient. Figure 13–14 shows this sequence of action. The first application (day 1) kills most of the insects but not the eggs. The eggs begin hatching immediately after treatment because no insecticidal residue is left by aerosols or smokes. Six days later, before these insects have matured to the stage when they can lay eggs, a second application of insecti-

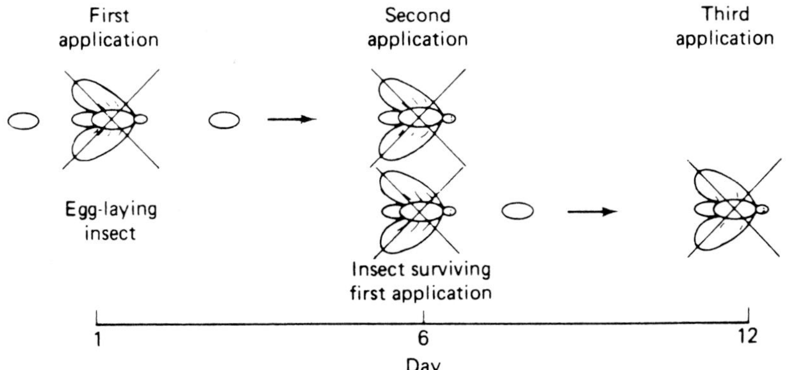

Figure 13–14

An illustration of the destruction of a population of insects having a seven-day life cycle by means of aerosol or smoke with no residual effect.

cide kills them. Insects that escaped the first application are also killed, but they have had a chance to lay a few eggs. These eggs hatch after day 6, and on day 12, before the new insects have laid eggs, they are killed by the third insecticide application, thus ending the population of insects.

If a spraying interval longer than the life cycle of the insect is used, eggs will always be present and the insect population will not be eliminated. Generally, life cycles increase in length with decreasing temperatures. An insecticide that leaves a residue capable of killing may be applied less frequently because it continues to kill for part of the interval between applications.

Pesticide application frequencies of five to seven days are common for the eradication of many types of insects and mites. Even a frequency as short as three days may be necessary for eradicating spider mites and whiteflies during hot weather. Systemic insecticides are to be considered separately since their long residual effectiveness eliminates the need for periodic application.

Pesticide Compatibility

Do not mix pesticides until you are certain they are safe together. Sometimes, two pesticides that are safe to use on a crop individually become toxic to the crop when mixed. Other times, mixing two pesticides reduces their effectiveness because of precipitation or clumping. The compatibility chart in Figure 13–15 indicates which pesticides should not be mixed. Further mixing precautions are to be found on the actual pesticide labels.

As a general rule, avoid mixing different kinds of formulations, such as wettable powders and emulsifiable concentrates. Avoid mixing most pesticides in alkaline solutions (pH above 7.0), such as the alkaline fertilizers. Never mix herbicides (weed killers) with any other pesticides. Use separate equipment for herbicides. An herbicide residue in any insecticide spray could cause extensive damage to a crop.

Plant Toxicity

When a pesticide is injurious to a plant species as a whole, recommendations will not be found on the label for that crop. There are, however, pesticides labeled for use on crops where there are a few cultivars that are injured by the pesticide. Lists of cultivars injured by specific pesticides can be found in some of the pest control manuals recommended for further reading at the end of this chapter and also at the beginning of Table 13–3. Whenever you are not certain about the plant toxicity of a pesticide, you should apply it to a small number of plants and wait one week to determine whether or not it is safe.

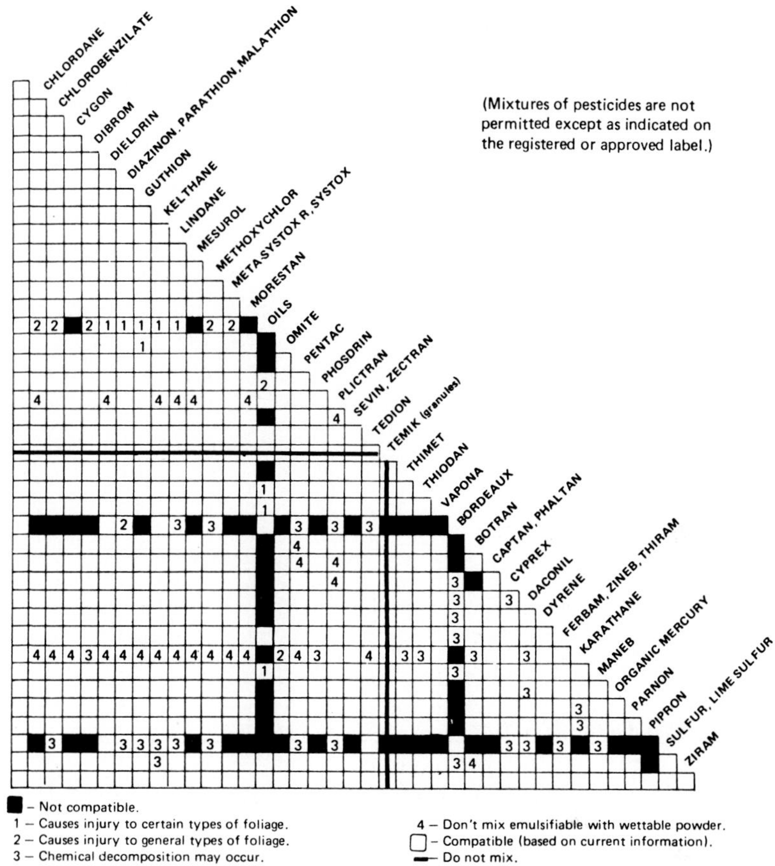

Figure 13–15

Compatibility chart for mixing insecticides, miticides, and fungicides. (*From* L. K. *Cutkomp, Minnesota State* Florists' *Recommendations for Greenhouse and* Floriculture Pest Control, 1973)

Shelf Life

Some pesticides are dated as to their effective life; many are not. Generally, after one year they should be inspected for symptoms of deterioration. The effectiveness of some pesticides is reduced or lost, while others may become toxic to plants. Emulsifying agents in EC formulations often become toxic. To help guard against this problem, pesticides should be dated when purchased and properly inventoried to ensure use of the older materials first. The visual symptoms listed in Table 13–5 indicate the need to dispose of a material.

Table 13–5

Visual Symptoms of Various Pesticide Formulations That Indicate It Is Time to Stop Using and Dispose of Pesticide

Formulation	*Visual Evidence of Deterioration*
Emulsifiable concentrates	When milky coloration does not occur with the addition of water and when sludge is present or any separation of components is evident in the container.
Oil sprays	When milky coloration does not occur with the addition of water.
Wettable powders	When lumping occurs and the powder will not suspend in water.
Dusts	Excessive lumping.
Granulars	Excessive lumping.
Aerosols	Generally effective until the opening of the aerosol dispenser becomes obstructed.

PESTICIDE SAFETY

Handling of pesticides is a very serious matter. Many of the materials are highly toxic to humans. Even where the immediate toxicity is not great, there is the risk of a long-term effect. Often the long-range effects are not known. All pesticides should be handled with an urgency of caution.

Pesticides serve an invaluable role in the greenhouse. The subtropical environment of the greenhouse and unlimited host-plant supply provide an ideal setting for insect development. Competition within the industry necessitates high-quality standards with minimal insect damage. A pest control program is necessary. While one should not fear pesticides, a healthy respect for them is essential.

The pesticide program should be in the hands of one or more employees who are carefully trained for the job. It should not be an odd job passed weekly to different personnel who are less familiar with pesticides and less qualified. Human life is at stake. There are a number of common sense rules to follow, which will be discussed next in logical order.

Storage Area

Store pesticides in a well-ventilated, locked closet or room to which children and other unauthorized people have no access. Be sure the temperature remains at

40–90°F (4–32°C). Place a warning sign on the door indicating that the room contains pesticides. Ideally, the sign should state: "Pesticide Storage, Authorized Personnel Only, In Case of Emergency Call. . . ." A list of the chemical contents of the room should be available. A floor plan of the building showing the location of the pesticide room and its contents should be provided for the local fire department. This will give them a better chance to protect themselves in the event of a fire. You must have a material safety data sheet (MSDS), which is provided by the manufacturer or supplier, for all hazardous chemicals received after September 23, 1987. Some states have adopted more stringent storage regulations.

Labels

Be sure that labels remain on all containers. Tape or glue them on if they become loose. Read the label before using any pesticide. It contains essential information. To use it for any other purpose is illegal. The toxicity rating, symptoms of poisoning, and antidote also are generally included. Rates and methods of application are listed as well. Failure to comply with them could lead to ineffectiveness, injury to the crop, or fines for improper use.

Training Program for Employees

It is required that employers develop a training program for their employees to inform them of the hazardous chemicals on site, how to protect themselves, and what to do if exposed. A training guide must be prepared and kept on site.

Poison Information Centers

Throughout the nation, there are poison information centers. These centers have personnel who can advise your physician as to action to take in the event of poisoning. Obtain the address and phone number of your local center and post it on the outside of your pesticide room. Collect a set of labels of the pesticides you use and keep them handy. In the event of poisoning, take the appropriate label and the address and phone number of your local poison information center with you to the physician. Since such poisonings are not common, valuable time is often lost in a hospital looking up the proper chemical identity of a pesticide and its antidote. The label and poison information center can provide this information.

Pesticide Containers

Keep pesticides in their original containers. Never transfer them to another container. If the label is lost from a container and there is any uncertainty about the contents, dispose of the material. Do not guess! Do not reuse pesticide containers. The slightest residue is potentially dangerous. Most people killed by pesticides are children. Several cases have occurred where pesticides were transferred to household containers such as soda bottles only to be found and drank by a child.

LD_{50}

Categories of toxicity of pesticides have been set forth in the Federal Insecticide, Fungicide, and Rodenticide Act. The toxicity of pesticides is quantitatively expressed as an LD_{50} value either for oral or dermal entry into the body. The former refers to ingestion through the mouth and the latter to absorption through the skin. In either event, LD_{50} refers to the amount of pesticide, expressed in milligrams (mg) per kilogram (kg) of body weight, that will kill 50 percent of a group of animals tested within 14 days of poisoning. These figures are fairly well applicable to humans. The lower the LD_{50} value, the more poisonous is the pesticide because less of it is required to kill. Listed in Table 13–6 are most of the available pesticides by toxicity category and their LD_{50} values. Note that packages in the highly toxic category must bear the words "Danger" and "Poison" as well as a picture of a skull and crossbones. Any time this designation is seen, exercise the ultimate in precaution. Note the LD_{50} values of pesticides you use and be sure your application personnel are aware of them.

Protective Clothing

When Category III (*Slightly Toxic*) pesticides are used that bear the word "Caution" on the label, you should wear long-legged trousers, a long-sleeved shirt, shoes, socks, and a wide-brimmed hat. Proper clothing and equipment to be used with Category II (*Moderately Toxic*) pesticides, which bear the word "Warning," include (in addition to the preceding) rubber gloves, goggles if required by label precautionary statement, and a cartridge or canister respirator if the label precautionary statement says "Do not breathe vapors or spray mists" or "Poisonous if inhaled." When Category I (*Highly Toxic*) pesticides are used that bear the words "Danger—Poison" plus a skull and crossbones, you should wear long-legged trousers, a long-sleeved shirt, rubber boots, a wide-brimmed hat, rubber gloves, goggles or face shield, and a canister respirator if the label precautionary statement says "Do not breathe vapors or spray mists" or "Poisonous if inhaled."

Rubber gloves and boots should be unlined since cloth linings will absorb pesticides and are difficult to wash. It is a good idea, in applying highly toxic pesticides, to wear waterproof coveralls extending from neck to wrists and ankles. It is well to keep the coveralls buttoned at the neck and outside the gloves and boots.

After application of pesticides, the outside of the gloves should be washed in a warm detergent solution before removing. This prevents contamination of the hands in the process of removing the gloves. The boots, hat, mask, and goggles should be washed next in a detergent solution. The coveralls need to be laundered after each use. Disposable waterproof coveralls and hats are now available and can be discarded after each use. Finally, the employee should take a thorough shower and use plenty of soap. It is for this latter reason that it is best to spray at the end of the day. If pesticide application is done early in the day, there is the temptation to wait until the end of the day to clean up. This prolongs exposure of the individual to any contamination, particularly if it is a warm day and the pores of the body are open.

Respirators and gas masks have covers or tape to place over the inlet when not in use. This prevents the absorption of gases and solids during storage that might use up the absorbent contained within. Masks, respirators, and clothing should never be stored in the pesticide room since they would be prone to absorb pesticide vapors.

Equipment

Manufacturers of equipment will provide safety checklists. They are mostly common-sense rules and should be followed. A number of accidents have occurred as a result of improperly maintained equipment. Old spray hoses in particular should be replaced before they burst and douse the operator.

Eating and Smoking

Never smoke, eat, or drink while preparing or applying pesticides. This provides a very likely avenue of entry for the pesticide into your body. Keep all foods and beverages out of and away from the pesticide storage room. Do not eat in the greenhouse where plants are routinely treated with pesticides. Set up a lunch and coffee-break area in a safe part of the work building where there is no chance of pesticide contamination.

Signs and Locks

At the time you begin to apply pesticides, place signs at the greenhouse entries forbidding entrance and indicating that pesticides have been applied. The signs should remain until it is safe to work on the plants again (see Tables 13–3 and 13–4). Signs are particularly necessary when aerosols, fogs, and smokes are used. These signs should indicate that fumigation is occurring. To avoid any chance of a problem, the greenhouse should be locked.

Table 13–6

Toxicity of Pesticides, Including Many Not Registered for Greenhouse Use[1]

Common Name of Chemical[2]	*Trade Name*	*Type of Compound*	*Acute*[3] *Oral (mg/kg)*	*Acute*[3] *Dermal (mg/kg)*
		Highly Toxic		
[Acute oral LD_{50} (to rats) from 0–50 mg/kg. The label of the majority of these pesticides shows the signal words "Danger—Poison" (printed in red) and the skull and crossbones. (From a taste to 7 drops could be lethal to a 150 lb person.)]				
Cyanides (Fum)	Cyanogas	Calcium cyanide	Extremely toxic	Extremely toxic
Chloropicrin (Fum)			LC_{50} 0.8 mg/liter	Severe irritation
Methyl bromide (Fum)			LC_{50} 1 mg/liter	Extremely toxic
Aldicarb (I)	Temik	Carbamate	0.93	2.5
TEPP (I)		Phosphate	1.05	2.4
Phorate (I)	Thimet	Phosphate	1–3	3.6
Cyclohexamide (F)	Acti-dione PM		2	Extremely toxic
Demeton (I)	Systox	Phosphate	2–6	8–14
Disulfoton (I)	Di Syston	Phosphate	2–7	6–15
Fensulfothion (I)	Dasanit	Phosphate	2–11	3–30
Mevinphos (I)	Phosdrin	Phosphate	4–6	4–5
Parathion (I)		Phosphate	4–6	7–21
Sulfotepp (I)	Dithio	Phosphate	5	8
Carbofuran (I)	Furadan	Carbamate	5	885
Fonofos (I)	Dyfonate	Phosphate	8–17.5	25
EPN (I)	EPN-300	Phosphate	8–36	25–230
Carbophenothion (I)	Trithion	Phosphate	10–30	27–54
Arsenic compounds (I)			10–50	Toxic
Azinphosmethyl (I)	Guthion	Phosphate	11–13	220
Methyl parathion (I)		Phosphate	14–24	67
Methomyl (I)	Lannate	Carbamate	17–24	1,500
Endosulfan (I)	Thiodan	Hydrocarbon	18–43	74–130
Methamidophos (I)	Monitor	Phosphate	18.9–21	118

Monocrotophos (I)	Azodrin	Phosphate	20	342
Phosphamidon (I)	Dimecron	Phosphate	20–22.4	107–143
Dioxathion (I)	Delnav	Phosphate	23–43	63–235
Mexacarbate (I)	Zectran	Carbamate	25–37	1,500–2,500
Methidathion (I)	Supracide	Phosphate	25–48	375
Ethion (I)	Nialate	Phosphate	27–65	62–245
Dinitro compounds (F,I,H)	DNOC	Dinitro phenol	30	150–600 (guinea pig)
Oxamyl (I,N,A)	Vydate		37	2,960 (rabbit)
Dieldrin (I)		Hydrocarbon	46–60	60–100
Coumaphos (I)	Co-Ral	Phosphate	56	860
Nicotine sulfate (I)		Alkaloid	83	285
Paraquat (H)			120	480

Moderately Toxic

[Acute oral LD_{50} (to rats) from 50–500 mg/kg. The label of these pesticides shows the signal word "Warning."]

Kerosene		Solvent	50 for comparison	
Rotenone (I)		Botanical	50–75	950+ (rabbit)
Pentachlorophenol (H,I)	PCP		50–140	Mild reaction
Dichlorvos (I)	Vapona	Phosphate	56–80	75–107
Oxydemeton-methyl (I)	Meta-Systox-R	Phosphate	65–76	250
Bux (I)	Bux-Ten	Carbamate	87–170	400 (rabbit)
Lindane (I)		Hydrocarbon	88–125	1,000
Arprocarb (I)	Baygon	Carbamate	95–100	1,000
Crotoxyphos (I)	Ciodrin	Phosphate	125	385 (rabbit)
Pirimicarb (I)	Pirimor	Carbamate	147	—
Chlorpyrifos (I)	Dursban	Phosphate	163	—
Chlordimeform (I)	Fundal & Galecron		162–170	255
Aromatic solvents		Solvent	170	—
Dimethoate (I)	Cygon	Phosphate	215	400–610
Fenthion (I)	Baytex	Phosphate	215–245	330
Chlordimeform hydrochloride (I)	Fundal & Galecron		225–280	4,000+
Naled (I)	Dibrom	Phosphate	250	800
Dichlonfenthion (N,I)	VP-13 Nemacid	Phosphate	250–270	6,000

Table 13–6 *(continued)*

Common Name of Chemical[2]	Trade Name	Type of Compound	Acute[3] Oral (mg/kg)	Acute[3] Dermal (mg/kg)
		Moderately Toxic *(continued)*		
Metaldehyde (M)		Hydrocarbon	250–1,000	—
Phosmet (I)	Imidan	Phosphate	300	3,160
Vorlex (Fum)	Vorlex		305	—
Diazinon (I)	Diazinon	Phosphate	300–400	455–500
Chlordane (I)		Hydrocarbon	335–430	690–840
Diquat (H)			400–440	500+
2,4,5-T (H)			481–500	Mild reaction
Fenithrothion (I)	Sumithion	Phosphate	500	1,300
Plictran (A)			540	2,000+
		Low Toxicity		
(Acute oral LD_{50} above 500 mg/kg. The label of these pesticides shows the signal word "Caution.")				
Carbaryl (I)	Sevin	Carbamate	500–850	4,000+
Petroleum solvents		Solvent	About 510	—
Crufomate (I)	Ruelene	Phosphate	548	3,000
Trichlorfon (I)	Dylox-Dipterex	Phosphate	560–630	2,000+
Ethylene dichloride (Fum)			670–890	3,890 (rabbit)
Formaldehyde	Formalin		800	Mild reaction
Metam-Sodium (Fum)	Vapam	Carbamate	820	800
Dicofol (A)	Kelthane	Hydrocarbon	809–1,100	1,000
Acephate (I)	Orthene	Phosphate	945	—
Chlorobenzilate (A)	Acaraben	Hydrocarbon	960–1,220	5,000+
Morestan (A,F)		Carbonate	1,100–1,800	2,000+
Ryania (I)		Botanical	1,200	4,000+ (rabbit)
Pyrethrum (I)		Botanical	1,345	2,060 (rabbit)
Ammonium sulfamate (H)	Ammate X		1,600–3,900	Mild reaction
Ronnel (I)	Korlan	Phosphate	1,940	5,000+
Temophos (I)	Abate	Phosphate	2,000	2,000

Kinoprene (I)	Enstar	Insect growth regulator	2,330	9,000 (rabbit)
Propargite (A)	Omite	Sulfite	2,500	—
Pentac (A)		Hydrocarbon	3,160	3,160+ (rabbit)
Trifluralin (H)	Treflan E		3,700–10,000	5,000
Tetrachlorvinphos (I)	Gardona, Rabon	Phosphate	4,000–5,000	5,000+ (rabbit)
Resmethrin (I)	SBP 1382	Synthetic pyrethroid	4,240	3,040+
Chloropropylate (A)	Acaralate	Hydrocarbon	5,000	10,200+ (rabbit)
Methoxychlor (I)	Marlate	Hydrocarbon	5,000	6,000+
Perthane (I)		Hydrocarbon	8,170	—
Benomyl (F)	Benlate	Carbamate	9,590	Little reaction
Tetradifon	Tedion	Hydrocarbon	14,700	10,000
Bacillus thuringiensis	Dipel, Biotrol, Thuricide	Bacteria	Harmless	Harmless

[1]From Gentile and Scanlon (1976).

[2]Letters in parentheses indicate the class of pesticide as follows: (A)—acaracide, (F)—fungicide, (Fum)—fumigant, (H)—herbicide, (I)—insecticide, and (M)—molluscicide.

[3]Acute poisoning—Severe poisoning that occurs after a single exposure to the pesticide. Chronic poisoning—Poisoning that occurs as a result of repeated exposures to small doses of the pesticide over a long period of time. LC_{50}—The air concentration that will kill 50 percent of test animals exposed for a period of 1 hour. Minimum of 14 days observation.

Disposal

Empty pesticide containers are potentially dangerous because of the difficulty of removing all residue from them. Each state has a set of rules for disposing of them. Contact your Cooperative Extension Service to learn what these rules are. This is especially important for disposing of pesticides that have deteriorated.

SUMMARY

1. Insects can constitute a major problem for greenhouse crops. An integrated pest management (IPM) approach should be taken to increase pest control effectiveness and minimize reliance on pesticides. Steps involve eradication of weeds in and around the greenhouse because these can harbor insects and disease. The greenhouse should be cleaned, and root media should be pasteurized prior to crop establishment. New plants introduced into the greenhouse should be checked for pests and treated if any are found. A constant surveillance, including the use of yellow sticky cards, should be kept for the appearance of pests in the greenhouse and careful notes should be recorded. The greenhouse environment may need to be altered to tip the advantage away from the pest to the crop. Finally, pest eradication measures may need to be taken. These can involve biological controls or pesticide application.
2. The major insects and related pests in greenhouses include aphids, fungus gnats, leaf miners, mealybugs, mites, scale insects, slugs, snails, thrips, whiteflies, and worms.
3. Biological control involves the release of predator insects, parasite insects and related organisms, or pathogenic microorganisms into the crop that seek out and destroy the pests. Several beneficial organisms are commercially available for this use today.
4. There are eight methods of pesticide application in the greenhouse. Aqueous spray application of pesticides is the most popular method. Mist application is similar and involves liquid preparations 10–20 times more concentrated than sprays but applied in considerably less volume. Application of dust formulations of pesticides is practiced to a limited degree. Spray, mist, and dust applications leave a residue on the plant surface that has a residual effectiveness. Other methods of application, including aerosol, fog, smoke, and volatilization disperse the pesticides throughout the greenhouse atmosphere, killing insects in hard-to-reach crevices and under benches, but have little or no residual activity. Systemic insecticides can be applied to the root medium or the plant. They are taken up into the plant and result in the death of insects and related pests feeding on the plant. These pesticides have long residual activities and can eliminate the need for other methods of application.

5. Greenhouse managers are legally bound to follow the approved uses for pesticides set forth on their labels. Since these are constantly prone to change, the manager must keep all literature up to date. Greenhouse pest control recommendations are continually updated by a number of state universities and state flower grower organizations.
6. Pesticides must be properly selected to ensure effectiveness and prevent plant injuries. Some combinations of pesticides are toxic to plants, while others become ineffective. A compatibility chart should be consulted. Many pesticides used alone are safe on one plant species but not on another. Some are safe for most cultivars of a crop but may injure a few other cultivars.
7. Proper timing of pesticide applications is important. Pesticides may be effective in some stages of an insect's life cycle but not in others, such as the egg or the pupa stages. A single application, therefore, does not eliminate the insect population. Additional treatments must be made at the correct time to catch the remaining insects in a vulnerable stage and before they progress to another resistant stage.
8. Human safety should be the major concern on each manager's mind. Safety precautions should include the following:
   - **a.** A labeled, well-ventilated, locked storage area for pesticides.
   - **b.** Labels on all pesticide containers, MSDS sheets for each, and the use of appropriate containers.
   - **c.** Posted address and telephone number of the nearest poison information center.
   - **d.** Familiarity of each pesticide applicator with the toxicity of each pesticide he or she handles.
   - **e.** Use of protective clothing during pesticide application.
   - **f.** Application equipment in a good state of repair.
   - **g.** No eating or smoking in areas where pesticides are being or have been applied.
   - **h.** Signs and possibly locks on all access doors to recently sprayed areas.
   - **i.** Proper disposal of pesticide containers and old pesticides.

REFERENCES

1. Anon. 1979. New spray technique promises better plant coverage. *Agrichemical Age* 23 (8):20–21.
2. ______. 1983. Pesticide recommendations for greenhouse ornamentals. Ontario Ministry of Agr. and Food. Pub. 381. Toronto, Ontario M7A 2B2, Canada.

3. ______. 1990. *North Carolina Agricultural Chemicals Manual.* College of Agr. and Life Sci., North Carolina State Univ., Raleigh, NC 27695.
4. Ascerno, M. E., D. M. Noetzel, and L. K. Cutkomp. 1984. Insecticide suggestions to control greenhouse and floriculture pests in 1984. Univ. of Minnesota Agr. Ext. Ser. Bul. 392. Univ. of Minnesota, St. Paul, MN 55108.
5. Baker, J. R., ed. 1978. Insects and related pests of flowers and foliage plants. North Carolina Agr. Ext. Ser. Bul. AG–136. North Carolina State Univ., Raleigh, NC 27695.
6. Ball, V. 1985. *The Ball Red Book,* 14th ed. Reston, VA: Reston Publishing.
7. Beasley, E. O., and W. A. Skroch. 1984. Equipment and methods for applying pesticides to trees, shrubs, and trellised vines. North Carolina Agr. Ext. Ser. Bul. AG–80. North Carolina State Univ., Raleigh, NC 27695.
8. Becker, P. 1974. Pests of ornamental plants. Ministry of Agriculture, Fisheries and Food. Bul. 97. Her Majesty's Stationery Office, 49 High Holborn, London, WC1V 6HB, England.
9. Bing, A., et al. 1983. Cornell recommendations for commercial floriculture crops. Part II. Pest control—diseases, insects, and weeds. New York State College of Agr. and Life Sci., Cornell Univ., Ithaca, NY 14853.
10. Coyier, D. L., and J. J. Gallian. 1982. Control of powdery mildew on greenhouse-grown roses by volatilization of fungicides. *Plant Disease* 66:842–844.
11. Gentile, A. G., and D. T. Scanlon. 1976. Floricultural insects and related pests—biology and control. Section 1. Specialty Manual Issue of the *Florigram.* Massachusetts Coop. Ext. Ser., Amherst, MA.
12. Heinz, K. M., and M. P. Parrella. 1990. Losing the battle with bugs? *Greenhouse Grower* 8 (2):36–40.
13. Hussey, N. W., and N. Scopes. 1985. *Biological Pest Control, the Glasshouse Experience.* Ithaca, NY: Cornell Univ. Press.
14. Lindquist, R. K. 1983. Preliminary experiment with an electrostatic applicator for insect and mite control on greenhouse-grown plants. *Ohio Florists' Assoc. Bul.* 639:4–6.
15. Miller, R. 1988. Making biological controls work for you. *Grower Talks* 52 (1):52–54, 56, 58–63.
16. Morgan, W. M., and M. S. Ledieu. 1979. *Pest and Disease Control in Glasshouse Crops.* The British Crop Protection Council, 74 London Rd., Croydon CRO 2TB, England.
17. Powell, C. C., and R. K. Lindquist. 1983. Insect, mite and disease control on commercial floral and foliage crops. Ohio Coop. Ext. Ser. Bul. 538. The Ohio State Univ., Columbus, OH 43210.
18. Tayama, H. K. 1989. Floriculture crops insect and mite control, disease control, growth regulator, and herbicide booklet. *Ohio Florists' Assoc. Bul.* 711.
19. Vittum, P. J., F. J. Campbell, W. J. Bennett, and G. W. Moorman. 1982. Pest management and growth regulators for commercial floriculture. Massachusetts Coop. Ext. Ser. SP–133. Univ. of Massachusetts, Amherst, MA.
20. Weekman, G. T., ed. 1983. Applying pesticides correctly. USDA and U.S. EPA. Published by North Carolina Agr. Ext. Ser., Raleigh, NC 29695.

CHAPTER 14

Disease Control

Infectious diseases of greenhouse crops are the downfall of the careless grower. Many diseases cannot be eradicated; at best, they can only be contained. Others cannot be contained, which means that the infected portion of the crop must be quickly identified and removed. As a whole, fungicides and bactericides are not nearly as effective as are insecticides and miticides.

Prevention plays a very important role in disease control. But even with the best of preventive programs, disease organisms will get a foothold in the greenhouse. Some disease organisms are transmitted in soil or groundwater and then are carried in on the bottom of a pot or the sole of a shoe. Some fungi such as the rusts and *Botrytis* produce windblown spores. If host plants are growing near the greenhouse, these spores can be blown into it. Your disease-prevention program depends upon that of other greenhouse ranges if you are purchasing seedlings or cuttings or, in some cases, even seed. Numerous pathogens are readily transported on these plant materials. Knowing the inevitability of disease, the manager must be careful to check daily for its presence in the same manner that he or she watches for insects and checks the need for water. The value of IPM (covered in Chapter 13) pertains equally well to disease control.

Much of what has been discussed for pest control is apropos of this discussion on control of disease organisms. The same application equipment is used, including sprayers, dusters, foggers, and smokes. Surfactants are important in WP formulations. LD_{50} values are assigned to fungicides, bactericides, and nematicides as well. These chemicals are to be found in the compatibility chart already presented (see Figure 13–15). In general, all of the safety rules governing insecticides and miticides pertain equally well to fungicides, bactericides, and nematicides.

DISEASES OF GREENHOUSE CROPS

There are numerous pathogenic diseases of greenhouse crops. They come under four general categories: viruses, bacteria, fungi, and nematodes (Figure 14–1). It is important to know the characteristics of each as well as the life cycles of specific pathogens in order to determine how to control them. Some require free water on the plant foliage in order to develop. Others require a very wet root medium or appear exclusively on purchased cuttings. Each of these requirements suggests a very effective way of controlling the pathogen.

Aside from introductory paragraphs, the following accounts of viruses, fungi, and nematodes are taken verbatim from the writing of Drs. M. L. Daughtrey and R. K. Horst, of the Department of Plant Pathology at Cornell University as presented in the 1991 recommendations for the integrated management of greenhouse florist crops (Part II: Management of pests and crop growth).

Viruses

Viruses are submicroscopic infectious agents that generally consist of particles composed of protein surrounding genetic material (RNA or DNA). Because plants do not produce antibodies, they neither recover from a virus infection nor become immune. Once a plant is infected, it may remain infected for life, even though the symptoms of disease become masked or the plants grow out of it under certain conditions. Thus, perennial plants and vegetatively propagated greenhouse plants carry the virus from one crop to the next with continuing loss to the disease.

Symptoms. The most common symptom of virus infection is stunting or dwarfing. Leaves may also show distinctive signs, most commonly color changes. Leaves may show spots, streaks, blotches, and rings of light green, yellow, white, brown, or black, or they may develop uniform yellow or orange coloration. Leaves also may change in size or shape, either puckering or developing rolled margins. Flowers may be dwarfed, deformed, streaked, faded, colored green instead of their usual color, or even changed into leafy structures. These are only a few of the more obvious symptoms caused by virus or viruslike causal agents. [See Figure 14–2]

Spread. Generally, viruses are not transmitted through seed although some, such as tomato ring spot and tobacco ring spot, which affect geraniums, are seed transmitted. A crop grown from seed can suffer serious loss if a virus disease (such as tomato spotted wilt virus) appears early and has an efficient means of spread. The next year, however, the crop will again start clean.

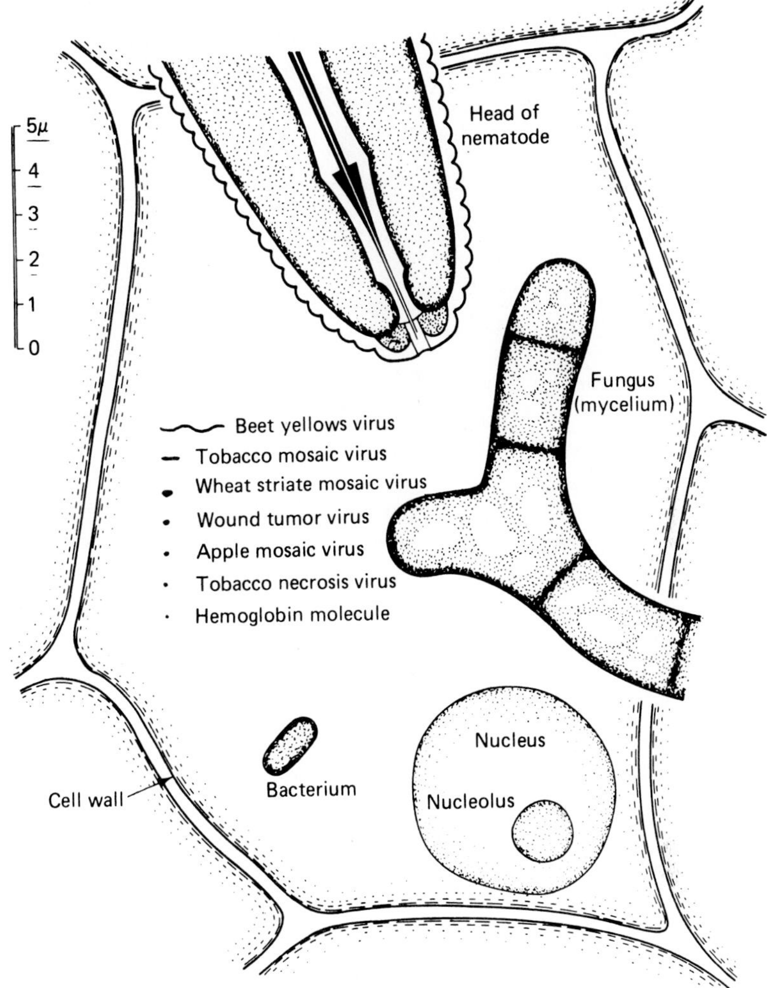

Figure 14–1

Schematic diagram of the shapes and sizes of certain plant pathogens in relation to a plant cell. (*From* G. N. *Agrios, Plant Pathology, Academic Press, New York,* 1969)

Although viruses can spread unaided from cell to cell in one plant, they require active assistance to spread from one growing plant to another and a wound through which to enter the plant. Most frequently, viruses are spread by insects feeding on a healthy plant after feeding on an infected one, by grafting with a scion from an infected plant, or by using infected stock plants as a source of cuttings.

Insect control can be critical to virus control in greenhouses. The current difficulty in controlling western flower thrips, for example, creates a potential danger of widespread tomato spotted wilt virus infections.

Figure 14–2

Mosaic virus of roses with its characteristic symptoms of leaf puckering and yellow discoloration. (*From R. K. Jones, Department of Plant Pathology, North Carolina State University, Raleigh,* NC 27695–7616)

Indexing Program. The use of pathogen-free propagating material is extremely important in any disease control program. Virus indexing is used to eliminate viral pathogens from propagative material of chrysanthemums, carnations, geraniums, orchids, lilies, hydrangeas, and foliage plants. Culture- and virus-indexed plant material is initially free of the internal pathogens for which the index is set up to check; however, such plant material is not disease resistant and requires a growing medium free of the designated pathogens and good cultural practices if the full potential of healthy plants is to be realized.

Virus indexing makes use of indicator plants or serological assays for each specific virus since many cultivars can act as "sleepers," that is, virus carriers that show no external symptoms. Sleeper varieties or cultivars are a tremendous threat since they can be responsible for a large amount of virus spread before the grower realizes there is a serious problem. When the plants are about to flower, the seriousness of the problem is realized in uneven plant growth and flowering time along with a reduction in flower quality.

Diseases of a few crops for which indexing programs have been developed are listed below.

Chrysanthemum
Viruses
- Chrysanthemum stunt
- Chrysanthemum mosaics
- Chrysanthemum aspermy
- Chrysanthemum chlorotic mottle
- Tomato spotted wilt

Vascular wilts
- Verticillium wilt
- Bacterial blight

Carnation
Viruses
- Carnation mottle
- Carnation ring spot
- Carnation mosaic
- Carnation streak
- Carnation etch-ring
- Necrotic fleck

Vascular wilts
- Fusarium wilt
- Phialophora wilt
- Bacterial wilt
- Slow wilt

Geranium
Viruses
- Tomato ring spot
- Tobacco ring spot
- Pelargomium flower break

Vascular wilts
- Bacterial blight
- Verticillium wilt

Tomato Spotted Wilt Virus (TSWV) TSWV is among the most serious threats to the greenhouse industry today. Its prominence began in the mid-1980s with the spread of the western flower thrips (WFT), which is the vector for it. Its host range is extremely broad, encompassing nearly 200 plant species in 40 plant families. Except for geranium, poinsettia, and rose, most greenhouse crops are very susceptible. The most highly susceptible crops appear to be impatiens, New Guinea impatiens, chrysanthemum, and gloxinia. A number of major outdoor vegetable and agronomic crops are susceptible. Thrips can pick the virus up from such outdoor crops and spread it into greenhouses that have been clean or have managed to eradicate it. Another source is plant material that is brought in from propagators. This source is augmented by the fact that the virus is able to lay dormant in plants. Such symptomless plants escape roguing but can later express the disease and become a source for spread to other plants. The disease may also arrive in thrips on young plant material. The disease is worldwide; therefore, it is not possible to obtain plant material from beyond its reach.

Symptoms of TSWV are numerous and overlap those of several other diseases (Figure 14–3). Visual identification of TSWV is further complicated by the variation in symptoms brought on by plant species, stage of plant development, and the greenhouse environmental conditions. The range of symptoms encompasses necrotic and chlorotic ringspots, veinal necrosis, leaf distortion, dark purple-brown sunken spots, stem browning, flower breaking, chlorosis, wilting, stunting, and plant death. Since there is no cure, plants need to be removed as soon as they are identified. Many crops in their entirety have been sacrificed in order to stop the disease from spreading. The main line of defense is through control of the thrips.

Bacteria

Bacteria are single-celled microorganisms. Bacterial diseases are difficult to control. A few bactericides exist. Control is primarily through prevention and elimi-

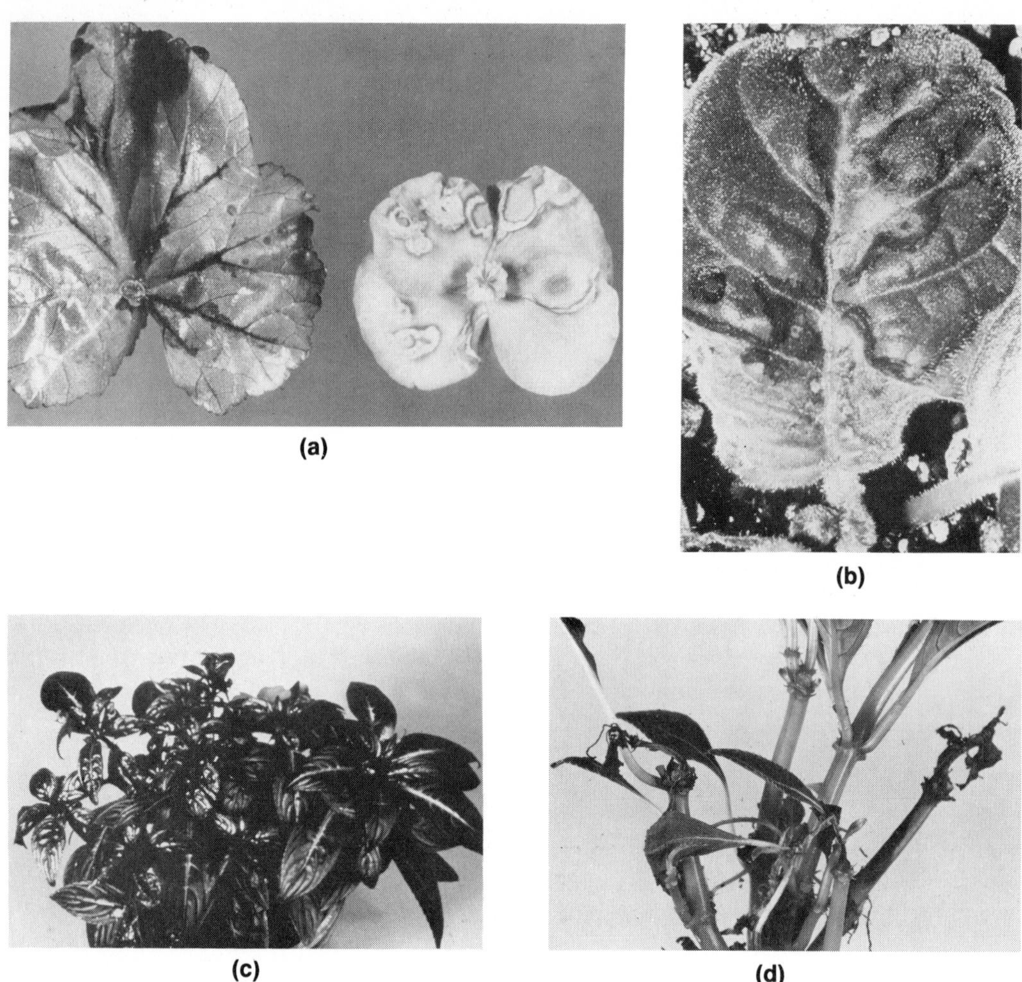

Figure 14–3

Some of the more common symptoms produced by tomato spotted wilt virus. (a) Elatior begonia with concentric rings in petals and veinal necrosis in leaves. (b) Gloxinia leaf displaying chlorosis and necrosis. (c) New Guinea impatiens plant showing a common pattern of infection with only one sector of the plant affected. Foliage on the left side is stunted and distorted. (d) Exacum plant with lesions on stems and young leaves. (*Photos courtesy of* R. K. *Jones and* J. W. *Moyer, Dept. of Plant Pathology, North Carolina State University, Raleigh, North Carolina* 27695-7616)

(a) (b)

Figure 14–4

Bacterial diseases: (a) bacterial leaf spot on Rieger begonia and (b) bacterial soft rot of the stem of a poinsettia cutting. (*From* D. L. *Strider, Department of Plant Pathology, North Carolina State University, Raleigh,* NC 27695–7616)

nation of infected plants. There are not as many bacterial diseases (Figure 14–4) as fungal diseases. Some of the more common bacterial diseases are bacterial wilt of carnation (*Pseudomonas caryophylli*); bacterial blight (stem rot and leaf spot) of geranium (*Xanthomonas pelargoni*); soft rot of cuttings, corms, and bulbs (*Erwinia chrysanthemi*); bacterial leaf spots such as on geranium and English ivy (*Xanthomonas hederae*); fasciation on crops including carnation, chrysanthemum, geranium, and petunia (*Corynebacterium fascians*); and crown gall on rose, chrysanthemum, and geranium (*Agrobacterium tumefasciens*).

Fungi

The fungal diseases are the most numerous and lend themselves best to control measures (Figure 14–5). Fungal organisms are much more complex than bacteria. They are multicellular organisms, often comprising several tissues. Some of the more important categories as described by Drs. Daughtrey and Horst follow.

Powdery Mildew

Powdery mildew, one of the most easily recognized of all plant diseases, is characterized by the presence of a whitish, powdery mildew growth on the surfaces of leaves, stems, and sometimes petals. The fungal threads (hyphae) and the spores (conidia), known as sporophores (conidiophores), that develop on short, erect branches are visible under a strong lens. Under some conditions, however, the

(a) (b) (c) (d)

Figure 14–5

Fungal diseases: (a) powdery mildew on rose; (b) *Botrytis* blight in the spore-forming stage on a poinsettia leaf under mist propagation; (c) damping-off of salvia seedlings; and (d) *Pythium* root rot of chrysanthemum (*left* and *right*) and normal plant (*center*). (*From* R. K. *Jones and* D. L. *Strider, Department of Plant Pathology, North Carolina State University, Raleigh,* NC 27695–7616)

threads are so sparse that the mildew can be detected only by examination under strong light with a good lens or dissecting microscope. In some cases, the mildew development is limited to small areas in which the leaf cells are killed and turn black.

The mildew spores are easily detached from the sporophores and carried by air currents to surrounding plants where they initiate new infections. On some plants, such as rose and delphinium, the young foliage and stems often become severely distorted in addition to being covered by the whitish mildew growth. Seriously affected plants may be of little value as cut flowers or potted plants.

Bioenvironmental Control. Unlike the spores of nearly all other fungi, powdery mildew spores can germinate and initiate infections at humidity levels far below those commonly encountered in the field or greenhouse. Development of mildew following infection, however, may be more rapid and luxurious at higher humidities. As a deterrent to mildew in greenhouses, ventilation and heating should be adjusted to avoid high-humidity conditions. Avoid syringing if possible; otherwise syringe in the morning of a bright day and dry plants rapidly. Heat at least one hour before sunset, and provide adequate ventilation. Horizontal air flow systems assist in powdery mildew management.

Chemical Control. Under some conditions, fungicides for mildew control are essential. Systemic and nonsystemic protectant materials are available for spray application (see Tables 14–2 and 14–3). In addition, sulfur can be vaporized by painting a slurry of sulfur in water on steam heating pipes or by heating pure sulfur in vaporizers. Regular use of sulfur as a preventative will usually keep powdery mildew from becoming a serious problem.

Botrytis Blight

The common gray mold fungus, *Botrytis cinerea,* attacks a wide variety of ornamental plants, probably causing more losses than any other single pathogen. The fungus causes a brown rotting and blighting of affected tissues. It commonly attacks the stems of geranium stock plants and wounds on cuttings. As a result of Botrytis infection, very small seedlings can be rotted, snapdragon stems can be girdled, and petal tissues of many plants, including carnations, chrysanthemums, roses, azaleas, and geraniums, can be spotted and ruined. The fungus is usually identified by the development of fuzzy grayish spore masses over the surface of the rotted tissues, although such sporulation will not develop under dry conditions.

Spores of *Botrytis* are produced on distinctive dark-colored, hairlike sporophores and are readily dislodged and carried by air currents to new plant surfaces. The spores will not germinate and produce new infections, however, except when in contact with water, whether from splashing, condensation, or exudation. Only tender tissues (seedlings, petals), weakened tissues (stubs left in taking cuttings, tissues infected by powdery mildew), injured tissues (bases of cuttings), or old and dead tissues are attacked on most crops. Active, healthy tissues, other than petals, seldom are invaded.

Bioenvironmental Control. Because high humidity is required for spore production and actual condensation is necessary for spore germination and infection, *Botrytis* can usually be controlled under glass by avoiding splashing and by heating and ventilating to prevent any condensation on the plant surfaces. Because the fungus readily attacks old or dead tissues and produces tremendous quantities of airborne spores, the importance of strict sanitation cannot be overemphasized. All old blossoms and dead leaves should be removed, and all fallen leaves and plant debris on or under the benches should be gathered and burned.

Chemical Control. Fungicides may be required under some greenhouse conditions, especially with highly susceptible crops such as exacum, geranium, poinsettia, and fuchsia (see Tables 14–2 and 14–3).

Root Rot Diseases

Rhizoctonia, Phytophthora, and *Pythium* not only cause damping-off of seedlings but together with *Thielaviopsis* are very important in causing root and basal stem rots of older plants. These three fungi are common inhabitants of soil and attack a wide range of plants. They are spread by the mechanical transfer of mycelia, sclerotia, or resting spores in infested soil particles (on flats, tools, pots, baskets, or in the end of the watering hose) or infected plant tissue.

Whereas sanitation measures are effective against all the root rot fungi, fungicides are more specific in their control benefits. The most important control measures are (1) the use of a light, well-drained soil mix; (2) thorough sterilization of the mix as well as the containers, tools, and benches that come in contact with the plants (see appendix tables 1 and 2); (3) the use of clean plants; (4) the enforcement of a sound sanitation program; and (5) the use of supplementary soil treatments with chemicals to minimize recontamination (see Tables 14–2 and 14–3).

Pythium Root Rot

Pythium causes a dark brown to black wet rot that makes roots soften and disintegrate. It typically attacks below the soil surface and may extend up into the base of the stem.

Bioenvironmental Control. *Pythium* is favored by cool, wet, poorly drained soils. Using a well-drained mix with sufficient air pore space and avoiding excessive levels of ammonium or soluble salts will minimize *Pythium* losses.

Rhizoctonia Root Rot

Rhizoctonia causes a drier root or stem rot. Affected tissues are brown or tan. It is favored by an intermediate range of moisture, neither too wet nor too dry. Cankers formed by *Rhizoctonia* usually appear at the soil line; roots are rarely affected in peat-lite mixes.

Bioenvironmental Control. Rhizoctonia disease is often favored by warm temperatures, so losses will typically occur during spring bedding plant production and summer pot plant propagation.

Thielaviopsis Root Rot

Thielaviopsis causes a drier stem lesion than *Rhizoctonia*, one that soon turns black because a large number of black spores of the fungus are produced in the lesion. It may also cause a very black root rot, but this is likely to occur only in mixes containing soil.

Bioenvironmental Control. The disease is not a problem in soil adjusted to pH 4.5 to 5.0.

Damping-Off Disease

Damping-off of seedlings, which is caused mostly by fungi, can be a complex of several diseases occurring separately or simultaneously. Most commonly, either *Rhizoctonia* or *Pythium* is involved. *Botrytis, Sclerotinia,* and *Alternaria* are also occasionally responsible for damping-off.

Preemergence Infection. Seed decay before germination or rot of seedlings before emergence is commonly caused by a water mold, usually *Pythium* or sometimes *Phytophthora.*

Postemergence Infection. Rot developing at the soil line after emergence, which causes the seedling to topple, is most commonly caused by *Rhizoctonia.* This is the conspicuous type of damping-off most frequently reported by growers. Older seedlings may be infected at the soil surface and yet remain upright. Transplanted seedlings remain hard and stunted and eventually die. In some cases, water molds (such as *Pythium*) invade the rootlets at the tips and progress upward to the stem, whereupon the plant dies.

Cultural Control. For all practical purposes, *Rhizoctonia* and *Pythium* do not have an airborne stage. Therefore, spread of both fungi depends upon the mechanical transfer of mycelia, sclerotia, or resting spores in infested soil particles (on flats, tools, baskets, or in the end of the watering hose) or infected plant tissue. Thus, if soil or another medium is steamed or chemically treated and care is taken to prevent recontamination, damping-off should be of little significance. Sowing seed in a layer of screened sphagnum, vermiculite, perlite, peat-lite mix, or other sterilized material also helps. However, some peat moss used in peat-lite mixes may carry these pathogens.

Chemical Control. Fungicide-treated seed is available for some crops. To avoid plant injury, it is best to rely on careful sanitation practices rather than on fungicide drenches to protect crops until after seedling emergence. Preplant mix incorporation of granular fungicide formulations may lead to phytotoxicity problems with some species, particularly if ingredients are not well distributed through the soil mix.

If experience has shown that particular plant species are plagued by damping-off, make spot applications of appropriate fungicides to just those species (see Tables 14–2 and 14–3).

If preventative fungicide treatments are made to all crops, pay careful attention to the appropriate dosage delivery for the size of the container and recognize that fungicides labeled for ornamentals are often not registered for use on vegetable seedlings.

Bacterial Blight of Geranium

Bacterial blight is caused by a bacterium specific to geranium, *Xanthomonas pelargonii*, which becomes systemic in plants. Leaf symptoms are either an overall tiny spotting or a wedge-shaped yellow area on a geranium leaf, often preceded by leaf wilting. The disease can cause black dieback of growing points and stem cankers at the base of the petioles. In hot humid weather, the bacteria spread from infected leaves into the stem, becoming systemic and killing the plant.

Only zonal and ivy geraniums will develop symptoms of this disease, although all geraniums—zonal, Regal, and ivy—may carry the bacteria. Hybrid "seed" geraniums can become badly diseased if they are grown with an infested cutting crop.

Xanthomonas-free material for cuttings is assured through careful culture indexing. Culture indexing is performed by specialists and involves removing thin slices obtained aseptically from the base of a cutting and placing the slices in a nutrient medium. Cultures of nutrient media showing any fungus or bacterial growth are discarded along with the cuttings from which the slices were removed.

Cultural Control. Grow culture-indexed cuttings only, and grow stock plants using individual tube watering systems. The organism is easily spread by splashing water. Subirrigation may spread the disease from root system to root system.

Verticillium Disease

Verticillium is a fungus capable of infecting a wide variety of ornamental plants; some of the more important are chrysanthemums, China asters, snapdragons, roses, geraniums, and begonias. Symptoms vary with the host.

Snapdragons can appear completely healthy until blossoms develop; then the foliage can suddenly wilt completely. The conductive tissues of some varieties can turn brown or purple, particularly the woody stem tissues.

With chrysanthemums, there is usually a marginal wilting of the leaves, followed by chlorosis and eventually death and browning of the leaves, which remain attached and hang down against the stem. These symptoms commonly develop at first on only one side of the plant and only after blossom buds have formed. Young, vigorous plants usually remain symptomless.

The buds on one or two branches of red-flowered varieties of greenhouse roses turn blue and fail to open; the leaves and the green stem tissues may become mottled, and when the stem is shaken, the leaves fall from the plant, and the stem dies. Additional shoots can develop from basal buds and go through the same sequence, though eventually a shoot may remain healthy. Usually there is no vascular discoloration.

With semituberous-rooted begonias, some yellowing of leaf margins can occur, but the most distinctive symptom is the development of an extremely shiny lower leaf surface.

The symptoms thus are quite variable, but the most characteristic ones are one-sided development, wilting and yellowing of leaf margins progressing upward from the lowest leaves, lack of leaf and stem lesions, and normal-appearing roots.

The fungus causing the disease invades the soil and may persist there for many years. Initial infection usually occurs through normal roots, and the fungus grows upward through the water-conducting (xylem) tissues. Infected plants of some types (for example, chrysanthemums) are usually not killed by the fungus and, during periods of rapid vegetative growth, can appear symptomless.

Cultural Control. Cuttings taken from symptomless diseased plants can carry the fungus internally and introduce the disease to new areas. Obtain planting stock only from a reliable dealer, and purchase chrysanthemums and geraniums from propagators who culture index all nucleus stock (see Bacterial Blight of Geranium for a description of culture indexing).

Chemical Control. Plant only in soilless mixes or in soils that have been steamed or treated with chloropicrin to eliminate *Verticillium*.

Nematode Diseases

Nematodes are very small, round worms sometimes called *eelworms*. For the most part, they cannot be seen by the unaided eye. Nematodes are present in essentially all soils, but many of the numerous types are not harmful. Nematode assays of soil samples will quite often reveal the presence of harmful types. It is not until a large population of these types builds up that crop injury occurs (Figure 14–6). Often, this buildup does not occur because of natural predators in the soil. Nematodes are rarely a problem in soil-less root media. They should not be a problem in soil-based root media if it is pasteurized. The following description of nematodes is by Drs. Daughtrey and Horst.

Root-Knot Nematode

Root-knot nematodes may cause plants to appear stunted and unthrifty and to wilt on warm days. When the root system is examined, galls are generally conspicuous and easily recognized. On some crops, root-knot nematodes may cause crop loss even when only a few galls are evident. The presence of root-knot nematodes may also increase the amount of plant injury from bacterial and fungal diseases, or it may break the resistance of plants to these diseases.

Galled plants will not perform as well as healthy ones, but adequate moisture and fertility may mask the difference in vigor between nematode-infested and healthy plants.

Six kinds of root-knot nematodes are recognized in the United States today. All have been identified on greenhouse crops in New York State, although only the northern root-knot nematode, *Meloidogyne hapla*, survives outdoors. Thus, the other five kinds are shipped into the state on plant material. The host ranges and host-parasite relationships may vary, but all have essentially the same life history.

Eggs of *Meloidogyne* are about twice as long as they are wide. They are usually found in a gelatinous mass about the posterior end of the female. Eggs hatch into small, slender

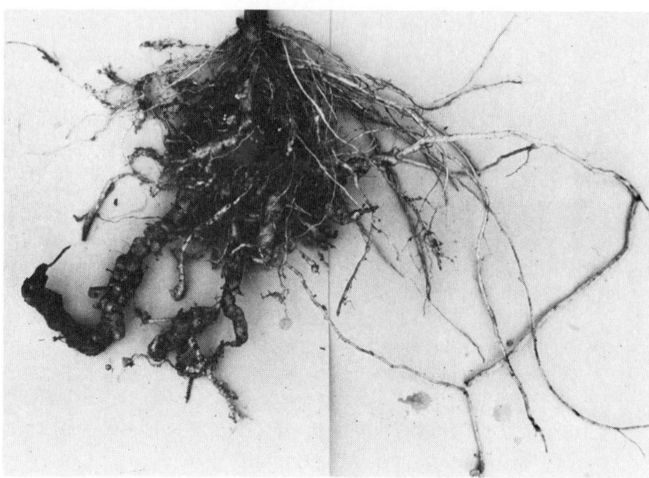

Figure 14–6

Symptoms of root-knot nematode on tomato roots. (*From* R. K. *Jones, Department of Plant Pathology, North Carolina State University, Raleigh,* NC 27695–7616)

worms (larvae) about 1/50 inch long. The larvae migrate through the soil seeking new roots, which they enter near the tip. Once inside the root, with its head located in what will become the vascular cylinder, the nematode does not change position. Stimulated by the nematode's saliva, nearby root cells develop into giant cells, which provide nourishment. Other cells adjacent to the nematode enlarge and increase in number, forming the familiar gall or knot. After the giant cells are functioning, the nematode goes through three molts (shedding of cuticle), becomes an adult female, and starts the cycle over. A female can lay as many as 2,000 eggs during her life, but the average is probably 200 to 500.

The temperature of the soil is critical in the development of the nematode. It takes about 17 days at 29 degrees C (85 degrees F) for females to develop from infective larvae to egg-laying adults, 21 to 30 days at 24 degrees C (76 degrees F), and 57 days at 16 degrees C (60 degrees F). Females fail to reach maturity at temperatures above 33 degrees C (92 degrees F) or below 15 degrees C (59 degrees F).

Spread within a greenhouse occurs through movement of infested soil or plant debris by man, water, and possibly wind. Migration of larvae through the soil is limited to perhaps a few feet per year.

There is no known cure for root-knot nematodes. With continued care, infected bed or bench plants can produce a good crop. Discard infected potted plants carefully to prevent spreading the nematode. Preplanting treatments of steam or fumigants effectively eliminate nematodes from soil, but be sure that infested crop residues are thoroughly decomposed.

Other Nematodes Affecting Roots

Other root-attacking nematodes can cause chlorosis and stunted and unthrifty growth of aboveground parts of the plant. Affected roots may be shortened, thickened, excessively branched to the point of becoming matted, and occasionally killed.

Foliar Nematodes

Leaf (foliar) nematodes cause deformity of young growth, leaf spots, and defoliation. The spots are first discernible on the lower leaf surface as yellowish or brownish areas, which eventually turn almost black. Although the lesions are small at first, with favorable temperature and moisture they may spread until much of the leaf is destroyed. Unlike other nematodes, foliar nematodes do not persist in the soil in the absence of living host-crop tissues.

On chrysanthemum plants, the leaf veins retard the spread of the nematodes through the leaf, causing the lesions to be V-shaped or angular. Infection begins on the lower leaves and progresses upwards.

On *Peperomia*, gloxinia, African violet, and Elatior begonias, the lesions are less definite in outline and infection may occur on any leaf.

DISEASE PREVENTION

The value of root-media pasteurization discussed in Chapter 6 can readily be seen. It also should be apparent that no resistance to pathogen reinfection is imparted to the root medium by pasteurization. A total program of sanitation is needed. Learn to integrate disease control into all the cultural operations of your business.

Sterilize Pots and Other Containers

All materials that have contacted another crop must be sterilized before coming into contact with a newly pasteurized root medium. In this list of materials are tools, flats, pots, wire or plastic supports for plants, and watering systems. Presented in Table 14–1 are a number of useful disinfectants and items that can be sterilized with each. Care should be taken in using formaldehyde because it burns the skin—wear gloves and an apron. Since bleaches will discolor clothing, an apron should be worn during their use.

Sterilize Potting Benches

Too often, because potting benches are used for work and storage, tools, motors, and supplies accumulate there. Dirt begins to settle between and around items, and soon it is impossible to sterilize the benches. Keep potting benches clear. Sweep them off after each use with a broom maintained just for that purpose. Do not use a broom that is also used on the floor. At the end of each week, it is a good idea to swab the benches off with a disinfectant or bleach.

Table 14–1

Common Disinfectants Used in the Greenhouse for Sterilizing Tools, Containers, and Other Materials That Come into Contact with Pasteurized Root Media

Disinfectant	*Rate*	*Application*
Sodium hypochlorite (household bleach)	1 part bleach (5.25% sodium hypochlorite) to 9 parts water	Tools—dip to wet all areas.
		Water system pipes—thoroughly wet with a sponge or rag.
		Flexible water tubes—soak until all interior surfaces are wet for 1 minute and rinse with water.
		Plastic or wire plant support—syringe (a proportioner may be used).
Formaldehyde (formalin)	1 part formalin (40% formaldehyde) to 100 parts water	Flats—soak in solution 30 minutes; rinse and aerate until fumes are gone.
		Pots (plastic and clay)—same as above.
Copper naphthenate	2% solution in Stoddard solvent (VarSol®)	Wooden benches, wooden flats—paint or dip and wait until dry to use.

Isolate Root-Media Storage

Bins for holding root-media components should be high enough so that groundwater does not flow into them. If they are in a location where dust from crop areas can blow into them, they should be covered.

Avoid Foreign Soil

People will sometimes naturally put one foot on the side wall of a bench when they are talking or surveying a greenhouse. This should not be done because soil on the bottom of their shoe will be scraped off into the bench. Such soil may have originated in another greenhouse range or in someone's garden. The chance of a disease organism being in it is quite high.

Foreign soil will undoubtedly be deposited on the greenhouse floor. One easy way in which it is spread to the bench is by the end of the watering hose. It is a natural impulse to drop the hose on the ground when one is done with it. A hose on the ground picks up soil, which is later flushed off all along the bench during watering. If the floor is contaminated, the whole crop may quickly become infected. A simple, inexpensive broom-handle clip can be nailed to the side of the bench near the water faucet, or a hook can be fashioned out of heavy wire. When the water is turned off, the hose end is hung up.

Clean Up Debris

Sometimes, a crop may become its own worst enemy. In a weakened state, it is more susceptible to a number of pathogens. Plant parts should never be cast where a disease organism developing in them can produce inoculum for the crop. Poorly rooted cuttings should never be thrown under the bench. In pinching the tops from plants or removing the lateral flower buds (disbudding), never throw these plant parts on the floor. Strap a cloth pouch around your waist for holding plant tissue. Disbud pot mums over a container into which the buds can fall (Figure 14–7). Do not expect employees to always go the extra yard for disease prevention. Devise systems whereby they can operate in accordance with sound principles of sanitation with little or no extra effort.

At the end of each crop, there is usually a percentage of plants or flowers left that do not meet the market standards. If another crop is not coming in directly behind the first one, it is tempting to leave rejected plants in the bench until all hope of sale is gone. Clean these plants out immediately! They are weak and will become even weaker as they are neglected. They constitute likely tissue to be infected and, once infected, are an excellent source of infection for other crops. During spring and fall, when evening condensation is common on plants, old flowers invariably become infected with *Botrytis*. It is nearly impossible to eradicate in old flowers.

Plant debris should be placed in a compost pile or dump far enough away from the greenhouse so that soilborne microorganisms, windblown spores, and insects contained in it cannot make their way back to the greenhouse.

Clean Stock

When you purchase seedlings or cuttings, you are relying on the sanitation program of another business. Select your plant sources by their reputation. An occasional pathogen or pest problem can come along with plants from the best of

Figure 14–7

A disbudding stand holds the pot mum at working height. As disbuds are removed and dropped, a funnel directs them into a basket. Plant tissue discarded on the floor provides a good host for disease organisms.

propagators. Inspect each lot of plants. If disease is present, isolate these plants and discard or treat them immediately.

If you propagate your own cuttings, maintain a careful disease-prevention program on the stock plants. Carefully inspect stock plants to avoid taking cuttings from any infected plants. If a knife is used for removing cuttings, periodically dip it in rubbing alcohol to sterilize it. Transport the cuttings in clean containers and work on a sterilized surface. If there is any doubt, keep the cuttings on clean newspaper.

Environmental Control

The life cycles of pathogens as discussed earlier suggest cultural procedures for reducing their incidence. Diseases such as *Botrytis* blight depend upon free water on the plant surface for spores to germinate. Free water often occurs as condensation. Warm air holds more water than cold air. During warm fall and spring days, the air picks up moisture. Evenings at these times of year are generally cold. As the air cools, its moisture-holding capacity drops until the dew point is reached and water begins to condense on any solid surface.

Condensation can be combated by three methods. Many growers keep the ventilators open an inch or so (or exhaust fans on at low capacity) when the heat comes on in the late afternoon. Cold air enters the greenhouse, while warm, moist air leaves. The cold, drier air entering is heated and further dried. Then, after 5–10 minutes, the ventilators are closed (or fans turned off). A warm, dry air now exists in the greenhouse. Moving air in a closed greenhouse is a second way of eliminating water on plant surfaces. The horizontal airflow system or the overhead polyethylene fan–tube system will minimize temperature differentials and cold spots where condensation is likely to occur. When extremely moist conditions exist in a greenhouse, it may be necessary to use a third method, which provides for an air exchange one or more times during the night. Controls can be purchased from greenhouse temperature-control equipment manufacturers that will, in accordance with a time clock or a relative humidity sensor, turn on the exhaust fans during the night. The fans remain on long enough to exhaust one volume of air. The heat loss is small since the mass of the exhausted air is small relative to the combined mass of the greenhouse structure, plants, root media, floor, and so on, which all hold heat inside the greenhouse.

Mildew is encouraged by high humidity. Ventilating during the early stages of heating and maintaining good air circulation will help control it. Humidity can further be reduced by watering early in the day when the warm air can absorb moisture from wet surfaces.

Spread of root-rot and damping-off pathogens depends upon mechanical transfer of the root medium in which they reside. Automatic watering helps out here because it minimizes the splashing and lateral transfer of soil that are associated with hand watering. It also eliminates the use of a nozzle, which may periodically touch the root medium along the bench.

A number of the root-rot and damping-off pathogens are enhanced by high root-media moisture levels. A well-drained root medium should always be used. Water should be applied only as needed. Watering too frequently encourages development of these diseases.

Weed Control

Weeds harbor insects and disease. The importance of eliminating weeds in and around the greenhouse was already stressed in Chapter 13. Various weeds can serve as a host for several pathogens that infect greenhouse crops.

FUNGICIDE AND BACTERICIDE RECOMMENDATIONS

The approach to disease control should be through the use of an IPM program. When preventive measures fail to hold the line and pesticides are required, surveillance will indicate the specific areas to be treated and number of applications. Diseases attacking specific greenhouse floral crops and their control recommendations are listed by crop in Table 14–2 (developed by R. K. Jones). Similar recommendations for greenhouse vegetable crops are found in Table 14–3 (developed by C. W. Averre and P. B. Shoemaker). These tables have been reproduced from the 1990 *North Carolina Agricultural Chemicals Manual.*

Specific crops that are particularly susceptible to soilborne root-rot and damping-off diseases and that are grown in an area where such diseases have been a problem can be protected by the use of fungicidal drenches. Truban® is effective against *Pythium* and *Phytophthora*, Aliette® against *Phytophthora*, Subdue® against *Pythium* and *Phytophthora*, benomyl against *Rhizoctonia* and *Thielaviopsis*, and Terraclor® against *Rhizoctonia.* These fungicides are mixed in water and are applied to the root medium in the fashion of a normal watering. Combinations are often used to give a broader spectrum of protection. Benomyl plus Truban® is a popular combination. Banrot® is a commercially available combination similar to benomyl plus Truban®. Upon planting, a new crop is drenched with one of these. Bedding plants, poinsettia, and Easter lily are some crops for which this practice is popular.

SUMMARY

1. Categories of pathogens causing plant diseases are viruses, bacteria, fungi, and nematodes.
2. Viruses are the smallest of the pathogenic organisms infecting plants and are similar in size and chemistry to the genetic material (DNA) contained in the nuclei of plant and animal cells. There are no pesticides for controlling viruses, and plants neither recover nor become immune to them. Control depends upon procurement of virus-free plants, insect control, and disposal of infected plants. The more common symptoms include stunting; distortion of leaves or flowers; and spots, streaks, blotches, or rings on leaves with yellow, white, brown, black, or orange discolorations. Viruses are most commonly

Table 14–2

Commercial Floral Crop Disease Control*

Crop	Disease	Pesticide & Formulation	Rate of Formulation	Schedule & Remarks
ANY CROP	Powdery mildew	fenarimol (Rubigan AS)	4-12 oz per 100 gal	Spray every 7-14 days.
AFRICAN VIOLET	Phytophthora rot and Phythium root rot	etridiazole (Truban 30 WP)	3 to 10 oz/100 gal/400 sq ft or ½ pt/6-inch pot	Apply additional water immediately after application. Repeat at 4- to 8-week intervals if needed.
		metalaxyl (Subdue 2E)	½ to 2 fl oz/100 gal/400 to 800 sq ft	Repeat every 1 to 2 months. Dot not apply rates of 1 3/5 to 2 fl oz/100 gal more often than once every 6 weeks.
	Botrytis blight	benomyl (Benlate 50 WP)	½ lb/100 gal	Spray every 7 to 10 days.
	Powdery mildew	benomyl (Benlate 50 WP)	¼ lb/100 gal ½ tsp/gal	Spray every 7 to 10 days or as needed.
AZALEA	Ovulinia petal blight	triadimefon (Bayleton 25 W)	4 to 8 oz/100 gal	Make one application as first flower buds show color. Spray later varieties as they show color.
	Leaf gall	zineb 75 W ferbam 76 W	2 tsp/gal 2 tsp/gal	Spray just before leaves unroll in spring and 10 days later.
	Phytophthora root rot	etridiazole (Truban 30 WP)	10 oz/100 gal/400 sq ft or ½ pt/6-inch pot	Water-in immediately after application. Repeat at 4- to 12-week intervals. Effective for disease prevention.
		metalxyl (Subdue 2 E)	1 to 2 2/5 fl oz/100 gal for 400 to 800 sq ft	Repeat applications every 2 to 4 months.
		fosetyl-Al (Aliette 80 WP)		
			1 to 2 lb/1000 sq ft ½ to 1½ pt/sq ft	Drench monthly.
	Phomopsis die-back	benomyl (Benlate 50 W)	½ lb/100 gal 1 tsp/gal	Spray older plants immediately after any summer pruning. Prune out any dead branches.
	Phytophthora root rot and nematodes	methyl bromide	2 lb/100 sq ft	Apply under tarp. Wait 1 to 3 weeks to plant.
	Powdery mildew	benomyl (Benlate 50 W)	½ lb/100 gal 1 tsp/gal	Spray at 10- to 14-day intervals at first sign of disease. Thorough coverage necessary.
		triadimefon (Bayleton 25 WP)	2 to 4 oz/100 gal	Spray as needed.
	Rhizoctonia web blight	benomyl (Benlate 50 W)	½ lb/100 gal 1 tsp/gal	Spray weekly in rooting bed or every 7 to 14 days during July and August outside.
		iprodione (Chipco 26019 50 WP)	1 to 2 lb/100 gal	Apply as a foliar spray during July and August every 7 to 14 days.
		chlorothalonil (Daconil 2787 W85)	1½ lb/100 gal 1 tbsp/gal	At first sign of disease or mid-July and repeat at 7- to 14-day interval until early September.
BEGONIA	Botrytis blight	benomyl (Benlate 50 WP)	½ lb/100 gal or 1 tsp/gal	Spray every 7 to 10 days (2 to 3 times per week during wet periods).

Table 14–2 *(continued)*

Crop	Disease	Pesticide & Formulation	Rate of Formulation	Schedule & Remarks
	Powdery mildew	benomyl (Benlate 50 WP)	½ lb/100 gal 1 tsp/gal	Spray every 7 to 14 days as needed.
		dinocap (Karathane 19.5 WP)	4 oz/100 gal	Spray every 7 to 14 days as needed. Apply with caution when temperature is above 85° F.
		sulfur (dust)	Follow label instructions	Do not apply sulfur when temperature is above 90° F.
CARNATION	Alternaria blight	zineb 75 WP	1½ lb/100 gal + spreader 2½ tsp/gal	Spray every 7 days.
		anilazine (Dyrene 50 WP)	1 lb/100 gal	Spray every 7 to 14 days after disease begins to appear.
	Gray mold (Botrytis)	chlorothalonil (Daconil 2787 75 WP)	1 lb/100 gal 2 tsp/gal	Spray every 7 to 14 days.
		benomyl (Benlate 50 WP)	½ lb/100 gal 1 tsp/gal	
		chlorothalonil (Termil)	3½ oz/10,000 cu ft	Fumigate every 7 to 14 days.
		iprodione (Chipco 26019 50 WP)	1 to 2 lb/100 gal	Spray every 7 to 14 days.
	Pythium and Phytophthora root rot	etridazole (Truban 30 WP)	4 to 6 oz/100 gal to 800 sq ft 1 tsp/4 gal to 30 sq ft	Apply at planting. Apply additional water immediately after application. Repeat at 4- to 8-week intervals if needed.
		metalaxyl (Subdue 2 E)	½ to 2 oz/100 gal to 800/sq ft	Start at transplanting and repeat at 1- to 2-month intervals if needed.
	Fusarium wilt	steam	180° F for 30 min under tarp	Use disease-free plants.
	Fusarium stem rot	benomyl (Benlate 50 WP)	½ lb/100 gal 1 to 2 tsp/gal	Use disease-free plants; spray every 7 to 14 days; keep humidity low.
CHRYSANTHEMUM	Stemphylium ray speck	chlorothalonil (Daconil 2787 75 WP)	1 lb/100 gal 2 tsp/gal	Spray every 7 to 14 days.
		chlorothalonil (Termil)	3½ oz/10,000 cu ft	Fumigate every 7 to 14 days.
	Gray mold	chlorothalonil (Daconil 2787 75 WP)	1 lb/100 gal 2 tsp/gal	Spray every 7 to 14 days after disease first appears.
		benomyl (Benlate 50 WP)	½ lb/100 gal 1 tsp/gal	Spray every 7 to 14 days after disease first appears.
		chlorothalonil (Termil)	3½ oz/10,000 cu ft	Fumigate every 7 to 14 days after disease first appears.
	Pythium root rot	etridiazole (Truban 30 WP)	4 to 6 oz/100 gal to 800 sq ft 1 tsp/4 gal to 30 sq ft	Apply at planting. Apply additional water immediately after application. Repeat at 4- to 8-week intervals if needed.
		metalaxyl (Subdue 2E)	½ to 2 fl oz 100/gal 400 to 800 sq ft	Repeat at 1 to 2 month intervals. Do not use 1 3/5 to 2 fl oz rates more often than every 2 weeks.
	Pythium, Fusarium and root parasitic nematodes	methyl bromide	1 to 2 lb/100 sq ft	Apply under cover 10 to 14 days prior to planting.
		steam	180° F for 30 min under tarp	

CHRYSANTHEMUM (continued)	Rhizoctonia root rot	benomyl (Benlate 50 WP)	½ to 1 lb/100 gal 1 tsp/gal	Drench immediately after planting. Use ½ pt per 6-inch pot.
	Phythium and Rhizoctonia root rot	etridiazole + thiophanate methyl (Banrot 40 WP)	6 to 12 oz/100 gal/400 sq ft; 6 to 12 oz/100 gal (½ pt/6 inch pot)	Re-treat at 4- to 12-week intervals.
	Fusarium wilt	benomyl (Benlate 50 WP)	¼ lb/100 gal	Drench at planting and repeat 2 weeks later. Use ½ pt per 6-inch pot.
		thiophanate methyl (Topsin M 70 WP)	1 lb/100 gal, use 1 to 2 pt/sq ft	Apply as drench immediately after transplanting.
EXACUM	Botrytis stem rot	benomyl (Benlate 50 WP)	½ lb/100 gal 1 tsp/gal	Drench plants just after potting and repeat every 7 to 10 days until plants begin to bloom.
		chlorothalonil (Daconil 2787 75 WP)	1½ lb/100 gal 1 tbsp/gal	
GERANIUM	Botrytis blight	benomyl (Benlate 50 WP)	1 tsp/gal	Spray every 7 to 10 days.
	Pythium blackleg	etridiazole (Truban 30 WP)	4 to 6 oz/100 gal to 800 sq ft 1 tsp/4 gal to 30 sq ft	Apply at planting. Apply additional water immediately after application. Repeat at 4- to 8-week intervals if needed.
		metalaxyl (Subdue 2E)	½ to 2 fl oz/100 gal/400 to 800 sq ft	Repeat every 1 to 2 months. Do not use 1 3/5 to 2 fl oz rates more than every 6 weeks.
	Rust	zineb 75 WP	2 tsp/gal	Spray every 7 to 10 days.
GLADIOLUS	Botrytis foliage blight	zineb 75 WP	1½ to 2 lb/100 gal 2½ to 3 tsp/gal	Spray every 7 to 10 days (during wet periods 2 to 3 days). Add spreader.
	Curvularia leaf spot	zineb 75 WP	1½ to 2 lb/100 gal 2½ to 3 tsp/gal	Same as for Botrytis.
		maneb 80 WP		
		mancozeb 80 WP		
	Fusarium corm rot	Busan 75 EC (10.2 lb/gal)	1 pt/100 gal	Soak corms 15 min. Prestorage plus preplant.
		benomyl (Benlate 50 WP)	1 lb/100 gal	
GLOXINIA	See African violet			
IRIS	leaf spot	chlorothalonil (Daconil 2787 75 WP)	1½ lb/100 gal 1 tbsp/gal	Spray every 10 to 14 days in spring.
KALANCHOE	Powdery mildew	benomyl (Benlate 50 WP)	½ lb/100 gal 1 tsp/gal	Spray every 7 to 14 days.
LILY (EASTER)	Gray mold Botrytis blight	benomyl (Benlate 50 WP)	½ lb/100 gal 1 tsp/gal	Spray every 7 to 14 days.
		chlorothalonil (Termil)	3½ oz/10,000 cu ft	Fumigate every 7 to 14 days. Do not apply when foliage is wet or temperature is above 75°F.
	Rhizoctonia root rot	See Chrysanthemum		
	Pythium root rot	etridiazole (Truban 30 WP)	3 to 10 oz/100 gal	Drench immediately after planting. Use ½ pt per 6-inch pot.
		metalaxyl (Subdue 2E)	½ to 2 fl oz/100 gal/400 to 800 sq ft	Repeat every 1 to 2 months. Do not use 1 3/5 to 2 fl oz rates more often than every 6 weeks.
	Pythium and Rhizoctonia root rot	See Chrysanthemum		

Table 14–2 *(continued)*

Crop	Disease	Pesticide & Formulation	Rate of Formulation	Schedule & Remarks
NARCISSUS	Basal rot (Prestorage and/or preplanting)	thiabendazole (Mertect 140-F)	30 fl oz/100 gal	Soak 15 to 30 minutes 24 to 48 hours after digging.
POINSETTIA	Botrytis blight	benomyl (Benlate 50 WP)	½ lb/100 gal or 1 tsp/gal	Spray every 7 to 14 days.
		chlorothalonil (Termil)	3½ oz/10,000 cu ft	Fumigate every 7 to 14 days. Do not apply when foliage is wet or temperature is above 75° F. For foliage only.
		iprodione (Chipco 26019 50 WP)	1 to 2 lb/100 gal	Spray every 7 to 14 days as needed.
	Rhizoctonia root rot and Thielaviopsis root rot	benomyl (Benlate 50 WP)	½ to 1 lb/100 gal 1 tsp/gal	Drench immediately after planting. Use ½ pt per 6-inch pot.
	Pythium root rot	etridiazole (Truban 30 WP)	3 to 10 oz/100 gal	Drench immediately after planting. Use ½ pt per 6-inch pot.
		metalaxyl (Subdue 2E)	½ to 2 fl oz/100 gal/400 to 800 sq ft	Repeat every 1 to 2 months. Do not use 1 3/5 to 2 fl oz rates more often than every 6 weeks.
	Pythium and Rhizoctonia root rot	See Chrysanthemum.		
ROSES (Greenhouse)	Powdery mildew	benomyl (Benlate 50 WP)	½ lb/100 gal 1 tsp/gal	Apply every 7 to 10 days as needed.
		triforine (Funginex 18.2% EC)	12 to 18 fl oz/100 gal	
		dodemorph (Milban 39% EC)	32 oz/100 gal	Spray every 10 to 14 days. For commercial use only. Some varieties may be sensitive.
		triadimefon (Bayleton 25 W)	1 to 2 oz/50 gal	Apply to runoff every 30 days.
		fenarimol (Rubigan AS)	4 to 12 oz/100 gal	Spray every 7 to 14 days.
		piperalin (Pipron LC)	¼ pt/100 gal	Spray at first sign of disease. Make one application as eradicant.
SNAPDRAGON	Rust or Cercospora leafspot	mancozeb 80 WP	1½ lb/100 gal 1 tbsp/gal	Spray every 10 to 14 days beginning at first appearance of disease. If severe disease develops spray every 7 days.
	Botrytis blight	See Carnation		
	Damping-off Preplant	steam	160° F for 30 minutes	Before planting under tarp.
		methyl bromide	2 lb/100 sq ft	Before planting, wait 7 days after removing tarp.
		etridiazole + thiophanate methyl (Banrot 8 G)	Mix 8 oz/cu yd of soil mixture	

	Damping-off Postplant	etridiazole (Truban 30 WP) + benomyl (Benlate 50 WP)	8 oz + 8 oz/100 gal for 400 sq ft	Drench at first sign of disease.
		etridiazole + thiophanate methyl (Banrot 40 WP)	4 to 8 oz/100 gal/ 800 sq ft	Re-treat at 4- to 8-week intervals.
	Powdery mildew	benomyl (Benlate 50 W)	½ lb/100 gal 1 tsp/gal	Spray every 10 to 14 days.
ZINNIA	Powdery mildew	benomyl (Benlate 50 WP)	½ lb/100 gal 1 tsp	Spray every 10 to 14 days.
Greenhouse flowering crops such as CHRYSANTHEMUM GERANIUM POINSETTIA SNAPDRAGON and ANNUALS	Pythium root rot	etridiazole (Truban 30 WP)	½ lb/100 gal	Drench as disease appears. Use disease-free seeds. Sanitation and prevention are most important.
		metalaxyl (Subdue 2E)	½ to 2 fl oz/100 400 to 800 sq ft	Repeat every 1 to 2 months. Do not use 1 3/5 to 2 fl oz rates more frequently than every 6 weeks.
	Rhizoctonia root rot	benomyl (Benlate 50 WP)	½ lb/100 gal	
		iprodione (Chipco 26019 50 WP)	0.4 lb/100 gal	Apply 1 to 2 pt/sq ft.
	Pythium and Rhizoctonia	Banrot	Follow label instructions	
Flowering Annuals except SALVIA and CARNATION	Damping-off	methyl bromide	2 lb/100 sq ft under tarp	10 to 14 days before planting. Follow cautions on label.
		steam	160° F for 30 min under tarp	Plant immediately after soil cools.
Flowering Annuals	Botrytis blight or gray mold	See Carnation		
	Powdery mildew	benomyl (Benlate 50 WP)	½ lb/100 gal	Spray at first appearance and at 10- to 14-day intervals.

*From Jones (1990). In *North Carolina Agricultural Chemicals Manual.* College of Agr. Life Sci., North Carolina State Univ., Raleigh, NC 27695–7603.

Table 14–3

Greenhouse and Covered Plantbed Vegetable Crop Disease Control Schedule*

Follow manufacturer's directions on label in all cases.

Information in the following table must be used in the context of a total disease control program. For example, many diseases are controlled by the use of resistant varieties, crop rotation, sanitation, seed treatment, and cultural practices. Always use top-quality seed or plants obtained from reliable sources. Seed are ordinarily treated by the seed producer for the control of seed decay and damping-off.

Most foliar diseases can be reduced or controlled by maintaining relative humidity under 90 percent, by keeping the air circulating in the house, and by avoiding water on the leaves.

CAUTION: The risk of pesticide exposure in the greenhouse is high; use protective clothing laundered daily or after each exposure; ventilate during application and use appropriate respirator

Commodity	Disease	Material	Formulation Rate/100 gal	Minimum Days		Method, Schedule and Remarks
				Harv.	Reentry	
GREEN-HOUSE	Sanitation	Solarization	140° F, 4 to 8 hrs for 7 days	—	—	Close up greenhouse during hottest and sunniest part of summer for at least 1 week. Greenhouse must reach at least 140° F each day. Remove debris and heat sensitive materials and keep greenhouse and contents moist; will not control pests ½" or deeper in soil; not effective against TMV.
		Added heat	180° F for 30 min	—	—	Remove all debris and heat-sensitive materials. Keep house and contents warm.
		methyl bromide 98%	3.0 lb/1,000 cu ft	—	—	Clean out greenhouse, moisten interior, close tightly, treat for 24 hours at 65° F or higher and ventilate.
	Fusarium crown and root rot[2] Wilts: Bacterial[1] Fusarium[1] Verticillium[1] Nematodes[1]	Steam, Vorlex, Vapam or chloropicrin	—	—	7 to 21	Preplant soil treatment. See table on sanitizing greenhouses and plant beds.
CUCUMBER	Sclerotinia	Botran 75 W	1.33 lb/100 gal water	0	1	Spray when disease first appears on affected areas. Repeat at 14-day intervals.
	Powdery mildew	Karathane 19.5 WD	4 to 8 oz/100 gal water	7	1	Spray when disease first appears. Repeat 5 to 10 days. Avoid hot days over 90° F.
	Nematodes	See under tomato	—	—	—	—
LETTUCE (leaf)	Botrytis	Botran 75 W	1.33 lb/100 gal water	14	1	Spray 7 days after transplanting and when plants are half mature.
RHUBARB	Botrytis	Botran 75 W	1.33 lb/100 gal water	3	1	Spray first appearance. Repeat weekly.
		captan 50 W	2.0 lb/100 gal water	5	4	
TOMATO	Botrytis Early blight Gray leafspot Late blight Leaf mold[1]	chlorothalonil—20% smoke generator (Exotherm termil)	3.5-oz can per 1000 sq ft	0	1	Smoke generator. Start program prior to disease appearance. Repeat treatments at weekly intervals.

	Botrytis Leaf mold Cercospora Phoma Sclerotinia	Benlate 50 W	0.5 to 1 lb/100 gal water	0	1	Spray on first appearance of disease. Repeat at 7- to 14-day intervals.
	Bacterial hollow stem	Clorox	1 pt/10 pt water	0	—	Leave 1-inch stumps when pruning. Dip knife in Clorox solution. Don't handle wet plants. Copper fungicide sprays may help.
		copper fungicides	See label	0	1	
	Botrytis	Dyrene 75 W	2.0 lb/100 gal water	0	1	Spray when disease first appears. Repeat weekly. Do not use after house is covered.
		Botran 75 W	1.0 lb/100 gal water	0	1	Spray when disease first appears. Repeat weekly. Spray stems only.
	Anthracnose Early and late blights Gray leaf spot Septoria leaf spot	maneb 4 F	4.5 to 6.1 fl oz 5000 sq ft	5	1	Spray when disease first appears. Repeat weekly. Do not use maneb on tender, young plants.
		maneb 80 W	1.5 lb/100 gal water	5	1	
		captan 50 W	2 to 4 lb/100 gal water	0	4	
	Sclerotinia	—	—	—	—	Botran and Benlate as used for control of Botrytis should give some control. Soil treatment effective.
	Southern blight (*Sclerotium rolfsii*)	Terraclor L	0.2% solution, 0.5 pt per plant	—	—	Cover soil at base of plant at transplating.
	TMV[1,2] (on seed)	sodium hypochlorite 5.25% solution (Clorox)	2 pints in 8 pints of water			Use 1 gallon of mix per pound of seed. Wash seed in it for 40 minutes, provide continuous agitation; air dry promptly.
	Viruses	Milk (skim)	—	—	0	Dip hands before handling plants. (See Plant Pathology Information Note 186.)
	Fusarium crown and root rot[2] Wilts: Bacterial[1] Fusarium[1] Verticillium[1] Nematodes[1]	Steam, Vorlex, Vapam or chloropicrin	—	—	7 to 21	Preplant soil treatment. See table on sanitizing greenhouses and plant beds.
	Southern blight	Terraclor 75 W	2.2 lb	—	—	Use 0.5 pint/plant. Transplant use only.
BEDDING PLANTS **broccoli** **cabbage** **cauliflower** **cucumber** **lettuce** **melons** **spinach** **squash**	Pythium damping-off	Ridomil 2E	2 to 4 pt/50 gal/acre (1 to 2 fl oz or 2 to 4 tbsp/150 sq yd of beds in 2 gal water)	—	—	Apply preplant in 50 gal water, incorporate lightly, or follow by ½-inch sprinkler irrigation.
tomato	Phytophthora Pythium	Ridomil 2E	4 to 8 pt/20 to 50 gal/acre	—	—	

[1] Resistance available. [2] Use sanitation, seed treatment.

spread by specific insects or through vegetative propagation by such means as grafting and cuttings.

3. Bacteria are single-celled microorganisms. Bacterial diseases are difficult to control since only a few bactericides exist. Again, control is mainly through elimination of infected plants as well as pasteurization of root media and sterilization of containers and tools. The number of bacterial diseases on greenhouse crops is small in relation to the number of fungal diseases. The more common symptoms of various bacterial diseases are wilting; stem rot; leaf spot; soft rot of cuttings, corms, or bulbs; fasciation; and crown gall.
4. Fungal pathogens comprise a large group of multicellular organisms. They are more successfully controlled than other categories of pathogens because there are a larger number of effective chemicals (fungicides). Pasteurization of root media and sterilization of containers and tools also play an important part in control. Some of the most common fungal diseases of greenhouse crops are powdery mildew, *Botrytis* blight, *Verticillium* wilt, and root rots including *Pythium*, *Rhizoctonia*, and *Thielaviopsis*. Control measures range from the reduction of high humidity around plants and free moisture on plants to the application of fungicides (both topical and systemic).
5. Nematode diseases are caused by small, round worms that are usually not visible to the eye. Nematodes abound in all soils; most are harmless. These pests penetrate plant roots, causing lack of vigor and stunting of the plant, shortened and thickened roots, and chlorosis of the foliage. Root-knot nematodes stimulate the development of giant root cells, which develop into galls or knots. Foliar nematodes infect leaves, causing yellowish or brownish spots and areas that enlarge and turn darker. Leaf death and sometimes abscission follows. Root-knot nematodes can be controlled only by discarding infected plants and pasteurizing the root medium. Other root-attacking nematodes can be controlled by postplanting root-media applications of chemicals.
6. The first, and very often the only, line of defense against diseases is prevention. For this reason, the IPM (integrated pest management) program is the most sensible approach. Purchase disease-free plants by dealing with reputable propagators. Periodically, pasteurize all root media and sterilize growing containers and tools. Prevent weed establishment in and around the outside of greenhouses. Clean up plant debris such as pinched-off plant tops and disbuds. Maintain proper air-circulating equipment, heating and ventilating practices, and watering practices to minimize the occurrence of free water on plants. Above all, keep a constant watch for initial disease development and take appropriate action when it occurs.
7. When disease does get a foothold, follow proper label recommendations for the use of an appropriate bactericide, fungicide, or nematicide. These pesticides fall under the same laws of usage as insecticides, and one must adhere strictly to instructions on the label. The same rules of safety apply, and similar

methods of application are used. Insecticides, miticides, and disease-control chemicals are often applied together.

REFERENCES

In addition to the references listed at the end of Chapter 13, the following are suggested.

1. Baker, K. F., ed. 1957. The U.C. system for producing healthy container-grown plants. Univ. of California Agr. Exp. Sta. and Ext. Ser. Manual 23. Berkeley, CA.
2. Daughtrey, M. L., and R. K. Horst. 1990. Biology and Management of diseases of greenhouse florist crops. In 1991 Recommendations for the integrated management of greenhouse florist crops. Part II. Management of pests and crop growth. New York State College of Agr. and Life Sci., Cornell Univ., Ithaca, NY 14853.
3. Forsberg, J. L. 1975. Diseases of ornamental plants. Univ. of Illinois Sp. Pub. No. 3. Urbana, IL.
4. Gould, C. J., and R. S. Byther. 1979. Diseases of *Narcissus*. Washington State Univ. Coop. Ext. Bul. 709. Pullman, WA.
5. ______. 1979. Diseases of tulips. Washington State Univ. Coop. Ext. Bul. 711. Pullman, WA.
6. Horst, R. K. 1983. *Compendium of Rose Diseases*. Amer. Phytopath. Soc., 3340 Knob Rd., St. Paul, MN 55121.
7. Horst, R. K., and P. E. Nelson. 1975. Diseases of chrysanthemum. New York State College of Agr., Cornell Univ. Info. Bul. 85. Ithaca, NY.
8. Jones, R. K., and R. C. Lambe, eds. 1962. Diseases of woody ornamental plants and their control in nurseries. North Carolina Agr. Ext. Ser. Pub. AG–286. North Carolina State Univ., Raleigh, NC 27695.
9. Nichols, L. P., and O. D. Burke. 1963. Diseases of commercial florists crops. Pennsylvania Agr. Ext. Ser. Cir. 519. The Pennsylvania State Univ., University Park, PA.
10. Nichols, L. P., and P. E. Nelson. 1976. Diseases. In Mastalerz, J. W., ed. *Bedding Plants: A Manual on the Culture of Bedding Plants as a Greenhouse Crop*, pp. 406–422. Pennsylvania Flower Growers' Assoc., 103 Tyson Bldg., University Park, PA 16802.
11. Pirone, P. P. 1970. *Diseases and Pests of Ornamental Plants*. New York: The Ronald Press Co.
12. Strider, D. L., ed. 1984. *Diseases of Floral Crops*. New York: Praeger Scientific.

CHAPTER 15

Postproduction Handling

Unlike potted plants, fresh flowers present a special problem. A fresh flower is still a living specimen even though it has been cut from the plant. Its maximum potential vase life, although acceptable in the marketplace, is short. There are many impinging forces that can interact to reduce fresh flower vase life—that is, the period of time during which fresh flowers possess aesthetic value. As an industry, we have not been highly successful in preserving the potential life of fresh flowers. As mentioned earlier, some 20 percent of harvested fresh flowers become unmarketable as they move through the market channel (harvesting, packaging, transporting, and selling). A very significant proportion of the remaining flowers are sold in a weakened condition, which leads to consumer dissatisfaction. Something must be done about poor-quality flowers if the fresh flower industry is going to be progressive. Fortunately, there are well-known solutions for the bulk of this problem. First, we need to take a look at why there is such a decline in the vase life of fresh flowers.

VASE LIFE

Cultural Influences

Basically, those forces that improve crop quality before and after harvest usually improve vase life. Light intensity is very important. A crop grown under dirty glass or during a period of inclement winter weather, such that light is a limiting factor for photosynthesis, will be low in carbohydrate content. Respiration continues after the flowers are harvested, but little photosynthesis occurs because light is limited in the packing house, florist shop, and consumer's home. When carbohydrates are low, respiration is very low and flower senescence (deterioration) occurs. Optimum light intensity during growth of the crop is very important to vase life.

The time of the day when flowers are harvested can be very important for some crops—for instance, roses. Carbohydrates build up during the day through photosynthesis and reach a peak in late afternoon. During the night, carbohydrates are utilized during respiration. Roses cut at 4:30 P.M. were found by Howland (1945) to last longer than those cut at 8:00 A.M.

Temperature also enters into the picture because it influences photosynthesis and respiration, which, in turn, influence carbohydrate accumulation. During hot periods of the year, crops sensitive to high temperatures, such as carnations and roses, have shorter vase lives because flowers contain low carbohydrate levels. When the temperature is raised to an adversely high level to force earlier flowering, the same problem occurs.

Nutrition of the crop likewise has an effect on flower longevity. Shortages or toxicities of nutrients that retard photosynthesis will reduce vase life. Deficiencies in a number of nutrients, including nitrogen, calcium, magnesium, iron, and manganese, result in a reduction in the chlorophyll content, which, in turn, reduces photosynthesis. The net result is a low carbohydrate supply for each flower. On the other hand, high levels of nitrogen at flowering time can have an adverse effect on keeping quality, particularly for carnations and roses.

Diseases and insects reduce the vigor of plants and directly reduce vase life. Diseases also reduce vase life indirectly: Injured tissue releases large quantities of ethylene gas, which hastens senescence of fresh flowers.

Cause of Vase-Life Decline

Fresh flowers deteriorate for one or more reasons. Five of the most common reasons for early senescence are as follows:

1. Inability of stems to absorb water because of blockage.
2. Excessive water loss from the cut flower.
3. A short supply of carbohydrate to support respiration.
4. Presence of diseases.
5. Negative effect of ethylene gas.

Inability to absorb water is a very common reason for premature wilting. The water-conducting tubes in the stem (xylem) become plugged. Bacteria, yeast, and/or fungi living in the water or on the flower foliage proliferate in the containers holding the flowers. These microorganisms and their chemical products plug the stem ends, restricting water absorption. They continue to multiply inside and eventually block the xylem tubes (Figure 15–1). Chemical blockage also can occur. Chemicals present in some stems, upon cutting, change into a gumlike material that blocks the end of the stem. This material is suspected to be composed of oxidized tannins in some plants, and in others it is unidentified.

Excessive water loss from flowers can lead to wilting and reduction in quality and vase life. After harvest, flowers should be removed from the field or greenhouse and refrigerated as soon as possible. Leaving the flowers out of water and in warm air or in warm drafts such as from a heater causes considerable damage. Flowers should be in water and under cool temperatures as much as possible from the time they are cut until they reach the final customer.

Low carbohydrates are another reason for flower deterioration. A low carbohydrate supply can occur as a result of improper storage temperature and handling. Respiration continues to be governed by temperature after harvest. Low temperatures reduce respiration and conserve carbohydrates, thereby prolonging quality and vase life. Each of the many stages in the marketing channel must be

Figure 15–1

A longitudinal section (1,500X magnification) of a rose stem showing the interior of water-conducting cells and a slime plug blocking some of the cells. Such slime plugs can be composed of microorganisms, particularly bacteria, and solidified compounds from the flower itself. (*Photo courtesy of* H. P. Rasmussen, *Department of* Horticulture, *Michigan State University*, E. *Lansing*, MI 48824)

watched. Flowers should be placed in cold storage as soon after harvesting as possible. They should be refrigerated during surface transport and during holding periods by the wholesaler and retailer. Serious damage occurs when flowers are left on a heated loading dock at the motor or airfreight terminal or when they are left sitting in a hot warehouse for a day or so.

The harmful effects of disease and pests, as well as the effect of ethylene, have already been pointed out. Fruits, especially apples, give off large quantities of ethylene gas, making it inadvisable to store lunches containing fruits in coolers. It has already been mentioned that ethylene is evolved from plant tissue, particularly injured and old plant tissue. Coolers should be kept clean of plant debris such as cut stems and leaves that might accumulate on the floor. Old unsalable flowers should be discarded.

Ethylene gas has many deleterious effects. Generally, it causes premature deterioration of flowers. It also causes sleepiness (the upward cupping of petals) of carnation flowers, which gives the flowers an appearance of wilting. This phenomenon is not reversible.

Preservatives for Extending Vase Life

Considerable research has been conducted over the past 30 years to find a preservative solution that will combat some of the causes of flower deterioration and reduction of vase life. One of the earliest home remedies called for table sugar (sucrose) plus aspirin, and sometimes a penny was added to the vase to provide copper as a bactericide. Another remedy used carbonated lemon soft drinks containing sugar. There is some value in these remedies, but aspirin is not readily soluble and the penny is essentially insoluble. Hence, the remedies supply sugar but do not control microbial growth.

Floral preservatives perform three functions:

1. They provide sugar (carbohydrate).
2. They supply a bactericide to prevent microbial growth and blockage of the water-conductive cells in the stem.
3. They acidify the solution. This function suppresses bacterial development and, through some unknown process, prevents wilting of flowers. It is suspected that the acidity helps prevent chemical blockage.

Various universities and the U.S. Department of Agriculture have developed successful preservatives (Figure 15–2). The most popular preservatives today contain 8-hydroxyquinoline citrate (8-HQC) and sucrose (common table sugar). Listed in Table 15–1 are preservative formulas for five fresh flowers. The 8-HQC is a bactericide and an acidifying agent. Besides suppressing bacterial development and lowering the pH, 8-HQC also prevents chemical blockage, thus

Figure 15–2

Floral preservative trials on gladiolus flowers. The flower on the left is in water, and the one on the right is in a preservative containing 600 ppm 8-hydroxyquinoline citrate plus 4 percent sucrose. (*Photo courtesy of* F. J. *Marousky, U.S. Department of Agriculture, Agricultural Research Service, Bradenton,* FL 33505)

aiding in the absorption of water. Sucrose taken up by the stem maintains quality and turgidity and extends vase life by supplementing the carbohydrate supply.

There are a number of commercial preservatives on the market, including products such as Floralife®, Petalife®, Oasis®, Rogard®, and Everbloom®. These work well. One can also purchase 8-HQC under the name *oxine citrate* from

Table 15-1

Floral Preservative Formulas for Five Fresh Flowers

	8–HQC			Sucrose		
Flower	*oz/10 gal*	*g/l*	*ppm*	*oz/10 gal*	*g/l*	*%*
Gladiolus	0.80	0.6	600	54	40	4
Carnation	0.27	0.2	200	27	20	2
Chrysanthemum*	0.27	0.2	200	27	20	2
Rose	0.27	0.2	200	27–42	20–30	2–3
Snapdragon	0.41	0.3	300	20	15	1.5

*Use this formula for other flowers in general.

florist supply companies and add sucrose to make the preservatives listed in Table 15–1.

The bactericide 8-HQC is not totally effective in preventing the buildup of bacteria in floral solutions. Chlorine is a very effective bactericide but dissipates quickly from solution unless provided in a slow-release form. Two slow-release forms sold extensively in products including bleaches, deodorizers, detergents, dishwashing compounds, and swimming-pool additives are DICA (sodium dichloroisocyanurate) and DDMH (1,3-dichloro-5,5-dimethylhydantoin). Both are highly effective bactericides for floral preservation of aster, carnation, gladiolus, gypsophila, and rose. Each is used at a concentration of 300 ppm (0.41 oz/10 gal, 0.3 g/l) in the place of 8-HQC (Marousky 1976). DICA or DDMH is used with sucrose at a concentration of 2 percent (27 oz/10 gal, 20 g/l). These chlorine compounds will bleach stems and leaves immersed in the preservative solution. They may also injure outer petals of roses, but this occurs after normal senescence of the flower begins. These disadvantages are outweighed by the superior bactericidal effects of these materials. They are particularly useful for gypsophila, which is exceptionally prone to bacterial buildup.

Floral preservatives are very effective in maintaining quality and extending longevity. On the average, they can double the vase life of cut flowers when compared to water. Snapdragons with a life expectancy of five to six days last up to twelve days in preservative. The life expectancy of roses can be extended from three to five days to seven to ten days. Carnations with a vase life expectancy of five days, after extensive shipping, have been shown to last twelve days in preservatives.

REFRIGERATED STORAGE

The most common system for handling harvested flowers is refrigerated storage, which involves the following sequential steps.

1. Flower stems should be cut with a sharp knife or shears to prevent crushing of stem and water-conduction cells.

2. The cut flowers should be placed in a preservative solution as soon as possible to prevent wilting. The flowers should not be allowed to be out of water while they are waiting to be transferred to the storage or grading rooms. If flowers are cut in the field, buckets containing solution can be brought out on trailers to hold the harvested flowers. Flowers cut in the greenhouse should not be left in the sun or out of water for more than a few minutes. One person should be assigned to carry these flowers to the grading room or storage cooler immediately. One chrysanthemum grower has installed a conveyor system to carry cut flowers to the grading room.

3. As soon as flowers arrive at the storage room, they should be placed in preservative solution inside the refrigerated storage room. If wilted, they should be placed in a warm preservative solution at room temperature until turgid. They should then be placed in the cooler.

4. The temperature of the refrigerated room should be 33–40°F (0.5–4°C). The lower the temperature the better because the respiration rate falls off with diminishing temperature. Low respiration rates have an effect similar to that resulting from adding sucrose to the preservative solution in that they conserve carbohydrates within the flower. A temperature range of 35–40°F (2–4°C) is usually encountered in flower coolers. Special attention should be paid to some flowers, such as orchids and gardenias, which cannot withstand low temperatures. If Catteleya orchids are stored below 50°F (10°C), they will show signs similar to frost injury (petal browning).

5. Air should be gently circulated inside the cooler only to the extent necessary to ensure uniform temperatures in all areas. Unprotected flowers placed in a direct air stream will be desiccated. Flowers immediately adjacent to a cooling coil may freeze even though the air temperature is above freezing. Since the coil itself is below the freezing point, radiant heat is lost from the flower to the coil, and the flower can be colder than the surrounding air.

6. Potential sources of ethylene gas should be avoided by keeping fruit and vegetables out of the cooler. Discard old flowers. Wash the inside of the cooler periodically.

7. Replace the preservative solution at two- to seven-day intervals. The preservative should be checked periodically for bacterial growth, which is apparent when the solution becomes cloudy. In spite of the bactericides in preservatives, microorganisms will develop and need to be eliminated periodically. To accomplish this, wash the buckets with a disinfectant such as bleach.

Refrigerated storage goes beyond this point, but from here on it becomes difficult to ensure that it is carried out properly. The flowers are sold to a wholesaler who, in turn, sells them to a retail shop. These people should continue to preserve the quality you have worked hard to maintain. The wholesaler and retailer should hold the flowers under refrigeration as you have. Whenever possible, flowers should be transported under refrigeration. Needless delays at shipping terminals should be avoided. Instruct the wholesaler and retailer to cut ½ inch (1.3 cm) from the base of the stems whenever it has been necessary to leave the flowers out of water for a period of time and then to place them in warm water at a cool air temperature to avoid the ends of the stems from drying out and restricting water movement.

Many growers, wholesalers, and retailers are of the opinion that these procedures, particularly the use of floral preservatives, are not necessary. Undoubtedly, they have partial evidence to support their view. However, if they could look at the whole market channel, they would realize they are wrong. It is too late for the retailer to get maximum effectiveness from a preservative if the grower or the wholesaler has failed to use one. Flowers left to wilt in the greenhouse while others are cut have already lost a significant portion of their quality and longevity. Precautions taken after this time will have diminished effects and at times may appear to be without effect. Very often, abusive handling is the main culprit in flower deterioration.

DRY STORAGE

Flowers can be held in refrigerated storage for one to three weeks, depending on the species. Refrigerated storage is more generally used as an aid for maintaining quality as flowers pass through the market channel. Dry storage is used when flowers must be held for periods longer than one to five days. Roses may be held in dry storage up to 18 days, chrysanthemums and carnations up to three weeks, and rooted cuttings of chrysanthemums and carnations for as long as six weeks. Gladioli do not store well.

Flower prices depend to a great degree upon market demand. Prices are high at holidays, but flowers cannot always be scheduled to bloom at each holiday. Dry storage offers a means of holding flowers without deterioration for a high-priced holiday market.

Only the best-quality flowers should be dry stored. Those of poor quality will have a short vase life, if any at all, when they are removed from storage. Flowers should be cut and packaged for storage immediately without being placed in water. Standard cardboard flower boxes are suitable, but a lining of polyethylene film should be placed in them to cover the flowers and seal in moisture (Figure 15–3). Desiccation can be a problem in long-term storage, especially when an absorbent container such as cardboard is used.

Figure 15–3

Bunches of pompon chrysanthemums being packed in a polyethylene cardboard carton. The polyethylene will be placed over the flowers, the lid placed on the box, and then it will be stored at 31°F (-0.6°C) for a period of up to three weeks. (*Photo courtesy of* F. J. Marousky, U. S. *Department of Agriculture, Agricultural Research Service, Bradenton,* FL 33505)

A common problem of dry storage is the presence of free water on the flowers, which encourages the development of disease. While flowers freeze only at temperatures below 29°F (−1.7°C), the free water will freeze at 32°F (0°C). Resulting ice crystals on the petals can be injurious. Boxes and flowers packed at warm temperatures develop condensation (free water) as the plants and air inside are cooled. Because of the polyethylene barrier, the water cannot escape. Disease, enhanced by this moisture, is a common cause of failure in dry storage. Boxes of flowers should be cooled open in a 38–40°F cooler (3.3–4°C) and then sealed and placed in a 31°F (−0.6°C) cooler.

Since most flowers freeze at 27–29°F (−3 – −2°C), it is essential that the temperature stay above this point. Flower life expectancy is lessened at 33°F (0.5°C) and drops rapidly at temperatures above this point. Many of the failures of this system have been due to high temperatures or fluctuating temperatures. Since the dry storage cooler should not be open too often, another cooler is needed for regular refrigerated storage. The 31°F (−0.6°C) cooler is often built inside the 35–40°F (2–4°C) cooler to provide for a more uniform temperature. Space should be left between boxes of flowers when they are placed in storage initially. Respiration is occurring, and this produces heat. A large stack of boxes can generate enough heat and provide sufficient insulation to prevent thorough cooling of the inner flowers. Leave space between each stack of boxes and between every other box in a stack to permit the absorption of heat by circulating cool air.

Flowers removed from dry storage need to be hardened. Cut 1/2 inch (1.3 cm) from the bottom of each stem. Place the flowers in a preservative solution inside a 38–40°F (3–4°C) cooler. Allow the flowers to become fully turgid before marketing them; this will take 12–24 hours. With proper handling, dry stored flowers should have reasonable quality and the same longevity as fresh flowers. Poor temperature control or disease will decrease quality and longevity.

Dry storage is used only to a limited degree by the industry and works best with chrysanthemums. Chrysanthemums, carnations, and roses are the crops to which it is primarily applied. Much more potential exists here than is being realized. The main reason for its low level of acceptance has probably been failures due to inept handling of the system.

BUD HARVESTING

Bud harvesting is a procedure that is used infrequently but is fairly well proven and has a tremendous potential. Carnations and chrysanthemums can be harvested and shipped in the bud stage, which cuts down greatly on their volume and hence lowers the cost of shipping. The wholesaler may then store the buds or open them immediately for resale. Once open, the flower has at least the same vase life potential as a mature harvested flower.

Bud harvesting enables a grower to produce more crops per year in the same greenhouse space. The grower must, of course, either provide space for opening these buds or pass along part of his or her production savings to the wholesaler or retailer who then must provide facilities and time for opening the buds. In any event, there is a significant increase in net return to the grower.

There are other advantages to this system. Buds are more immune to handling injuries and ethylene toxicity, making a higher-quality final product possible. As in the case of mature harvested flowers, buds will dry store very well, enabling one to build up inventory for higher-priced market dates. Bud harvesting is not a new concept for all crops since roses, gladioli, irises, tulips, and peonies have always been cut in the bud stage.

Carnations are cut when from 1/2 to 1 inch (13–25 mm) of petal color is showing (Figure 15-4). Standard chrysanthemums are cut when the buds are 2 inches (51 mm) in diameter. Buds at this stage can be placed directly into dry storage, or they can first be shipped under ice or refrigeration in a box and then be put into dry storage. When needed, buds are removed from the storage box, 1/2 inch (13 mm) of stem is cut off, and they are placed in a floral preservative solution. The buckets of buds are held in an opening room at 70–75°F (21–24°C) until the buds are fully open. A low light intensity is provided in the opening room. Carnation buds open in two to three days and chrysanthemum buds in seven to nine days. The open flowers may be held under refrigeration in the preservative solution, or they may be sold directly. The quality and longevity of these flowers have been reported to be superior to that of flowers harvested at maturity.

(a)

(b)

Figure 15–4

(a) Carnation buds cut at three stages of maturity: (*left*) petals just showing, (*center*) ¼ inch (6 mm) of petals showing, and (*right*) ¾ inch (19 mm) of petals showing. (b) The same buds after three days in an opening solution. The youngest buds will require seven to eight days total opening time, the intermediate buds four to five days, and the oldest buds three days. The oldest buds are ready for retail use after three days in the opening solution. For greatest efficiency of growing and postproduction handling time, the buds should be harvested when ¾ inch (19 mm) of petals is showing. (*Photos courtesy of* F. J. *Marousky*, U. S. *Department of Agriculture, Agricultural Research Service, Bradenton*, FL 33505)

Bud harvesting is becoming important. Growers who ship flowers great distances, across North America or from other countries, recognize its value and find it necessary to use this system. Greater cooperation among growers, wholesalers, and retailers will foster it even more.

SILVER THIOSULFATE (STS)

Silver has a bactericidal activity. On the strength of this point, silver has been tested as a component of floral preservatives. Vase life of carnations has been increased with silver (Kofranek and Paul 1972; Halevy and Kofranek 1977). However, when silver is applied in the form of a soluble salt (most commonly silver nitrate), the silver is only slightly absorbed by cut flowers. Most is wasted, and results are limited. It was found in 1978 that silver in the complex form of silver thiosulfate (STS) is readily taken up and translocated in plants and cut flowers (Veen and van de Geijn 1978). It is very active in this form in preventing postproduction problems. Silver acts as an antagonist of ethylene (Beyer 1976), thereby blocking the aging effects of ethylene. Some problems that are reduced are curling of carnation petals (sleepiness), abscission of petals and florets of numerous plants, drooping and epinasty (twisting) of poinsettia leaves, and a general rapid decline in cut flower condition.

STS must be formulated by the grower as follows (Cameron et al. 1981):

1. Dissolve either 120 g (4.25 oz) of prismatic sodium thiosulfate pentahydrate ($Na_2S_2O_3{\bullet}5H_2O$) or 80 g (2.8 oz) of anhydrous sodium thiosulfate ($Na_2S_2O_3$) in 1 pint of water.
2. Dissolve 20 g (0.7 oz) of silver nitrate ($AgNO_3$) in 1 separate pint of water.
3. Slowly pour the silver nitrate solution into the sodium thiosulfate solution while rapidly stirring. Some acceptable browning of this concentrated STS solution may occur.
4. The concentrated STS solution is diluted before use according to the requirements of the plant being treated. When 1 fluid ounce of concentrated STS is diluted in 1 gallon of water, the concentration becomes 108 ppm silver, which is equivalent to 332 ppm (1 mM) STS.

The metric equivalent to this preparation is as follows:

1. Dissolve 100 g of prismatic sodium thiosulfate pentahydrate or 63 g of anhydrous sodium thiosulfate in 500 ml of water.
2. Dissolve 17 g of silver nitrate in 500 ml of water.
3. Mix the silver nitrate solution into the sodium thiosulfate solution.

4. Use 10 ml of the concentrated STS solution in each liter of water to achieve a concentration of 108 ppm silver, which is equivalent to 332 ppm (1 mM) STS.

An exciting use for STS has been for extending vase life of carnations (Reid et al. 1980). Studies have shown that vase life can be doubled. The concentration of STS to use depends on the length of time stems are left in it. Reid and Staby (1981) developed a graph relating the required concentration for any given desired exposure time. Three effective alternatives from their work include a 10-minute pulse with 4 mM STS at room temperature, a one-hour pulse with 2 mM STS at room temperature, or an overnight (20-hour) treatment with 1 mM STS in a cool room at 32–35°F (0–2°C).

STS treatment shows promise of increasing vase life of a number of other cut flowers, including delphinium, *Dendrobium* orchid, enchantment lily, gerbera, *Mathiola* (stock), and snapdragon. The vase lives of gladiolus and rose are not improved by STS; however, the quality of gladiolus flowers is improved. STS used in combination with floral preservatives further increases vase life beyond that of the floral preservative or the STS alone.

Foliar sprays of STS in combination with 0.1 percent of the spreader-sticker Tween 20® have been shown to prevent abscission of flowers or flower parts from several pot plant crops. A common problem of seedling geraniums has been "shatter," the premature dropping of petals. Shatter is particularly troublesome during shipping and marketing. It has been shown that sprays of 0.5 mM STS to entire geranium plants or 2.0 mM STS to the buds only of other plants result in complete prevention of petal drop three weeks later, when plants are placed in a market environment for six days, while plants sprayed with water drop florets continuously during the six days (Cameron and Reid 1983). Sprays should be timed to coincide with the appearance of color in the first florets (Miranda and Carlson 1981). There is an indication that geranium plants sprayed with STS are more susceptible to *Pythium* root rot. *Calceolaria* plants sprayed to runoff with 0.5 mM STS and, one week later, moved to a laboratory where they were exposed to 1 ppm ethylene for two days or to four days of simulated transport at 77°F (25°C) in the dark show dramatic improvement over plants sprayed with water. Flower drop in plants treated with STS can be reduced from 91 percent to 36 percent in the ethylene test and from 83 percent to 22 percent in the transport test (Cameron and Reid 1983). Bracteole drop from bougainvillea plants brought on by water stress can be greatly minimized by sprays of 0.5 mM STS (Cameron and Reid 1983). Zygocactus are also very prone to flower drop during transportation and marketing. Sprays of 2.0 mM STS to plants in the tight-bud stage almost completely prevent flower drop during exposure to two days at 0.5 ppm ethylene or to four days in the dark at 80°F (27°C) (Cameron and Reid 1981; Cameron et al. 1981).

Poinsettia plants placed in sleeves for shipping purposes can develop droopy bracts and epinastic (twisted) leaves. This apparently results from a buildup of ethylene in the sleeve released from the mechanically stressed plant tissues

(Sacalis 1977). These problems have been significantly reduced by spraying plants with a 3 mM solution of silver ions 24 hours before placing them in the sleeves (Saltveit and Larson 1981). These problems, however, can be minimized by using more porous paper or fiber rather than solid plastic sleeves and by using the sleeves for the least time possible (Staby et al. 1979). Complete correction can usually be obtained by allowing plants to stand for a period of time after sleeve removal and before selling.

THE FUTURE

We can look for some very fascinating developments in the future with regard to postproduction handling. For some time now, fruit has been stored in "controlled atmosphere" (CA) systems. Crisp, fresh apples stored from September to June are the products of this system. The merits of the system in relation to flower storage are being tested. In such a system, flowers would be stored at low temperatures in an atmosphere very low in oxygen (1–3 percent) and high in CO_2 (2–5 percent). The low oxygen and high CO_2 levels further reduce the rate of respiration.

Hypobaric (low-pressure) storage is a much newer idea. Fruits, vegetables, or flowers are placed in a sealed chamber, and a vacuum is established in the chamber down to a pressure of about 50 mm of mercury (6.7 kPa). The chamber is constructed to maintain a vacuum, yet allow fresh air to be swept through it. The chamber is also cooled to a low temperature. As the chamber is evacuated, the oxygen content is reduced to a level that sharply reduces respiration. Ethylene gas evolved by the plant tissue is quickly removed by the flowing air.

There is tentative evidence that these systems will play a role in the future of floriculture. More testing is needed before low-pressure storage is realized.

SUMMARY

1. The five common factors that reduce vase life of harvested fresh flowers are the inability of stems to absorb water due to blockage by microbial organisms or solidified chemicals; excessive water loss from the cut flower; a low supply of carbohydrate to support respiration; the presence of pathogenic diseases; and the buildup of ethylene gas derived particularly from fruit or from injured and deteriorating plant material.
2. Maximum vase-life potential is achieved by producing high-quality flowers rich in carbohydrate; preventing the occurrence of diseases before and after harvest; harvesting at the proper stage; placing flowers in a floral preservative immediately upon cutting and maintaining them in such a preservative throughout the marketing channel; keeping cut flowers at a low temperature of 33–40°F (0.6–4°C) whenever possible during handling and marketing; and

preventing the buildup of ethylene gas around stored flowers by removing injured and old plant material and keeping fruit out of the storage cooler.

3. Floral preservatives can double the vase life of fresh flowers when compared to water. Generally, they provide sugar to supplement the carbohydrate supply in the flower, a bactericide, and an acidifying agent that suppresses bacterial development in the storage water. Sucrose (table sugar) is a common source of sugar, and 8-hydroxyquinoline citrate is often used as the bactericide and acidifying agent.

4. Refrigerated storage of flowers in preservative solution works well for periods of a few days, as is often necessary during the marketing period. Dry storage of flowers can be used when they must be held for a longer period—up to 18 days for roses and three weeks for chrysanthemums and carnations. Freshly cut, turgid flowers are placed in polyethylene-lined cartons without water, and the cartons are held in a 31°F (−0.6°C) cooler. Flowers cut in this manner have essentially the same longevity after removal as flowers handled in the more conventional manner.

5. Some flowers, such as roses, irises, and tulips, have traditionally been cut in the bud stage, while others, such as carnations and chrysanthemums, are customarily harvested in an open stage. These latter crops can also be harvested in the bud stage with a considerable reduction in the culture time required in the greenhouse. Harvested buds may be shipped and/or stored at this stage. Ultimately, they are placed in an opening solution, similar to a floral preservative, at room temperature. Carnation buds open in two to three days, and chrysanthemum buds open in seven to nine days. A savings in production expense and shipping cost can be realized, and less flower injury is sustained during shipping.

6. Silver thiosulfate (STS) has recently found application as a fresh flower preservative for carnation, delphinium, *Dendrobium* orchid, enchantment lily, gerbera, *Mathiola*, and snapdragon. The vase life of carnations can be doubled. In this form, silver effectively moves into the flower and blocks the effects of ethylene. Research shows that abscission of flowers or floral parts can be delayed by sprays of STS for a number of crops including bougainvillea, *Calceolaria*, geranium, and zygocactus. There is an indication, however, that STS sprays can render geranium plants susceptible to *Pythium* root rot.

REFERENCES

1. Ball, V., ed. 1985. *The Ball Red Book*, 14th ed. Reston, VA: Reston Publishing.
2. Beyer, E., Jr. 1976. A potent inhibitor of ethylene action in plants. *Plant Physiol.* 58:268–271.

3. Boodley, J. W., and J. W. White. 1969. Post-harvest life. In Mastalerz, J. W., and R. W. Langhans, eds. *Roses,* pp. 78–92. Pennsylvania Flower Growers' Assoc., New York State Flower Growers' Assoc., Inc., and Roses, Inc.

4. Cameron, A. C., and M. S. Reid. 1981. The use of silver thiosulfate anionic complex as a foliar spray to prevent flower abscission of zygocactus. *HortScience* 16:761–762.

5. ______. 1983. Use of silver thiosulfate to prevent flower abscission from potted plants. *Scientia Hort.* 19:373–378.

6. Cameron, A. C., M. S. Reid, and G. W. Hickman. 1981. Using STS to prevent flower shattering in potted flower plants—a progress report. Flower and Nursery Report for Commercial Growers (Fall 1981). Univ. of California Coop. Ext. Ser.

7. Carpenter, W. J., and D. R. Dilley. 1975. Investigations to extend cut flower longevity. Michigan Agr. Exp. Sta. Res. Rep. 263.

8. Halevy, A. H., and A. M. Kofranek. 1977. Silver treatment of carnation flowers for reducing ethylene damage and extending longevity. *J. Amer. Soc. Hort. Sci.* 102:76–77.

9. Howland, J. E. 1945. A study of the keeping quality of cut roses. *Amer. Rose Annual* 30:51–66.

10. Kofranek, A. M., and A. H. Halevy. 1972. Conditions for opening cut chrysanthemum flower buds. *J. Amer. Soc. Hort. Sci.* 97:578–584.

11. Kofranek, A. M., and J. L. Paul. 1972. Silver impregnated stems aid carnation flower longevity. *Florists' Review* 151 (3913):24–25.

12. Marousky, F. J. 1970. New methods for improving keeping quality for gladiolus, roses and chrysanthemums. *Florists' Review* 145 (3770):67, 116–119.

13. ______. 1976. Control of bacteria in vase water and quality of cut flowers as influenced by sodium dichloroisocyanurate, 1,3-dichloro-5,5-dimethylhydantoin, and sucrose. ARS-S-115. USDA, Washington, D.C.

14. Mastalerz, J. W. 1969. Low temperature dry storage. In Mastalerz, J. W., and R. W. Langhans, eds. *Roses,* pp. 150–156. Pennsylvania Flower Growers' Assoc., New York State Flower Growers' Assoc., Inc., and Roses, Inc.

15. Miranda, R., and W. H. Carlson. 1981. How to stop petal shattering in hybrid seed geranium. *Grower Talks* 45 (7):18–22.

16. Reid, M. S., J. L. Paul, M. B. Farhoomand, A. M. Kofranek, and G. L. Staby. 1980. Pulse treatments with silver thiosulfate complex extend the vase life of cut carnations. *J. Amer. Soc. Hort. Sci.* 105:25–27.

17. Reid, M. S., and G. L. Staby. 1981. "Super" carnations—a concept. *Canadian Florist, Greenhouse and Nursery* 76 (1):40, 42, 44, 46, 48.

18. Robertson, J. L., and G. L. Staby. 1976. Economic feasibility of once-over bud harvest of standard chrysanthemums *HortScience* 11:159–160.

19. Sacalis, J. 1977. Epinasty and ethylene evolution in petioles of sleeved poinsettia plants. *HortScience* 12:388.

20. Saltveit, M. E., and R. A. Larson. 1981. Reducing leaf epinasty in mechanically stressed poinsettia plants. *J. Amer. Soc. Hort. Sci.* 106:156–159.

21. Staby, G. L., J. L. Robertson, D. C. Kiplinger, and C. A. Conover. 1976. *Proc. National Floricultural Conference on Commodity Handling*. Ohio Florists' Assoc., 2001 Fyffe Ct., Columbus, OH 43210.

22. Staby, G. L., J. F. Thompson, and A. M. Kofranek. 1979. Post-harvest characteristics of poinsettias as influenced by handling and storage procedures. *Florists' Review* 165:86–87, 136–139.

23. Veen, H. 1983. Silver thiosulfate: An experimental tool in plant science. *Scientia Hort.* 20:211–224.

24. Veen, H., and S. C. van de Geijn. 1978. Mobility and ionic form of silver as related to longevity of cut carnations. *Planta* 140:93–96.

CHAPTER 16

Marketing

There is as much science, technology, and art applied to floral crops after harvest as before. Storage, packaging, transportation, design, advertising, marketing, and servicing can all be involved in flower or plant handling after harvest. The input can be sufficiently great to justifiably raise the final retail price to several times the level of the wholesale price. Failure to properly market a crop can negate the efforts that have gone into producing a quality crop.

Marketing actually begins with the planning of the crop. It entails a market-demand evaluation to ensure that the correct crops, sizes, colors, and so forth are grown to meet market needs. Cultural schedules are developed to finish the crop at a potentially profitable time. All too often growers become concerned entirely with maximizing the use of bench space and lose sight of the market demand and selling price of the crop. Once a crop is properly planned, the more obvious steps of marketing begin at harvest time.

PACKAGING

It requires skill to harvest fresh flowers at the proper stage of maturity. This topic is covered in detail in books on flower crop production and will not be discussed here. It is sufficient to note that, with the exception of roses, there is a degree of latitude in the stage of development at which the flower must be cut. The exact stage depends upon the length of time and type of handling in the market channel. European and Colombian carnations are often harvested in a tight stage (with guard petals upright) to facilitate shipping and lengthen vase life. Carnations grown for local consumption are generally harvested open (guard petals horizontal or lower) to minimize handling time. Standard chrysanthemums can be similarly harvested in the bud stage, as described in Chapter 15.

Floral products are packaged in conventional unit sizes. Roses and carnations are packaged in bunches of 25, while the number is 10 for standard chrysanthemums, snapdragons, gladioli, tulips, daffodils, irises, and most other fresh flowers. Pompon chrysanthemums are bunched according to weight with 9 ounces (255 g) being common. Generally, the stems are 30 inches (76 cm) long and not less than five stems are included in a bunch. The weight of the bunch varies with different growers. Bunches of fresh flowers are often placed in a plastic sleeve to protect the blooms, and the stem ends are bound with a rubber band or string. Bunches so wrapped are placed in cardboard containers for refrigerated storage or shipping. Colors are not mixed in individual bunches, nor are the types of flowers mixed within a carton. Different-colored bunches are conventionally mixed within the carton in whatever proportion they are produced. The wholesaler and retailer are expected to take them in this ratio to guarantee a market for all. Communication is required between grower and wholesaler for the system to work.

Potted plants are usually sold individually to full-service florists. Some of the larger suppliers of mass markets package potted plants in cardboard cartons in varietal proportion so that they can be more easily stacked in trucks, handled, and inventoried, especially if they are distributed from the central warehouse of a chain store.

Potted plants are often placed in a plastic or paper sleeve just prior to shipping. The sleeve compacts the foliage, reducing the amount of valuable shipping space required by each plant. It also protects the plant from damage during handling. Some growers take advantage of the sleeve as a strategic place to advertise their company and to offer cultural suggestions.

Packaging will play a very important role in the future, particularly for those growers servicing the mass market. Plants are already being marketed in complete enclosures that nearly eliminate evaporation and the need to water them during the period of marketing. The enclosure consists of clear plastic for viewing the plant and for transmission of light for photosynthesis. Some make use of cardboard for the frame, a handle, and a place to advertise. Fresh flowers also may be packaged to prolong shelf life. Such packaging enables control of the atmosphere within and extends life. The location of packaging (grower, wholesaler, retailer) will depend upon comparative costs and returns of the alternatives. Packaging is a fertile area that the grower should consider.

GRADES AND STANDARDS

There has been considerable controversy over grading. Opponents cite hidden factors such as the increased cost of handling. Proponents see grading as a means of discouraging poor quality in the marketplace and achieving financial remuneration for quality. It could also go a long way toward nurturing consumer satisfaction.

Most fresh flower producers use a grading system. One problem, however, is the diversification of grading systems among growers and even the shifting of standards by an individual grower as average flower sizes change throughout the year. If grades could be standardized for all growers, it would be a great benefit for wholesalers and retailers. Ultimately, what benefits the market system and the consumer usually brings benefits to the grower.

Standardized grading could give both the marketer and the consumer a means for judging and demanding the quality they are willing to pay for. It would give the grower a tangible objective and measuring stick for achieving a better product. Greater consumer satisfaction should lead to increased product demand. Higher-quality production and handling would help reduce flower loss in the market channel, which could be helpful in reducing the final selling price of flowers. Obviously, marketers must get involved in this aspect also.

Grading standards have been developed for some fresh flowers. Although a single national set of standards has not been established for roses, nearly all growers grade by stem length. Increments of 2, 3, or 4 inches (51, 76, or 100 mm) are used to separate grades, with the most common being 3 inches and beginning at a minimum length of 9 inches (23 cm). Flowers with weak stems, blemished foliage, off-color blooms, or bullhead blooms are sold as a utility grade. The Society of American Florists (SAF) has been instrumental in developing grades for carnations (Table 16–1).

A set of standards has been developed for green plants (Gaines 1977). Green plants in particular should be graded to protect the consumer as well as the grower of quality plants. Green plants are grown in a favorable environment relatively rich in nutrients and sunlight. They are then utilized, hopefully for many years, in a rather marginal indoor environment. A period of acclimatization must be provided by the grower for these plants to make the transition successfully. Acclimatization can be costly since it entails a period of slow growth when nutrients and light are reduced. Growers who do not acclimatize their crops may realize a profit in the short run, but in the long run the industry is hurt by consumer dissatisfaction. Standards for green plants should take into account such handling so that it is encouraged and rewarded.

Standards did not exist for flowering pot plants until recently. In 1987, the Produce Market Association (PMA) made the decision to promote the development of grades and standards. They joined forces with the Society of American Florists. The first set of guidelines was released in 1989 and covered azalea, chrysanthemum, lilies, and poinsettia. Standards for African violet, gloxinia, *Kalanchoe,* and all other bulb crops should be completed in 1990 and all remaining crops by the mid-1990s.

The standards are voluntary, and it is hoped that they will never be absolutely binding. Differences in taste exist across regions. Desired pot plant height is

Table 16–1

Society of American Florists' Standards for Carnation Grades[1]

	Blue Grade (Fancy) (1)	Red Grade (Standard) (2)	Green Grade (Short) (3)
Minimum length[2]	22 in. (56 cm)	17 in. (43 cm)	12 in. (30 cm)
Minimum flower diameter[3]	Tight[4] 2 in. (51 mm)	1¾ in. (44 mm)	No requirement
	Fairly tight 2½ in. (64 mm)	2¼ in. (57 mm)	
	Open 3 in. (76 mm)	2¾ in. (70 mm)	

[1]Flowers in the blue, red, and green grades should be full, symmetrical, free of insects, disease, mechanical injury, and free of bloom defects such as slab side, bullhead, blow heads, singles, sleepy appearance, splits, and discoloration. The stems should be of sufficient strength so that they do not deviate more than 30 degrees from the horizontal plane when held 1 inch (2.5 cm) above the minimum length of the grade with the natural curvature down. Any flowers with these defects are either sold at a lower price or are discarded.

[2]Length measured from top of bloom to cut end of stem.

[3]The flower diameter is the greatest dimension of the petals measured through the center of the bloom. The guard petals of open blooms are held horizontally when size is determined.

[4]*Tight*—guard petals up, center petals up but fluffed. *Fairly tight*—guard petals horizontal, center petals up and fluffed. *Open*—guard petals are horizontal or lower, center petals are out or down.

taller in the western regions of the United States than in the East. The consumer preference is for an 18–20 inch (46–51 cm) pot mum in California; on the East Coast, a 14–16 inch (36–41 cm) plant (measured from base of pot to top of plant) is preferred. Included in the standards are height, minimum width of the top of the plant, number and developmental stage of buds, condition of foliage and roots, strength of stems, and the presence of a care tag. Separate standards are developed within each species of plant for various grades in accordance with pot size. For example, poinsettia grades include "small" for 4–4.5 inch (10–11 cm) pots, "medium" for 5–5.5 inch (13–14 cm) pots, "large" for 6–6.5 inch (15–17 cm) pots, "extra large" for 7–8.5 inch (18–22 cm) pots, and "jumbo" for 10 inch (25 cm) pots. (A complete set of standards may be purchased. Write to PMA, 1500 Casho Mill Rd., Newark, DE 19714.)

When the grower has finished grading and packing fresh flowers or potted plants, it is generally his or her task to ship them to the wholesaler or retailer. Green plants are an exception as they are often shipped by the grower at the retailer's expense or are picked up directly by the wholesaler or retailer.

THE MARKET SYSTEM

Consumers exist wherever people live—in cities, towns, and villages scattered throughout the states and provinces. Floral production, however, is more centralized. This is particularly true of the fresh flower industry. The heaviest concentration of gladioli comes from Florida; carnations, from Colorado and California; and spray-type chrysanthemums, from Florida and California. The trend is not as well established for flowering plants, but the vast majority of green plants come from Florida, California, and Texas. Under such circumstances, a complex marketing system is necessary (Figure 16–1).

The marketing system serves the functions of gathering together the various floral products of many diverse growers, of bringing these within reach of consumers both close to and distant from the producers, and of developing a consumer awareness and desire to purchase the floral products.

Fresh Flowers

The floral marketing system has several components. There are a number of possible channels within the system. Fresh flowers pass through the most extensive channel, thus providing us with a good overview of the whole system. In The Netherlands, fresh flowers and flowering plants are customarily brought to an auction where they are purchased by wholesalers. Such auctions have appeared in America on a limited scale in the past 15 years. The broker quite often serves as an alternative to the auction in America. In this situation, an individual firm purchases flowers or plants from growers to fill orders it has received from wholesalers or large retail florists. Most often, the broker is located in the region of concentrated production such that crops can be examined to match them to the various grade and quality levels demanded by clients. The wholesalers served are scattered at considerable distances from the production area. It is this breach between grower and wholesaler that creates the need for auctions and brokers. The broker system is popular in the fresh flower production area of California as well as in the green plant production areas of Florida and California.

Traditionally, fresh flowers in America have passed directly from the grower to the wholesaler. Often, the wholesaler is a commission wholesaler, one who takes flowers on consignment. This means that the grower is paid for flowers that the wholesaler sells but not for those that he or she fails to market. The commis-

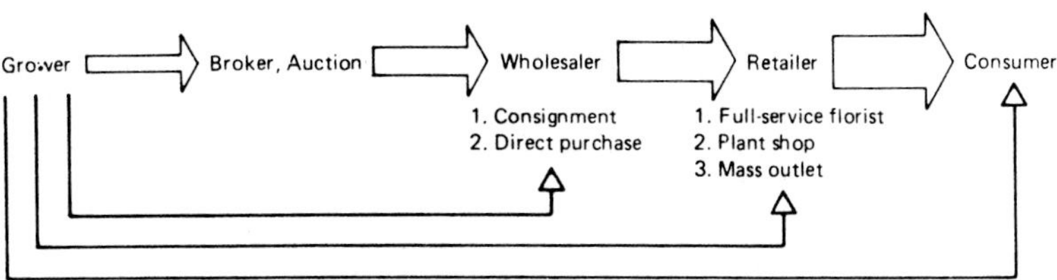

Figure 16–1

Channels through which fresh flowers flow from the grower to the final consumer.

sion wholesaler sells the flowers at a wholesale price and then takes a commission of about 25 percent from this price, returning the remainder to the grower.

Recently, a trend has been developing for wholesalers to buy flowers outright from the grower or broker. This system is more expedient where flowers are mass-produced in an area and wholesaled at a great distance away. Although the wholesaler appears to assume all the risk, this is not the case. Flower losses can be reflected in lower returns to the grower or higher prices to the consumer. The latter affects consumer demand, which hurts the grower.

Wholesalers sell flowers to retailers. Some retailers travel to the wholesale house to make their purchases; others are serviced by trucks operated by the wholesaler. Wholesale florists quite often stock supplies needed by retail florists. Included are such items as ribbon, net, vases, and wreaths, which are used in the daily operation of a full-service retail flower shop. The inventory may be larger, including plastic flower arrangements and giftwares to be sold directly by the retail florist.

Most of the sales are made over the phone by salespeople employed by the wholesale florist. When the orders are filled, the remaining space on the truck is filled with flowers and merchandise that will probably be sold along the route (Figure 16–2). Each florist is generally serviced twice a week, often by more than one wholesaler. These truck routes serve a very valuable role for retail florists who are located in remote areas. The wholesale florist likewise plays a valuable role for the retail florist near transportation facilities. The wholesaler brings together hundreds of items from numerous sources for the retailer's use. This saves the retailer considerable time and expense as well as the problem of overstocking on items that must be purchased in case lots and soon become outdated. The wholesaler makes it his or her business to keep abreast of changing tastes in supplies, which further benefits the retailer.

There are various types of retailers, as anyone who purchases flowers or plants is well aware. Traditionally, we think of the full-service florist shop, where there is a designer to arrange flowers and an available delivery service. Plant shops and flower boutiques are becoming more numerous. These are cash-and-carry outlets where plants and flowers may be purchased. Sometimes, simple arrangements of flowers are offered, mainly for home decoration, but delivery service is not provided. A number of full-service florists operate such shops as well. Mass-market retail outlets have become a very large business. Close to half the production of the United States passes through these outlets. These are the cash-and-carry stands, wagons, and minishops that are located in high-traffic areas within supermarkets, department stores, discount stores, shopping malls, airports, and on street corners. The markup is generally 30–40 percent. Therefore, when a plant sells for \$1.00, the mass-market outlet retains \$0.30–\$0.40, while the grower receives \$0.60–\$0.70.

A subtle difference (often misunderstood) exists between two systems for setting the retail price. *Markup* refers to a percentage of the retail price,

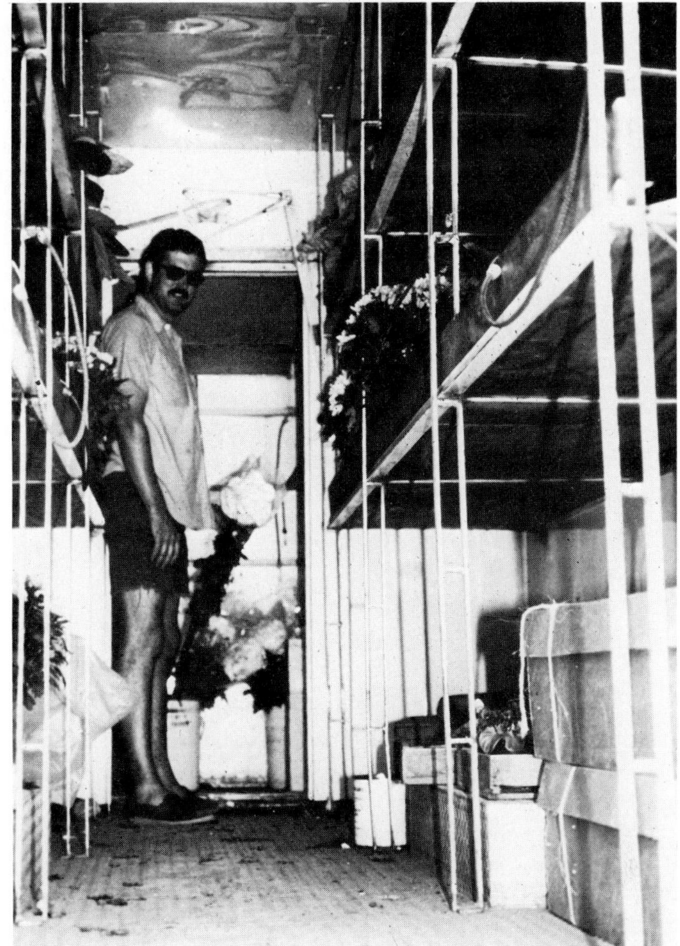

Figure 16–2

The interior of a wholesaler's truck used for delivering fresh flowers and potted plants to full-service retail florists. Although not common, a small refrigerated room for fresh flowers is located at the forward part of this truck.

while *mark-on* relates to a percentage of the wholesale price. To illustrate the difference, assume that you as grower receive \$1.00 each for your potted plants. One retail outlet using a 33 percent markup charges its customers \$1.50 per plant: \$1.00 (wholesale price) ÷ (1 − 0.33) = \$1.49. A second outlet using a 33 percent mark-on charges \$1.33 per plant: 1.33 × \$1.00 (wholesale price) = \$1.33.

Flowering Pot Plants

Flowering plants are sold through auctions in The Netherlands. As a rule, in America they are sold directly to retail outlets by growers. Flowering plant growers are generally situated near population centers. Long-distance transportation does not enter into the picture as extensively as in the fresh flower case. The typical flowering plant grower would operate one or more trucks for delivery purposes and have his or her own sales department. Plants are generally delivered within a radius of one working day's travel. There has been a feeling in the past that potted plants are too heavy to transport the distances that fresh flowers are shipped. To a degree this is true since potted plants cannot generally be shipped by air as many of the fresh flowers are. However, in recent years, some very large pot plant ranges have developed to supply the mass market. Such ranges successfully deliver plants 500 or more miles by truck. Success is dependent upon having fewer delivery points per truck, larger orders per stop, and stores that can accommodate large trucks. Insulated trucks are used that are heated in winter and cooled in summer.

Green Plants

Green plants are produced most extensively in Florida, California, and Texas, which dictates the need for a marketing system as described for fresh flowers. Many of these plants pass through brokers to wholesalers. A significant group of green plant wholesalers turns out to be growers operating in close proximity to the retail market. While the basic line of green plants is the tropicals, which in spite of transportation are most economically produced in subtropical regions, there are some green plants that can be produced economically in close proximity to the market. The local grower–wholesaler business combination allows the flexibility needed to develop this potential.

Wholesalers truck their plants from Florida or California to their greenhouse range, where they are held until they can be marketed to retailers along their truck routes. The greenhouse is necessary for holding these plants since a considerable length of time may pass before some are sold. The greenhouse also affords an opportunity to supplement the line of plants with some that can be produced more profitably than bought. There are yet other plants that are purchased in early stages of growth and are finished locally. The grower–wholesaler business combination is working out well for the green plant industry.

Direct Sales

Locally produced fresh flowers are in high demand when they are produced continuously throughout the year and at a high level of quality. There is some effort on the part of retailers to trade directly with such sources. With a modest effort, a grower can establish a market without passing through the wholesaler. This system is used particularly by smaller growers. New growers of fresh flowers, and more often of potted plants, sometimes sell directly to the final consumer. This allows them to enter into two businesses for little more overhead than that of the growing operation. Funds are generated faster this way. This system works well when the extra labor can be provided by the owner, assuming that there is not a more profitable use for his or her labor at the time. This is at best a temporary system, and soon a decision must be made as to whether to operate one or both businesses.

There are a number of large full-service retail outlets and some mass-market retailers who operate their own production ranges. Care must be taken to keep separate records on each business, lest one should exist at the expense of the other. Quite often, the retail outlet is the more successful of the two, in which case it might be better to purchase flowers and plants from another source.

Flower Auctions

Flower auctions exist where there is concentrated production some distance away from the retail market. The Dutch flower auctions are perhaps the most famous (Figure 16–3). Flower production, concentrated in a few regions of a small nation, The Netherlands, supplies retail markets through Europe and America. To make the distribution system efficient, growers send fresh flowers and plants to an auction, where they are purchased by the wholesalers who, in turn, distribute them to retailers throughout Europe. This adds an extra link between the grower and the wholesaler in the distribution chain illustrated in Figure 16–1, but in so doing it brings wholesalers into contact with hundreds of growers who would otherwise be unreachable.

Flower auctions in The Netherlands and Canada also exist because of the practices of some wholesalers who played growers off against one another. Growers by definition are in a weak market position because of the perishability of their product. By uniting in a producer's cooperative, individuals strengthen their market position.

Dutch auctions charge the grower/members a commission of about 5 percent. The buyer pays about 0.3 percent service costs. This does not necessarily increase the retail price over that in a system without a flower auction since the job of the wholesaler is made more efficient by the auction.

A typical auction functions as follows. Flowers or plants are delivered by the grower to the auction, where they are set out on display. Early in the day, wholesalers peruse each lot to assess quality and condition. In so doing, they decide which lots they wish to purchase and how much they are willing to pay. Later in the morning, wholesalers take their assigned seats in the auction room as pictured in Figure 16–4. Each lot of plants is brought one at a time before the wholesalers. The clock at the front of the room indicates the identification number of the

Figure 16–3

The exterior and interior views of the United Flower Auctions in Aalsmeer, The Netherlands. This is the largest flower auction in the world with approximately 4,000 members. Such auctions serve as a distribution channel between growers and wholesalers. (*Photos courtesy of United Flower Auctions Aalsmeer, Aalsmeer, The Netherlands*

Figure 16–4

One of many auction rooms in the United Flower Auctions in Aalsmeer, The Netherlands, where over two billion flowers and plants are sold each year. (*Photo courtesy of* United Flower Auctions Aalsmeer, Aalsmeer, The Netherlands)

grower of the plants and the lot number of the plants. An auction employee holds the plants for all to see, and the auctioneer gives a brief assessment of the plants. The sale begins when the clock pointer, set on 100, is released and begins its descent in price. The value of each unit on the clock's scale of 0 to 100 is denoted on the clock—whether it be 1, 5, 10, 25, or 100 Dutch cents. When the pointer comes down to the price a wholesaler is intending to pay, he or she presses a desk button that stops the clock and electrically records his or her identification number and the price on the clock at that point. The wholesaler finalizes the sale by indicating the quantity of the lot he or she wishes to purchase. In a matter of a few hours, all of the day's sales are made.

This system works rapidly. As many as 700 transactions can be made per clock per hour. The interests of both seller and buyer are served. If the buyer waits for an exceptionally low price, he or she may lose the chance to purchase the plants desired. If he or she bids too soon, a needlessly high price is paid. Each lot of plants is judged independently, and its price is established accordingly. The principle of supply and demand expresses itself in this system.

When sales are finished, flowers or plants are moved from their display area to loading docks where the trucks of the various wholesalers are waiting. Even this process is often mechanized. Carts are loaded according to purchaser and are moved automatically along tracks to the loading area. When the day ends, the auction house is ready to repeat its cycle.

Three auctions have opened in Canada in recent years in Montreal, Toronto, and Vancouver, and two have opened in the United States on Long Island, New York, and in San Diego. Concentrated production at a distance from scattered markets played a role in the establishment of these auctions, particularly the Toronto and San Diego auctions. Wholesalers and retailers alike make purchases in these auctions.

ADVERTISING

The need for advertising varies. A grower who sells to one wholesaler or to a few wholesalers will generally have little motivation to advertise. The grower of a centralized crop such as green plants in Florida or fresh flowers in California will probably be interested in new wholesale outlets. This grower often advertises in the various florist trade papers.

The retailer has the greatest need for advertising. Unfortunately, cost may be a deterrent. Those who do advertise generally find it profitable. Newspaper ads are most commonly used. Radio spots are also valuable, particularly toward the weekend and in connection with a gardener's program. Television has been used by some and can have a far-reaching effect when done properly. Mailing lists have provided a very successful avenue of communication with the consuming public for many retailers.

It is not the intent of this book to take more than a cursory look at retail marketing. While the major burden of advertising rests on the retailer, the grower is not without obligation. The allied supply industry, growers, wholesalers, and retailers, are all parts of one system that culminates in the sale of floral products to the consumer. It has been demonstrated in the floral industry that advertising effectively increases the demand for these products. This ultimately benefits all segments of the industry; thus, all should share in the advertising program. Shared advertising is often practiced in other businesses. The Coca Cola® sign, so often used to display the name of a restaurant, is paid in part by the Coca Cola Company. Advertisements for a given product, regardless of the retail outlet, will carry the same logo (sketch, picture, and so on). The logo is developed and provided at the expense of the producer. The advertising cost for many items presented by the local supermarket in its newspaper ads is borne by the producer of the products.

There are national and international advertising programs in the floral industry. The floral wire services collect a percentage of the gross wire sales of their member retail florists and use these funds for wide-range advertisement. The individual retail florists expend additional funds for local advertising. Through the centralized program of the wire houses, expensive but highly effective advertising media can be used. National television and major magazine ads are procured. Billboard space is contracted. Consumer information literature is underwritten, such as the booklet *Professional Guide to Green Plants* sponsored by Florists' Transworld Delivery Association.

The closest the floral industry comes to a properly shared advertising program is seen in the efforts of the American Florists' Marketing Council (AFMC) of the Society of American Florists (SAF). This organization carries on a national advertising program with funds derived from all segments of the floral industry on a voluntary basis. The AFMC is running advertisements in national magazines and newspapers such as *U.S. News and World Report, Redbook, Sports Illustrated,* and the *Wall Street Journal,* as well as radio spot ads on the ABC, CBS, and NBC television networks. In addition, they prepare and offer at cost in-store display banners, newspaper advertisement mats ready to submit to the newspaper once the retailer's name and address are inserted, radio spot scripts, and truck and billboard signs. The overall program is having a positive effect on increasing the floral market but needs to be much larger in light of the potential market.

Floral growers have an obligation to share the overall marketing responsibility of the industry. There are several things they can do:

1. Financially support cooperative advertising programs such as the AFMC.
2. Explore the possibility of and, when warranted, work with wholesalers and retailers in local promotional programs.
3. Establish communications with the wholesale and retail segments of the industry through membership in their organizations, attendance at their conventions, and reading of their literature.

Much of the potential of the floral industry is dependent upon a greater degree of cooperation among the diverse businesses making it up. A major problem in the industry today is lack of unity, as seen in separate grower, wholesaler, and retailer organizations, meetings, literature, and attitudes. Such disunity can hurt even at the individual grower's level. Wire services periodically feature specific fresh flowers and plants in their promotional programs. Grower alerts are issued long in advance of the promotion date, but many growers are not tuned in. This has a negative effect in the marketplace since the promotional item falls into short supply and prices rise adversely. It can be disadvantageous to the growers, who find themselves heavy on nonpromotional items and short on those in demand. Through interindustry communication, it should be possible to use promotional programs as a means for coping with inadvertent overproduction and periods of low market demand and for establishing consumer demand for products and product forms, thus rendering larger profit to the grower, greater ease of handling in the market channel, and increased consumer satisfaction.

There are other ways growers can play a role in the overall promotional or advertising program. They must concern themselves with consumer satisfaction. This can be done by selecting plant varieties that stand up best in the region in which they are marketed. Fuchsias are beautiful almost anywhere in the spring but are a disappointment to consumers in hot climates when the heat of summer arrives. Such sales should be discouraged, and in their place crops adapted to the situation should be promoted. The grower has a responsibility to make such decisions and to educate the retailer. It is the further responsibility of the grower to produce plants of high quality, free of insects and disease. Whether consumers relate plant failure to the grower or to themselves, the main effect is the erosion of the desire to make a subsequent purchase.

The consuming public has an underlying desire for information. This is often as important as the product itself. The grower should provide identification and cultural information with each unit sold. Plastic stakes are available with such information for many types of pot plants. If not available, one could have such stakes made or could attach an information sheet to the plant or have the information printed on the plastic sleeve if used.

The grower's responsibility to educate does not stop here. He or she must pass information along to the retailer as to how the product is to be handled during marketing. The grower should also supply information that the retailer can pass along to the consumer. This responsibility is particularly important in the mass-market channels, where merchandisers often have little experience in handling plants. Some larger growers supplying mass markets have found it advantageous to work with the management in chain stores in training their produce managers to properly handle floral products.

There are no binding laws forcing a grower to participate in advertising or promotional programs. Advertising as discussed thus far falls under two categories: (1) *brand-name advertising,* in which the advertising firm is directly promoting its own products; and (2) *generic advertising.*

In brand-name advertising, for example, Nelson the Florist advertises poinsettias for Christmas so that the townspeople will buy from him rather than from the supermarket. The effects of such advertising are relatively easy to evaluate. The fact that most retailers and wholesalers engage in it is testimony to its success.

Generic advertising promotes flowers and plants in general without reference to any brand names. Its purpose is to expand the total market. The AFMC program is an example of this type of advertising or promotion. It is difficult to evaluate the usefulness of such advertising since the effects are indirect. A large producer servicing the mass market over an expansive region will probably sense an effect and feel that the expenditure returns a profit. A smaller grower, particularly one selling to full-service retail florists, may not feel that it is profitable. This is a business decision that must be made by each firm; however, too few businesses have realistically considered generic advertising. It would be better for the floriculture industry as a whole if more businesses were involved.

SUMMARY

1. Packaging of fresh flowers has been standardized by convention. A set number or weight of flowers constitutes a bunch. Bunches are shipped in cardboard cartons, the number contained within depending upon the grade. Potted plants were customarily sold individually and often in plastic sleeves. It is common today for potted plants to be shipped in cardboard cartons and to be sold in the multiple contained within a carton. The number in a carton depends on the pot size, type of plant, and the grower. Pot plant packaging is new and not standardized.

2. Grades and standards exist for some fresh flowers and are just now being established for potted plants. Grading is a voluntary program that is practiced by many growers. It would be advantageous to the floral industry and the consumer if all growers adhered to a single grading system. Today, many systems are in use.

3. Fresh flowers are usually purchased from growers by wholesalers who, in turn, sell them to retailers. Brokers and auctions are playing an increasing role in moving fresh flowers from growers to wholesalers.

4. Potted flowering plants are generally sold directly by growers to retailers. Potted green plants often pass through a broker and a wholesaler en route to the retailer.

5. Flower auctions are popular in Europe and have recently opened in Canada and the United States. They serve well as a channel between growers and wholesalers when production is concentrated and located at a considerable distance from the retail market.

6. Advertising, as in any other business, is critical to the floral industry. Any increase in consumer demand has the potential to benefit all segments of this industry. While the heaviest investment in advertising is made by retailers, the burden is shared by wholesalers, growers, and allied trades as well. The American Florists' Marketing Council (AFMC) of the Society of American Florists (SAF) carries out a promotional program enhanced by voluntary contributions from all of the industry. Considerably more promotional effort must be made by the floriculture industry before it comes up to the standards of most other industries. Growers can do their part by supporting existing national promotional programs, by joining in local promotional programs with wholesalers and retailers, by communicating more extensively with the wholesaling and retailing groups, by supplying technical information to retailers to aid them in handling floral products and better advising the consumer, and by producing high-quality plants well acclimated to the consumer's environment so that satisfaction is guaranteed.

REFERENCES

Numerous popular and academic books exist on marketing. As a student, one should consider a course in marketing essential.

1. Berninger, L. M. 1982. *Profitable garden center management*, 2d ed. Reston, VA: Reston Publishing.
2. Gaines, R. L. 1977. *Guidelines to Foliage Plant Specifications for Interior Use*. Apopka, FL: Florida Foliage Association.
3. Laurie, A., D. C. Kiplinger, and K. S. Nelson. 1979. *Commercial flower-forcing*, 8th ed., chap. 14. New York: McGraw-Hill.
4. Nichols, R., and G. Sheard, eds. 1975. Post harvest physiology of cut flowers. *Acta Hort.* No. 41.
5. Pfahl, P. B. 1973. *The Retail Florist Business*, 2d ed. Danville, IL: Interstate Printers & Publishers.
6. Society of American Florists' Grades and Standards Committee. Standard grades for carnations. Soc. Amer. Florists, 901 N. Washington St., Alexandria, VA 22314.
7. Staby, G. L., J. L. Robertson, D. C. Kiplinger, and C. A. Conover. 1976. *Proc. National Floricultural Conference on Commodity Handling*. Ohio Florists' Assoc., 2001 Fyffe Ct., Columbus, OH 43210.

CHAPTER 17

Business Management

Management and labor are distinctly different activities. *Management* is the directing of labor, time, and materials. *Labor* is the execution of plans developed. The owner of small greenhouses often finds it necessary to be a laborer as well as a manager. This is alright as long as he or she never loses sight of the need to manage. Without proper management, an owner–manager expends a great deal of effort with little return, the attitude of the labor force deteriorates, and the business fails to meet its goals. This situation is unstable and ultimately leads to failure.

Management efforts must be applied to planning the expenditure of labor, time, and materials and must allocate these expenditures properly to crop production and to marketing. As the greenhouse range grows in size, the integration of production and the subsequent marketing of this production become complex, and responsibilities such as purchasing materials, handling billing and payments, bookkeeping, and even correspondence in general become great enough to distract the manager from production and marketing operations. At this point, a business affairs office with its own staff is warranted, as well as additional managerial personnel.

BUSINESS STRUCTURE

Managers themselves must be properly organized and managed in order for a business to succeed. The general manager is at the top of the managerial ladder. He or she is responsible for all departments. The manager of each department answers directly to the general manager. It is important that each department manager be held responsible for his or her assignment and the work of employees below him or her. At the same time, each employee should answer to one person only.

The labor of a greenhouse production business falls into four general categories (Figure 17–1):

1. The efforts directly involved in producing crops come under the production department.
2. The marketing department solicits orders, packages the crop, and delivers and performs whatever other services might be required at the point of sale.
3. The engineering department maintains the physical plant and equipment. It has the further task of custom-building facilities and equipment such as benches in the greenhouse, racks for the trucks, and so on.
4. The business affairs department handles affairs such as record-keeping for tax and cost accounting purposes, billing, purchasing, and payroll administration.

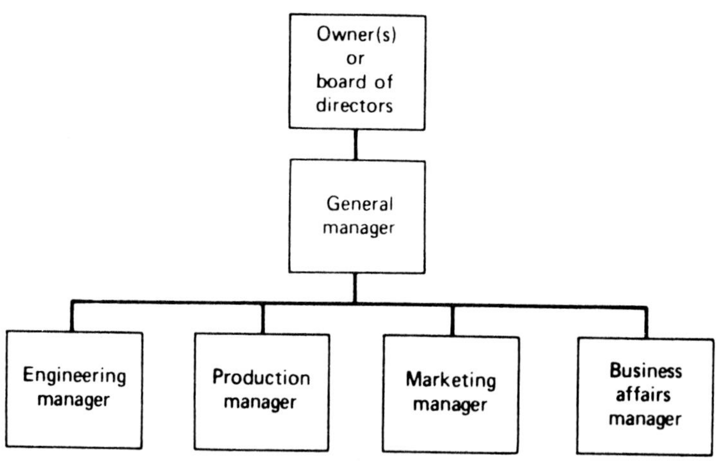

Figure 17–1

A typical managerial structure of a greenhouse business. The owner(s), in the case of a single proprietorship or partnership, or the board of directors of a corporation, carry the full responsibility for the business. The manager of each of four departments takes orders directly from a general manager, who takes orders from the owner. All labor within a department answers directly to the management of that department. The four common departments are engineering (repairs and construction), production, marketing, and business affairs.

Full responsibility for the business is held by the owner. The owner of a small business often fills the various management roles as well. In this case, he or she serves two roles and is entitled to the manager's salary and whatever profits are left over. The small business has few employees, and direct communication can be maintained between each employee and the owner. Although the functions of the four departments exist, separate managers are not required. The owner is the general manager and also the manager of each department.

When the business grows in size, it becomes impractical for the owner to manage all functions. The owner assesses his or her talents and interests and continues to manage one or more departments. Personnel are employed to manage the other departments. For example, the general manager of the company might continue to serve as manager of the engineering and marketing departments. The general manager hires a business affairs manager, who at first manages and carries out the tasks of this department alone and later supervises a number of clerks subsequently hired. The general manager also hires a production manager to manage the labor force involved in growing the crops. The two new managers take their orders directly from the general manager, who is the owner in this case. Each employee receives his or her orders from his or her department manager and not from the general manager.

Further expansions may increase the workload of the general manager to the point where the owner serves only in that capacity. Engineering and marketing managers may then be hired. Perhaps at this time, the size of the production department has become too great for a single manager to effectively handle. Submanagers (often called growers) might be hired to manage production sections. The submanagers take orders from the production manager, and, in turn, the employees under them take orders only from them. Production sections are defined by logic. If the greenhouse business is situated in two locations, each might constitute a section. If potted plants and fresh flowers are grown, it is logical to place each in its own section since the physical facilities (bench type and arrangement, planting area, and so on) differ.

The owner may enter into other business ventures, such as wholesale marketing, retailing, or even an unrelated business. The establishment of another business may possibly require all of his or her attention, in which case the role of the general manager of the greenhouse business should be relinquished. At this point, he or she no longer draws a managerial salary but does receive the profits.

Two or more owners in partnership must organize in such a manner that the business is commanded with a single voice. Duality of command is constantly open to discrepancy and undermines productivity. One partner might serve as general manager, while the other serves below him or her as manager of one or more departments. In another arrangement, one owner may be a silent partner; the other, a general manager. Both partners share in the profits according to their initial agreement, but the managing partner generally draws in addition a salary in accordance with his or her managerial input. There are many ways to organize a partnership, but the important point is that a unified line of command is established and that the agreement between partners is in writing.

The owners of a corporation are the stockholders. A number of greenhouse businesses are corporations. Obviously, each owner cannot be allowed to give orders. Stockholders' meetings are periodically convened to decide the objectives and methods of operation of the corporation. A board of directors is set up to represent all the stockholders. The board of directors communicates in a single voice with the general manager of the company.

A proper balance of management and labor must be achieved. Management is costly, as the students of floriculture well know, since it is these positions they ultimately seek. But indiscriminate reduction of the management force can be even more costly because it leads to a breakdown in communications and inefficiency of resource utilization. The owner must watch the profit-and-loss statement and weigh it against the operational efficiency of his or her business to determine the proper time to adjust the management force. Presented in Table 17–1 are the average number of people in various management positions and typical salaries received in 1980 for six categories of flowering pot plant firms. These firms encompass three sizes (20,000, 100,000, and 400,000 ft^2) and two market channels (the mass market and full-service florists).

LABOR MANAGEMENT

Labor management begins with personal management. To manage others, one must manage one's own life in such a way as to develop traits of leadership. Leadership, coupled with financial and other personal inducements, should provide the motivation needed for workers to carry out their job assignments.

Leadership

A leader is one who through practice comfortably exhibits traits of self-motivation and perseverance that will provide the impetus to stimulate activity when there is a resistance to move ahead. He or she must provide the motivation when the task becomes wearisome and success seems out of reach. A leader must naturally maintain traits of integrity and justice. These qualities gain respect, without which leadership cannot exist. A just system gives the worker a sense of security and an inducement to render an honest day's service for an honest day's wage. Justice calls for setting aside personal prejudices and relationships to see that each individual is judged on his or her own merits. It calls for a just reward where earned and constructive criticism or assistance where needed. A leader must have empathy, for it is only through compassion and understanding that the myriad of gaps in personality and position of the workers can be bridged. Unless some common ground can be found, communication is not possible.

Table 17–1

Typical Annual Salaries and Number of People in Various Management Positions in Each of Three Greenhouse Firm Sizes Producing Pot Plants for Either the Mass Market or the Full-Service Flower Shops[1]

	Mass Market			*Flower Shop*		
Position	*Number*	*Salary*	*Total Cost*	*Number*	*Salary*	*Total Cost*
20,000 ft² Firm Size:						
General mgr.	1	$15,000	$ 15,000	1	$15,000	$ 15,000
Salespeople	0.80	10,000	8,000	1.33	12,000	15,960
Sec-bookkeeper	0.40	9,000	3,600	0.50	9,000	4,500
Total cost			$ 26,600			$ 35,460
100,000 ft² Firm Size:						
General mgr.	1	$25,000	25,000	1	$25,000	$ 25,000
Prod-maint-lab mgr.[2]	1	20,000	20,000	1	20,000	20,000
Growers	1	15,000	15,000	2	15,000	30,000
Salespeople	1.33	12,000	15,960	2	20,000	40,000
Sec-bookkeeper	0.75	9,000	6,750	1	9,000	9,000
Total cost			$ 82,710			$124,000
400,000 ft² Firm Size:						
General mgr.	1	$35,000	$ 35,000	1	$35,000	$ 35,000
Asst. general mgr.				1	25,000	25,000
Production mgr.	1	25,000	25,000	1	25,000	25,000
Growers	5	15,000	75,000	6	15,000	90,000
Labor mgr.	1	25,000	25,000			
Maint. mgr.				1	20,000	20,000
Maint. people	2	10,000	20,000	3	10,000	30,000
Sales mgr.	1	25,000	25,000	1	25,000	25,000
Salespeople	6	14,500	87,000	9	22,000	198,000
Sec-bookkeeper	1.5	10,000	15,000	3.5	10,000	35,000
Total cost			$307,000			$483,000

[1]From Brumfield, Nelson, Coutu, Willits, and Sowell (1981).
[2]Production–maintenance–labor manager.

Elements of Success

The manager who has the qualities of leadership must organize his or her efforts in such a way as to achieve success. Success depends upon a goal, a plan, faith, and perseverance.

Goal The manager must establish the success of the business as his or her primary goal. This can be spelled out in many ways. It may be a monetary figure that the business should achieve by some point in time, a volume of production for the existing greenhouse area, a prespecified lower level of crop loss, a projected level of quality, an expansion in business size, or the adoption of new crops into the production scheme. If the manager is not the owner, it is important that his or her goals coincide with those of the owner. A business in the free enterprise system can afford to reimburse employees financially only in proportion to their contribution toward the financial goal of the business.

When the manager sets a goal, it must be explicit as in a dollar value of income, a certain number of pots, or a definite percentage of flowers in the premium grade. When a specific quantity is set as the goal, the manager is able to determine where he or she is in relation to the goal. With this knowledge, all efforts can be apportioned to reach the goal. The goal is very important. Without it, a course of action cannot be plotted. Some years ago, contestants of quiz shows were interviewed some 10 years after they had won large sums of money. They were asked to show their positive achievements as a result of the unexpected sum of money that had entered their lives. More than 9 out of 10 failed to show any lasting value derived from the money. On the contrary, many found themselves in a poorer lot of life as a result. Loss of initiative, complacency, inability to adapt back to a lower material level of life when the funds were depleted, and other such problems took their toll. Divorce was a common result. The problem stemmed from acquisition of money without a goal to direct its proper use. It is unusual when one can properly manage that which he or she is incapable of earning. If the contestants had a realistic goal and a plan for using the acquired money, it is very likely that it would have improved their lot in life.

Plan A goal alone is not enough to bring success. Just as one does not drive to an unfamiliar destination without a road map, a goal is not attained without a plan. Plans are sometimes demanded of us, as in the case of arranging a loan. Lending agencies demand a proforma as part of the application to see how the money is to be used and what the chances of success and repayment are. This same planning should enter into all operations of the greenhouse range.

Before a plan is drafted, the objective should be researched. The manager should obtain literature in order to establish a background. He or she should communicate with other firms that have successfully undertaken this objective. Suppliers of materials required for the objective are another good source of information. Finally, the manager should integrate this knowledge into his or her own past experience and logic and sit down to formulate a plan.

The plan must encompass a timetable. A reasonable timetable is a weapon against procrastination. The plan should earmark primary objectives within the goal for periodic review and secondary objectives for setting up daily work plans. Each objective must have a stated date of accomplishment.

Crop production depends upon a number of straightforward operations performed on a precise schedule. A good program has the misleading appearance of monotony. A chrysanthemum range, for instance, has its recurring three-month cycle of planting, pinching, lighting, shading, disbudding, watering, fertilizing, spraying, and harvesting. A new manager can quickly settle into a state of boredom and, in the absence of a plan, can begin to perform operations late or miss them altogether. Monotony is quickly replaced with an almost impossible task of saving the crop. The astute manager seeks to establish a simple plan of culture that meets all the needs of the plant on schedule. He or she then satisfies the need for adventure and creative outlet through an appreciation for the plant and an attention to detail.

Even the best plans do not hold up forever. Most change begins subtly. The keen manager develops a sense for where insects or disease might first appear and develops a recognition of the infinitesimal changes in plant appearance signaling encroaching disorder. In short, he or she heads off conflict before the need arises to fight a battle. It is an ever-changing challenge that can be met only when the gross physical requirements of the crop are guaranteed in a plan.

Faith Goals and plans require a degree of faith. If the manager harbors doubt in his or her ability to accomplish the plan, it tends to feed on itself and grow in his or her mind. The feeling is inadvertently transmitted to the workers, who will magnify it and reflect it back. Doubt is self-destructive and can be countered only by faith.

Everyone has doubts at one time or another. Doubt can be minimized by practicing an attitude of positive thinking. Doubts that still exist can be disposed of through a process of autosuggestion.

We form impressions from everything we do, see, hear, or feel. These impressions may be negative or positive. There is no middle ground. Information received by our conscious faculties feeds into our subconscious. Our minds are at work day and night gathering evidence to support conclusions we have drawn.

When we entertain the idea of failure, we begin to see evidence around us that would suggest failure. When we anticipate success, our minds tend to blank out evidence that would suggest failure and recognize evidence supporting impending success. Our faith in success is thereby strengthened. This, in turn, causes us to gravitate toward an environment in which answers exist for the needs of our goal; thus, it nurtures our ability to draft a plan.

Our attitudes are readily communicated even without speech. An attitude of direction and self-confidence attracts other positive-thinking people. This is important because one rarely solves all of his or her problems independently. Each member of a group contributes a different perspective and additional information. The greenhouse manager should never "go it alone." He or she should seek a relationship with positive-thinking people at the state university and among the management of other greenhouses, as well as with allied tradespeople, community business people, and civic groups. All conceivable types of information and perspectives eventually come to bear on greenhouse management.

Perseverance Besides a goal, a plan, and faith, success requires perseverance. Very often, one's first plan will fail. If you give up at this point, then you will not be a successful manager. Each apparent failure has a lesson contained in it that points the way to an improved plan. People who press on after repeated failures invariably succeed.

The effective manager comes to learn that success is a journey and not a destination. While a plan for the culture of a crop must be simple and precise, it must also be continuously altered to accommodate changing cultivars, climate, market dates, automation, and so forth. Maintenance of faith requires constant practice of positive thinking. Above all, to realize viable goals, a manager must continuously develop a perspective on the business firm he or she serves, the floriculture industry, the labor force, and the needs of society as a whole.

Manager–Employee Relationship

Assuming that the labor force has an adequate level of skill and motivational potential, its accomplishments will depend upon the manager. The labor force must be aware of the managerial structure, know the goals toward which they work, be delegated sufficient authority to accomplish their jobs, understand the system by which they are to be evaluated, and be assured of recognition for their efforts.

Management Structure As previously discussed, each employee must answer to only one superior. Such a system gives continuity to the chain of command so that the firm's goals are not altered or diluted. It also minimizes confusion in the minds of employees so that each can more fully apply himself or herself to the task. To maintain such a system, each employee should be made aware of the overall structure of management. Although the structure demands that each employee takes orders from his or her immediate superior, there should also be a system for higher appeal in the event that an employee feels unfairly treated by a superior. Such a system guards the employee against unfair treatment and at the same time allows the firm to identify improper management.

Goals People seek to improve their self-esteem. Some attain self-esteem by serving in a managerial role; others, by implementing plans of the firm that they deem to be of value. In either event, the employee seeks to have a part in a worthwhile goal. No matter how mundane one's role may be, each employee can relate to the overall mission if he or she is properly motivated.

Each individual, therefore, should be made aware of the goals in which he or she participates, their values to the firm or to society, and the importance of his or her part in the plan. This is an easy task for the manager in floriculture because the product is one that brings pleasure to people. It enriches their lives, improves the human environment, helps to heal wounds, adds to the pitch of emotional experiences, and expresses sentiments more aptly than words. Flowers, like their artistic and recreational counterparts, bring added meaning to life beyond that of survival.

The manager should point out the goals of the firm. The properly motivated employee takes pride in the growth of the firm for which he or she works. Greenhouse owners have found to their surprise a spirit of exhilaration among employees during periods of greenhouse expansion. One would think that in such a period of added stress just the opposite mood would take over; however, a feeling of accomplishment prevails because workers are participating in goal-setting. The firm that is living off its depreciation (running into the ground) is one in which management of the labor force is difficult, if not impossible.

Finally, the manager must clearly inform each employee of the task he or she is to achieve as part of the overall goal. The task should be spelled out in detail, and a deadline should be given. It is important that the manager have the employee repeat the work assignment to eliminate any misconceptions. No doubt should exist in the employee's mind as to what is expected. This puts the employee in a position to apply all his or her resources directly to accomplishing the task. Any doubt in the objective will dilute an employee's efforts.

Where the chain of command is long, involving perhaps owner, general manager, production manager, and several subproduction managers, it is wise to post a long-range set of production plans for periodic reference by all concerned. Some growers have devised graphical ways of doing this, as seen in Figure 17–2. Such a visible plan aids the managers in maintaining their responsibilities and in briefing their employees.

Delegation of Authority Without some level of authority, an employee cannot organize his or her own activity. The manager must always assume full responsibility for the tasks performed by those under his or her command but must also delegate authority to subordinates. Such authority may cover decisions of priority, purchases, and labor assistance. This authority permits the employees to organize their efforts for greater efficiency and to proceed without the minute-to-minute supervision of the manager.

Delegation of authority becomes more important as the number of employees answering to a manager increases. It often turns out to be one of the most difficult roles for the manager to perform. It can be difficult to relinquish authority over applications of growth regulators or pesticides when the stakes are so high and the responsibility for avoiding error still rests on the manager. If such author-

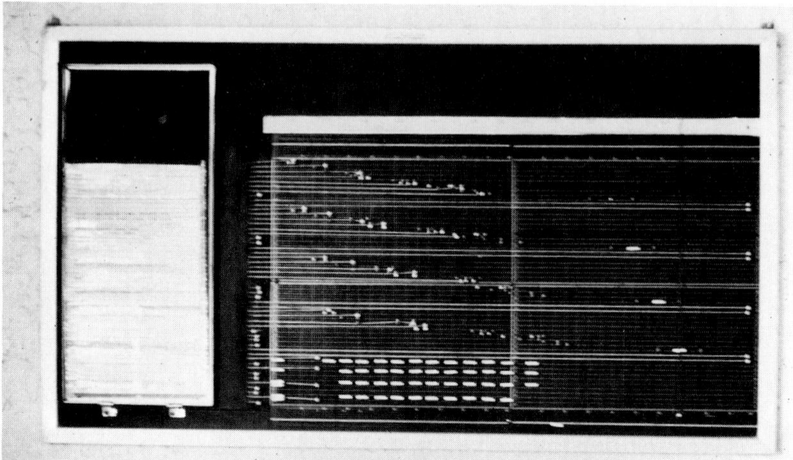

Figure 17–2

A production schedule chart in the management office of the Royal Carnations Co. in Bogotá, Colombia. Each row represents a production area and has holes for each week of the year. Numbered pegs are inserted in holes for the weeks when an operation is to be executed for that production area. The number refers to the operation, and a detailed set of instructions for the operation can be found in the pages at the left side of the board.

ity is not relinquished, however, the manager may not be able to attend to responsibilities of even higher priority.

Evaluation The employee should know at the outset how performance will be evaluated. Such a system gives employees a chance to gauge their performance. They have a chance to improve performance before being reprimanded and to pace themselves. The evaluation system is equally valuable for the manager because it provides a means for guiding the professional development of the employee and thereby further assuring that one's responsibilities as a manager are met.

A set of standards for the employee's work should be established. This might include, in the case of disbudding pot mums, the loss of not more than one terminal bud for each three pots, a time allocation of three minutes per pot, no unnecessary breakage of foliage, placement of all disbuds in a receptacle, and orderly replacement of the pot and watering system after disbudding.

The method of evaluation should be set. The person planting cuttings might be given a set of labels bearing his or her name so that one can be placed in each section in which this person plants. Periodically, the manager checks the planting operation, complimenting those who have performed well and correcting those who have not performed well.

It is advisable to set up a periodic meeting with each employee to review performance. This serves as a reminder to the employee to give some attention to his or her efforts, and it gives the manager an easy means to communicate a judgment without unduly alarming the employee.

Some managers reserve comments for times when job performance is poor. Some employees may understand that no comment is a vote of confidence, but most are unable to respond to this system. A periodic evaluation system circumvents the problem of lack of recognition.

Sometimes, it helps to provide an overall record of accomplishment. For example, a grower might post a chart in the center of the flower production area. Data could be added weekly to graphs showing the total production for the week, the proportion of the total represented in each flower grade, and the quantity of loss due to neglect on the part of labor. This system would provide all employees with a continuous evaluation of the range as a whole and would tend to encourage higher performance.

Reward As employees, we work primarily for pay. Rarely do we feel that we have enough. Increased pay is a stimulus for improved performance, but increases must be handled equitably. If poor evaluation of performance or favoritism enters into the system of pay raises, it has a negative effect on performance.

At times, financial recognition of superior service is not possible. This does not nullify the need for an evaluation and reward system. People are social beings and as such are very concerned about recognition. The manager must make it his or her business to notice good performance and to express appropriate appreciation. At the same time, the manager must be certain to notice and help correct poor performance. Both are an integral part of the system for encouraging performance.

Working Conditions

Working conditions are as important as the manager–employee relationship for encouraging good performance. Consider your own feelings when walking along a street in a town with no trees or plantings and with noisy traffic passing a few feet away versus walking along a pedestrian mall landscaped with lawn and planters and overhung by trees. Without realizing it, many greenhouse ranges develop into a harsh, repelling environment that brings about negative feelings in the employees. How much stimulation is there to plant seedlings neatly and at the precise depth when all around are weeds, trash, and unrepaired greenhouses?

Facilities The greenhouses, headhouse, rest rooms, and surroundings should be orderly and clean. It was pointed out earlier that this is an important part of insect and disease control. It is also important to proper management. A harmonious environment suggests a state of finesse, which, with a little encouragement by the manager, can be achieved.

A job is not finished until it is cleaned up. Tools, empty cartons, and so forth should always be in their proper places. Greenhouse aisles, headhouse, and areas around the greenhouse should be clear. Aside from the negative messages that such messes impart, they also present hazards and a physical barrier to efficient operation.

There should be a program of preventive maintenance for all equipment to ensure that jobs will always be done on schedule. A little paint on a tank before it rusts, grease on a bearing before it freezes, or a tune-up on a rototiller before it stops will prevent breakdowns that could snowball into a stoppage of many other operations.

Each human has an internal rhythm. When the pace of his or her work is geared to this rhythm, efforts are minimized and productivity is maximized. Disruptions in the form of ambiguous orders, undue changes in orders, and equipment breakdown break the work momentum. It is fatiguing and depressing to the employee.

Work facilities should be respectable. Human dignity dictates that bathroom facilities be provided. If the very being of an individual does not command respect, why should his or her productivity be any different? A pleasant area for eating and taking breaks also should be provided. A brief repose at mid-morning, noon, and mid-afternoon benefits the firm as well as the employee. A tired employee is not productive.

There are many other aspects of the physical facilities that warrant attention if the manager simply puts himself or herself in the position of the employee. Worthwhile improvements are those that prevent needless fatigue and facilitate work efficiency. Rubber mats on the floor and, under some circumstances, chairs are an asset to progress. Convenient centralization of tools and supplies also increases efficiency. The range layout as a whole should be formulated with efficiency in mind. A flat site and ridge-and-furrow greenhouses rather than separate structures permit automation and minimize walking effort. Service buildings on the north side, midway along the greenhouses, minimize travel distance. Permanently plumbed pesticide lines, local steam outlets for pasteurization, and central fertilizer proportioning equipment improve efficiency. Conveyor systems for moving flowers, potted plants, and supplies to or from production areas should be considered.

Product Quality The demand for low-quality products is small. The profitability of such production is low at best. Some years ago, it was stated in the *Florist and Nursery Exchange* that Mr. Larry Taylor of Denver Wholesale Florist found on a year-round average that it took 1.8 standard-grade (second) carnations or 3.5 short-grade or 7.5 design-grade of 11 split-calyx blooms to equal the profit of one fancy-grade (first) bloom.

Aside from market price, product quality is important to personnel management. It affects the same principle of the employee relating to the firm. When one knows that he or she is part of a quality production scheme, the incentive exists to try to meet these standards in his or her own work.

Education Most people take pleasure in learning. It is flattering to an employee when the firm thinks enough of him or her to provide an education along with the job. Actually, there is a mutual advantage since employees who understand the why and what of their tasks have the potential to make better workers. They are in a position to reason out better ways of doing the job and how to solve a problem when the job is not proceeding smoothly.

Education in a small firm need not consist of anything more than the manager's talking with employees as they work. They should be given an appreciation of the various cultural procedures involved in a crop and how they interrelate. Employees should be aware of the quality standards required by the market. They should know the problems that can arise from mistakes such as insect or disease establishment, excessively high or low temperatures, improper photoperiod control, the wrong planting depth, nutritional disorders, and overwatering. Worthwhile employees welcome such knowledge and use it to better themselves within the firm and to assist the manager in meeting his or her responsibilities.

Larger firms, in addition to the procedure just discussed, sometimes make use of training sessions for their employees. These may be held on the premises of the firm and be conducted by management within the firm or by instructors hired from outside. Outside services are available for topics such as management and marketing. Visits from university personnel, allied trade representatives, or competitive greenhouse operators can be a very valuable source of information. If possible, the general manager should arrange an opportunity for key personnel to meet with such individuals. One cannot help but be impressed by the professional manner in which Colombian growers receive such visitors. Preparation is apparent in the complete involvement of the management staff and the organized quest for information by each staff member.

Numerous meetings are sponsored each year by industry organizations, state universities, and other state and federal agencies. These meetings are an excellent educational opportunity for the owner and his or her key employees. Many state universities with a horticultural or plant science department conduct annual or semiannual floricultural short courses of one to three days' duration. Commodity groups such as Roses, Inc., and Professional Plant Growers' Association sponsor meetings. The Society of American Florists, the Produce Marketing Association, and various wire services hold meetings, with topics ranging in scope from the grower to the wholesaler to the retailer. Many other wholesaler and retailer associations also sponsor meetings.

Most of the organizations mentioned publish newsletters containing current floral news items as well as technical subjects. Growers should definitely get on the mailing list of the horticulture department at their local state university. They should join their local flower growers' association as well as a national growers' association. Many growers join associations in other states as a means of expanding their sources of information and ideas. Information derived from these organizations should be passed down through the firm by one or another of the methods discussed earlier.

PRODUCTION MANAGEMENT

Record-Keeping

The grower who does not keep records is committed to repeat the same errors over and over. Every business must keep records for income tax purposes. With a little more thought and effort, a set of records can be developed for cost accounting purposes. *Cost accounting* is a system for assessing the costs of conducting a business. The costs of each input—labor, utilities, and material—are determined and compared to a reasonable proposal of costs. The overall profitability of the business is determined.

To know at the end of a year that a business made a profit is not enough. Some crops may have been profitable, while others were marketed at a loss. Certain grades of fresh flowers or sizes of pot plants may have contributed little or nothing to the profit. It could be that one market channel was more profitable than another. These differences must be known, or else the poorer alternatives may be allowed to increase out of proportion to the better alternatives. Cost accounting provides a tool for comparing the cost of producing units. The units may be different crops, different sizes of a given crop (bedding plants in 1¾ inch versus 3 inch pots), different market dates for a given crop, or different methods for producing and marketing a crop.

Cultural Records Before growing a crop, one should decide which records to keep. One set will be financial, including costs of items such as plants, containers, root media, labor, utilities, and so forth. The other set of records is cultural in nature. Cultural records are maintained for the purposes of (1) providing a plan for duplicating successful crops and (2) giving an accounting from which the cause of errors in the culture of the crop can be determined and then corrected in the next crop.

Long before a crop is planted, a cultural schedule should be written, listing dates and labor budgets for operations such as root-media preparation, planting, syringing, fertilization, pesticide application, pinching, pruning, chemical growth regulation, disbudding, anticipated harvest period, and cleaning up. This cultural schedule should be maintained in the general manager's office. The information should be duplicated on a cultural schedule record sheet to be hung in the greenhouse at the location of the crop being grown (Figure 17–3). The cultural schedule record sheet serves as a daily reminder to the production manager as to the various operations that must be performed.

When each operation is performed, the date is entered on the cultural schedule record sheet in the greenhouse and the name of the performing employee is entered. Should an unscheduled operation or an alteration in a scheduled operation be necessary, a description of the operation is entered in the record. At the end of each day, the entries are verified and initialed by the manager overseeing the operations.

Plant Environment Records A second set of culture-related records contains the plant environment records, including temperatures inside and outside the

Greenhouse section		Benches	Crop	Cultivar	
IV		9-15	Cut Mums	Nob Hill	
Date scheduled	Date accomplished	Operation		Employee	Mgr. initials
3-7		Plant 7" x 8"			
3-7		Fertilize, half strength			
3-7		Start lighting at night			
3-14		Fertilize and spray			
3-21		Fertilize and spray			
3-28		Pinch			
3-28		Fertilize and spray			
4-4		Fertilize and spray			
4-11		Fertilize and spray			
4-18		Fertilize and spray			
4-18		Start shading			
4-19		Prune plants back to 2 or 3 shoots			
4-25		Fertilize and spray			
5-2		Fertilize and spray			
5-9		Fertilize and spray			
5-16		Fertilize and spray			
5-23		Fertilize and spray			
5-30		Fertilize and spray			
5-30		Disbud			
6-6		Fertilize and spray			
6-13		Spray			
6-20		Spray			
6-24		Harvest			

Figure 17–3

A typical cultural schedule record placed at the end of a bench in the greenhouse. All planned cultural operations are entered on the record prior to planting the crop. As the operations are performed, the actual dates, any changes in descriptions, and the names of employees performing the operations are entered. The manager verifies the record with his or her initials.

greenhouse, solar radiation, root-media nutrient analyses, foliar analyses, insect and disease occurrence, and visual observations. Temperature should be recorded in the greenhouse to determine whether the desired temperatures have been maintained. Deviations from both low-temperature and high-temperature phases have an adverse effect on plant growth and prevent efficient use of energy. Such records give an assessment of the quality of the heating and cooling equipment and indicate breakdowns. They can prevent the erroneous conclusion, when the crop matures at the wrong time, that the schedule is incorrect. To change the cultural schedule in this case would only lead to a second mistimed crop. Recording thermometers with a seven-day record are available for this purpose (priced from $200). One should be placed in the aspirated control box in each zone of the greenhouse range. The seven-day graphs should be kept chronologically in a notebook. The computerized environmental control systems of today can provide a record of temperature and other factors controlled.

Inside temperatures give an indication of the condition of the temperature-control equipment, while outside temperatures are a reflection of fuel and electrical consumption. A record of outside temperatures can be obtained from your local branch of the National Weather Service. Data are gathered at several points in each state and are published. The grower should keep a record of daily minimum and maximum temperatures, heating degree days, and solar radiation. The winter-temperature and heating-degree-days data are useful in determining whether the fuel bill for one winter will be representative of successive years. These data also can be used to determine what proportion of the total fuel bill to allot to each crop grown during the heating season. This is important information for cost accounting. Summer-temperature data can be used in a like manner. Extremes in summer temperature result in crop delay and poor quality. Such records permit proper assessment of the blame.

Solar radiation values indicate the amount of light reaching the earth's surface and thereby indicate when light is a limiting factor. When growth is limited by insufficient light, increases in temperature, fertilization, or CO_2 level are ineffective and a waste of money. Records such as those for solar radiation give an indication of which factor is limiting to growth, thereby enabling the grower to decide whether or not the alteration of environmental factors will be profitable.

The periodic root-media tests and foliar analysis reports should be saved chronologically by crop. These are also valuable in determining the limiting factors to growth and thereby explaining exceptionally good or poor growth. As mentioned in Chapter 8, these records are also used for establishing the fertilization program itself.

All states have agricultural extension agents who can identify insect and disease problems. Some states have insect and disease clinics where samples can be sent for identification. Whenever an insect or disease problem is identified, it should be reported in the plant environment records. These factors again explain poor quality and yield.

Production Records The third set of culture-related records needed by the general manager are the production records. These records are gathered throughout the growth period of the crop. The production manager should assess the condition of each crop weekly and enter this assessment into the production record. For a crop such as gloxinia, the width of a dozen typical plants might be measured and the average value entered into the record. The average height of a chrysanthemum crop could be measured and recorded. Visual observations also should be recorded, considering factors such as form, leaf color, leaf size, stem thickness, and appearance of chlorosis or necrosis.

These types of information allow for the comparison of the present crop with previous crops. A problem such as phosphorus deficiency, which is not apparent to the eye in early stages, can be identified through a smaller-than-normal growth measurements. By looking at a poor crop in retrospect, the stage of growth when trouble first occurred can be identified. The cultural record and plant environment records can then be checked to find the cause of the problem. In most cases, when the cause can be found, it can be corrected in subsequent crops.

The production record should also include the number of blooms or pots harvested, the date, and the grade or quality. These records are needed for cost accounting and are used in the same manner as the earlier growth measurements just described.

Financial Records Just as cultural records must be gathered so that cultural mistakes can be identified, assessed, and corrected, financial records must be collected for improving the procedures for conducting business.

Income. Income should be recorded by crop. It is important to further subdivide income by date of sale, market outlet, and grade of product. Such a breakdown allows for comparison of relative profitability of season, market outlets, and grades.

Expenses. All inputs into the production and marketing of each crop must be identified. Each input is then quantified in a monetary value and entered as an expense. Some expenses are easily identified with a given crop, such as cuttings, pots, planting labor, disbudding labor, and trucking to market. These are known as *variable costs* because their magnitude varies with the size of the crop and from one crop to another. Other costs are known as *fixed costs* because they will continue even when production stops. Examples are interest on the loan for buildings and equipment, taxes, insurance, and management salaries. There are yet other costs that appear to fall between fixed and variable. These are *semifixed costs,* which increase as production increases but which are not directly related to the number of units produced. Fuel, electricity, and lower-level management costs are examples of semifixed costs. They increase with increasing production but are not directly related to a pot of mums or a bunch of roses.

Variable costs permit the most sensitive cost analysis. The method of record-collecting sometimes determines whether an expense can be treated as variable, fixed, or semifixed. Labor will be at best a semifixed cost if only the total number of hours worked per week is recorded. When the number of hours expended on each crop is recorded, it can be treated as a variable cost since the labor per unit of production can be determined. Labor in the former case would be divided by the total area in production, regardless of whether the crop was pot mums or poinsettias. Since each square foot of production area carries the same expense, a comparison of the cost of production or the profitability of pot mums and poinsettias would not take into account labor, one of the largest expenses. A comparison in the latter case, where labor was accurately related to each crop, would permit an accurate comparison of the crops.

Labor could be even further identified by operation. W. W. Grimmer (1975), in his booklet *Greenhouse Cost Accounting*, breaks labor down into 50 categories (Table 17–2). Each employee is required to fill out a time sheet at the end of each day, identifying the quantity of time spent, the crop, and the labor operation category (Figure 17–4). The manager verifies these sheets. From these sheets, the total labor input for each operation of each crop can be calculated.

This type of variable expense record permits comparisons within a crop. Alternative methods may be studied, such as manual pinching of azalea versus chemical pinching. Such a record also indicates where the greatest expenses lie so that the possibilities for their reduction can be studied.

Fixed Expenses. Detailed expense records by crop are very important but not always possible. The first letters of each of the five common fixed expenses spell DIRTI; these expenses are known as the "DIRTI Five" and include depreciation, interest, repairs, taxes, and insurance.

Depreciation is a means of allocating the costs of fixed assets such as buildings, vehicles, machinery, and so on. For purposes of cost analysis within the firm, the cost of an asset is depreciated over the useful life expectancy of the asset. If a glass greenhouse is anticipated to serve a useful function for 20 years, then for straight-line depreciation its purchase price is divided by 20 to determine the annual depreciation cost. This allows one to allocate the proper cost of greenhouses to a given crop. The loan for the greenhouse may be for only 10 years. In this case, the amount of annual repayment of the principal on the loan is twice the amount of the depreciation. Depreciation is generally calculated over a shorter period of time than its useful life for income tax purposes. This permits a greater tax break in early years when the dollar is worth more.

Depreciation is not a savings fund to be used for replacing equipment or buildings. It is money already spent for the original equipment and buildings. As such, it is a business expense that can be deducted from sales revenue for determining taxable income. A separate fund should be set aside for asset replacement if so desired.

Interest is the cost to the business for using money to set up and run the business. The interest cost exists whether the money was borrowed from a commercial lending institution or was provided by the owner. If the owner puts up the money to establish the business, he or she must expect to receive interest for this money from the business. Otherwise, the interest that could have been made by investing the money elsewhere is lost. This is known as an *opportunity cost.* To get an accurate picture of the profitability, interest on all borrowed money must be entered as an expense.

Table 17–2

Code of Labor Operations in a Greenhouse Business*

Production Labor (by Crop and Operator Number)	*Nonproduction Labor (by Operator Number Only)*
1 Propagation	50 R & M buildings
2 Seeding	51 R & M greenhouses
3 Grafting	52 R & M benches
4 Transplanting	53 R & M steam and water
5 Mixing soil	54 R & M electrical
6 Potting	55 R & M boiler room
7 Moving plants	56 R & M machinery
8 Jeep operation	57 R & M trucks and tractors
9 Weeding	58 Shade—remove shade
10 Pinching	59 Sales—pick orders
11 Disbudding	60 Sales—wrap
12 Water and syringe	61 Sales—pack
13 Cultivate soil	62 Sales—load trucks
14 Mulch	63 Trucking—delivery
15 Stake and tie	64 Trucking—around plant
16 Black cloth shading	65 Fire boilers
17 Pruning	66 Temperature control
18 Grading pot plants	67 Stock room
19 Cutting flowers	68 Laboratory
20 Grading cut flowers	69 General miscellaneous labor
21 Fertilizing	70 Supervision
22 Fumigating	71 Office
23 Spraying	72 New construction
24 Dusting	73 Grounds maintenance
25 Sterilizing	
26 Cleaning up	

*From Grimmer (1975).

Daily Time Sheet

Name ____________________

Clock number ______________

Date ____________________

Operator no.	Crop	Hours	For office use only

Approved by: ______________ Checked by: __________

Figure 17–4

A daily time sheet to be filled out by each employee and verified by the manager for the purpose of assessing labor as to crop and type of operation. (*From Grimmer*, 1975)

Repairs to facilities and equipment will be required periodically. Maintenance also falls into this category since it is a logical expense for keeping repairs realistic.

Property taxes are a fixed expense. They include taxes paid to municipal, county, and state governments.

Insurance on facilities and equipment is a fixed expense. Labor-related insurance is not included here but comes under the expense category of labor.

Other fixed expenses include management salaries, the services of accountants and attorneys, travel to technical meetings or to business appointments relating to the business in general, organizational dues, contributions, entertainment, and office expenses. Of these, management salaries bear close scrutiny.

When the owner is the manager, there is a temptation to consider management salary as profit. This should not be done since it interferes with cost accounting. An unrealistically low cost of production emerges and cannot be maintained as the range expands beyond the size that the owner can manage alone. The manager should consider what a hired manager would be paid to do the job and enter it as an expense. The owner should realize that an employee could be hired to replace him or her, thereby freeing the owner to derive income from another endeavor. This type of thinking might set the stage for a more profitable use of time.

The lower levels of management come close to a variable expense. Often, growers are assigned to specific jobs. As greenhouses are added, more growers are hired. If a direct relationship can be established between crops and grower input, then their salaries can be considered a valuable expense.

Variable Expenses. These expenses are the easiest to identify. Each increases directly as the number of units produced increases. In this category are labor, plants, seeds, and growing supplies such as pots, root media, labels, pesticides, growth regulators, and fertilizers.

Fuel can be a variable expense if some measure of consumption is kept relative to crops. The weekly number of heating degree days could be used to determine the fuel consumption attributed to each week of the heating season. Within each week, the fuel cost could be proportioned to each crop according to area occupied and inside temperature maintained. This is too large a bill to be treated as a fixed expense.

Electricity could be treated in the same manner. The greater part of total consumption may be accounted for during the summer by cooling and during the winter by photoperiodic lighting.

Sales expenses should take into account packaging materials (sleeves, labels, and cartons), packaging labor, delivery labor, and sales labor. In a large operation where separate office personnel and telephones are used for sales, these expenses can also be listed under sales and can possibly be relegated to crops.

Labor has already been discussed. As indicated, labor of production and marketing should be treated as a variable expense as much as possible.

Expense Comparison. It is difficult to state a general cost of production or marketing. There is a different set of figures for each crop. There are also great differences among categories of growers. A small business may have a relatively high labor bill but low equipment expense compared to a large automated business. The relative relationship of each expense to the total can be seen in the circle graph in Figure 17–5. This is a composite of a study of several categories of fresh flower and pot plant growers in Wisconsin and Michigan. The study indicated that the sales expense for the growers surveyed is low and would probably run at least 25 percent for the industry as a whole.

Cost Analysis

The records thus far gathered are in two general categories—cultural and financial. The cultural records can serve to set a consideration of the financial records into perspective. Before the accounting office settles down to a cost analysis of a crop that has shown no profit, the cultural records should be studied. Failure may

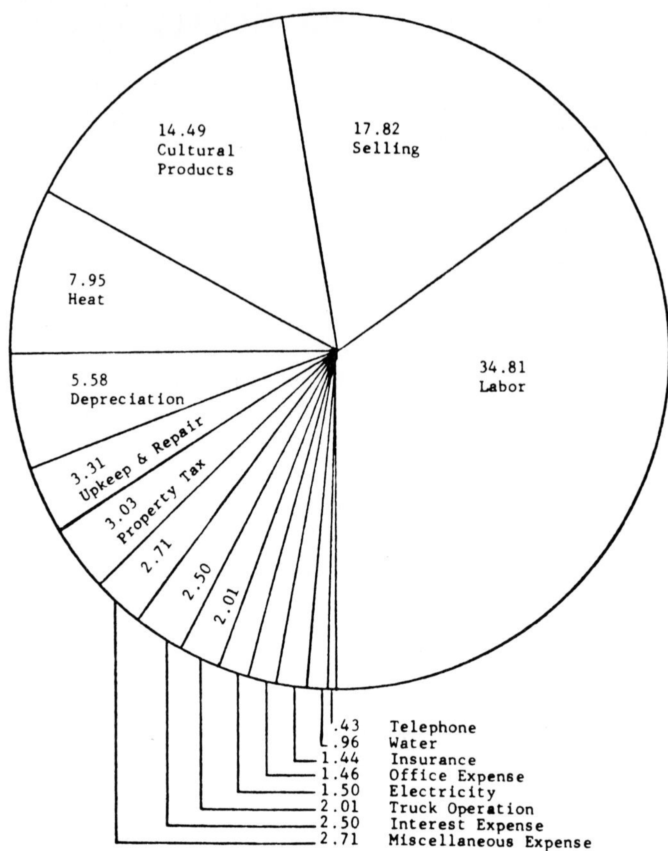

Figure 17–5

The relationship of each production and marketing expense to the total expense. (*From Grimmer,* 1975)

be due to one of such diverse factors as managerial error in executing the cultural schedule, uncontrolled disease, or boiler failure. In any case, assessment and correction of the problem are cultural considerations. An analysis of expenses and revenue will do little to shed light on the problem.

Profit or Loss Assessment After the cultural records have been studied, and barring any unduly large cultural problem, cost analysis becomes an important operation. A cost analysis statement (Table 17–3) is developed for each crop to determine the profitability of each. The statement further serves to pinpoint the causes of expense and sources of revenue.

Fixed expenses are commonly determined on a per-square-foot-of-bench basis, and the crop is assessed according to the area it occupies. Variable expenses

Table 17–3

Cost Analysis Sheet for an Individual Crop Listing Expenses, Revenues, and Profit or Loss

Crop__________ Greenhouse Section__________ Date__________

EXPENSES

Fixed and Semifixed

Depreciation (facilities and equipment)	______	
Interest	______	
Repairs and maintenance (facilities and equipment)	______	
Taxes	______	
Insurance	______	
Office expenses	______	
Telephone	______	
Accounting and legal fees	______	
Travel and dues	______	
Management salaries	______	
Automotive	______	
Miscellaneous	______	
Variable		
Seed	______	
Cultural supplies	______	
Labor	______	
Fuel	______	
Electricity	______	
Sales costs	______	
	Total Expenses	______

REVENUES

Grade	Units	Unit Price	Total

Total Revenues ______

PROFIT OR LOSS ______

are assigned directly to the crop. Revenue may be identified by flower grade for fresh flower crops. If more than one market channel is used, and pricing differs, revenue is entered according to market channel. Cost analysis by crop permits the grower to determine which crops are most profitable at various times of the year. It gives him or her an opportunity to determine the more profitable market dates in spite of seasonal changes in expenses such as fuel. It can be a difficult task to determine workable combinations and rotations of crops for greenhouse culture. Without this type of cost analysis, serious error may be made.

In determining the profitability of a crop, one must add in the fixed costs associated with vacant bench space that is associated with the crop. This may occur during the early culture of a crop such as bedding plants, when plants are in the seedling or cutting stages. Vacant space is held for spacing of plants as they develop. The rotation in which bedding plants and poinsettias are grown makes use of greenhouse space in the spring and fall but leaves considerable space open in the summer. Often, this space cannot be fully utilized because the market demand for floral products is low at this time and the length of time between the bedding plant and poinsettia crops is too short to grow many crops. Fixed expenses continue and must be met for the empty space during this period.

Planning for Profit Increase Profit depends on the management of expenses and the production of revenue. Many things can be done to increase revenue. Many methods have already been introduced in reference to various greenhouse operations.

The market price of fresh flowers varies with supply and demand; however, there are well-established annual patterns. A price curve can be developed from market reports given in weekly trade papers. Quite often, land-grant university libraries maintain some of these. The firm should subscribe to such literature and develop a record of its own. Flowering pot plant prices are fairly stable, but demand varies considerably. There are times when part of the crop cannot be sold. Even if this were not the case, the percentage of pots not sold due to form or condition would tend to decrease during a period of peak demand. Whether the increased demand affects price or the percentage of the crop sold, the result is an increase in revenue.

Crop rotations should be designed to maximize bench utilization as long as they do not result in crops of low profitability. The grower with a bedding-plant–poinsettia rotation might look into propagating poinsettia cuttings during the summer. If this were not profitable for the grower's own use alone, the selling of cuttings might be considered. Even though this is the same plant that he or she grows in the fall, the grower must consider it as a separate crop for cost analysis purposes. The sales price of the cuttings used within the business is the price the business would normally pay for these. Profits for the propagation business are then calculated from this point.

Greenhouse productivity also can be maximized by the physical arrangement of the growing space. Benches running the length of the greenhouse will occupy about 67 percent of the floor space, while peninsular benches may cover 75 percent of available space. The former benches are often more practical for fresh flowers, but a pot plant grower will benefit more from the latter arrangement. Movable benches that make use of some of the aisles also should be considered.

The system of growing pot plants on a paved floor offers even a greater advantage for increasing revenue. Hanging basket plants grown over aisles permit nearly 100 percent utilization of greenhouse space. Increased use of greenhouse space is important because it reduces the fixed costs per unit of growing space. This concept should be pursued as long as it is not offset by another input such as labor. Conceivably, the aisles could become too narrow or the blocks of plants too wide to allow for efficient use of labor. Such relationships can be established through cost analysis of trial crops.

Revenue can be increased by producing higher-quality products if one is not currently meeting the market standards. *There is always a demand for quality.* Low-quality produce is generally dumped first. Even for flowering pot plants, there is a range of prices. The grower of high quality can usually command a higher price for his or her products. This is most pronounced for fresh flowers, which are priced according to grade. The cultural records should suggest factors in the greenhouse environment that are limiting growth as well as errors in the cultural schedule. A fresh coat of paint, reflective material on the north wall, clean glass, and proper plant spacing can improve light intensity, which is often limiting in the winter. Repair or replacement of heating and cooling equipment, the injection of CO_2 into the greenhouse atmosphere, better sanitation, improved drainage of the root medium, and many other factors discussed in this book should be considered for increasing quality. There is little profit in the floriculture industry for low-quality producers.

Cutting fresh flowers in the bud stage shortens the length of time the crop is in the bench, thus permitting a higher volume of production. Greenhouse space is replaced by opening room space in the grower's service building or, even more preferably, the marketplace. The substitution of space and gain in time have been shown to be profitable.

Revenue is tied into the choice of a market channel. Prices can vary among the different outlets. The speed of payment is quite variable. Most large mass-marketing chains have a reputation for prompt payments; uncollected debts are not common. A rapid cash flow permits growers to minimize the amount of money to be borrowed and thereby minimizes interest expense. Slow receipt of payment and bad debts are a real problem for some growers.

Raising prices to increase revenue usually does not work for the flower grower. A modest increase might be supported by exceptional quality or superior service. Any extensive increase opens the door for competitive growers. To a degree, flower growers are price takers rather than price setters.

Another step in improving profits is that of managing (reducing) expenses, which can be a very elusive challenge. Growers tend to react to sudden changes and overlook other more important, subtle changes. A good system of cost analysis can prevent this problem.

Professor A. O. Voigt (1976) of Pennsylvania State University presented an interesting analysis of a grower's situation. Even though the monetary figures are out of date, the principle is of value. The fuel cost for producing a 6 inch poinsettia rose \$0.065 from a cost of \$0.06 in 1972 to a cost of \$0.125 in 1974. The industry as a whole was deeply alarmed at the doubling in fuel costs, and many felt that such prices might eventually put them out of business. Strong support developed for research into methods of energy conservation and alternative energy sources—and justifiably so. But what about the other expenses? While the cost of fuel doubled by rising \$0.065, the grower's total production and marketing costs rose \$0.54 in the same period. The cost of cuttings alone increased by a larger amount than did the fuel, and the total labor bill increased \$0.07 per pot.

Fuel prices are a real challenge for the grower, but they are not the only problem. Considerable attention should be given to labor, marketing expenses, and cultural supplies, which are larger expenses that are also rising rapidly (see Figure 17–5). The cost of supplies can be significantly reduced by ordering in large quantities to take advantage of volume discounts. A common complaint of the companies supplying greenhouse materials (seed, pesticides, fertilizers, pots, and so on) is that growers tend to buy as needed. Discounts of 5–15 percent are passed up by failing to consolidate orders to cover three- to four-month operating periods. This is the length of time of a typical crop. The discounts are possible in part because supply companies may have the order shipped direct from the manufacturer rather than from their own warehouse. Extra handling and warehousing costs are avoided.

Worse than the loss of discounts are the additional shipping charges. Small orders may be assessed at minimum freight rates. A large order could be shipped for the same freight cost. Whole truckloads or carloads have a lower per unit freight rate than partial loads. This may be seen in a higher rate or in a single fixed charge for a partial load. For heavy materials, the freight bill can equal the cost of the materials. Freight savings are very worthwhile but often overlooked.

Cash discounts are often overlooked because of their small apparent size. A 2 percent discount for payment within 20 days equates to better than 36 percent annual interest. There are slightly more than eighteen 20-day periods in a year, and within each period 2 percent is collected. Even though the interest is collected only once on a given purchase, a greenhouse firm is making purchases throughout the year. If the firm's cash flow is low, such that the cash discount is rarely received, then the firm may be paying 36 percent more for materials than is necessary.

An empirical profitability study was made by P. J. Kirschling and F. E. Jensen (1974) at Rutgers University for 4 inch (10 cm) pot mums in a model double-layer polyethylene greenhouse range. The range encompassed 17,664 ft^2 (1,640 m^2) of bench space and was situated on a 1 acre (0.4 ha) lot of land. Three crops of pot mums were considered per year with no production in the summer. Production costs were developed for this model. The effect of changes in the wage rate and in the marketable percentage of the crop on profitability were calculated as shown in Table 17–4. From such a table, the market price necessary to yield a specified profit can be readily ascertained.

Kirschling and Jensen further calculated the effect that a 1 percent increase in various factors could have on profit (Table 17–5). Considering the 100 percent

Table 17–4

Estimated Annual Entrepreneurial Profits[1] from a Plastic Greenhouse Operation Model Producing Three Crops of 4 Inch (10 cm) Chrysanthemums[2]

	Percentage of Crop Marketable				
Wage Rate	*80*	*85*	*90*	*95*	*100*
$2.00	$11,117	$16,505	$21,913	$27,311	$32,709
2.50	6,103	11,502	16,900	22,298	27,696
3.00	1,090	6,488	11,887	17,285	22,811
3.50	−3,923	1,475	6,873	12,271	17,670
4.00	−8,936	−3,538	1,860	7,258	12,656

[1]Entrepreneurial profits are defined as total revenues less total expenses except management cost. Sales price per pot is $0.65.

[2]Adapted from Kirschling and Jensen (1974).

rise in fuel cost mentioned earlier, a profit drop of 218 percent would be anticipated, based on the 2.18 percent reduction in profit per 1 percent rise in fuel cost reported in Table 17–5. This could be offset by an 8.1 percent rise in the price received per plant, which would raise the price from $0.60 to $0.649 (218 percent profit decline divided by 26.90 percent profit rise per 1 percent increase in price per plant = 8.1 percent required increase in price per plant).

The figures presented in Table 17–5 apply only to its specific model and are not to be used by other firms. Each firm must develop its own change-sensitivity chart. The progressive grower will invariably develop detailed expense records. These will provide the data needed to calculate the effect that an increase or decrease in an expense factor will have on profit. Armed with this information, the progressive grower is in a position to pinpoint the production operation most critical to profits and then to do something about improving the condition of this operation.

The point cannot be emphasized too strongly that successful ownership or management of a greenhouse business for someone else depends as much upon a knowledge of business principles as it does upon a technical knowledge of crop production. A person entering or already in the greenhouse business should consider supplementing his or her knowledge with courses in accounting, personnel management, business law, and marketing.

Computer Assistance

Most people agree with the principles of record-keeping and cost analysis set forth in this chapter; however, few greenhouse firms have an adequate system. Greenhouse managers feel that it is difficult to devise and establish an adequate

Table 17–5

Sensitivity[1] of Changes in Economic Profit to 1 Percent Increases in Some Factors of Production of Chrysanthemums in 4 Inch (10 cm) Pots in a Plastic Greenhouse Operation Model[2]

Factor (Increased by 1 Percent)	*Economic Profit (Change in Percent)*
Price received per plant ($)	+26.90
Yield, percent of crop marketable	+24.63
Production materials expense ($)	−7.17
Production labor (person-hours)	−5.25
Labor wage rate ($)	−5.25
Equipment investment ($)	−4.18
Management cost ($)	−3.93
Cuttings ($)	−3.81
Packaging costs ($)	−2.28
Fuel ($)	−2.18
Interest rate on the money (%)	−0.97

[1]Levels of 60¢ per plant, $2 per hour, 95% yield, and $15,000 management cost were assumed for the sensitivity analysis.

[2]From Kirschling and Jensen (1974).

record-keeping system and that it is time-consuming to maintain one. This has, in the past, been partly true.

Today, however, the computer greatly lessens the burden. The computer is actually a file and a calculator. The cultural, plant environment, production, and financial records described earlier in this chapter can be entered into a computer at any frequency rather than onto papers in a file drawer. The computer has the capability of recalling any specific records with minimal operator input. One might wish to contrast the variable costs of producing pot mums versus gloxinias. Records for the years in which they have been collected can be immediately retrieved. Singling out an individual year, averaging several years, or expressing the variable costs on a per-pot or per-square-foot-of-bench-area basis are among numerous options that can be obtained in moments with simple commands. Data may be tabulated or presented in graphic form. Analyses of the retrieved data can be easily handled to arrive at management decisions. All of these operations could be performed without a computer, but the time required would generally discourage it.

The computer gives even greater assistance since the planned cultural operations and greenhouse space allocations can be entered prior to planting. The computer can then be used to generate work schedules for each day. At the end of a year, unused bench space can be plotted out to study plans for better utilization of this space.

Word-processor software programs can make the daily work of the office staff more efficient. Form letters can be typed only once. Correspondence with similar content can have only the differences typed. While many greenhouse firms have computerized their business office affairs, far fewer have computerized monitoring and control of the plant environment. The day is rapidly approaching when it will be necessary for greenhouse firms to have two computer systems—one for the business office and a second for greenhouse environmental control.

SUMMARY

1. There are four general categories of operations within the greenhouse business: crop production, marketing, engineering, and business affairs. Each department has a manager, and over all four is a single general manager. The general manager answers to the owners. In a large business, there may be submanagers in each department. In a small business, the owner may serve as general manager as well as manager of each department.
2. A manager's ability to govern the affairs of others depends upon an ability to manage himself or herself. A manager must conduct himself or herself in a manner that fosters leadership. This includes self-motivation, perseverance, integrity, and a sense of justice. Further, he or she must operate according to the rules of success. These entail establishment of worthwhile goals, development of precise plans, unfaltering faith in his or her ability to achieve the goals, and relentless perseverance.
3. An effective manager–employee relationship calls for several situations. Employees must be aware of the management structure so that they know clearly the source of orders and to whom they are to answer. Each employee must know the goals of the firm and the specific portion of each that he or she is to perform. The employee must have sufficient authority to work out the accomplishment of assignments. Finally, there must be a system of evaluation by which the employee's performance is appraised, and there must be a just system of reward or constructive criticism.
4. Working conditions have a bearing on labor management. The physical facilities should be neat to encourage orderly work. Proper bathroom and eating facilities demonstrate respect for the employee and increase the chance that such respect is transferred by the employee to his or her job. Preventive maintenance and timely repair of equipment and facilities reduce discord in the employee's efforts. Efficient arrangement of work areas, supplies, and equipment averts needless expenditures of energy. Production of quality crops evokes a spirit of pride that the employee transfers into his or her work. Most employees look upon an educational experience provided by the employer as a desirable benefit. Such provision also has great benefit to the firm because it improves the employee's ability to carry out his or her mission.

5. Production management is absolutely dependent upon record-keeping, for without it one is destined to repeat errors. Cultural records serve to identify causes of cultural errors and are used as the framework for improved crop-production plans. Financial records, including sources of revenue and expense, provide the tools for an analysis of marketing and business affairs in general.

6. The use of records goes well beyond the realm of income tax returns and the analysis of past performance. Records are used for profit planning. Profits depend upon management of expense and production of revenue. Records provide the basis for cost analysis of alternative production operations, which, in turn, has a bearing on expenses. They provide the basis for assessing the effect that increases in selling price have on profits. Most important, such analyses identify the relative effects of various expenses and revenues on profit, thereby providing a system of priorities in the effort to obtain increased profits.

REFERENCES

1. Bange, G. A., E. E. Bender, and G. A. Stevens. 1972. Planning and accounting for profit in floriculture. Univ. of Maryland Agr. Exp. Sta. MP 806.
2. Boyd, R. M., T. D. Phillips, T. M. Blessington, and S. P. Myers. 1982. Costs of producing selected floricultural crops. Mississippi Agr. and Forestry Exp. Sta. AEN Res. Rep. 133.
3. Brumfield, R. G., P. V. Nelson, A. J. Coutu, D. H. Willits, and R. S. Sowell. 1981. Overhead costs of greenhouse firms differentiated by size of firm and market channel. North Carolina Agr. Res. Ser. Tech. Bul. 269.
4. Griffith, H. V., and R. N. Payne. 1969. An analysis of pot chrysanthemum production methods, direct costs and space use. Oklahoma State Univ. Agr. Res. Bul. B–670.
5. Grimmer, W. W. 1975. *Greenhouse Cost Accounting.* Gateway Technical Institute, 3520 30th Ave., Kenosha, WI.
6. Hill, N. 1960. *Think and Grow Rich.* Greenwich, CT: Fawcett Publications.
7. Jarvesoo, E. 1977. Cost of producing flowers in Massachusetts. Univ. of Massachusetts Coop. Ext. Ser. C–136.
8. Kirschling, P. J., and F. E. Jensen. 1974. Profitability of pot chrysanthemum production under glass greenhouses. New Jersey Agr. Exp. Sta. AE 351.
9. ______. 1974. Profitability of pot chrysanthemum production under plastic greenhouses. New Jersey Agr. Exp. Sta. Bul. 835.
10. Mueller, F. J., and G. I. Prater. 1969. Greenhouse management cost control and profit planning. *Proc. 1963 WSU Greenhouse Institute.* Univ. of Washington, Seattle, WA.
11. Nelson, K. S. 1973. *Greenhouse Management for Flower and Plant Production.* Danville, IL: The Interstate Printers and Publishers.
12. Peale, N. V. 1974. *You Can If You Think You Can.* Greenwich, CT: Fawcett Publications.

13. Perry, D. B., and J. L. Robertson. 1980. An economic evaluation of energy conservation investments for greenhouses. Ohio Agr. Res. and Devel. Cen. Res. Bul. 1114.
14. Reynolds, R. K., and W. R. Luckham. 1979. *Business Management Techniques for Nurserymen*. Reston, VA: Environmental Design Press.
15. Schwartz, D. J. 1965. *The Magic of Thinking Big*. Englewood Cliffs, NJ: Prentice-Hall.
16. Voigt, A. O. 1976. Are growers confusing energy problems with problems caused by poor marketing? *Florists' Review* 158:23, 78–80.
17. Voigt, A. O. 1978. *Business Analysis of Pennsylvania Retail Florists*. The Pennsylvania State Univ., University Park, PA.

Glossary

Abortion The partial or complete arrest of a developing tissue, as in embryos, buds, and so forth.

Abscission The separation of leaves, flowers, fruits, or other plant parts from the plant, generally following the formation of a separation layer of cells.

Actinomycetes A group of microorganisms apparently intermediate between bacteria and fungi and classified as either.

Aerated steam pasteurization Using a mixture of air and steam that is adjusted to a temperature below that of steam (212°F, 100°C) for pasteurizing root media.

Aeroponics A system for growing plants with their roots suspended in air. Water and nutrients are misted onto the roots.

Apical dominance The suppression of lateral shoot development by the apical bud (shoot tip).

Asset Any item of value or resource. Assets of a business include cash, amounts owed to the business by its customers for goods and services sold to them on credit, merchandise held for sale by the business, supplies, equipment, buildings, and land.

Auxin A group of hormones that induces growth through cell elongation.

Azalea pot A pot with equivalent inside rim diameter of but only three-quarters the depth of a standard pot.

Bactericide An agent or preparation used for killing bacteria.

Bacterium (plural *bacteria*) A unicellular plant that lacks chlorophyll and multiplies by fission.

Bedding plants A wide range of plants that are propagated and cultured through the initial stages of growth by commercial growers and are then sold for use in outdoor flower and vegetable gardens.

Blindness The condition of a plant stem evidenced when the bud stops developing. It is a frequent problem of roses during low-light periods.

Blown head A bloom that is excessively open.

Bluing The objectionable development of a blue pigment in flower petals, usually after harvest.

Boiler horsepower A quantity of heat equal to 33,475 Btu.

Bract A more or less modified leaf subtending a flower or belonging to an inflorescence.

Bracteole A secondary bract, as one upon the pedicel of a flower.

Btu (British thermal unit) The amount of heat required to raise the temperature of 1 pound of water 1°F at or near its point of maximum density.

Bulk density The mass per unit bulk volume. For example, bulk density of a soil-based medium in a dry state might be 70 pounds per cubic foot.

Bullhead A flower whose short petals, particularly at the center, give it a blunt, broad appearance. Also, a flower whose excess number of petals gives it a blunt, broad appearance.

Calyx A term referring to the sepals collectively. It is the first of the series of floral parts and is usually green and leaflike but may be colored like the petals.

Cambium A zone or cylinder of meristematic (dividing) cells located between xylem and phloem tissues in plants. The cambium cells divide to form new xylem and phloem cells.

Cation exchange capacity (CEC) A measure of the ability of an absorbing material such as a root medium to hold exchangeable cations such as various fertilizer nutrients including ammonium nitrogen, potassium, calcium, magnesium, iron, manganese, zinc, and copper. It is generally measured in milliequivalents per 100 cubic centimeters (me/100 cc) of dry absorbing material, and a value of 6–15 me/100 cc is considered ample for greenhouse root media. A root medium with low CEC does not retain nutrients well and consequently must be fertilized often.

CEC *See* Cation exchange capacity.

Chelate A chemical complex that will hold or bind a metal. Metals that are commonly chelated for agricultural use are less subject to tie-up in adverse root-media environments. These metals include iron, manganese, zinc, and copper.

Chloropicrin Tear gas. A chemical used for pasteurizing greenhouse root media. It is not as popular as methyl bromide but can be used in carnation root media.

Chloroplast A specialized body (organelle) in the cytoplasm of some plant cells that contains chlorophyll.

Chlorosis The state in which normally green plant tissue is lighter green and possibly yellow due to the loss of chlorophyll or the failure of chlorophyll to form.

Chord A support member of the greenhouse frame that is under tension.

Clay A mineral component of soils consisting of particles less than 0.002 mm in diameter.

Closed cultural system Any method for growing plants in which the nutrient solution is recirculated. Nutrients are not allowed to leach from the pot or bench to the ground.

CO_2 The chemical formula for the gas carbon dioxide.

Conduction heat loss Heat lost by transmission through a barrier such as the covering of a greenhouse.

Conidiophore A specialized hypha on which one or more conidia are produced.

Conidium (plural *conidia*) An asexual fungus spore formed from the end of a conidiophore.

Container capacity The maximum amount of water a root medium can hold against the force of gravity when this root medium is in a container that has open drainage holes in its base.

Convection heat loss Loss of heat from the greenhouse as it moves in air convection currents to the greenhouse covering, then through the covering by conduction, and finally away from the outside of the covering.

Convection heater A heater that does not contain a heat exchanger. Heat leaves the heater in the smoke. The smoke is carried the length of the greenhouse in a pipe that serves as an exchanger as heat passes through its walls to the greenhouse air.

Corporation A legal entity, separate and distinct from the persons (stockholders or shareholders) who own it. The corporation has all the rights and responsibilities of a person and may buy, own, and sell property; sue and be sued; and enter into contracts with both outsiders and its own shareholders. The most important advantage of the corporate form is its responsibility for its own acts and debts and the freedom of its owners from liability for either.

Cost accounting The use of the cost data of producing a given product for the purpose of assessing and controlling those costs. Since a knowledge of costs and controlling costs is vital to good management, a large greenhouse firm often engages the services of a cost accountant.

Critical night length The length of darkness less than which a short-night plant or more than which a long-night plant will undergo a photoperiodic response. The critical night length varies with plant species and even sometimes with cultivars within a species.

Cross-fluted cellulose pad An evaporative cooling pad composed of laminated sheets of fluted (corrugated) cellulose impregnated with insoluble antirot salts, rigidifying saturants, and wetting agents. Pores are oriented diagonally through the pad in two directions, crossing each other.

Crown bud A flower bud whose development has ceased. It sometimes develops the appearance of a crown. Generally, this cessation of development breaks apical dominance, resulting in the development of side shoots. Crown buds may be caused by excessively low or high temperatures or in long-night plants by a series of short nights while the flower bud is developing.

Cultivar A cultivated variety. A cultivar usually has less variation within it than does a botanical variety.

Curtain wall The nontransparent lower portion of the side walls of a greenhouse.

Cuticle A nonliving waxy layer covering all plant cells that are in contact with air. Although this layer protects plant cells from drying, water and nutrients can slowly penetrate it, as in the case of foliar fertilization.

Cutting The portion of a plant removed for the purpose of asexual propagation. It may be part of a stem, a leaf, or part of a root, depending on the species of plant to be propagated. Commercial cultivars of chrysanthemums, for example, are propagated by removing terminal stem pieces and placing the lower inch of them in a rooting medium in a moist environment to induce new root formation.

Cyclic lighting An alternative method of applying light during the night to achieve the photoperiodic effect of long days. The customary lighting period is divided into a number of subperiods, each comprised of a duration of light followed by darkness. The total duration of light can be reduced by as much as 80 percent. Where three hours of light are customarily applied, six consecutive cycles of 5 minutes of light and 25 minutes of darkness can be substituted, thereby reducing electrical consumption greatly.

Damping-off A disease caused by a number of fungi, mainly *Pythium*, *Rhizoctonia*, and *Phytophthora*. The symptoms include decay of seeds prior to germination; rot of seedlings before emergence from the root medium; and development of stem rot at the soil line after emergence, causing seedlings to topple.

Day-neutral plant A plant that does not respond to the relative lengths of light and darkness in the daily cycle.

Depreciation Decline in value of an asset due to such factors as wear or obsolescence.

Desiccation The process of drying. Desiccation of plants results from a lack of water. High levels of soluble salts in the root medium cause desiccation of roots by preventing water from entering the roots.

Detergent *See* Surfactant.

DIF The difference between day and night temperature computed by subtracting the night temperature from the day temperature. By controlling DIF, the length of stem internodes (overall plant height) can be controlled. For many crops, the lower the DIF value is, the shorter the plant will be.

Disbudding The process of removing flower buds from a plant stem, generally to improve the size of the remaining bud or buds. In most cases, the terminal flower bud is retained and all of the lateral (side) flower buds are removed.

Disease A plant is said to be diseased when it develops a different appearance or changes physiologically from the normally accepted state. These differences are called symptoms. Disease can be caused by unfavorable environmental conditions such as temperature extremes, insects, or pathogenic organisms such as nematodes, fungi, bacteria, or viruses.

Distribution tube A clear plastic tube with holes along either side that is installed along the length of a greenhouse to provide uniform distribution of air within the greenhouse.

Dry matter That portion of the plant remaining after water has been driven off. For purposes of foliar analysis, leaves are generally dried for one day at a temperature of 158°F (70°C).

Eave A component of the greenhouse frame to which the side wall and roof are connected.

Ebb-and-flow system A cultural system in which containerized plants are grown in a watertight bench top. When watering is required, nutrient solution is pumped into the bench to a depth of 0.5–0.75 inch (13–19 mm). The solution is drawn into the root medium by capillarity. When the pot is thoroughly wet, after about 10–15 minutes, the nutrient solution is drained from the bench to a holding tank where it is stored until needed by the crop again. This is a closed cultural system.

Employee One who works for wages or salary in the service of an employer.

Employer One who employs another individual.

Emulsifiable concentrate (EC) A liquid pesticide preparation in which the pesticide is dissolved in oil and that contains an emulsifying agent to render the oil miscible in water.

Emulsifying agent A chemical that when added to two immiscible liquids renders them miscible.

Epinasty That state in which the more vigorous growth of the upper surface of an organ (as in an unfolding leaf) causes a downward curvature.

Equinox The two times of the year when day and night are of equal length everywhere on the earth. The sun is closest to the equator. The vernal equinox occurs about March 21; the autumnal equinox, about September 23.

Even-span greenhouse A greenhouse both of whose roof slopes are of equal length and angle.

Excelsior pad A pad comprised of curled shreds of wood, generally aspen wood, that is used for evaporative cooling of greenhouses.

Facultative long- and short-night plants Plants that do not require a night length longer or shorter than a given critical length for a response to occur, but that will respond faster if the dark period is longer or shorter respectively than a critical length.

Fan-and-pad cooling A system for cooling greenhouses used during the warm months of the year. Warm air expelled through exhaust fans in one wall is replaced by air entering through wet pads on the opposite wall. The entering air is cooled by the evaporation of water in the pad.

Fan–tube cooling A system for cooling greenhouses used during the cool months of the year. Cold air entering through a louver high in the gable of the greenhouse is directed along the length of the greenhouse through a clear plastic distribution tube. Pairs of holes spaced equidistant along the length of the tube's opposite vertical walls permit uniform air distribution throughout the greenhouse.

Fasciation A malformation in plant stems resulting in an enlarged and flattened stem, as if several stems were fused.

Fertigation The combined application of watering and fertilizer such that fertilizer solution is applied every time the plants require water.

Fertilizer proportioner (Also known as a *fertilizer injector.*) Equipment used to inject concentrated fertilizer solution into a water line to result in a desired dilution prior to plant application.

Fixation The process or processes in a soil by which certain chemical elements essential for plant growth are converted from a soluble or an exchangeable form to a much less soluble or to a nonexchangeable form.

Fixed costs Costs of conducting business that are not directly related to the number or type of items produced. Interest on a greenhouse mortgage, for example, is fixed because it remains unchanged if poinsettias are grown rather than azaleas, or even if no crop is grown.

Flat A container used in greenhouses and nurseries for purposes such as germinating seeds or for holding several small plant containers. Flats are commonly constructed from wood or plastic. They are variable in size but commonly approximate 21 inches (53 cm) long by 11 inches (28 cm) wide by 2.5 inches (6 cm) deep.

Floramull® A white water-absorbing synthetic urea formaldehyde type of resin produced by BASF Corporation. It is an amendment used in root media for its high water-holding capacity; it holds water to the extent of approximately 50 percent of its volume.

Floor heating Application of heat in or near the floor of a greenhouse.

Floriculture The art and science of growing and utilizing those plants valued for their aesthetic characteristics other than woody plants used in outdoor landscape.

Flowering plants Greenhouse crop plants grown in a pot and sold in the flowering state.

Fog cooling A system for cooling greenhouses in which fog is generated inside the greenhouse. As the fog droplets evaporate, heat is absorbed, thus cooling the air.

Foot-candle (fc) A unit of illumination equal to the direct illumination on a surface everywhere 1 foot from a uniform point source of 1 international candle. It is equivalent to 10.76 lux.

Forced-air heater A heater containing a heat source, a heat exchanger, and a fan for expelling the heated air.

Fresh flowers Flowers marketed subsequent to being cut from commercial crops.

Fritted nutrients Nutrients, usually potassium or micronutrients, contained in a solid, finely ground glass powder. The glass slowly dissolves in the root medium, releasing nutrients over an extended period of time.

FRP (fiberglass-reinforced plastic) A type of panel used as the transparent covering on some greenhouses.

Fungicide An agent or preparation used for killing fungi.

Fungus An undifferentiated plant lacking chlorophyll and conductive tissues.

Gibberellins A category of hormones that stimulate growth through cell division or elongation or both.

Glasshouse A term used more commonly in Europe to designate a structure used for growing plants that has a transparent cover and an artificial heat source. The equivalent American term is *greenhouse*.

Gravelculture A system for growing plants in a root substrate consisting exclusively of gravel.

Greenhouse A structure used for growing plants that has a transparent covering and an artificial heat source.

Greenhouse range A term referring collectively to two or more greenhouses at a single location that belong to the same business entity.

Green plants Commercial crop plants grown in a pot and sold primarily for the aesthetic value of their foliage.

Headhouse A work-building in close proximity to or attached to a greenhouse. This facility might be used for purposes such as a workshop, storage area, pesticide room, potting area, or eating area. This building may also be referred to as a *service building*.

Herbicide A chemical used for killing weeds.

Hormone An organic substance produced in one part of the plant and translocated to another part where in small concentrations it regulates growth and development.

Horticulture The art and science of growing fruits, vegetables, flowers, and woody ornamentals as well as spice, medicinal, and beverage plants.

Host plant A plant that is invaded by a parasite and from which the parasite obtains its nutrients.

Humus The relatively stable fraction of the soil organic matter remaining after the major portion of added plant and animal residues have decomposed.

Hydroponics The culture of plants in a root substrate consisting exclusively of water and dissolved nutrients.

Hypha (plural *hyphae*) A single branch of the mycelium that makes up the body of a fungus.

IAA (indole-3-acetic acid) A naturally occurring auxin produced in apical meristems of both roots and shoots.

IBA (indole-3-butyric acid) A synthetically produced auxin.

Infiltration heat loss Loss of heated air from the greenhouse through cracks.

Inoculum The pathogen or its parts that can cause disease; that portion of individual pathogens that are brought into contact with the host.

Insecticide An agent or preparation used for killing insects.

Internode The portion of a plant stem between two nodes. The node is the portion of the stem where one or more leaves are attached.

Interveinal Pertaining to the space between the vascular tissue (veins) on a leaf.

IPM (integrated pest management) A holistic approach for managing pests including insects and related animals, pathogenic diseases, and weeds. Components of the program can contain restriction of pest entry into the cultural area, establishment of environmental conditions unfavorable to the pest at hand, biological control, and, only when necessary, the use of chemical pesticides.

Lap sealant A clear sealing material forced into the space formed between two overlapping panes of glass.

Larva The immature, wingless, and often wormlike form in which some insects hatch from the egg and in which they remain through increase in size and other minor changes until they assume the pupa or chrysalis stage.

Lean-to greenhouse A greenhouse built against the side of another structure such that it has only one sloping roof.

Loam A textural class name for soils having reasonably balanced amounts of sand, silt, and clay. Loam soils can contain 7–28 percent clay, 28–50 percent silt, and less than 52 percent sand.

Logo A word, slogan, or sketch used to convey a thought. A logo is often used in advertising programs—for example, *Say It with Flowers* or the cougar on a Mercury automobile advertisement.

Long-night plant A plant that undergoes photoperiodic response, such as flowering, only when the night length is greater than a critical length.

Lumen The unit of light equal to the light emitted in a unit solid angle by a uniform point source of 1 international candle.

Lux The international unit of illumination, being the direct illumination on a surface that is everywhere 1 meter from a uniform point source of 1 international candle. It is equal to 1 lumen per square meter, or 0.0929 foot-candles.

Management The making of decisions that affect the profitability of a business.

Mark-on The percentage of the wholesale price added on to the wholesale price in order to cover overhead and profit and to arrive at a retail price.

Markup The percentage of the retail price added on to the wholesale price to cover overhead and profit. An item purchased for $1 and selling for $2 has a markup of 50 percent and a mark-on of 100 percent.

Mass marketing In the field of floriculture, the sale of floral products through high-traffic outlets such as supermarkets, discount stores, department stores, sidewalk stands, and shops in shopping malls.

Meristem A tissue composed of embryonic, unspecialized cells actively or potentially involved in cell division. An apical meristem is a meristem located at the apex (tip) of a shoot or root.

Methyl bromide A chemical commonly used for pasteurizing greenhouse root media. It should not be used in carnation root media.

Miticide An agent or preparation used for killing mites.

Mycelium The hypha or hyphae that make up the body of a fungus. Mycelium are the microscopic threadlike strands that make up the body of a fungus.

NAA (naphthalene acetic acid) A synthetically produced auxin.

Necrosis The state of being dead and discolored.

Nematicide An agent or preparation used for killing nematodes.

NFT (nutrient film technique) The culture of plants in a system where a thin film (a few millimeters deep) of nutrient solution is circulated through a trough that also contains the plant roots. It is a specialized form of hydroponics.

Open cultural system Any system for growing plants in which nutrient solution is allowed to pass through the root zone and out into the environment.

Opportunity cost The value of other opportunities (alternatives) given up in order to produce or consume any good; that which must be forfeited when alternative *A* is abandoned in order to pursue alternative *B*.

Organelle One of several types of small structures within plant or animal cells that is bounded by a membrane. The chloroplast is one type of organelle in which photosynthesis occurs.

Ovipositor A prominent structure projecting from the posterior end of females of some insects that is used to deposit eggs.

Pasteurization The selective destruction of some, but not all, living microorganisms. Root media are pasteurized to eliminate harmful disease organisms and to retain the beneficial microorganisms.

Pathogen An entity (fungus, bacterium, nematode, virus) that can incite disease.

Peat The organic remains of plants that have accumulated in places where decay has been retarded by excessively wet conditions. There are many types of peat, some desirable and others not, used for greenhouse root media.

Peat humus Peat that is at an advanced stage of decomposition in which the original plant remains are not identifiable. It is not generally a desirable form of peat for greenhouse root media because of its rapid rate of decomposition and its occasionally high rate of ammonium nitrogen release.

Peat moss Peat consisting predominantly of slightly humified (decomposed) *Sphagnum* moss species. Horticultural peat moss contains over 75 percent sphagnum moss.

Pedicel Stem of one flower in a cluster.

Perimeter heating system A row of heating pipe or pipes just inside the perimeter walls of a greenhouse.

Perlite A siliceous volcanic rock that is crushed and heated to 1,800°F to cause it to expand into lightweight (about 6 pounds per cubic foot) particles with closed air-filled cells. Perlite is used as a substitute for sand when a lightweight root medium is desired.

Pesticide An agent or preparation used for killing living organisms that are a nuisance or are harmful to crops.

Petiole The stalk or stemlike portion of a leaf.

Photoperiodism The response of a plant or animal to the relative length of day and night. The response in plants can take on many forms, including flowering, changes in leaf shape or internode length, and bulb or tuber formation.

Photosynthesis The manufacture of carbohydrate from carbon dioxide and water in the presence of chlorophyll, using light energy and releasing oxygen.

Phytotoxic Toxic to plants.

Pinching Removal of the top of a vegetative plant stem in order to cause it to form several branches.

Plug seedlings Seedlings produced and contained in a small cohesive volume of root medium. This unit of root medium is known as a *plug*.

Polyethylene A plastic material used in the greenhouse industry in the form of thin films for covering greenhouses. It is an inexpensive substitute for glass. Generally, two layers are used—an outer layer 6 mils (6 one-thousandths of an inch) thick and an inner layer either 4 (0.10 mm) or 6 (0.15 mm) mils thick.

Pompon chrysanthemums A term used in this book to denote the chrysanthemum cultivars grown with several flowers on each stem. The term *spray chrysanthemum* is more commonly used.

Potable Drinkable.

Precipitation The process whereby a dissolved substance comes out of solution to form a solid. The solid substance is a *precipitate*.

Pressuring fan A fan in the end of the clear plastic greenhouse distribution tube that forces heater air, exterior cold air, or interior warm air through the tube, depending on whether the system is being used for heating, cooling, or air circulation, respectively.

Proprietorship A business owned by a single individual.

Pupa The intermediate, usually quiescent, stage assumed by many insects after the larval stage and maintained until the adult stage.

Purlin A component of the greenhouse frame running the length of the greenhouse just below the roof covering that connects the trusses together.

PVC (polyvinyl chloride) A plastic material available in corrugated sheets. This material was used for covering greenhouses during the 1960s, but, because of its rapid deterioration from ultraviolet light, it has virtually disappeared from the greenhouse industry.

Radiant heat loss The radiation of heat from a warm body, such as plants in a greenhouse, to a cooler body, such as the covering on the greenhouse or the sky and earth outside.

Rafter A frame component spanning the space between the eave and the ridge. Unlike a sash bar, glass is not attached to it.

Reglaze To replace the glass or the glazing compound that seals the glass on a greenhouse.

Respiration Those biochemical processes in the plant or animal that result in the consumption of oxygen and carbohydrate, the evolution of carbon dioxide, and the release of energy. Respiration has the reverse effect of photosynthesis.

Revenue Income; return from investment.

Ridge A component of the greenhouse frame to which the upper portion of the two roof slopes are connected.

Ridge-and-furrow greenhouses Two or more greenhouses connected to each other along their length at the eave. In this case, the eave becomes a gutter, or furrow. The common side wall is eliminated in each greenhouse. Such greenhouses are less expensive to heat and easier to automate than an equivalent area of separate greenhouses.

Rock wool A fibrous material used for thermal and acoustical insulation as well as a root medium for plants. It is made from melted rock that can be basalt or limestone, sometimes in combination with iron slag. The hot liquid is spun and cooled into long fibers. The fibers may be formed into granules for use in potting media, blocks for plant propagation, or large slabs for growing finished crops of vegetables and fresh flowers.

Root medium (plural *root media*) A suitable substrate in which plant roots can grow. It consists of one or more mineral and/or organic components mixed together. This term is most commonly used in the greenhouse and nursery circles of agriculture.

Sand A soil mineral particle measuring 0.05–2.0 mm in diameter.

Sandculture The culture of plants in a root substrate consisting exclusively of sand.

Sash bar The bar to which glass is attached in a greenhouse.

Senescence The process of growing old; aging.

Sepal One of the components of the calyx.

Shatter When used to describe a floral condition, this term refers to the dropping or abscission of petals.

Short-night plant A plant that undergoes a photoperiodic response, such as flowering, only when the night length is less than a critical length.

Sill The portion of the greenhouse that rests on the curtain wall and to which the side wall sash bars are attached.

Silt A mineral component of soils consisting of particles measuring 0.002–0.05 mm in diameter.

Slab-side (also known as *cling-side*) A flower that has failed to open symmetrically. The petals on part of the circumference are still straight up, while the remaining petals have opened in a normal fashion.

Sleepiness A condition in flowers in which petals curve upward, giving the appearance of a wilted condition. It is commonly caused by ethylene gas after harvest.

Soil The upper, heavily weathered layer of the earth's crust that supports plant life. It is a mixture of mineral and organic materials.

Solenoid valve An electrically activated valve that controls the flow of gases or liquids. Such valves can be activated by a time clock to control the flow of water in automated greenhouse watering systems.

Solstice The two times of the year when the sun is farthest from the equator (closest to the poles). In the Northern Hemisphere, the summer solstice occurs about June 22 and the winter solstice about December 22.

Split A flower having a split calyx, in which the petals protrude from the split. It is a common problem of carnations.

Spore The reproductive unit of fungi consisting of one or more cells; analogous to the seed of green plants.

Sporophore A hypha or fruiting structure bearing spores.

Spreader-sticker *See* Surfactant.

Standard chrysanthemums Cultivars of chrysanthemum customarily grown with one large flower on each stem.

Sterilization The destruction of all living organisms. Greenhouse tools and growing containers are periodically sterilized to eliminate harmful organisms including pathogenic diseases, insects, nematodes, and weeds.

Strap leaves Leaves whose margins are partially or completely missing such that the leaf is narrower than normal, often resembling a strap.

Strut A support member of the greenhouse frame that is under a compression force.

Surfactant A chemical used to alter the surface properties of liquids. Surfactants are added to pesticide sprays to reduce the surface tension over the plant leaf surface. Without a surfactant, complete coverage of the leaf surface often is not achieved. Surfactants used for these purpose include *spreader-stickers, wetting agents*, and *detergents*. Surfactants are also used to enhance the initial wetting of root media containing relatively dry peat moss, which tends to be waxy and water-repellant.

Symphillid A small, translucent to white, many-legged arthropod that ranges up to 1/4 inch (6 mm) in length and that feeds on the roots of plants.

Systemic Spreading internally throughout the plant body. Some pesticides are systemic, as are some pathogens.

Texture The relative proportion of various sizes of mineral particles in a given soil or root medium.

Transpiration The loss of water from plant tissue in the form of vapor.

Tropism A growth response or bending toward or away from a stimulus. Geotropism is in response to gravity; roots grow toward, and shoots away from, the center of the earth's gravity. Phototropism is in response to light; shoots tend to grow toward light.

Trough culture A closed system for growing potted plants in which a single row of pots is placed in a watertight trough arranged on a slight incline. Nutrient solution is pumped to the high end of the trough. It flows by gravity around the bases of the pots to the low end where it is channeled to a holding tank. Solution is drawn into the root medium by capillarity. The solution is reused each time the crop requires watering.

Truss A compound component of the greenhouse frame spanning the width of the greenhouse and consisting of rafters, chords, and struts that are welded or bolted together.

Ultralow volume When used to describe pesticide application to plants, this term refers to the application of a very low volume of liquid pesticide formulation per unit area. When less than 5 gallons is used per acre (47 1/ha), the application is referred to as *low volume*; below 1 gallon per acre (9.5 1/ha), it is referred to as *ultralow volume.*

Uneven-span greenhouse A greenhouse with one roof slope longer than the other, generally for the purpose of adaptation to a hillside.

Unit heater A forced-air heater. Unit heaters are usually mounted overhead in a greenhouse. They may contain a firebox or receive heat in the form of steam or hot water from a boiler elsewhere.

Variable cost A cost that increases proportionately with each additional unit produced and ceases if no units are produced. The cost of pots, root media, and plants are variable costs; the mortgage on the greenhouse range is not a variable cost but rather a fixed cost because it continues even if no plants are produced.

Vascular tissue Tissue in the root, stem, leaf, or flower stem including phloem for conducting organic substances throughout the plant, xylem for conducting water and nutrients primarily from the roots to the shoot, and supporting fiber cells. Vascular tissue in leaves is often called *veins.*

Vase life The length of time that a cut flower retains its aesthetic value after it has been placed on display.

Veinal Pertaining to the vascular tissue (veins) or the tissue immediately above the vascular tissue in a leaf.

Ventilator A glazed panel attached to the greenhouse with hinges that permit opening for ventilation purposes.

Vermiculite A micaceous mineral that exfoliates (expands by separation of the many layers composing it) when heated. It is used in the expanded state as a lightweight component of greenhouse root media. Its desirable properties include a light bulk density of 7–10 pounds per cubic foot, a relatively high cation exchange capacity of 19–23 me/100 g, and a high water-holding capacity.

Vermiculaponics The culture of plants in a root substrate consisting exclusively of vermiculite.

Wettable powder In floriculture, an agricultural chemical formulated generally in talc or dry clay. It is suspended in water by continual mixing and is applied as a spray or root-media drench.

Wetting agent *See* Surfactant.

Whole-firm recirculation A closed circuit system encompassing an entire firm. Effluent from all benches or beds is channeled to a treatment pond. There, it is often treated for pathogens, analyzed, and nutritionally altered prior to being recirculated through the crops.

Witch's broom A symptom of boron deficiency in a plant. A witch's broom consists of a large number of shortened plant stems situated parallel and close to one another to give the appearance of the straws in a broom.

Xylem A tissue in the plant that transports water and nutrients upward from the roots to the foliage. Cells connected from end to end form xylem tubes. Vessels are the predominant xylem cells in flowering plants and have open ends. Tracheids predominate in the conifer (pines, etc.) xylem; rather than having open ends, they have pits along their sides connecting to adjacent tracheid cells. Vessel and tracheid cells are nonliving at the time they carry out the function of water and nutrient transport.

Index